OXFORD EARLY CHRISTIAN STUDIES

General Editors

Gillian Clark   Andrew Louth

THE OXFORD EARLY CHRISTIAN STUDIES series includes scholarly volumes on the thought and history of the early Christian centuries. Covering a wide range of Greek, Latin, and Oriental sources, the books are of interest to theologians, ancient historians, and specialists in the classical and Jewish worlds.

Ancient Traditions of the Virgin Mary's Dormition and Assumption

STEPHEN J. SHOEMAKER

OXFORD
UNIVERSITY PRESS

OXFORD

UNIVERSITY PRESS

Great Clarendon Street, Oxford OX2 6DP

Oxford University Press is a department of the University of Oxford.
It furthers the University's objective of excellence in research, scholarship,
and education by publishing worldwide in

Oxford New York

Auckland Bangkok Buenos Aires Cape Town Chennai
Dar es Salaam Delhi Hong Kong Istanbul Karachi Kolkata
Kuala Lumpur Madrid Melbourne Mexico City Mumbai Nairobi
São Paulo Shanghai Taipei Tokyo Toronto

Oxford is a registered trade mark of Oxford University Press
in the UK and in certain other countries

Published in the United States
by Oxford University Press Inc., New York

© Stephen J. Shoemaker 2002

The moral rights of the author have been asserted
Database right Oxford University Press (maker)

First published 2002

British Library Cataloguing in Publication Data

Data available

Library of Congress Cataloging in Publication Data

Data applied for

ISBN 0–19–925075–8

1 3 5 7 9 10 8 6 4 2

Typeset in Imprint
by Regent Typesetting, London
Printed in Great Britain
on acid-free paper by
Biddles Ltd,
Guildford and King's Lynn

დედასა და მამასა
For Mom and Dad

Staunst du nicht, wie sanft sie ihm entging?
Fast als wär sie's noch, nichts is verschoben.
Doch die Himmel sind erschüttert oben:
Mann, knie hin und sieh mir nach und sing.

Rainer Maria Rilke, *Das Marien-Leben*,
'Vom Tode Mariae, III'

PREFACE

In many ways this is a book that I had hoped not to write. That is not to say that I have not enjoyed doing so, for I have. Nevertheless, it was my initial intention to produce an altogether different study of early Dormition narratives when first taking up this corpus of traditions. This book owes its existence to my doctoral dissertation, which I defended at Duke University in 1997 under the title, 'Mary and the Discourse of Orthodoxy: Early Christian Identity and the Ancient Dormition Legends'. As this title suggests, the dissertation was a somewhat different enterprise than the present volume. Yet it too was not the dissertation that I had hoped to write. It was my initial intention to produce a study of the early Dormition traditions that detailed their position in the culture and society of the early Byzantine Near East. Although I was able to achieve a fraction of this goal in the dissertation, as my studies of the Dormition traditions have progressed I have continually struggled with the need for a detailed study of the basic facts of these narratives, including such matters as the relations among these highly variegated traditions, their approximate dates, their relations to the emergent cult of the Virgin, and their theological positioning within the diversity of late ancient Christianity, among other details.

Early in my studies of the Dormition traditions, Simon Mimouni's exhaustive work, *Dormition et assomption de Marie: Histoire des traditions anciennes*, was published (1995). It was my hope that this volume could fill my need, but I am very sorry to say that it did not. Although Mimouni's study is to be commended for its enormous scope and attention to detail, it is in my opinion fundamentally flawed in its approach to the traditions, as this study will frequently make clear. Unfortunately for my purposes, Mimouni's study served only to make already murky waters even more cloudy, particularly for the reader otherwise unfamiliar with these traditions. More importantly, however, Mimouni's study completely up-ended the significant scholarship on the early Dormition traditions that Antoine

Wenger had begun and Michel van Esbroeck has been continuing. The work of these two scholars, based on careful literary and philological study of the various traditions, is without question the most useful analysis that I have encountered.

In this regard, van Esbroeck's series of studies on the Dormition traditions (now collected in his *Aux origines de la Dormition de la Vierge: Études historique sur les traditions orientales*) offered more promise. Nevertheless, as anyone who has read these articles can attest, van Esbroeck's studies often assume a great deal on the part of their readers. It can frequently be frustrating for uninitiated readers to follow the details of their arguments, unless they are familiar with all the various sources and issues that van Esbroeck has engaged elsewhere, many of which will be rather obscure to the average scholar of late antiquity. This is particularly the case with van Esbroeck's brief article 'Les Textes littéraires sur l'assomption avant le Xe siècle', which I have found more valuable than any other single work in studying these traditions. In this extremely compressed article, van Esbroeck outlines the various traditions and presents two stemmata that diagram the literary relations among the different narratives quite accurately. Nevertheless, the article gives only the slimmest argumentation for its important and perceptive conclusions, leaving readers who are otherwise innocent of the Dormition traditions to take a great deal on faith. Moreover, while I strongly agree with van Esbroeck concerning certain fundamentals, in the following pages I offer a considerably different interpretation of the ancient Dormition traditions and their history.

Nor were these the only two options available for understanding these ancient traditions. As the reader of this book will soon discover, a variety of hypotheses have been advanced concerning the nature of the early Dormition traditions, most of which I have found even more problematic. In view of these circumstances, I decided that I would write a book to bridge this gap, providing a basic introduction to these traditions, with the hope of eventually being able to follow it with the book that I had initially wanted to write, resting my studies of these traditions' cultural significance on the foundations laid in this volume. I have also included a number of translations, some of them quite lengthy, to assist in the introduction of this unnecessarily obscure corpus. The idea to include these translations was initially suggested by my first readers, the members of my dissertation committee, who in reading my work expressed some frustration at the inability to access easily the narratives that I was discussing. I hope that these translations will help to open up these fascinating traditions to a much broader audience than they have yet received.

At this point, then, I would like to thank the members of my dissertation committee not only for this helpful suggestion, but for the multitude of good advice they have provided me for the past ten years. Above all others, I must thank my *Doktormutter*, Elizabeth Clark, who has not only been an outstanding mentor and friend, but also deserves the credit for initially suggesting the early Dormition traditions as a topic of research. I am also deeply indebted to Orval Wintermute, who patiently guided my first steps in many of the languages required to undertake this project, as well as to the other members of my dissertation committee, Bart Ehrman, Dale Martin, and John Oates, whose gifts as both teachers and scholars have nurtured my own scholarship. In addition, I wish to thank my colleagues in the graduate programme, particularly John Lamoreaux and Andrew Jacobs, at Duke for their numerous, otherwise unacknowledged contributions to the gradual development of the present work.

I especially wish to thank my most valued colleague and friend, Melissa Aubin, not only for her considerable contributions to this work, but especially for her companionship and her support. Special thanks are also due to Derek Krueger, who more than anyone else helped this project to get off the ground, and to Susan Ashbrook Harvey, who kindly shared with me both her encouragement and her unpublished work on the Syriac Dormition traditions. At a later stage, Philip Sellew similarly made an important contribution, also by sharing his unpublished work and by offering helpful comments on my then work in progress. Walter Ray has been a valued dialogue partner almost from the start, particularly with regard to the liturgical traditions of Jerusalem and the newly discovered 'Kathisma' church in particular. News of the 'new' Kathisma church's discovery broke just as the ink was drying on my dissertation, and I owe an enormous debt to the church's excavator, Rina Avner, who personally introduced me to the site while I was in

Jerusalem and quite generously shared with me the unpublished results of the most recent (and final) excavations. I should also like to thank Michel van Esbroeck for generously providing me with copies of several forthcoming articles and certain other of his writings that proved very difficult to obtain.

Moreover, I wish to thank Dumbarton Oaks for the generous financial support of a Junior Fellowship and the opportunity to utilize its outstanding Byzantine collection while completing my dissertation in 1996–7. Likewise, the valuable conversation and helpful advice of the various scholars then in residence improved this dissertation considerably, including particularly Alexander Alexakis, John Birkenmeier, Barbara Crostini, Leslie Dossey, Yizhar Hirschfeld, Alexander Kazhdan, William Macomber, Irfan Shahid, and Jean-Pierre Sodini. While in Washington, I was warmly welcomed by scholars at the Catholic University of America's Institute for Christian Oriental Research. Of these, I thank especially David Johnson for providing me with reproductions of certain Coptic manuscripts at an early stage in this project, Janet Timbie for her comments on my edition of the Ps.-Evodius homily, and Monica Blanchard for kindly allowing me the privilege of sitting in on her 'Introduction to Old Georgian', a language which has proved crucial for the study of these traditions.

Also I wish to thank the National Endowment for the Humanities for a fellowship in the year 1999–2000, which supported my stay at the W. F. Albright Institute for Archaeological Research in Jerusalem, where I completed this book. I am very grateful to the Albright and its staff, as well as to the American Schools of Oriental Research, for the opportunities both to utilize the numerous resources of which it avails its residents and to enrich myself with the Albright's extensive educational programme of speakers and site excursions in the Holy Land. In conjunction with my stay at the Albright, I would like to thank in particular Douglas Edwards, Eric Meyers, Yorke Rowan, and Robert Schick for their contributions to this study.

I should additionally like to thank the libraries and staff of the École Biblique and the Studium Biblicum Franciscanum for allowing me to use their collections during my stay in Jerusalem. I am also indebted to the Armenian Studies program at the Hebrew University of Jerusalem, and I thank Konstantine

Lerner, Daniel Stoekl, and Michael Stone for various contributions to this study. I am especially grateful to Professor Stone for allowing me to participate in his Classical Armenian seminar and for his hospitality in general during my year in Jerusalem.

I owe a special debt to Andrew McGowan for initially putting me in contact with Andrew Louth, and I would like to thank Professor Louth and Gillian Clark for agreeing to publish this volume in the Oxford Early Christian Studies series. Their comments, and those of Sarah Boss, who served as an anonymous reader, considerably improved the final product. When at last the book reached Oxford University Press, Hilary O'Shea, Enid Barker, Lucy Qureshi, Lavinia Porter, and Sylvia Jaffrey offered much assistance and showed great flexibility in bringing a work with so many languages and fonts into print.

Finally, my greatest debt is imperfectly acknowledged in the dedication. I cannot begin to thank my parents for all that they have done. They have been simultaneously both my biggest fans and toughest critics, striking the difficult but crucial balance that good parents must. For this and for so much else, I am altogether grateful.

S.J.S.

Eugene
November 2001

CONTENTS

LIST OF FIGURES

ABBREVIATIONS

Patristic texts are cited according to the systems of abbreviation outlined in G. W. H. Lampe (ed.), *A Patristic Greek Lexicon* (Oxford: Oxford University Press, 1961) (for Greek) and Albert Blaise and Henri Chirat, *Dictionnaire latin–français des auteurs chrétiens* (Paris: Librairie des Meridiens, 1954) (for Latin). Biblical and rabbinic texts are cited according to the list of abbreviations given in the *Journal of Biblical Literature*, 107 (1988): 579–96.

CCG   Corpus Christianorum, Series Graeca
CCL   Corpus Christianorum, Series Latina
CCSA Corpus Christianorum, Series Apocrypha
CSCO Corpus Scriptorum Christianorum Orientalium
CSEL Corpus Scriptorum Ecclesiasticorum Latinorum
GCS   Die griechischen christlichen Schriftsteller der ersten drei Jahrhunderte
NHS   Nag Hammadi Studies; Nag Hammadi and Manichaean Studies
PG   *Patrologia Graeca*, ed. J. P. Migne, *et al.* (Paris, 1857–)
PL   *Patrologia Latina*, ed. J. P. Migne, *et al.* (Paris, 1844–)
PO   Patrologia Orientalis
SC   Sources chrétiennes
TU   Texte und Untersuchungen zur Geschichte des altchristlichen Literatur

Introduction

The end of the Virgin Mary's life remains a relatively uncertain moment in the Christian story. Despite decades of research and the Vatican's concerted efforts to resolve the matter during the past century, culminating in the 1950 dogma of the Virgin's Assumption, the topic remains an unclear point of the early Christian tradition. Indeed, even the Vatican's 1950 definition fails to clarify such a basic matter as whether or not the Virgin actually died before departing this world. In the Vatican's defence, it must be said that the first four Christian centuries are surprisingly reticent on the subject of Mary's 'death', although what little evidence there is does seem to indicate that, in contrast to the ambiguity of the modern Assumption dogma, Mary did in fact die. Our understanding of the end of Mary's life improves considerably, however, once we reach the late fifth and sixth centuries, when there was suddenly an efflorescence of diverse traditions, both narrative and liturgical, all celebrating the Virgin's departure from this world. This sudden proliferation of traditions calls for an explanation: something about this topic and its narrative traditions must have resonated with the issues and concerns of the early Byzantine world. Although it is my intention to address in a future volume the intriguing question of why these legends found such great appeal during the period from 450 to 600, before tackling such a topic we must first come to grips with the complicated nature of the corpus itself. Before we can hope to interpret these traditions coherently within their broader context, we require a better understanding of the traditions themselves, including particularly the relations between different narratives and the nature of their early history and development in general.

These are the aims of the present study: to bring a measure of clarity and coherence to this tangled mass of traditions by identifying the earliest, exploring the connections among them, and unravelling the nature of their earliest development. Such work is made necessary by the often intimidating diversity of these traditions: in fact rather than resolving the issue of how Mary departed this life, the abundance of fifth- and sixth-century traditions merely complicates the matter further. Only a very few themes are common to all (or almost all) the earliest narratives, and these include Mary's death in Jerusalem; the involvement of at least a few of the apostles; Christ's reception of his mother's soul; the transfer of Mary in body and/or soul to Paradise; and the imagined hostility of the Jews towards Mary.[1] While this suggests a rather basic outline that may represent the earliest stage of these traditions, beyond this slim core the differences pile up very quickly. The list of variants is unfortunately too vast to catalogue here, but a quick comparison of the appended translations will give the reader a good sense of the diversity represented in the earliest traditions. Nevertheless, a select few of these differences were significant for the formulation of the 1950 dogma, and consequently they have held a firm grasp on the direction of much previous scholarship and will necessarily be important foci of the following discussions.

Of the various disagreements among the narratives, no issue has attracted more attention, and likewise generated more confusion, than the moment of Mary's death and its theological significance as described in these narratives. The overwhelming interest in this topic was generated primarily by the Vatican's 1950 definition, in view of which many scholars turned to the earliest traditions to garner support for the dogma, both before and since its proclamation. At the heart of the modern Assumption dogma lies a belief that Mary, at the end of her life, received 'prematurely' the final reward of the just, which others of the just will receive only at the end of time, at the Last Judgment. But if a few of the earliest narratives seem to express this view, others do not. The majority, however, as we will see, are quite ambiguous on this matter and thus not at all suited to fit within the sharp lines drawn by modern dogmatic discourse.

---

[1] On the latter point, one can now see Stephen J. Shoemaker, ' "Let Us Go and Burn Her Body": The Image of the Jews in the Early Dormition Traditions', *Church History*, 68 (1999), 775–823.

The ancient narratives are neither clear nor unanimous in either supporting or contradicting the modern dogma on this point, a situation that has often invited modern scholarship to manipulate the early history of these traditions in the service of this modern dogma.

The varied representation of Mary's ultimate fate in these narratives requires that we clarify some theological terms, in order that we may better understand both the diversity of the early Dormition narratives themselves and their complex relationship with the modern dogmatic formula. For instance, in many Dormition narratives, the Virgin's body and soul are only temporarily separated, usually for three or four days, after which she is, like her son, resurrected and taken bodily into heaven, where she presently exists as a living witness to the reward that awaits all the just at the end of time. Since this conclusion corresponds more or less with the modern dogma of the Virgin's bodily Assumption, I will occasionally refer to traditions representing this view as 'Assumptionist'. Other early narratives, however, omit any mention of Mary's resurrection or bodily Assumption; these generally conclude with Christ's descent to receive his mother's soul, followed by the transfer of her body to a hidden place where it awaits reunion with her soul at the end of time. Inasmuch as these narratives do not express the modern theological concept of Mary's bodily Assumption, I will from time to time identify such traditions as 'Assumptionless', so as to distinguish them from the Assumptionist traditions. When referring collectively to all the traditions of the end of Mary's life, however, whether Assumptionist, Assumptionless, or otherwise, I will consistently use the term 'Dormition traditions', both because all the narratives include an account of the Virgin's 'Dormition'[2] and because the Byzantine tradition itself refers collectively to the Assumptionist and Assumptionless traditions using the single term κοίμησις, 'the Dormition'.[3]

Nevertheless, in spite of adopting such theological terminology, I will be the first to admit, and even insist, that this

---

[2] i.e. the scene in which Christ receives his mother's soul and takes it to heaven.

[3] See e.g. Martin Jugie, AA, *La Mort et l'assomption de la Sainte Vierge: Étude historico-doctrinale,* Studi e Testi, 114 (Vatican City: Biblioteca Apostolica Vaticana, 1944), 185–94.

theological bifurcation of the early traditions is highly over-determined in much scholarship. In fact, such a strict division among the narratives would probably not have been made in the first place, but for the impact of the modern Assumption dogma on the study of these traditions. Many of the earliest traditions simply do not fit in either of these theological categories, and consequently, this issue presents a poor criterion for organiz-ing the various traditions, despite its frequent implementation in modern scholarship. Time and again scholars have proposed an understanding of these traditions and their early history that rests primarily on their theological differences, often ignoring or even contradicting other evidence, such as literary relations. In contrast to this frequent approach, this study will present a case for classifying and studying the earliest narratives primarily on the basis of their literary history and relationships, as an alternative to the predominantly theological orientation of much previous scholarship. This is certainly not the first effort to investigate the corpus according to these terms: on the contrary, many have laboured in this area before me, making the pres-ent study feasible. Nevertheless, a reassessment of these tradi-tions and their early history is especially needful at the present moment, particularly in the light of relatively recent discoveries unknown to prior scholarship. Moreover, the literary history of these traditions has often been ignored and even distorted by scholarship taking a more theological approach to them. It is primarily in an effort to restore these traditions to an under-standing that rests more firmly on their literary history that I offer this study.

One particular consequence of the overemphasis on theo-logical themes has been a variety of efforts to account for the diversity of these traditions according to a developmental model of either dogmatic evolution or decline over time. In such a view, the various theological positions represented in the early Dormition narratives correspond to a related progression in the history of Christian thought, according to which one interpreta-tion of the end of Mary's life is replaced by another. As opinions with regard to Mary's death changed, it is supposed, there was need to produce new narratives that would embody a particular dogmatic position. Some, for instance, have maintained that the Assumptionist traditions reflect an earlier tradition, which only later degenerated into the Assumptionless traditions that fail to narrate Mary's Assumption. Others, however, posit a development of dogma in the spirit of John Henry Newman, arguing that the original simplicity of the Assumptionless traditions eventually gave rise through a process of unilinear development to the Assumptionist traditions, which represent a more complex understanding of the primitive deposit of faith. Nevertheless, historical evidence in favour of either developmental model is extremely limited. Since the earliest exemplars of each dogmatic tradition appear at approximately the same moment, the turn of the sixth century, there is no historical basis for maintaining that either theological position precedes the other. On the contrary, the nature of the earliest traditions themselves strongly suggests the existence of multiple 'origins', which together have given rise to the complex diversity of the traditions as we now find them. The progressive development of each narrative type out of another, which it ultimately displaces, extending back to a single origin, seems comparatively unlikely.

Another important difference in the earliest traditions that has been the focus of much previous scholarship is the location of Mary's house. While the overwhelming majority of the traditions situate Mary's house somewhere in the Jerusalem area, a significant group of narratives identifies a second house in Bethlehem, where a number of events take place. Additionally, a few early narratives seem to suggest the location of Mary's house at the foot of the Mount of Olives, in contrast to its later association with Mt. Zion. Certain scholars have sought to correlate each of these variants with the early liturgical and archaeological evidence for the cult of the Virgin in Jerusalem, in an attempt to link changes in liturgical practice with the theological and narrative diversity of these traditions. In this way, it is sometimes argued that the development of Marian veneration in Jerusalem parallels and thus can confirm the narrative and theological development that is proposed to explain the diversity of the early Dormition traditions. Nevertheless, a clear understanding of both the early liturgical traditions and the related archaeological remains demonstrates the improbability of such hypotheses. It is to this end that I devote considerable attention to the cult of Mary in late ancient Jerusalem, incorporating both very recent archaeological discoveries and several liturgical sources that have often been underutilized in previous discussions of this phenomenon. The result is a fresh reassessment of earliest development of the Marian cult in Palestine, which, although valuable in its own right, is of particular importance for understanding the early history of the Dormition narratives.

A further issue that must be addressed in regard to the early history of the Dormition traditions is the question of their 'originary' milieu. With surprising frequency one meets the assertion that the traditions of Mary's Dormition had their origin among the opponents of the council of Chalcedon (451). Nevertheless, this commonly held view is simply not supported by the current state of our evidence. On the contrary, the earliest narratives seem deliberately to avoid taking a position on the debates over Christ's humanity and divinity that issued from the council of Chalcedon. Instead, they are larded with the sort of theological commonplaces that were acceptable to those on both sides of this debate, while the language and formulae of the controversy over Chalcedon are completely absent. On a few occasions, one even finds theological formulae representative of various efforts to heal the theological rift occasioned by Chalcedon. Not only then is there no evidence to support an anti-Chalcedonian origin, but the contents of the narratives themselves seem to contradict such a hypothesis.

On the other hand, many of the very earliest narratives are filled with various 'heterodox' theologoumena that are rather peculiar for the early Byzantine context into which these narratives first emerged. These include, among other things, Christ's identification as a 'Great Angel', a persistent emphasis on secret and often soteriological knowledge, and even reference to a common gnostic creation myth. There is widespread agreement that these themes are indications of an earlier existence somewhere outside the mainstream of proto-orthodox Christianity.[4] While many scholars have argued for a Jewish-Christian origin, this is improbable for various reasons, and it seems that positing some sort of contact with gnostic Christianity (but not

---

[4] In regards to my use of the terms 'orthodox' or 'proto-orthodox', see the discussion in Bart D. Ehrman, *The Orthodox Corruption of Scripture: The Effect of Early Christological Controversies on the Text of the New Testament* (New York: Oxford University Press, 1993), 3–25, and esp. 11–13, where the use of these terms in discussing early Christianity is well explained.

necessarily a gnostic origin) can best account for the unusual theology of these early narratives. Several among the second generation of extant narratives openly express their discomfort with this aspect of the earlier traditions, and the authors of these narratives feel the need to explain for their readers that they have sanitized the earlier traditions for their protection, an editorial cleansing that is quite evident in the earliest transmission of these legends during the sixth and early seventh centuries.

Finally, one of the primary obstacles to the study of these traditions has been their preservation in numerous ancient languages, and specifically the fact that many have not been translated into English, and in some cases not into any modern language. In an effort to remedy this situation the present study includes translations of six important early Dormition traditions, gathered in appendices at the end of the volume. The first of these is probably the earliest extant Dormition narrative, which, despite its importance, has not previously been translated into English, nor, in its totality, into any modern language. This narrative, witnessed by several fifth-century Syriac fragments, is known in its entirety only from a complete Ethiopic version, although fragments also survive in other languages, including Georgian and Coptic. In the first appendix I have translated the Ethiopic version, presented in synopsis with translations of all the known fragments. In reading this translation, one will immediately notice the difficult nature of this text, which is a consequence of its unfortunately poor preservation in the Ethiopic, where the language is very irregular and occasionally even non-sensical. This condition presents numerous problems for translation and may in part account for the long-standing neglect of this important apocryphon. In rendering this narrative into English, I have tried whenever possible to use idiomatic English, brushing over most of the endemic grammatical irregularities, but when on occasion the sense of the text breaks down completely, I have tried to express the Ethiopic as literally as possible. Moreover, I have throughout made an effort to represent the Ethiopic as closely as possible in English, preserving such awkward stylistic features as hendiadys and the waw consecutive. The decision to translate in this fashion was determined primarily by the fact that this is the apocryphon's first translation into English, as well as by the similar nature of many earlier translations of other ancient Dormition narratives. By adopting a similar style, the reader can more easily compare the different narratives in English. As such, the narrative is intended primarily for academic readers, rather than as a literary translation.

The remaining narratives are significantly less complicated from a translator's viewpoint. They are for the most part free of the irregularities that plague the first narrative, and I have similarly tried in each case to represent the original as clearly as possible in English, adopting a style that may in some cases seem wooden, but may more easily be compared with earlier translations and the originals. The second translation presents the earliest extant Greek narrative, a text very closely related to the first narrative. This relationship provides the main reason for including this narrative, which, in addition to its general antiquity, evidences many of the same heterodox themes found in the Ethiopic narrative, confirming their presence in the earliest layer of the tradition. The remaining four narratives were all chosen to represent the different narrative types present among the earliest Dormition traditions. The first two narratives are the earliest exemplars of a particular narrative type, and the third and fourth are early representatives of a second major narrative family. The fifth translation represents a third narrative type, while the final translation does not belong to any of the three main narrative types. Instead, the final narrative is included as the earliest example of various 'atypical' Dormition narratives from the earliest period, of which there are several. It is hoped that these translations will assist the reader in following the arguments in this study, as well as opening up this literary tradition, long the domain of specialists in various ancient languages, to a broader readership.

The Earliest Dormition Traditions: Their Nature and Shape

On the Feast of All Saints, 1 November 1950, the See of St Peter exercised its rather recently identified privilege of defining doctrine infallibly by pronouncing the theological dogma of the Virgin's bodily Assumption. In the words of Pius XII's encyclical, *Munificentissimus Deus*, this dogma affirms that:

According to His general rule, God does not will to grant the full effect of the victory over death to the just until the end of time shall have come. And so it is that the bodies of even the just are corrupted, and that only on the last day will they be joined, each to its own glorious soul. Now God has willed that the Blessed Virgin Mary should be exempted from this general rule. She, by an entirely unique privilege, completely overcame sin by her Immaculate Conception, and as a result she was not subject to the law of remaining in the corruption of the grave, and she did not have to wait until the end of time for the redemption of her body.[1]

Coming as the result of nearly a century of effort, mostly French and Italian, the decision was immensely popular with the faithful masses but was a matter of concern to some theologians, both at the time and in the years preceding the definition.[2] Prior to

[1] Pius XII, 'Munificentissimus Deus', *Acta Apostolicae Sedis*, 42 (1950), 754; trans. Joseph C. Fenton, 'Munificentissimus Deus', *The Catholic Mind*, 49 (1951), 65.

[2] It was perhaps most notably a concern to those theologians actively engaged in ecumenical dialogue, who feared that the definition would bring an end to Catholic–Protestant dialogue: Paul E. Duggan, 'The Assumption Dogma: Some Reactions and Ecumenical Implications in the Thought of English-Speaking Theologians' (STD diss., International Marian Research Institute,

the definition, for instance, certain German Catholic scholars, perhaps most notably J. Ernst, had challenged the dogma's definability on historical grounds.[3] Consequently, a papal committee was established and charged with investigating whether or not the Assumption ought to be defined as a dogma of the church. The result was a body of scholarship determined to locate the Dormition traditions, and more specifically a tradition of the Virgin's Assumption, as close to the apostolic age as is possible, in an effort to lend historical support to the papal definition. This effort marks the birth of modern, critical study of the ancient Dormition traditions.

The results of this campaign were rather disappointing, as evidenced particularly by the voluminous studies of Martin Jugie, who (together with Carolus Balić) was charged with combing the earliest Christian centuries in search of historical evidence supporting the definition of this dogma.[4] Despite years of research, the historical record has still yielded no clear witness to the Virgin's Dormition and Assumption from the earliest church. Rather surprisingly, the early centuries of Christianity, as they are preserved for us today, maintain a profound silence regarding the end of Mary's life. The pre-Nicene Fathers show complete disregard for this event, not even mentioning her death, and only at the end of the fourth century does this gap in the early Christian tradition first generate any visible concern.[5]

University of Dayton, 1989), 11. For a specific example, see Karl Rahner, 'Zum Sinn des Assumpta-Dogmas', in *Schriften zur Theologie* (Einsiedeln: Benziger, 1967), 239–52.

[3] As cited in Joseph Duhr, SJ, *The Glorious Assumption of the Mother of God*, trans. John Manning Fraunces, SJ (New York: P. J. Kennedy & Sons, 1950), pp. ix–x.

[4] The sum of Jugie's work is found in Martin Jugie, AA, *La Mort et l'assomption de la Sainte Vierge: Étude historico-doctrinale*, Studi e Testi, 114 (Vatican City: Biblioteca Apostolica Vaticana, 1944). Balić's work consisted primarily in collecting significant fragments from the Fathers that touched on the Dormition and Assumption: Carolus Balić, OFM, *Testimonia de Assumptione Beatae Virginis Mariae ex omnibus saeculis. Pars prior: ex aetate ante concilium tridentine* (Rome: Academia Mariana, 1948). Regarding their roles (and Jugie's in particular) in researching the dogma's history, see Duggan, 'The Assumption Dogma', 57–63.

[5] For a short but pithy consideration of the patristic literature on this topic see Walter J. Burghardt, SJ, *The Testimony of the Patristic Age Concerning Mary's Death* (Westminster, MD: The Newman Press, 1957).

As with the events of Mary's birth and childhood, the writings of the New Testament are similarly silent regarding the end of Mary's life. Yet for one reason or another, while the early Christians rather swiftly produced narratives of the Virgin's early life, they were not so quick in supplying accounts of her death. Already by the second century, Christians had begun to circulate stories of the Virgin's life before the Annunciation,[6] but evidence of a similar concern with the details of her life after her son's ascension does not emerge for several more centuries.

This long and profound silence surrounding the end of Mary's life first arouses concern only late in the fourth century, when Epiphanius of Salamis pauses momentarily during his energetic refutation of the heretics in the *Panarion* to reflect on the disquieting fact that he can find no authorized tradition about how the Virgin's life ended.[7] Despite Epiphanius' close contacts with Palestine, where the cult of the Virgin's tomb would soon

---

[6] The primary example is the *Protevangelium of James* (C. Tischendorf, ed., *Evangelia Apocrypha*, 2nd edn. (Leipzig: 1876; repr. Hildesheim: Georg Olms, 1966), 1–50). For the date see Wilhelm Schneemelcher, ed., *New Testament Apocrypha*, rev. edn., 2 vols., trans. and ed. R. McL. Wilson (Philadelphia: Westminster, 1991), i. 423.

[7] A few Patristic authors, some possibly predating Epiphanius, note Mary's death as a matter of fact, generally in the context of Mary remaining a virgin until her death: (Ps.-) Ephrem, *Hymni de beata Maria*, 15. 2 (J. Lamy, ed., *S. Ephraemi Syri hymni et sermones*, 4 vols. (Mechliniae: H. Dessain, 1882–1902), ii. 583), The authenticity of these hymns is disputed: see Edmund Beck, 'Die Mariologie der echten Schriften Ephräms', *Oriens Christianus*, 40 (1956), 22. See also, however, Burghardt's criticism of Beck's judgement: *Testimony*, 44 n. 4. Similar testimony may be found in (Ps.-)Origen, *comm. in Io.*, frg. 31 (E. Preuschen, ed., *Origenes Werke*, iv. *Der Johanneskommentar*, GCS 10 (Leipzig: J. C. Hinrichs, 1903), 506); regarding the inauthenticity of this passage see Ronald E. Heine, 'Can the Catena Fragments of Origen's Commentary on John be Trusted?' *Vigiliae Christianae*, 40 (1986), 118–34, esp. 120 and 130. See also Severian of Gabala, *creat. 6* (PG 56. 498). Finally, there is similar testimony in Augustine, *Tract. eu. Io.* 8. 9 (R. Willems, ed., *Tractatus in evangelium Ioannis*, CCL 36 (Turnhout: Brepols, 1954), 88), where he attributes Mary's death to original sin (!) (note that elsewhere Augustine explains that Mary was without sin, 'out of honor to the Lord': Augustine, *Nat. et grat.* 36. 42 (C. F. Urba and J. Zycha, eds., *De natura et gratia liber*, CSEL 60 (Leipzig: G. Freytag, 1913), 263–4)). Contrary to some suggestions, Gregory of Nyssa, *virg.* 14 [13] (V. W. Callahan, J. P. Cavarnos, and W. Jaeger, eds., *Gregorii Nysseni Opera*, viii pt. 1, *Opera Ascetica* (Leiden: E. J. Brill, 1952) 306–7) does not refer to the Virgin's death: clearly in this passage it is Christ and not Mary's virginity that defeats death.

develop, he professes a complete ignorance of the Virgin's final days. This is not for want of searching, however: Epiphanius reports that he has carefully investigated the matter and uncovered several possibilities, but ultimately he cannot decide which of these alternatives bears the truth. Epiphanius begins by addressing the biblical tradition, apologizing that the Scriptures are silent on this matter 'because of the overwhelming wonder, not to throw men's minds into consternation'.[8] Despite this apology, Epiphanius quickly turns to the New Testament for clues as to how the Virgin's earthly life may have come to a close. He first considers Symeon's prophecy that 'a sword shall pierce your own soul too',[9] thinking that this might suggest Mary's death as a martyr. Then Epiphanius turns to chapter 12 of John's Apocalypse, which describes 'a woman clothed with the sun, with the moon under her feet, and on her head a crown of stars',[10] who gave birth to a son. When attacked by 'the dragon', she was 'given the two wings of the great eagle, so that she could fly from the serpent into the wilderness, to her place where she is nourished for a time, and times, and half a time'.[11] His attacks thwarted, the dragon then turns to persecute her children. This passage, Epiphanius proposes, may indicate that Mary did not die as other human beings, but somehow remained immortal, although he makes clear his own uncertainty and refrains from advocating this view.[12]

Many other exegetes across the centuries have not shared Epiphanius' caution, interpreting this 'woman clothed with the sun' as a reference to Mary's immortality and Assumption. This reading has been especially popular with certain Roman Catholic

---

[8] Epiphanius, *haer.* 78, 11. 2–3 (ed. Karl Holl; J. Dummer, 2nd edn., *Epiphanius: Ancoratus und Panarion*, 3 vols., GCS 25, 31 (2nd edn.), 37 (2nd edn.) (Leipzig: J. C. Hinrichs, 1915; Berlin: Akademie Verlag, 1980, 1985), vol. iii (GCS 37), 462; trans. Frank Williams, *The Panarion of Epiphanius of Salamis*, NHS 36 (Leiden: E. J. Brill, 1994), 609).

[9] Luke 2: 35. This and all subsequent biblical citations are from the NRSV, unless otherwise noted.

[10] Rev. 12: 1.

[11] Rev. 12: 14.

[12] Epiphanius, *haer.* 78. 11. 4 (Holl/Dummer, *Epiphanius*, iii (GCS 37), 462, 17–19), 'Perhaps this [Rev. 12: 13–14] can be applied to her; I cannot decide for certain, and I am not saying that she remained immortal. But neither am I saying that she died.' Williams, *Panarion*, 609.

thinkers who, faced with the scandalous lack of any formal testimony regarding the end of the Virgin's life in the earliest
Christian writings, have sought to identify here an implicit testimony to the Virgin's Assumption.[13] Nevertheless, this biblical
passage in no way answers the general absence of early witnesses
to the end of Mary's life: Epiphanius is the first known writer to
propose (tentatively) such an interpretation, and he fails to tell us
whether anyone had actually ever advocated the identification of
the Virgin with the 'woman clothed with the sun', leaving the
distinct possibility that he may have first drawn this tentative
connection on his own. Although this exegesis would subsequently become quite popular and has endured even to this
day, there is no evidence of its existence before Epiphanius. On
the contrary, the early church unanimously identified this
apocalyptic woman with the church.[14] For the most part this
hermeneutic trend continues in later patristic literature, where
the Virgin is only infrequently identified with this apocalyptic
woman, an interpretation that was first advocated (excluding
Epiphanius) in a fifth-century sermon of Quodvultdeus, and in
the East only in the early sixth-century commentary on the
Apocalypse by Oecumenius.[15]

Ultimately Epiphanius cannot himself decide if either of these
two biblical traces is trustworthy, and, hedging his bets, he concludes: '[I] am not saying that she remained immortal. But
neither am I affirming that she died.'[16] This is in fact the general
tenor of his entire discussion of the matter: throughout he very
carefully avoids endorsing any of the possibilities he raises,
merely noting their existence and some of the evidence in favour
of each position. This does not necessarily mean, however, that
when Epiphanius was completing his *Panarion* (*c.*377) there

---

[13] Jugie, *La Mort*, 12–14, 33.

[14] Hilda Graef, *Mary: A History of Doctrine and Devotion*, i. *From the
Beginnings to the Eve of the Reformation* (New York: Sheed & Ward, 1963), 27–8:
Graef describes this interpretation as belonging especially to 'modern times'.

[15] Quodvultdeus, *Sermones de symbolo* 3. 1 (R. Braun, ed., *Opera Quodvultdeo
Carthaginiensi episcopo tributa*, CCL 60 (Turnhout: Brepols, 1976), 349). Oecumenius, *Apoc.* (H. C. Oskier, ed., *Commentary of Oecumenius of Tricca on
the Apocalypse*, University of Michigan Humanistic Series, 23 (Ann Arbor:
University of Michigan Press, 1928), 135–6).

[16] Epiphanius, *haer.* 78. 11. 2–3 (Holl/Dummer, *Epiphanius*, iii (GCS 37),
462; trans. Williams, *Panarion*, 609).

were as of yet no developed traditions about the end of the Virgin's life in circulation; it merely reveals that there was no authoritative or orthodox tradition (in his view) to which he could turn. Quite to the contrary, Epiphanius' indecisive reflections themselves suggest that some difference of opinion had already arisen among Christians as to whether Mary actually died or remained immortal, a difference which Epiphanius could not resolve through recourse to either biblical or church tradition. There appear to have been at least three basic options in circulation by the late fourth century, which Epiphanius identifies as follows:

The holy virgin may have died and been buried—her falling asleep [αὐτῆς ἡ κοίμησις] was with honor, her death in purity, her crown in virginity. Or she may have been put to death—as the scripture says, 'And a sword shall pierce through her soul'—her fame is among the martyrs and her holy body, by which light rose on the world, [rests] amid blessings. Or she may have remained alive, for God is not incapable of doing whatever he wills. No one knows her end.[17]

As usual, Epiphanius here carefully avoids taking a position on what was for him an undefined point of dogma; instead, he chooses to report several distinct possibilities without embracing one or the other. That certain Christian groups actually espoused some of these opinions at this time is almost certain. A number of post-Nicene writers mention Mary's death, usually in context of Mary having remained a virgin until she died,[18] while belief in Mary's martyrdom is corroborated by Ambrose, who seeks to refute this 'error' as having no foundation either in Scripture or tradition.[19] In regard to the possibility that Mary did not die, Epiphanius is the first witness to such a tradition, since there is no obvious parallel to this view in either contemporary or later sources: although the early Dormition traditions clearly imagine Mary's 'death' to have been in some sense special, they are quite insistent on the reality of her death as important proof of her son's consubstantiality with humanity.[20]

---

[17] Epiphanius, *haer.* 78. 23. 9 (Holl/Dummer, *Epiphanius*, iii (GCS 37), 474; trans. Williams, *Panarion*, 619). [18] See n. 7 above.

[19] Ambrose, *Luc.* 2. 61 (C. and H. Schenkl, eds., *Expositio evangelii secundum Lucam*, CSEL 32. 4 (Leipzig: G. Freytag, 1902; repr. New York: Johnson Reprint Co., 1962), 74).

[20] On this fact, see e.g. Édouard Cothenet, 'Marie dans les Apocryphes', in

As various modern investigators have returned to Epiphanius' ancient quandary, they have found themselves confronted more or less with the same options that met Epiphanius at the end of the fourth century. In general, however, these modern investigators have not remained as 'impartial' as was Epiphanius in his cautious and non-partisan report of the various possibilities uncovered by his research. Martin Jugie, for instance, after decades of researching the matter on the Vatican's behalf, emerged as a modern champion of Mary's immortality, a view which he laboured to promote in his publications as the earliest (and thus, true) view regarding the end of Mary's life.[21]

It was surely no coincidence that this was more or less the direction taken by the Vatican in its decision to pronounce the Assumption dogma. In view of the striking absence of early historical evidence, the Vatican proceeded to establish the Assumption dogma primarily on a dogmatic rather than a historical basis. It was determined that despite the complete lack of any historical evidence for early belief in the Virgin's Assumption, the dogma should still be proclaimed on the basis of other already well-established dogmas, all of which implied that Mary

Hubert du Manoir, SJ (ed.), *Maria: Études sur la Sainte Vierge*, 7 vols. (Paris: Beauchesne et ses Fils, 1952–66), vi. 145.

[21] Jugie argued (*La Mort*, 70–6) that a homily *In Simeonem et Annam* attributed to a certain 'Timothy of Jerusalem' witnessed to a tradition about the end of the Virgin's life, and more specifically, her immortality, from the end of the 4th or the beginning of the 5th cent. He dated the text by this otherwise unknown author to this period based on the absence of any mention of Mary's Jerusalem tomb (a legend that he incorrectly believed began to take shape only around 550; for more on this, see the following chapter), the absence of any anti-Nestorian polemic, and the use of παρθένος instead of θεοτόκος. Bernard Capelle, however, has convincingly shown that the homily was composed sometime between the 6th and 8th centuries (Bernard Capelle, 'Les Homélies liturgique de prétendu Timothée de Jérusalem', *Ephemerides liturgicae*, 63 (1949), 5–26). Jugie, however, was unconvinced: see his *L'Immaculée Conception dans l'Écriture sainte et dans la tradition orientale*, Collectio Edita Cura Academiae Marianae Internationalis, Textus et Disquisitiones, Bibliotheca Immaculatae Conceptionis, 3 (Rome: Academia Mariana/Officium Libri Catholici, 1952), 74–5 n. 3. According to my knowledge, there is, as of yet, no critical edition of this text, but a critical edition of the relevant passage may be found in Othone Faller, SJ, *De priorum saeculorum silentio circa Assumptionem b. Mariae virginis*, Analecta Gregoriana, Series Facultatis Theologicae, 36 (Rome: Gregorian University, 1946), 27. For the complete text, see PG 86. 237–54, where this passage occurs at 245.

did not in fact actually die, but remained immortal.[22] Two of these dogmas had already been identified by the early Byzantine church fathers: Mary's Divine Maternity and Perpetual Virginity. Germanus of Constantinople (715–30), for instance, reasoned that as the 'Mother of Life', it was indeed impossible that Mary should die: 'death will not boast of you, because you have borne Life in your womb'.[23] Likewise, Germanus argued this point from Mary's Perpetual Virginity, maintaining that because her body had been transformed by this 'into the highest life of incorruptibility . . . it was impossible that this body be subdued by the murderous confinement of the tomb'.[24] To this the Western Church would later add the dogmas of the Immaculate Conception and Original Sin, which together suggested Mary's immortality: if Mary was immaculately conceived and therefore did not possess original sin, then it was necessary that she was bodily assumed and did not taste death, since she lacked that which causes human beings to die.[25] In the light of such

[22] A good explanation of this dogmatic reasoning is to be found in Caspar Friethoff, OP, 'The Dogmatic Definition of the Assumption', *The Thomist*, 14 (1951), 41–58, esp. 42–3. See also Duggan, 'Assumption Dogma', 13.

[23] Germanus of Constantinople, *Homily on the Dormition II* [*or*. 8] (*PG* 98. 361C). This and all other translations are, unless otherwise specified, my own. See also John of Damascus: 'How shall the realm of death receive her? How shall corruption dare to assault that body once filled with life? These things do not belong to her; they are foreign to both the soul and body of the one who bore God. Death saw her and was afraid.' John of Damascus, *Homily on the Dormition II* [*hom*. 9. 3] (P. Voulet, ed., *Homélies sur la nativité et la dormition*, SC 80 (Paris: Les Éditions du Cerf, 1961), 132–3; trans. Brian E. Daley, SJ, *On the Dormition of Mary: Early Patristic Homilies* (Crestwood, NY: St Vladimir's Seminary Press, 1998), 207).

[24] 'Your virginal body is utterly holy, utterly pure, truly the dwelling-place of God, and because of this it endures and does not know earthly dissolution. Transformed, even though it is human, into the highest life of incorruptibility, this body is intact and supremely glorious, of a perfect life and sleepless, because it was impossible that this body be subdued by murderous confinement of the tomb, as it was the vessel that received God and a temple animated by the most holy divinity of the Only-Begotten.' Germanus, *Homily on the Dormition I* [*or*. 6] (*PG* 98. 345B).

[25] 'Now God has willed that the Blessed Virgin Mary should be exempted from this general rule. She, by an entirely unique privilege, completely overcame sin by her Immaculate Conception, and as a result she was not subject to the law of remaining in the corruption of the grave, and she did not have to wait until the end of time for the redemption of her body.' Pius XII, 'Munificentissimus Deus', 754; translation: Fenton, 'Munificentissimus Deus', 65.

dogmatic reasoning then, and at the urging of Jugie in particular, the 1950 definition deliberately left open the question of the Virgin's actual death.

The Vatican's statement, however, is somewhat more careful than was Jugie himself, and like Epiphanius, the 1950 definition similarly falls short of asserting Mary's immortality, presumably because there is such strong consensus in the earliest Dormition traditions that Mary's death was necessary in order to ensure her son's consubstantiality with humanity. The resulting tension has made for an often ambiguous relationship between Roman Catholic scholarship and the earliest Dormition traditions.[26] For instance, many Roman Catholic theologians have spurned these 'apocryphal' traditions, and appealing to the inclusion of the 'Transitus Mariae' among the list of apocrypha condemned by 'Pope Gelasius', they frequently have argued that these apocrypha already stand under an ancient papal censure.[27] But others, including Jugie's 'successor' Antoine Wenger and various scholars at the Studium Biblicum Franciscanum in Jerusalem, have taken a more positive approach to these ancient legends, recognizing their critical importance for any possibility of understanding the earliest beliefs regarding the end of Mary's life. They are, as Wenger explains, 'streams from murky waters, but occasionally they bear in their muddy waters flecks of gold that will never be tarnished'.[28]

Nevertheless, the spectre of *Munificentissimus Deus* always looms large in these and other studies of the ancient Dormition

[26] See e.g. Jugie, *La Mort*, 167–71, where he concludes that the apocrypha are of no 'historical' value, and while they may tell us something about later developments in Marian piety, they are in no way indicative of a tradition of Mary's Dormition and Assumption that reaches back to the apostles. It is perhaps worth noting that this conclusion may have been inspired by their emphasis on Mary's death, which contradicted Jugie's own immortalist faith.

[27] e.g. Joseph Duhr, SJ, *Glorious Assumption*, 36. Although these theologians invest the decree with Papal authority, its author was not Pope Gelasius, but an otherwise unknown Christian of sixth-century Gaul. See Schneemelcher, *New Testament Apocrypha*, i. 38. For a critical text and a more detailed argument, see Ernst von Dobschütz, *Das Decretum Gelasianum de libris recipiendis et non recipiendis*, TU 38. 4 (Leipzig: J. C. Hinrichs, 1912), esp. 334–57. See also Jugie, *La Mort*, 167–71.

[28] Antoine Wenger, AA, *L'Assomption de la T. S. Vierge dans la tradition byzantine du VIe au Xe siècle*, Archives de l'orient chrétien, 5 (Paris: Institut Français d'Études Byzantines, 1955), 67.

traditions, even many that set out to be deliberately non-confessional. As may be expected, Wenger, who, like his mentor Jugie, was an Assumptionist priest, was particularly concerned to identify traditions of the Virgin's bodily Assumption that were as early as possible. In doing so, Wenger employed traditional philology, and it is very much to his credit that, despite his unconcealed prejudice, his analysis of the texts then at his disposal is very reliable and relatively unbiased. In addition to publishing several key texts, Wenger's work resulted in a stemma diagramming the patterns of textual influence and filiation among approximately twenty of the early Dormition narratives.[29] In many ways this labour has laid the foundation for critical study of these traditions, and several of Wenger's hypotheses have been confirmed by subsequent discoveries. But perhaps Wenger's most important contribution was his determination that the strikingly diverse traditions of Mary's Dormition and Assumption arise from 'a great variety of original types',[30] rather than being the result of a progressive modification of a single, original tradition. His recognition of this fact is evident particularly in the decision to include in his stemma only certain early narratives that are clearly joined by close literary relations, rather than attempting to create stemma including all the then known narratives.

This diversity of 'original types', however, has been only infrequently recognized by other students of these traditions, even in quite recent studies. Various scholars of the Studium Biblicum Franciscanum in Jerusalem, for instance, including Bellarmino Bagatti, Emmanuele Testa, and Frédéric Manns (among others), collectively share a somewhat similar view that the origins of the Dormition traditions lie in certain Palestinian Jewish Christians, whose practice and theology were quite distinct from the Gentile church that is much better known from our ancient sources.[31] Bagatti, who is in some sense the founder

[29] This stemma is found ibid. 66, and it forms the basis of the first of van Esbroeck's two stemmata, published in his 'Les Textes littéraires sur l'assomption avant le Xe siècle', in François Bovon (ed.), *Les Actes apocryphes des apôtres* (Geneva: Labor et Fides, 1981), 270.

[30] Wenger, *L'Assomption*, 17.

[31] See, however, the important recent criticism of this group of scholars by Joan E. Taylor, *Christians and the Holy Places: The Myth of Jewish-Christian Origins* (Oxford: Clarendon Press; New York: Oxford University Press, 1993),

of this school of interpretation, argued that during or shortly after the apostolic age a group of Jewish Christians in Jerusalem preserved an oral tradition about the end of the Virgin's life. This 'original' version is more or less known today from certain of the earliest Dormition apocrypha, a select group of narratives that all, rather unsurprisingly, express a rather clear belief in the Virgin's bodily Assumption, thus offering historical support for the modern dogma.[32] Testa has in some sense expanded on Bagatti's initial theory, extending its historical scope to include an account of the Dormition legends' subsequent development within the 'church of the Gentiles'. In this way, Testa orders the different literary types (which will be identified below) in chronological succession, explaining how these primitive

where she challenges their rather speculative theories regarding the importance of these hypothetical Jewish Christians. Regarding the traditions of Mary's death and her tomb, see esp. 202–4. Manns presents a slightly different view from the others, according to which the 'original' tradition was produced by a member of a Johannine 'rabbinic school' with Jewish-Christian tendencies, similar to the Jewish rabbinic schools of Shammai and Hillel. See Frédéric Manns, OFM, *Le Récit de la dormition de Marie (Vatican grec 1982), Contribution à l'étude de origines de l'exégèse chrétienne*, Studium Biblicum Franciscanum, Collectio Maior, 33 (Jerusalem: Franciscan Printing Press, 1989), esp. 115–19. A brief summary of Manns' argument may be found in his article 'La Mort de Marie dans les textes de la Dormition de Marie', *Augustinianum*, 19 (1979), 507–15.

[32] Bellarmino Bagatti, OFM, 'Ricerche sulle tradizioni della morte della Vergine', *Sacra Doctrina*, 69–70 (1973), 186–94; idem, 'La morte della Vergine nel Testo di Leucio', *Marianum*, 36 (1974), 456–7. An excellent summary of Bagatti's work on the Dormition traditions can be found in Lino Cignelli, OFM, 'Il prototipo giudeo-cristiano degli apocrifi assunzionisti', in Emmanuelle Testa, Ignazio Mancini, and Michele Piccirillo (eds.), *Studia Hierosolymitana in onore di P. Bellarmino Bagatti*, ii. *Studi esegetici*, Studium Biblicum Franciscanum, Collectio Maior, 23 (Jerusalem: Franciscan Printing Press, 1975), 259–77. Bagatti summarizes the Mariology of these supposed Palestinian Jewish Christians in his *Alle origini della chiesa*, i. *Le comunità giudeo-cristane* (Vatican City: Libreria Editrice Vaticana, 1981), 66–8. See also Ignazio Mancini, OFM, *Archaeological Discoveries Relative to the Judaeo-Christians: Historical Survey*, trans. G. Bushell, Publications of the Studium Biblicum Franciscanum, Collectio Minor, 10 (Jerusalem: Franciscan Printing Press, 1970), 159. In this English summary of the Franciscan school's studies of the 'Church from the Circumcision', Mancini notes that Jean (Cardinal) Daniélou, who very much approved of Bagatti and Testa's work, cited their interpretation of the early Dormition traditions along these lines as an important demonstration of the Assumption dogma's antiquity.

traditions were reshaped by the 'Gentile church' after it adopted
the original form of the legend from the descendants of the
original Jerusalem community sometime in the fourth or fifth
century. Thus, the single, original tradition of the early Jewish
Christians, which records the Virgin's bodily Assumption, was
altered in successive stages according to certain doctrinal needs
of the 'church of the Gentiles', resulting in the theological and
narrative diversity of the traditions as they stand today.[33]

An altogether different development of dogma has been proposed by certain others, including most recently the prolonged
argument by Simon Mimouni in favour of an alternative evolution of these traditions. Although portions of Mimouni's work
have been published separately in various articles, these have
mostly been gathered together with additional material in his
Dormition et Assumption de Marie.[34] Like many other scholars
before him, Mimouni identifies three main literary traditions,
which are roughly the same as those described below in the
present chapter. In approaching these distinct traditions, however, Mimouni has revived an older theory proposed in 1961
by Édouard Cothenet, who in turn drew his inspiration from
the earlier work of Donato Baldi and Anacleto Mosconi.[35] Like
Bagatti and Testa, this group of scholars interprets the different
literary types as successive forms of what amounts to a single

---

[33] Emmanuele Testa, OFM, 'L'origine e lo sviluppo della *Dormitio Mariae*',
Augustinianum, 23 (1983), 249–62. Testa presents a more detailed argument
for his position in 'Lo sviluppo della "Dormitio Mariae" nella letteratura, nella
teologìa e nella archeologìa', *Marianum*, 44 (1982), 316–89. It should be noted
that many of Testa's conclusions are not well supported by the textual evidence
and are highly speculative in general.

[34] Simon C. Mimouni, *Dormition et assomption de Marie: Histoire des traditions anciennes*, Théologie Historique, 98 (Paris: Beauchesne, 1995). See also,
idem, 'La Fête de la dormition de Marie en Syrie à l'époque byzantine', *The
Harp*, 5 (1992), 157–74; idem, 'Genèse et évolution des traditions anciennes
sur le sort final de Marie. Étude de la tradition litteraire copte', *Marianum*,
42 (1991), 69–143; idem, ' "Histoire de la Dormition et de l' Assumption de
Marie": Une nouvelle hypothèse de recherche', *Studia Patristica*, 19 (1989),
372–80; idem, 'La Tradition littéraire syriaque de l'histoire de la Dormition et
de l'Assomption de Marie', *Parole de l'Orient*, 15 (1988–9), 143–68.

[35] Cothenet, 'Marie dans les Apocryphes'; Donato Baldi, OFM and Anacleto
Mosconi, OFM, 'L'Assunzione di Maria SS. negli apocrifi', in *Atti del congresso
nazionale mariano dei Fratei Minori d'Italia (Roma 29 aprile–3 maggio 1947)*,
Studia Mariana, 1 (Rome: Commissionis Marialis Franciscanae, 1948), 75–125.

tradition, with one narrative type displacing its predecessor as changes occurred in Christian dogma. But in contrast to the theories of the Jerusalem friars, with their emphasis on a primitive belief in the Assumption, Mimouni and his predecessors have argued that belief in the Virgin's Assumption is the final dogmatic development, rather than the point of origin, of these traditions. That is, from an originally Assumptionless tradition, the narratives have gradually evolved to affirm a belief in Mary's Assumption. Mimouni proposes in his study to confirm this theory with the 'objective' testimony of liturgical history and archaeology, but as we shall see in subsequent chapters, these phenomena in no way afford the support that Mimouni claims, and the sort of linear, successive development that Mimouni and others have supposed is not at all indicated by the earliest traditions, which, on the contrary, testify against it.

Despite his occasional criticisms of the dogmatic prejudices guiding many previous scholars, Mimouni's work is without doubt the most theologically oriented study yet to have appeared. By this I do not mean that it is beholden to the faith claims of a particular community, but rather that the study is from start to finish controlled by Mimouni's (ultimately) theological conviction that the belief in Mary's Dormition without an Assumption is original, and that belief in her Assumption only developed at a later time, arguing that the 'more complex' belief in the Assumption must have evolved from the 'more simple'.[36] Moreover, theology is the organizing principle of the entire investigation: the narratives are not classified and studied on the basis of their literary relations, but instead according to whether or not they are seen to espouse the dogma of the Assumption. In fact, Mimouni wilfully rejects the often undeniable evidence of literary relations, evidence which he himself at times acknowledges, in favour of a theologically oriented classification. As we will have occasion to see in subsequent chapters, Mimouni does not hesitate to separate texts that from a literary point of view are identical in the name of theology. Even when their identity is unmistakable (by his own admission), Mimouni rejects this relation in order to make the corpus conform to his understanding of a dogmatic evolution. As he himself professes on several

---

[36] See e.g. Mimouni, *Dormition*, 19 n. 49.

occasions, such literary relations are neither significant nor a suitable means of classifying the texts: Mimouni clearly prefers dogma.[37] But as this study will demonstrate, such dogmatic organization is questionable in itself, and not only because it so unabashedly contradicts the literary history of these traditions. It is especially problematic because for the most part such classification imposes the categories and distinctions of modern discourse surrounding the Assumption of Mary onto the ancient narratives.[38] As will be shown in Ch. 3, these categories do not fit the ancient data well, and Mimouni has often had to twist certain narratives in order make them fit into one or another of his categories.

In various other ways *Munificentissimus Deus* lurks in the background of Mimouni's study, which is somewhat surprising, given Mimouni's criticism of the dogmatic concerns that have influenced much previous scholarship.[39] Yet because the connections with *Munificentissimus Deus* in this instance are not quite so explicit as in many other cases, they are not immediately obvious, perhaps even to Mimouni. It is not a matter of 'negative' influence, as one might at first glance suspect. While one could superficially interpret Mimouni's 'anti-Assumptionist' historiography as a critical response both to the dogma and the pro-Assumptionist stance of much previous scholarship, in all fairness, this is not the tone of Mimouni's work. Instead, the relationship between Mimouni's work and the modern dogma is even more complex and comes primarily as a consequence of Mimouni's font of inspiration.

Although Mimouni frequently describes his approach as 'une nouvelle hypothèse de recherche', it is basically Édouard Cothenet's hypothesis revived and somewhat refined,[40] and this

---

[37] 'A notre avis la présence de thêmes littéraires dans un texte n'est pas signifiante.' Simon C. Mimouni, 'Histoire de la Dormition et de la Assomption de Marie: Recherche d'histoire littéraire' (Thèse de diplôme, École Pratique des Hautes Études, Section des Sciences Religieuses, 1988), 102. See also his criticism of Michel van Esbroeck's work in idem, *Dormition*, 49: 'Cette classification repose sur des thématiques littéraires. Or, la présence de thèmes littéraires dans un texte ne paraît pas suffisante.'

[38] See Mimouni, *Dormition*, 13–21, where he develops his categories of analysis primarily on the basis of 19th- and 20th-century theology, relying on Jugie in particular.   [39] Ibid. 6.

[40] Mimouni acknowledges something of this debt following his description of

source bears the hidden link between Mimouni's proposed reconstruction and the 1950 dogma. An examination of Cothenet's original presentation of this model for understanding the early Dormition traditions reveals that, like so many others, it too has a definite theological agenda with regard to the Assumption dogma, a tendency that Mimouni's work seemingly inherits, unwittingly, from its ancestor. Published in a 7-volume collection of essays by Roman Catholic scholars on 'la Sainte Vierge' (complete with 'Nihil Obstat' and 'Imprimatur'), Cothenet's discussion of the ancient Dormition apocrypha concludes with significant reflection on how his reconstruction of their earliest history relates to the modern dogma of the Assumption. In his remarks Cothenet poses a strong challenge to Jugie's decision that the Dormition apocrypha are historically worthless and in no way represent an apostolic tradition.[41] As noted above, Jugie's dismissal of the apocrypha was crucial for maintaining his own theological views, since the earliest narratives clearly attest to Mary's death and tomb. Since these data conflicted with his own immortalist belief, Jugie argued that these traditions were rather late, and not worthy of much consideration from a dogmatic viewpoint. But Cothenet argues instead that the earliest apocrypha belong to the late second century, and consequently that the origin of these traditions can probably be traced back to the original 'apostolic deposit of faith', of which the first apocrypha are themselves a development.[42]

On the basis of the early apocrypha, Cothenet proposes that while belief in Mary's Assumption was not a component of this initial deposit, belief in the Assumption was nevertheless a logical development of this kernel of tradition, which establishes a continuity between the Assumption dogma and the teaching of the primitive church. The earliest apocrypha, according to Cothenet, described only Mary's Dormition and knew nothing of her Assumption. From this origin, however, the traditions first passed through an intermediate narrative form, which was a

Cothenet's work: 'On peut considérer que la typologie établie par É. Cothenet est directement à l'origine de l'hypothèse de travail qui sera proposée', *Dormition*, 48–9.

[41] Jugie, *La Mort*, 167–71.
[42] Cothenet, 'Marie dans les Apocryphes', 144–5, 148.

dogmatic hybrid, and eventually developed into their final narrative form, which clearly articulates the Virgin's bodily Assumption. In this way, Cothenet explains, the early apocrypha 'manifest how, under the influence of the Holy Spirit, the Church has become progressively aware of Mary's total glorification'.[43] Thus, the Dormition apocrypha are, in Cothenet's view, evidence of the sort of dogmatic development that has often been espoused in modern Roman Catholicism. These apocrypha, as Cothenet interprets them, demonstrate that belief in the Assumption stands as an authentic development of the original apostolic deposit, a doctrine that, although it was not first articulated perhaps for centuries, was implicit in this initial deposit of faith.[44]

Although Mimouni himself does not develop his research in this direction, the influence of such theological thinking is evident in the sort of dogmatically oriented approach that he takes. His concern with demonstrating the discrete, successive evolution from one dogmatic position to another clearly owes a great deal to the more confessionally oriented research of his predecessors, who sought in the development of dogma assurances of more 'recent' beliefs. But this is not the only way in which the events of 1950 have impacted Mimouni's thinking. As we will see when discussing the 'original' milieu[x] of these traditions in the final chapter, Mimouni's speculation regarding the catalyst that sparked this dogmatic development also conceals the lingering influence of *Munificentissimus Deus*.

In drawing attention to the looming presence of this papal decree in much previous study of the Dormition traditions, it is not my intention to belittle what is otherwise often very fine scholarship, as I have attempted to indicate, when such praise is indeed due. Rather, it is important that this influence be recognized for what it is, so that we may develop new interpretations

---

[43] Cothenet, 'Marie dans les Apocryphes', 146–8.

[44] This theology of the 'development of doctrine', especially as it impacts the early church, is perhaps best exemplified in the work of John Henry Cardinal Newman, who writes: 'The absence, or partial absence, or incompleteness of dogmatic statements is no proof of the absence of impressions of implicit judgments, in the mind of the church. Even centuries might pass without the formal expression of a truth, which had been all along the secret life of millions of faithful souls.' 'The Theory of Developments in Religious Doctrine', in *Conscience, Consensus, and the Development of Doctrine* (New York: Image Books, 1992), 13.

that take a somewhat less dogmatic approach to the corpus. Moreover, I do not mean to imply in pointing out the theological biases of my predecessors that I intend to follow with an interpretation of the early Dormition tradition that will somehow transcend this 'limitation', freeing these traditions at last from their theological 'confinement'. Quite to the contrary, my understanding of the Dormition traditions has been shaped by particular theological and ideological concerns, commitments from which no scholar is ever free. I do not propose to give an 'objective' account of the Dormition narratives, but one that is necessarily engaged with them, yet at the same time, one that maintains a critical coherence with the historical evidence.

Ideologically, this study is inspired by a concern to identify diversity in the early Christian tradition and to emphasize differences, rather than homogenize them. Moreover, in contrast to certain other scholars and theologians, I do not understand these differences as deviations from or developments of some original truth, but rather as sacrifices to the emergence of 'orthodoxy', a totalizing discourse that silenced many of these dissonant notes in the process of harmonizing Christian doctrine. This study seeks in part to hear once again, strange though it may sound to our ears, the unusual loss of modality effected as the competing traditions of ancient Christianity are enabled to sound simultaneously, as well as to expose the process by which certain traditions were silenced and others transposed in the creation of a discourse of orthodoxy. In developing this approach, I will emphasize the diversity of the early Dormition traditions, arguing in particular for their diverse origins and parallel development, as first proposed by Wenger, as well as exhuming the peculiar, and quite heterodox, milieu which seems to have birthed many of the earliest traditions.

THE ANCIENT TRADITIONS OF MARY'S DORMITION AND ASSUMPTION

The primary focus of this study will be on those Dormition narratives that came into existence before the Islamic conquest of the Near East in the middle of the seventh century. There are several reasons for drawing this boundary, not the least of which is to make this rather considerable corpus somewhat more manageable. Other less arbitrary reasons, however, suggest this as a useful limit for investigating the earliest history of these traditions. On the one hand, the Islamic conquest brought drastic changes to the late ancient Near East, and although one would not want to overemphasize the difference between the early Byzantine and early Islamic Near East, the events of the seventh century were pivotal for the history of Christianity in this region. More importantly, however, the Dormition traditions themselves also suggest such a divide. There is a striking difference between the pre-Islamic Dormition apocrypha and homilies, and the middle Byzantine homilies that followed, written by such luminaries of the church as John of Damascus, Andrew of Crete, and Germanus of Constantinople. These post-Islamic homilies are more encomiastic and less narrative than their predecessors: they very briefly and cautiously sketch the narratives of the ancient traditions, replacing their detail with much theological reflection and rhetorical praise of the Virgin.[45] Consequently, we will treat here the earliest stage of the Dormition traditions, as represented in the pre-Islamic narratives, which will be collectively referred to as the 'ancient' Dormition traditions.

In moving backwards from this date, we are unfortunately limited by the state of our sources. As the beginning of this chapter has made clear, there is no evidence of any tradition concerning Mary's Dormition and Assumption from before the fifth century. The only exception to this is Epiphanius' unsuccessful attempt to uncover a tradition of the end of Mary's life towards the end of the fourth century, and his failure confirms the otherwise deafening silence. The fifth century itself also has very little to offer, until the very end, when the first fragments of a Dormition narrative appear, as well as limited indications from a few independent sources that confirm a sudden interest at this time in the end of Mary's life. Perhaps the earliest of these external witnesses is the *Acts of John* by Ps.-Prochorus, an early Byzantine retelling of the apostle's wondrous deeds that focuses especially on John's activity on Patmos but incorporates many

---

[45] See e.g. Brian E. Daley, SJ, *On the Dormition of Mary: Early Patristic Homilies* (Crestwood, NY: St Vladimir's Seminary Press, 1998), 27–35.

extracts from the earlier, second-century *Acts of John* as well.[46] In a somewhat disputed passage, the text briefly mentions the end of the Virgin's life as having occurred sometime before the dispersal of the apostles.[47]

While this passage may very well be one of the earliest witnesses to the Dormition traditions, it is somewhat difficult to establish an accurate date for Ps.-Prochorus' *Acts of John*, and, since the narrative is extant in around 150 manuscripts with numerous variants, it is often problematic to distinguish ancient material from later interpolations. Most scholars agree that this orthodox rehabilitation of John's ministry was probably composed sometime during the fifth century, with the intention of superseding the older, somewhat heterodox *Acts of John*. But there is no similar consensus as to which of the many variants belong to this earliest version of the text.[48] Richard Lipsius, for instance, the text's editor, regards this reference to Mary's death as an interpolation, while Eric Junod and Jean-Daniel Kaestli consider the passage authentic and in fact rely on it as the primary means of dating the original text.[49] According to the two latter scholars, the indication that Mary's death took place sometime before the dispersal of the apostles is a strong pointer to the tradition's antiquity, since the early Dormition traditions generally describe a time after the apostles were already scattered throughout the world, a fact necessitating their miraculous travel to the Holy Land to be with the Virgin at her departure

[46] According to Junod and Kaestli, it is not a matter of Ps.-Prochorus having a copy of the ancient *Acts of John* in front of him, but rather he knows these fragments from oral traditions or other texts that have drawn on the *Acts of John*. Eric Junod and Jean-Daniel Kaestli, *L'Histoire des actes apocryphes des Apôtres du IIIe au IXe siècle: Le cas des Actes de Jean*, Cahiers de la revue de théologie et de philosophie, 7 (Lausanne: La Concorde, 1982), 111.

[47] 'Now that his [the Holy Spirit's] grace has come upon us all, let us seek after nothing except what has been commanded by the master, especially because the mother of us all has departed this life.' Ps.-Prochorus, *a. Io.* (Theodor Zahn, ed., *Acta Joannis* (Erlangen, 1880; repr. Hildesheim, 1975), 3–4).

[48] Zahn, *Acta Joannis*, p. lix; Richard A. Lipsius, ed., *Die apokryphen Apostelgeschichten und Apostellegenden*, 2 vols. (Brunswick, 1883–90; repr. Amsterdam: Philo Press, 1976), i. 406–7; Eric Junod and Jean-Daniel Kaestli, eds., *Acta Iohannis*, 2 vols., CCSA 1–2 (Turnhout: Brepols, 1983), ii. 749.

[49] Lipsius, *Die apokryphen Apostelgeschichten*, i. 407; Junod and Kaestli, *Acta Iohannis*, ii. 749.

from this world.[50] Consequently, it is rather unlikely that this dissonant passage would be interpolated at a later time, when the Dormition traditions had grown quite strong and uniform; rather, its omission from a number of manuscripts on account of its contradicting an established tradition is much more likely. In all probability then, this passage and the remainder of Ps.-Prochorus' narrative were composed sometime during the fifth century, before the Dormition traditions in the forms that we know them had gained a firm hold on the imagination of the early Christian mainstream.

Another important early witness, from around the same time or probably a little later, is the so-called *Tübingen Theosophy*, an apologetic text composed around 500, whose contents are known to us only through an eighth-century Byzantine epitome.[51] From this epitome we know that the *Theosophy*'s author made use of several apocrypha, including a work described as γεννήσεως καὶ ἀναλήψεως τῆς ἀχράντου δεσποίνης ἡμῶν θεοτόκου, 'the birth and assumption of our lady the immaculate Theotokos'.[52] Although this work has been strangely ignored in previous studies of the ancient Dormition traditions, it forms a valuable witness to the existence of these traditions in written form before the turn of the sixth century.[53] There is some question as to whether the *Theosophy* here refers to one or two works, but for the reasons given by Pier Franco Beatrice, I am convinced that this passage refers to a single work, more or less.[54] In our earliest Syriac manuscripts, from the late fifth and sixth centuries, the narration

[50] Certain early Coptic texts are the only exceptions to this pattern, but even in these Coptic traditions only a few of the apostles are involved, and it seems that the others have already dispersed. Ps.-Melito's *Transitus* places the Dormition only two years after the Ascension, but the apostles have nevertheless already dispersed. It would appear that the occurrence of the Dormition after the dispersal of the apostles and their miraculous reunion quickly became cornerstones of the Dormition traditions.

[51] Pier Franco Beatrice, 'Traditions apocryphes dans la *Théosophie de Tübingen*', *Apocrypha*, 7 (1996), 109–10; idem, 'Pagan Wisdom and Christian Theology According to the *Tübingen Theosophy*', *Journal of Early Christian Studies*, 3 (1994), 403–4.

[52] *Tübingen Theosophy*, 4 (Hartmut Erbse, ed., *Theosophorum Graecorum Fragmenta* (Stuttgart: Teubner, 1995), 2–3).

[53] Beatrice, 'Traditions apocryphes', 113–14, comments on the peculiar absence of this witness from previous scholarship.

[54] Ibid. 114–15. I very sharply disagree with Beatrice, however, concerning

of Mary's Dormition is prefaced by the *Protevangelium of James* and the *Infancy Gospel of Thomas*, all three of which seem arranged into a single unit that transmits the birth and Assumption of Mary.[55] This recognition is particularly important, since it signals the existence of a particular type of Dormition narrative in the late fifth century, about which more will be said below.

Roughly contemporary with the *Tübingen Theosophy* is the Ps.-Dionysian corpus, which also bears witness to the traditions of Mary's Dormition. While its actual author remains a mystery, scholars think that this collection of mystical writings originated in western Syria sometime around the year 500.[56] In the following passage from *On the Divine Names*, this unknown author refers to what appears to be the Virgin's Dormition: 'As you know, we and he and many of our holy brothers met together for a vision of that mortal body, that source of life, which bore God [ἐπὶ τὴν θέαν τοῦ ζωαρχικοῦ καὶ θεοδόχου σώματος συνεληλύθαμεν]. James, the brother of God, was there. So too was Peter, that summit, that chief of all those who speak of God.'[57] Martin Jugie strongly objected to the interpretation of this passage as a witness to Mary's Dormition, since it contradicted his immortalist views. He maintained instead that the 'body' to which the author

the particular type of Dormition narrative to which the *Theosophy* refers. Although Beatrice begins by linking this reference to the Syriac Six Books, with which it should be linked, he ends up with the conclusion that the fragments probably refer to the *Obsequies/Liber Requiei* narrative, since this appears to be the earliest. It seems that Beatrice is led astray by an assumption that the different types of the Dormition narratives stand in chronological succession to one another, and thus only the one, 'original' type, represented in the *Obsequies/Liber Requiei*, could be extant at this time.

[55] William Wright, 'The Departure of My Lady Mary from this World', *The Journal of Sacred Literature and Biblical Record*, 6 (1865), 417; Agnes Smith Lewis, ed., *Apocrypha Syriaca*, Studia Sinaitica, XI (London: C. J. Clay & Sons, 1902), x. This pattern is also exemplified by Göttingen MS syr. 10.

[56] See the discussion of the date in Paul Rorem and John C. Lamoreaux, *John of Scythopolis and the Dionysian Corpus: Annotating the Areopagite*, Oxford Early Christian Studies (Oxford: Clarendon Press; New York: Oxford University Press, 1998), 9–11.

[57] Ps.-Dionysius the Areopagite, *d. n.* III, 2 (Beate Regina Suchla, ed., *Corpus Dionysiacum*, i. *Pseudo-Dionysius Areopagite De divinis nominibus*, Patristische Texte und Studien, 33 (Berlin/New York: Walter de Gruyter, 1990), 141; trans. Colm Luibhéid (and Paul Rorem), *Pseudo-Dionysius: The Complete Works*, The Classics of Western Spirituality (New York: Paulist Press, 1987), 70).

here refers is most likely the Eucharist, rather than Mary, and only in later centuries did writers (incorrectly, in his opinion) come to identify this 'body' with the Virgin.[58] Consequently, this passage has not figured very significantly in many subsequent discussions of the earliest traditions of Mary's departure from this life. But subsequent studies of the Dionysian corpus have shown that Jugie's rather rough dismissal was undeserved.

In particular, more recent scholarship has demonstrated that the identification of this 'life-giving body that bore God' with the Virgin's is somewhat earlier than was commonly thought in Jugie's time. A passage from the *Scholia* on the Dionysian corpus, an early commentary on the writings of Ps.-Dionysus, explains that 'by "source of life which bore God" [the author] means the body of the holy Theotokos who at that time fell asleep [κοιμηθείσης]'.[59] Like others of his day, Jugie attributed these *scholia* to Maximus the Confessor, but recent investigations have shown that most of these comments, including this one in particular, were actually written by John of Scythopolis, sometime between 537 and 543.[60] Thus we may be rather certain that, even if this meaning was perhaps not the author's original intention, within a few decades of the initial appearance of the Dionysian corpus, this passage had come to be understood as a reference to the Virgin's Dormition.

Also from approximately this same time are the different versions of the Coptic *Gospel of Bartholomew*, an apocryphon that most scholars would date to sometime in the fifth or sixth century.[61] Of the three extant recensions, two are very fragmentary, but we are fortunate that one of the fragmentary versions and the complete version both briefly describe the Virgin's Dormition.[62] Since the fragmentary versions are

---

[58] Jugie, *La Mort*, 99–101.

[59] John of Scythopolis [Ps.-Maximus the Confessor], *schol. d. n.* 3 (PG 4. 236; trans. Rorem and Lamoreaux, *John of Scythopolis*, 199–200).

[60] Rorem and Lamoreaux, *John of Scythopolis*, esp. 39 and 272.

[61] Schneemelcher, *New Testament Apocrypha*, i. 537; J. K. Elliott, *The Apocryphal New Testament* (Oxford: Clarendon Press, 1993), 652.

[62] The two fragmentary versions have been published in Pierre Lacau, ed., *Mémoires publiés par les membres de l'institut français d'archéologie orientale du Caire*, ix. *Fragments d'apocryphes coptes* (Cairo: Imprimerie de l'institut français d'archéologie orientale, 1904), version A: 25–32 (Copt.) and 33–7 (Fr.); version B: 43–66 (Copt.) and 67–77 (Fr.). The complete version (C) has been published

generally judged to be somewhat earlier than the complete manuscript, I give here the version of the episode as found in the fragments, although the version from the complete text is not very different:

And he said to her, 'When you have gone forth from the body, I will come to you myself with Michael and Gabriel. We will not allow you to have fear in the face of Death, whom the whole world fears. I will bring you to the places of immortality, and you will be with me in my kingdom. And I will place your body under the tree of life, where a cherub with a sword of fire will watch over it, until the day of my kingdom.[63]

Here Christ promises his mother that at her death, he will come to meet her, sparing her from seeing the terrifying face of Death when her soul goes forth from the body. In many of the earliest Dormition narratives, Mary is very concerned about having to face the powers of Death when leaving the body, but she reassures herself of her son's promise to meet her soul himself. Later in these same narratives, when Mary dies, Christ in fact comes with his angels to meet his mother, so that powers of Death do not beset her soul as it leaves her body, and he takes her body to rest in Paradise beneath the Tree of Life, as the *Gospel of Bartholomew* foretells.[64] Like the *Tübingen Theosophy* then, the *Gospel of Bartholomew* seems to be aware of certain early Dormition traditions that survived unto the present, namely, the 'Palm of the Tree of Life' traditions, the first of several that we will now discuss.

These four witnesses merely confirm, however, what we know more directly from the Dormition narratives themselves, since the earliest exemplars of these appear at approximately the same time, the late fifth and early sixth centuries. The sudden appearance of these traditions at this moment identifies this time as the era when the various traditions of the end of Mary's life first became an important component of the now well-preserved

in E. A. W. Budge, ed., *Coptic Apocrypha in the Dialect of Upper Egypt* (London: British Museum, 1913), 1–49 (Copt.) and 179–215 (Eng.).

[63] *The Gospel of Bartholomew* (Lacau, *Mémoires*, 58 (Copt.) and 72 (Fr.); see also the complete version in Budge, *Coptic Apocrypha*, 15 (Copt.) and 192 (Eng.)). Regarding the priority of the fragments, see Schneemelcher, *New Testament Apocrypha*, i. 537.

[64] This can be seen in the narratives translated in Appendices A and B, for instance.

'orthodox mainstream' of ancient Christianity. Although there are indications that some of these narratives had a prior existence somewhere outside this mainstream, as will be seen in the final chapter, the end of the fifth century was the moment when these traditions were first embraced by the varieties of Christianity that were emerging as victorious from the ideological conflicts of early Christianity.

As if a reflection of Christianity's primitive diversity, not one, but several different traditions appear at this time, and each of these distinct narratives types is represented among the earliest extant narratives. In addition to two major textual families, there is also a significant sub-family, as well as a substantial number of atypical narratives, these being accounts that do not belong to one of the main textual families, but instead present a more or less unique account of the end of Mary's life. There is near unanimity among scholars regarding the existence of these three literary types, but interpreters have often disagreed over the relationships among these different families and, occasionally, regarding the appropriate classification of individual narratives within these families. These issues, however, will be addressed in the third chapter, and for now, it will suffice to describe the various narrative types, on which there is substantial agreement, and to identify those narratives within each family that likely belong to the period here under consideration, the period before the Islamic conquest of the Near East.

A. The 'Palm of the Tree of Life' Traditions

The largest of the two major textual groupings is often known as the 'Palm of the Tree of Life' family, so called because of the importance that these traditions ascribe to a certain 'Palm' taken from this mythical tree (see Fig. 1). The literary relations among the various members of this family are rather well established, owing primarily to Wenger's groundwork, in which he created a stemma including all the traditions from this textual family that were known at his time.[65] Michel van Esbroeck has since updated

---

[65] This stemma is found in Wenger, *L'Assomption*, 66. Much of the textual commentary in Wenger's study describes the basis for this stemma. Wenger himself built on the previous others working primarily on the Latin and Irish versions, including J. Rivière, 'Le Plus Vieux "Transitus" latin et son dérivé

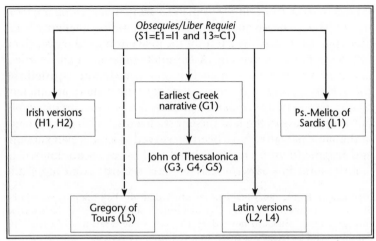

FIG. 1. Basic outline of the ancient Palm traditions and their literary relations

Wenger's stemma by including a number of more recently published texts, but as van Esbroeck's stemma indicates, the original insights of Wenger have not been challenged, only confirmed, by these subsequent discoveries.[66]

The earliest witness to these literary traditions, and perhaps the earliest extant Dormition narrative, is preserved in a set of Syriac fragments, dated by paleography to the late fifth and early sixth centuries. Identified in the earliest fragment as the *Obsequies of the Holy Virgin*, these fragments were published in the middle of the nineteenth century by William Wright.[67] The

grec', *Recherches de théologie ancienne et médiévale*, 8 (1936), 5–23; Bernard Capelle, 'Les Anciens Récits de l'Assomption et Jean de Thessalonique', *Recherches de théologie ancienne et médiévale*, 12 (1940), 209–35; John D. Seymour, 'Irish Versions of the Transitus Mariae', *Journal of Theological Studies*, 23 (1921–2), 36–43; R. Willard, 'The Testament of Mary: The Irish Account of the Death of the Virgin', *Recherches de théologie ancienne et médiévale*, 9 (1937), 341–64.

[66] This stemma is found in van Esbroeck, 'Les Textes', 270.

[67] William Wright, ed., *Contributions to the Apocryphal Literature* (London: Williams & Norgate, 1865), ܡܣܘ-ܡܢ (Syr.) and 42–51 (Eng.); for date see 6, 10–11. Note also that Wright has elsewhere dated the earliest of these fragments to the beginning of the 6th century: idem, *Catalogue of the Syriac Manuscripts of the British Museum Acquired Since the Year 1838*, 3 vols. (London, 1870), i. 369. Mimouni bases much of his study on a belief that these fragments belong to the

fragments describe scattered episodes from much a longer narrative of Mary's death and resurrection, including a lengthy fragment partially detailing a tour of the heavens that Mary received
following her resurrection. A complete version of this earliest
narrative survives only in an Ethiopic translation, entitled the
Liber Requiei, and in those sections for which there are ancient
Syriac parallels, the *Liber Requiei* is seen to be a remarkably
faithful witness to the late ancient traditions.[68] Other fragments
of the same narrative have been preserved in a Georgian version,
and fragments of a closely related early version are known in
Coptic, some in a papyrus that has only recently come to light.[69]

'Bethlehem' family described below, rather than the Palm family. As will be
demonstrated in Ch. 3, Mimouni's classification of these fragments is incorrect
and misleading. See also now Mary Clayton, 'The Transitus Mariae: The
Tradition and Its Origins', *Apocrypha*, 10 (1999), 76–82.

[68] Victor Arras, ed., *De Transitu Mariae Aethiopice*, 2 vols., CSCO 342–3
(Louvain: Secrétariat du CorpusSCO, 1973), i. A lengthy fragment of this
narrative was earlier edited in A. van Lantschoot, 'Contributions aux actes de s.
Pierre et de s. Paul', *Le Muséon*, 68 (1955), 17–46 and 219–33. Because the *Liber
Requiei* had not yet been published, van Lantschoot was unable to identify the
fragment with these traditions. The faithfulness of the *Liber Requiei* to these
ancient versions is demonstrated in Ch. 3 below, as well as by the appended
translation of the *Liber Requiei* and these fragments. See also Arras, *De Transitu*,
i. 75–105 (Lat.) regarding the *Liber Requiei* as a bearer of the earliest traditions,
and also Clayton, 'Transitus Mariae', 74–85. Wenger was able to predict the
existence of such a narrative based on his knowledge of the earliest Palm traditions, and consequently his commentary on these is also valuable for understanding the relation of the *Liber Requiei* to the other early representatives of the
Palm family (*L'Assomption*, 17–95).

[69] Georgian fragments: Michel van Esbroeck, 'Apocryphes géorgiens de la
Dormition', *Analecta Bollandiana*, 92 (1973), 55–75; these have also been edited
in Tamila Mgaloblišvili, ed., ქართული მრავალთავი (*K'larjuli mravaltavi
[The Klardjeti Homiliary]*), Zveli kartuli mcerlobis zeglebi, 12 (Tbilisi:
'Metsnieba', 1991), 420–5. Coptic fragments: E. Revillout, ed., *Évangile des
douze apôtres*, PO 2. 2 (Paris: Librairie de Paris/Firmin-Didot et Cie, 1907),
174–83. Other Coptic fragments have recently been published by Philip Sellew,
'An Early Coptic Witness to the *Dormitio Mariae* at Yale: P. CtYBR inv. 1788
Revisited', *Bulletin of the American Society of Papyrologists*, 37 (2000), 37–69.
A preliminary edition was made by Leslie S. B. MacCoull, 'More Coptic Papyri
from the Beinecke Collection', *Archiv für Papyrusforschung*, 35 (1989), 25–35,
with plate 4, an edition now superseded by Sellew's. I thank Professor Sellew
for sharing his work with me before its publication. There is, however, a
peculiar problem with the Yale Coptic fragments: although several of the fragments preserve extremely close parallels to the other early Palm narratives, the
order of the first several fragments is opposite to that of the other Palm narra-

An abbreviated version of this earliest narrative survives in a sixth-century Greek version, edited by Wenger. As Wenger has demonstrated in the commentary to his edition, a narrative very similar to this one formed the basis for John of Thessalonica's early seventh-century homily for the Dormition.[70] John of Thessalonica's homily itself was delivered sometime between 610 and 649 placing it at the very end of the period under primary consideration.[71]

In addition to these eastern witnesses, there are numerous western narratives belonging to the Palm family (which is the only literary tradition attested in the West), and many of these also preserve early traditions. Although these narratives have often significantly abbreviated the fuller, eastern witnesses that were presumably their sources, in their totality they offer important confirmation regarding the antiquity of much that is found in the more verbose eastern accounts. Among the various Latin narratives, the *Transitus* attributed to Ps.-Melito of Sardis is perhaps the earliest, dated almost universally to the fifth century, primarily on the basis of its topographical dissimilarity with the later tradition, in particular, its location of Mary's house on the Mount of Olives.[72] Nevertheless, a number of other Latin

tives (for more on this, consult the notes to translation of the Ethiopic *Liber Requiei* in this volume). The order in the papyrus text is unquestionable, being clearly established by the artefact itself. There is no obvious explanation for this divergence, and one can only guess that the original Coptic manuscript may have preserved excerpts or was a rather free composition that drew on the earlier traditions of the Palm narrative. The fact that the final three fragments do not find close parallels with the early Palm narratives could also indicate either of these possibilities.

[70] Wenger, *L'Assomption*, 210–41 (text) and 17–67 (commentary).

[71] John of Thessalonica, *dorm. BMV A & B*, (Martin Jugie, AA, ed., *Homélies mariales byzantine (II)*, PO 19. 3 (Paris: Librairie de Paris/Firmin-Didot et Cie, 1926), 344–438); the first version (pp. 375–405) is the earliest, while the second is a later, interpolated version, which none the less occasionally bears important witness to the earliest traditions. John was metropolitan of Thessalonica, 610–49.

[72] Text: Monika Haibach-Reinisch, ed., *Ein neuer 'Transitus Mariae' des Pseudo-Melito* (Rome: Pontificia Academia Mariana Internationalis, 1962). On the 5th-century date, see Faller, *De priorum saeculorum silentio*, 42–63; H. Lausberg, 'Zur literarischen Gestaltung des Transitus Beata Mariae', *Historisches Jahrbuch*, 72 (1935), 46; Wenger, *L'Assomption*, 90–1; Haibach-Reinisch, *Ein neuer 'Transitus Mariae'*, 45–7; D. M. Montagna, 'Appunti critice sul Transitus B. V. Mariae dello Pseudo-Melitone', *Marianum*, 27

versions are important for understanding the earliest history of this literary family, including especially two texts published by

(1965), 184. Jugie (*La Mort*, 112) concludes, on the basis of the narrative's identification of Mary's house on the Mount of Olives, that it must have been written by 550 at the latest. Mimouni (*Dormition*, 272) acknowledges that a 5th-century date is in fact the scholarly consensus, but he challenges this dating based on his theory of dogmatic development from the Dormition to the Assumption. Since Ps.-Melito describes the Virgin's Assumption, on this basis alone Mimouni assigns the narrative to the late 6th or 7th century. Nevertheless, unless one shares Mimouni's presuppositions regarding the development from Dormition into Assumption, he provides no other argument for such a late date. For reasons that will be made clear in Ch. 3, this sort of dogmatic evolution is not supported by the evidence, and thus this is not a credible reason for dating Ps.-Melito's narrative to this time. See also the remarks of Michel van Esbroeck specifically on this point in 'Some Early Features in the Life of the Virgin', *Marianum* (2001) (forthcoming). Mary Clayton, in her recent study of the Old English Dormition narratives, has similarly argued for a late 6th or 7th century date for Ps.-Melito: *The Apocryphal Gospels of Mary in Anglo-Saxon England*, Cambridge Studies in Anglo-Saxon England, 26 (Cambridge: Cambridge University Press, 1998), 85. In doing so, however, she suddenly relies primarily on Mimouni, agreeing with his observation that the 'advanced character of the text in doctrinal terms' suggests such a date (I fail to see how the existence of 8th-century manuscripts favours this later dating, as Clayton additionally suggests). For Mimouni, any reference to 'more advanced dogma' means belief in the Assumption, which he believes to be a later development. Clayton's assent to Mimouni's argument in this instance is particularly odd, since throughout the introduction to her study, as well as in a recent article ('Transitus Mariae'), she has persistently criticized Mimouni, precisely on the point of positing such a dogmatic evolution and dating texts accordingly. For Clayton suddenly to rely on both Mimouni's work and his method here is both surprising and inconsistent. Consequently, her arguments for dating Ps.-Melito to the late 6th or 7th century are not convincing. Furthermore, her assertion that 'there is little justification for such an early date' (*Apocryphal Gospels*, 72) is misleading. The primary reason for dating the work to the late 5th century is, as indicated above, the remarkable topographical dissimilarity between Ps.-Melito and the remainder of the Dormition traditions: namely that Ps.-Melito locates the Virgin's house 'near the Mount of Olives', an identification attested in no other Dormition tradition and at odds with the traditions locating her house on Zion and her tomb near Gethsemane (for more on this, see Ch. 2). Moreover, this narrative's indication that Mary was living with John at the time of her death stands at odds with the other early Dormition traditions, according to which John had already gone forth to preach the Gospel with the other apostles at this time. Finally, the narrative's prologue identifies it as a response to earlier heterodox works on the same subject, which indicates that this is one of the earliest 'orthodox' narratives. Clayton fails to address these points, all of which suggest the antiquity of Ps.-Melito's narrative.

Wilmart and Wenger respectively.[73] Gregory of Tours also gives an important précis of these early traditions in his *In gloria Martyrum*.[74] Finally, there is an early Irish version, preserved in two different recensions, that was probably translated sometime before 712. This text, in spite of its considerable geographic distance, is a key witness to the earliest traditions from the eastern Mediterranean, which probably reached Ireland early on via traffic through Spain.[75]

The basic outline of these Palm narratives runs as follows. Mary is met on the Mount of Olives by an angel who announces her impending death and gives her a palm from the Tree of Life. In several of the earliest narratives, the angel recounts some of his past acts, as a demonstration of his authority, including events from the Holy Family's flight to Egypt and the time of Israelite captivity in Egypt. Mary then returns to her house in Jerusalem, where she calls together her friends and family to inform them of her impending death. At this point, the apostles are miraculously transported from the ends of the earth, to which they had formerly dispersed. John arrives first, alone, and in the

[73] A. Wilmart, ed., *Analecta Reginensia: Extraits des manuscrits Latins de la Reine christine conservés au Vatican*, Studi e Testi, 59 (Vatican: Biblioteca Apostolica Vaticana, 1933), 323–62; Wenger, *L'Assomption*, 245–56. The importance of these two narratives for understanding the earliest history of these traditions is made clear by Wenger, ibid. 17–95.

[74] B. Krusch, ed., *Gregorii Episcopi Turonensis miracula et opera minora*, 2nd edn., Monumenta Germaniae Historica, Scriptores Rerum Merovingicarum, 1. 2 (Hanover: Impensis Bibliopolii Hahniani, 1969), 39 and 43.

[75] One of these versions has been published with translation by C. Donahue, ed., *The Testament of Mary: The Gaelic Version of the Dormitio Mariae together with an Irish Latin Version*, Fordham University Studies, Language Series, 1 (New York: Fordham University Press, 1942). On the date, see pp. 25–7. A translation of the second version has been published by Máire Herbert and Martin McNamara, eds., *Irish Biblical Apocrypha* (Edinburgh: T. & T. Clark, 1989), 119–31. On the Irish link to the East in late antiquity through Visigothic Spain, see J. N. Hillgarth, 'The East, Visigothic Spain, and the Irish', *Studia Patristica*, 4 (1961), 442–56. Hillgarth identifies a process of literary transmission from the East to Ireland through Visigothic Spain. This cultural connection with the East owed its existence to a late ancient trade route running from the eastern Mediterranean through the straits of Gibraltar to Ireland and south-west Britain. The existence of this trade pattern is known from remains of eastern Mediterranean pottery found in Ireland and northern Britain: see Charles Thomas, *The Early Christian Archaeology of North Britain* (London: Oxford University Press, 1971), 22–5.

earliest versions Mary entrusts him with certain secret items
and/or sayings, as well as the palm. The rest of the apostles
follow shortly thereafter, and Peter is clearly identified as the
leader of the apostles. During the night before she dies, Peter
delivers a lengthy discourse to those who have gathered, and
when morning arrives, Mary prepares herself for death. Those
present are miraculously put to sleep, except only for the apostles
and three virgins, who witness Christ's arrival with a company
of angels. Christ then receives in his hands Mary's soul, which
appears as an infant clothed in white, and he hands her soul
over to Michael. The apostles then carry Mary's body outside
the city to a tomb at the foot of the Mount of Olives, beside
the garden of Gethsemane. During her funeral procession, however, the Jewish leaders plot to destroy the Virgin's body. Yet
when they attempt to carry out their plan, they are all stricken
with blindness, with one exception, a man named Jephonias,
who rushes her funeral bier and attempts to upset it. As soon
as Jephonias grasps the bier, an angel cuts off his hands, and
only by his conversion and prayers to the Virgin are they
restored. Then, Jephonias re-enters Jerusalem, and when he
reports what has happened, only those Jews who repent and
believe have their sight restored. Meanwhile, the apostles
continue on towards the tomb, and reaching it, they place the
Virgin's body inside. The apostles then sit awaiting Christ's
return outside the tomb, and when Paul asks the others to teach
him the 'mysteries' that Christ had taught them, a debate erupts
over how the Gospel should be preached. Several days after
Mary's death Christ returns, and, after vindicating the Pauline
version of the Gospel, he takes the body, along with the apostles,
to Paradise, where the Virgin's body and soul are rejoined.
Following this description of the Virgin's resurrection, the
earliest Palm narratives conclude with a tour of the places of
final reward and punishment before the apostles are returned
to earth, the Virgin remaining resurrected in the garden of
Paradise.

It is almost certain that these traditions were first written
down in Greek, although Syriac cannot be completely ruled out.
The transmission of these traditions in different versions and
languages presents a substantial number of variants that are best
explained by a Greek original lying behind the various extant

versions.[76] In favour of Syriac, one can appeal to the fact that the earliest witnesses to this tradition are the late fifth-century fragments published by Wright, to which Frédéric Manns adds a list of variants that he believes indicate a Semitic original.[77] Altogether, Manns' list is not as convincing as the evidence favouring a Greek original: not only are the variants fewer and often less significant, but they have been compiled based only on comparison of the *Liber Requiei* with the early Greek narrative published by Wenger. The indications of a Greek original, by contrast, arise from a comparison of all the early witnesses to the Palm tradition, from Irish to Georgian, a point that Manns neglects to consider. Moreover, an alternative explanation can be identified for those variants in the *Liber Requiei* that seem to arise from a Semitic context. Rather than indicating a Semitic original, these variants probably reflect the subsequent transmission of the *Liber Requiei* through Semitic languages, perhaps through Syriac or Arabic, or even Ethiopic itself. While Mann's list may perhaps indicate that the Ethiopic translation of the *Liber Requiei* was not made directly from a Greek original (although by no means should we rule this possibility out), these variants are easily explicable by transmission through Syriac or Arabic, both of which were primary sources of Ethiopic translations.[78]

[76] Arras has identified many such indicators of a Greek original in his brief commentary on the *Liber Requiei: De Transitu*, i. 75–105. A list of some of these is given by Frédéric Manns, *Le Récit*, 80–1. See also Michel van Esbroeck, 'Bild und Begriff in der Transitus-Literatur, der Palmbaum und der Tempel', in Margot Schmidt (ed.), *Typus, Symbol, Allegorie bei den östlichen Vätern und ihren Parallelen im Mittelalter* (Regensburg: Verlag Friedrich Pustet, 1982), 333–51, esp. 340–1; Mgaloblišvili, კლარჯული მრავალთავი, 474; and Mario Erbetta, *Gli apocrifi del Nuovo Testamento*, i pt.2. *Vangeli: Infanzia e passione di Cristo, Assunzione di Maria* (Casale: Marietti, 1981), 422–3 n. 2.

[77] Manns, *Le Récit*, 81–2. This is, of course, with the aim of attributing the origin of these traditions to an early Jewish-Christian group. For more on this topic, see Ch. 4.

[78] On the translation of texts from Syriac and Arabic, see Edward Ullendorff, *The Ethiopians: An Introduction to Country and People* (London: Oxford University Press, 1960), 138–9, 146. Translations from Greek and Syriac occurred primarily in the Axumite period, from the late 4th or early 5th century through the 7th century, while translations from Arabic (primarily Egyptian) belong generally to the medieval period. My suspicion would be that the *Liber Requiei*, like the books of *Jubilees* and *1 Enoch*, was translated during this earlier period, when biblical and ancient apocryphal material was first translated.

One particular point of comparison among the earliest Palm traditions that suggests their initial composition in Greek is the particular word used to designate the 'palm' in a given narrative. After the Jew Jephonias is healed by the apostles, they give him a piece from this palm with which he is to restore sight to those of his people who are willing to believe. In the earliest Greek traditions, this object is referred to as a θαλλεῖον ἐκ τοῦ βραβείου,[79] 'a branch from the palm'. This is a somewhat unusual usage of the word βραβεῖον, which is commonly used in reference to a 'prize' or a 'wand' or 'baton' that is given as a prize. Paul and other early Christian writers frequently use βραβεῖον in reference to the 'prize' awaiting Christians in the next life or for the martyr's crown. In the context of the early Dormition traditions alone, however, the term has been interpreted as a 'palm', for which one would normally expect to find the word φοῖνιξ.[80] The early Latin (and Irish) texts are quite explicit in identifying this object as a 'palma',[81] but in an often ignored fragment, the Syriac *Obsequies* describe this object as a ܩܠܐܕܐ ܡܢ ܗܕܐ ܫܒܛܐ, 'a branch from this staff' or 'rod'.[82]

---

[79] See John of Thessalonica, *dorm. BMV A* 13 (Jugie, *Homélies mariales byzantine (II)*, 401); Wenger's text, however, omits the word θαλλεῖον, reading only ἐκ τοῦ βραβείου instead (Wenger, *L'Assomption*, 238–9). But comparison with John's homilies, as well as the other early representatives of the Palm family, suggest that Wenger's text originally read as above: see *Liber Requiei* 76 (Arras, *De Transitu*, i. 45 (Eth.) and 29 (Lat.)) and the *Obsequies* (Wright, *Contributions*, 15), among others.

[80] See Lampe, *A Patristic Greek Lexicon*, Liddell-Scott-Jones, *A Greek–English Lexicon*, and Sophocles, *Greek Lexicon of the Roman and Byzantine Period*, s.v. βραβεῖον. The only lexicographical indication that the word can mean 'palm' is given by Lampe, and he cites only John of Thessalonica's homily on the Dormition as evidence of this usage. Gehard Kittel, *Theological Dictionary of the New Testament*, trans. Geoffrey W. Bromley, s.v. βραβεῖον, also notes that in early Christian literature the term had become an alternative expression for the martyr's crown.

[81] Sometimes a 'ramus palmae' (Haibach-Reinisch, *Ein neuer "Transitus Mariae"*, 66), but more often simply 'palma' (ibid. 82; Wenger, *L'Assomption*, 245; Wilmart, *Analecta Reginensia*, 354). The Irish reads 'pailm' (Donahue, *Testament of Mary*, 48).

[82] Wright, *Contributions*, 15; the fragment has probably been ignored since Wright failed to translate it. ܫܒܛܐ is a word generally meaning 'rod, staff, or sceptre', although it can potentially also mean 'stick' or even 'branch'; Wright identifies it as a 'staff' in his summary of the passage: see J. Payne Smith, *A Compendious Syriac Dictionary*, and R. Payne Smith, *Thesaurus Syriacus*, s.v. ܫܒܛܐ.

This variant from the earliest extant manuscript is significant for a number of reasons. On the one hand, it raises questions about the very nature of the object in question. In each of the early Palm narratives we are told that Peter took a 'branch' from this object and gave it to Jephonias so that with it he might heal those who had become blinded: but does he take this from a palm branch or from some sort of staff having palm leaves affixed to it?[83] It is interesting to note in this regard that while a palm often features prominently in Western depictions of the Dormition (where the language is quite clear), it is not represented in Eastern iconography.[84] The ambiguity of the Eastern narratives might find an explanation in the religious traditions of the ancient Near East, according to which kings and other authorities (such as Moses) held as a symbol of their authority a rod or staff that was in fact believed to be a branch from the Tree of Life. In many of these traditions, the Tree of Life was believed to be a date palm as it is here in the earliest Dormition traditions.[85] In the early Dormition narratives then, we might understand that such a staff had been sent from heaven in order to honour the Virgin in the events of her death. The narratives inform us that the angel brought this object from the heavens specifically so that the apostles would carry it in her funeral

[83] The question of this βραβεῖον's nature has been raised only, to my knowledge, by Leopold Kretzenbacher, *Sterbekerze und Palmzweig-Ritual beim 'Marientod': Zum Apokryphen in Wort und Bild bei der κοίμησις, dormitio, assumption der Gottesmutter zwischen Byzanz und dem mittlealterlicher Westen*, Österreichische Akademie der Wissenschaften, Philosophisch-Historische Klasse, Sitzungsberichte, 667 (Vienna: Verlag der Österreichischen Akademie der Wissenschaften, 1999), 17, where rather than asking the question, he dismisses it, asserting 'Es ist wesentlich, zu betonen, daß es sich bei unseren βραβεῖον / *bravium* nur um einen Palmzweig ("aus dem Paradiese") handelt.' Kretzenbacher does not, however, give any sort of an explanation for his conclusion. Moreover, he appears to indicate that in some Greek text or another the βραβεῖον is specified as 'τὸ δε ἦν κλάδος βαΐων φοινίκων', but I am unaware of any such instance: no reference is given. In general, this study does not present the ancient Dormition narratives very clearly or accurately.

[84] Ibid. 18.

[85] See Geo Widengren, *The King and the Tree of Life in Ancient Near Eastern Religion (King and Saviour IV)*, Uppsala Universitets Årsskrift, 1951: 4 (Uppsala: A. B. Lundequistska bokhandeln, 1951), 20–41; and E. O. James, *The Tree of Life: An Archaeological Study*, Studies in the History of Religions, Supplements to Numen, 11 (Leiden: E. J. Brill, 1966), 93–129.

procession, seemingly as a 'royal' emblem of sorts intended to represent her dignity as the mother of the 'king'. This processional function could potentially suggest such a staff, instead of a palm leaf, here being used as a royal standard of sorts.

Admittedly it is not altogether certain exactly what sort of object is being imagined here, but the ambiguity itself is highly significant for determining the language of origin. In this case, as in so many others, the variants in the different traditions can best be explained by positing a Greek original. If the word βραβεῖον holds potential for reading either 'palm leaf' or 'wand', then the divergent traditions may take their origin from the ambiguity of this Greek word, thereby suggesting a Greek original. Likewise the use of ܬܠܚܐ in the Syriac fragments to describe the 'palm-branch' points in this direction. The word ܬܠܚܐ is a Greek loanword (from θαλλός) not regularly used in Syriac, which normally uses the words ܣܘܟܐ or ܣܘܟܬܐ for 'branch', and occasionally even more specifically in reference to a palm-branch.[86] Now were these fragments initially composed in Syriac, one would expect to find one of these Syriac expressions, rather than a Greek word that is not usually part of the Syriac vocabulary. Consequently, the text's transcription of this Greek word, instead of using a Syriac word, suggests that the Syriac version was made from Greek *Vorlage* that contained the word θαλλός here, a word closely related to θαλλεῖον, as found in the earliest Greek Dormition narratives.

This is, however, only one of many indicators that these traditions derive from a Greek source, and even if we may not be entirely certain what such an *Urtext* may have looked like, the sum of the evidence strongly suggests a Greek origin for the Palm narratives. From this we may conclude with some confidence that these traditions antedate their initial appearance in the late fifth-century Syriac fragments, although we cannot be certain by how much.

Richard Bauckham has made an effort to date the earliest Palm narratives more precisely based on the apocalypse that brings the

---

[86] ܬܠܚܐ does not have a lexical entry in any of the various Syriac dictionaries that I have consulted, including R. Payne Smith, *Thesaurus Syriacus*. This is fairly solid indication that θαλλός is not one of the many Greek words that became a part of the standard Syriac vocabulary, and consequently that its appearance here is significant.

earliest narratives to a close, which he names the *Obsequies* apocalypse, after the title given to the fifth-century Syriac fragments that are its earliest witness. Through comparison of this apocalypse with other late ancient apocalyptic traditions, Bauckham concludes that the Palm narratives probably first took shape at least as early as the fourth century. This is particularly suggested by the close relationship between the *Apocalypse of Paul*, written around 400 CE, and the *Obsequies* apocalypse, which parallel each other in two main sections.[87] The first of these describes the punishments allotted to four individual sinners who held church offices, and the second reports the cries of the damned for mercy, the intercession of Paul and Michael, and the Saviour's grant of weekly respite for the damned. The comparison of these two passages suggests a literary dependence between these two texts, and the preponderance of the evidence appears to indicate the priority of the *Obsequies* apocalypse.

In the first place, Paul's vision of the four clerical sinners is the only instance in the *Apocalypse of Paul* where the punishments of specific individuals, as opposed to groups of sinners, are described. This would seem to indicate that the *Apocalypse of Paul* has here used a source, whose focus on these four individuals has been preserved. Moreover, in the *Obsequies* apocalypse, discussion of the specific punishments allotted to the damned is limited to only these four clerical sinners: there is no further discussion of additional punishments, as there is in the *Apocalypse of Paul*. These peculiarities are most easily explained by supposing that the *Apocalypse of Paul* has borrowed the episode involving the four clerical sinners from the *Obsequies* apocalypse, expanding on it by adding the further descriptions of punishments inflicted on groups of sinners. The alternative, that

---

[87] See *Apoc. Paul.* 34–6, 43–4 (Montague Rhodes James (ed.), *Apocrypha Anecdota*, Texts and Studies, II. 3 (Cambridge: The University Press, 1893), 29–30, 34–6. In a recent article Pierluigi Piovanelli isolates the composition of the *Apocalypse of Paul* within the period 395–416 CE: 'Les Origines de l'*Apocalypse de Paul* reconsidérées', *Apocrypha*, 4 (1993), 37–59. Most importantly, however, Piovanelli convincingly puts to rest a popular theory that there was an earlier version of the *Apocalypse of Paul*, written before 240, that later on was reworked into the version that has survived. The most recent representative of this view is Claude Carozzi, *Eschatologie et au-delà: Recherches sur l'*Apocalypse de Paul (Aix-en-Provence: Université de Provence, 1994), 165–73, although I do not find Carozzi's arguments convincing.

the *Obsequies* apocalypse has for one reason or another adopted only this unique scene from the *Apocalypse of Paul*, is comparatively less likely.[88]

The priority of the *Obsequies* apocalypse is also indicated by the different forms of Christ's response to Michael's pleas for mercy in the two texts. As Bauckham explains, Christ's response in the *Obsequies* apocalypse that the sinners are God's creation is a traditional form, evidenced in much earlier literature, while the form in the *Apocalypse of Paul*, lacking this emphasis, represents an innovation.[89] In regard to this difference, Bauckham notes that 'it is possible that the Obsequies Apocalypse is dependent on the Apocalypse of Paul and on the traditional form [of Christ's response] known independently, but it is somewhat easier to suppose that the Apocalypse of Paul is dependent on the Obsequies Apocalypse'.[90] Bauckham further observes that length of respite granted to the damned in these two texts additionally points to the priority of the *Obsequies* apocalypse. In the *Apocalypse of Paul*, the damned are given respite of a day and a night (Sunday) every week as a result of Paul's pleas, while in the *Obsequies* apocalypse, Mary and the apostles' collective intercessions secure only three hours of respite for the damned each week. As Bauckham concludes, this difference strongly suggests the priority of the *Obsequies* apocalypse: '[I]t seems odd that, if the concession in the Apocalypse of Paul were already known and used by the author of the Obsequies Apocalypse as his source, he should attribute to the intercessions of Mary and the

---

[88]   Richard Bauckham, *The Fate of the Dead: Studies on Jewish and Christian Apocalypses*, Supplements to Novum Testamentum, 93 (Leiden: Brill, 1998), 344–5. Cothenet too commented on the relationship between the early Dormition traditions and the *Apocalypse of Paul*, leading him to argue for a 3rd century origin: Cothenet, 'Marie dans les Apocryphes', 127–9.

[89]   *Liber Requiei* 94 (Arras, *De Transitu*, i. 55 (Eth.) and 36 (Lat.)): 'Do you love them more than the one who created them, or will you be more merciful to them than the one who gave them breath?'; *Apoc. Paul.* 33 (James, *Apocrypha Anecdota*, 29; trans. Elliott, *Apocryphal New Testament*, 634): 'Are you more merciful than God? For though God is good, he knows that there are punishments, and he bears patiently the human race, allowing each one to do his own will.'; *Apoc. Paul.* 40 (James, ed., *Apocrypha Anecdota*, 33; trans. Elliott, *Apocryphal New Testament*, 636): 'Are you more merciful than the Lord God, who is blessed forever, who has established judgment and sent forth every man to chose good and evil in his own will and do what pleases him?'

[90]   Bauckham, *Fate of the Dead*, 345–6.

apostles only three hours out of the twenty-four granted by Paul's intercession.'[91]

Finally, Mary's presence in Paradise at the close of the *Apocalypse of Paul* is an important additional point, overlooked by Bauckham, that appears to indicate the priority of the *Obsequies* apocalypse. The general narrative structure of the *Apocalypse of Paul* is identical to that of the *Obsequies* apocalypse. Paul, like Mary, is first taken to Paradise, from which he ventures forth to visit the places of the damned and intercede on their behalf. Following this, Paul and Mary each return to Paradise where they are greeted by the patriarchs and other biblical figures. Interestingly enough, however, in the *Apocalypse of Paul* the first person to greet Paul after his return to Paradise is the Virgin Mary.[92] This seems to indicate the *Apocalypse of Paul*'s knowledge of the ancient Dormition traditions, and, by consequence, its use of the *Obsequies* apocalypse. I am unaware of any ancient tradition describing Mary's presence in Paradise separately from the traditions of her Dormition,[93] and thus it seems rather likely that the *Apocalypse of Paul* has borrowed this tradition from the ancient Dormition traditions. Given this apparent awareness of the Dormition traditions, together with the assemblage of evidence identified by Bauckham, it begins to seem rather likely, as opposed to just merely possible, that the *Obsequies* apocalypse antedates the *Apocalypse of Paul* and was one of its sources.[94] If

[91] Ibid. 346.

[92] *Apoc. Paul.* 46 (James, ed., *Apocrypha Anecdota*, 37–8).

[93] The Greek and the Ethiopic *Apocalypse of the Virgin*, two texts of uncertain date, describe Mary's journey through the other world, but these are clearly later than the two texts here under consideration: see Bauckham, *Fate of the Dead*, 333–40. In *Ascens. Is.* 11. 2–16 (Paolo Bettiolo and Enrico Norelli, eds., *Ascensio Isaiae*, 2 vols., CCSA 7–8 (Turnhout: Brepols, 1995), i. 119–23), Isaiah has a vision of Christ's birth from Mary during his tour of the heavens, but this is clearly a vision of future events, rather than the actual presence of Mary somewhere in the heavenly realms.

[94] The *Obsequies/Liber Requiei* also shares with the *Apocalypse of Paul* an interest in the righteous and wicked angels that come upon a recently deceased soul. Although the two texts use similar language in describing their actions on the newly departed soul, the account in the *Obsequies/Liber Requiei* is *much* shorter than that in the *Apocalypse of Paul*, and the latter's more extensive version cannot be explained simply by literary dependence on the former. See *Liber Requiei* 40 (Arras, *De Transitu*, i. 23 (Eth.) and 15 (Lat.)); van Esbroeck, 'Apocryphes géorgiens', 60–1; *Apoc. Paul.* 11–18 (James, ed., *Apocrypha*

this is in fact the case, we may date the composition of the *Liber Requiei/Obsequies* narrative to the fourth century, at the latest, and as will be seen in the final chapter, the doctrinal peculiarities of this narrative confirm this as a *terminus ante quem* for the earliest Palm traditions.

B. The Bethlehem Traditions

The second major group of narratives is generally known as the 'Bethlehem' traditions, a name that is earned by their location of many important events in Bethlehem instead of in Jerusalem, the latter being the exclusive setting of the other early Dormition narratives (see Fig. 2). These traditions were largely ignored in Wenger's foundational work, but Michel van Esbroeck has recently produced a stemma that diagrams the literary relations among the earliest narratives of this textual family.[95] Only a few of these narratives fall within the period here under consideration, but representatives of this tradition first appear, like the earliest Palm traditions, in the late fifth and early sixth centuries, the moment when the Dormition traditions in general first become visible. The earliest of the Bethlehem narratives is probably a work known as the Six Books, which is evident in two early Syriac manuscripts, as well as in a number of later Syriac manuscripts and Arabic and Ethiopic versions.[96] The earliest of

_____

Anecdota, 14–21). Note, however, that in her comparison of the *Apocalypse of Paul* with the *Apocalypse of Zephaniah*, Martha Himmelfarb concludes the following: 'The Apocalypse of Paul is much more expansive that the Apocalypse of Zephaniah. The three sins and punishments of the Apocalypse of Zephaniah are only a small fraction of the many in the Apocalypse of Paul. . . . The vision of souls leaving the body is more developed and carefully balanced in the Apocalypse of Paul than in the Apocalypse of Zephaniah.' Both of these comparisons mark the *Apocalypse of Paul*, she argues, as a later work than the *Apocalypse of Zephaniah* (*Tours of Hell: An Apocalyptic Form in Jewish and Christian Literature* (Philadelphia: University of Pennsylvania Press, 1983), 151). Comparison between the *Apocalypse of Paul* and the *Obsequies/Liber Requiei* using identical criteria suggests the same: the *Obsequies/Liber Requiei* describes only four sins and punishments, and its account of what happens to the souls as they leave the body is much less developed than in the *Apocalypse of Paul*.

[95] van Esbroeck, 'Les Textes', 273.

[96] The Syriac manuscripts are listed in Mimouni, *Dormition*, 91–2 n. 64. Arabic: Maximillian Enger, ed., اخبار يوحنّا السليح في نقلة امّ المسيح) *Akhbâr Yûhannâ*

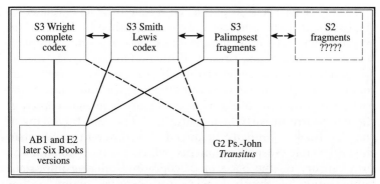

FIG. 2. Basic outline of the ancient Bethlehem traditions and their literary relations

these manuscripts is an Egyptian palimpsest, dated by its editor, Agnes Smith Lewis, to the late fifth century or perhaps the beginning of the sixth, based on paleography.[97] Unfortunately, this manuscript is badly damaged in large sections, for which Smith Lewis has supplied readings from a much later Syriac manuscript (copied in 1857); nevertheless, those sections that are still legible in the palimpsest preserve a very early version of this narrative. Another early version of the Six Books narrative is known from a complete manuscript edited by William Wright, dated to the later sixth century by paleography.[98] Although these two versions are quite similar, they are not identical, as is the case with the *Obsequies* fragments and the Ethiopic *Liber Requiei*, mentioned above. There are significant differences between these two early recensions of the Six Books, and as Simon Mimouni's work has emphasized, it is important to distinguish carefully between the two versions.[99]

as-salîh fi naqlat umm al-masîh), id est Joannis apostoli de transitu Beatae Mariae Virginis liber (Eberfeld: R. L. Friderichs, 1854). The Ethiopic version is translated in Appendix D.

[97] Smith Lewis, *Apocrypha Syriaca*, ܡܝܡܪܐ (Syr.) and 12–69 (Eng.); for date, see ibid. p. x.

[98] Wright, 'Departure', 417–48, and 7 (1865), 108–60; for date, see 417. I am presently preparing a new edition of this version of the Six Books, based on more recent manuscript discoveries, including a second manuscript from the 6th century that has preserved this text in its entirety

[99] Mimouni, *Dormition*, 102–3, although Mimouni has perhaps overemphasized the differences at the expense of vast and considerable similarities.

There are also several published Syriac fragments related to
the (more or less) complete versions published by Wright and
Smith Lewis. The most important of these are four palimpsest
folios from Mt. Sinai, preserved in the famous Syriac manuscript no. 30, whose underwriting also preserves extensive fragments of the Old Syriac version of the Gospels and is one of the
earliest manuscripts of the Gospels in any language, copied in
the late fourth or early fifth century.[100] The four fragments of
the Six Books originally belonged to a different codex than
the Old Syriac Gospels fragments, which has been dated to the
fifth century on the basis of paleography, offering important
confirmation of Smith Lewis's fifth-century dating of her
palimpsest codex.[101] These fragments were published without
translation as an appendix to Smith Lewis's publication of her
palimpsest codex described above.[102] Other palimpsest fragments of the Six Books have been identified in the Sinai collection, but these have not been published, since, as Smith Lewis
reports, 'these portions all coincide with some part of the older
texts, but the variants are too slight to be worth recording'.[103]

Note, however, the version of the Six Books edited by E. A. W. Budge has been
omitted from this discussion because its manuscript (and text it would seem) is
of a much later date, the 13th or 14th century (E. A. W. Budge, ed., *History of
the Blessed Virgin Mary and the History of the Likeness of Christ which the Jews of
Tiberias Made to Mock at* (London: Luzac & Co., 1899)).

[100] Robert L. Bensly et al., *The Four Gospels in Syriac* (Cambridge: The
University Press, 1894), pp. xv–xvii; Smith Lewis, *Apocrypha Syriaca*, iii;
eadem, *Catalogue of the Syriac MSS. in the Convent of S. Catharine on Mount
Sinai*, Studia Sinaitica, I (London: C. J. Clay & Sons, 1894), 47. Note that
Smith Lewis does *not* describe the palimpsest fragments as illegible in her
catalogue, as Mimouni reports (*Dormition*, 92 n. 64); instead, she merely notes
that the palimpsest's date is illegible. Regarding the date of the Old Syriac
Gospels fragments, see Arthur Vööbus, *Early Versions of the New Testament:
Manuscript Studies*, Papers of the Estonian Theological Society in Exile, 6
(Stockholm: Estonian Theological Society in Exile, 1954), 74; and Bruce M.
Metzger, *The Early Versions of the New Testament: Their Origin, Transmission,
and Limitations* (Oxford: Clarendon Press, 1977), 38.

[101] Bensly, *Four Gospels*, pp. xv–xvii; Smith Lewis, *Apocrypha Syriaca*, p.
iii; for date, see ibid.

[102] Ibid. ܡܘܡ–ܩ; These fragments are translated in Appendix C.

[103] Bensly, *Four Gospels*, pp. xv–xvii; Smith Lewis, *Apocrypha Syriaca*, p. iii.
See Margaret Dunlop Gibson, *Catalogue of the Arabic MSS in the Convent of
S. Catharine on Mount Sinai*, Studia Sinaitica, III (London: C. J. Clay & Sons,
1894), 102, 125; although one of the manuscripts is listed as missing in the catalogue, Smith Lewis notes that later on it reappeared.

The four Sinai palimpsest folios preserve a version of the Six Books having parallels with the more complete narratives published by both Wright and Smith Lewis, although in general they have more affinity with the latter than the former.[104] Three of the folios preserve the conclusion to Book 4 and the beginning of Book 5, a passage that is missing from the palimpsest codex edited by Smith Lewis. This makes them valuable witnesses to what may have once stood in these missing pages. Moreover, the narrative in these fifth-century folios is very close to the nineteenth-century manuscript of the Six Books that Smith Lewis used to fill the gaps in her ancient codex, offering important confirmation that her selection of this manuscript for this purpose was appropriate.[105] Nevertheless, while the palimpsest folios are generally quite close to Smith Lewis's codex version, the two are not always identical. This observation is very important for understanding the nature of the various ancient witnesses to the Six Books traditions. For instance, Simon Mimouni has suggested, as noted above, that there were two versions of the Six Books circulating in late antiquity, exemplified in the versions published by Smith Lewis and Wright. Nevertheless, in the light of these palimpsest fragments, and their affinities with both early manuscripts, it would seem more likely that we are dealing with a relatively free tradition that had not yet crystallized into one particular form or another.[106]

As much is also indicated by two additional Syriac fragments from the Six Books traditions, both of which were published by

[104] *Contra* Mimouni, *Dormition*, 91–2 n. 64, who appears to identify these fragments as witnesses to the same version published by Wright.

[105] Again, *contra* Mimouni, *Dormition*, 101–2, who criticizes her for this decision. He seems to suggest that she should have used Wright's narrative, but based on the significant differences between these two versions, this would not have been a good solution.

[106] Mimouni (*Dormition*, 102–3) makes much of a supposed difference between one narrative in six books (Wright) and another in five books (Smith Lewis). Nevertheless, this distinction cannot bear the weight that is placed on it, since the ancient manuscript published by Smith Lewis clearly identifies itself as being in fact Six Books: Smith Lewis, *Apocrypha Syriaca*, ܟܐ (Syr.) and 17 (Eng.). The division into five books, as opposed to six, is seen only in the 19th-century manuscript with which Smith Lewis has completed her edition—this is not a feature of the ancient manuscript. Moreover, the four 5th-century palimpsest folios also identify themselves as having once been 'Six Books': ibid. ܡ, ܡܚ.

Wright in the same volume as the *Obsequies* fragments. These
fragments come from significantly later manuscripts, one from
the ninth or tenth century[107] and the other copied in 1197.[108]
Despite van Esbroeck's potentially misleading identification
of these fragments as if they comprise a single text, they are, as
Mimouni correctly points out, in fact two entirely separate fragments from unrelated manuscripts.[109] Like the four Sinai palimpsest folios, the affinities of these two fragments with the other
early versions of the Six Books are obvious, but so too are the
differences. The first fragment relates the opening scenes of the
Six Books narratives, corresponding roughly with the first half
of Book 2; the second fragment (copied 1197) represents a little
more than the second half of Book 3, describing a debate between
the 'believers' and 'unbelievers' and Jephonias' failed attempt to
destroy the Virgin's body, the latter being an important feature
of Bethlehem narratives as well as the Palm traditions. This
second fragment offers a considerably expanded version of the
events as related in Wright's manuscript, but in comparison to
Smith Lewis's version, the details are rather compressed. Before
reaching its conclusion, however, this fragment is interrupted,
and when the text resumes, we find it in the midst of narrating
the Virgin's transfer to Paradise, in an account which has no
parallel in the other published versions of the Six Books, nor in
any other known narrative.

Despite the considerable youth of these fragments, both van
Esbroeck and Mimouni regard them as preserving perhaps the
earliest version of the Bethlehem traditions, a version that was
later reworked in the more complete versions published by
Wright and Smith Lewis.[110] There is little reason to think this,
however. While there is no compelling reason to conclude prima
facie that these fragments preserve a significantly later version of
the narrative, simply on the basis of their relatively late manuscripts, neither is there convincing evidence (in my opinion) of
their antiquity. Consequently, these fragments clearly do not

---

[107] Wright, *Contributions*, ܠ‑ܠ (Syr.) and 18–24 (Eng.); for date, see 8.

[108] Ibid. ܠ‑ܐ (Syr.) and 24–41 (Eng.); for date, see 10.

[109] See van Esbroeck, 'Les Textes', 266, and the discussion in Mimouni,
Dormition, 90–1.

[110] See van Esbroeck, 'Les Textes', 266, 273; and Mimouni, *Dormition*, 72,
87–90.

command the special attention that the early manuscripts edited by Wright and Smith Lewis do, and while they will by no means be disregarded in this study, they will be considered primarily as later, if closely related, witnesses to the same traditions preserved in the more ancient manuscripts.

The only other narrative from this textual family that undoubtedly belongs to the period before the Islamic conquest is the Greek *Discourse on the Dormition* attributed to St John the Theologian. This medieval 'best-seller', as van Esbroeck describes it, is extant in over 100 different Greek manuscripts, as well as in Georgian, Arabic, Latin, and Church Slavonic versions. Konstantin Tischendorf prepared a critical edition of the Greek version, based on five of the earliest known manuscripts, but a team of scholars is presently engaged in producing a much more complete edition that will supersede Tischendorf's earlier work.[111] In comparison with the Syriac traditions, the earliest manuscripts preserving this narrative are rather late (tenth century), making for some uncertainty regarding the work's date. But as Mimouni has convincingly argued, certain liturgical indications in this narrative, when compared with what we know otherwise regarding the earliest Marian feasts, suggest a date sometime in the late fifth or early sixth century.[112] In terms of its contents, this early Greek version is very close to the Six Books traditions, but its narrative is significantly more condensed.

A basic outline of the earliest Bethlehem traditions, and the Six Books traditions more particularly, is as follows. The Virgin had a custom of praying at the tomb of Christ, which was a source of great annoyance to the Jewish leaders. Consequently, the Jews convinced the Roman authorities to post watchmen preventing her from continuing this practice. When Mary later attempts to pray at the tomb, the Jews tell her to leave Jerusalem for her house in Bethlehem. Having previously learned of her impending death from an angel at the tomb, Mary willingly

---

[111] Konstantin Tischendorf, ed., *Apocalypses Apocryphae* (Leipzig: Herm. Mendelssohn, 1866), 95–110. The new edition is slated to appear as *Dormitio Mariae, auctore Iohanne apostolo*, in the series Corpus Christianorum, Series Apocryphorum, edited by S. Mimouni, B. Outtier, M. van Esbroeck, and S. Voicu.

[112] Mimouni, *Dormition*, 124; see also van Esbroeck, 'Les Textes', 269. The early development of the cult of the Virgin is the subject of Ch. 2.

leaves her house in Jerusalem and goes to Bethlehem. There she is joined by the apostles, who travel from the ends of the earth by miraculous means. While in Bethlehem, Mary performs many healings and again attracts the unfortunate attention of the Jewish authorities in Jerusalem, who fear that Mary will destroy the entire Jewish nation. Therefore, the Jewish leaders persuade the Roman authorities to send a force of soldiers against Mary and the apostles in Bethlehem. Before the soldiers reach Mary's house, however, Mary and the apostles are warned by the Holy Spirit and transported through the air back to the Virgin's Jerusalem house. When the soldiers attempt to enter Mary's house, they find no one there. Then when the Jewish leaders find Mary and the apostles back in Jerusalem, they attempt to burn Mary's house, but when they try, a fire blazes forth from its doors, killing many of the Jews. Following this, the Roman governor organizes a debate between the 'believers' and 'unbelievers', in which he judges the outcome in favour of the 'believers'. In some of the narratives, the Roman governor, after he himself has recognized the truth of the Christian faith, orders the Jews to reveal the location of the implements of crucifixion, which they have cleverly disguised as Jewish 'relics'. Then the apostles carry the Virgin Mary, who is still living, out from the city to her tomb near Gethsemane, and as they are carrying her, the Jews plot to burn Mary's body. One of them, Jephonias, attacks her bier. When Jephonias grabs the bier, an angel cuts off his arms, which are left dangling from the bier, and only through the wonder-working power of the Virgin Mary are his limbs eventually restored. While the apostles minister to Mary at her tomb, Christ appears to receive his mother's soul. Following her soul's departure from the body, the narratives give a set of liturgical instructions. After this, some narratives conclude with the translation of Mary's body into Paradise, where it awaits reunion with her soul at the general resurrection. Such narratives omit any mention of her bodily resurrection or Assumption. But other narratives in this tradition, including both Wright's complete version and the Sinai palimpsest folios, continue to describe her resurrection in Paradise and a subsequent tour of the places of reward and punishment, in an account something like the Virgin's Assumption as narrated in many of the early Palm traditions.

In addition to all this, the various versions of the Six Books begin with an intriguing preface, explaining how these traditions were found after having been lost for some time. 'Certain men on Mount Sinai', were are told, were 'concerned', and because of this they wrote to bishop Cyrus (Cyriacus/Kyriakos) of Jerusalem, enquiring about a 'book of my Lady Mary, how she departed from this world'.[113] Although we are strangely uninformed as to just what was troubling these three men, their actions suggest that they were concerned, like Epiphanius, that they did not know a tradition concerning the end of Mary's life. When their letter reached Jerusalem, it was read before 'the whole people', but no one could find the book. Instead, they found a book in which James, the first bishop of Jerusalem, wrote with his own hand that the book of Mary's departure from this world was written in 'six books', each one by two of the apostles, and that John the young, Peter, and Paul know where they are, because they carried the books with them from Jerusalem. Bishop Cyrus then replied to the men of Sinai that the book of Mary's departure had not been found, but that, based on James's letter, they might find it in Rome or Ephesus. Cyrus asked in addition that, if the volume were found, a copy be sent to Jerusalem. Various enquiries were made, and eventually some men went to Ephesus, where they prayed in 'the house of St John'. While they were sleeping, John appeared to them and gave them the book of Mary's departure, with instructions that it be made known that the book was sent 'in order that there may be a commemoration of the Lady Mary, the mother of God, three times in the year'. The book they received was written in 'Hebrew, Greek, and Latin', although as the preface concludes we are told that 'this volume was translated from Greek into Syriac at Ephesus.'

This preface is intriguing for a number of reasons, but most important for our purposes are the story's indication that memory of these traditions had been 'lost' and its explicit identification of a Greek original. The first point is an important confirmation of what we have already seen: the overwhelming

---

[113] The two earliest versions are preserved in Wright, 'Departure', ‏ܣܘ‎ (Syr.) and 131–3 (Eng.); and Smith Lewis, *Apocrypha Syriaca*, ‏ܟ–ܠܐ‎ (Syr.) and 15–19 (Eng.). Part of this story is also witnessed by one of the 5th-century palimpsest folios: ibid. ‏ܩ‎.

silence of the early (proto-orthodox) Christian tradition on this subject, as well as a growing concern over this deficiency, as we have already seen in Epiphanius. Similar apologies for the late appearance of the Dormition traditions are found in Ps.-Melito's *Transitus* and John of Thessalonica's homily, both of which express concern regarding the long absence of any Dormition tradition from orthodox Christian discourse.[114] The primary value of these candid admissions lies in their confirmation of modern scholarship's inability to identify any significant traditions concerning the end of Mary's life from before the fifth century. The Christian writers of late antiquity themselves warn us that we should not expect to find very much on this subject from earlier centuries, at least not anything that Epiphanius or some other orthodox Christian writer would want to report. This does not mean that we should not expect to find any early traditions at all, only that we should not expect to find them among the well-preserved remnants of proto-orthodox Christianity. As we will see in Ch. 4, there is much to suggest that there were in fact earlier traditions of the end of Mary's life, but that these narratives were long 'unknown' to proto-orthodox writers because they were theologically heterodox: both Ps.-Melito and John of Thessalonica rather frankly attest to this fact. Indeed, one of the most remarkable aspects of the earliest visible history of these traditions is the hurried effort to sanitize many of the earliest texts, in an effort to make them safe for orthodox consumption.

The explicit identification of a Greek source for these traditions more or less obviates the question of their original language. The existence of a Greek archetype is elsewhere confirmed by the *Tübingen Theosophy*, which appears to refer to a Greek version of this narrative.[115] As already noted, the *Tübingen Theosophy* mentions a work with the title, 'the birth and assumption of our lady the immaculate Theotokos'. This title very likely refers to an early version of the Six Books, since the earliest manuscripts preserving this narrative preface their account of Mary's Dormition and Assumption with copies of the

---

[114] Ps.-Melito, *Transitus Mariae*, prologue (Haibach-Reinisch, *Ein neuer Transitus*, 64–5); John of Thessalonica, *dorm. BMV A* 1 (Jugie, *Homélies*, 376–7).

[115] See above and Beatrice, 'Traditions apocryphes', 114–15.

Protevangelium of James and the *Infancy Gospel of Thomas*, all three of which together described the birth and Assumption of Mary. Nevertheless, the indication that the narrative was extant in three languages may be unreliable: otherwise, we might ask why the translation into Syriac was made from the Greek instead of the Hebrew. In all probability, the existence of Greek, Hebrew, and Latin versions is merely meant to signal the polyglot nature of the apostolic preaching, and the privileging of Greek as the source from which one would translate if given a choice also says something about the linguistic milieu in which these traditions first came to light.[116] In any case, we may with some confidence take faith in the narrative's statement of its origins, leaving us in a position similar to the Palm narratives.[117] Prior existence in a Greek archetype assures us that these narratives are at least somewhat older than their earliest exemplars, and thus the traditions probably date to the first half of the fifth century at the latest.

Richard Bauckham attempts to date the Six Books narratives more precisely by analysing their apocalyptic conclusion, repeating his efforts with the Palm traditions. Through comparison with various apocalyptic 'tours' from early Judaism and Christianity, Bauckham proposes that the Six Books narrative is probably 'from the fourth century at the latest, but perhaps considerably earlier'.[118] He bases his determination solely on the fact that in the Six Books apocalypse the dead have not yet received their reward or punishment. Although Bauckham acknowledges that this view continues to be found in texts as late as the fifth century CE, he explains that it is not present in any other apocalypse later than the mid-second century CE. He then continues to speculate that the *Urtext* on which both the Palm and Bethlehem traditions depend originally contained this Six Books apocalypse. Later on, the Palm narratives, he suggests, replaced this primitive apocalypse with a new version, primarily to eliminate

---

[116] For more on the changing attitudes in the Syriac-speaking world with regard to Greek language and culture, see Sebastian Brock, 'From Antagonism to Assimilation: Syriac Attitudes to Greek Learning', in Nina G. Garsoïan, Thomas F. Mathews, and Robert W. Thomson (eds.), *East of Byzantium: Syria and Armenia in the Formative Period* (Washington: Dumbarton Oaks, 1982), 17–34.

[117] See also Mimouni, *Dormition*, 94–5.

[118] Bauckham, *Fate of the Dead*, 346–60, esp. 358–60.

the archaic representation of the dead as having not yet received their reward or punishment.

While Bauckham's findings are indeed intriguing, they are not altogether convincing. In contrast to his very compelling suggestions regarding the *Obsequies/Liber Requiei* and its apocalypse, his reasoning in this case rests on a single argument that itself relies on some questionable assumptions. On the one hand, there is no compelling reason to suppose that the Palm and Bethlehem traditions derive from a common *Urtext*, as I will demonstrate in Ch. 3. Moreover, as Bauckham himself admits, there is evidence of belief that the dead have not yet received their reward or punishment in non-apocalyptic literature from as late as the fifth century. Had Bauckham cast his net even more broadly, he would have found that this idea persists in Byzantine theological literature, where it is in fact the predominant view.[119] In the light of the persistence of this belief, we cannot eliminate the possibility that these ideas have influenced the Six Books apocalypse at a later time. Moreover, other features of the Six Books narratives seem to militate against an origin in the fourth century, let alone earlier. These include the references to Judas Kyriakos, a character borrowed from the fifth-century legends of the True Cross; the inclusion of a narrative of the discovery of the True Cross; inclusion of material from the fifth-century *Doctrina Addai*; and a monastic community on Mt. Sinai, among other things.[120] While these features may in fact all be later additions to a more primitive Six Books tradition or Bauckham's hypothetical *Urtext*, they should nevertheless caution us about

[119] Antoine Wenger, 'Ciel ou Paradis: Le Séjour des âmes, d'après Phillipe le Solitaire, Dioptra, Livre IV, Chapitre X', *Byzantinische Zeitschrift*, 44 (1951), 560–1; Jean Daniélou, 'Terre et paradis chez les pères de l'église', *Eranos-Jahrbuch*, 22 (1953), 448; Jean Delumeau, *History of Paradise: The Garden of Eden in Myth and Tradition*, trans. Matthew O'Connell (New York: Continuum, 1995), 31–2. See also *Oxford Dictionary of Byzantium*, s.v. 'Paradise'.

[120] Regarding Judas Kyriakos, see Wright, 'Departure', ܩ (Syr.) and 131 (esp. n. *m*) (Eng.) and Jan Willem Drijvers, *Helena Augusta: The Mother of Constantine the Great and the Legend of Her Finding of the True Cross*, Brill's Studies in Intellectual History, 27 (Leiden: E. J. Brill, 1992), 165–80. Concerning the date of the *Doctrina Addai*, see ibid. 153–4; Schneemelcher, *New Testament Apocrypha*, i. 493. On the beginnings of the Sinai community around the middle of the 4th century, see Derwas Chitty, *The Desert a City: An Introduction to the Study of Egyptian and Palestinian Monasticism Under the Christian Empire* (Oxford: Basil Blackwell, 1966), 168.

pushing the date too early. This is, however, the narrative tradition referenced by the *Tübingen Theosophy* of *c*.500, and since these traditions are extant in fifth-century Syriac translations that were made from an earlier Greek version, we can be relatively safe in identifying a *terminus ante quem* in the early fifth century.

C. The Coptic Traditions

It is to some extent debatable whether or not the Coptic Dormition traditions form a narrative type unto themselves. Van Esbroeck, for instance, includes them as a special subgroup of the Palm traditions, within which they 'occupent une place à part'.[121] While some of the earliest Coptic traditions have strong and obvious links to the Palm traditions, others are remarkably distinct and from a literary point of view are best understood as being atypical narratives. These narratives, for instance, do not mention the Palm, nor do they describe the miraculous reunion of the apostles, only a few of whom are present in certain early accounts. Moreover, the events of Mary's departure from this life are greatly condensed in the Coptic tradition when compared with many other early narratives, a feature allowing more room for religious polemics. Already then it should be clear that unlike the previous two families, the Coptic traditions are not joined by literary relations: on the contrary, from a literary point of view they represent a diverse assortment of narratives. What identifies them as a unit, however, is a consistent and distinctive liturgical pattern manifest in all the different Coptic narratives, in spite of their literary diversity, as well as in current Coptic (and Ethiopian) practice (see Fig. 3).

Essentially without exception, the earliest Coptic traditions locate the Virgin's departure from this life on 21 Tobe (16 January), a date that also holds the feast of Mary's Dormition in both the ancient and the modern Coptic Church. In a few of the earliest narratives, this is the only feast that is acknowledged.[122]

---

[121] van Esbroeck, 'Les Textes', 272; see also the stemma on p. 270.

[122] The only possible exception to this being the fragment published by Revillout, *Évangile des douze apôtres*, 174–83. Although this fragment includes the 16 Mesore feast (see below), the 21 Tobe feast is not indicated. Nevertheless, this is almost certainly an accident of the text's incomplete preservation, and in

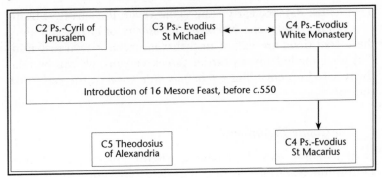

FIG. 3. Basic outline of the ancient Coptic traditions and their literary relations

These earliest accounts conclude with Mary's funeral, following the separation of her body and soul, without any kind of resurrection or Assumption. Mary's body is on this same day 'removed' from this world (and in some accounts placed in Paradise); in contrast to many early Dormition traditions, and the later Coptic traditions especially, there is no post-mortem reunion of Mary's body and soul in the heavenly realms that might be taken to indicate her bodily Assumption.

Other early Coptic narratives, however, attest a second feast, celebrating the Virgin Mary's Assumption on 16 Mesore (9 August). Perhaps the most important of these (because it can be dated) is the homily on the Dormition by Theodosius of Alexandria. Although Coptic literature abounds with pious forgeries, there is every reason to think that this is an authentic work of Theodosius that was, as its prologue informs us, delivered 'in the final year of his life', namely, 566 or 567.[123]

the parts no longer extant, we would probably find mention of the 21 Tobe feast. See Mimouni, *Dormition*, 185. Note that both feasts are indicated in the rather similar fragments published by H. G. E. White, ed., *The Monasteries of the Wadi 'n Natrûn*, i. *New Coptic Texts from the Monastery of Saint Macarius* (New York: The Metropolitan Museum of Art, 1926), 55–8.

[123] Theodosius of Alexandria, *Homily on the Assumption*, prologue (F. Robinson, ed., *Coptic Apocryphal Gospels*, Texts and Studies, IV (Cambridge: Cambridge University Press, 1896), 90–1). Concerning the homily's authenticity, see the introduction to Marius Chaine's edition of the text: 'Sermon de Théodose, Patriarche d'Alexandrie, sur la Dormition et l'Assomption de la Vierge', *Revue de l'Orient Chrétien*, 29 (1933–4), 273–6.

From this we know that by the mid-sixth century, Coptic liturgical practice had come to include two separate celebrations of the end of the Virgin's life: a feast of her Dormition on 21 Tobe and a feast of her Assumption on 16 Mesore. This schedule has made a rather dramatic impact on subsequent accounts of the end of Mary's life: these narratives insert a period of 206 days between Mary's Dormition and her Assumption. After placing Mary's lifeless body in the tomb, the apostles return to Jerusalem, and for the next 206 days they regularly visit the tomb and offer songs and prayers to the Virgin, as Christ had instructed them. When 16 Mesore finally arrives, the apostles go to the tomb, where they witness together Mary's resurrection and bodily Assumption into heaven.

These liturgical and narrative patterns provide the main criteria for defining the boundaries of the otherwise diverse Coptic Dormition traditions. More importantly perhaps, these liturgical developments allow us to date a few of the early Coptic narratives with a fair amount of certainty. The earliest feast of Mary in the Coptic tradition was a feast of the Memory of Mary, celebrated on 21 Tobe. The Memory of Mary was a commemoration of Mary's role in the Nativity that was celebrated throughout the eastern Mediterranean on various dates in different locales. Sometime before the early sixth century, however, this feast changed into a celebration of Mary's Dormition, both in Egypt and elsewhere. Then, in the Coptic church, as indicated by Theodosius' homily, a second feast was added sometime around the middle of the sixth century, a celebration of Mary's Assumption on 16 Mesore that has continued uninterrupted until the present day.[124] Consequently, those narratives that are ignorant of this liturgical change, and describe instead the removal of the Virgin's body on 21 Tobe, were almost certainly composed before the mid-sixth century. Narratives including the second feast, however, are not necessarily later compositions, at least not in their entirety: in some cases older traditions may have been updated to reflect contemporary practices, with a few

---

[124] A discussion of the early Coptic liturgical tradition may be found in Simon Mimouni, 'Genèse et évolution', 123–33. See also Bernard Capelle, 'La Fête de l'Assumption dans l'histoire liturgique', *Ephemerides Theologicae Louvanienses*, 3 (1926), 37–8. For more detail on the development of the earliest Marian liturgies, see Ch. 2.

minor changes, and we know that in at least one instance such
liturgical revision did in fact occur.

There are three Coptic narratives lacking any awareness of
the 16 Mesore feast, and this, together with their indication that
the Virgin's body was removed from this world on 21 Tobe,
identifies them as having been composed before the middle of
the sixth century. The first of these is a homily falsely attributed
to Cyril of Jerusalem, which affords a rather brief narration of
the Virgin's Dormition, involving only the apostles John, Peter,
and James. This is prefaced by a quick rehearsal of the Virgin's
life and a refutation of the opinion, apparently held by some,
that the Virgin was a spiritual 'power' (ⲆⲨⲚⲀⲘⲒⲤ) who had
descended into the world.

Also from before the mid-sixth century are two closely
related but distinct homilies on the Dormition that have been
falsely ascribed to Evodius of Rome. Of these homilies, one is
additionally extant in two different versions, the more recent of
which has been revised to reflect the liturgical changes described
above. In the light of their common attribution to Evodius, it
seems best to distinguish each of these three texts according to
the particular monastery that has preserved it, in order to avoid
confusion.[125]

The first of these homilies is known primarily in manuscripts
from the monastery of St Michael in the Fayyum (now in the
Pierpont Morgan collection), and consequently we will refer
to this text as the 'St Michael homily (St Mich.)'.[126] This
homily begins with an encomium on the Virgin, after which it
indulges in a substantial anti-Jewish harangue, followed by a
rather hurried narration of Mary's Dormition that concludes
with the removal of her unresurrected body on 21 Tobe. Unlike
Ps.-Cyril's narrative, however, all the apostles are present,
together with the '72' disciples, at a time just before their dispersal.[127]

---

[125] For further discussion of the relations among these three different but
related texts, see Stephen J. Shoemaker, 'The Sahidic Coptic Homily on the
Dormition of the Virgin Attributed to Evodius of Rome: An Edition of Morgan
MSS 596 & 598 with Translation', *Analecta Bollandiana*, 117 (1999), 241–51.

[126] Published in Shoemaker, 'Sahidic Coptic Homily on the Dormition'. A
translation of this homily is included in Appendix E.

[127] Luke 10: 1, 7. The number 72 (as opposed to 70) is a textual variant
preserved in the Sahidic version, among other early witnesses.

The second homily ascribed to Evodius is known in a fragmentary Sahidic version and a complete Bohairic version. Although the two versions have much in common, they occasionally diverge, particularly on the matter of Mary's Assumption on 16 Mesore. Consequently, we also need to distinguish these two versions according to their monastic pedigree. Since the Sahidic version is known only in fragments from the White Monastery, we will refer to this version as the 'White Monastery homily (W. Mon.)'.[128] Likewise, since the Bohairic version is known only in a manuscript from the monastery of St Macarius, this has been designated as the 'St Macarius homily (St Mac.)'.[129] Only the complete St Macarius version (Bohairic) preserves the homily's beginning, which, like the St Michael's homily, begins with an encomium and anti-Jewish polemic, the former being somewhat similar to the opening of the St Michael homily, the latter, rather different and briefer. The homily's narration of the Virgin's Dormition, which is also extant in the White Monastery version (Sahidic), provides a somewhat more detailed narration than the St Michael homily.

Despite some not insignificant points of contact, the St Macarius and White Monastery versions are quite distinct from the St Michael's homily, while the St Macarius and White Monastery versions themselves are very closely related to one another. Nevertheless, the St Macarius and White Monastery versions diverge most significantly regarding the conclusion to Mary's life and the related issue of the 16 Mesore feast of her Assumption. In the White Monastery homily, as in the St Michael's homily, the Virgin's unresurrected body is removed from this world on 21 Tobe. But in the St Macarius homily, Mary's body is placed in the tomb on 21 Tobe, where it remains for 206 days until its resurrection and Assumption on 16 Tobe. From this we may conclude that the White Monastery fragments represent a early version of a second homily attributed to Evodius that, like the St Michael's homily, was initially

---

[128] The bulk of these fragments have been published in Robinson, *Coptic Apocryphal Gospels*, 67–89. Concerning these and additional fragments, see Shoemaker, 'Sahidic Coptic Homily on the Dormition', 242 n. 6 and 243 n. 9.

[129] Published by Paul de Lagarde, ed., *Aegyptiaca* (Göttingen: A. Hoyer, 1883; repr. Osnabruck: O. Zeller, 1972), 38–63. There is an English translation by Forbes Robinson in *Coptic Apocryphal Gospels*, 44–67.

composed sometime before the liturgical changes of the mid-sixth century. The complete St Macarius homily, on the other hand, represents a later revision of the White Monastery homily, which aimed primarily at bringing this tradition up to date with contemporary liturgical practice.

Two further Coptic witnesses are also revealing of the earliest development of the Dormition narratives, Theodosius of Alexandria's *Homily on the Dormition*, which we have already mentioned, and a handful of fragments that are closely related to the narrative preserved by the Syriac *Obsequies* and Ethiopic *Liber Requiei*.[130] These fragments, in the light of their literary relations to the earliest members of the Palm family, are obviously important witnesses to the early Palm traditions, from a literary standpoint. But because they share the liturgical pattern of the Coptic tradition, including its 206-day interval, they are usually classified together with the other Coptic narratives.[131] The same is also true of Theodosius' homily, whose narrative, he informs, was borrowed from an ancient Jerusalemite source that he had come across in the library of St Mark in Alexandria.[132] From a literary vantage, Theodosius' homily is clearly related to the Palm traditions, but despite these strong literary ties, Theodosius' homily is the earliest source reflecting the complete liturgical pattern that gives the otherwise unrelated Coptic narratives their identity as a specific group of traditions. Consequently, it too is to be classed among the Coptic traditions. Finally, it is not without interest that Theodosius identifies the origin of his narrative source in Jerusalem, a fact that may suggest a link between the early history of these traditions and the Holy City. A possible Jerusalemite origin is further suggested by the prologue to the Six Books narratives, the Hagiopolite setting of the narratives themselves, and

---

[130] The largest fragment (in Sahidic) was published by Revillout, *Évangile des douze apôtres*, 174–83. Other Bohairic fragments have been published in White, *Monasteries of the Wadi 'n Natrûn*, 55–8.

[131] The fragments published in Sellew, 'An Early Coptic Witness to the *Dormitio Mariae*', do not bear witness to this liturgical pattern, so we have discussed them above in the context of the Palm narratives.

[132] Theodosius of Alexandria, *Homily on the Assumption* (Chaine, 'Sermon de Théodose', 282 (Copt.) and 304 (Fr.); note that this passage is omitted from Robinson's text and translation).

the related development of the cult of the Virgin, her tomb, and other sites in the Jerusalem area, which is the subject of Ch. 2.

D. The Atypical Traditions

Moving beyond these three literary types, we encounter a rather motley collection of texts, and aside from a few common narrative features, such as the Jewish assault on Mary's funeral procession (which appears in every Dormition narrative but one), these narratives do not evince literary relations with any other early Dormition narratives, including each other. The earliest of these atypical narratives is probably a homily on the Dormition by Jacob of Serug, which identifies itself as a work delivered before a church council in Nisibis in 489.[133] Martin Jugie challenged the homily's authenticity, arguing from the relative youth of its manuscript tradition, but it seems more likely that Jugie in fact objected more to its explicit indication of the Virgin's death and burial, since he is often quite generous with other, more problematic texts that appear to support his own immortalist view.[134] In the years since Jugie's early work, however, a rather strong consensus has emerged that the homily is in fact authentic, a point demonstrated particularly by its remarkable topographic dissimilarity with the rest of the Dormition traditions.[135]

[133] Published by Paul Bedjan, ed., *S. Martyrii, qui et Sahdona, quae supersunt omnia* (Leipzig: Otto Harrassowitz, 1902), 709–19. A Latin translation from a different manuscript has been published by Anton Baumstark, 'Zwei syrische Dichtungen auf das Entschlafen der allerseligsten Jungfrau', *Oriens Christianus*, 5 (1905), 82–125 esp. 91–9. A good introduction to this homily may be found in Thomas R. Hurst, 'The "Transitus" of Mary in a Homily of Jacob of Sarug', *Marianum*, 52 (1990), 86–100. A translation may be found in Appendix F. Another English translation has recently been published by Mary Hansbury, *Jacob of Serug: On the Mother of God* (Crestwood, NY: St Vladimir's Seminary Press, 1998), 89–100.

[134] Martin Jugie, 'La mort et l'assomption de la Sainte Vierge dans la tradition des cinq premiers siècles', *Échos d'Orient*, 25 (1926), 283. Jugie is far more generous, for instance, regarding the homily *In Simeonem et Annam* attributed to 'Timothy of Jerusalem' (see n. 21 above) or certain rather dubious variants in the *Acts of John* by Ps.-Prochorus (see *La Mort*, 89; see also the remarks in van Esbroeck, 'Les Textes', 280–1).

[135] Jacob locates Mary's tomb 'on that mountain of Galileans' (ܟܕ ܗܘ ܛܘܪ ܕܓܠܝܠܝܐ), Jacob of Serug, *Homily on the Dormition* (Bedjan, *S. Martyrii*, 714). As both Jugie (*La Mort*, 84 n. 3) and Mimouni (*Dormition*, 106) explain, the

In all likelihood then Jacob composed this homily in the late fifth century, as the homily's prologue indicates, and certainly before his death in 521. The homily describes the events of the Virgin's death, burial, and entry into heaven in a unique and highly poetic account, but there is no question of Mary's bodily Assumption in its narrative. Despite the wishful thinking of some modern interpreters, there is no indication of her bodily presence in heaven, and only the translation of her soul is described:[136]

> The heavenly assemblies led with their cries of 'Holy'
> to the glorious soul of the mother of the Son of God.
> The fiery Seraphim were surrounding the soul that was
> translated . . .[137]

Some scholars have additionally seen this text as evidence of

'mountain of the Galileans' is the Mount of Olives. This identification arises from a Jerusalemite tradition designating the Mount of Olives as the mount of the Galileans. No one knows for certain the source of this tradition. Anton Baumstark suggests Mt. 28: 16 as the source ('Die leibliche Himmelfahrt de allerseligsten Jungfrau und die Lokaltradition von Jerusalem', *Oriens Christianus*, 4 (1904), 376), and indeed there is a tradition, beginning in the 6th century, that identifies the Mount of Olives with the mountain 'in Galilee' on which Christ appeared to the eleven. An alternative explanation suggests that the name is due to the ancient practice of Galilean Jews, who would camp here when coming to participate in the Jerusalem feasts. Today the name is still attached to a Greek Orthodox complex, Viri Galilaei, originally built on the mountain in 1881 as a residence for the Patriarch of Jerusalem. Inside, one can find a Byzantine chapel erected on the spot where the angel informed the Virgin of her impending death (Eugene Hoade, OFM, *Guide to the Holy Land* (Jerusalem: Franciscan Printing Press, 1984), 253).

[136] Ortiz de Urbina incorrectly asserts that Jacob 'cantat assumptionem gloriosam Mariae corpore et anima'. Ignatius Ortiz de Urbina, SJ, *Patrologia Syriaca*, 2nd edn. (Rome: Pont. Institutum Orientalium Studiorum, 1965), 109. Elsewhere he explains that because Jacob's homily mentions the Virgin's 'coronation', 'tendríamos toda la razón de suponer una coronación posterior a la resurrección del cuerpo de su Madre': idem, 'Maria en la patristica siriaca', *Scripta de Maria*, 1 (1978), 92. I do not find this argument very convincing. Faller has also proposed that her Assumption is being celebrated (*De priorum saeculorum silentio*, 20–2), but A. Raes has convincingly argued to the contrary (A. Raes, SJ, 'Aux origines de la fête de l'Assomption en Orient', *Orientalia Christiana Periodica*, 12 (1946), 271–2).

[137] ܕܒܗ ܐܬܗ ܗܘܢ ܚܝ̈ܠܐ ܫܡ̈ܝܢܐ ܡܩܕܫܝܢ ܠܗ̇: ܠܢܦܫܐ ܫܒܝܚܬܐ ܕܐܡܗ ܕܒܪ ܐܠܗܐ ܀ ܟܕ ܚܕܝܪ ܗ̈ܘܘ ܠܗ̇ ܠܢܦܫܐ ܗ̇ܝ ܕܐܬܦܢܝܬ ܣܪ̈ܦܐ ܕܢܘܪܐ: Jacob of Serug, *Homily on the Dormition* (Bedjan, *S. Martyrii*, 718).

an early liturgical celebration of the Dormition among Syriac-speaking Christians, and in the light of other evidence, notably the liturgical calendars found in the early Syriac Dormition apocrypha, this remains a distinct possibility.[138]

Another atypical narrative probably from the period here under consideration is the homily on the Dormition by Theo-teknos of Livias. In Greek the text is known only from a single manuscript, edited by Wenger in his volume on the early Byzantine Dormition traditions, although there is also an Arabic version, still unedited, from which Wenger has completed several lacunae.[139] The homily's author is identified as an oth-erwise unknown bishop, Theoteknos, who lived in the small town of Livias, at the foot of Mount Nebo, just across the Jordan river from Jericho. Since there ceased to be a bishopric in Livias sometime before 649, we may be fairly certain that Theoteknos delivered his homily sometime before this year, perhaps around the turn of the seventh century, if not slightly earlier.[140] Like Jacob of Serug's homily, and the various Greek homilies that would later follow it, Theoteknos' homily consists more in panegyric than in the complex narrative details that characterize the earliest Dormition apocrypha. In contrast to Jacob's hom-ily, however, Theoteknos' oration clearly describes the Virgin's Assumption, which he refers to as her ἀνάλημψις, a word not normally used in Greek, which strongly prefers either κοίμησις (Dormition) or μετάστασις (removal) for this event, even in narratives where Mary's resurrection and bodily Assumption eventually follow.[141]

Another atypical narrative from the early medieval period that may have originated before the Arab conquest is found in the rather unique account of the Virgin's Dormition preserved by the Armenian homiliary tradition. The work appears to have been originally composed in Armenian, although there are some

---

[138] Most notably, Baumstark, 'Zwei syrische Dichtungen', 83–5. See also Raes, 'Aux origines de la fête', 262–74; and Mimouni, *Dormition*, 106–7. Faller also supposes the existence of a feast, although he incorrectly identifies the object of its celebration in the Virgin's Assumption (see n. 136 above).

[139] Wenger, *L'Assomption*, 272–91; see also ibid., 'Théoteknos de Livias, Addendum', for the witness of the Arabic version.

[140] Ibid. 99–103.

[141] Jugie, *La Mort*, 184.

indications that Greek and/or Syriac sources may have been used.[142] The account has some limited similarities with the Palm traditions, among which van Esbroeck has classified it, but the differences are striking enough that it is probably better understood as an atypical account that may have drawn some of its material from the Palm tradition.[143] The narrative's age has been a matter of disagreement, some having suggested a sixth-century origin, with others favouring a date sometime much later in the Middle Ages, perhaps as late as the ninth or tenth century.[144] Nevertheless, more recent work allows us to conclude that this Dormition narrative was probably composed sometime before the mid-eighth century. Although a number of manuscripts have preserved this narrative, one in particular identifies 747 CE as a likely *terminus ante quem*. The manuscript in question was copied only around the turn of the thirteenth century, but its colophons identify it as a copy of an earlier manuscript, which had been written in 747 by a certain Salomon of Makhenots. The thirteenth-century manuscript, however, clearly includes some items not belonging to its eighth-century archetype, since some of its contents were themselves composed after 747. This poses, as Mimouni has noted, the rather difficult task of distinguishing the manuscript's more recent texts from those that were present in its early medieval model.[145] But Michel van Esbroeck has with

---

[142] Esayi Tayetsʻi, ed., Երանելւոյն Նիկոդիմոսի առաջեալ յաղագս ննջմանն Մարիամու Աստուածածնի եւ Միշտ Կուսին (A Narration concerning the Dormition of the Theotokos and Ever-Virgin Mary by the Blessed Nicodemus)', in Անկանոն գիրք Նոր Կտակարանաց (*Ankanon girkʻ Nor Ktakaranatsʻ [Apocryphal Books of the New Testament]*), Tʻangaran haykakan hin ew nor dprutʻeantsʻ, 2 (Venice: I Dparani S. Łazaru, 1898), 451–78. A German translation made from different manuscripts (without Armenian text) was published by Paul Vetter, 'Die armenische dormitio Mariae', *Theologische Quartalschrift*, 84 (1902), 321–49. Regarding the language of composition, see ibid. 324–5.

[143] van Esbroeck, 'Les Textes', 270. In a different article, van Esbroeck says of this piece in comparison to other early versions, 'La narration des faits est bien sûr parallèle, mais la rédation est entièrement différente': idem, 'Étude comparée des notices byzantine et caucasiennes pour la fête de la Dormition', in *Aux origines de la Dormition de la Vierge: Études historique sur les traditions orientales* (Brookfield, VT: Variorum, 1995), 3.

[144] Sixth cent.: Vetter, 'Die armenische dormitio Mariae', 325; medieval: Jugie, *La Mort*, 155; Erbetta, *Gli apocrifi*, 524.

[145] See the discussion in Mimouni, *Dormition*, 325–6.

a fair amount of certainty identified many of the works that were included in this earliest homiliary. Through an extensive comparison of the medieval Armenian homiliaries, van Esbroeck has successfully identified many of the items that in all probability belong to the homiliary of 747, and this early Armenian Dormition narrative is located within this archetypal collection.[146] Thus while we cannot be altogether certain of the narrative's origin before the Islamic conquests, van Esbroeck's investigations make this a likely possibility.

A stray Georgian fragment, preserved in the early Georgian homiliaries may also belong to the period here under consideration, although it is difficult to be sure. The brief text describes the Virgin's funeral procession and burial, and although van Esbroeck has classified it among the Palm traditions, it clearly presents a distinct version of these events. Mention is made, however, of Mary's death on Mount Zion, and as will be seen in Ch. 2, this is a strong indication that the text is not earlier than the late sixth century. A *terminus ante quem* is guaranteed only by the date of its tenth-century manuscript.[147]

E. The Late Apostle Tradition

A number of later Dormition narratives, all of them atypical, include an episode in which one of the apostles arrives late and does not witness the events of the Dormition. According to this tradition, one of the apostles, who is often identified as Thomas, is delayed in making his journey to Jerusalem for Mary's Dormition. He arrives sometime after her burial has taken place, and when the others tell him all that has transpired, the belated apostle generally asks to see for himself. In order to satisfy him, the apostles reopen Mary's sealed tomb. When they look into the tomb, however, they do not find Mary's body. They discover

---

[146] Van Esbroeck, 'Étude comparée', 3; idem, 'La Structure du répertoire de l'homéliaire de Mush', in G. B. Jahykyan (ed.), Միջազգային Հայերենագիտական գիտաժողով. Զեկուցումներր *(Mijazgayin hayerenagitakan gitazhoghov: zekuts'umner [International Symposium on Armenian Linguistics: Proceedings])* (Yerevan: Haykakan SSH GA Hratarakch'ut'yun), 282–306.

[147] This fragment is discussed, together with the two Georgian fragments mentioned above, in van Esbroeck, 'Apocryphes géorgiens', 55–9. This particular text of the fragment is found at 62–4.

instead certain relics, initially Mary's funeral robe, and in later traditions, her girdle as well.[148] These are of course the famous Constantinopolitan relics of the Virgin (about which more is said below), which established Mary's special bond with the imperial capital (at least in the minds of its inhabitants). The 'late apostle' tradition most likely developed as an explanation for the discovery of these relics, and this motif was incorporated into the Dormition traditions only at a later point in their history, sometime between 550 and 750. Nevertheless, an origin sometime before 650 seems likely (but not certain), meaning that some of these narratives may potentially belong to the period here under consideration.[149] Although van Esbroeck has for some reason assigned the following narratives (with one exception) to the Bethlehem tradition, any points of contact with this group are extremely minimal, and consequently these traditions are best regarded as a group of independent narratives, unrelated even to one another, that share the common theme of the late apostle.

Perhaps the most famous of these traditions is a brief work known as the *Euthymiac History*. This legend was interpolated into the second of John of Damascus' homilies on the Dormition at an early point in their transmission, where it is identified as a quotation from 'the third book of the *Euthymiac History*, chapter 40'. Its inclusion in these, 'the most celebrated of all the ancient homilies for the feast of the Dormition', ensured that it was the most widely circulated of the late apostle traditions.[150] The *Euthymiac History*, as quoted in John's homily, describes an incident that is supposed to have occurred during the events of the council of Chalcedon. While Juvenal and the other bishops of Palestine were present for the council, the imperial couple, Pulcheria and Marcian, enquired about the relics of the Virgin Mary, asking that Mary's remains be sent to the imperial capital,

---

[148] On the somewhat later development of the girdle relic, see the discussion in Mimouni, *Dormition*, 624–8.

[149] Wenger, *L'Assomption*, 136–9; Mimouni, *Dormition*, 552–61.

[150] The interpolation of this legend at an early stage in the transmission of John's homilies was convincingly argued by Jugie, *La Mort*, 159–67. Quotation is from Daley, *On the Dormition*, 21. The most recent edition of these homilies utilized 152 manuscripts, many of which include this insertion: Bernard Kotter, ed., *Die Schriften des Johannes von Damaskus*, v. *Opera homiletica et hagiographica* (Berlin: Walter de Gruyter, 1988), 461–555; the *Euthymiac History* is found at 536–9.

in order to protect it. In response, Juvenal briefly narrates the events of Mary's Dormition, explaining why there are actually no bodily relics to be had. There is, however, he tells them, another kind of relic that he could send. Three days after Mary's burial, Juvenal explains, the apostle Thomas finally reached Jerusalem, and, having missed the events of Mary's Dormition, he requested that the tomb be reopened, so that he might pay his respects (not out of doubt, I might emphasize). When the apostles opened the tomb, they were startled to find no body, but instead only Mary's funeral robe. Juvenal then concludes by referencing the passage from Ps.-Dionysius' *The Divine Names* discussed above, after which the imperial couple requests that Juvenal send them the garment. When Juvenal returns home to Jerusalem, he fulfils their request, and Marcian and Pulcheria enshrined the robe in the church of Blachernae, the Constantinopolitan church that housed this famous relic. It is difficult to date this tradition, and we do not know whether it arose sometime before or after the Islamic conquest. We know only that the legend developed sometime between 550 and 750, making it a potential witness to the earliest development of the Dormition traditions.

A similar difficulty with dating problematizes many of the other late apostle traditions as well. Two potentially early narratives are preserved in Armenian, and another in Georgian, although it is likely that all three were originally composed in Greek. The first of these narratives is a homily on the Dormition, known only in Armenian and falsely ascribed to John Chrysostom. The text's editor, Michel van Esbroeck, has proposed that this is a work of the fourth century, written by John II of Jerusalem, but this is extremely unlikely.[151] The homily

---

[151] Michel van Esbroeck, 'Une homélie arménienne sur la dormition attribuée à Chrysostome', *Oriens Christianus*, 74 (1990), 199–233; regarding the attribution to John II of Jerusalem, see esp. 205–8. Mimouni's explanation of the various problems with this attribution is quite convincing: *Dormition*, 333–5. Nevertheless, van Esbroeck repeats this claim in 'Some Early Features in the Life of the Virgin'; and 'L'Homélie Ա𝑟𝑎𝑟𝑖𝑧 𝑎𝑟𝑎𝑟𝑎ծ𝑛𝑔, ses attributs et sa métamorphose', *Hask*, NS 6 (1994), 54–5, but I still do not find it very convincing. Note that the homily edited in the latter article is very closely related to the Ps.-Chrysostom homily, as is the homily published in Thamar Dasnabedian, 'Une homélie arménienne sur le transitus de la Mère de Dieu et sur son image', *Bazmavep*, 1–4 (1992), 217–35; repr. in *La Mère de Dieu: Études sur l'Assomption et sur l'image de la très-sainte Mère de Dieu* (Antelias: Catholicossat Armenien de Cilicie, 1995), 73–102.

commences with an encomium to the Virgin, a genre especially characteristic of the later Greek homiletic tradition, as well as the homilies of Jacob of Serug and Theoteknos of Livias. The second half of the homily rather quickly narrates the life of the Virgin, concluding with a description of her Dormition. Although there is little evidence that can date this homily precisely, its indication that Mary was living with her parents, in their house, at the time of her death is at variance with the rest of the Dormition traditions. This striking dissimilarity suggests that the text was probably composed before the Dormition traditions had become both standardized and widespread.[152] Consequently, we will consider it among the traditions arising before the Islamic conquest.

Another late apostle text, also known in Armenian, purports to be a letter from (Ps.-)Dionysius the Areopagite to Titus, and since this text is not a part of the traditional Dionysian corpus, it is, in effect, a double forgery.[153] Its main purpose is to elaborate on the *Divine Names'* reference to Mary's Dormition that was discussed above. In this narrative, one of the apostles arrives late, after the Virgin's death and burial, but in contrast to the other late apostle traditions, no relics are discovered, only the absence of the Virgin's body. Without any question this narrative was produced after the composition of the Dionysian corpus itself. Thus it was probably written sometime after 550, although we cannot identify a *terminus ad quem* with any certainty, other than the date of its earliest manuscript (1194).

---

[152] This is well discussed by Mimouni, *Dormition*, 334–5.

[153] Garegin Sruandzteants', ed., Թուղթ Դիոնեսիոսի Արիսպագացւոյ (The Letter of Dionysius the Areopagite), in Հանգ եւ նորոգ պատմունիւն վասն Դաւթի եւ Մովսեսի խորենացւոյ (*Hnots' ew norots' patmut'iwn vasn Dawt'i ew Movsesi Khorenats'woy* [History of the Old and New concerning David and Moses Khorenatsi]), (Constantinople: Tpagrut'iwn E. M. Tntesean, 1874), 110–15. There is also a German translation based on a different manuscript by Paul Vetter, 'Das apocryphe Schreiben Dionysius des Areopagiten an Titus über die Aufnahme Mariä', *Theologische Quartalschrift*, 69 (1887), 133–8. This article has also been published in an Armenian version, which includes the Armenian text of this letter that Vetter used for his translation: Paul Vetter, 'Ապականրական Թուղթ Դիոնեսիոսի Արիսպագացւոյ առ Տիտոս վասն ննջման Մարեմայ (The Apocryphal Letter of Dionysius the Areopagite to Titus concerning the Dormition of Mary)', in J. Dashian (ed.), Հայկական աշխատասիրութիւնք (*Haykakan ashkhatsirut'iwnk* [Armenian Studies]), Azgayin matenadaran, 17 (Vienna: Mkhit'arean Tparan, 1895), 11–17.

Finally, there is a Dormition narrative attributed to Basil of Caesarea, known in a Georgian translation, which also includes the traditions of Thomas's late arrival and the subsequent discovery of Mary's empty tomb and funeral shroud.[154] This narrative is especially peculiar in its combination of motifs from both the Palm and Bethlehem traditions, including both the presence of the Palm and a house of Mary in Bethlehem, for instance. Presumably on account of the latter, van Esbroeck has identified this text as one of the Bethlehem traditions, although it is much better classified as an atypical narrative that has combined elements from the two major literary traditions. As we will see in the following chapter, this narrative preserves important liturgical traditions, and primarily on this basis we can identify it as probably a seventh-century composition.[155]

F. *The Traditions of Constantinople and Ephesus*

Before bringing this chapter to a close, at least brief mention must be made of the traditions of the end of Mary's life associated with the cities of Constantinople and Ephesus. In the case of the former, it is somewhat incorrect to speak of any 'Dormition' traditions, since the Marian traditions of the imperial capital focused more on the relics of her robe and girdle than on her empty tomb. Nevertheless, since these relics eventually appear in certain Dormition narratives, as just noted, it will be useful to make some mention of the entirely different tradition of the robe's discovery that was circulating in contemporary Constantinople. Rather than employing the device of the late apostle to explain the robe's invention, the imperial capital during the fifth, sixth, and seventh centuries embraced an alternative set of traditions that were uniquely its own, the so-called legend of Galbius and Candidus. This narrative, whose earliest recension Wenger has convincingly assigned to the late fifth century, tells the tale of Galbius and Candidus, two converts

---

[154] Michel van Esbroeck, 'L'Assomption de la Vierge dans un Transitus Pseudo-Basilien', *Analecta Bollandiana*, 92 (1974), 128–63.

[155] The identification of Zion with the death of Mary suggests an origin sometime after the late 6th century, and the narrative's liturgical programme cannot be from after 700, at which time one of its main churches ceased to function.

from Arianism who travel from Constantinople to the Holy Land.[156] While they are travelling through Palestine on their way to Jerusalem, a Jewish woman offers them hospitality, and they stay the night in her house. As they settle in, Galbius and Candidus notice a small, inner room filled with sick and possessed people who were receiving healing. After persuading their hostess to dine with them, they get her drunk and trick her into revealing the nature of the object in this room. She tells them that the room contains a robe once belonging to the Virgin Mary, which has been in her family for generations. It is kept in a special coffer and has been passed down from one of her ancestors, who was one of Mary's attendants. Galbius and Candidus ask to be allowed to sleep in the inner room with the coffer, and their hostess grants their request. During the night, the two men carefully measure the coffer and take note of its details, with the intent of eventually stealing it. In the morning, Galbius and Candidus thank the woman for her hospitality and depart for Jerusalem, where they have an exact duplicate of the woman's coffer made. On their way back to Constantinople, they return to the woman, who again offers them lodging for the night, allowing them to sleep in the room with the coffer and its robe as before. In the middle of the night then, Galbius and Candidus switch their replica for the real coffer and its relic, and in the morning, when they leave, they take with them the Virgin's robe, bringing it to Constantinople.

As one can see, the story of Galbius and Candidus is not in any way a Dormition narrative, and consequently, neither it nor the relics of Constantinople themselves will receive much treatment in this study beyond this brief discussion. Nevertheless, this narrative is the earliest known account of the Virgin's robe and its discovery, a legend that initially did not circulate much beyond the city of Constantinople, where it appears to have been the predominant Marian tradition in late antiquity. Elsewhere in the early Byzantine empire, it seems, the early Dormition traditions were instead the legends of choice, as manifest in their rapid diffusion throughout the regions and languages of the empire and beyond. But likewise, these Dormition traditions are

---

[156] Edition and translation: Wenger, *L'Assomption*, 294–311. Regarding the date, see ibid. 111–36. Mimouni, after re-evaluating Wenger's conclusions, agrees with his assessment: *Dormition*, 604–17.

themselves strangely absent from the literature of the imperial capital for over a century after their initial appearance in the provinces. All of this suggests that these were two 'rival' Marian traditions in late antiquity: one centred in Constantinople and focused on the origin of the city's prized relics, and another, known throughout the provinces, which told the end of Mary's life, in a way that more or less precluded the existence of any Marian relics by the removal of her body from this world.

The first evidence of the Dormition traditions having made any impact in the imperial capital comes with the emperor Maurice's decision, at the very end of the sixth century, to establish the commemoration of Mary's Dormition on 15 August throughout the empire.[157] There is also a *Life of the Virgin* attributed to Maximus the Confessor which, if authentic, would date to approximately the same time, probably composed early in his career, when he was living in the capital city (before 626). This text, preserved only in Georgian translation, is probably the earliest complete life of the Virgin, pulling together traditions from the infancy gospels, the New Testament, and the Dormition apocrypha to produce a complete narrative of the Virgin's life.[158] Although I have heard whispers questioning the *Life*'s authorship, I have not yet seen a challenge in print. The text's editor Michel van Esbroeck argues rather convincingly for its authenticity, and no less an authority on Maximus than Hans Urs von Balthasar quickly vouched for its authenticity.[159] Subsequent studies by Simon Mimouni and Aidan Nichols have also affirmed van Esbroeck's attribution, although some recent studies of Maximus have oddly avoided this text and the issue of its authorship entirely.[160] As van Esbroeck demonstrates, for

---

[157] Nicephorus Callistus, *Historia ecclesiastica* I. 17, 28 (PG 147. 292).

[158] Maximus the Confessor, *Life of the Virgin* (Michel van Esbroeck, ed., *Maxime le Confesseur, Vie de la Vierge*, 2 vols., CSCO 478–9 (Louvain: Peeters Press, 1986). Regarding the place of this composition in Maximus' life, see ibid. pp. XXXI–XXXII.

[159] Michel van Esbroeck, 'Some Earlier Features in the Life of the Virgin'.

[160] van Esbroeck, *Maxime le Confesseur*, pp. III–XXXVIII (Fr.). After critically analysing each of van Esbroeck's arguments Mimouni concludes: 'On ne peut donc que difficilement réfuter, et par conséquent refuser, les propositions de M. van Esbroeck.' Simon Mimouni, 'Les *Vies de la Vierge*: État de la question', *Apocrypha*, 5 (1994), 216–20. See also Aidan Nichols, OP, *Byzantine Gospel: Maximus the Confessor in Modern Scholarship* (Edinburgh: T. & T.

instance, this *Life* includes an early version of the Galbius and Candidus legend, and the *Life* itself reports that it utilized apocryphal sources (as opposed the later homiletic traditions) for its account of Mary's Dormition, both of which support its composition in the early seventh century.[161]

More than a century passes before we find an account of the Virgin's Dormition that may be unquestionably associated with Constantinople, namely the two homilies composed by Patriarch Germanus of Constantinople (715–30).[162] It would perhaps be wrong to overemphasize the longstanding silence on this subject in the culture of the imperial capital by insisting, for instance, that these legends were completely unknown or deliberately ignored. Nevertheless, the absence of these traditions in Constantinople, at a time when they had become so widespread and popular in the provinces, is certainly telling, and this neglect of the Dormition traditions might possibly be attributed to a greater concern in Constantinople for the powerful Marian relics that made the Virgin a very real presence within the city.[163]

Finally, there is another set of traditions that identify Ephesus, rather than Jerusalem, as the city where the Virgin Mary departed this life. While these Ephesus traditions may be more familiar to many readers, they are substantially later than the traditions that locate the end of the Virgin's life in Jerusalem

---

Clark, 1993), 111–19. This work is strangely unacknowledged, for instance, in Andrew Louth, *Maximus the Confessor* (New York: Routledge, 1996); idem, 'Recent Research on St Maximus the Confessor: A Survey', *Saint Vladimir's Theological Quarterly*, 42 (1998), 67–84.

[161] Van Esbroeck, *Maxime le Confesseur*, pp. XVI, XXVI–XXVIII; Maximus the Confessor, *Life of the Virgin*, 2 (ibid. 4 (Geor.) and 3 (Fr.)). See also Mimouni, 'Les *Vies de la Vierge*', 218. By way of contrast, Epiphanius the Monk's *Life of the Virgin*, composed at the end of the 8th century, explicitly draws on John of Thessalonica's and Andrew of Crete's homilies in order to narrate the end of Mary's life, as the *Life* itself makes explicit: PG 120. 188. This would seem to indicate that the life attributed to Maximus was composed somewhat earlier, and on this basis at least is likely to be authentic.

[162] Germanus of Constantinople, *Homilies on the Dormition I & II* [*or.* 6 & 8] (PG 98. 340–72).

[163] On the importance of these relics from a Constantinopolitan viewpoint, see especially Vasiliki Limberis, *Divine Heiress: The Virgin Mary and the Creation of Christian Constantinople* (New York: Routledge, 1994) and Averil Cameron, 'The Theotokos in Sixth-Century Constantinople', *Journal of Theological Studies*, NS 29 (1978), 79–108.

and are not evident before the end of the ninth century. Their source no doubt lies in the early Christian tradition of the apostle John's mission to Ephesus, a tradition often affirmed by the Dormition traditions themselves.[164] On the basis of Christ's instructions from the cross to his mother and the 'Beloved Disciple', 'Woman, here is your son. . . . Here is your mother',[165] many must have assumed that after Christ's death, his mother was entrusted to the care of the Beloved Disciple. Since tradition has identified this disciple with John, it was further understood that Mary would have accompanied him on his mission to Ephesus to live out her final days there.[166] Nevertheless, the earliest evidence of any such belief appears only in the late ninth century, in a Syriac manuscript copied in 874, which reports that Mary accompanied John to Ephesus, where she died and was buried.[167] Three more Syriac writers from the twelfth and thirteenth centuries attest to this tradition, but this is the sum of all the premodern evidence that may be marshalled on behalf of this tradition.[168] Despite such meagre evidence, beginning in the seventeenth century and for much of the eighteenth century, many scholars favoured the tradition of Mary's death in Ephesus. They argued that the existence of a church dedicated to Mary in Ephesus, in which the third ecumenical council met, and a letter from the council associating Ephesus with both John

---

[164] When John comes to Mary's house, it is frequently noted that he travelled there from Ephesus.

[165] John 19: 26–7.

[166] Many of the early Dormition traditions are aware of the potential conflict among these traditions, and when John arrives, Mary reminds him that Christ left her in his care. In his own defence, John reminds Mary (and the reader) that he did care for her as he was ordered, by leaving behind a servant. John explains that this was the only possible solution, since he was also commanded by Christ to go forth and preach the Gospel. See esp. *Liber Requiei*, 42–3, in Appendix A.

[167] French translation is given in Michel van Esbroeck, 'Deux listes d'apôtres conservées en syriaque', in René Lavenant, SJ (ed.), *Third Symposium Syriacum 1980*, Orientalia Christiana Analecta, 221 (Rome: Pont. Institutum Studiorum Orientalium, 1983), 15–24, esp. 22–3. See also the article by Filbert de la Chaise, OFM Cap., 'A l'origine des récits apocryphes du "Transitus Mariae"', *Ephemerides Mariologicae*, 29 (1979), 77–90, where he argues (unconvincingly) on behalf of the Ephesus tradition. De la Chaise also refers to a manuscript in which Moshe bar Kepha attests to this tradition: ibid. 81.

[168] These are identified and discussed in de la Chaise, 'A l'origine des récits', 81–2.

and the Virgin Mary authenticated the Ephesus tradition. Nevertheless, these arguments have since been dismissed and are no longer taken seriously.[169]

The tradition of Mary's house in Ephesus, however, as separate from the question of her tomb, has witnessed some dramatic developments over the course of the past two centuries, even if these may not hold much in the way of historical significance. This tradition was enlivened by the famous visions of a nineteenth-century nun, Catherine von Emmerich (d. 1824) who, although she never left her native Germany, repeatedly received visions of the Virgin Mary living her final days in a house near Ephesus.[170] Inspired by her visions, a group of priests from Izmir set out with spade in one hand and Catherine's detailed descriptions in the other, and in the hills above the ruins of Ephesus they discovered the foundations of an ancient house, remarkably, just as Catherine had described it.[171] Despite this modern 'miracle', however, there remains virtually no historical evidence of an ancient tradition that the Virgin's earthly life had its end in Ephesus. The earliest evidence of such belief is significantly more recent than the Jerusalem traditions, and the very limited medieval evidence for this tradition is for some peculiar reason limited almost exclusively to the Tur Abdin region, now in south-eastern Turkey.

CONCLUSIONS

Having rather quickly surveyed the earliest literary evidence of traditions concerning the end of the Virgin Mary's life, we may now draw the rather general conclusion that the end of the fifth century saw the initial emergence of these traditions into the mainstream of orthodox Christian discourse from an otherwise uncertain past. That these traditions had some sort of a prior existence is quite clear, not only from the sheer volume and diversity of the traditions that suddenly appear, but also from the fact that many of the earliest extant narratives are themselves

---

[169] See the discussion in Mimouni, *Dormition*, 586–8.

[170] Although none other than Jugie notes the 'caractère suspect' of these visions. *La Mort*, 96.

[171] A tomb, also described by Emmerich, has not been found.

translations from earlier Greek texts that must have been in circulation no later than the early fifth century. Very little, if anything, is known for certain about the prior history of these traditions, although there has been a fair amount of speculation regarding their origins, particularly regarding a genesis within some sort of Jewish Christianity. When these narratives finally do appear, however, they manifest a striking diversity, including several well-developed narrative traditions and a handful of atypical traditions, all of which come suddenly and simultaneously into view. This variety has invited several scholars to propose an evolutionary typology, according to which one type of narrative evolves from and displaces another, in a linear succession, a topic that will be discussed fully in Ch. 3.

In the chapters that follow, I will, as many have before me, address both the diversity of this corpus and the question of its prehistory. The former issue must be considered first, since it will determine whether we ought to look for a single origin for these traditions or, alternatively, for several distinct origins underlying these diverse narratives. From this point we can begin to unravel some of the puzzling clues that the earliest narratives afford regarding their earliest milieux. Many of the earliest narratives are in fact quite heterodox from the vantage of early Byzantine orthodoxy, and the process of theological revision now visible in the narratives of the sixth and seventh century shows a considerable concern to recast these narratives to fit their new theological context. Other early narratives, however, are quite orthodox and stood in need of much less rewriting. Yet even these betray a keen awareness that these traditions have long been absent from the orthodox mainstream of Christianity, a void that is explained by such devices as the 'global' search undertaken by the monks of Sinai at the opening of the earliest Bethlehem narratives. Before turning to consider these matters, however, we must consider the rather complex body of cultic evidence that relates to this literary corpus, and as we will find, the early liturgical and archaeological evidence confirms, among other things, that the late fifth and sixth centuries were the time in which these traditions about the end of Mary's life first entered into orthodox Christian thought and practice.

2

The Ancient Palestinian Cult of the Virgin and the Early Dormition Traditions

The nascent cult of the Virgin in late ancient Palestine is unquestionably intertwined with the early narratives of Mary's Dormition and Assumption.[1] At the very moment when the various Dormition narratives first appear, many of the locations featured in the legends were simultaneously becoming the focus of organized veneration and were incorporated into the annual liturgical calendar of Jerusalem. Consequently, any investigation of the earliest Dormition traditions must also take into consideration the development of these related liturgical practices. On the one hand, these liturgical traditions are important to understand in their own right, since they are, unquestionably, ancient traditions about the end of the Virgin Mary's life. Simply because these are non-narrative sources does not mean that they are any less a part of this corpus of traditions. Nevertheless, our primary interest in this study is to understand the early history of the different narrative traditions, and for this purpose, an understanding of the earliest liturgical traditions is highly desirable. As we have just seen in the preceding chapter, in discussing the Coptic traditions, an understanding of liturgical history can often help to date and understand better certain early narratives. Moreover, as the homilies of the Coptic traditions should also remind us, many of the earliest narratives were designed with a liturgical purpose: homilies predominate, but many so-called apocrypha can be instead identified (and some even identify

[1] An earlier version of this chapter was previously published as Stephen J. Shoemaker, 'The (Re?)Discovery of the Kathisma Church and the Cult of the Virgin in Late Antique Palestine', *Maria: A Journal of Marian Studies*, 2 (2001), 21–72.

themselves) as liturgical readings.[2] Jacob of Serug's homily, for instance, may very well have been delivered for a feast of the Virgin, and the early Six Books apocrypha explicitly identify themselves as liturgical readings, providing a calendar of Marian feasts together with a mandate that 'the volume of the decease of the Blessed One [Mary]' be read at each of these feasts.[3] Likewise, certain of the earliest Palm traditions bear evidence of possible division for liturgical use, and John of Thessalonica's homily was delivered to initiate the celebration of the feast of the Dormition on 15 August in that city.[4] For these reasons especially, the ancient Marian liturgies of Jerusalem have always formed an important component of the study of the early Dormition traditions, often utilized by scholars to organize and date the literary traditions, with varying results.

In addition, recent archaeological discoveries make a re-evaluation of these liturgical traditions particularly needful at this moment. The most important of these is clearly the (re)discovery of the ancient church of the Kathisma, or 'Seat', of the Theotokos, a large fifth-century Marian church that excavators have gradually brought to light over the course of the past decade. This church is the first known centre of organized Marian cult in the Holy Land. Our earliest sources indicate that the Kathisma church was built to commemorate the spot where, according to the *Protevangelium of James*, the Virgin descended from an ass and rested before giving birth to Christ. Although it

---

[2] Simon C. Mimouni, 'La Lecture liturgique et les apocryphes du Nouveau Testament: Le Cas de la Dormitio grecque du Pseudo-Jean', *Orientalia Christiana Periodica,* 59 (1993), 403–25; idem, 'Les Transitus Mariae sont-ils vraiment des apocryphes?' *Studia Patristica,* 25 (1993), 122–8.

[3] William Wright, 'The Departure of my Lady Mary from this World', *The Journal of Sacred Literature and Biblical Record,* 6 (1865), ܝ (Syr.) and 153 (Eng.); Agnes Smith Lewis, ed., *Apocrypha Syriaca,* Studia Sinaitica, XI (London: C. J. Clay & Sons, 1902), ܟܐ–ܣ (Syr.) and 61 (Eng.).

[4] Regarding the earliest Palm traditions, see the headings that have been inserted into the *Liber Requiei* (88: Victor Arras, ed., *De Transitu Mariae Aethiopice,* i. CSCO 342–3 (Louvain: Secrétariat du CorpusSCO, 1973), 52 (Eth.) and 34 (Lat.)) and the *Obsequies* (William Wright, ed., *Contributions to the Apocryphal Literature* (London: Williams & Norgate, 1865), ܩ (Syr.) and 47 (Eng.)), which may be indications of liturgical usage. On John's homily, and its later liturgical usage as well, see Simon Mimouni, *Dormition et assomption de Marie: Histoire des traditions anciennes,* Théologie Historique, 98 (Paris: Beauchesne, 1995), 135–6, 146.

appears from this and other indicators that the site of the
Kathisma was originally associated with the celebration of the
Nativity, by the beginning of the fifth century, this church had
become an important centre of Marian cult. It was long thought
that the Kathisma church had been excavated in the late 1950s
during the excavations at Ramat Rahel, just to the south of
Jerusalem. In 1992, however, salvage excavations made necessary by the effort to widen the main Jerusalem–Bethlehem road
revealed the existence of a large church, just a few hundred
metres south of Ramat Rahel, near the monastery of Mar Elias.
In the summer of 1997 another emergency excavation was
performed after the church's foundation was damaged by construction workers laying pipe for the nearby settlement at Har
Homa. Finds brought to light during this second season, as
well as a recently completed third season, have convinced the
excavators that this new church is in fact the ancient church of
the Kathisma, and that the church at Ramat Rahel, only a few
hundred metres to the north, was previously misidentified.

  This recent discovery, possibly to be identified with the
Kathisma church, calls for a fresh study of the ancient Marian
shrines of Jerusalem and their related liturgies, primarily during
their formative period between the fifth and seventh centuries.
In reassessing these phenomena, this chapter will first consider
the material remains evident of Marian veneration, including the
two primary Marian churches, the Kathisma and Mary's tomb,
as well as various *eulogiai* indicative of the vitality of Marian
piety in Byzantine Palestine. The chapter will then conclude
with an investigation of the Marian liturgies of ancient Jerusalem, examining a number of ancient liturgical texts that are
preserved only in Georgian and were either unknown or underutilized in many previous discussions of the Marian liturgies
of ancient Palestine. These documents, together with more
familiar liturgical sources, can help us to understand better the
earliest development of the cult of the Virgin and the changing
relationships among the various early Marian shrines in late
ancient Jerusalem.

THE ANCIENT CHURCH OF THE KATHISMA AND THE ORIGINS OF THE PALESTINIAN CULT OF THE VIRGIN

In 1347 CE, Niccolò da Poggibonsi, an Italian Franciscan, recorded what appears to be the last known sighting of the Kathisma church, or at least, what were presumably some of its remains. In his catalogue of the holy sites of Palestine, the *Libro d'Oltramare*, Niccolò describes his journey from Jerusalem to Bethlehem, coming first upon the monastery of Mar Elias, which, he notes, stands midway between Jerusalem and Bethlehem on the main road, as it still does today. Near this monastery, Niccolò explains, 'there was once a church on the plain, about a crossbow's shot toward Jerusalem, but now it is not there, except for some brick pavement, resembling a mosaic'.[5] Approximately fifty years later, a Russian pilgrim named Grethinos could only report having seen a rock, two kilometres south of Mar Elias, on which the Virgin Mary had once supposedly sat, when she paused to rest before giving birth nearby,[6] as the apocryphal *Protevangelium of James* describes the events of the Nativity. By

[5] Niccolò da Poggibonsi, OFM, *Libro d'Oltramare* (Alberto Bacchi, ed., *Libro d'Oltramare*, 2 vols., Scelta di curiosita letterarie inedite o rare dal secolo XIII al XVII, Dispensa, 182–3 (Bologna: G. Romagnoli, 1881), i. 210.

[6] Grethinos the Archimandrite, *Pilgrimage of Grethinos the Archimandrite* 15 (Sophia Khitrovo (trans.), *Itinéraires russes en Orient*, Publications de la Société de l'Orient latin, Série géographique, 5 (Geneva: J-G. Fick, 1889), 181). Grethinos locates this rock in a pea field, full of rocks in his day. The field, however, is in the wrong spot: past Mar Elias, and even past Rachel's tomb. We can see, however, in an earlier Russian pilgrimage account, a separation between the (remains of the) church of Mary at the mid-point between Jerusalem and Bethlehem and the location of her descent from the ass. In the pilgrimage account of Daniel the Abbot (1106–8), Daniel notes in moving from Jerusalem to Bethlehem that 'there was once a church and monastery of the Holy Mother of God', which stood in the approximate location of the ancient Kathisma, 'but now they are destroyed by pagans'. From there, it is another two 'versts' to the tomb of Rachel, and finally one more 'verst' to the place where Mary descended from the ass. This brings us into Bethlehem, and what has presumably occurred here is an attempt to harmonize the two divergent Nativity traditions of the *Protevangelium of James* and the canonical gospels. Daniel the Abbot, *The Life and Journey of Daniel, Abbot of the Russian Land* 45–6 (Klaus-Dieter Seemann, ed., *Хожение [Khozhdenie]: Wallfahrtsbericht*, Slavische Propyläen, 36 (Munich: W. Fink, 1970), 62; trans., John Wilkinson, Joyce Hill, and W. F.

the time of Felix Fabri's famous pilgrimages to the Holy Land, in the late fifteenth century, only the 'rocky places' where the tired Virgin once sat to rest remained to be seen.[7] With this it seems that what was once perhaps the most impressive Marian shrine of Palestine had become hidden beneath the earth, a testament, perhaps, to its apocryphal origin.

Nevertheless, in spite of its medieval disappearance, the existence of this church continued to be known from these and other literary sources. Generally known as the 'Kathisma of the Theotokos', or the 'Seat of the God-Bearer', as the Greek translates, the church was apparently built to commemorate the spot halfway between Jerusalem and Bethlehem, where, according to the second-century *Protevangelium*, the Virgin rested before giving birth in a nearby cave.[8] The first text to draw our attention to this site, other than the *Protevangelium*, is the Jerusalem Armenian Lectionary, a calendar representing the Holy City's liturgical practices sometime in the period 420–40. Without either naming or even indicating the existence of a church on this spot, the Armenian Lectionary outlines readings for a feast of Mary the Theotokos celebrated at the mid-point of the Jerusalem–Bethlehem road.[9] The lectionary also fails to identify this location with the tradition from the *Protevangelium*, informing us only that a feast of Mary was celebrated here on 15 August, a date that later came to be associated with the celebration of Mary's Dormition and Assumption, a transformation about which more will be said later in this chapter.

There are no other witnesses to the Kathisma church for about a hundred years, until the early sixth century, when a certain Theodosius compiled a pilgrimage guide known as the *De situ*

Ryan, *Jerusalem Pilgrimage 1099–1185*, Works Issued by the Hakluyt Society, 2nd series, 167 (London: The Hakluyt Society, 1988), 143).

[7] Felix Fabri, OP, *Evagatorium in Terrae Sanctae, Arabiae et Egypti peregrinationem*, 3 vols., ed. C. D. Hassler, Bibliothek des Literarischen Vereins in Stuttgart, 2–4 (Stuttgart: sumtibus Societatis literariae stuttgardiensis, 1843–9), i. 429.

[8] *Protev.* 17. 1. 3 (Konstantin Tischendorf, ed., *Evangelia Apocrypha*, 2nd edn. (Leipzig: 1876; repr. Hildesheim: Georg Olms, 1966), 33).

[9] A. Renoux, ed., *Le Codex arménien Jérusalem 121*, 2 vols., PO 35. 1 and 36. 2 (Turnhout: Brepols, 1971), ii. 354–7. For the date, see ibid. i. pp. 166–72.

terrae sanctae, written sometime between 520 and 530.[10] Like
the Armenian Lectionary, Theodosius' guide also fails to indicate explicitly the presence of a church at this site, but it does
clearly identify the location with the *Protevangelium*'s tradition
of Mary's pause, also mentioning the existence of a rock on
which the Virgin sat to rest, thereby blessing it. But by the time
of Theodosius' visit, in the early sixth century, this rock was no
longer to be found at the midpoint of the Jerusalem–Bethlehem
road, a circumstance that Theodosius attributes to recent events.
According to his account, this blessed stone attracted the interest of a certain Urbicus, who had been a Roman administrator
in Palestine during the reign of Anastasius (491–518), some
twenty years before Theodosius compiled his guide. Urbicus,
he informs us, ordered that the stone be cut into an altar and
shipped to Constantinople. But this relic, unlike so many others,
refused to be taken from the Holy Land to the imperial city and
could not be moved beyond the St Stephen's gate in Jerusalem.
When Urbicus eventually recognized the futility of his efforts,
he ordered that the stone, at this point already made into an
altar, be taken to the church of the Holy Sepulchre, where in
Theodosius' day it could still be found behind Christ's Tomb.
It would seem that something of this nature may actually have
happened, since the rock is not a feature of subsequent Kathisma
traditions, at least not for another 900 years, when it rather suddenly reappears in Grethinos' account of his pilgrimage, made
around 1400. Even then, Grethinos does not find the rock in the
correct spot, but instead identifies a rock about two kilometres
further south, beyond the present site of Rachel's tomb.[11]

   The first explicit notice of a church built to commemorate
this tradition comes only from two related lives of Theodosius
the Coenobite composed in the mid-sixth century by Theodore
of Petra and Cyril of Scythopolis. These *Vitae* both describe
the generosity of a woman named Ikelia, a governor's wife and
later a deaconess, who during the reign of Juvenal financed the

---

[10] Theodosius, *De situ terrae sanctae* (P. Geyer, ed., *Itineraria et alia Geo-
graphica*, CCL 175 (Turnhout: Brepols, 1965), 119); composed sometime
between 518 and 538: John Wilkinson, *Jerusalem Pilgrims Before the Crusades*
(Warminster: Aris & Phillips, 1977), 5; Johann Gildemeister, *Theodosius de situ
Terrae Sanctae im ächten Text und der Brevarius de Hierosolyma vervollstäandigt*
(Bonn: Adolph Marcus, 1882), 9.   [11] See n. 6 above.

construction of a church dedicated to Mary on this spot, sometime around the year 450. According to Theodore's account, the monk Theodosius was sent by his superior to live at the church known as the Old Kathisma, which lay along the main Jerusalem–Bethlehem road.[12] To this Cyril of Scythopolis adds that, after Ikelia's death, the 'community of pious ascetics' at the church of the Kathisma elected Theodosius first as their steward (οἰκονόμος) and eventually as the superior (ἡγούμενος) of the monastery.[13] By the mid-fifth century then, the tradition of Mary's rest along the Jerusalem–Bethlehem road was marked not only by the church of the Kathisma, but also by a monastic community attached to the church.

When archaeologists excavating at Ramat Rahel in the 1950s discovered a large basilical church (13.5m × 20m) and monastery from the fifth century (see Fig. 4), they quickly determined that they had uncovered remains of the long-lost Kathisma church and monastery.[14] Their decision was quite reasonable: the site lies just east of the Jerusalem–Bethlehem road, approximately 4km from both ancient cities, which our sources identify as the location of the ancient Kathisma church. Furthermore, the stratigraphy of the structure isolates its construction to sometime during the fifth century, in agreement with Ikelia's reported foundation of the Kathisma church around 450.[15] The

---

[12] Theodore of Petra, *v. Thds.* (H. Usener, ed., *Der heilige Theodosius, Schriften des Theodoros und Kyrillos* (Leipzig: Teubner, 1890), 13–14).

[13] Cyril of Scythopolis, *v. Thds.* (Eduard Schwartz, ed., *Kyrillos von Skythopolis*, TU 49. 2 (Leipzig: J. C. Hinrichs, 1939), 236).

[14] See the excavation reports published in Y. Aharoni, 'Excavations at Ramath Rahel, 1954: Preliminary Report', *Israel Exploration Journal*, 6 (1956), 102–11, 137–57, esp. 107–11; idem, *Excavations at Ramat Rahel*, 2 vols., Serie archeologica, 2 and 6 (Rome: Universita degli studi, Centro di studi semitici, 1962 and 1964), esp. P. Testini, 'The *Kathisma* Church and Monastery', i. 73–91, and idem, 'The Church and Monastery of the "Kathisma"', ii. 101–6.

[15] Pottery from the 4th century was discovered in the church's foundation and a coin from the reign of Anastasias I (491–518) in the church itself (Aharoni, 'Excavations at Ramath Rahel', 110, 155–6). The excavators' conclusions have recently been reconfirmed by Jodi Magness, *Jerusalem Ceramic Chronology, circa 200–800 CE*, Journal for the Study of the Old Testament/American Schools of Oriental Research Monographs, 9 (Sheffield: Sheffield Academic Press, 1993), 116–17. Magness also identifies the presence of pottery from the late 5th century in the monastery, indicating a *terminus ante quem* for the church and monastery: ibid. 107.

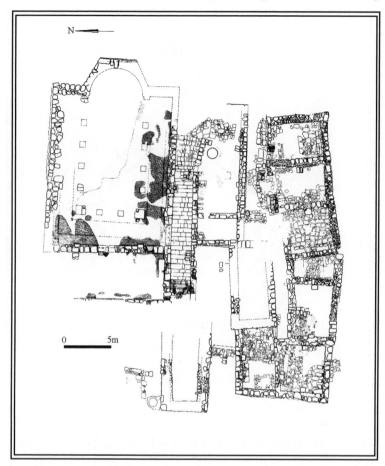

FIG. 4. The fifth-century church and monastery at Ramat Rahel (the 'Old Kathisma') (after Y. Aharoni, *Excavations at Ramat Rahel*, 2 vols., Serie archeologica, 2 and 6 (Rome: Universita degli studi, Centro di studi semitici, 1962 and 1964), fig. 39)

architecture of the building finds parallels in a number of other fifth-century churches, and its mosaic pavements exemplify a common decorative pattern of this period.[16] Consequently, for almost half of a century, the identification of this structure with the ancient church of the Kathisma stood unquestioned.

[16] Aharoni, *Excavations at Ramat Rahel*, i. 77–86.

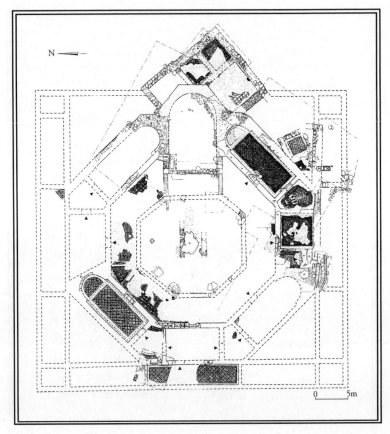

FIG. 5. The 'Mar Elias' church (The 'New Kathisma') (after Rina Avner, 'ירושלים מר אליאס—כנסיית הקתיסמה', *Hadashot Arkheologiyot*, 108 (1998), 139–42)

A recent discovery, however, has cast doubt on this once rather easy assumption. In 1992, efforts to widen the Jerusalem–Bethlehem highway led to a salvage excavation in which the foundations of a large, octagonal church (43m × 52m) were uncovered, approximately 350m north of the monastery of Mar Elias (see Figs. 5 and 6).[17] The Mar Elias church (as I will call it) lies near an old cistern identified by local tradition as the 'Bir al-

---

[17] The report for this first season has been published by Rina Avner, 'Jerusalem, Mar Elias', *Excavations and Surveys in Israel*, 13 (1993), 89–92.

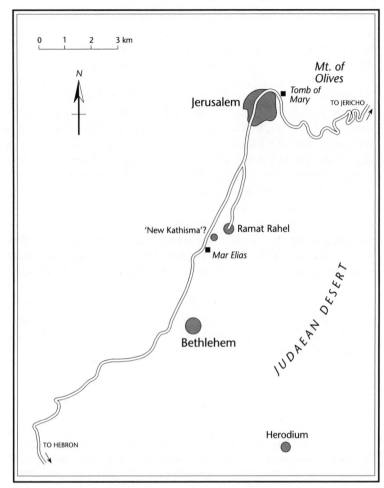

Fig. 6. Marian shrines of fifth-century Jerusalem (after Y. Aharoni, 'Excavations at Ramath Rahel, 1954: Preliminary Report', *Israel Exploration Journal*, 6 (1956), fig. 1)

Qadismu', or the 'well of the Magi', a cistern that is also, it should be noted, relatively near the Ramat Rahel church, whose remains lie only few hundred metres north-west of the new Mar Elias church.[18] Work on the Mar Elias church was

[18] See e.g. A. M. Schneider, 'Die Kathismakirche auf Chirbet Abu Brek', *Journal of the Palestine Oriental Society*, 14 (1934), 230–1, which enlists the

unfortunately suspended before its remains could be fully excavated, until the autumn of 1997, when construction workers laying pipe for the controversial settlement at Har Homa damaged the church's foundation, necessitating a rescue excavation. This time, archaeologists from the Israel Antiquities Authority were able to excavate a significant portion of the church, which they date to the fifth century, revealing a large rock, about 2 × 4m, in the centre of the church.[19] While the architecture of the Mar Elias church is somewhat more unusual than that of the Ramat Rahel church, the design of three concentric octagons finds very close parallels in the fifth-century churches at Mt. Gerazim and Capernaum.[20] Its floor mosaics are also quite unusual, finding their closest parallels in the Dome of the Rock, but these mosaics are early eighth-century additions that were installed when the church was converted into a mosque at this time.[21] Based on these discoveries, the excavators have concluded that this church was in fact the church of the Kathisma, rather than the church at Ramat Rahel, just a few hundred metres to the north. This identification is supported, they argue, by the large rock at the centre of this church, which, as we have already noted, certain accounts identify as an important feature of the Kathisma traditions.[22]

nearby well as evidence in favour of the Ramat Rahel church's identification with the ancient Kathisma.

[19] The report for this second season has been published by Rina Avner, 'ירושלים, מר אליאס—כוסיית הקתיסמה', *Hadashot Arkheologiyot*, 108 (1998), 139–42. An English translation will, it is hoped, soon appear in *Excavations and Surveys in Israel*, 21. Note also that a third season of excavation was just completed as this chapter was being written, winter 1999–2000, and Avner has informed me that during the most recent season coins from the 5th century were found beneath the lowest of the three floors, and 6th-century coins above, thus confirming the date.

[20] Yitzhak Magen, 'The Church of Mary Theotokos on Mt. Gerazim', in Yoram Tsafrir (ed.), *Ancient Churches Revealed* (Jerusalem: Israel Exploration Society, 1993), 83–9; Virgilio Corbo, OFM, 'The Church of the House of St. Peter at Capernaum', ibid. 71–6.

[21] In the second season, it was recognized that the floor had three different levels: two as a church, and a third floor that was put in place when the church was converted into a mosque: Avner, 'ירושלים, מר אליאס—כוסיית הקתיסמה'. The excavator, Rina Avner, has informed me that coins from the early Islamic period have been found beneath the uppermost level of the floor, dating the present mosaics to the time of the church's conversion into a mosque.

[22] Avner, 'ירושלים, מר אליאס—כוסיית הקתיסמה'; eadem, 'Birth Pangs on the

The result of this new discovery is that we are now confronted with two fifth-century churches, within a few hundred metres of each other, in the approximate location of the ancient Kathisma church, both of which have been identified as this church by their excavators. Various news organs quickly reported the new Mar Elias church as the long-lost church of the Kathisma, announcing that the excavations would continue, in an effort to develop the site for the anticipated throngs of millennial pilgrims.[23] In all the excitement, the lowly church of Ramat Rahel and its monastery have been almost, if not completely, forgotten. Nevertheless, it seems that this edifice should be reintroduced to the current discussion of the ancient Kathisma traditions. Indeed, it would appear that the newly discovered church raises far more questions than it answers. For instance, if we accept the Mar Elias church as the Kathisma, then what was the church and monastic complex at Ramat Rahel? Alternatively, is it possible that the Ramat Rahel church is in fact the ancient Kathisma, as it was identified for decades, while the Mar Elias church was intended to commemorate something else? Or is it somehow possible that both of these churches were built to commemorate the Virgin's *ante partum* pause? Unfortunately, there are no easy answers to these questions, and since the archaeology of the two structures cannot decide, we must seek clarification in the rather complex tangle of textual witnesses to the ancient church of the Kathisma.

As noted above, the excavators of the Mar Elias church have proposed that the enormous rock unearthed at the centre of their church favours its identification with the Kathisma, a line of reasoning accepted by many, including the Greek Orthodox Patriarchate (which owns the property and plans to develop the site for pilgrims). At first glance, there is much to favour this conclusion. Although neither the *Protevangelium* nor the

Bethlehem Road (in Hebrew)', *Judea and Samaria Research Studies: Proceedings of the Eighth Annual Meeting 1998* (Kedumim-Ariel: The Research Institute, College of Judea and Samaria 1999), 155–60; English summary, pp. XVIII–XIX.

[23] This final process was just getting started, albeit somewhat belatedly, in the spring of 2000. It is possible, however, that the present *intifada* has disrupted these developments, since the Mar Elias church lies just over the Green Line in Palestinian territory.

Armenian Lectionary mention Mary's sitting or the rock, there is the testimony of Theodosius' pilgrimage guide regarding a holy rock on which the Virgin once rested. In the light of this one might consider the matter rather easily resolved, but this is not the full extent of Theodosius' witness. As already mentioned, Theodosius continues to describe the removal of the rock from its original location along the Jerusalem–Bethlehem road. Although Urbicus, the Byzantine official, was not successful in bringing the rock to Constantinople, the stone was in fact, according to Theodosius, displaced and turned into an altar, which in the early sixth century could be found in the church of the Holy Sepulchre. This is the first and last mention of the rock of Mary's Kathisma in any text until the Russian Grethinos reports having seen this rock some 2km to the south, around the year 1400.

If this creates at least some doubt regarding the identification of the Mar Elias church with the church of the Kathisma, then what alternatives might exist for understanding this newly discovered church? One is suggested by the late sixth-century pilgrimage guide attributed to a certain Antony of Placentia, also known as the 'Piacenza Pilgrim'. This guide, probably written between 560 and 570, describes the holy sites along the Jerusalem–Bethlehem road, first noting the place called 'Ramah', at the third mile from Jerusalem, where Rachel's body lies.[24] Just beyond this 'Ramah' of 'Rahel' (which must be the

---

[24] (Ps.-)Antoninus Placentius, *Itinerarium* (P. Geyer, ed., *Itineraria et alia Geographica*, CCL 175 (Turnhout: Brepols, 1965), 137); for the date, see Celestina Milani, *Itinerarium Antonini Placentini: Un viaggio in Terra Santa del 560–570 d.C.* (Milan: Vita e Pensiero, 1977), 36–8. The location of Rachel's tomb is a matter concerning which there is some question. In the first place, there are two conflicting traditions from the Hebrew Scriptures, one locating her tomb near its traditional site, outside Bethlehem, and another (more accurate) tradition locating the tomb to the north of Jerusalem (where ancient Ramah was in fact located: for more on this matter, see *The Anchor Bible Dictionary*, s.v. 'Rachel's Tomb'). G. Lombardi, *La tomba di Rahel*, Pubblicazioni dello Studium Biblicum Franciscanum, Collectio Minor, 11 (Jerusalem: Franciscan Printing Press, 1971) discusses the history of the traditional tomb near Bethlehem, as well as claiming to identify Rachel's actual tomb to the north of Jerusalem, near 'ain Farah (which Lombardi identifies as the biblical Ephrathah).

Nevertheless, from the first century CE onwards, both Jewish and Christian sources agree that Rachel's tomb lay somewhere between Jerusalem and

source of the modern 'Ramat Rahel' (?)), the Piacenza Pilgrim reports the presence of a large rock in the middle of the road, from which poured forth an inexhaustible supply of sweet water. This miraculous rock, his guidebook explains, owes its origin to the Virgin's presence, but the context in this instance is the flight to Egypt, rather than the *Protevangelium*'s account of the Nativity and its traditions of Mary's rest. As the Holy Family was fleeing to Egypt, the pilgrimage guide explains, Mary rested in this spot, and when she grew thirsty, the rock poured forth water for her to drink. The wonder was believed to have continued until the late sixth century, when the Piacenza Pilgrim saw the miraculous waters, along with a church standing at the midpoint of the Jerusalem–Bethlehem road to commemorate the rock and its miracle.

Is it possible then that the Mar Elias church, with its large rock and nearby 'well of the Magi', may actually have been designed to commemorate these traditions rather than those of the *Protevangelium*, as the Piacenza Pilgrim would seem to indicate?[25] A few details could seem to point in this direction, including an alternative tradition of Mary's roadside rest that circulated in late ancient Christianity. The legend of the Holy Family's flight into Egypt is perhaps best known from the *Gospel of Ps.-Matthew*, a Latin composition of the late sixth or seventh century, which drew on an earlier source in recounting the Holy Family's trip to Egypt.[26] Similar versions of this legend were

Bethlehem, following the tradition that (incorrectly) located the site of ancient Ramah between the two cities. The tomb's precise location within this area, however, varies somewhat in the early Christian pilgrim literature. Epiphanius Hagiopolita (*c*.800), for instance, locates Rachel's tomb at the second mile from Jerusalem (but without reference to 'Ramah'): *Itinerarium*, 4 (Herbert Donner, ed., 'Die Palästinabeschreibung des Epiphanius Monachus Hagiopolita', *Zeitschrift des Deutschen Palästina-Vereins*, 87 (1971), 70 (Grk.) and 84 (Germ.)). Adamnan (*c*.685) describes a site that agrees with the tomb's traditional (and present) location: Adamnan, *De locis sanctis* 2. 7 (Denis Meehan, ed., *Adamnan's De locis sanctis*, Scriptores Latini Hiberniae, 3 (Dublin: Dublin Institute for Advanced Studies, 1958), 78-9.

[25] An early exploration of the relations among the Kathisma traditions, the Rachel traditions, and the traditions of the flight into Egypt was made by Gustav Klameth, *Die neutestamentlichen Lokaltraditionen Palästinas in der Zeit vor den Kreuzzügen*, Neutestamentliche Abhandlungen, 5. 1 (Münster: Aschendorffsche Verlagsbuchhandlung, 1914), 60–71.

[26] *The Gospel of Ps.-Matthew*, 20–1 (Jan Gijsel and Rita Beyers, eds., *Libri de*

in fact already circulating in the Christian East by the late fifth century, as the earliest traditions of the Virgin Mary's Dormition and Assumption bear witness.[27] Certain of these narratives describe an episode in which the Virgin becomes thirsty while resting from the journey to Egypt, and a spring miraculously gushes forth to quench her thirst. Although the various narratives usually set these events in an unspecified desert location, it would seem from the report of the 'Piacenza Pilgrim' that by the late sixth century certain Christians had identified these traditions with a miraculous rock and spring found at the midpoint of the Jerusalem–Bethlehem road, both of which are present at the Mar Elias church.

Moreover, a prominent feature of the structure itself also suggests a possible connection with these events: one of the floor mosaics depicts a large palm tree, flanked by two smaller palms, all of which are laden with fruit. This is, as the excavator, Rina Avner has explained, a rather unusual composition whose only known artistic parallel is found in the wall mosaics of the Dome of the Rock.[28] Yet even though this mosaic dates from the time of the church's conversion into a mosque, as the excavators have recently concluded,[29] the image also resonates strongly with the

nativitate Mariae, 2 vols., CCSA 9–10 (Turnhout: Brepols, 1997), i. 458–70). For date and regarding the use of a source for the flight to Egypt, see ibid. i. 11, 59–67.

[27] This episode is preserved in the following early narratives of Mary's Dormition: *Liber Requiei* 5–9 (Arras, *De Transitu*, 3–4 (Eth.) and 2–3 (Lat.)); Michel van Esbroeck, 'Apocryphes géorgiens de la Dormition', *Analecta Bollandiana*, 92 (1973), 69–73; Charles Donahue, ed., *The Testament of Mary: The Gaelic Version of the Dormitio Mariae together with an Irish Latin Version*, Fordham University Studies, Language Series, 1 (New York: Fordham University Press, 1942), 28–31. Regarding the early circulation of this story in the East, see also Michel van Esbroeck, 'Bild und Begriff in der Transitus-Literatur, der Palmbaum und der Tempel', in Margot Schmidt (ed.), *Typus, Symbol, Allegorie bei den östlichen Vätern und ihren Parallelen im Mittelalter* (Regensburg: Verlag Friedrich Pustet, 1982), 335–41.

[28] Avner, 'Birth Pangs on the Bethlehem Road'. Avner presented a compelling presentation of the relations between this church and the Dome of the Rock in a paper delivered at the 1998 meetings of the Society of Biblical Literature in Orlando. Further explorations regarding the relationship of this new Kathisma church and the Dome of the Rock have recently been made by Michel van Esbroeck in 'Die Quelle der Himmelfahrt Muhammeds vom Tempel in Jerusalem aus', in *Deutscher Orientalistentag in Bamberg März 2001* (forthcoming).   [29] See n. 21 above.

literary traditions of the flight into Egypt that the Piacenza Pilgrim associates with this spot. These stories begin when a fatigued Mary spots a tall palm in the distance and persuades Joseph to let her rest for a while under its shade. While sitting under the tree, Mary notices that it, like the trees in the mosaic, is fruitful, and she expresses a desire to eat from its fruit. In the earliest extant version of this legend, known from a fifth-century Dormition narrative, preserved identically in Georgian and Ethiopic versions,[30] Joseph is somewhat put off by what he perceives as Mary's complaints, and he explodes in a tirade, complaining that all their troubles are her fault, because she failed to guard her virginity, ranting further that this child is not even his, and that he should be at home with his real family, whom he has been forced to abandon. The infant Jesus then intervenes (in his clearly dysfunctional and very non-traditional family), and after mildly chastising Joseph, he orders the palm tree to bend down and offer its bounty to his parents, who then take and eat its fruit. As its reward, Christ returns the tree to the Garden of Eden, thereby concluding the episode. In the light of this tradition, it may be that the mosaic of the fruit-laden palm, apparently the only pictorial mosaic uncovered in the Mar Elias church,[31] was meant to commemorate the Holy Family's legendary feeding from this tree, thus drawing the church within the traditions of the Flight to Egypt, as the Piacenza Pilgrim explicitly identifies it.

The connection of the Holy Family's flight to Egypt with Herod's slaughter of the innocents in Bethlehem may have suggested the localization of these events nearby. In particular, the Gospel according to Matthew explicitly associates both of these events with Rachel's lamentations in Ramah (Mt. 2: 18; citing Jer. 31: 15). Although the actual site of Ramah, where Rachel died in childbirth, almost certainly lay just to the north of Jerusalem, the Hebrew Scriptures preserve an alternative tradition locating Rachel's death and tomb between Jerusalem and Bethlehem (Gen. 35: 16–20). The early Christian and Jewish traditions consistently opt for this latter tradition, locating the

---

[30] See n. 27 above; regarding the antiquity of the version in this narrative, see Ch. 3.

[31] As determined from the plan published in Avner, 'ירושלים, מר אליאס—כוסייח הקתיסמה', 139–42.

tomb of Rachel (and Ramah) to the north of Bethlehem, towards Jerusalem. In the light of Matthew's connection between the flight into Egypt and the region north of Bethlehem, an early Christian tradition seems to have developed that the Holy Family first fled to the north when they departed Bethlehem.[32] Admittedly, it does seem a bit odd for the Holy Family initially to have fled north, Egypt of course lying to the south of Bethlehem, but perhaps we must assume, as this early Christian tradition may have, that rather than opting for a fast getaway, Mary and Joseph had to sneak out the back in order to avoid the notice of Herod's henchmen.

The tradition of a sacred spring near this spot is persistent throughout the Middle Ages, but later authors estimate its significance variously, many identifying the spring as the 'well of the Magi', in agreement with what has become the modern tradition.[33] This tradition undoubtedly had its origin in medieval Palestine, sometime after the destruction of both churches and when Greek had yielded to Arabic, thus transforming the Greek 'kathisma-seat' into the Arabic 'qadismu-holy'.[34] None the less, it remains entirely possible that the Mar Elias church was originally built to commemorate the events described in the late ancient traditions of the flight into Egypt, while the actual Kathisma church stood somewhere nearby, perhaps on the hill just to the north, at Ramat Rahel. As memories faded and buildings disappeared, the name of the Kathisma church apparently shifted its association from the ancient church to this nearby spring, which was eventually understood as 'qadismu' by the local Arabic-speaking Christians. Thus these ancient Marian traditions were transformed by accidents of language into the more recent tradition of the well of the Magi.

Nevertheless, the association of this church with flight of the Holy Family is merely one possibility, and one which is

[32] See n. 24 above.

[33] The various medieval and early modern witnesses to this tradition may be found scattered among the sources collected in Donatus Baldi, OFM, *Enchiridion Locorum Sanctorum* (Jerusalem: Typis PP. Franciscanorum, 1935), 119–207.

[34] The relation between the ancient and modern place-names was first discussed by K. von Reiss, 'Kathisma Palaion und der sogenannte Brunnen der Weisen bei Mar Eljas', *Zeitschrift des Deutschen Palästina-Vereins*, 12 (1889), 19–23.

admittedly not completely persuasive, particularly in the light of the Piacenza Pilgrim's occasional 'originality' on this and other matters.[35] Another more attractive option, in my opinion, is to regard both churches as having been the church of the Kathisma, one an older church and the other more recently built. The possible existence of two Kathisma churches has occasionally been considered in scholarship on the earliest Marian liturgies of the Holy City, even before the second, nearby church was unearthed.[36] There are several indications of this in the literature, and although no single item can be considered decisive, together they make the prospect of two churches somewhat likely. Perhaps the most suggestive of these clues are the two previously mentioned lives of Theodosius the Coenobite. The first of these, by Theodore of Petra, informs us that near the beginning of Theodosius' monastic career, his superior sent him to live at the church and monastery known as the Old Kathisma, (ἐν τῷ λεγομένῳ Παλαιῷ Καθίσματι) a designation which, as many have noted, seems to imply the existence of a 'New Kathisma', from which it was distinguished.[37] This New Kathisma, it is supposed, would have been the church financed by Ikelia, and this may in fact be the large church discovered by the recent excavations. The possibility of two Kathisma churches is further substantiated by Cyril of Scythopolis' life of Theodosius, where he rather unambiguously notes that Theodosius was sent to live with Ikelia and her community of ascetics at a time when she was still having the Kathisma church built.[38] The Old Kathisma then, would presumably refer to the smaller church at Ramat Rahel, along with its attached monastic community, where

[35] See Wilkinson, *Jerusalem Pilgrims*, 6: 'He mentions a great many places and practices of which we have no other evidence, and although occasionally confused and inaccurate he conveys more vividly than any other writer from our period the variety of experience which makes up a pilgrimage.'

[36] See, e.g. Wilkinson, *Jerusalem Pilgrims*, 163b; Mimouni, *Dormition*, 522 n. 154.

[37] Theodore of Petra, *v. Thds.* (Usener, *Der heilige Theodosius*, 13–14). On the implication of a New Kathisma, see Mimouni, *Dormition*, 522 n. 154, and J. T. Milik, 'Notes d'épigraphie et de topographie palestiniennes', *Revue Biblique*, 67 (1960), 571.

[38] ἀλλὰ λαβὼν αὐτὸν τῆι μακαρίαι καὶ ἐν ἁγίοις παρέθετο Ἰκελίαι τὴν τοῦ Καθίσματος τῆς θεοτόκου ἐκκλησίαν τὸ τηνικαῦτα οἰκοδομούσηι. Cyril of Scythopolis, *v. Thds.* (Schwartz, *Kyrillos von Skythopolis*, 236).

Theodosius and Ikelia lived at the time when the New Kathisma was being built.

Such a reconstruction also finds support in the earliest liturgical traditions of Jerusalem, as preserved in the fifth-century Armenian Lectionary, whose traditions, again, have been convincingly assigned to the period between 420 and 440. As already noted, among its various commemorations the lectionary includes a programme for the feast of the Memory of Mary, to be celebrated on 15 August at the third mile from Bethlehem, the site of the Kathisma, where the Virgin was supposed to have rested. At this time, however, before 440, Ikelia's Kathisma church had not yet been built, raising the question of where this feast was celebrated. Although the lectionary does not specify the existence of a church here, this is not particularly meaningful: the lectionary generally fails to do so for liturgical stations outside Jerusalem, giving only their geographic location instead.[39] While there is the rather unlikely possibility that the feast was conducted in the open air, alongside the road near the third milestone, it seems more likely that some sort of a church stood on or near this spot, providing an altar in order to celebrate the liturgy.[40] This church, I propose, may have been the church at Ramat Rahel, the Old Kathisma that was succeeded by Ikelia's New Kathisma, which can perhaps be identified with the impressive octagonal church discovered near Mar Elias.

Both of these alternatives are admittedly speculative, yet given the present state of our evidence I do not think that we can approach these monuments with a great deal more certainty. I admit a tentative preference for the latter explanation, the possibility that there were two Kathisma churches, particularly since it fits well with the earliest literary witnesses. Nevertheless, the issue of the rock still remains: what is it doing in the New Kathisma church if, as Theodosius reports, it had been removed near the turn of the sixth century? Was it perhaps never even removed at all, despite Theodosius' near contemporary report? Was it perhaps later 'repatriated'? Rina Avner, the excavator,

[39] I thank Walter Ray for this observation.

[40] Wilkinson, *Jerusalem Pilgrims*, 168b, draws a similar conclusion with regard to Rachel's tomb: although there is not clear evidence of a church here, a feast is specified in the Jerusalem Georgian Lectionary, and, as Wilkinson notes, the celebration of a liturgy there would have required some sort of an altar.

suggests the possibility that only a portion of the rock was taken, which would not necessarily contradict Theodosius' report.[41] On the other hand, we might ask why the Old Kathisma church at Ramat Rahel appears to have had no rock. One possible explanation is that the tradition of a holy rock developed only after the Old Kathisma had already been built. This would appear to be the indication of our earliest sources, from the *Protevangelium* to the lives of Theodosius the Coenobite, none of which make any mention of a rock. It would seem that only Mary's rest was commemorated at this stage, without any special rock on which she rested. Not until 530 do we first hear of any rock associated with this tradition. Perhaps this later identification of a particular rock with Mary's resting place was in part the impetus for constructing a new, larger church at the bottom of the hill. Alternatively, a new church may have been necessitated by an increase in pilgrimage traffic, or it may be that a combination of such factors provoked the construction of a new church. The presence of an ancient road connecting the two sites offers strong support for this hypothesis, suggesting that the older coenobium, which continued to function, was related to the pilgrimage shrine on the hill below.[42]

Nevertheless, the possible connections of this church with the flight to Egypt remain intriguing, even if they are somewhat complicated. Perhaps somehow these two identifications are not mutually exclusive. It certainly appears that both interpretations were somehow simultaneously viable within the sixth century, as the differing opinions of Theodosius and the Piacenza Pilgrim attest. It would also seem that this may have been true of the seventh and eighth centuries as well, if we consider the Nativity traditions that have been preserved in the Qur'an. Christ's birth as described in the Qur'anic Sura Mary appears to be a conflation of both these early Christian traditions of Mary's rest.[43] After

[41] This was suggested to me in a personal communication. Theodosius does not, however, say that this is what happened. Nevertheless, as Avner has explained to me, the fact that the rock is slightly off-centre in the present remains of the structure suggests that part of the original rock has been removed. Yet even if this is the case, the long silence of the later pilgrimage accounts with regard to the rock remains.

[42] Again, I thank Rina Avner for making me aware of this road in a personal communication.

[43] Klameth, *Neutestamentlichen Lokaltraditionen*, 70, also notes the

having withdrawn from her family, Mary is met by an angel, who announces that she will give birth. Then, as the pains of childbirth overcame her, she took herself to rest beneath a palm tree, and a voice from 'below' said to her, 'Do not despair. Your Lord has provided a brook that runs at your feet, and if you shake the trunk of this palm-tree it will drop fresh ripe dates in your lap.'[44] Clearly here the two Christian traditions of Mary's rest have been joined: to the earliest tradition of Mary's rest before giving birth have been added the traditions from the flight to Egypt, according to which Mary was miraculously refreshed by the fruit of a palm tree and the waters from a spring that spontaneously gushed forth. Although the church of the Kathisma is naturally unmentioned in the Qur'anic account, it would seem that it may have played a role here, since this church is, to my knowledge, the only point that joins these two Christian traditions. Nevertheless, much remains uncertain regarding the significance of these two churches in Christian late antiquity, and we may only hope that additional research and continued excavation and discussion will shed further light on this subject in the coming years.

THE CHURCH OF MARY IN THE VALLEY OF JOSAPHAT AND THE TOMB OF THE VIRGIN

Equally important for understanding the origins of Marian veneration in Palestine is the ancient church of Mary in the Wadi Kidron, next to the Garden of Gethsemane, which tradition identifies as the location of the Virgin's cenotaph (see Fig. 7). Although Byzantine and Crusader churches once stood above the present sanctuary, these have been completely effaced and are now known exclusively from literary sources.[45] Excepting only the present façade and stairway, both of which are of

interesting connection between these three traditions, long before the discovery of the second church.

[44] Qur'an 19: 22–5 (N. J. Dawood, trans., *The Koran with a Parallel Arabic Text* (London: Penguin Books, 1994), 305).

[45] Our knowledge of these structures has been gathered in B. Bagatti, M. Piccirillo, and A. Prodomo, OFM, *New Discoveries at the Tomb of Virgin Mary in Gethsemane*, Studium Biblicum Franciscanum, Collectio Minor, 17 (Jerusalem: Franciscan Printing Press, 1975), 56–82. The ancient church has been described and analysed, ibid. 11–55.

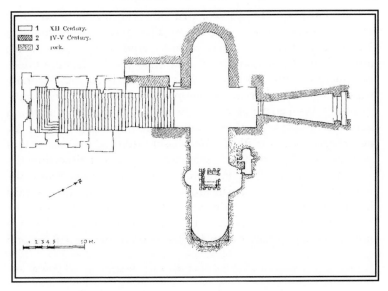

FIG. 7. The church of Mary's tomb (after B. Bagatti, M. Piccirillo, and A. Prodomo, OFM, *New Discoveries at the Tomb of Virgin Mary in Gethsemane*, Studium Biblicum Franciscanum, Collectio Minor, 17 (Jerusalem: Franciscan Printing Press, 1975), 21)

Crusader origin, the earliest church is all that remains to be seen today. Much of this cross-shaped chapel has been carved into the rock that originally surrounded the traditional tomb of Mary, and the loculus itself has been isolated in a manner reminiscent of Christ's tomb in the church of the Holy Sepulchre. A second tomb may be entered through the church's northern wall, only a few metres from the Virgin's tomb, a further indication of the ancient usage of this place. Following a flood in February 1972, the church underwent major restoration, enabling Bellarmino Bagatti and other archaeologists from the Studium Biblicum Franciscanum to examine carefully the earliest features of the church and its tomb, many of which are ordinarily invisible or inaccessible. Based on these studies, Bagatti determined that the church had in fact been carved into an ancient necropolis, whose tombs are consistent with a first-century dating, although the church itself is a later construction, dating most probably to sometime in the fifth century.[46]

[46] Ibid. 57–8. More recently, see also Ronny Reich, Gideon Avni, and Tamar

The date of the church's construction is known more precisely from various literary sources.[47] The Jerusalem Armenian Lectionary provides a fairly reliable *terminus post quem*, since although it seems to know the church of the Kathisma, it does not mention the church of Mary in Gethsemane, strongly suggesting its appearance sometime after the lectionary's composition. We can be certain, however, that the church was in existence by 451 from the witness of a sixth-century Coptic text, a *Panegyric on Macarius of Tkōw*, falsely ascribed to Dioscorus of Alexandria. An important segment of this text describes the events consequent to Patriarch Juvenal's return from the Council of Chalcedon to the Holy City and his decision to establish the Chalcedonian definition of Christ's two natures in one hypostasis as the orthodox faith in Palestine. His decision was not entirely popular, to say the least; upon his arrival, a mob

Winter, *The Jerusalem Archaeological Park* (Jerusalem: Israel Antiquities Authority, 1999), 116–19. A 5th-century tombstone was found inside the church, concerning which see Sylvester J. Saller, OFM, 'The Tombstone Inscription in the Church of Mary's Tomb at Gethsemane', in Virgilio Corbo, OFM, *Richerche archeologiche al Monte degli Ulivi*, Publicazioni dello Studium Biblicum Franciscanum, 16 (Jerusalem: Tip. dei Padri Francescani), 76–80.

[47] A very few interpreters have argued for a much earlier date, referencing especially the 10th-century *Annals* of the Alexandrian Patriarch Eutychius, where he notes that 'King Theodosius the Great also built the church of Gethsemane in the Holy City, where the tomb of holy Mary is, which was destroyed by the Persians, when they destroyed the churches in the Holy City. It remains in ruins to this day.' *Annales*, 222 (M. Breydy, ed., *Das Annalenwerke des Eutychios von Alexandrien*, CSCO 471–2 (Louvain: Peeters, 1985), 88. 12–14 (Arab.) and 73 (Germ.); in the Antiochene recension: L. Cheikho, ed., *Eutychii Patriarchae Alexandrini Annales*, 2 vols., CSCO 50–1 (Louvain: L. Durbecq/ CSCO, 1954, 1960), i. ١٥٢). The church in question, however, is not the church of the Virgin's tomb, but rather the church of Gethsemane (today the Basilica of the Agony/Church of All Nations), which lay on the opposite side of the garden. From the Patriarch of Jerusalem Sophronius (634–8), as well as other sources, we know that the Church of the Virgin's tomb was not destroyed and left in ruins by the Persians (Sophronius of Jerusalem, *carm.* 20 (PG 87. 3824AB)). It continued to exist well into the Middle Ages. The church of Gethsemane, however, is known to have been destroyed, a fact confirmed by archaeological evidence of a fire. The Virgin's tomb is mentioned here only to specify the location of a church that was no longer standing. On the two churches, see Robert Schick, *The Christian Communities of Palestine from Byzantine to Islamic Rule: A Historical and Archaeological Study*, Studies in Late Antiquity and Early Islam, 2 (Princeton: The Darwin Press, 1995), 352–4.

opposed to the Chalcedonian statement of faith gathered in protest at 'the shrine of holy Mary in the valley of Josaphat'.[48] The outcome was an unhappy one: Juvenal dispatched imperial troops to retake the church from his opponents.

Although this text was written approximately a hundred years after these events took place and its author was a known forger, this report has every indication of being genuine.[49] Its witness to the church of Mary in the valley of Josaphat is confirmed by two early pilgrimage guides, the *De situ terrae sanctae* of Theodosius, composed between 520 and 530, and the *Brevarius de Hierosolyma*, an anonymous guide that dates to sometime around 500. Theodosius attests to the existence of a church dedicated to Mary in the valley of Josaphat, without explicitly identifying it as her tomb.[50] The *Brevarius*, however, a slightly earlier text, is quite explicit, telling us that 'the basilica of St Mary is there [in Jerusalem], and her tomb is there'.[51] While the *Brevarius* fails to specify the location of the church of Mary's tomb within Jerusalem, this passage almost certainly refers to the church of Mary in the valley of Josaphat, since we know of no other church in Jerusalem dedicated to the Virgin at this early date. Moreover, the construction of the Nea or 'New' church of the Theotokos in Jerusalem strongly suggests the existence of an earlier, 'Old' church dedicated to Mary, a role probably filled by the church

---

[48] Ps.-Dioscorus of Alexandria, *Panegyric on Macarius of Tkōw* 7. 5 (David Johnson, ed., *A Panegyric on Macarius, Bishop of Tkōw, Attributed to Dioscorus of Alexandria*, CSCO 415–16, Scriptores Coptici, 41–2 (Louvain: Peeters, 1980), 49–50 (Copt.) and 38 (Eng.)). The entire episode, including the slaughter of Juvenal's opponents by the soldiers, is recounted in ibid., 7.1–8.16 (ibid., 45–70 (Copt.) and 34–54 (Eng.)).

[49] The events are also known from Zachariah of Mitylene's *Ecclesiastical History* 3. 3 (E. W. Brooks, ed., *Historia Ecclesiastica Zachariae Rhetori vulgo adscripta*, 2 vols., CSCO 83–4, 87–8, Scriptores Syrii 3. 5–6 (Louvain: E Typographeo I.-B. Istas, 1919–24), i. 155–7 (Syr.) and 107–8 (Eng.)); and Cyril of Scythopolis, *v. Euthym.* 27 (Schwartz, *Kyrillos*, 41–5). These sources do not, however, mention the church of Mary here in question.

[50] Theodosius, *De situ terrae sanctae* (Geyer, Itineraria, 119).

[51] *Brevarius de Hierosolyma* 7 (R. Weber, ed., *Itineraria et alia Geographica*, CCL 175 (Turnhout: Brepols, 1965), 112). Regarding the date see Mimouni, *Dormition*, 565–6. See also the discussion of pilgrimage guides in Michel van Esbroeck, 'Les Textes littéraires sur l'assomption avant le Xe siècle', in François Bovon (ed.), *Les Actes apocryphes des apôtres* (Geneva: Labor et Fides, 1981), 277–82.

near Gethsemane. Although the Nea was consecrated only in November 543, its construction was begun under the Patriarch Elias (494–516), which would comport with the existence of a Gethsemane church in the fifth century.[52]

It is noteworthy that the *Panegyric on Macarius of Tkōw* and Theodosius do not identify the Gethsemane shrine with the Virgin's tomb. Likewise, the *Brevarius* fails explicitly to locate the church of Mary's tomb in Gethsemane, although it clearly attests to the tomb's presence in Jerusalem. While it seems undeniable that there was a church dedicated to Mary near the garden of Gethsemane by the mid-fifth century, and also that Mary's tomb was venerated in Jerusalem by the close of the fifth century, some scholars have disputed the identity of the tomb with the Gethsemane church of Mary. Even though these scholars will generally concede the existence of the Gethsemane church of Mary in the fifth century, they argue that the association of this church with the Virgin's tomb is a secondary development, belonging to the later sixth century.[53]

There is in fact some limited indication that this site may originally have been identified as the location of Mary's house, rather than her tomb, and a number of scholars have advocated the view that the Gethsemane church was originally built to commemorate Mary's house. The primary witnesses to this tradition are identified in two late fifth-century sources, the narrative of the Virgin's Dormition attributed to Melito of Sardis, and possibly the *Acts of John* attributed to Prochorus, although the witness of the latter is rather complicated and dubious, and generally unworthy of the authority with which it

---

[52] Procopius of Caesarea, *aed.* 5. 6. 1–2 (Jacobus Haury, ed., revised by Gerhard Wirth, *Opera Omnia*, iv (Leipzig: Teubner, 1964), 162) and Cyril of Scythopolis, *v. Sab.* 177. 15–20 (Schwartz, *Kyrillos*, 175–8). See also the discussion in Hughes Vincent and F.-M. Abel, *Jérusalem: Recherches de topographie, d'archéologie et d'histoire*, ii. *Jérusalem Nouvelle* (Paris: J. Gabalda, 1926), fasc. 4, 912–15. The significance of this 'New' church of Mary was first proposed by Anton Baumstark, 'Die leibliche Himmelfahrt der allerseligsten Jungfrau und die Lokaltradition von Jerusalem', *Oriens Christianus*, 4 (1904), 380. For more on this topic, see Mimouni, *Dormition*, 512–14.

[53] See e.g. Mimouni, *Dormition*, 577–8, where Mimouni concludes that 'l'existence à Gethsémani d'une église dédiée à Marie est incontestable'; nevertheless, Mimouni maintains that its identification with the tomb was not made before the middle of the sixth century.

has occasionally been invested.[54] The *Transitus* of Ps.-Melito, however, the more credible of the two sources, indicates that at the time of her death, Mary was living with John in his parents' house next to the Mount of Olives.[55]

It was primarily on this basis that Martin Jugie first championed the idea that the earliest traditions located Mary's house near Gethsemane, and consequently, that the fifth-century church of Mary referred to in the *Panegyric on Macarius of Tkōw* is to be identified with her house rather than her tomb. Because the tradition of Mary's tomb was more or less contrary to Jugie's theological prejudices, namely, his conviction that the Virgin did not die but remained immortal, he identified the tradition locating Mary's house in Gethsemane as earlier than the tradition of the tomb. Consequently, Jugie maintained that the Gethsemane church was originally constructed in the fifth century to commemorate Mary's house, and only much later did it become associated with her tomb. This reconstruction enabled Jugie to brand the tradition of Mary's tomb as a later 'corruption' of the truth concerning the end of her life, which, as he believed, did not in truth include her death, but only her immortal translation into Heaven.[56]

Jugie's theologically motivated decision has had a lasting impact on the interpretation of this monument's earliest significance, to the effect that later scholars have often favoured the antiquity of the house tradition over the tomb tradition, even

---

[54] Ps.-Melito of Sardis, *Transitus Mariae* 1 (Monika Haibach-Reinisch, ed., *Ein neuer 'Transitus Mariae' des Pseudo-Melito* (Rome: Pontificia Academia Mariana Internationalis, 1962), 66); regarding the *Acts of John* by Ps.-Prochorus, see Martin Jugie, AA, *La Mort et l'assomption de la Sainte Vierge: Étude historico-doctrinale*, Studi e Testi, 114 (Vatican City: Biblioteca Apostolica Vaticana, 1944), 89, where he discusses a rather late variant from a few manuscripts that report this tradition. See also van Esbroeck, 'Les Textes', 281, where he too notes that the witness of Ps.-Prochorus does not deserve the high regard in which Jugie holds it.

[55] Ps.-Melito, *Transitus* 1 (Haibach-Reinisch, *Ein neuer 'Transitus Mariae'*, 66).

[56] See Jugie, *La Mort*, 85–92. Regarding Jugie's role in researching the dogma's definability and his 'Immortalist' belief regarding the Virgin Mary, see Paul E. Duggan, 'The Assumption Dogma: Some Reactions and Ecumenical Implications in the Thought of English-Speaking Theologians' (STD diss., International Marian Research Institute, University of Dayton, 1989), 57–63; and Mimouni, *Dormition*, 497.

without sharing Jugie's commitment to Mary's immortality.[57] In upholding this position, however, interpreters have persistently overlooked significant evidence that strongly favours the shrine's early association with the Virgin's tomb. Perhaps the most important and unavoidable of these indications is the presence of the tomb itself and the construction of the earliest church within an ancient necropolis. It is hard to imagine that one could fail to notice these facts, but it has frequently been done.[58] Indeed, it is incontrovertible that the tombs are basic elements of the ancient structure, and it seems most unlikely that they were later added to what was originally a church built in commemoration of Mary's house. Nor does it seem probable that a church commemorating Mary's house would have been carved out of an ancient necropolis. While the super-suspicious might suppose an elaborate ecclesiastical scheme to forge an ancient tomb and necropolis at the site sometime during the sixth or seventh century, this seems rather extreme.

Moreover, even if we were lacking this clear archaeological evidence of the tomb itself, literary witnesses from the close of the fifth century strongly suggest the identification of the Gethsemane church with Mary's tomb. The ancient Dormition narratives, for instance, indicate as much, and as we have seen in the preceding chapter, the earliest of these date, at the latest, to the second half of the fifth century. The earliest narratives from both the Palm and Bethlehem traditions locate the events of Mary's death at her Jerusalem house, which lies *within* the

---

[57] e.g. Mimouni, *Dormition*, 473–548, who has recently advanced Jugie's position, while nevertheless raising some criticisms of Jugie's formulation of it. An important recent exception to this view is van Esbroeck, 'Les Textes', 277–82, who has argued that the church was from its beginning associated with the tomb. This position had previously been argued, along slightly different lines, by Donato Baldi, 'I santuari mariani in Terra Santa', *Liber Annus*, 3 (1952–3), at 258–60. A. Raes, SJ, 'Aux origines de la fête de l'Assomption en Orient', *Orientalia Christiana Periodica*, 12 (1946), 262–74, argues that the church was not identified with the tomb until the middle of the 6th century, yet without embracing the tradition of Mary's house advocated by Jugie.

[58] This has been done most recently by Simon Mimouni, who maintains that the ancient church, the same one that Bagatti has analysed, was built to commemorate the Virgin's house and not her tomb, this despite the fact that he himself elsewhere asserts that 'sur le plan archéologique, il ne fait pas de doute que la tomb fouilée par B. Bagatti date du Ier siècle de notre ère'. Mimouni, *Dormition*, 571–8, esp. 576.

city of Jerusalem, as is attested by the fact that the apostles must 'go out' from the city to bury her.[59] This indication clearly pre-cludes the location of her house in Gethsemane, which lay out-side Jerusalem's walls.[60] Although the earliest Coptic narratives are not so specific with regard to the location of Mary's house, they are none the less quite explicit in identifying the valley of Josaphat as the location of her tomb.[61] Thus we find that all three major literary traditions of Mary's Dormition speak against a fifth-century identification of the church of Mary in the valley of Josaphat with her house instead of her tomb.

To these narratives may also be added the weight of the pilgrimage guides discussed above. As already noted, the *Brevarius* reports that a church of Mary had been built in Jerusalem at the site of her tomb, and although it does not explicitly specify the tomb's location near Gethsemane, this is strongly implied by the tomb's appearance in a list comprised of other sites in the Gethsemane area, such as the valley of Josaphat and the place where Christ was betrayed.[62] More importantly, however, the church of Mary in Gethsemane is the only known Marian shrine in the Holy City at the time that the *Brevarius* represents. Since then we know from the Dormition narratives and the *Brevarius* that Mary's tomb was venerated somewhere in Jerusalem by the late fifth century, it is logical to assume that the fifth-century Gethsemane church, which had been carved into a tomb complex near Gethsemane, was from its origin conceived as the church of the tomb.[63]

[59] See van Esbroeck, 'Les Textes', 280. Smith Lewis, *Apocrypha Syriaca*, ⟶ﬞ (Syr.) and 50–1 (Eng.); Wright, 'Departure', ﬞ⟶ (Syr.) and 148 (Eng.); *Liber Requiei* 70 (Arras, *De Transitu*, 41 (Eth.) and 27 (Lat.)); Wenger, *L'Assomption*, 232–3.

[60] With the exception only of Ps.-Melito's narrative, which alone specifies this location.

[61] Ps.-Evodius of Rome, *Homily on the Dormition* (St Mich.) 22 (Stephen J. Shoemaker, 'The Sahidic Coptic Homily on the Dormition of the Virgin Attributed to Evodius of Rome: An Edition from Morgan MSS 596 & 598 with Translation', *Analecta Bollandiana*, 117 (1999), 278–9); Ps.-Cyril of Jerusalem, *Homily on the Dormition* 51 (Antonella Campagnano, ed., *Ps. Cirillo di Gerusalemme: Omelie copte sulla Passione, sulla Croce e sulla Vergine*, Testi e Documenti per lo Studio dell'Antichita, LXV (Milan: Cisalpiono-Goliardica, 1980), 190–1).

[62] *Brevarius de Hierosolyma* 7 (Weber, ed., *Itineraria*, 112).

[63] Although Theodosius does not identify this church with Mary's tomb, as

Towards the end of the sixth century, however, the Piacenza Pilgrim gives, as he or she from time to time does, a somewhat individual assessment of the Gethsemane shrine's significance, identifying it as the site of her house, where she went forth from the body. Although later versions of this itinerary would add mention of her tomb as well, this is clearly the hand of a later editor.[64] Yet this witness comes at a time when even advocates of the priority of the house tradition concede that the Gethsemane church has become identified with Mary's tomb.[65] And so once again we find that it is no simple matter to identify the early Marian shrines of Palestine. It may in fact be that there was an early tradition locating Mary's house in this area (in addition to the separate tradition of her tomb). We would then assume that this house tradition was effaced in the early seventh century, when our sources unanimously begin to locate Mary's house (and the site of the Dormition) on Mount Zion.[66] Nevertheless, the rather limited witnesses to Mary's Gethsemane house only vaguely locate her dwelling somewhere in the Gethsemane area, and while these traditions are undoubtedly both interesting and important, they are hardly sufficient evidence for determining that this house tradition was the basis for the construction of the church of Mary in the valley of Josaphat. When compared with the witness of the early Dormition traditions and the *Brevarius*, as well as the rather convincing presence of ancient tombs within the present structure, it seems almost certain that the fifth-

Mimouni points out, neither does his guide support Mimouni's case for identifying the church with Mary's house (as he seems to indicate), since it equally fails to make any mention of Mary's house. The same is also true of the *Panegyric on Macarius of Tkôw*, which Mimouni similarly identifies as a 'source favorable' to the tradition of Mary's house in Gethsemane: this fails equally to identify this church with either her house or tomb. See Mimouni, *Dormition*, 506–8.

[64] Antoninus Placentius, *Itinerarium* 17 (Geyer, *Itineraria*, 137 (1st recension); 163 (2nd recension)). Recensions indicating Mary's tomb have been published by Milani, *Itinerarium Antonini Placentini*, 300; and T. Tobler and A. Molinier, eds., *Itinera Hierosolymitana*, 2 vols. (Geneva: J.-G. Fick, 1889), i. 100). On the relation of these other recensions to the earliest recension, see Wilkinson, *Jerusalem Pilgrims*, 6–7.

[65] See e.g. Mimouni, *Dormition*, 577–8.

[66] More on the Zion church and its significance for the early Marian liturgies of Jerusalem may be found below, but see also the discussion in Mimouni, *Dormition*, 533–47.

century shrine of Mary in Gethsemane was from the beginning a church commemorating her tomb. Any tradition regarding the location of Mary's house in this area was probably separate from the ancient necropolis that tradition identifies as the site of her tomb.

CHRISTIAN *EULOGIAI* AND THE PALESTINIAN CULT OF THE VIRGIN

The Christian *Eulogiai* from Byzantine Palestine form an appropriate bridge between the discussions of material remains and liturgical practice, since they truly belong to both categories. *Eulogiai* were small tokens, 'souvenirs' if you will, that Christian pilgrims carried with them when they returned home from various shrines and holy sites that they had visited. These small items included such things as earth from a sacred place, small images of holy persons or events, lamps, ampullae, or small flasks containing holy water or oil collected at the shrine, or even cloth that had come into contact with relics or some other holy object. These items were much more than mere mementos, however. They were believed somehow to bear in themselves the holiness of the place that had been visited, allowing the pilgrim to capture some of the shrine's power and bring it into his or her home. One of the earliest literary sources for understanding this practice is the Piacenza Pilgrim, who reports taking holy oil from Christ's tomb, which gave its bearer a 'blessing' (*benedictio*; εὐλογία in Greek). But many of the items themselves identify this as their function, bearing inscriptions such as 'a blessing of the Lord from the Holy Places'.[67] Thus the modern name for such objects

---

[67] A good general discussion of this phenomenon may be found in Gary Vikan, *Byzantine Pilgrimage Art*, Dumbarton Oaks Byzantine Collection Publications, 5 (Washington: Dumbarton Oaks, 1982). See esp. 10–13, where Vikan notes that the *eulogia* was 'not a memento to evoke memories, but rather a piece of portable, palpable sanctity which possessed and could convey spiritual power to its owner'. The Piacenza Pilgrim's description of this practice may be found in Antoninus Placentius, *Itinerarium* (Geyer, *Itineraria*, 164). Examples of ampullae bearing this inscription and other similar inscriptions may be found in Peter Thomsen, 'Die lateinischen und griechischen Inscriften der Stadt Jerusalem', *Zeitschrift des Deutschen Palästina-Vereins*, 44 (1921), 125–30, nos. 215–20.

derives from their ancient function: *eulogiai* were small objects obtained at various shrines that continued to confer the blessings of the holy places on their bearers even after they had returned home.

The archaeological record has yielded a fair number of such objects related to the Palestinian cult and shrines of the Virgin Mary during the period here under consideration. Without doubt the most noteworthy of the Marian *eulogiai* from the Holy Land is a clay token recently discovered at Bet She'an, which, despite significant damage, can be seen to depict the Virgin's Dormition (see Fig. 8).[68] This remarkable discovery is at present the earliest known artistic representation of Mary's Dormition, preceding by some 400 years the tenth and eleventh-century ivories from Constantinople that had long held this honour.[69] While these ivories depict the Dormition according to what has become its canonical form, the 2.7cm (diameter) token presents a simpler representation, confirming the suspicions of art historians that non-canonical forms must have existed at an earlier time, probably portraying the scene in a more abbreviated form.[70] The token depicts the nimbed Virgin lying on her funeral bed, head to the left, with three nimbed, bearded figures facing front above her head. At her feet one can see portions of a fourth nimbed figure who, bent over and gazing down, touches her feet with its left hand. L. Y. Rahmani, who first published the token, has also discerned traces of a fifth, upright figure, probably Christ, who appears to be 'supporting an object to its upper left', which was likely the soul of Mary.[71] Finally, in the centre of the token, above the Virgin's supine

---

[68] L. Y. Rahmani, '*Eulogia* Tokens from Byzantine Bet She'an', '*Atiqot*, 22 (1993), 113–15; and Gideon Foerster and Yoram Tsafrir, 'City Center (North); Excavations of the Hebrew University Expedition', *Excavations and Surveys in Israel*, 11 (The Bet She'an Excavation Project (1989–1991)) (1993), 19–20. I thank Professor Jean-Pierre Sodini for drawing my attention to this object, his advice on its interpretation, and his encouragement to incorporate this sort of material in my investigation.

[69] *Reallexikon zur byzantinischen Kunst*, s.v. 'Koimesis'; Christa Schaffer, *Koimesis, Der Heimgang Mariens: Das Entschlafungsbild in seiner Abhängigkeit von Legende und Theologie*, Studia Patristica et Liturgica, 15 (Regensburg: Kommissionsverlag Friedrich Pustet, 1985), 62–5.

[70] *Reallexikon zur byzantinischen Kunst*, s.v. 'Koimesis'.

[71] Rahmani, '*Eulogia*', 113.

FIG. 8. Sixth-century eulogia token from Bet She'an (Scythopolis) depicting the Virgin's Dormition (Courtesy of the Israel Antiquities Authority)

body, stands a monogram for *Μαρία*. This simplified image of the Dormition differs in only a few details from the middle Byzantine ivories. Most notably, unlike the ivories, the token shows the Virgin lying flat, rather than with her head propped up, and it omits the small footstool usually in front of her bed, as well as several of the apostles. Also missing are the censer ordinarily carried by Peter, and the angels who almost always accompany Christ. Rahmani suggests that some of these omissions may be due to a lack of space on the token, which seems a very convincing explanation.

Unfortunately this token was not found *in situ*, but in deposits from the Mamluk period (1263–1516). Other criteria, however, allow the token to be dated to sometime before 614. Five similar tokens were found at Bet She'an, and their stratigraphy places them between 540 and 614. Rahmani explains that the Dormition token is 'so similar in form, material, style, and execution'[72] to these other tokens it should be similarly dated within this period. Rahmani's hypothesis is otherwise confirmed by comparison with similar objects found throughout the late ancient and medieval Near East, particularly since such tokens are not known to have been fashioned in clay outside the fifth to seventh centuries. The phenomenon was at its peak in sixth-century Syro-Palestine, and appears to have met its demise sometime after the loss of this region to the invading Muslims in the seventh century.[73] Although pilgrimage to the Holy Land does not altogether cease in the face of this political obstacle, it does wane considerably,[74] and when pilgrimage in northern Syria was reinvigorated in the tenth century with the Byzantine reconquest of this region, *eulogia* tokens were once again fashioned, deliberately according to the late ancient styles, but no longer from clay and almost always from lead.[75] Thus, a date sometime before 614 seems reasonable on the basis of the token's artistic form.

Nevertheless, Rahmani's attempt to date the token based on comparison of its content with the earliest literary traditions of the Virgin's Dormition is not as successful. Rahmani argues that the earliest Dormition legends can confirm a sixth-century date, basing his conclusions on St Michael's absence from the *eulogia* token's depiction.[76] Rahmani claims, incorrectly, that the tradition of Christ receiving Mary's soul into his hands and then

[72] Rahmani, '*Eulogia*', 114.

[73] Vikan, *Byzantine Pilgrimage Art*, 39–40.

[74] On pilgrimage to the Holy Land after the Arab conquest, see Franca Mian, *Gerusalemme città santa: Oriente e pellegrini d'Occidente (sec. I~IX/XI)* (Rome: Il Cerchio, 1988), 241–8, and Schick, *Christian Communities*, 109.

[75] Vikan, *Byzantine Pilgrimage Art*, 40.

[76] Rahmani, '*Eulogia*', 117 nn. 13–14.

transferring it to Michael is a later accretion to the Dormition legends, first attested only in the 'late sixth century', in the *Transitus* of Ps.-Melito, after which time it begins to appear in all our texts. The earliest texts, Rahmani maintains, simply depict Christ as transferring the Virgin's soul directly into heaven himself, without Michael's assistance. This, so the argument goes, is the stage of the legends reflected in the Bet She'an token, and thus it must be very early.

There are, however, numerous difficulties with this argument, the first of which is that, in addition to Michael, many other facets of the canonical portrayal are absent, a fact which is perhaps most easily explained by Rahmani's own suggestion, that there was simply not enough room on the token for a 'complete' depiction.[77] Moreover, the text that Rahmani identifies as affording the earliest evidence of St Michael's involvement, the *Transitus* of Ps.-Melito, is generally regarded as one of the earliest texts, probably belonging to the late fifth century rather than the late sixth, as Rahmani proposes.[78] In fact, the earliest extant Dormition narrative, the late fifth-century Syriac fragments of the *Obsequies*, demonstrates that the tradition of Christ handing over his mother's soul to Michael is at least as old as any other known traditions about the end of Mary's life.[79]

[77] As Rahmani himself essentially explains elsewhere: 'The context of the scene so far described and the surviving portion of the upper central figure seem consistent with that figure's identification as Jesus carrying the *eidolon* (the personification of Mary's soul), as in the later representations. If this is so, this would have taken up most of the missing upper right part of the token and left scarcely any space in which the angel Michael, descending to receive Mary's soul, might have been shown.' Rahmani, '*Eulogia*', 113.

[78] Dated by almost universal consensus to the late 5th century: see Othone Faller, SJ, *De priorum saeculorum silentio circa Assumptionem b. Mariae virginis*, Analecta Gregoriana, Series Facultatis Theologicae, 36 (Rome: Gregorian University, 1946), 42–63; H. Lausberg, 'Zur literarischen Gestaltung des Transitus Beata Mariae', *Historisches Jahrbuch*, 72 (1935), 46; Antoine Wenger, *L'Assomption*, 90–1; Haibach-Reinisch, *Ein neuer 'Transitus Mariae'*, 45–7; D. M. Montagna, 'Appunti critice sul Transitus B. V. Mariae dello Pseudo-Melitone', *Marianum*, 27 (1965), 184. See also the discussion in Ch. 1.

[79] This fragment was left untranslated by Wright and not published with the edited text, but separately in the introduction with several other fragments: 'And when Mary had said these things, her spirit went forth from her body. And in their presence, grace surrounded her face. Then our Lord took her soul and placed it between Michael's hands. And he wrapped it in a pure garment whose splendor a mortal could not describe.' Wright, *Contributions*, 14.

While it is true several early texts do omit Michael's reception of the Virgin's soul,[80] the absence of this motif from the pilgrimage token can in no way provide a secure date, given the simultaneous existence of traditions including this episode.[81] Therefore while the token can be dated to approximately the sixth century according to its form, the date unfortunately cannot be further refined according to its content. Rahmani is probably correct in his estimation that the token originated from the church of Mary in the valley of Josaphat, probably being a souvenir of someone's pilgrimage to her tomb.[82] As such, the token forms an intriguing witness to the function of this particular shrine in the sixth-century Jerusalemite cult of the Virgin, providing further material evidence (in addition to the tomb itself) that this church was originally linked with Mary's death.

Other, similar Marian *eulogiai* have survived from Byzantine Palestine, but these unfortunately lack any obvious connection with a particular shrine and thus can only attest to the general vitality of the cult of the Virgin in sixth-century Palestine. Among these are several other *eulogia* tokens depicting the Virgin Mary, each of these similarly dated to the sixth century. One of these tokens is also from Bet She'an, while five more from an unknown provenance (although probably Palestinian) are presently in the British Museum's collection. The tokens

[80] Rahmani correctly cites in his favour the *Transitus* of Ps.-John, which he dates 550–80, and the Coptic narratives. He also mentions 'Gr. Vat. Cod. 2072', which is a MS of John of Thessalonica's homily for the Dormition. Nevertheless, this text does not support his case, clearly stating, Ἡμεῖς δὲ οἱ ἀπόσ-τολοι ἐθεασάμεθα τὴν ψυχὴν Μαρίας παραδεδομένην εἰς χεῖρας Μιχαὴλ (Martin Jugie, ed., *Homélies mariales byzantine (II)*, PO 19. 3 (Paris: Firmin-Didot et Cie, 1925), 396), exactly the same as found in the early Greek Dormition narrative edited by Antoine Wenger, a version of which John used as a source (Wenger, *L'Assomption*, 232–3). Wright's version of the Six Books also omits the scene of Christ handing the Virgin's soul over to Michael, but it omits Christ's reception of her soul as well: Wright, 'Departure', ܠ (Syr.) and 152 (Eng.).

[81] In addition to the *Obsequies* and John of Thessalonica's homilies discussed above (see nn. 79, 80), other early examples of this motif from the earliest Greek and Latin traditions include: Wenger, *L'Assomption*, 232–3; A. Wilmart, OSB, ed., *Analecta Reginensia: Extraits des manuscrits Latins de la Reine christine conservés au Vatican*, Studi e Testi, 59 (Vatican: Biblioteca Apostolica Vaticana, 1933), 344; Ps.-Melito 8 (Haibach-Reinisch, *Ein neuer 'Transitus Mariae'*, 76).

[82] Rahmani, '*Eulogia*', 115.

portray a central figure flanked by two bearded men, and although there is some uncertainty regarding the identification of the central figure, it seems very likely that this represents the seated Virgin holding her son. This interpretation is particularly indicated by the British Museum tokens, which are better preserved than the Bet She'an token, and as Rahmani has shown, other similar representations from the same period confirm this reconstruction.[83] Since these images convey a rather generic depiction of Mary, in contrast to the Dormition token for instance, these tokens may be associated with the Palestinian cult of Mary only generally. Consequently, they may have had their origin at any one of the Holy Land's several Marian shrines, including the Kathisma, Mary's tomb, or even the Nea church, about which we will have more to say in the final section. There is, however, one possible exception: Peter Thomsen reports a fifth-century silver medallion from Jerusalem bearing the inscription 'Εὐλογία τῆς θεοτόκου τῆς πέτρας (καὶ) ουδαμο' (A blessing of the Theotokos of the rock (and) no one/no where/in no way [?]).[84] The inscription is quite puzzling, but it could perhaps refer to the rock at the mid-point of the Jerusalem–Bethlehem road, which was a focus of the ancient traditions surrounding the Kathisma church. Although there is no way to be certain, this mention of the Theotokos and a rock is quite intriguing in the light of the early Marian traditions of the Jerusalem area.

There are also numerous late ancient oil lamps whose inscriptions identify them as Marian *eulogiai*. These lamps are of a particular type, known as 'slipper lamps', a variety that, although found throughout Palestine, appears to have a special association with Jerusalem, which is thought to have been the centre of their production. Many of these lamps bear a Greek inscription around their filling hole, and a number read '*ΤΗΣ ΘΕΟΤΟΚΟΥ*' ('of the Theotokos'). Comparison with other similar objects suggests supplying the word '*ΕΥΛΟΓΙΑ*' ('blessing'), which is generally thought to be implied in the case of such inscribed objects.[85] It is thought that these were lamps purchased by the

[83] Ibid. 109–10.

[84] Thomsen, 'Die lateinischen und griechischen Inscriften', 125, no. 214.

[85] On these lamps and their function, see the recent article by Jodi Magness, 'Illuminating Byzantine Jerusalem: Oil Lamps Shed Light on Early Christian

faithful with the intent of bringing the 'blessing of the Theotokos' into their homes when the lamps were lit. Other similar lamps bear inscriptions invoking the blessings of St Elias or the light of Christ, and almost all of these originate from the Jerusalem area. The inscriptions on these lamps in all probability identify them with a particular shrine in Jerusalem, the shrine of St Elias or the tomb of Christ in the case of the latter two inscriptions, or one of Jerusalem's Marian shrines for those lamps bearing an inscription invoking the Theotokos.[86] As with the tokens discussed above, however, it is not certain which of Jerusalem's Marian shrines was the source of these sanctifying lamps: the Kathisma, the tomb, and the Nea all present possibilities.

While most of these objects cannot be linked with a specific Marian shrine, they are nevertheless important evidence of a lively Marian cult in late ancient Palestine. For one thing, they show that in addition to the annual liturgical feasts discussed below, Marian veneration in Palestine involved the more

Worship', *Biblical Archaeology Review*, 24/2 (March/April 1998), 40–7, 70–1. Published examples of such lamps may be found in Stanislao Loffreda, OFM, *Lucerne Bizantine in Terra Santa con Iscrizioni in Greco*, Studium Biblicum Franciscanum, Collectio maior, 35 (Jerusalem: Franciscan Printing Press, 1989), 123–8; Sylvester J. Saller, OFM, *Excavations at Bethany (1949–1953)*, Publications of the Studium Biblicum Franciscanum, 12 (Jerusalem: Franciscan Press, 1957), 178; R. A. S. Macalister and J. Garrow Duncan, *Excavations on the Hill of Ophel, Jerusalem, 1923–25*, Palestine Exploration Fund Annual, 1923–1925, vol. 4 ([London]: Published by order of the committee, 1926), 195; *Palestine Archaeological Museum Gallery Book*, iii. *Persian, Hellenistic, Roman, Byzantine Periods* (Jerusalem: n.p., 1943), 91, no. 1674; Thomsen, 'Die lateinischen und griechischen Inscriften', 130, no. 222.

Thomsen also notes the existence of another such lamp found in Aleppo; published by J.-B. Chabot, 'Deux *Lychnaria* chrétiens avec inscriptions greques', *Journal Asiatique*, series 9, 16 (1900), 271–2. Only one of these lamps is actually a *eulogia*, not two as Thomsen reports: the inscription on the second lamp records the name of its manufacturer, according to Chabot. Chabot notes that the inscriptions on these lamps are quite different from similar Palestinian lamps, and in the case of the lamp bearing its maker's name, this may be the case. The other lamp, however, bears the inscription εὐλογία τῆς θεοτόκου μεθ' ἡμῶ[ν]. Contrary to Chabot's observation, this is quite typical of the *eulogia* lamps that we are discussing, and it may in fact be that this Marian lamp is of Jerusalemite origin.

[86] See Saller, *Excavations at Bethany*, 178–9; Magness, 'Illuminating Byzantine Jerusalem'.

'private' forms of piety evident in the production and consumption of *eulogiai*. These remains also indicate something of the
vitality of these shrines during 'ordinary time', that is, outside
the context of the feast days signalled in the lectionaries and
other early liturgical sources. In addition to these formal, struc-
tured celebrations, Marian veneration was something that was
a part of people's everyday lives, that brought the Virgin and
her blessings to live with them in their homes, by means of
the various types of *eulogiai*. These lamps, tokens, flasks, etc.,
are revealing material traces of the dynamic piety that once
flourished amidst the now silent rocks and at present lies distilled
in the terse outlines of the ancient lectionaries.

THE ORIGINS, SHAPE, AND DEVELOPMENT OF
MARIAN CULT IN LATE ANCIENT JERUSALEM

The shrines of the Kathisma and the Virgin's tomb together
formed the matrix for the beginnings of the cult of the Virgin
in late ancient Palestine. The earliest Marian feast for which
there is any significant evidence is the feast of the Memory of
Mary (also called Memory of the Virgin and Memory of the
Theotokos), a feast that was celebrated in Palestine as well as
elsewhere in the Byzantine empire, beginning in the early fifth
century, even before the important events of the council of
Ephesus in 431.[87] In Palestine, the Memory of Mary was originally celebrated on 15 August at the church of the Kathisma, as
already indicated above.[88] In other parts of the empire, however,
the feast's date varied: in Constantinople and Syria the Memory
of Mary was observed on 26 December, while the Egyptian
church marked the feast on 16 January.[89] The Syrian and
Constantinopolitan date, 26 December, is today observed as the
Memory of Mary by the Eastern Orthodox churches, but the
Coptic and Palestinian variants did not disappear altogether.
Instead, the nature of these feasts was transformed, and they
both survive today as major Marian feasts. The Egyptian feast of

---

[87]   The early evidence for this feast in Eastern Christianity has been collected
and well presented by Mimouni, *Dormition*, 371–471.

[88]   See n. 9 above.

[89]   Mimouni, *Dormition*, 429.

16 January became a commemoration of the Virgin's Dormition, observed only by the Copts and their Ethiopian cousins,[90] while 15 August, the Jerusalem feast date, later came to be recognized as the feast of the Virgin Mary's Dormition and/or Assumption. The initial transformation of the 15 August feast into a feast of Mary's Dormition and Assumption took place in Palestine, where it was probably effected some time around the beginning of the sixth century. A little bit later, near the end of the sixth century, the Emperor Maurice gave official sanction to this commemoration of the end of Mary's life, establishing its celebration on 15 August throughout the Christian world.[91]

Although the sixth century saw several other important developments in the Palestinian cult of the Virgin, including the introduction of the feasts of the Annunciation, the Nativity of Mary, and the Presentation of Mary, these celebrations will be bracketed from the present discussion, since it simply is not possible to cover every aspect of early Marian cult in detail.[92] Instead, we will continue to focus on the primitive Marian shrines of Palestine, the related feast of the Memory of Mary, and the relation of both to the emergence of a liturgical commemoration of Mary's Dormition. In taking this view we will consider primarily the changing nature of this early feast, as it developed into a commemoration of the end of Mary's life, as well as the shifting relations among Jerusalem's Marian churches and their connection with changes in liturgical practice.

In its earliest discernible form, the commemoration of Mary at the Kathisma church on 15 August was clearly not the celebration of Mary's departure from this world that it would later become. Rather, the earliest sources relevant to this shrine and its feast of the Memory of Mary indicate that its initial associations were with the Nativity and the Virgin's role in the incarnation and birth of Christ, and not with the end of her life. As is the

---

[90] See Shoemaker, 'Sahidic Coptic Homily', 245–7. A rather detailed consideration of the Coptic liturgical tradition may be found in Simon Mimouni, 'Genèse et évolution des traditions anciennes sur le sort final de Marie: Étude de la tradition littéraire copte', *Marianum*, 42 (1991), 123–33.

[91] Nicephorus Callistus, *Historia ecclesiastica* 1. 17, 28 (PG 147. 292).

[92] All three of these feasts were introduced around the middle of the 6th century. For bibliography, see Mimouni, *Dormition*, 376–7.

case for the related feasts in Egypt, Syria, and Constantinople, the earliest witnesses indicate a celebration of Mary's maternity and virginity, themes that continue to characterize the modern celebration of Memory of Mary in the Eastern Orthodox world on 26 December, the day following the feast of the Nativity.[93] Since the site of the Kathisma church itself appears to derive its initial significance from the events of the Nativity as described in the second-century *Protevangelium of James*, it is not at all surprising to find that its primary liturgical celebration was originally linked with the birth of Christ. The earliest witness to both the Kathisma church and the nature of its feast is the fifth-century Armenian Lectionary, whose readings attest to the feast's association with the Nativity: the lection from the Hebrew Scriptures is Isaiah 7: 10–16 ('Behold, a virgin shall conceive', as the Christians were reading it); the Epistle reading is Galatians 3: 29–4: 7, in which Paul emphasizes redemption by God's son, 'born of a woman'; and the Gospel text is the beginning of Luke's birth narrative, 2: 1–7, which describes Mary's birthing of Christ. Each of these verses then emphasizes the birth of Christ from Mary, a theme that is confirmed by other early sources relevant to the church of the Kathisma and the feast of the Memory of Mary.

Contemporary with the Armenian Lectionary are two homilies by Hesychius, a priest of the Jerusalem diocese during the first half of the fifth century. The first of these, Homily 5, was probably delivered on 15 August, 431, 432, or 433 in the church of the Kathisma; the oration celebrates the Virgin's role in the Nativity, referring on four separate occasions to the biblical texts specified for the feast in the Armenian Lectionary.[94] The second homily, Homily 6, probably pronounced several years earlier, does not reveal these same textual links, but like the former homily, its theme is initially Mary's role in the Nativity,[95] a

---

[93] Raes, 'Aux origines', 268–9.

[94] Edited with extensive commentary by Michel Aubineau, ed., *Les Homélies festales d'Hésychius de Jérusalem*, 2 vols., Subsidia Hagiographica, 59 (Brussels: Société des Bollandistes, 1978–80), i. 118–69; see also Mimouni, *Dormition*, 392–3.

[95] Edited with extensive commentary by Aubineau, *Les Homélies festales d'Hésychius*, i. 170–205; see also Mimouni, *Dormition*, 393–5. I would agree with Mimouni (against Aubineau) that this homily was probably delivered for the Feast of the Memory of Mary. Although it focuses particularly on the

subject that eventually yields to a considerable anti-Jewish harangue, the like of which is unfortunately not uncommon in Marian piety.[96] Also from this same milieu comes a homily by Chrysippus of Jerusalem, himself a Jerusalemite priest of the mid-fifth century. Chrysippus' homily shares much with Homily 5 of the elder priest Hesychius, so much so that some have argued for some sort of literary dependence, while others have suggested that the similarities may instead derive from the liturgical order for the feast. Although Chrysippus' homily was delivered to the monastic community of the St Euthymius lavra, and not at the Kathisma church, it nevertheless confirms the themes of Mary's role in the Nativity that were the early focus of the feast of the Memory of Mary on 15 August.[97]

In addition to these Greek homilies, there are a number of important sources surviving only in Georgian translation (from Greek originals) that illustrate the changing roles of both the Kathisma shrine and its feast in the Christian liturgies of late ancient Jerusalem. While it may strike some readers as a bit peculiar that early Palestinian liturgical practice is known primarily from Caucasian, and especially Georgian, sources, this is not as odd as it may at first glance appear. Relations between Jerusalem and the Caucasus in the early medieval period were remarkably strong, and this is nowhere more evident than in the important liturgical connections between the Jerusalem church and both Georgian and Armenian Christianity.[98] In the case of

Annunciation, it cannot be for this feast since it did not yet exist in Jerusalem. Instead, Aubineau suggests its delivery for the feast of the Epiphany, which was at this time the equivalent of the feast of the Nativity in Jerusalem, the latter being introduced only in the 5th century by Juvenal. The date 25 December, for instance, is not listed as a celebration of the Nativity in the Armenian Lectionary. See the brief discussion in Mimouni, *Dormition*, 433–8, where he convincingly explains the reasons for identifying this homily with the Memory of Mary.

[96] On this topic, see Stephen J. Shoemaker, ' "Let Us Go and Burn Her Body": The Image of the Jews in the Early Dormition Traditions', *Church History*, 68 (1999), 775–823.

[97] See the discussion in Mimouni, *Dormition*, 395–7. The homily has been edited by Martin Jugie, AA, ed., *Homélies mariales byzantines (II)*, PO 19. 3 (Paris: Librairie de Paris/Firmin-Didot et Cie, 1926), 336–43.

[98] See Robert W. Thomson, 'Jerusalem and Armenia', *Studia Patristica*, 18 (1985), 77–91; Annegret Plontke-Lüning, 'Über einige Jerusalemer Einflüsse in Georgien', in Ernst Dassmann and Josef Engemann (eds.), *Akten des XII. Internationalen Kongresses für Christliche Archäologie, Bonn 1991*, Jahrbuch

the Georgian church, the connection with Jerusalem and Palestine remained especially strong in the light of a shared commitment to the Christology of the Council of Chalcedon, and there was a significant Georgian presence in medieval Palestine, particularly in its monastic communities. Consequently, Georgian is an extremely important language for the study of early medieval Palestine, particularly with regard to its Christian inhabitants.[99] Since Georgian literature has done so much to preserve the history of Palestinian Christianity during this period in many other regards, it is not at all surprising to find that Georgian translators and scribes have preserved much of the period's liturgical practice as well. The Georgian communities at the monasteries of Mar Saba and Mt. Sinai in particular deserve credit for preserving much of the ancient Jerusalem liturgies that would otherwise be lost.

Nevertheless, there is even more to this connection than the Georgian presence in the Holy Land and the general value of Georgian translations for medieval Palestinian history. As Tamila Mgaloblišvili has recently demonstrated in her edition and study of the Klardjeti homiliary, the liturgical practices of early medieval Georgia are directly dependent on the late ancient

---

für Antike und Christentum, Ergänzungsband, 20 (Münster, Germany: Aschendorffsche Verlagsbuchhandlung, 1995), 1114–18. On the liturgy specifically, see also Charles Renoux, 'La Fête de l'assomption dans le rite arménien', in A. M. Triacca and A. Pistoia (eds.), *La Mère de Jésus-Christ et la communion des saints dans la liturgie* (Rome: Edizioni Liturgiche, 1986), 235–53; idem, 'De Jérusalem en Arménie: L'heritage liturgique de l'église arménienne', in Thomas Hummel, Kevork Hintlian, and Ulf Carmesund (eds.), *Patterns of the Past, Prospects for the Future: The Christian Heritage in the Holy Land* (London: Melisende, 1999), 115–23.

[99] See esp. Sidney Griffith, 'From Aramaic to Arabic: The Languages of the Monasteries of Palestine in the Byzantine and Early Islamic Periods', *Dumbarton Oaks Papers*, 51 (1997), 30–1. See also idem, 'The Monks of Palestine and the Growth of Christian Literature in Arabic', *The Muslim World*, 78 (1988), 14–17; Robert P. Blake, 'La Littérature grecque en Palestine au VIII siècle', *Le Muséon*, 78 (1965), 367–80. On the Georgian presence in early medieval Palestine, see G. Peradze, 'An Account of the Georgian Monks and Monasteries in Palestine', *Georgica*, 1 (1937), 181–246; Amnon Linder, 'Christian Communities in Jerusalem', in Joshua Prawer and Haggai ben-Shammai (eds.), *The History of Jerusalem: The Early Muslim Period, 638–1099* (New York: New York University Press, 1996), 147–52.

liturgies of Jerusalem. The calendar embedded in this tenth-century Georgian collection of liturgical readings is clearly derived from the calendar preserved in the eighth-century Jerusalem Lectionary, many of whose traditions belong to earlier centuries.[100] Michel van Esbroeck, who has also studied the earliest Georgian homiliaries, has similarly demonstrated the close relationship between these liturgical collections and the pre-Byzantine liturgy of Jerusalem.[101] Other Georgian scholars who have studied the various manuscript witnesses to the Georgian homiliary tradition have concluded even more specifically that these homily collections were compiled in the seventh century, based on the liturgical practices of the Holy City at this time.[102] Perhaps even more striking, however, is the effort to mimic the liturgical stations of Jerusalem in the medieval Georgian capital, Mtskheta. The various churches of Mtskheta were occasionally called by the names of several important Jerusalem shrines, in an attempt to replicate the Hagiopolite pattern of worship in the Georgian capital.[103] As a result of this effort to reproduce the Jerusalem liturgies in medieval Georgia, Georgian liturgical sources are particularly revealing of Jerusalemite practice in late antiquity and the early Middle Ages, making them of the utmost importance for understanding its development.

One of the most important of these early Georgian sources is also among the most neglected, the Jerusalem Georgian 'Chant-book' or 'Tropologion', known in Georgian as the 'Iadgari'.[104]

---

[100] Tamila Mgaloblišvili, ed., კლარჯული მრავალთავი *(K'larjuli mravalt'avi [The Klardjeti Homiliary])*, Zveli k'art'uli mcerlobis zeglebi, 12 (Tbilisi: Mec'niereba, 1991), 469–73, 478–88.

[101] Michel van Esbroeck, *Les Plus Anciens Homéliaires géorgiens: Étude descriptive et historique*, Publications de l'Institut orientaliste de Louvain, 10 (Louvain-la-Neuve: Universite catholique de Louvain, Institut orientaliste, 1975), 325–49.

[102] M. Maisuradze, *et al.*, ათონის მრავალთავი *(At'onis mravalt'avi [The Athos Homilary])* (Tbilisi: Georgian Academy of Sciences, K. Kekelidze Institute of Manuscripts, 1999), 284–5.

[103] Mgaloblišvili, კლარჯული მრავალთავი, 486.

[104] While some scholars (Garitte, van Esbroeck) refer to this work as a 'Menaion', its editors have identified it as a 'Tropologion', an earlier, more rudimentary liturgical manual containing only hymns: Hélène Métrévéli, Ts. Tchankieva, L. Khevsouriani, 'Le Plus Ancien Tropologion géorgien', trans. Michel van Esbroeck, *Bedi Kartlisa*, 39 (1981), 54. See also *Oxford Dictionary*

This early collection of liturgical hymns exists in several tenth-century manuscripts from Mt. Sinai, which preserve two distinct versions, the earliest of which concerns us present-ly.[105] Although this oldest version of the Jerusalem Georgian Chantbook was probably composed around 600, the liturgical calendar that structures its hymns is significantly earlier, probably reflecting liturgical practices in Jerusalem during the 560s.[106] A copy of what is probably the Greek original for this Georgian translation has recently come to light among the newly discovered Sinai manuscripts (found in 1975), in an eighth- or ninth-century manuscript.[107] Presumably the publication of this remarkable new manuscript will improve our understanding of the ancient Palestinian liturgies; in the near future, it is to be hoped.

Most significant for the present purpose is the Chantbook's indication of a commemoration of Mary's Dormition and Assumption on 15 August. With this, the Chantbook presents the earliest evidence of this date's association with the events of Mary's death. Although the Chantbook describes the feast with the rather generic term 'Feast of Mary' (მარიამობასა), the various hymns for the feast demonstrate that this was indeed a celebration of the Virgin's Dormition.[108] The feast's location is

---

of Byzantium, s.v. 'Menaion'. Presumably, this designation is confirmed by the recently discovered Greek version, which is described as a 'Tropologion' (see below, n. 107). I have followed Peter Jeffery in referring to this book in English as a 'Chantbook', even though this is not a translation of either the Greek or Georgian (which themselves have different meanings): see Peter Jeffery, 'The Sunday Office of Seventh-Century Jerusalem in the Georgian Chantbook (Iadgari), A Preliminary Report', *Studia Liturgica*, 23 (1993), 52–3, esp. n. 4.

[105] Regarding the different versions of the Jerusalem Georgian Chantbook, see Hélène Métrévéli, 'Les Manuscrits liturgiques géorgiens des IXe–Xe siècles et leur importance pour l'étude de l'hymnographie byzantine', *Bedi Kartlisa*, 35 (1978), 46–8.

[106] Jeffery, 'Sunday Office', 56–60.

[107] See the brief discussion in Paul Géhin and Stig Frøyshov, 'Nouvelles découvertes sinaïtiques: à propos de la parution de l'inventaire des manuscrits grecs', *Revue des Études Byzantines*, 59 (2000), 178–9.

[108] *Jerusalem Georgian Chantbook* (E. Metreveli, C. Cankievi, and L. Xevsuriani, eds., უძველესი იადგარი (*Uzvelesi Iadgari [The Oldest Chantbook]*), Zveli k'art'uli mcerlobis zeglebi, 2 (Tbilisi: Mec'niereba, 1980), 266–75). The first hymn, for instance, begins: 'You went forth from the world, O virgin Theotokos, to the eternal light . . .' (გარდაიცალე სოფლით, ლდრთოისძმობელო ქალწულო, ნათელსა დაუსრულებელსა).

unfortunately unspecified, but its observance at Mary's tomb seems very likely. On the basis of the oldest Jerusalem Chantbook then, we can be assured that the Memory of Mary's transformation into a celebration of Mary's Dormition had already taken place by the middle of the sixth century. At present we do not know more specifically when this change took place, and it was probably a gradual rather than a sudden change. A transformation beginning sometime around the turn of the sixth century seems likely, particularly in the light of the sudden interest in the events of the Dormition and Assumption that emerges around this time. Moreover, comparison with the liturgical traditions of Egypt and Syria supports this approximate time, since both these regions knew celebrations of the Virgin's Dormition and/or Assumption during the early sixth century, even though the feasts were observed on different dates.[109]

The probable context of this change has been identified in the celebration of the feast of the Memory of Mary at the tomb of the Virgin, where the feast gradually took on an association with the events of her death. Ordinarily, a saint's feast day was observed on his or her *dies natalis*, that is, on the day when the saint had died and was consequently reborn in heaven. The Virgin Mary's earliest feast, however, was an anomaly: instead of commemorating her earthly death and heavenly rebirth, it was a celebration of her Divine Maternity and the events of the Nativity. The absence of a feast honouring Mary's death was probably felt, and consequently the commemoration of her departure from this life was attached to her traditional feast day, in conformity with the practice of other saints' cults. The probable celebration of the Memory of Mary at the Virgin's Gethsemane tomb, in addition to its celebration at the church of the Kathisma, no doubt made such a change seem all the more natural. Thus it is generally supposed that the feast of the Memory of Mary, for many years the only Marian feast, eventually moved in a direction that

---

[109] These changes are discussed in some detail in Stephen J. Shoemaker, 'Mary and the Discourse of Orthodoxy: Early Christian Identity and the Ancient Dormition Legends', Ph.D. diss., Duke University, 1997, 27–44. See also idem, 'Sahidic Coptic Homily', 245–7; Mimouni, 'Genèse et évolution, 123–33; idem, 'La Fête de la dormition de Marie en Syrie à l'epoque byzantine', *The Harp*, 5 (1992), 157–74.

made it more typical of a saint's feast day, almost certainly sometime before the middle of the sixth century, when a new celebration of Mary's Divine Maternity emerged in the feast of
Annunciation.[110]

The next significant source, chronologically, is the Jerusalem
Georgian Lectionary, mentioned briefly above. This is a liturgical manual similar to the Armenian Lectionary, except that it
describes the practices of the Holy City at a later stage, reflecting
developments of the period between 450 and 750.[111] Although
the calendar is extant for the entire year, it is not known from
a single complete manuscript, having been pieced together from
various fragmentary witnesses, one of which dates from the
beginning of the seventh century. Most of the manuscripts, however, were copied in the tenth and eleventh centuries, and dating
much of the material is problematic, as indicated by the 300-year
window within which the text's traditions are located. While
many of the Georgian Lectionary's traditions represent practices
from the earlier part of this period, others are undeniably later
developments.

At the stage represented in the Georgian Lectionary, the feast
of 15 August had already become a celebration of the Virgin's
death or 'translation', and the site of its commemoration had
likewise changed from the church of the Kathisma to the Virgin's
tomb in Gethsemane.[112] The feast of the Memory of Mary, however, did not disappear; it was instead moved ahead two days,
when it continued to be observed on 13 August at the church of

---

[110] See the dicussions in Jugie, *La Mort*, 174; Mimouni, *Dormition*, 378, 463;
Capelle, 'La Fête de la Vierge', 28–9; and Raes, 'Aux origines', 274 n. 1.

[111] Michel Tarchnischvili, ed., *Le Grand Lectionnaire de l'église de Jérusalem*,
2 vols. CSCO 188–9, 204–5 (Louvain: CSCO, 1959–60). Regarding the date
and for a general description of this source, see John F. Baldovin, *The Urban
Character of Christian Worship: The Origins, Development, and Meaning of
Stational Liturgy*, Orientalia Christiana Analecta, 228 (Rome: Pont. Institutum
Studiorum Orientalium, 1987), 72–3. Helmut Leeb, *Die Gesänge im Gemeingottesdienst von Jerusalem (vom 5. bis 8. Jahrhundert)*, Wiener Beiträge zur
Theologie, 28 (Vienna: Verlag Herder, 1970), 23–33, provides a more detailed
discussion, and emphasizes the many indicators of the Lectionary's antiquity,
such as archaic language and usage of the earliest Georgian biblical translation.

[112] Tarchnischvili, *Le Grand Lectionnaire*, ii. 30–1 (Geor.) and 27–8
(Lat.). The feast's new focus is indicated particularly by the Troparion for the
feast, whose incipit is რაჟამს მიიცვალე დგრთოისჰ: 'When the Virgin was translated . . .'

the Kathisma.[113] This is significant because it marks the beginning of a trend with regard to the feast of the Dormition that
will be seen in later witnesses to the early Jerusalem liturgical
calendar. During the seventh century, it appears that the celebration of Mary's Dormition was extended to comprise more
than just a single day, eventually expanding to include a five-day
liturgical cycle involving all Jerusalem's major Marian shrines.
The Georgian Lectionary's inclusion of a second feast is the first
step in this direction. Presumably, concern to somehow preserve
observance of the primitive feast was an impetus for this initial
expansion, but later sources reveal that a Memory of Mary in
mid-August was soon forgotten in the Holy City's observance.
Nevertheless, traces of the original feast's emphasis on Mary's
role in the Nativity continue to be manifest, as the next source in
particular demonstrates.

A somewhat later stage in the development of Hagiopolite
celebration of the Dormition is evident in one of the earliest
Georgian homiliaries, the tenth-century Klardjeti homiliary,
mentioned briefly above. This manuscript contains a variety
of homilies, some of which are otherwise unknown, as well as
a handful of apocrypha that were used for liturgical reading,
covering the second half of the liturgical year. Consequently,
the homiliary is also in some sense a calendar, since its structure
reveals the liturgical organization of the year, and it is primarily, but not exclusively, on the basis of this calendar that the
collection's dependence on ancient Jerusalem liturgical practice
is well established.[114] With regard to Jerusalem's earliest Marian
feasts, two things in particular stand out from this assemblage of
readings. Firstly, the celebration of the Memory or Dormition
and Assumption of Mary has been expanded to include a third
feast on 14 August, a feast that is absent from the Georgian
Lectionary's liturgical programme. Much more striking, however, is the rather interesting content of the readings for these
three days: several of them clearly combine material appropriate
for both the feast of the Memory of Mary and the Feast of the
Dormition and Assumption, raising the possibility that in their
present state they somehow reflect a period of transition, when
the nature of the 15 August feast was still being transformed.

---

[113] Tarchnischvili, *Le Grand Lectionnaire*, ii. 29–30 (Geor.) and 26 (Lat.).
[114] See nn. 100 and 101 above.

The first reading for this liturgical cycle is a lection from the 'words of the prophet Jeremiah', whose superscription identifies it as a reading for 13 August, in commemoration of the 'gathering in Bethlehem, when the apostles led the Theotokos forth from Bethlehem to Zion'.[115] The reading consists of an extended, interpolated quotation from the 'Life of Jeremiah', a brief writing preserved in Greek among the *Vitae Prophetarum*.[116] The bulk of this reading concerns the events of the Nativity and the typology of Mary as the Ark of the Covenant, themes that seem more resonant with the Memory of Mary than a celebration of her Assumption. Like the various other documents associated with the Memory of Mary, the reading emphasizes the Virgin's role in the Nativity, leading Michel van Esbroeck to conclude that the feast of the Memory of Mary was the reading's original context. This would make a certain amount of sense, given that 13 August was according to the Georgian Lectionary the new date assigned to the Memory of Mary, after 15 August had become a celebration of her Dormition and Assumption.[117] Nevertheless, van Esbroeck further notes that in its present state this lection also has unmistakable associations with the Virgin's Dormition. On this basis van Esbroeck concludes that this reading was once a reading for the feast of the Memory of Mary that has since been rewritten to commemorate the end of the Virgin's life, and in the light of this he has included this reading in his catalogue of the earliest Dormition traditions.[118]

Nevertheless, Simon Mimouni has objected to van Esbroeck's classification of this reading as a Dormition tradition, maintaining that the piece has no connections with the Dormition beyond

---

[115] Michel van Esbroeck, 'Nouveaux apocryphes de la Dormition conservés en Géorgien', *Analecta Bollandiana*, 90 (1972), 366: კრებაი ბეთლემს ოდეს მოციქულთა ღმრთისმშობელი ბეთლემით სიონდ წარჰყვანდა. Although this text is also available in Mgaloblišvili's edition of the Klardjeti homiliary (Mgaloblišvili, კლარჯული მრავალთავი, 409–10), I have referred to van Esbroeck's edition since it is more widely available.

[116] These quotations have been taken from *Vitae Prophetarum* 2. 8–19 (Theodor Schermann, ed., *Prophetarum vitae fabulosae indices apostolorum discipulorumque Domini Dorotheo, Epiphanio, Hippolyto aliisque vindicate* (Leipzig: Teubner, 1907), 72–4). This excerpt includes approximately ⅔ of the original text.

[117] Tarchnischvili, *Le Grand Lectionnaire*, ii. 29–30 (Geor.) and 26 (Lat.).

[118] van Esbroeck, 'Nouveaux apocryphes', 364–5. See also idem, 'Les Textes', 268.

its title in the manuscript and thus should not be counted among these traditions.[119] Although this is a fair indication of the strong contacts between the reading and the feast of the Memory of Mary, Mimouni's assessment of the lection is incorrect. The reading has very obvious connections with the Virgin's Dormition, including particularly the occasion of the Virgin's transport from Bethlehem to Zion, which is not only indicated in the reading's superscription, but also is repeated in the body of reading.[120] This presumably refers to an event described in a few of the early Dormition traditions, in which prior to Mary's Dormition, she and the apostles miraculously pass through the air from her house in Bethlehem to her house in Jerusalem, which later tradition came to locate on Mt. Zion.[121]

Even more clear, however, is the reading's unmistakable reference to Mary's 'transfer from earth into heaven'.[122] Not only then does the lection's text commemorate a specific event from the early Dormition narratives, but it also unambiguously refers to Mary's *transitus* from this life to the next. This is especially evident in the reading's exegesis of passages from the 'Life of Jeremiah' and the Hebrew Scriptures, both of which are interpreted as prefiguring the Virgin's Assumption:

And the prophet said: '*His coming will be a sign to you*, for the other children at the end of world.[123] *And no one will bring forth the hidden Ark from the rock, except the priest Aaron*, the brother of Mary [Mariam]. *And no one will disclose the tablets in it, and no one will read them, except the lawgiver Moses, the chosen of the Lord.' And at the resurrection of the dead, the ark will first arise from the rock and will be placed on Mount Sinai*, so that the prophet David's saying will be fulfilled, in which he says, 'Arise, O Lord, into your resting place, you and the Ark of your holiness [Ps. 131: 8]', which is the holy Virgin Mary [Mariam], who passes from this world to the presence of God.[124]

[119] Mimouni, *Dormition*, 302–3.

[120] van Esbroeck, 'Nouveaux apocryphes', 367 (Geor.) and 369 (Lat.).

[121] See e.g. Wright, 'Departure', ܚܒܐ (Syr.) and 142–3 (Eng.); and Tischendorf, *Apocalypses Apocryphae*, 104–5. On the relatively late identification of Zion as the site of the Virgin's 'death', see below as well as Mimouni, *Dormition*, 533–47.

[122] van Esbroeck, 'Nouveaux apocryphes', 367 (Geor.) and 369 (Lat.) ესე დღეს ბეთლემით სიონდ წარგზავნების, და დღეს ქუეყანით ზეცად მიივალების.

[123] This is a very puzzling phrase: მერმეთა მათ ყრმათაი აღსასრულსა სოფლისასა.

[124] van Esbroeck, 'Nouveaux apocryphes', 367 (Geor.) and 369 (Lat.). The

This passage, which comprises a significant portion of the reading, is clearly (*contra* Mimouni) aimed at a commemoration of the Virgin's Assumption. Nevertheless, it must be emphasized that much of the reading's remaining content focuses instead on Mary's role in the Nativity, rather than the events of her death. This dual emphasis suggests a liturgical text that is in transition, reflecting themes of both the earlier feast of the Memory of Mary and the emerging commemoration of her Assumption on this same day.

Perhaps the most intriguing indicator of the reading's liturgically composite nature is its use of Psalm 131: 8 (LXX), a verse identified by the Armenian Lectionary as one of the readings for the feast of the Memory of Mary.[125] The function of this verse is particularly striking, since it creates a rather graceful bridge between the two traditions: originally belonging to the ancient liturgy of the Memory of Mary, here the verse speaks to a rather different context, in which the Lord has brought to rest with him the 'Ark of his holiness'. As the reading itself makes abundantly clear, this Ark is a typology of the Virgin, who has arisen into the 'resting place', where she is now in the presence of God. Indeed, this verse is one of the few biblical 'witnesses' to the Assumption of the Virgin adduced by the Vatican's 1950 definition of this dogma, the papal encyclical *Munificentissimus Deus*.[126] Thus, this lection has cleverly reworked material from the older celebration of the Memory of Mary, articulating it in the new liturgical context of her Dormition and Assumption.

Although this text in many ways seems to reflect a time when the focus of the 15 August feast was first beginning to change, probably the early sixth century, in its present state the reading reflects a somewhat later stage in the history of Jerusalem's Marian traditions. While the core of the lection may perhaps date from an earlier time, its topography suggests that the form preserved in the Klardjeti homiliary is from the late sixth or early seventh century, at the earliest. This is especially indicated by

italicized passages have been identified by van Esbroeck as quotations from the 'Life of Jeremiah', which is extant in Greek.

[125] Renoux, *Le Codex arménien Jérusalem 121*, ii. 354. It is not, however, indicated in the Georgian Lectionary.

[126] Pius XII, 'Munificentissimus Deus', *Acta Apostolicae Sedis*, 42 (1950), 763.

the reading's connection of Zion with the end of Mary's life, an association that is explicitly made only from this time onward. A basilica is known to have stood on Zion since the late fourth century, with some scholars even proposing the rather speculative existence of a Jewish-Christian synagogue on the same spot between the late first century and the basilica's contraction under Patriarch John (387–417).[127] The basilica, however, whose existence is quite certain, appears initially to have been associated with the events of the Last Supper and Pentecost, rather than with any aspect of the Virgin Mary's life. There is in fact no clear association of Zion with the Marian traditions of Jerusalem before the first decades of seventh century, when Sophronius, in his *Anacreontic Hymns*, refers to a stone on Zion, where the Virgin lay down and died.[128] In spite of this silence, however, the earliest Dormition traditions could seem to imply, without clearly stating, the association of this general location with the end of Mary's life. Various narratives from the late fifth and early sixth centuries attest that after the Virgin's death, Christ instructed the apostles to go out from the city towards the left, and bring Mary's body to the tomb prepared for her in Gethsemane.[129] While these early narratives all fail to specify Zion as the starting point of Mary's funeral procession, Christ's directions do seem to imply her death at some place in the area of Mount Zion. This is admittedly rather slim evidence for an earlier tradition of Mary's death on Zion, and a more cautious dating would locate the Georgian lection for 13 August in its present form sometime after the turn of the seventh century. Nevertheless, the core of this reading may very well reflect a much earlier stage, when the 15 August feast was still a hybrid of the Memory of Mary and the Dormition.

Another topographical peculiarity of this reading is the mention of Bethlehem in the reading's superscription. This

---

[127] See e.g. Bargil Pixner, 'Church of the Apostles Found on Mt. Zion', *Biblical Archaeology Review*, 16/3 (1990), 16–35 and 60; Simon Mimouni, 'La Synagogue "judéo-chrétienne" de Jérusalem au Mont Sion', *Proche-Orient chrétien*, 40 (1990), 215–324. Against such views, see the excellent work by Joan E. Taylor, *Christians and the Holy Places: The Myth of Jewish-Christian Origins* (Oxford: Clarendon Press, 1993), esp. 207–21.

[128] Sophronius of Jerusalem, *carm.* 20 (PG 87. 3821A).

[129] See e.g. *Liber Requiei* 70 (Arras, *De Transitu*, 41 (Eth.) and 27 (Lat.)); Wenger, *L'Assomption*, 232–3. See also van Esbroeck, 'Les Textes', 280.

could potentially be understood as identifying a liturgical station in Bethlehem, as could the superscription of the reading that immediately follows: '14 August. The assembly of the Holy apostles in Bethlehem, when the Holy Theotokos passed away. The reading before the feast: the homily of St. John Chrysostom.'[130] There is, however, no other evidence of Bethlehem's use as a liturgical station for the Virgin's August feasts. Although one might immediately think of the Kathisma shrine, to my knowledge this church is never identified by any source as being in Bethlehem: on the contrary, its location is always specified as 'on the Bethlehem road, at the Kathisma, at the third mile, in the village of Betophor (or Betebre/Petophor)',[131] Jerusalem of course being the point of geographic reference. This village indicated is not a reference to Bethlehem, but most likely to the modern village of Sur Bahir, which lies about 1km to the east of both Ramat Rahel and the Mar Elias church.[132] Moreover, Bethlehem's mention in both superscriptions clearly seems to have a purpose other than the identification of a liturgical station. Rather than referring to the feast's location, these superscriptions identify their occasion, in the first instance, the Virgin's transport with the apostles from Bethlehem to Jerusalem, and in the second, the gathering of the apostles at Mary's house in Bethlehem and the eve of the great feast.[133] The chronology here is admittedly out of the order indicated by the Bethlehem narratives: the gathering of the apostles in Bethlehem should precede the miraculous journey from Bethlehem to Zion, after which the apostles should be in Jerusalem, on the eve of the Virgin's Dormition. Nevertheless, this problem in no way tips the balance in favour of understanding Bethlehem as a liturgical station, since it too fails to resolve the issue. Thus, while the Klardjeti homiliary is an important witness to the evolution of the 15 August feast into a celebration

---

[130] Mgaloblišvili, კლარჯული მრავალთავი, 410.

[131] See Tarchnischvili, *Le Grand Lectionnaire*, ii. 29 (Geor.) and 26 (Lat.); Gérard Garitte, *Le Calendrier palestino-géorgien du Sinaiticus 34 (Xe siècle)*, Subsidia Hagiographica, 30 (Brussels: Société des Bollandistes, 1958), 84.

[132] Milik, 'Notes d'épigraphie', 571–2; Aharoni, *Excavations at Ramat Rahel*, i. 75–6.

[133] Likewise the superscription for 15 August refers not to the location of the feast, but to the 'Passing of the Holy Theotokos': Mgaloblišvili, კლარჯული მრავალთავი, 413.

lasting several days, it does not provide us with information regarding the liturgical stations for the feast. These were perhaps lost when the traditions were transferred from Jerusalem to south-western Georgia, where the proper stations were no longer available, nor as important for the local celebration.

As the second superscription indicates, the Klardjeti homiliary follows the 13 August lection from the 'Life of Jeremiah' with a homily of (Ps.-)Chrysostom for 14 August. This homily in turn is followed by several readings for the feast of the Dormition on 15 August which include the following: a second homily attributed to Chrysostom, a Georgian version of (Ps.-)John's narrative of Mary's Dormition (G2), two fragments of the *Liber Requiei*, and a third, otherwise unknown fragment describing Mary's Dormition. Of these additional readings, the two homilies attributed to Chrysostom are the most significant for understanding the liturgical development of the 15 August feast.[134] Both these homilies are known only in Georgian (but in several manuscripts), and, like the reading for 13 August, they have the appearance of liturgical hybrids, emphasizing themes appropriate for both the Memory of Mary and the Virgin's Dormition and Assumption. According to Bernard Outtier, there is little chance on stylistic grounds that they are actually works of Chrysostom, but comparison with other similar homilies suggests their composition in late ancient Palestine, probably in Jerusalem.[135] Mgaloblišvili also argues for such a provenance, on the basis of their inclusion in the earliest Georgian homiliaries and their related liturgical indications, both of which point to a probable origin in fifth- or sixth-century Jerusalem.[136]

---

[134] Printed texts of both homilies from two (of several) separate manuscripts may be found in Mgaloblišvili, კლარჯული მრავალთავი, 410–13 and 425–8; and Akaki Šanize, ed., სინური მრავალთავი 864 წლისა (*Sinuri mravaltavi 864 c'lisa [The Sinai Homiliary of the Year 864]*), Zveli k'art'uli enis kat'edris šromebi, 5 (Tbilisi: T'bilisis Stalinis saxelobis saxelmcip'o universitetis gamomc'emloba, 1959), 199–202 and 202–5 (the order of the homilies is inverted from that of the Klardjeti homiliary, and both readings are assigned to 15 August. No other readings are included for this date). French translations of both homilies, with commentary and information concerning additional manuscripts, may be found in Bernard Outtier, 'Deux homélies pseudo-chrysostomiennes pour la fête mariale du 15 Août', *Apocrypha*, 6 (1995), 165–77.

[135] Outtier, 'Deux homélies', 176–7.

[136] Mgaloblišvili, კლარჯული მრავალთავი, 477.

Like the other items mentioned so far, these sermons place strong emphasis on Mary's role in the Nativity, a theme that, as already noted, was especially characteristic of the celebration of the feast of the Memory of Mary. Likewise the homilies both exhort their audiences to 'keep the feast of the Memory of the Holy Theotokos'[137] and 'rejoice in the Memory of the Holy Virgin',[138] which probably are direct references to the commemoration of this feast. Nevertheless, both homilies also make significant reference to the Virgin's Assumption, as one would expect given their usage for this liturgical cycle in the Klardjeti homiliary. In the light of such indications, Outtier concludes that these homilies were originally composed for the Memory of Mary, but in their present state have been adapted for use at the feast of Mary's Dormition and Assumption. This is indeed a likely proposal, but one might also consider the possibility that these homilies were produced in an atmosphere of liturgical transition, and rather than revealing two redactional layers, they may simply reproduce the fusion of traditions occasioned by the transformation of the 15 August feast.

On the whole, Outtier's hypothesis seems more likely. In each homily, material relevant to the Virgin's Assumption is positioned at the beginning and end of the oration, while the core of both readings is devoted exclusively to celebrating the Virgin's role in the Nativity. This pattern suggests that both works were originally composed for the feast of the Memory of Mary, as it was celebrated in fifth-century Jerusalem. Once the 15 August feast had been transformed into the feast of the Dormition and Assumption, it was felt necessary to 'correct' these homilies to agree with later practice by inserting these otherwise intrusive references to the Virgin's Dormition and Assumption. This seems particularly clear in the case of the homily designated for 15 August (Outtier's first homily). Outtier has identified the existence of a 'first conclusion', which presumably brought the original homily to a close.[139] A lengthy section dedicated to Mary's Assumption follows this first conclusion, completing the oration with a conclusion of its own. As

---

[137] კდლესასწაულობდეთ საჰსენებელსა წმიდისა ღმრთისმშობელისასა, ibid. 427.
[138] ვიშუებდეთ ჰსენებასა წმიდისა ქალწულისასა, ibid. 428.
[139] See Outtier, 'Deux homélies', 167–8 and 171.

Outtier suggests, this is a probable indication that material relevant to the Assumption has been appended to an earlier homily
originally designed for the feast of the Memory of Mary, which
focused on Mary's role in the Nativity and finished with the first
conclusion. If this hypothesis is correct, then the cores of these
two homilies belong to the traditions related to the Memory of
Mary and the Kathisma church, probably having been composed in fifth-century Palestine.[140]

THE EMERGENCE OF A STATIONAL MARIAN LITURGY IN EARLY MEDIEVAL JERUSALEM

It would seem that the final development of the Jerusalem
cult of the Virgin, before its eventual standardization to reflect
Byzantine practice, was a sequence of successive feasts, extending over the five days 13–17 August. The expansion of the
original 15 August feast into a liturgical cycle extending over
a course of several days is first anticipated by the Georgian
Lectionary's transfer of the Memory of Mary to 13 August,
a phenomenon also witnessed in the three-day cycle of the
Klardjeti homiliary. While these witnesses offer only faint hints
of a stational, progressive liturgy in Jerusalem centred on the
15 August feast, such practice is well known from other early
medieval Georgian sources. A stational liturgy is a mobile form
of worship, in which services are held at a designated shrine, in
or near a city, on a designated feast day.[141] The programme for
such a stational liturgy, lasting for five days and centred around
the end of Mary's life, is given by the tenth-century Palestinian
Georgian liturgical calendar preserved at Mount Sinai. A similar
pattern is also evidenced in an early Dormition narrative attributed to Basil of Caesarea, extant only in Georgian, and in the
more recent version of the Jerusalem Georgian 'Chantbook' or
'Tropologion'.[142]

---

[140] See Outtier, 'Deux homélies', 177.

[141] Baldovin, *Urban Character of Christian Worship*, 36–7.

[142] Garitte, *Le Calendrier palestino-géorgien*, 84–5; Michel van Esbroeck,
'L'Assomption de la Vierge dans un Transitus Pseudo-Basilien', *Analecta
Bollandiana*, 92 (1974), 161–2. Regarding the versions of the Georgian Chant-
book, see Metreveli, 'Les Manuscrits liturgiques géorgiens', 46–8.

The Palestinian Georgian Calendar is one of the most important witnesses to the liturgical traditions of Jerusalem in the
early Middle Ages. Although the manuscript is presently found
among the rich collection of Georgian manuscripts at Mt. Sinai,
a colophon alerts us that the calendar was actually produced in
the famous monastery of Mar Saba, whose practice it represents.
Although the calendar occasionally draws on a Byzantinizing
liturgical source, for the most part it reflects the organization of the liturgical year in the Holy Land before its eventual conformation to the Byzantine pattern.[143] In the Georgian
Palestinian Calendar, the feast of 15 August has expanded into a
five-day celebration of the Virgin, a practice that is also attested
in the *Transitus* of Ps.-Basil. Although there are some minor
differences in the two calendars,[144] these two texts describe a
stational liturgy that was enacted over the course of five (or perhaps four) days in mid-August, connecting all the Holy City's
major Marian shrines in a commemoration of the Virgin's
Dormition and Assumption (see Fig. 9). The progressive celebration began on 13 August at the church of the Kathisma, where
it apparently continued on 14 August as well. The following day,
15 August is named 'the feast of Mary', the standard designation for the feast of the Dormition in Georgian, and although the
specific location is not given, we may assume from the Georgian
Lectionary's earlier witness that this feast was celebrated at the
Virgin's Gethsemane tomb, as one would expect.[145] The location
of the 16 August feast, identified as 'the exaltation of the Virgin',
is also unspecified in the calendar. Finally, this liturgical cycle
concluded at the Nea Church in Jerusalem, where the sequence
was completed on 17 August.

The more recent version of the Georgian Jerusalem Tropologion or Chantbook confirms the existence of this liturgical
pattern. This version, or perhaps we should say versions, is
preserved by several tenth-century manuscripts from Sinai,

---

[143] Garitte, *Le Calendrier palestino-géorgien*, 15–37.

[144] The *Transitus* of Ps-Basil differs in that it does not specify the location
or significance of the feasts, and it is one day shorter, beginning on 14 August
rather than 13 August, as in the Sinai calendar. It does not, however, offer any
information that contradicts the Sinai calendar, other than omitting the first
feast.

[145] Tarchnischvili, *Le Grand Lectionnaire*, ii. 30 (Geor.) and 27 (Lat.).

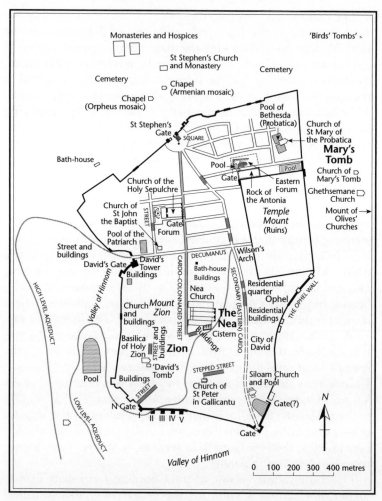

FIG. 9. Byzantine Jerusalem, showing Marian shrines (after Ephraim Stern (ed.), *The New Encyclopaedia of Archaeological Excavations in the Holy Land* (New York: Simon & Schuster, 1992), 769)

although its composition probably dates to the seventh or eighth century.[146] Presumably, however, its calendar is somewhat older, as was the case with the oldest version of the Chantbook. As will be seen, it is almost certain that this stational liturgy was

[146] Métrévéli, 'Les manuscrits liturgiques géorgiens', 48.

practised during the seventh century. Each of the five August feasts is attested by these liturgical manuals, as Garitte has indicated in his commentary on the Palestinian Georgian Calendar.[147] Each of these celebrations is identified as a Marian feast, and the hymns designated for the first four celebrations indicate their commemoration of the Virgin's Dormition. Only the final feast, for 17 August, lacks specific identification with Mary's Dormition. Nevertheless, this may not be significant. The catalogue on which we are dependent for our knowledge of the unpublished Chantbook manuscripts gives the incipits for only a few of any given festival's hymns, and if the complete contents of these liturgical manuals were known, we might find that the hymns for 17 August also have Mary's Dormition as their theme. In contrast to the Georgian Calendar, the Chantbook does not specify locations for the 13 and 14 August feasts, but the 16 August feast is identified as a commemoration of 'Mary's leading forth from Zion to Gethsemane', making this a commemoration of her funeral and burial, which according to early tradition had travelled this route. Both the Calendar and the Chantbook agree, however, on the location of the 17 August feast at the Nea.[148]

In his commentary on the Palestinian Georgian Calendar, Garitte raised some doubt regarding the feast of 14 August, which the Calendar associates with the Virgin only by a supralinear insertion. Garitte expressed additional concern because he could find the feast attested in only one of the early Chantbook manuscripts that he had examined. Although the existence of a vigil for the 15 August feast seemed rather likely to him, Garitte was puzzled by its absence from the Georgian Lectionary and the 'primitive' text of the Palestinian Georgian Calendar.[149] Nevertheless, we now know that the 14 August feast is present in at least two additional tenth-century manuscripts of the Chantbook from Sinai, bringing the total to three.[150] Moreover, both

---

[147] Garitte, *Le Calendrier palestino-géorgien*, 301–5.

[148] E. Metreveli, *et al.*, ქართულ ხელნაწერთა აღწერილობა, სინური კოლექცია *(K'art'ul xelnacert'a agceriloba, sinuri kolek'c'ia [Description of Georgian Manuscripts, Sinai Collection])*, 3 vols. (Tbilisi: Mec'niereba, 1978), i. 28, 52, 83, 105, 122, 159, 181–2, 210–11, 235.

[149] Garitte, *Le Calendrier palestino-géorgien*, 301–2.

[150] The feast is attested in MSS Sin. georg. 1, 14, and, 65: see Metreveli, *et al.*, ქართულ ხელნაწერთა აღწერილობა, i. 28, 52, 211. Perhaps Garitte missed two

the Klardjeti homiliary and the *Transitus* of Ps.-Basil attest to a 14 August feast in honour of the Virgin, and while its absence from the other sources is indeed peculiar, this collection of witnesses reassures us that the 14 August feast was in fact a part of the pre-Byzantine Jerusalem liturgies in the early Middle Ages. In any case, the presence of this complete liturgical cycle among the early witnesses to the Georgian Chantbook is, as both Garitte and van Esbroeck noted, important evidence of its antiquity, suggesting its observance in the seventh century.[151]

Other related factors suggest that this liturgical formation is representative of Jerusalem practice beginning in the late sixth or early seventh century, although it is rather difficult to establish a very certain *terminus ante quem*. The stational character of the early Jerusalem liturgy is well known and is at least as early as Egeria's visit sometime between 381 and 384, when she was witness to the progressive liturgies of the Holy City.[152] But the development of this Marian cycle is clearly later, given its absence from both the Armenian and Georgian Lectionaries. Its introduction sometime after the middle of the sixth century is further indicated by its inclusion of the Nea church, which was inaugurated by Justinian in 543,[153] but an upper date for this church is much more difficult to determine. Several sources report the Nea's destruction during the seventh-century Persian occupation, including the *Capture of Jerusalem*, an eyewitness account of the Persian conquest and rule.[154] Nevertheless, the

of these witnesses to the 14 August feast because he was using the inferior catalogues of N. Marr and I. Dzavakhišvili, which consisted only of the field notes taken by these two scholars during their expedition to Sinai in 1902: see Michel van Esbroeck, 'Le manuscrit sinaïtique géorgien 34 et les publications récentes de liturgie palestinienne', *Orientalia Christiana Periodica*, 46 (1980), 129.

[151] Garitte, *Le Calendrier palestino-géorgien*, 301–5; van Esbroeck, 'Les Textes', 285.

[152] Baldovin, *Urban Character of Christian Worship*, 55–64.

[153] Vincent and Abel, *Jérusalem*, ii. pt. 4. 911–19; Nahman Avigad, 'The Nea: Justinian's Church of St. Mary, Mother of God, Discovered in the Old City of Jerusalem', in Yoram Tsafrir (ed.), *Ancient Churches Revealed* (Jerusalem: Israel Exploration Society, 1993), 128–35.

[154] The *Capture of Jerusalem* has been preserved both in Georgian and in Arabic: Gérard Garitte, ed., *La Prise de Jérusalem par les Perses en 614*, CSCO 202–3 (Louvain: Secrétariat du CorpusSCO, 1960), 78–9 (Geor.) and 52 (Lat.); and idem, *Expugnationis Hierosolymae A.D. 614*, 2 vols., CSCO 340–1, 347–8 (Louvain, Secrétariat du Corpus SCO, 1973–4), i. 102 (Arab.) and 68 (Lat.);

Nea church is listed in the *Commemoratorium de casis Dei*, a catalogue of Jerusalem's churches made in 808 for the emperor Charlemagne. Although there are certain complications with the witness of this latter source (often unacknowledged), its confident identification of the Nea means that we must read the testimony of these earlier sources regarding the Nea's destruction with a fair amount of caution.[155]

ii. 146 (Arab.) and 99 (Lat.). See the discussion of this text in Robert L. Wilken, *The Land Called Holy: Palestine in Christian History and Thought* (New Haven: Yale University Press, 1992), 218–24. Other witnesses to the Nea's destruction are discussed in Moshe Gil, *A History of Palestine, 634–1099*, trans. Ethel Broido (Cambridge: Cambridge University Press, 1992), 440. Gil seems to favour the evidence suggesting the Nea's destruction in the early 7th century, particularly in the light of the fact that it is absent from the later pilgrim literature, with only the exception discussed in n. 155 below. But on the other hand Schick (*Christian Communities of Palestine*, 332–3) argues that, although the church must have been damaged, any destruction must have been slight, since the church was used by Patriarch Sophronius for Christmas services in 634, when it was not possible to travel to Bethlehem, on account of the Islamic incursions in the Holy Land, and also because the Nea is included in the *Commemoratorium de casis Dei*. Problems with the later source, however, are discussed in n. 155 below.

[155] The *Commemoratorium de casis Dei* reports the existence of twelve clergy at the church: Titus Tobler, ed., *Descriptiones Terrae Sanctae ex saeculo VIII. IX. XII. et XV.* (Leipzig: J. C. Hinrichs'sche Buchhandlung, 1874), 78. More complicated, however, is a later reference to 'Ipsa ecclesia sancta Mariae, quam ille terrae motus (evertit) et in terram demersit, habet mensuram de ambobus lateribus in longo dexteros XXXVIIII, in una fronte XXXV, per medium in adverso XXXII, in longo per medium L' (ibid. 83). Although this is often taken as a reference to the Nea church (see e.g. Schick, *The Christian Communities of Palestine*, 333; Wilkinson, *Jerusalem Pilgrims*, 166), the description follows immediately after a description of the tomb of Mary in the preceding paragraph. Consequently, it would seem that 'ipsa ecclesia santae Mariae' would refer to the same (*ipsa*) church of Mary that had just been mentioned, namely, the church of the tomb in the valley of Josaphat. There is no indication that the author has suddenly switched to a description of the Nea, and so, taken in itself, the text appears to describe the demolished state of the church of Mary in the valley of Josaphat.

Nevertheless, this passage is quite problematic: as various commentators have apparently noted, however strongly the text may suggest it, this cannot be an accurate description of the church of Mary's tomb. Even if the author is referring to the upper Byzantine church, the passage is still problematic, since there is otherwise no evidence for the destruction of either church at this time, and, on the contrary, a pilgrimage account from 870 attests that both churches at the tomb were still standing (Bagatti, *New Discoveries*, 18). So, if this is in fact a reference to the Nea, which goes against the clear indication of the text, then

The Kathisma church, however, is more useful for our purposes. If we may assume that the Mar Elias church is in fact the Kathisma church, or more precisely, the new Kathisma church that was utilized for the first of these successive feasts, then we can reasonably estimate that this stational liturgy was in place sometime before 700, since excavation of the Mar Elias church has determined that the building was transformed into a mosque during the first half of the eighth century.[156] In the alternative case that the Ramat Rahel may have been the church of the Kathisma, this date is not affected. Excavation of Ramat Rahel has shown that its settlement was greatly diminished after the Islamic conquest. At that time the church was converted into living quarters, and not long thereafter, by the middle of the eighth century, the site appears to have been abandoned.[157] Thus it seems rather likely that the stational liturgy described in these documents represents the practice of Jerusalem in the seventh century, if not in the later sixth century as well.

The absence of Mt. Zion from this liturgical programme is one

the Nea was in ruins in the year 808 ('thrown down by the earthquake and engulfed by the earth'; Wilkinson, *Jerusalem Pilgrims*, 138). Wilkinson himself suggests that the church was probably destroyed by an earthquake in 746 (ibid. 166).

Here is the catch: if, according to this reading, the Nea lay in ruins when the author of the *Commemoratorium* saw it, then the *Commemoratorium* cannot be invoked as evidence against the church's destruction, since it attests, on the contrary, that the church had been destroyed when its author visited. In this sense, the *Commemoratorium* is in full agreement with our earlier sources. The only disagreement is over the means of destruction, and in this case, it may be better to trust a native eyewitness (the author of the *Capture of Jerusalem*) than a Latin visitor who saw only the ruins. Nevertheless, the *Commemoratorium*'s indication of twelve clergy at this church that has been 'engulfed by the earth' is peculiar, as is the Nea's use by Sophronius for Christmas in 634. The latter may have been an ad-hoc use of what was in fact a ruined church when other options were not available, but the former is very puzzling. Finally, the measurements given by the *Commemoratorium* are not completely consistent with the excavated remains of the Nea, describing a somewhat smaller edifice (see Vincent and Abel, *Jérusalem*, ii. pt. 4. 918 n. 7). There does not appear to be an easy answer to these problems, but I suggest that the *Commemoratorium* is not entirely worthy of the authority with which it has been invested in this matter.

[156] Avner, 'Birth Pangs', p. XIX.

[157] Aharoni, 'Excavations at Ramath Rahel', 110; see also Magness, *Jerusalem Ceramic Chronology*, 117–18.

final factor to consider: as noted above, Zion is not clearly identified as the location of the Virgin's death or associated with her veneration until the first decades of the seventh century. Several of these Georgian sources place a strong emphasis on the tradition of Mary's death on Zion, the most obvious example being the liturgical reading for 13 August, which in its super-scription and the lection itself mentions the Virgin's transfer from Bethlehem to Zion by the apostles. Ps.-Basil's Dormition narrative also makes frequent reference to Mary's constant com-memoration on Zion, but there is no obvious connection between this emphasis and the events referred to in the liturgical reading for 13 August.[158] These references to Zion could indicate that a stational Marian liturgy developed only after Zion had become a part of Jerusalem's Marian traditions, around the turn of the seventh century. Nevertheless, there is other evidence suggest-ing the contrary: Zion is absent from the Palestinian Georgian Calendar, which makes no connection between any of the Marian feasts of 13–17 August and the sanctuary on Mt. Zion. As Simon Mimouni has noted, the Palestinian Georgian Calendar's failure to mention Zion suggests that, despite the somewhat later date of its manuscript, the calendar may represent the liturgical prac-tices of the Jerusalem church before the inclusion of Zion. This would identify the origin of this stational liturgy sometime in the second half of sixth century, but probably after the completion of the Nea.[159]

In the light of this important difference, it is difficult to esti-mate Zion's significance for dating these practices. On the one hand, Zion's mention by Ps.-Basil's narrative and the lection for 13 August locates the production of these works, in their present form at least, probably sometime after the sixth century. But on the other hand, Zion's absence from the Palestinian Georgian Calendar could suggest the inauguration of this mobile liturgy sometime before Zion had acquired significant Marian associa-tions, perhaps in the second half of the sixth century. While such an argument from silence is admittedly not always the most reliable, it is nevertheless suggestive of a date. More importantly, however, it conforms with various other indicators mentioned above that identify the practice of these liturgical traditions

---

[158] e.g. van Esbroeck, 'L'Assomption de la Vierge', 129, 137, 142–3.
[159] Mimouni, *Dormition*, 304–5, esp. n. 17.

during the seventh century, including both archaeological evidence and the seventh-century Georgian Chantbook. Thus we may conclude rather tentatively, but with some degree of probability, that this stational liturgy was first implemented in Jerusalem sometime during the period between 550 and 650, and that it passed more or less out of use sometime shortly after 700, when the Kathisma church ceased to be available as a liturgical station.[160]

CONCLUSIONS

The development of the ancient cult of the Virgin in Palestine follows along the path of the stational liturgy that was to be its eventual formation. Marian veneration in the Holy Land began, as did the annual festivities, at the early fifth-century church of the Kathisma, which stood halfway between Jerusalem and Bethlehem, to the east of the main road. Sometime later, probably in the late fifth century, the centre of Marian cult gradually shifted to the church of Mary's tomb next to Gethsemane, in the valley of Josaphat, which was the second station of this mobile celebration. Finally, with the completion of the Nea basilica in 543, this imposing Marian shrine became a third focus of Marian veneration in the Jerusalem area. While it seems unlikely that this church ever eclipsed the tomb of the Virgin as the focus of Marian cult, it nevertheless represents the final development of the Palestinian cult of the Virgin, being the last major shrine to be built, as well as the terminus of the stational liturgy that was practised in early medieval Jerusalem. Although it is uncertain when this pattern of worship was finally disrupted, it seems that following the Kathisma church's abandonment or conversion into a mosque (depending on which church one chooses) in the early eighth century, the possibilities for such a mobile liturgy would be severely limited, although it may have continued in some modified form. In any

---

[160] Mimouni (*Dormition*, 306) similarly dates the origin of this liturgical formation. Van Esbroeck has argued for an earlier date, around 500 in *Les Plus Anciens Homéliaires géorgiens*, 343–4, but Mimouni has correctly demonstrated the problems with van Esbroeck's argument: *Dormition*, 304–5.

case, this stational liturgy can be identified as the final shape of the ancient Palestinian cult of the Virgin, before its eventual Byzantinization, a set of practices that probably disappeared gradually as late antiquity slowly transformed into the Middle Ages.

3

Rival Traditions of Mary's Death: The Independent Origins of the Ancient Dormition Traditions

The significant variety and complexity evidenced in the ancient Dormition traditions has long posed a daunting obstacle to their historical study. In order to appreciate the impact and position of these traditions in the world of Mediterranean late antiquity, it is not enough simply to know the nature and content of each component. Before we can apprehend how this material connects with various aspects of late ancient culture and society, we must first come to an understanding of how the different traditions relate amongst themselves. In taking up this challenge, many previous scholars have produced various developmental theories of either dogmatic 'evolution' or 'decline' to explain the diversity of these traditions, as already noted in the first chapter. Such hypotheses understand the different narrative types as evidence of a linear, typological progression, in which one sort of narrative grows out of and replaces an earlier type. Nevertheless, these developmental typologies have generally not been well grounded in the literary history of the traditions, privileging instead the 'theology' of a given narrative, and particularly its presentation of Mary's Assumption. That is, a particular narrative, or even group of narratives, is evaluated not on the basis of literary connections shared with other similar narratives, but instead, narratives are classified within a given typology primarily according to their (perceived) theological positions regarding the Assumption of the Virgin Mary.

As we have already seen in the first chapter, there is some diversity of opinion concerning Mary's ultimate fate in the earliest traditions: some narratives clearly describe Mary's resurrection and bodily Assumption, while others merely report her Dormition, followed by the miraculous disappearance of her body. Using this theological (as opposed to narrative) difference as the primary criterion of their typology, certain scholars have divided up the Dormition traditions according to whether or not they appear to support the doctrine of the Assumption, often ignoring or misrepresenting clear literary relationships that suggest an altogether different organization of the earliest traditions. Prominent examples of such developmental approaches to the early Dormition traditions may be found in the two major studies of these traditions published during the previous century. Martin Jugie, for instance, envisioned a pristine 'immortalist' tradition that then declined into the corruptions evident the various apocrypha and liturgical traditions (i.e. the tomb), although some kernel of the original 'truth' remains to be seen in those narratives where Mary's bodily Assumption follows after her death. Mimouni, on the other hand, presents a no less theological model, yet one that moves more or less in the opposite direction: an original tradition expressing only the Virgin's Dormition has evolved through a theologically intermediate stage to issue in the more recent tradition that clearly expresses belief in the Virgin's bodily resurrection and Assumption.

A major problem with such approaches, however, is that the criteria employed in determining whether a given narrative is either 'pro-' or 'anti-'Assumption are largely the terms of modern theological discourse, developed during the conversations that led to the 1950 definition of the Virgin's Assumption. As will be demonstrated in this chapter, these modern categories are poorly suited for analysis of the ancient traditions, and for this and many other reasons, literary analysis presents a more useful approach to the material. Moreover, I will argue here for a polygenetic understanding of the earliest Dormition traditions, which views the different narrative traditions as products of multiple and distinct origins. The narrative diversity of these traditions, rather than being the result of successive developments stretching back in a row to a single origin, is instead a testament to their discrete and parallel descent from several distinct narrative archetypes. There are, to be sure, various interesting points of contact among all (or almost all) the diverse narratives, such as the Jewish assault on Mary's funeral procession and the location of Mary's house in Jerusalem, but these connections are few and far between. Although these common features may provide some very limited indications of an original tradition underlying the presently extant traditions, such information is very small when compared with the significant diversity of the earliest narratives. Consequently, we must assume that while there may at some point have been a single 'original' tradition, beyond only a few details, this tradition is now lost, and sometime well before the earliest Dormition traditions come into view around the end of the fifth century, several different narrative types had already developed, of which the now extant narratives are later descendants.

Such an approach to these traditions, it must be confessed, is not entirely original. As mentioned in Ch. 1, Antoine Wenger had already in the 1950s advocated the idea that the literary and theological diversity of the ancient Dormition traditions is best explained by the existence of a 'great variety of original types', rather than by the progressive modification of a single original tradition.[1] More recently, Michel van Esbroeck has also taken such an approach, evident in his decision to schematize the different early narratives in two completely separate stemmata. Nevertheless, neither of these authors has taken it upon himself to argue extensively in favour of multiple origins, leaving the field open for more recent work such as Mimouni's, which can rightly disregard this viewpoint as undemonstrated. In an effort to fill this gap, this chapter will present an argument for the polygenesis of the Dormition traditions. Several factors suggest the existence of multiple origins, including the almost simultaneous appearance of each literary tradition around the turn of the sixth century. Related eschatological and liturgical traditions equally complicate the identification a particular literary tradition as primitive, and the significant diversity of eschatological belief and liturgical practice itself presents a likely context for

---

[1] Antoine Wenger, AA, *L'Assomption de la T. S. Vierge dans la tradition byzantine du VIe au Xe siècle*, Archives de l'Orient Chrétien, 5 (Paris: Institut Français d'Études Byzantines, 1955), 17.

the independent development of rival Dormition traditions. Although the silence of the first five centuries makes any conclusion about the origins of the Dormition traditions somewhat tentative, given the present state of our evidence, their independent origins seem relatively certain.

Before proceeding, however, I wish to repeat an important disclaimer made in the Ch. 1. I do not pretend to offer here a 'non-theological' or 'value-free' account of the early Dormition traditions, which would somehow avoid the 'distorting' influence of various theological commitments that is so evident in much previous scholarship. On the contrary, my conclusions arise from a conviction that the origins of the Christian tradition as a whole were diverse rather than singular, approaching early Christian culture as a 'discourse of heterodoxy', rather than adopting the traditional Christian 'discourse of orthodoxy', which imagines 'truth' to be both singular and original. Such a traditional discourse of orthodoxy underlies each of the various developmental interpretations, according to which they argue that the now diverse traditions arise from a single deposit of truth, and only later did this original tradition either degenerate into various heretical expressions (Jugie) or, alternatively, evolve into an increasingly complex understanding of the initial 'revelation' (Mimouni, following Cothenet). According to either view, truth lies at the origin, and such a discourse of orthodoxy has led many scholars to obscure the diversity of the earliest Dormition traditions in the attempt to identify a theologically authoritative origin. In contrast to these approaches, my interpretation arises from a conviction that no single deposit of orthodoxy existed in the early church, and that the origins of the Christian tradition are characterized by competition among numerous theological rivals, each of which strove against the others for dominance. Although many of the opinions that would subsequently comprise Christian orthodoxy admittedly existed from these earliest times, they often stood initially as merely one conviction among many. Only after their victorious emergence from the ideological conflicts of late antiquity did the later tradition invest them with the rarefied authority of 'orthodoxy'.[2]

---

[2] Such a view of Christian origins has been expounded, perhaps most famously, in Walter Bauer, *Orthodoxy and Heresy in Earliest Christianity*, trans. eds. Robert A. Kraft and Gerhard Krodel (Philadelphia: Fortress Press, 1971).

AGAINST THE PRIORITY OF AN ASSUMPTIONLESS
TRADITION: THE *OBSEQUIES*, THE *LIBER REQUIEI*,
AND THE PALM TRADITIONS

The main problem confronting any attempt to order the various narrative types in a chronological sequence is the simple fact that the earliest exemplars of each type appear at almost exactly the same historical moment. The Syriac apocrypha published by Wright and Smith Lewis demonstrate the initial appearance of both the Bethlehem and Palm traditions simultaneously. The paleography of the various Syriac manuscripts dates both the *Obsequies* (the earliest extant Palm narrative) and the Six Books (the earliest extant Bethlehem narrative) to approximately the turn of the sixth century.[3] Likewise, the earliest texts of the Coptic tradition are roughly contemporary with these Bethlehem and Palm narratives: changes in the Coptic liturgical celebration of the Dormition and Assumption during the mid-sixth century allow us to date several narratives to the beginning of the sixth century, as explained in the first chapter. Finally, to this can be added the 'atypical' homily of Jacob of Serug, written and delivered just before the turn of the sixth century, presenting us with a total of four distinct and roughly contemporary narrative types and no clear evidence of any one significantly antedating the others.

The span of roughly fifty years (at most), during which each of these four types first appeared, leaves very little time for any sort of a doctrinal evolution from one type into the next.[4] Consequently, on the basis of their earliest appearances, the various narrative types are best understood as coexistent, rival traditions

---

[3] *Obsequies*: William Wright, ed., *Contributions to the Apocryphal Literature of the New Testament* (London: Williams & Norgate, 1865), 11; William Wright, *Catalogue of the Syriac Manuscripts of the British Museum Acquired Since the Year 1838*, 3 vols. (London, 1870), i. 369. Six Books: Agnes Smith Lewis, ed., *Apocrypha Syriaca*, Studia Sinaitica, XI (London: C. J. Clay & Sons, 1902), p. x; William Wright, 'The Departure of my Lady Mary from this World', *The Journal of Sacred Literature and Biblical Record*, 6 (1865), 417–48 and 7 (1865), 417.

[4] See also Michel van Esbroeck's brief yet important response to Mimouni in 'Some Early Features in the Life of the Virgin', *Marianum* (2001) (forthcoming).

of Mary's Dormition, with none having a substantial claim to priority over the others, and with no evidence of any tradition having developed or decayed from the others. Although such development may possibly have occurred sometime before the first exemplars come into view, no one has yet found any convincing evidence to suggest this. We know only that each of these traditions first appears at approximately the same time, with no reliable means of distinguishing any narrative type as earlier than the others.

In spite of this daunting obstacle, Simon Mimouni has attempted to argue for a developmental typology of the Dormition traditions, presenting what is by far the most elaborate and sophisticated explanation of these traditions to date. This is achieved, however, only by subverting the evidence afforded by the literary history of these traditions to a theory of theological development. In his various studies, Mimouni argues, following Édouard Cothenet, that the earliest traditions about the end of Mary's life did not include a belief in her bodily resurrection and Assumption. Consequently, all those narratives lacking this feature may be identified as the earliest traditions, even if literary relations may suggest otherwise.

Since in Mimouni's view all the Bethlehem traditions lack an account of Mary's Assumption, he identifies these as the earliest traditions. I will occasionally refer to these traditions collectively as the 'Assumptionless' traditions, since, according to Mimouni, they are distinguished primarily by their failure to narrate the Virgin's Assumption. By way of distinction, the Palm traditions clearly attest to a belief in Mary's resurrection and bodily Assumption, and thus I will from time to time refer to these corporately as the 'Assumptionist' traditions. Since these narratives do in fact record Mary's bodily Assumption, which Mimouni considers as a later development in Christian dogma, Mimouni regards the Palm narratives (with a few important exceptions) as having come into existence more recently than the Bethlehem traditions. In between these two corpora (in terms of development), Mimouni identifies the Coptic traditions, whose awkward inclusion of the Virgin's Assumption in the mid-sixth century marks the moment of transition from the 'simpler' dogmatic position of the earliest stage to the more complex belief in the Assumption, evident in the more recent Palm tradition.

This argument centres around Mimouni's rather complicated supposition that

diachrony does not exclude synchrony. But synchrony supposes diachrony, in the sense that the doctrines of the Dormition and the Assumption could coexist, but that this coexistence supposes that the Dormition appeared before the Assumption, and not at the same time. Parallel or simultaneous origins seem difficult to conceive: a religious tradition takes birth from a question, in this case the final lot of Mary; it develops by expanding, and, the Assumption is an expansion of the Dormition.[5]

This principle is the basis of Mimouni's argument for the priority of both the Bethlehem traditions and their (purportedly) Assumptionless theology, and the bulk of his study aims to rearrange historical evidence, and most notably the literary history of these traditions, to comply with this presupposition.

Mimouni's axiom, however, is laden with unproven assumptions and contradicted, in my view, by the literary relations of the earliest narratives themselves.[6] Among other things, it is not self-evident that religious traditions always develop by expanding, nor that 'synchronic' coexistence necessarily requires 'diachronic' development. Moreover, Mimouni is not at all clear as to why he considers parallel or simultaneous origins unlikely: the various gospel traditions, both canonical and uncanonical, provide a compelling example of the simultaneous development of different religious traditions in answer to the same 'question'. On the other hand, one could mount an interesting counter-argument that religious traditions frequently 'develop' by restricting their content rather than by expanding it, as the

---

[5] Simon C. Mimouni, *Dormition et assomption de Marie: Histoire des traditions anciennes*, Théologie Historique, 98 (Paris: Beauchesne, 1995), 19 n. 49. Note that for Mimouni the term 'Dormition' refers exclusively to the Assumptionless traditions.

[6] One could, for instance, according to the same principle similarly maintain that the Bethlehem traditions arose later, since the location of the Virgin's house in Jerusalem alone is 'more simple', while the inclusion of a second house in Bethlehem (in addition to the Jerusalem house) is 'more complex', suggesting an evolution in which the Palm traditions were prior, and the Bethlehem traditions secondary. The synchronic existence of the two houses would thus presuppose that the Jerusalem house appeared before the Bethlehem house. Mimouni does not, however, apply the same logic in this instance, since he maintains the priority of the Bethlehem traditions.

early Christian centuries and their ecumenical councils would attest. It is often in the attempt to eliminate 'new' developments, 'heresies', that religious traditions have 'developed': according to such a view, the diachronic development of Christian orthodoxy would necessitate the prior 'synchronic' coexistence of both orthodoxy and various heterodoxies. Such is very much the Byzantine view, for instance, according to which 'there is no development in the *content* of the faith', but doctrinal developments and conciliar statements 'define issues of doctrine only to exclude the wrong interpretations proposed by heretics'.[7]

These and other more theoretical objections are not addressed by Mimouni's study, perhaps in part because it is so anxious to address the rather obvious difficulties posed by the literary history of the early Dormition traditions. Chief among these are the Syriac fragments of the *Obsequies*, a Palm narrative that is widely regarded as the earliest extant Dormition narrative.[8] Not only does this present a problem for viewing the Palm traditions as later developments, but the longest fragment of this earliest known narrative recounts what is almost certainly the Virgin's Assumption. Although the passage in question breaks off before reaching its conclusion, it describes the Virgin's resurrection and transport to Paradise in a manner so typical of the other Assumptionist narratives from the Palm tradition that it clearly must also be classified as such.[9] Since this is generally regarded as being both early and Assumptionist, its existence presents a substantial obstacle to Mimouni's interpretation of the earliest Dormition traditions. Somehow he must confront the fact that the earliest extant witness is in fact a narrative that appears to describe the Assumption.

Mimouni does not challenge the *Obsequies'* early date, which has been rather well established by Wright's careful eye. Instead, he seeks refuge in the possibilities afforded by the text's fragmentary nature, restating Cothenet's earlier proposal that before the complete text reached its conclusion, the Virgin was 'unresurrected', thus precluding her actual bodily

---

[7] John Meyendorff, *Byzantine Theology*, 2nd edn. (New York: Fordham University Press, 1979), 10.

[8] Its only competition would come from Smith Lewis's version of the Six Books (S3) which is perhaps of equivalent age.

[9] Wright, *Contributions*, ܪܥܘ‑ܡܢ (Syr.) and 43–8 (Eng.).

Assumption.[10] Mary's resurrection, these two scholars suggest, was merely temporary, effected only so that she could visit the places prepared for the just and the wicked after the final judgement. At the end of her apocalyptic tour, Mary was returned to Paradise and supposedly 'unresurrected' to await the general resurrection in a disembodied state. This corresponds, Cothenet and Mimouni explain, to the early Christian and Jewish conception of Paradise as a place where the disembodied souls of the elect await the general resurrection, and therefore Mary's presence in Paradise following her death is not unusual, nor does it indicate her Assumption.[11]

Nevertheless, as we will see in the final section of this chapter, this was not the only conception of Paradise available to early Christian writers, nor is the eschatological significance of Paradise in these narratives always such a simple matter, as this explanation presumes. There was in the ancient Mediterranean an alternative view of Paradise as the final resting place of the just, and many of the early Dormition narratives appear to make use of this idea, rather than the view singled out by Cothenet and Mimouni. From this perspective, the Virgin's presence in Paradise would clearly mark her Assumption, although as will be seen, the understanding of Paradise articulated in many of the earliest narratives is in fact extremely complex and often contradictory.

Moreover, the matter of Mary's supposed 'unresurrection' is itself highly speculative. Although both Cothenet and Mimouni assert that this 'unresurrection' is attested by the earliest Six Books narratives, this simply is not the case. In making this claim, Mimouni depends on Cothenet, who himself reiterates Martin Jugie's misreading of the earliest Syriac, Ethiopic, and Arabic versions of the Six Books.[12] Jugie maintained that in these early Bethlehem narratives the Virgin's resurrection was merely temporary, but there is in fact no

[10] This solution was first suggested by Édouard Cothenet ('Marie dans les Apocryphes', in Hubert du Manoir, SJ (ed.), *Maria: Études sur la Sainte Vierge*, 7 vols. (Paris: Beauchesne et ses Fils, 1961), vi. 124–5) and is repeated by Mimouni (*Dormition*, 81–2).

[11] Cothenet, 'Marie', 124–8; Mimouni, *Dormition*, 82–5.

[12] Martin Jugie, AA, *La Mort et l'assomption de la Sainte Vierge: Étude historico-doctrinale*, Studi e Testi, 114 (Vatican City: Biblioteca Apostolica Vaticana, 1944), 122–3.

indication of such an 'unresurrection' in the early Dormition narratives.[13] The only possible exception to this would be the *Life of the Virgin* published by E. A. W. Budge, which does describe Mary's 'unresurrection', but this narrative is preserved by a rather late manuscript, and is of questionable worth for understanding the ancient traditions.[14] With regards to the early Six Books narratives, Jugie infers Mary's unresurrection from a statement that the Virgin's soul was sent to the 'mansions' or the 'treasury' of the Father. The Six Books narratives relate this event, however, at the precise moment when Mary's soul departs her body and is taken away. Following this, her soulless body is taken to Paradise, where it is then reanimated, with absolutely *no* indication of its subsequent unresurrection. Instead, it would seem that these narratives have understood Mary's disembodied soul as temporarily residing in the 'mansions' or 'treasures' of the Father while her inanimate body was being transported to Paradise. Then, once Mary's body reached Paradise, her soul was restored to it in her resurrection, after which point her soul was presumably no longer in the 'mansions' or 'treasures' of the Father. At no point after her resurrection is there any indication in these narratives that her body and soul were again separated.[15]

Yet even if one might by some chance be convinced that such a temporary resurrection is described or suggested in certain narratives of the Bethlehem tradition, these clearly are not the traditions to which the *Obsequies* fragments are joined by literary

[13] See also Mary Clayton, *The Apocryphal Gospels of Mary in Anglo-Saxon England*, Cambridge Studies in Anglo-Saxon England, 26 (Cambridge: Cambridge University Press, 1998), 38, and now eadem, 'The Transitus Mariae: The Tradition and Its Origins', *Apocrypha*, 10 (1999), 76–82. Clayton notes both that unresurrection is not found in the early Six Books narratives, and that Cothenet and Mimouni have misrepresented the contents of these narratives.

[14] E. A. W. Budge, ed., *History of the Blessed Virgin Mary and the History of the Likeness of Christ which the Jews of Tiberias Made to Mock at* (London: Luzac & Co., 1899), 122 (Syr.) and 131 (Eng.). This narrative is from a manuscript of the 13th or 14th century, copied in 1890; although its traditions depend on the Six Books narratives, they clearly transmit a more recent and garbled version. Consequently, there is no reason that we should read the contents of the much later narrative into the earlier versions.

[15] For more on this matter, see the discussion below. One may also consult the Ethiopic version, translated in Appendix D.

relations.[16] The utter lack of any kinship between these earliest Syriac fragments and the Six Books narratives makes rather
dubious the proposal by Cothenet and Mimouni that the missing
conclusion of the *Obsequies* fragments may be supplied from the
earliest Bethlehem narratives.[17] This is demonstrated particularly by some relatively recent discoveries, which in all fairness
were unknown to Cothenet as he was first developing his hypothesis. The most important piece of new evidence is the Ethiopic
Liber Requiei, which preserves a complete version of the narrative witnessed only partially in the Syriac *Obsequies* fragments.
The identity of these two narratives is unmistakable: in the
passages where both versions are extant, the Ethiopic reproduces
the ancient Syriac narrative with remarkable accuracy, as can
be seen in the appended translation (Appendix A). Georgian
fragments of the same narrative are also extant, and while none
of these correspond to the *Obsequies* fragments, the Georgian
fragments, like their Syrian siblings, are astonishingly close
to the complete Ethiopic version.[18] Other close relatives of

---

[16] Note, for instance, that Jugie did not identify the *Obsequies* fragments as
having described Mary's unresurrection in their complete form: this narrative,
he writes, 'explicitly signals' the Virgin's resurrection and Assumption (*La
Mort*, 108–9).

[17] See also Clayton, *Apocryphal Gospels*, 38, eadem, 'Transitus Mariae', 76–
82.

[18] The three main *Obsequies* fragments parallel *Liber Requiei* 19–21, 32–5,
and 81–92 (Victor Arras, ed., *De Transitu Mariae Aethiopice*, 2 vols., CSCO
342–3, 351–2 (Louvain: Secrétariat du CorpusSCO, 1973), i. 10–11, 18–20,
48–54 (Eth.) and 7–8, 12–13, 32–6 (Lat.)). More damaged fragments, published
without English translation, parallel *Liber Requiei* 67, 72–3, 76, and 80 (ibid.
39–40, 42, 44–5, 48 (Eth.) and 26–9, 31 (Lat.)). The Georgian fragments parallel *Liber Requiei* 5–12 and 37–40 (ibid. 3–7, 21–4 (Eth.) and 2–5, 14–16 (Lat.)),
but do not find any parallels among Wright's fragments: Michel van Esbroeck,
'Apocryphes géorgiens de la Dormition', *Analecta Bollandiana*, 92 (1973),
55–75.
Mimouni also signals the existence of several Palestinian Syriac fragments of
this narrative from the 7th or 8th century, preserved in the Cairo Geniza that
parallel *Liber Requiei* 45–6 and 50–2 (Mimouni, *Dormition*, 76). According to
Mimouni, two of these have previously been published in Agnes Smith Lewis
and Margaret Dunlop Gibson, eds., *Palestinian Syriac Texts from Palimpsest
Fragments in the Taylor-Schechter Collection* (London: C. J. Clay & Sons, 1900),
75–6 (paralleled by *Liber Requiei* 45–6 and 51–2 respectively (Arras, *De
Transitu*, i. 27–8, 31–2 (Eth.) and 18, 20–1 (Lat.)). I have consulted these
very fragmentary texts and cannot determine on the basis of what has been
published the exact relation between them. Presumably, C. Kessler, who has

the *Obsequies* include the Irish apocrypha and Wenger's early Greek text, among the many other narratives of the Palm group, all of which share an unmistakable description of the Virgin's Assumption. Since the *Obsequies* clearly belong to this literary tradition, it seems altogether likely that the *Obsequies* similarly concluded with the Virgin's Assumption.[19] This is particularly indicated by the complete Ethiopic version, which carries to completion the same description of the Virgin's death and resurrection found in this earliest Syriac fragment. In the uninterrupted Ethiopic version, the Virgin is not unresurrected, which is a sure sign of her Assumption,[20] and there is every reason to believe that the *Obsequies*, in its complete form, concluded similarly.[21]

Nevertheless, one might at this point raise doubts regarding the reliability of *Liber Requiei* as a faithful witness to the ancient traditions of the fifth century, and with some cause, given its preservation only in manuscripts of the fourteenth and fifteenth centuries.[22] Nevertheless, the rather recent date of

provided Mimouni's information, has more carefully consulted all these fragments.

The existence of these Syriac fragments would, however, seem to belie Mimouni's argument that the *Obsequies* fragments cannot possibly report an Assumption, because as such they would be the only Assumptionist texts in the Syriac tradition (Mimouni, *Dormition*, 82). If these fragments are the same text as the *Liber Requiei*, then they are fragments of an Assumptionist Syriac text extant during the 7th or 8th century (at the latest), and as such they would seem to confirm strongly the identity of the *Obsequies* with the *Liber Requiei*, which Mimouni seeks to efface.

[19] The extensive annotations by Arras, *De Transitu*, i. 75–105 (Lat.) make these relations very clear.

[20] *Liber Requiei* 84–101 (Arras, *De Transitu*, i. 49–59 (Eth.) and 33–41 (Lat.)).

[21] The fact that the *Liber Requiei* has probably preserved a very ancient version of narrative strengthens this conclusion. See Michel van Esbroeck, 'Les Textes littéraires sur l'assomption avant le Xe siècle', in François Bovon (ed.), *Les Actes apocryphes des apôtres* (Geneva: Labor et Fides, 1981), 270. Its antiquity is suggested by the remarkable similarity of the sections common to both the *Liber Requiei* and the *Obsequies* and also by the heterodox tendencies preserved by the *Liber Requiei*, as will be seen in Ch. 4. In fact, some have suggested that this might be the text of 'Leucius' against which Ps.-Melito rails (Arras, *De Transitu*, i. p. v (Lat.)), or at least a close relative (van Esbroeck, 'Les Textes', 271).

[22] See A. van Lantschoot, 'Contribution aux Actes de S. Pierre et de S. Paul', *Le Muséon*, 68 (1955), 17 (14th–15th century); Arras, *De Transitu*, p. V (Lat.) (15th century).

these manuscripts is not as discouraging as it may at first glance appear: Ethiopic manuscripts from before the sixteenth century are extremely rare, and only a handful have survived from the fourteenth and fifteenth centuries. By comparison then, the *Liber Requiei* is preserved in some of the earliest extant Ethiopic manuscripts.[23] In actuality, this circumstance is not at all different from that of other late ancient apocrypha known primarily from recent Ethiopic manuscripts, including *1 Enoch*, the *Ascension of Isaiah*, the book of *Jubilees*, and the *Apocalypse of Peter*. The earliest complete witnesses to these apocrypha appear in only a handful of Ethiopic manuscripts from the fifteenth and sixteenth centuries: although there are significantly earlier fragments of all three apocrypha in various languages, we are, as with the *Liber Requiei/Obsequies* narrative, dependent on much later Ethiopic manuscripts for our complete knowledge of the ancient traditions.[24] In each of these instances, scholars have asked similar questions regarding the reliability of the Ethiopic versions as witnesses to the ancient texts, and they have resolved the matter by comparing the ancient fragments of these apocrypha with the parallel passages in the complete Ethiopic versions.

In the case of *Jubilees*, comparison with the Hebrew fragments from Qumran has confirmed that 'the Ethiopic manuscripts

---

[23] Edward Ullendorff, *The Ethiopians: An Introduction to Country and People* (London: Oxford University Press, 1960), 140–1.

[24] The Ethiopic manuscripts for each of these three apocrypha are listed in the following sources: *1 Enoch*: Michael A. Knibb, ed., *The Ethiopic Book of Enoch: A New Edition in Light of the Aramaic Dead Sea Fragments*, 2 vols. (Oxford: Clarendon Press, 1978), ii. 23–7; *Ascension of Isaiah*: James H. Charlesworth, ed., *The Old Testament Pseudepigrapha*, 2 vols. (Garden City, NY: Doubleday, 1983), ii. 144; *Jubilees*: James C. VanderKam, *Textual and Historical Studies in the Book of Jubilees*, Harvard Semitic Museum, Harvard Semitic Monographs, 14 (Missoula, MT: Scholars Press, 1977), 13–15; *Apocalypse of Peter*: Dennis D. Buchholz, *Your Eyes Will Be Opened: A Study of the Greek (Ethiopic) Apocalypse of Peter*, Society of Biblical Literature Dissertation Series, 97 (Atlanta: Scholars Press, 1988), 119–39.

The different versions of each apocryphon (in addition to Ethiopic) are as follows: *1 Enoch*: Greek and Aramaic (see discussion in Knibb, *Ethiopic Book of Enoch*, ii. 6–21); *Ascension of Isaiah*: Greek, Latin, Slavonic, and Coptic (see Charlesworth, *Pseudepigrapha*, ii. 144–6); *Jubilees*: Hebrew, Latin, Greek, and Syriac (the latter two consist mostly of collected citations from later sources; see VanderKam, *Textual and Historical Studies*, 1–11); *Apocalypse of Peter*: two distinct Greek versions (Buchholz, *Your Eyes Will Be Opened*, 139–55).

reproduce the Hebrew original with remarkable, though not complete precision', and thus the Ethiopic version can be studied as a reliable witness to the ancient version.[25] Likewise, the fifth- or sixth-century Greek fragment of the *Ascension of Isaiah* shows that the complete Ethiopic version has faithfully preserved its ancient source.[26] The situation with *1 Enoch* is more complicated, but a comparison with the early fragments also indicates that the Ethiopic version has faithfully preserved the ancient version that was its source. In contrast to *Jubilees*, the comparison of the Ethiopic version of *1 Enoch* with the Aramaic fragments from Qumran have not shown the Ethiopic version to be a reliable witness to the earliest, Aramaic version.[27] Although there is a general agreement between the two versions in most instances, there are numerous instances of minor disagreements.[28] Nevertheless, a similar comparison of the Aramaic with the late ancient Greek fragments reveals that many of these do not agree with the Qumran fragments, and that a rather distinct Greek version of *1 Enoch* existed in late antiquity. Comparison of the Ethiopic *1 Enoch* with this Greek version has shown that the Ethiopic version reliably transmits this late ancient Greek version that was its source.[29] Thus, even if the Ethiopic version

[25] See the extended comparison in VanderKam, *Textual and Historical Studies*, 18–95; the quotation is on p. 95.

[26] See Charlesworth, *Pseudepigrapha*, ii. 144; and R. H. Charles, ed., *The Ascension of Isaiah* (London: Adam & Charles Black, 1900), pp. xiv–xv. Charles's edition presents the Ethiopic text in synopsis with the Greek, Latin, and Slavonic (in Latin trans.) fragments, and from this the faithfulness of the Ethiopic to the Greek and first Latin versions can readily be seen. The second Latin version and Slavonic version preserve a distinct recension.

[27] See J. T. Milik, 'Problèmes de la littérature hénochique à la lumière de fragments araméens de Qumran', *Harvard Theological Review*, 64 (1971), 333–78; idem, ed. (with Matthew Black), *The Books of Enoch: Aramaic Fragments of Qumrân Cave 4* (Oxford: Clarendon Press, 1976).

[28] Knibb, *Ethiopic Book of Enoch*, ii. 13.

[29] Concerning the relation of the Greek and Ethiopic versions, see Matthew Black, ed. (in consultation with James C. VanderKam), *The Book of Enoch, or, 1 Enoch: A New English Edition with Commentary and Textual Notes*, Studia in Veteris Testamenti Pseudepigrapha, 7 (Leiden: E. J. Brill, 1985), 3–6; see also Knibb, *Ethiopic Book of Enoch*, ii. 15–21. It should be noted that there is some debate surrounding the language of the Ethiopic translation's source. Black (*Book of Enoch*, 3–6) argues for a Greek *Vorlage*, which is the predominant opinion. Knibb (*Ethiopic Book of Enoch*, ii. 37–46) discusses the various evidence favouring an Aramaic *Vorlage*, but concludes that in the present state

of *1 Enoch* does not reliably attest to the Aramaic version that once circulated at Qumran, it has nevertheless preserved well the ancient Greek version that was its model.

The *Apocalypse of Peter* presents a similarly complicated situation, but one that likewise attests to the reliability of its Ethiopic version as a witness to the ancient text. Although this apocryphon was already known from multiple references to it in early Christian literature, the first actual fragment of the apocalypse was recovered only in 1886, with the discovery of an eighth-century manuscript from an Egyptian grave. This manuscript preserves about half the *Apocalypse of Peter* as we now know it, and its discovery occasioned much scholarly attention.[30] Things suddenly became complicated, however, with the publication of a pseudo-Clementine text from an Ethiopic manuscript in 1910: although the text's editor did not completely recognize it for what it was, M. R. James immediately identified the *Apocalypse of Peter* embedded in this Ethiopic text. The problem, however, was that this Ethiopic version was markedly different from the previously discovered Greek version, raising the question of which version more accurately represents the earliest text.[31]

Many scholars continued to favour the antiquity of the Greek version, since, after all, this was both the earliest manuscript and the language of the apocryphon's origin. But James, following his identification of the *Apocalypse of Peter*'s Ethiopic version, immediately published an argument identifying the Ethiopic as having best preserved the ancient version in a series of articles that many still recognize today as the best discussion of this problem. By comparing the Ethiopic with a then recently discovered second Greek fragment from the third or fourth century, as well as with the ancient citations, James

---

of our knowledge we cannot determine whether the source of the Ethiopic translation was Greek or Aramaic, or perhaps both. In any case, the question is not especially relevant to the present matter: the Ethiopic version is faithful to the ancient version extant in three of the four Greek fragments, whether or not the translation was done from the Greek or an otherwise unknown witness to this version in Aramaic. It is extremely unlikely that the Ethiopic was translated from the Aramaic version that was present at Qumran.

[30] Buchholz, *Your Eyes Will Be Opened*, 20–104, 139–45.
[31] Ibid. 104–13, 119–39.

demonstrated the antiquity of the Ethiopic version.[32] James's conclusions were subsequently confirmed when another Greek fragment, from the same third- or fourth-century manuscript as the previous one, came to light in 1924. Together these two Greek fragments bear witness that there were two different Greek recensions of the *Apocalypse of Peter* in antiquity, and that the Ethiopic version is a faithful witness to the earliest of these two versions.[33] Although in places the Ethiopic version is muddled, it is likely that in these sections a translator or copyist either did not understand or did not like what he or she was reading. Excepting these few instances, the Ethiopic version of the *Apocalypse of Peter* is regarded as having accurately preserved the ancient version of this apocalypse.[34]

In each of these instances the comparison of a much more recent Ethiopic version with ancient fragments has vouched for the reliability of the Ethiopic versions as reliable transmitters of ancient texts, thus reaffirming the text-critic's maxim: *recentiores non deteriores*. Moreover, these four examples provide strong evidence for the general reliability of Ethiopic translations as witnesses to ancient apocrypha that antedate the manuscripts preserving them by 1,000–1,500 years. This characteristic is noted by Richard Bauckham in his recent study of the *Apocalypse of Peter*, where he writes:

There is the general consideration that the Ethiopic translation of apocryphal texts seems, as a general rule, to be faithful translation, and such works were not usually adapted or modified in the Ethiopic tradition. This contrasts with some other languages in which apocryphal works have been transmitted—such as Slavonic and Armenian—where creative development of the text has often taken place in those traditions. Of course, the Ethiopic may well include erroneous translations and textual corruptions—and in the case of the Apocalypse of Peter these are certainly present—but deliberate adaptation of the text is rare.[35]

---

[32] Buchholz, *Your Eyes Will Be Opened*, 104–13, 145–56; M. R. James, 'A New Text of the Apocalypse of Peter', *Journal of Theological Studies*, 12 (1911), 36–55, 157, 362–83, 573–83.

[33] Buchholz, *Your Eyes Will Be Opened*, 152–6; Richard Bauckham, *The Fate of the Dead: Studies on Jewish and Christian Apocalypses*, Supplements to Novum Testamentum, 93 (Leiden: Brill, 1998), 162–3.

[34] Buchholz, *Your Eyes Will Be Opened*, 376–431; Bauckham, *Fate of the Dead*, 162–5. [35] Bauckham, *Fate of the Dead*, 163.

Nevertheless, we need not rely on such precedent alone, since we can apply to *Liber Requiei* the same test that has verified the antiquity of these other Ethiopic translations. We are fortunate in possessing numerous ancient witnesses that may be compared with the *Liber Requiei*, a significantly greater sample, in fact, than we have for *Jubilees*. When we compare the ancient versions to the Ethiopic *Liber Requiei*, we discover that it too is a reliable transmitter of the ancient traditions that were its original source. The main witnesses in this case are the Syriac *Obsequies* fragments of the late fifth or early sixth century, and as the synoptic translation in Appendix A makes unmistakably clear, the *Liber Requiei* has faithfully transmitted this earliest extant Dormition narrative. The remarkable agreement of the *Liber Requiei* with the Georgian fragments also confirms the reliability of the Ethiopic version.

Still, one may wonder about those sections of the *Liber Requiei* for which there is no Syriac or Georgian parallel: did the ancient narrative include all this additional material, and if so, how reliably does the *Liber Requiei* transmit the remainder of its contents? Although this is a slightly more difficult problem, it is nevertheless also easily resolved. In order to answer these questions, one must undertake an extensive comparison with the other early representatives of the Palm tradition, including especially Wenger's early Greek text, John of Thessalonica's homily, the early Latin versions, and the early Irish versions. Fortunately, this task has already been accomplished by Victor Arras, the *Liber Requiei*'s editor, who has published the results in an appendix to his Latin translation.[36] Arras's commentary confirms accuracy of the *Liber Requiei* as a representative of the ancient tradition: in fact, looking back to Wenger's earlier work, we find that Wenger more or less predicted the existence of a text like the *Liber Requiei* some twenty years before it was actually brought to light.[37] The table in the final appendix to the present volume has collected each of the important ancient parallels to the various sections of the *Liber Requiei*, and rather than going over each of these in detail here, I will leave it to interested

---

[36] Arras, *De Transitu*, i. 75–105 (Lat.).

[37] See esp. his stemma (Wenger, *L'Assomption*, 66), where he includes a 'source grecque perdue', which is probably the ancient Greek source behind the *Liber Requiei*.

readers to investigate the matter on their own, since the relationships are usually fairly obvious.[38]

There are some narrative details in the *Liber Requiei* that differ
slightly from the other early Palm narratives, but most of these
are easily explained by their dogmatically questionable nature.
These variants embrace themes that were not acceptable according to the limits of early Byzantine theological discourse. As we
will see in the following chapter, most of these differences are
attributable to the efforts of more recent, 'orthodox' redactors,
who both attest and object to the theologically heterodox content
that they found in the earliest narratives that were their sources.
Rather than impeaching the *Liber Requiei*'s reliability as a transmitter of ancient traditions then, these variants instead attest to
the antiquity of the version it has preserved. Our main problem
with using the *Liber Requiei* to access the earliest traditions is not
its faithfulness to the ancient traditions, but rather its opacity in
certain sections, as the appended translation will unfortunately
disclose. In many such instances, however, comparison with the
earliest Palm narratives can help to reconstruct the general sense,
if not the actual meaning, of the Ethiopic version.

On the other hand, comparative study of the *Liber Requiei* also
reveals that a large section of the narrative as it is now preserved
does not belong to the ancient tradition. An entirely separate
work, known in its independent state as the *History of Peter and
Paul*, has been inserted near the conclusion of the *Liber Requiei*'s
early Dormition narrative, accounting for approximately 25 per
cent of the narrative as it is presently preserved (sections 105–
31). *The History of Peter and Paul*, which describes the two
apostles' struggles against the Devil, first in Rome and then in
India, is not a part of the ancient Dormition traditions, and it is
known to have circulated independently in Arabic and Karshuni
versions during the Middle Ages.[39] In contrast to the remaining

---

[38] If they are not so, then one may additionally consult Arras's commentary.
[39] Arabic version edited by Agnes Smith Lewis, with accompanying English
translation in Agnes Smith Lewis, ed., *Acta Mythologica Apostolorum*, 2 vols.,
Horae Semiticae, 3–4 (London: C. J. Clay & Sons, 1904), 150–64 (Arab.) and
175–92 (Eng.). She dates this manuscript between the 12th and 15th centuries
(ibid. p. x). In addition to Smith Lewis's Sinai codex, there is another copy in
the Mignana collection (van Lantschoot, 'Contributions', 18–21), and a
Karshuni version, edited by A. van Lantschoot, 'Contribution aux Actes de S.
Pierre et de S. Paul, II.—Recension Karsuni des Actes de S. Pierre et S. Paul',

contents of the *Liber Requiei*, there is no ancient witness (or any other witness, for that matter), indicating that this tradition was joined with the traditions of Mary's Dormition in antiquity. There is no evidence for the existence of *The History of Peter and Paul* before the Middle Ages, and its existence as an independent narrative at this time speaks against its inclusion in the ancient Dormition traditions. There is instead every reason to assume that in the *Liber Requiei* we find two literary traditions that were merged at a later date.[40] *The History of Peter and Paul* has been incorporated into this ancient Dormition narrative precisely at the point where other early Palm traditions refer to an incident in which Peter and Paul had to contend with the Devil before Jesus could reveal the mysteries of the cosmos to Paul. The details of their contentions are not described in the ancient Palm narratives: only the successful outcome is reported. Consequently, it seems most likely that *The History of Peter and Paul* was inserted into the *Liber Requiei*'s otherwise ancient narrative during the Middle Ages by someone who recognized that this account of Peter and Paul's contention with the Devil was well suited to fill out the somewhat disappointingly brief mention of this event in the ancient Dormition traditions.

Nevertheless, this insertion should not raise concern over the reliability of the remaining contents of the *Liber Requiei*, since a similar situation is found in the case of the *Apocalypse of Peter*. One will recall that the Ethiopic version of the *Apocalypse of Peter* is in its present state embedded within a larger pseudo-Clementine narrative. It was this narrative frame that prevented its initial editor from completely recognizing the significance of what he was publishing. Only after its publication did M. R. James recognize the text for what it is, a very ancient version of

Le Muséon, 68 (1955), 219–33. The Karshuni is considerably briefer and takes place only in Rome. Van Lantschoot has published a similar story from some Coptic palimpsest fragments in 'Les Textes palimpsest de B. M., Or. 8802', *Le Muséon*, 41 (1928), 225–47. In his edition of the Coptic fragments, van Lantschoot identified the Coptic text with Smith Lewis's Arabic version, but in his later publication of the Ethiopic and Karshuni fragments, he retracts this claim. Although the Ethiopic version from the *Liber Requiei* is remarkably close to the Arabic, it would seem that the Karshuni is not much closer than the Coptic.

[40] See also Michel van Esbroeck, 'La Première Église de la Vierge bâtie par les apôtres', *Festschrift Paul Devos* (forthcoming).

the *Apocalypse of Peter* joined with what is probably a medieval Arabic pseudo-Clementine composition.[41] In spite of the hybrid nature of this Ethiopic version, the *Apocalypse of Peter* has been preserved completely intact and almost entirely unmodified, and 'we can be sure that the text of the Apocalypse of Peter itself has not been affected by this later continuation of it'.[42]

After the completion of *The History of Peter and Paul*, the *Liber Requiei* itself comes to a close with a brief tour of Paradise that is also unparalleled by any of the other early Palm narratives. In contrast to the inserted *History of Peter and Paul*, however, the antiquity of this apocalyptic section seems rather likely. As Richard Bauckham notes in his recent study of the apocalyptic conclusions to the various early Dormition traditions, comparison with ancient 'cosmic tour' traditions in general and the literary history of the Palm traditions themselves suggest that this section belongs to the earliest traditions. On the one hand, Bauckham has charted a tendency of late ancient apocalyptic to reduce such cosmic tours to tours of hell only. This would conform with what we find elsewhere in the early Palm narratives, as the early Irish version demonstrates. Likewise, Bauckham observes that the later Palm traditions tend to abbreviate the earlier traditions, a pattern that is probably explained by their adaptation for liturgical usage.[43] On both of these accounts it seems probable, although not certain, that the tour of Paradise that concludes the *Liber Requiei* belongs to the earliest traditions.

In the light of the close literary relationship between the *Liber Requiei* and the early Syriac fragments, namely, their virtual identity, it is rather puzzling that Mimouni decided to classify the *Obsequies* fragments among the Bethlehem traditions. The judgement of scholarship is nearly unanimous in recognizing the identity of the *Liber Requiei* and the *Obsequies* fragments, as well

---

[41] Buchholz, *Your Eyes Will Be Opened*, 122–3, 376–86; Bauckham, *Fate of the Dead*, 162–3.

[42] Bauckham, *Fate of the Dead*, 162–3; see also Buchholz, *Your Eyes Will Be Opened*, 376–86, where the same conclusion is reached.

[43] Ibid. 344, 361. On the liturgical usage of the early Dormition traditions, see Simon C. Mimouni, 'Les Transitus Mariae sont-ils vraiment des apocryphes?' *Studia Patristica*, 25 (1993), 122–8; idem, 'La Lecture liturgique et les apocryphes du Nouveau Testament: Le Cas de la Dormitio grecque du Pseudo-Jean', *Orientalia Christiana Periodica*, 59 (1993), 403–25.

as the strong literary relations between the latter and the early texts of Palm tradition,[44] relations that not even Mimouni has ventured to deny outright. In fact, in a moment of guarded confession, hidden in a footnote, he admits the indisputable literary relationships among the *Obsequies*, the *Liber Requiei*, and Wenger's early Greek text: 'In effect, when one puts these three texts in relation, one is obliged to note that, from a literary point of view, they undeniably maintain affinities.'[45] As an example, he provides a synopsis of the Virgin's resurrection in Paradise according to each of these three texts, and since this is the issue with which we are presently concerned, I have reproduced it here, but to be sure, similar examples demonstrating the close relations of these texts could *easily* be multiplied, as the translations in the appendices should make clear.

---

[44] See e.g. Clayton, 'The Transitus Mariae', 76–82; Bauckham, *Fate of the Dead*, 342; Arras, *De Transitu*, i. 75–105 (Lat.); van Esbroeck, 'Les Textes', 270–1; idem, 'Apocryphes géorgiens', 55–7; Wenger, *L'Assomption*, 53–8, 66; Jugie, *La Mort*, 108–16, 139–50; R. Willard, 'The Testament of Mary: The Irish Account of the Death of the Virgin', *Recherches de Théologie ancienne et médiévale*, 9 (1937), 341–64; John D. Seymour, 'Irish Versions of the Transitus Mariae', *Journal of Theological Studies*, 23 (1921–2), 36–43; Charles Donahue, ed., *The Testament of Mary: The Gaelic Version of the Dormitio Mariae together with an Irish Latin Version*, Fordham University Studies, Language Series, 1 (New York: Fordham University Press, 1942), 12–21, 25–6; Frédéric Manns, OFM, *Le Récit de la dormition de Marie (Vatican grec 1982), Contribution à l'étude de origines de l'exégèse chrétienne*, Studium Biblicum Franciscanum, Collectio Maior, 33 (Jerusalem: Franciscan Printing Press, 1989), 46–51 and *passim*; Emmanuele Testa, OFM, 'Lo sviluppo della "Dormitio Mariae" nella letteratura, nella teologìa e nella archeologìa', *Marianum*, 44 (1982), 316–18; Mario Erbetta, *Gli apocrifi del Nuovo Testamento*, i. pt. 2, *Vangeli: Infanzia e passione di Cristo, Assunzione di Maria* (Casale: Marietti, 1981), 422; Jean Gribomont, OSB, 'Le Plus Ancien *Transitus* Marial et l'encratisme', *Augustinianum*, 23 (1983), 240.

The only exceptions would be Cothenet, Baldi, and Mosconi, who classified the *Obsequies* with the other Syriac apocrypha but were unaware of both the *Liber Requiei* and the Georgian fragments, both of which seem to make the *Obsequies'* relationship to the Assumptionist Palm tradition undeniable.

[45] Mimouni, *Dormition*, 83 n. 37.

S1. *Obsequies*[46]	E1. *Liber Requiei*[47]	G1. Wenger's Greek[48]
And after these things our Lord made a sign to Michael, and Michael answered in the voice of a mighty angel. And the angels descended on three clouds; and the number of angels on each cloud was 1000 angels, singing praises before Jesus. And our Lord said to Michael, 'Let them bring Mary's body to the clouds.' And when Mary's body entered the clouds, our Lord said to the apostles, 'Come near to the clouds.' And when they came into the clouds, they were singing with the voice of angels. And our Lord told the clouds to depart for the gate of Paradise. And when they entered Paradise, Mary's body went to the tree of life. And they brought her soul and made it enter into her body. And immediately our Lord sent the angels away to their places.	Then our Lord gave a sign to Michael, and Michael spoke with the voice of faithful angels. And they descended on three clouds, and the number of angels on a cloud appeared to be ten thousand angels in the presence of the Saviour. And our Lord said to them: 'Let them bring the body of Mary into the clouds.' And when the body had been brought, our Lord said to the apostles that they should draw near to him. And they ascended individually into the cloud, and they were singing with the voice of angels. And our Lord told the clouds to go to the East, to the region near Paradise. And when they arrived together in Paradise, they placed the body of Mary beside the tree of life. And they brought her soul and placed it upon her	Then he made a sign to Michael in a truly angelic voice, and the clouds descended to him. And the number of angels on each cloud was a thousand angels, and they uttered praises before the Saviour. And the Lord told Michael to take the body of Mary up onto the cloud and to set it down in Paradise. And when the body was taken up, the Lord told the apostles to come closer to it. And when they came onto the cloud, they were singing with the voice of angels, and the Lord commanded the clouds to depart for the East, to the regions of Paradise. And when they came to Paradise, they placed the body of Mary under the tree of life. And Michael brought her holy soul, and they placed it in her body. And the Lord returned

[46] Wright, *Contributions*, ⲥⲟⲩ̄ⲗ̄ⲓ (Syr.) and 46–7 (Eng.).
[47] *Liber Requiei* 89 (Arras, *De Transitu*, i. 53 (Eth.)).
[48] Wenger, *L'Assomption*, 240.

body. And our Lord	the apostles to their
dismissed his angels	places for the
to their places.	conversion and
	salvation of
	humankind.[49]

Despite the candour of Mimouni's footnote, and its admission of the 'undeniable' literary affinities among these texts, the body of his text persistently struggles to efface these literary relationships, which are on the top half of the very same page judged 'debatable'.[50] This apparent contradiction is consistent, however, with Mimouni's explicit rejection of literary relationships as a means of classifying texts, determining to rely instead on a narrative of dogmatic evolution to organize the material,[51] as he himself explains in this case: 'these two texts, the Greek and the Ethiopic, putting forth a belief in the Assumption, can only be compared with difficulty to the Syriac text, which bears witness to belief in the Dormition'.[52] With this conclusion, Mimouni's subordination of literary relations to dogma has reached its zenith: despite his own recognition of these 'undeniable' literary affinities, Mimouni forcefully uproots the *Obsequies* from its proper literary context, the Assumptionist Palm traditions, and attempts to graft it to the rather dissimilar, Assumptionless Bethlehem traditions. While this may resolve Mimouni's perceived dogmatic conflict, a similar comparison of the Virgin's resurrection in the *Obsequies* and the other Syriac apocrypha shows just how unlikely his classification is from a literary point of view.

[49] Wenger's text concludes here, but the other two (and many members of this textual family) continue with strikingly similar accounts of a visit by the Virgin and the apostles to the places of punishment.

[50] Mimouni, *Dormition*, 83.

[51] Perhaps most strongly stated in ibid. 49, where in criticizing the work of Michel van Esbroeck, Mimouni writes: 'Cette classification repose sur des thématiques littéraires. Or, la présence de thèmes littéraires dans un texte ne paraît pas suffisante. Une typologie, en effet, peut difficilement être établie uniquement sur la présence ou l'absence de thèmes littéraires dans des écrits.' Van Esbroeck's typology fails, in his opinion, because 'elle conduit à des contresens, aussi bien du point de vue topologique, ce qui n'est pas trop grave, que du point de vue doctrinal, ce qui est plus gênant'. Note especially the emphasis on the importance of doctrine above other criteria.

[52] Mimouni, *Dormition*, 83.

S1. *Obsequies*[53]	S2. Syriac Fragments[54]	S3. 'The Six Books'[55]
And after these things our Lord made a sign to Michael, and Michael answered in the voice of a mighty angel. And the angels descended on three clouds; and the number of angels on each cloud was 1000 angels, singing praises before Jesus. And our Lord said to Michael, 'Let them bring Mary's body to the clouds.' And when Mary's body entered the clouds, our Lord said to the apostles, 'Come near to the clouds.' And when they came into the clouds, they were singing with the voice of angels. And our Lord told the clouds to depart for the gate of Paradise. And when they entered Paradise, Mary's body went to the tree of life. And they brought her soul and made it enter into her body. And immediately our Lord sent the angels away to their places.	. . . and assemblies of spiritual beings, whose troops were without numbers, and their ranks without end, who were coming and praising, band by band; and every tongue in its own language was crying glory; and they were hovering over the blessed Mary. And the chariots were coming last, one of Moses, and one of Enoch, and one of Elias; and then the blessed chariot of our Lord was coming after them. And heaven and earth were praising on that day; and the dead, who were buried, gave glory from their graves. And a pleasant and sweet odour went forth from the highest heavens of His glory to all parts of creation. And they carried the blessed one to Paradise with this glory, and her holy body was placed	When the blessed one was placed in the Paradise of Eden and was crowned with this great glory, and the apostles had departed in all directions, our Lord Jesus came to his mother in the Paradise of Eden. And the chariots of the angels descended from heaven in infinite numbers, and the Paradise of Eden was covered, and all the mountains that were around it. And the sound of nothing was heard save the voice of those saying, Holy! Holy! Holy! And when our Lord came to my Lady Mary, he called to her and said: 'Mary, rise.' And straight-away she was restored to life and worshipped Him. And our Lord Jesus said to her: 'To show you the glory of my Father's house I am come to thee.' The blessed Mary said to Him: ''Tis well, Rabbuli.' And Elias

---

[53] Wright, *Contributions*, ‎ܠܒ‎ (Syr.) and 46–7 (Eng.).

[54] Ibid. ‎ܡܠܒ‎ (Syr.) and 39–40 (Eng.).

[55] Wright, 'Departure', ‎ܟܒ–ܡܒ‎ (Syr.) and 156 (Eng.).

there. And when she
was carried up and
reached the gate of
Paradise, the sword
that surrounds
Paradise was taken
away, and the holy
one went in with
glory that is
unspeakable into
Paradise, the
celestials and
terrestrials being
intermingled. And
they placed her in
boundless light amid
the delicious trees of
the Paradise of Eden;
and they exalted her
with glory on which
the eye of flesh is not
able to gaze. And our
Life-giver stretched
out His hand and
blessed Mary; and
He was raised up
from beside her to
His glorious Father,
and his promise is
life to all those who
believe in Him.

the Prophet came to
our Lord and to my
Lady Mary, and
Enoch and Moses
and Simon Cephas:
these came at the
beck of our Saviour
to the Paradise of
Eden.[56]

As one can see, from a literary standpoint, there is very
little to link the *Obsequies* fragments with the apocrypha of the
Bethlehem tradition, while comparison with the early versions
of the Palm tradition reveals an almost verbal agreement. It
remains then to consider whether the supposed dogmatic contradiction identified by Mimouni is sufficiently strong that we
should overlook the unambiguous testimony of literary relations
in favour of maintaining dogmatic harmony. It is clear that we

[56] Following this, in Wright's S3 text, Mary is given the 'grand tour' of
Paradise, accompanied by Elias, Enoch, Simon Cephas, and John the young.

should not, since this presumed dogmatic contradiction is, in fact, imagined. One need only consider the frailty of the circular logic used to invent it. Beginning with the relatively uncertain conclusion to the *Obsequies*, Mimouni supposes that as the complete narrative drew to a close, the Virgin was 'unresurrected', an ending supplied by comparison with the early apocrypha of the Bethlehem tradition, some of which perhaps envision such an occurrence (although doubtfully), without explicitly describing it. From this hypothetical ending, it follows that in its complete state, the *Obsequies* did not record the Virgin's Assumption, and therefore it must be classified among the other Assumptionless narratives. When Mimouni subsequently comes to consider the literary relations between the *Obsequies* and the remainder of the Dormition traditions, he finds, as have numerous scholars before him, that it 'undeniably shares affinities' with the narratives of the Palm tradition. Nevertheless, Mimouni rejects the significance of these literary relations, insisting that they are outweighed by the *Obsequies*' failure to report an Assumption. On this basis he classifies the *Obsequies* within the textual tradition of the otherwise unrelated Bethlehem traditions, which in turn, he claims, justifies the initial appeal to these traditions to complete the missing conclusion. At this point the circle is complete. Comparison with the Bethlehem apocrypha suggests the Virgin's unresurrection and the lack of an Assumption. This lack of an Assumption overrides the 'undeniable' literary relations between the *Obsequies* and the Assumptionist Palm traditions, prompting its classification with the Assumptionless Bethlehem narratives. In turn, this classification is adduced to justify the initial comparison of the *Obsequies* with the Bethlehem tradition. Such dizzying argumentation is not in the end very persuasive.

This circle can for the most part be avoided if instead we approach the problem by beginning from the other direction. Rather than beginning with a hypothetical conclusion to the *Obsequies* and evaluating any apparent literary relations in view of this theoretical ending, as Mimouni has done, one could instead begin with the evidence of literary relations. On the basis of these relations then, one could make a more informed judgement regarding the now lost completion to the *Obsequies*. Following this method, one would first recognize that the *Obsequies* is very closely related to the texts of the Palm tradition, all of which record the Virgin's Assumption and none of which describe her unresurrection. Moreover, we find that an almost identical version of the same text has been preserved by the Ethiopic *Liber Requiei*, in which the Virgin is also permanently resurrected, clearly indicating her Assumption. On this basis, it stands to reason that in the *Obsequies*, as in the related texts of the Palm tradition, the Virgin's resurrection in Paradise is not temporary but permanent, and therefore a sign of her Assumption.

The *Obsequies* then, according to this understanding, is our earliest witness to a belief in the Virgin's Assumption, which had certainly arisen sometime before the late fifth or early sixth century, when our version of the *Obsequies* was copied. At approximately this same time, the earliest exemplars of both the Coptic and Bethlehem traditions first appear, as does the idiosyncratic version of the end of the Mary's life recorded in Jacob of Serug's homily. Therefore, the literary history of the early Dormition traditions affords no evidence that a primitive Assumptionless tradition, or any single literary or dogmatic tradition preceded and somehow gave rise to the others. On the contrary, it would seem that at the moment of their initial emergence from an uncertain past, around 500, there were already at least four separate traditions in circulation, each presumably with its own origin. Thus, the earliest known state of these traditions was one of synchronic coexistence, and the literary relations among the early traditions afford no evidence for a diachronic, typological, and dogmatic evolution.

TOPOGRAPHY, LITURGY, AND THE QUESTION OF ORIGINS

In the effort to identify an original tradition among the various types of Dormition narratives, scholars have often sought to correlate the related liturgical and archeological data from the emerging cult of the Virgin with the topographical diversity of the different narratives. These geographic variants are believed by some to hold the key to understanding the transitions from one narrative type into the next. With this in mind, interpreters have frequently sought to establish a liturgical evolution for the

Feast of the Dormition in Palestine,[57] charting its celebration from primarily one shrine to the next and then using this outline as a guide for reconstructing the orderly dogmatic and narrative evolution of these legends.[58] Unfortunately, however, these liturgical and archeological data are neither as clear nor as forthcoming as these efforts would generally have them appear.

For instance, some scholars have argued that the priority of the Assumptionless Bethlehem traditions is demonstrated by their mention of Mary's house in Bethlehem, maintaining that the Bethlehem house corresponds in some way to earliest Marian liturgical celebrations at the Kathisma church.[59] Again Mimouni provides both the most recent and thorough exposition of this position, but his argumentation is highly problematic and dubious. Although there was unquestionably a liturgical celebration of the Memory of Mary at the Kathisma church by the early fifth century (at the latest), this does not in any way indicate the antiquity of the Bethlehem narratives. In fact, as seen in the preceding chapter, there is simply no evidence for a Bethlehem station in the Marian liturgies of ancient Palestine. The only possible exception to this would be the superscription of the Klardjeti Homiliary's reading for 13 August, which refers to the gathering of the apostles in Bethlehem and their flight through the air from Bethlehem to Zion, events that precede Mary's Dormition in some of the Bethlehem narratives.[60] Nevertheless, as already noted in the preceding chapter, the reading gives no indication of a station in Bethlehem, and everything else about the reading (and those that follow for 14 August) points toward a celebration at the Kathisma church. This location is further

[57] Although this feast is often just as much, if not more, a celebration of the Virgin's Assumption, following Eastern Christian practice I will refer to this feast as the Feast of the Dormition ($\kappa o i \mu \eta \sigma \iota s$). This is also consistent with the practice of referring to all the traditions of the end of the Virgin's life collectively as the 'Dormition' traditions.

[58] In particular, Cothenet, Mimouni, and van Esbroeck have adopted this approach, but to markedly different ends. For the latter, see in particular 'Le Culte de la Vierge de Jérusalem à Constantinople aux 6e–7e siècles', *Revue des Études Byzantines*, 46 (1988), 181–90, where the various shrines associated with the Virgin's Dormition are correlated with various stages in the struggle between monophysites and Chalcedonians in the Holy Land.

[59] e.g. Mimouni, *Dormition*, 57–8. See also Cothenet, 'Marie', 119 n. 200.

[60] Michel van Esbroeck, 'Nouveaux apocryphes de la Dormition conservés en Géorgien', *Analecta Bollandiana*, 90 (1972), 366.

suggested by both the Jerusalem Georgian Lectionary, which explicitly identifies the Kathisma church, and not Bethlehem, as the location of the 13 August feast.[61] Even Mimouni, in his analysis of the piece, agrees that its cultic setting was the Kathisma.[62]

Thus, the history of Mary's Palestinian cult in no way suggests a connection between any of its celebrations and a house of Mary in Bethlehem. Mimouni attempts to get around this problem by maintaining that the Kathisma church was constructed 'on the place where the [Bethlehem Dormition] tradition situates the house of Mary'.[63] But this is totally unfounded speculation and in no way demonstrates the antiquity of those traditions mentioning a house of Mary in Bethlehem. There is, to my knowledge, no tradition, ancient, medieval, or modern, identifying the Kathisma church with a house of the Virgin (or the events of the Dormition narratives, for that matter).[64] Nor can the simple existence of this church equidistant to both Jerusalem and Bethlehem in any way favour the precedence of the Virgin's Bethlehem house in relation to the Jerusalem-centred traditions.

Elsewhere in his quite substantial study, Mimouni softens his initial claim to the following: 'one could reasonably estimate that the house of Mary in Bethlehem was located in this place [the Kathisma]'.[65] Of course, the problem with this is that one could 'reasonably estimate' any number of things, especially in the

---

[61] Michel van Esbroeck, *Analecta Bollandiana*, 90 (1972), 364–5, where van Esbroeck similarly argues that this reading belonged to celebrations that took place at the church of the Kathisma.

[62] Mimouni, *Dormition*, 302–3.

[63] Mimouni, *Dormition*, 57. In support of this claim, he footnotes Bernard Capelle, 'La Fête de la Vierge à Jérusalem au Ve siècle', *Le Muséon*, 56 (1943), 1–[3]3, but in the entirety of this article, I do not find evidence of Capelle advancing this interpretation, and even if Capelle were to have made this connection, it would seem that it could be little more than the opinion of this erudite liturgical scholar. See also, Mimouni, *Dormition*, 528–30, for a more detailed (but unsuccessful) attempt to argue this point.

[64] This is borne out by Mimouni's discussion of the various literary attestations to this shrine, none of which afford any indication that either the Kathisma or its site are to be identified in any way with a house of the Virgin Mary: ibid. 519–26. The only connection between the Kathisma and the Dormition traditions is made in the later liturgical practices, which locate the beginning of the 5-day feast of Mary's Dormition at the Kathisma on 13 August.

[65] Ibid. 529.

absence of much solid evidence. In fact, the same piece of evidence, the Kathisma church, could quite reasonably be construed as demonstrating precisely the opposite, that the house of Mary was originally located in Jerusalem, not Bethlehem. Equally near to Jerusalem and definitely a part of the Jerusalem liturgical calendar, the Kathisma church is just as much evidence for the priority of the Jerusalem house traditions as it is for the Bethlehem house tradition. Only the spot's connection with the Nativity in the *Protevangelium of James* serves to draw it into the sphere of Bethlehem, but this point cannot tip the balance in favour of Mary's Bethlehem house, since it clearly links the church with the events of the Nativity, rather than a house of the Virgin or the end of her life.[66] As noted in the previous chapter, the feast of the Memory of Mary was at its earliest visible stage primarily a commemoration of the Virgin's role in the Nativity, having absolutely nothing to do with any of her potential houses. It is quite clear that the Kathisma's significance lay not in an association with traditions of the Virgin's house or the end of her life, but with events of Nativity that the *Protevangelium* describes as occurring just outside Bethlehem. There is simply no evidence suggesting the shrine's connection with the Virgin's Bethlehem house, a tradition completely unknown outside the early Dormition narratives of the Bethlehem type. But even in these narratives, the Virgin's Bethlehem house is clearly located inside the city of Bethlehem, and not halfway to Jerusalem, where the Kathisma church stood.[67]

Moreover, without exception, the Bethlehem narratives all identify two houses belonging to the Virgin, one in Bethlehem

---

[66] *Protev.* 17. 1. 3 (Konstantin Tischendorf, ed., *Evangelia Apocrypha*, 2nd edn. (Leipzig: 1876; repr. Hildesheim: Georg Olms, 1966), 33).

[67] For instance, the Bethlehem narratives report that the Bethlehemites became provoked as they observed the unusual events that were taking place at the Virgin's house, a development that is not very likely if the house was some three miles north of the city: 'And certain men of Bethlehem, when they saw the signs which were done, came to the house of the blessed one. And the people of Bethlehem saw the disciples when they were ministering in the upper chamber; and they saw the clouds coming and dropping down a gentle dew on all Bethlehem.' Wright, 'Departure', ܪܚ (Syr.) and 141 (Eng.). A similar passage is found in Smith Lewis, *Apocrypha*, ܘ (Syr.) and 33 (Eng.). There are numerous other passages in these texts to indicate that the house was *in* Bethlehem and not halfway to Jerusalem.

and another in Jerusalem, a fact that Mimouni's study has obscured. In each of the early Dormition narratives, including all the Bethlehem traditions, the Virgin is dwelling in her Jerusalem house as the story begins, and it is here that she completes her earthly life.[68] Only certain narratives, the

[68] Even Cothenet, whose typology Mimouni has basically adopted, recognizes that 'l'habitation de Marie à Bethléem apparaît comme un doublet de l'habitation à Jérusalem'. Cothenet, 'Marie dans les Apocryphes', 119. Mimouni admits that this is the case only for AB1, G2, and L8. See *Dormition*, 345–7. Those texts which according to Mimouni include *only* a Bethlehem house and *do not* mention a Jerusalem house are S2, S3, E2, E3, AB2, AB3, AB5, and AB10 (ibid. 346). I am puzzled by this inaccurate claim: on examination of the texts in question, this is simply not the case, and all these narratives note a Jerusalem house as well.

The Syriac texts clearly indicate two houses, concerning which see the discussion that follows. Both Ethiopic texts attest this 'doublet': in addition to the Bethlehem house, recognized by Mimouni, both E2 and E3 describe a house belonging to the Virgin that is unquestionably located in Jerusalem. As the narrative opens, the Virgin is living in this Jerusalem house, and after a brief sojourn in her Bethlehem house, she returns to the Jerusalem house for the story's conclusion. See E2: Marius Chaine, ed., *Apocrypha de Beata Maria Virgine*, 2 vols., CSCO 39–40 (Rome: Karolus de Luigi, 1909), 25–6 and 37–8 (Eth.) and 21 and 32 (Lat.), and E3: Arras, *De Transitu*, i. 93–4 (Eth.) and 61 (Lat.). Note, however, that there is some slight confusion in E3 concerning the Virgin's residence at the narrative's opening. Here she supposedly returns from Golgotha to Bethlehem (instead of Jerusalem as in every other text) and then announces her intention to depart for Bethlehem! (Arras, *De Transitu*, i. 86–7 (Eth.) and 56 (Lat.).) Her decision to relocate to Bethlehem would of course make more sense if the text had originally described an initial return to her Jerusalem house, as in the other versions of the Bethlehem tradition. In any case, the narrative's conclusion is explicitly located in Mary's Jerusalem house.

AB5 is unedited but is available in a French translation by Louis Leroy, 'La Dormition de la vierge (tradition du manuscrit arabe de Paris no. 150, fol. 157)', *Revue de l'Orient Chrétien*, 15 (1910), 162–72. This translation locates events at houses in both Jerusalem and Bethlehem, but neither house is ever specifically designated as belonging to the Virgin. Each house is always referred to as 'la maison où se trouvait la Vierge pure' (165, 167). The edition of AB2 and AB3 has eluded my grasp, and AB10 is still unedited. Consequently, I have not been able to consult them, but their descriptions by A. van Lantschoot ('L'Assomption de la Sainte Vierge chez les Coptes', *Gregorianum*, 27 (1946), 508–9, 511–12, and 514–16) and Gabriele Giamberardini, OFM (*Il culto mariano in Eggito*, i. Sec. I–VI, 2nd edn., Pubblicazioni dello Studium Biblicum Franciscanum, Analecta, 6 (Jerusalem: Franciscan Printing Press, 1975), 173–4 and 176–7), which seem to be Mimouni's sources of information (see *Dormition*, 218, 223, and 225), give no indication that these texts locate the Virgin's house only in Bethlehem. If in fact they do, and Mimouni has seen these texts, then he inexplicably fails to present evidence of this fact.

Bethlehem traditions, add an additional Bethlehem house, which serves as the site of the apostles' miraculous reunion during the Virgin's brief sojourn in Bethlehem to avoid persecution by the Jews. Considering the Syriac apocrypha, which are our earliest witnesses to the Bethlehem traditions, this pattern becomes clear. At the beginning of the sixth-century narrative published by Wright, for instance, Mary is in Jerusalem, and the 'people of Jerusalem' persuade the Roman governor to banish her from the city. Then, we are told, 'she sent and called all the women of the quarter in which she dwelt [in Jerusalem], and said to them: "Fare ye well, for I am going to Bethlehem, to the house which I have there." '[69] So as the narrative begins, Mary is dwelling in Jerusalem, presumably in a house, which she is forced to leave for her second house in Bethlehem. Then, after the reunion of the apostles, the entire party is flown through the air to Mary's house in Jerusalem, and when a Jewish mob attempts to come against them at the Bethlehem house, they find no one there. Determined to rid themselves of Mary, the 'people of Jerusalem' then make an effort to burn down her Jerusalem house, but when they attempt to open its doors, they are consumed by a fire that blazes forth from the house.[70] Thus, it is clear that this narrative envisioned two houses belonging to the Virgin, one in Jerusalem and another in Bethlehem.

The roughly contemporary version published by Smith Lewis affords a rather detailed description of Mary's Jerusalem house: 'the house, where the Blessed one dwelt in Jerusalem, had been bought by Joseph the carpenter from the household of Caleb the Sadducee, and it was near to the house of Nicodemus'.[71] It was here that Mary summoned her Jerusalemite neighbours and told them: 'Go in peace, I am going to Bethlehem, to the house which I have there.'[72] When a mob later comes against the Virgin and the apostles in Bethlehem, they escape in a miraculous flight through the air to 'the house of the Lady Mary, which she had at Jerusalem', to which she inevitably returns in all the narratives of this type for the conclusion of her earthly life.[73] Even the

---

[69] Wright, 'Departure', ܪ (Syr.) and 135 (Eng.).

[70] Ibid. ܡܐ‑ܠܐ (Syr.) and 142–3 (Eng.).

[71] ܢܠܬܐܪܟ ܪܐܬ‑ܢܒܐܠ ܚܢ ܕܐܡ ܪܡܠܡܐ ܪܐܬܐܙ, Smith Lewis, *Apocrypha,* ܠܐ (Syr.) and 23 (Eng.).   [72] Ibid.

[73] ܢܠܬܐܪܟ ܚܠ ܪܐܡ ܕܐܪܟܐ ܪܐܠܐܪܟ ܢܒܬܢ ܚܒܬܢ ,ܚܬܐܙ ܚܕܐܒ, ibid. ܒܡ (Syr.) and 37 (Eng.).

later Syriac fragments edited by Wright initially locate Mary's house in Jerusalem,[74] and when the Jews order her to leave the city, she replies, 'I have no desire to dwell longer in your city [Jerusalem]. . . . Then she called to the women of her neighborhood in Jerusalem, and said to them: "The Jews say to me that they will not permit me to dwell in Jerusalem, and therefore I am going forth to Bethlehem to my house." '[75]

A complete survey of the ancient Dormition traditions would confirm this bilocal pattern as invariably characteristic of the Bethlehem traditions, as well as establish the failure of any tradition to mention the Virgin's Bethlehem house without also including her Jerusalem house.[76] It should be noted that this fact actually speaks rather strongly *against* the Bethlehem tradition's antiquity and *for* the priority of the tradition of Mary's Jerusalem house. Inclusion of the Jerusalem house by every narrative mentioning a house seems a rather strong indication that this tradition was primitive enough to effect the basic structure of each of the three main narrative types, as well as some of the early independent narratives.[77] Furthermore, the appearance of the Bethlehem house in only a limited number of narratives, and always in the shadow of the Jerusalem house, suggests its insertion alongside an already established Jerusalem tradition, although admittedly, this is not the only possible explanation. Conceivably, the Bethlehem tradition could represent an equally ancient yet less influential tradition, but as the tradition of the Virgin's Bethlehem house is completely unknown outside the Dormition traditions, there is nothing particularly suggestive of this possibility.[78]

---

[74] Wright, *Contributions,* ܠܚ (Syr.) and 20 (Eng.).

[75] Ibid. ܠ (Syr.) and 20–1 (Eng.) (translation slightly modified). The text identifies Mary's Jerusalem house, the house to which she returns before leaving Jerusalem and to which she eventually returns, as ܐܘܚܕ (ܠܚ (Syr.)), and Mary herself calls the Bethlehem house ܠܕ ܪܚܘܐ (ܠ (Syr.)). Thus according to this text, they are clearly both her houses.

[76] See e.g. n. 68 above.

[77] Specifically, the homilies of Theoteknos of Livias (G8) and Ps.-Chrysostom (AM3).

[78] Although Mimouni produces several alleged literary, liturgical, and archeological attestations in favour of the Bethlehem tradition's priority (*Dormition*, 519–28), in reality these witnesses have absolutely nothing to do with a tradition of the Virgin's Bethlehem house, but concern instead the Kathisma church, which they *do not* connect in any way with a house of the Virgin.

If forced to make a judgement then, the Jerusalem house tradition in fact has the stronger claim to priority, a conclusion particularly suggested by the Bethlehem tradition's inclusion of Mary's Jerusalem house. The Virgin's Bethlehem house is never attested in the absence of her Jerusalem house, while the Jerusalem house is frequently mentioned independently, facts strongly suggestive that the Bethlehem tradition is secondary. It would make sense to assume that when the tradition of the Bethlehem house eventually arose, the Jerusalem tradition was already sufficiently entrenched that even those texts wishing to recognize the tradition of a Bethlehem house could not omit inclusion of the Virgin's well-known Jerusalem house. The importance of the Jerusalem tradition is also expressed by the fact that the Bethlehem narratives persistently set the most significant events of Mary's Dormition at the Jerusalem house, including only a brief excursion to the Bethlehem house. Although admittedly this is not the only possible explanation, it nevertheless seems a rather likely hypothesis.

Ultimately, it would seem that at some level even Mimouni cannot totally deny the force of this evidence, and although it completely contradicts the fundamental assumptions of his study, towards the end of the work we suddenly find him endorsing the priority of the tradition of Mary's Jerusalem house as if it somehow supported his thesis.[79] Here Mimouni suggests that during the first half of the fifth century, the Marian cult in the Holy City centred around the church of Mary in the valley of Josaphat, which he identifies with her house.[80] But following the council of Chalcedon, Mimouni believes that this Marian shrine fell under the control of the council's opponents, as Mimouni claims is indicated by Ps.-Dioscorus' *Panegyric on Macarius of Tkōw*. As noted in Ch. 2, this text reports that the church of Mary in Gethsemane had become a rallying point for anti-Chalcedonian resistance immediately after the council, from which Mimouni concludes that the shrine fell into 'monophysite' hands.[81] Based on this assumption, Mimouni

---

[79] Mimouni, *Dormition*, 515–16, 530–2.

[80] Against this identification of Gethsemane with her house, see the remarks in Ch. 2.

[81] Mimouni, *Dormition*, 531; Ps.-Dioscorus of Alexandria, *Panegyric on Macarius of Tkōw* 7. 5 (David Johnson, ed., *A Panegyric on Macarius, Bishop of*

suggests that the pro-Chalcedonian patriarch, Juvenal, who was in power only by imperial might, responded to his loss of authority at this ancient Marian shrine with an attempt to establish the cult of the Virgin at a site which would be firmly under Chalcedonian (and his) influence. He quickly initiated construction on the church of the Kathisma at the mid-point between Jerusalem and Bethlehem, a location already famous for its role in the events of the Nativity. Since the Gethsemane church commanded great respect as the site of Mary's house, Juvenal looked to complete his plan by manufacturing a similar tradition for his rival church, in the hopes of endowing it with instant authority.[82] This act in turn gave rise to the Dormition traditions locating the Virgin's house in Bethlehem.

All of this, however, is for the most part historical fiction, and it can be more or less disproved. Although we shall have more to say about the relation of Chalcedon to the early history of the Dormition traditions in Ch. 4, it is worth noting here that if one continues to read Ps.-Dioscorus' account, Juvenal arrives at the church with 400 soldiers who, at Juvenal's command, (unwillingly) slaughtered his opponents and retook the church. Thus it seems rather unlikely that Juvenal lost control of this shrine and needed to build a new one: the *Panegyric on Macarius of Tkōw*, at least, does not attest to this.[83] But rather shockingly, Mimouni's proposal here clearly contradicts his fundamental hypothesis, namely that those Dormition traditions mentioning a Bethlehem house are the earliest. Perhaps Mimouni has here begun to doubt his own theory and has come to recognize, at least partially, the strength of the evidence for the priority of the Jerusalem tradition.[84] In any case, Mimouni's proposal regarding Juvenal's

---

Tkōw, Attributed to Dioscorus of Alexandria, CSCO 415–16 (Louvain: Peeters, 1980), 49–50 (Copt.) and 38 (Eng.)).

[82] Mimouni, *Dormition*, 531–2.

[83] The entire episode is described in Ps.-Dioscorus, *Panegyric on Macarius of Tkōw* 7. 1–8. 16 (Johnson, *Panegyric on Macarius Tkōw*, 45–70 (Copt.) and 34–54 (Eng.)). See also Lorenzo Perrone, 'Christian Holy Places and Pilgrimage in an Age of Dogmatic Conflicts: Popular Religion and Confessional Affiliation in Byzantine Palestine (Fifth to Seventh Centuries)', *Proche-Orient Chrétien*, 48 (1998), 16–17, where Perrone offers a similar interpretation of these events.

[84] 'Comme l'église de Gethsémani abritrait une tradition mariale relative à sa maison, il [Juvenal] créa une tradition similar pour l'église du Kathisma.' Mimouni, *Dormition*, 531–2.

construction of the Kathisma completely undermines his developmental typology: if his hypothesis of the Kathisma's post-Chalcedonian origin were correct, then the Bethlehem house is clearly the more recent of the two traditions, and its inclusion would mark narratives composed in the wake of this development. The Jerusalem-only narratives, in this instance, would most likely be the earliest, since they are unaware of this development. This unacknowledged contradiction raises serious complications for the understanding of the early history of these traditions as Mimouni describes it in his study.

Also problematic with Mimouni's theory of the Kathisma's origin is the fact that the doctrinal alignments supposed by this hypothesis do not exactly comport with the wide diffusion of the Bethlehem narratives throughout the anti-Chalcedonian world both in late antiquity and the Middle Ages,[85] nor with the anti-Chalcedonian origin that Mimouni elsewhere attributes to these legends.[86] Mimouni would have us believe that from a polemical, pro-Chalcedonian origin, the Bethlehem tradition somehow quickly entered into anti-Chalcedonian circles, where it first appears in the early Syriac apocrypha of the sixth century. In the light of this evidence, Mimouni's hypothesis must somehow account for the rapid and enthusiastic monophysite adoption of a Chalcedonian propaganda narrative, presumably designed to promote a 'counterfeit' Chalcedonian shrine at the expense of the more ancient, 'genuine' shrine controlled by the opponents of Chalcedon. This contradiction is to some degree mitigated by the popularity of the Greek *Transitus* of Ps.-John (G2), a Bethlehem narrative that was widely used by Eastern Chalcedonians, which demonstrates that the Bethlehem traditions at least were not the exclusive property of Chalcedon's opponents.[87] But even so, one is left wondering why the resistance to Chalcedon would so quickly embrace what amounts to a fundamentally pro-Chalcedonian tradition.

Presumably in answer to this problem, Mimouni offers the following explanation: the early Bethlehem traditions express

---

[85] van Esbroeck, 'Les Textes', 269.

[86] Mimouni, *Dormition*, 665.

[87] van Esbroeck calls this text a 'best-seller', and notes that there are over 100 known Greek manuscripts preserving this text. van Esbroeck, 'Les Textes', 269.

their anti-Chalcedonian leanings by refusing to mention the actual cultic centre of this Chalcedonian tradition, the Kathisma church. This clever hypothesis serves double duty by simultaneously explaining the failure of these texts to identify the Virgin's house explicitly with the Kathisma church. But even if this 'misrepresentation' of the Virgin's house as being in Bethlehem rather than at the Kathisma is understood as some form of anti-Chalcedonian resistance, it still does not really explain why this tradition, supposedly of Chalcedonian origin, is so well preserved in anti-Chalcedonian circles,[88] nor does it explain why the 'Chalcedonian' *Transitus* of Ps.-John does not 'correctly' locate the house at the Kathisma. For instance, why did the opponents of Chalcedon not respond with a fervent insistence on the antiquity and authenticity of the Gethsemane shrine, purportedly under their control, thereby attacking, rather than adopting, the attempted fraud of the heretics? These and other questions are left unanswered in Mimouni's interpretations of the early topographical and liturgical traditions, and thus he ultimately fails to justify his claim that the tradition of Mary's Bethlehem house is primitive and therefore distinguishes the earliest traditions of the end of the Virgin's life.

Thus, in the absence of any historical evidence suggesting the antiquity of Bethlehem tradition, we can confidently conclude that mention of the Virgin's Bethlehem house is not a reliable criterion with which to distinguish the earliest Dormition narratives. On the contrary, the sum of the evidence seems to favour the view that this was probably a secondary development and therefore, if anything, a probable mark of later narratives. Even Mimouni's own hypotheses eventually seem to concede tacitly that the inclusion of a Bethlehem house would indicate a version of the Dormition that developed only sometime after the establishment of the 'rival' Kathisma church in the second half of the fifth century. In the light of this it might be tempting to conclude that those Dormition traditions that fail to include a Bethlehem house are the earliest, but this is not altogether certain: other possibilities exist. Consequently, it is perhaps best to conclude simply that, as with the doctrinal differences, the liturgical traditions of Jerusalem and topographical variants of the early

---

[88] One version of the Six Books (S3), published by Budge, actually has a Nestorian provenance.

Dormition traditions cannot reliably establish the priority of one tradition over the others.

A GARDEN CLOSED AND REOPENED: LATE ANCIENT PARADISE TRADITIONS AS EVIDENCE OF INDEPENDENT ORIGINS

In spite of the narrative diversity that characterizes the early Dormition traditions, these legends converge remarkably in regards to Mary's ultimate fate: almost without exception they conclude with Mary's transfer in body and/or soul to the Garden of Paradise following her death. Beyond this initial point of agreement, however, the accounts diverge quickly, offering various assessments of the Virgin's return to the Garden and its eschatological significance. In some instances, Mary's restoration to Paradise is seen as her attainment of the final reward awaiting all the just, while in other traditions, Mary's presence in Paradise is merely representative of the intermediate state presently shared by the righteous departed, who will together receive their final reward only on the day of resurrection, at the end of time. In most cases, however, the theological importance of Mary's presence in Paradise is rather difficult to assess, since the eschatological function of Paradise is either unclear or confused. This is particularly true of the many of the earliest narratives, from the fifth and sixth centuries, in which the reader follows Mary on an extensive tour of the heavenly realms, where the Garden of Paradise is seen in its relation to other districts within the eternal Kingdom. The images of Paradise that emerge from these apocalyptic visions are diverse and complex, and in this diversity the Dormition legends reflect a variety of eschatological opinion that is witnessed more broadly in the religious traditions of late antiquity.[89] I propose that the diversity of eschatological belief in the early Christian tradition, rather than any kind of ordered dogmatic development, can account for the theological differences regarding Mary's final state that are encountered in the earliest Dormition traditions. Instead of

---

[89] The apocalypses of the early Dormition traditions have recently received their first serious study within the broader context of ancient apocalyptic in Richard Bauckham *Fate of the Dead*, 332–62.

positing a linear evolution from one theological position to another, we may instead identify the source of the early Dormition narratives' theological diversity in the different understandings of Paradise and its eschatological purpose that were current in late antiquity.

In this regard, two major trends can be identified, although there are numerous variations involving one or both of these possibilities, as the early Dormition narratives themselves bear witness. On the one hand, many ancient writers understood Paradise as being the eternal resting place of the righteous, where after their resurrection, the elect would receive their final reward. Alternatively, other writers considered Paradise to be a place where disembodied souls awaited the general resurrection, after which they would move on in both body and soul to their ultimate dwelling place. Depending on which eschatological tradition informed one's thinking, Mary's final presence in Paradise would have a different meaning. For those who understood Paradise to be the final resting place of the elect, Mary's present existence there would reflect what modern dogma names her 'Assumption'. Alternatively, if one viewed Paradise merely as a waiting place for souls, then Mary's presence there would not be in any sense special, but rather typical of the blessed departed, who together in Paradise await their final reward. In this way, the apocalyptic and eschatological traditions of late antiquity can help us both to organize and comprehend the theological diversity of the early Dormition traditions, providing an alternative to the modern dogmatic categories utilized by much previous scholarship.

Whether overtly or tacitly, scholars have repeatedly read the Dormition traditions through the lens of modern Roman Catholic dogmatics, classifying the various narratives according to the terms of the 1950 definition.[90] Unfortunately, however, the rather precise categories of modern dogmatic discourse are often a poor fit for the complexity manifest in the early Dormition narratives, occasionally leading these interpreters to distort the contents of some narratives, in an effort to make them conform to the modern categories. At the heart of this matter

[90] This is most evident in Mimouni's work, where it is basic to his entire approach: see e.g. Mimouni, *Dormition*, 7–21, 57–68. This emphasis is also characteristic of the works of Jugie, Baldi and Mosconi, Wenger, and Cothenet.

lies a concern with whether or not a given narrative identifies
Paradise with the 'concept of Heaven as theologically defined',
that is, does it identify Paradise as the eternal dwelling place
of the righteous. The emphasis on this particular point is very
much with an eye towards the modern Assumption dogma. If
a given narrative can be understood to identify Paradise with
this 'theological Heaven', a view not uncommon in late ancient
literature, then the account is usually classed among those
in agreement with the Vatican's dogma. In this case, Mary's
presence in the Garden is seen as reflecting her 'unique privilege',
according to which, in the words of the Assumption definition,
'she did not have to wait until the end of time for the redemption
of her body'.[91] On the other hand, if a particular text is seen to
describe Paradise as merely a temporary waiting place for souls,
and not the final abode of the resurrected elect, also a common understanding, then modern interpreters class it among
those traditions opposed to the doctrine of the Virgin's bodily
Assumption. In each case, an effort is generally made to align
these narratives with one of these understandings of Paradise
and, by consequence, with a particular opinion on the modern
dogma. Such a binary approach is unfortunately not well suited
to these literary traditions, since they do not draw these lines so
clearly as contemporary thought would have them.

Mimouni and Cothenet, for instance, in their efforts to invent
an evolutionary typology, have both struggled to conform the
fifth-century *Obsequies* to a particular understanding of Paradise
and its eschatological purpose, in the light of which they can
then argue for its association with the Bethlehem traditions and
their Assumptionless conclusion. In the *Obsequies*, they argue,
Paradise is not understood as the final resting place of the elect;
consequently, Mary's presence in Paradise at the fragment's
end is not to be read as evidence of belief in her Assumption.[92]
Cothenet and Mimouni both insist that in the *Obsequies* '[Para-
dise] is not Heaven in the theological sense of the term, but the

---

[91] Pius XII, 'Munificentissimus Deus', *Acta Apostolicae Sedis*, 42 (1950),
754; trans. Joseph C. Fenton, 'Munificentissimus Deus', *The Catholic Mind*,
49 (1951), 65.
[92] Mimouni, *Dormition*, 82, 84–5; idem, 'La Tradition littéraire syriaque de
l'histoire de la Dormition et de l'Assomption de Marie', *Parole de l'Orient*, 15
(1988–9), 150–3; Cothenet, 'Marie dans les Apocryphes', 124–9.

earthly paradise whose foundations are on the earth, and the enclosure, whence flow four rivers, reaching up to heaven.'[93] Following a well-established ancient tradition, these scholars identify Paradise more or less with the ancient Jewish notion of 'Sheol', a place where disembodied souls awaited eventual reunion with their bodies at the final judgement.[94] The concept of such a waiting place was popular in certain circles of ancient Judaism and Christianity, where it was variously conceived. In some instances, a single waiting place is shared by the souls of the just and the wicked alike, while other texts describe two separate locations, each providing the just and the damned a foretaste of their final fate.[95] Writings that adopt the latter scheme often name the waiting place of the righteous 'Paradise', and if we may count the *Obsequies* among this group, this would invite the conclusion that Mary's existence in Paradise does not truly reflect her Assumption. Understood in this context, her presence there does not anticipate the final reward of the elect, but is merely typical of the departed elect who await the final judgement in an intermediate place.

The earliest known Christian to articulate this concept of Paradise is Tertullian, who identifies Paradise as one of two waiting places prepared for the souls of the faithful departed. The first of these, Sheol or Hades, holds the vast majority of departed souls, but for the martyrs alone, God has reopened Paradise, so that they might enjoy its pleasures as they await the final judgement. 'Heaven' is yet another place, which will be opened only at the end of time to serve as the final home of the elect.[96] Similar understandings of the afterlife were expressed by Hippolytus of Rome, Hilary of Poitiers, Ambrose, and Jerome,

---

[93] Cothenet, 'Marie dans les Apocryphes', 125. See also Mimouni, *Dormition*, 82.

[94] Cothenet, 'Marie dans les Apocryphes', 125–8; Mimouni, *Dormition*, 82–5. See also Bauckham, *Fate of the Dead*, 53–4, 86–7; and Martha Himmelfarb, *Tours of Hell: An Apocalyptic Form in Jewish and Christian Literature* (Philadelphia: University of Pennsylvania Press, 1983), 108.

[95] This diversity is well described by Richard Bauckham, 'Visiting the Places of the Dead', *Proceedings of the Irish Biblical Association*, 18 (1995), 78–93; idem, 'Early Jewish Visions of Hell', *Journal of Theological Studies*, NS, 41 (1990), 355–85; and now idem, *Fate of the Dead*, esp. 49–96.

[96] Tertullian, *An.* 55–6 (J. H. Waszink, ed., *Tertulliani Opera*, pt. 2, *Opera Montanistica*, CCL 2 (Turnhout: Brepols, 1954), 861–5).

among others.[97] Origen too stands in this tradition but has made it his own, describing Paradise as a classroom for souls, where for a time they receive instruction in the course of their ascent to God.[98] Although details can vary from author to author, at the heart of this tradition lies the notion of Paradise as a temporary resting place for the elect, where they await final entrance to their eternal dwelling place, usually named 'Heaven'.

Eventually, this tradition of Paradise as a waiting place would gain wide acceptance and establish itself as the dominant eschatological perspective in Byzantium,[99] but in late antiquity it still faced fierce competition. There was in this earlier period a vibrant counter-tradition identifying Paradise with the final resting place of the just, i.e. 'Heaven in the theological sense of the term'.[100] As the Jewish apocalyptic tradition well attests, this belief was strongly rooted in late ancient Judaism.[101] The *Fourth*

---

[97] Jean Delumeau, *History of Paradise: The Garden of Eden in Myth and Tradition*, trans. Matthew O'Connell (New York: Continuum, 1995), 28.

[98] Origen, *princ.* 2. 11. 6 (Henri Crouzel and Manli Simonetti, eds., *Origène. Traité des Principes*, 5 vols., SC 252–3, 268–9, 312 (Paris: Les Éditions du Cerf, 1978, 1980, 1984), i. 408). See also Lawrence R. Hennessey, 'The Place of Saints and Sinners after Death', in Charles Kannengeisser and William L. Peterson (eds.), *Origen of Alexandria: His World and His Legacy* (Notre Dame: University of Notre Dame Press, 1988), 295–312.

[99] Antoine Wenger, 'Ciel ou Paradis: Le Séjour des âmes, d'après Phillipe le Solitaire, Dioptra, Livre IV, Chapitre X', *Byzantinische Zeitschrift*, 44 (1951), 560–1; Jean Daniélou, 'Terre et paradis chez les pères de l'église', *Eranos-Jahrbuch*, 22 (1953), 448; Delumeau, *History of Paradise*, 31–2.

[100] J. Edward Wright, *The Early History of Heaven* (New York: Oxford University Press, 2000), 188–9.

[101] Bauckham, *Fate of the Dead*, 86–8. Nevertheless, a number of apocalyptic texts consider Paradise as a temporary resting place rather than a final destination: these are described by Delumeau, *History of Paradise*, 23–7. Contrary to Delumeau, however, the *Fourth Book of Ezra* does not identify Paradise as a waiting place for souls. While it does mention such a place, it is not identified with Paradise; Paradise is instead the name for the *final* home of the elect (see n. 103 below and Bauckham, *Fate of the Dead*, 88). His interpretation of the *Ethiopic Apocalypse of Enoch* also does not do justice to the text's ambiguity on this and other issues (see e.g. Ephrem the Syrian, *Hymns on Paradise*, trans. Sebastian Brock (Crestwood, NY: St Vladimir's Seminary Press, 1990), 49, where Brock finds *Ethiopic Enoch* an example of the tradition that Paradise is 'both the primordial and the eschatological state at the end of time'). Moreover, Delumeau has perhaps overlooked an important witness to the Paradise-as-Sheol tradition in the *Vision of Ezra* 58–9 (Otto Wahl, ed., *Apocalypsis Esdrae—*

Book of Ezra (2 Esd.), for instance, a text probably composed in Palestine around 100 CE,[102] records a vision of the final judgement, when 'the pit of torment shall appear, and opposite it the Paradise of delight', places where the damned and elect respectively will spend eternity.[103] The closely related *Syriac Apocalypse of Baruch* (2 Baruch),[104] also from Palestine and of approximately the same age, similarly reports that following the resurrection and judgement, 'the extents of Paradise will be spread out for them [the righteous]'.[105] Both recensions of the *Slavonic Apocalypse of Enoch* (*2 Enoch*) also share this view, stating that after the judgement, the righteous will have 'a great indestructible light, and Paradise, great and incorruptible'.[106] Elsewhere in this same text, when Enoch actually visits this Paradise, he notes that this place is 'where rest is prepared for the righteous'.[107]

Certain of the church fathers, such as Epiphanius and Gregory of Nyssa, share a similar understanding of Paradise as the ultimate destiny of the elect,[108] but Ephrem is by far the best

---

Apocalypsis Sedrach—Visio beati Esdrae, Pseudepigrapha Veteris Testamenti Graece, 4 (Leiden: E. J. Brill, 1977), 58–9).

[102] Charlesworth, *Pseudepigrapha*, i. 520.

[103] *Fourth Book of Ezra*, 7. 36 (ff.) (Robert Weber, OSB, *et al.* eds., *Biblia sacra iuxta vulgatam versionem*, 3rd edn. (Stuttgart: Deutsche Bibelgesellschaft, 1983), 1945; translation: B. M. Metzger, in Charlesworth, *Pseudepigrapha*, i. 538).

[104] The two probably share a common source. Charlesworth, *Pseudepigrapha*, i. 617.

[105] *Syriac Apocalypse of Baruch*, 51. 11 (Michael Kmosko, ed., *Liber Apocalypseos Baruch Filii Neriae*, Patrologia Syriaca, 1/2 (Paris: Firmin-Didot et Socii, 1907), 1152, 23–4; trans. A. F. J. Klijn, in Charlesworth, *Pseudepigrapha*, i. 638).

[106] *Slavonic Apocalypse of Enoch*, 65. 10 (F. I. Anderson, trans., in Charlesworth, *Pseudepigrapha*, i. 192–3: the translation was made from Library of the Academy of Sciences of the USSR, Leningrad MSS 13. 3. 25 and 45. 13. 4; a critical text may be found in A. Vaillant, ed., *Le Livre des secrets d'Hénoch* (Paris: Institut d'études slaves, 1952), where the passage occurs on p. 62, but this edition is somewhat problematic (see Charlesworth, *Pseudepigrapha*, i. 93–4)).

[107] *Slavonic Apocalypse of Enoch*, 42. 3 (Anderson, in Charlesworth, *Pseudepigrapha*, i. 168–9; Vaillant, *Le Livre des secrets*, 106). See also Bauckham, *Fate of the Dead*, 87–8.

[108] Epiphanius, *haer*. 64. 47. 1: 'Paradise, from which, in the person of our first ancestor, we were expelled, is obviously a particular place on this earth, set

patristic source for this eschatology, and all the more so since in this instance we are dealing with ancient Syriac texts.[109] Moreover, Ephrem's notion of Paradise shares with the early Palm traditions the 'paradox' that Paradise is simultaneously both terrestrial and celestial. In contrast to some other early Christian writers, Ephrem does not distinguish between the earthly Paradise, from which Adam was expelled, and an eschatological Paradise; rather, for Ephrem, Paradise is a place simultaneously both in Heaven and on earth, standing at the intersection of these two spheres.[110] Ephrem describes Paradise as a mountain, whose physical connection with the earth is perhaps most obvious in the first of his *Hymns on Paradise*,[111] where he describes the gradual descent of Adam and his family along its slopes as their sins

apart for the untroubled rest and residence of the saints' (Karl Holl, ed.; J. Dummer, 2nd edn., *Epiphanius: Ancoratus und Panarion*, 3 vols., GCS 25, 31 (2nd edn.), 37 (2nd edn.) (Leipzig: J. C. Hinrichs, 1915; Berlin: Akademie Verlag, 1980, 1985), ii. (GCS 31), 472; trans., Frank Williams, *The Panarion of Epiphanius of Salamis*, NHS 36 (Leiden: E. J. Brill, 1994), 172). Regarding Gregory, see Daniélou, 'Terre', 445–50; he notes there is some ambiguity, but finds Gregory's *hom. opif.* a rather solid witness that 'the paradise of the first Adam' is also 'the place of eschatological beatitude' (447).

[109] For the influence of earlier Jewish thinking on Ephrem's conception of Paradise, see Nicholas Séd, 'Les Hymnes sur le Paradis de Saint Ephrem et les traditions juives', *Le Muséon*, 81 (1968), 455–501. Séd concludes that Ephrem's description of Paradise derives from traditions preserved by 'Semitic Christians' centred in Edessa. These traditions have a Jewish origin in the period 'between the apocrypha of the Old Testament and the redaction of the first midrashic collections. These primitive elements probably come from the oral *Torah* of Judaism' (501).

[110] Delumeau, *History of Paradise*, 30–2; Brock, in Ephrem, *Hymns*, 51. This was also Epiphanius' view: see n. 108 above. As Bauckham notes, the location of 'such mysterious places as the places of the dead at the furthest extremities of the earth' is a very ancient notion, present in both the *Odyssey* and the *Epic of Gilgamesh*: Bauckham, *Fate of the Dead*, 84.

[111] Ephrem's description of Paradise is, however, often paradoxical, and some interpreters have sought in the light of this to mitigate Ephrem's use of terrestrial terms, noting that although Paradise is on earth, it is nevertheless located 'outside time and space as we know them' (Brock, in Ephrem, *Hymns*, 54; see also Daniélou, 'Terre', 451). See e.g. Ephrem, *Hymns on Paradise* 11. 4 (Edmund Beck, ed., *Des Heiligen Ephraem des Syrers Hymnen de Paradiso und Contra Julianum*, CSCO 174–5 (Louvain: CSCO, 1957), 47 (Syr.) and 43 (Germ.)). See also Robert Murray, *Symbols of Church and Kingdom: A Study in Early Syriac Tradition* (Cambridge: Cambridge University Press, 1975), 306–10.

accrue, making them unworthy of being in close proximity to God,[112] who resides on the summit.[113] Between the *Shekhina*, the divine presence, and the remainder of Paradise lies the Tree of Life,[114] beneath which are 'the heights'.[115] The Tree of Knowledge separates 'the heights' from the lowest level of Paradise,[116] and the Cherub with his sword guards the boundary between the Garden and the lower slopes of the mountain,[117] dividing Paradise proper into three regions, with the 'lower slopes' lying just outside its bounds.[118]

Within this Paradise, humanity had its origin, and to this same terrestrial Paradise, the righteous will at the end of time return, restoring humanity to its original, intended state. In a strophe from his *Hymns on Paradise*, Ephrem clearly outlines this process of the initial placement in the Garden, the expulsion, and then the final restoration:

> When Adam
> was in all things complete,
> then the Lord took him
> and placed him in Paradise.
> The soul could not enter there
> of itself and for itself,
> but together they entered,
> body and soul,
> pure and perfect to that perfect place—
> and together they left it, once they had become sullied.

---

[112] Ephrem, *Hymni de paradiso* 1. 10–11 (Beck, *Hymnen de Paradiso*, 3 (Syr.) and 3 (Germ.)).

[113] Ibid. 2. 11. 6 (ibid. 7 (Syr.) and 7 (Germ)).

[114] Ibid. 3. 2 (ibid. 9 (Syr.) and 8–9 (Germ.)). On the trees of Paradise, see Tryggve Kronholm, 'The Trees of Paradise in the Hymns of Ephraem Syrus', *Annual of the Swedish Theological Institute*, 11 (1978), 48–56.

[115] Ephrem, *Hymns on Paradise*, 2. 11. 5–6 (Beck, *Hymnen de Paradiso*, 7 (Syr.) and 7 (Germ.)).

[116] Ibid. 3. 3 (ibid. 9 (Syr.) and 9 (Germ.)).

[117] Ibid. 4. 1. 6 (ibid. 13 (Syr.) and 12 (Germ.)).

[118] Brock supplies a chart outlining the structural equivalencies, noted by Ephrem, of these levels with the various parts of the Temple, Ark, Sinai, and human beings: Ephrem, *Hymns*, 53. At times, however, Ephrem refers to the 'lower slopes' as also being part of Paradise, e.g. ibid. 2. 11. 5 (Beck, *Hymnen de Paradiso*, 7 (Syr.) and 7 (Germ.)). On this, see Ignatius Ortiz de Urbina, SJ, 'Le Paradis eschatologique d'après Saint Ephrem', *Orientalia Christiana Periodica*, 21 (1955), 467–8.

From all this we should learn
    that at the Resurrection they will enter again together.[119]

From this we learn not only that Paradise is the ultimate destination of the righteous, but also that it cannot be entered by the
naked soul. Lacking its body, the soul must await the time of the
final judgement, when, rejoined to its body, it will enter Paradise
in the company of the saints. Implicitly, then, there must be
some place where the righteous souls are gathered together
in anticipation of their restoration, and Ephrem does indeed
identify such a place: it is the 'lower slopes' of Paradise. Here,

> in the delightful mansions
>   on the borders of Paradise
> do the souls of the just
>   and righteous reside,
> awaiting there
>   the bodies they love,
> so that, at the opening
>   of the Garden's gate,
> both bodies and souls might proclaim,
>   amidst Hosannas,
> 'Blessed is He who has brought Adam from Sheol
>   and returned him to Paradise in the company of many.'[120]

Therefore, at the end of time, when the dead are restored to their
bodies, the righteous will enter into paradise, with

> the lowest parts for the repentant,
>   the middle for the righteous,
> the heights for those victorious,
>   while the summit is reserved for God's Presence.[121]

Thus, the 'righteous' will spend eternity in the 'middle' parts
of Paradise, which are actually the lowest section of the Garden
proper, enclosed by the Cherub and his sword, and the 'heights',

---

[119] Ephrem, *Hymns on Paradise* 8. 9 (Beck, *Hymnen de Paradiso*, 35 (Syr.) and
32 (Germ.); trans. Brock, *Hymns*, 134).

[120] Ibid. 8. 11 (Beck, *Hymnen de Paradiso*, 35 (Syr.) and 33 (Germ.); trans.
Brock, *Hymns*, 135). For further discussion of 'Sheol' in Ephrem's thought, see
Edmund Beck, OSB, *Ephraems Hymnen über das Paradis*, Studia Anselmiana,
26 (Rome: Herder, 1951), 90–5.

[121] Ephrem, *Hymni de paradiso*, 2. 11. 5–6 (Beck, *Hymnen de Paradiso*, 7
(Syr.) and 7 (Germ.); trans. Brock, *Hymns*, 89).

the area between this lower region and the *Shekhina*, is reserved
for the martyrs. The 'lower slopes' of Paradise, according to
Ephrem, will at this time become the final resting of the 'repent-
ant', those sinners who were not quite worthy to dwell in Paradise, but equally were not deserving of Hellfire:

> Blessed is the sinner
>   who has received mercy there
> and is deemed worthy to be given access
>   to the environs of Paradise;
> even though he remains outside,
>   he may pasture there through grace.[122]

So at the end of time, when the faithful receive their bodies and
re-enter Paradise, the place in which their souls had previously awaited resurrection will become the eternal home of those
deserving neither Heaven nor Hell, a sort of 'Limbo', 'where
those who have found mercy can receive chastisement and
forgiveness'.[123]

This conception of the earthly and eschatological Paradise
articulated in Ephrem's *Hymns on Paradise* differs significantly
from the model used by Cothenet and Mimouni to interpret
the early Dormition traditions, and although Ephrem's hymns
offer a particularly vivid example of this view, it is by no means
unique.[124] According to Ephrem and various other ancient
sources, the terrestrial Paradise from which Adam was expelled
is to be the final resting place of the elect. At present, Paradise
is empty, and the souls of the just await their final resurrection
in another location.[125] According to this conception of Paradise,

---

[122] Ephrem, *Hymni de paradiso*, 10. 14. 1–3 (Beck, *Hymnen de Paradiso*, 45 (Syr.) and 42 (Germ.); trans. Brock, *Hymns*, 153).

[123] Ibid. 10. 14. 6 (Beck, *Hymnen de Paradiso*, 45 (Syr.) and 42 (Germ.); tran. Brock, *Hymns*, 153).

[124] See Séd, 'Les Hymnes', 501.

[125] Javier Teixidor ('Le Thème de la descente aux enfers chez Saint Éphrem', *L'Orient Syrien*, 6 (1961), 25–40) has argued that Paradise is not completely empty in Ephrem's understanding, but instead that Ephrem envisions Adam as presently existing in Paradise in a resurrected state, as a passage from Ephrem could seem to suggest (*Hymni de Paradiso* 4. 6. 5–6 (Beck, *Hymnen de Paradiso*, 14 (Syr.) and 13 (Germ.))). Ephrem's reference here, however, seems to be primarily to the 'New Adam', rather than the 'Old'. When after his resurrection, Christ re-entered Paradise in the flesh, he in effect brought 'Adam' back into Paradise. As humanity had once been expelled from Paradise in Adam, so in the

Mary's resurrection there would be a truly unique event, an anticipation of the blessed state awaiting the elect at the end of time, and one frequently encounters just such an understanding of Paradise in the earliest Dormition traditions. Yet this is by no means the only view: certain Dormition narratives clearly suppose a version of the Paradise-as-Sheol tradition, while others, including many of the earliest narratives, do not clearly fit either category, presenting hybrid or contradictory views of Paradise. In the light of this range of possibilities then, it seems quite likely that these different eschatological views, rather than any kind of dogmatic development, underlie the diverse fates ascribed to Mary at the conclusion of the various Dormition narratives.

The fact of the matter is that in most of the earliest extant Dormition narratives, the eschatological purpose of Paradise is rather confused and muddled, making their classification according to modern dogmatic categories particularly complicated. Such is the case, for instance, in the earliest Palm narratives, the *Obsequies* and the *Liber Requiei*. As demonstrated above, we can with a fair amount of certainty look to the *Liber Requiei* for the lost conclusion to *Obsequies*, and in instances where other early Palm narratives confirm the witness of the *Liber Requiei*, it is almost undeniable that these traditions represent the earliest known stage of the Palm traditions. According to the longest of the *Obsequies* fragments, Mary's body was brought after her death to the Garden of Paradise, where it was resurrected beneath the Tree of Life, in the presence of the

human being that was joined to God, it has finally re-entered. 'Adam', in the sense of fallen humanity, has been returned to Paradise by Christ's, the New Adam's, resurrection. By resurrecting his body and taking it into Paradise, he has 'cosmically' resurrected and restored 'Adam' to Paradise, both in actuality and in potential. Note that in the preceding strophe, Ephrem writes that 'Through Mary Adam had another robe', which makes more apparent this collapsing of all humanity into 'Adam', particularly the 'New Adam', Christ (ibid. 4. 5. 4 (Beck, *Hymnen de Paradiso*, 13 (Syr.) and 13 (Germ.); trans. Brock, 99; see also the note IV.5 on p. 191)). This interpretation is all the more likely in the light of Ephrem's unambiguous assertion elsewhere that Paradise is presently empty (e.g. ibid. 5. 11 (Beck, *Hymnen de Paradiso*, 18 (Syr.) and 13 (Germ.))). On this see also Beck, *Ephraems Hymnen*, 34–6, Sebastian Brock, *The Luminous Eye: The Spiritual World Vision of Saint Ephrem the Syrian*, rev. edn., Cistercian Studies, 124 (Kalamazoo, MI: Cistercian Publications, 1992), 88–9, and Brock in Ephrem, *Hymns*, 55–6.

apostles. Following her resurrection, Christ obliged his mother and the apostles with a tour of the heavenly places, in an account similar to the one that would later circulate separately in the Byzantine world under the title the *Apocalypse of the Virgin*.[126] Although the Syriac fragments are unfortunately interrupted just as this excursion begins, the account is continued in the Ethiopic version and, much more succinctly, in the closely related early Irish versions.[127] The tour begins with a visit to the places of punishment, where Mary and the apostles witness various fates allotted to the damned. Drawing on traditions evident in the second-century *Apocalypse of Peter*, as well as in such roughly contemporary texts as the *Apocalypse of Paul*, this ancient version of Dante's *Inferno* describes the different torments prepared for the wicked, explaining how each is suited to their particular crimes.[128]

The Virgin successfully intercedes on behalf of the damned, securing for them three hours of respite every Sunday, after which the party returns to the Tree of Life in Paradise, where the apocalypse continues. Unfortunately, the Irish parallels cease at this point, and the episode that follows is not known from other early Palm narratives, although it seems likely that such a return to Paradise would have concluded the tour of Hell described above.[129] Upon re-entering Paradise, Mary is greeted by the souls of Abraham, Isaac, Jacob, and David, along with the souls of many others who had been 'brought from death to life by his resurrection and placed in the Paradise of the living'. The list of names is exclusively male, excepting only Elizabeth, who was

---

[126] For more on these traditions, see Bauckham, *Fate of the Dead*, 332–62 and Simon C. Mimouni, 'Les *Apocalypses de la Vierge*: État de la question', *Apocrypha*, 4 (1993), 101–12. Bauckham correctly notes against Mimouni (who follows Wenger) that the *Obsequies* apocalypse and the *Apocalypse of the Virgin* are separate texts.

[127] Syriac fragment published in Wright, *Contributions*, ܪܘܚܐ (Syr.) and 46–8 (Eng.). See the parallels and continuation in *Liber Requiei* 88–103 (Arras, *De Transitu*, 52–60 (Eth.) and 34–9 (Lat.)); Donahue, *Testament of Mary*, 50–5; and Herbert and McNamara, *Irish Biblical Apocrypha*, 129–31.

[128] Concerning these related early Christian apocalypses, see Himmelfarb, *Tours of Hell*, esp. 8–29. Concerning the relation of the *Apocalypse of Paul* to the *Obsequies* apocalypse, see Bauckham, *Fate of the Dead*, 344–6, where he tentatively argues that the *Apocalypse of Paul* is probably dependent on the *Obsequies* apocalypse, contrary to what has often been supposed.

[129] The reasons for this omission were given above: see n. 43.

present to meet the Virgin, despite the fact, we are told, that 'there was another place for the women'.[130] No further explanation is given as to what this 'other place' might be, but it seems clear that this narrative imagined some sort of gender separation in the heavenly realms. It may be that the Garden of Paradise was thought to be reserved for men alone, the souls of women being assigned to some other corner of heaven. Alternatively, the text may envision a divided Paradise, in which the souls of men and women were separated from one another inside the Garden. In either case, the narrative reaches its conclusion in this male territory, whether that be the entire Garden or only a part of the Garden, and Mary's establishment here after her death crosses this gender boundary, a transgression presumably allowed in the light of her supremely exalted status.

Also noteworthy in this account is the explicit identification of the inhabitants of Paradise as 'souls', indicating their existence there in a disembodied state. This is not altogether surprising, given the popular ancient view that Paradise was a place where the souls of the righteous awaited the resurrection; nevertheless, it presents quite a contrast with the preceding descriptions of the places of punishment, in which the souls of the wicked are clearly embodied. Some have mouths and hands that burn with flames; others are bound and continually pelted by demons with stones, prompting the Virgin to wonder why their bones do not crumble into dust. If the elect exist in Paradise without their bodies, it seems clear that the damned already have theirs, complete with mouths, hands, and bones. Although the early Irish texts confirm that Mary's vision of the embodied damned belongs to the earliest traditions, unfortunately they do not narrate her reception in Paradise by the 'souls' of the patriarchs. Elsewhere in the *Liber Requiei*, however, in a passage with clear parallels from the other early Palm narratives, there is further suggestion that the disembodied souls of the elect presently await their resurrection in the Garden of Paradise. As much is intimated by the Great Angel (who is also Christ) as he describes for Mary what will happen when she comes forth from the body:

---

[130] ጠባሕቱ፡ ባዕድ፡ መካኖን፡ ለአንስት፡ *Liber Requiei* 66 (Arras, *De Transitu*, i. 59 (Eth.) & 39 (Lat.)).

And when you depart from the body, I will come myself on the fourth day; for this extra day is allowed, because our Saviour arose on the third day. And not only will I lead you away on the fourth day, but all those who keep the words of our Saviour. I will come again to those and lead them away to the Paradise of joy. Their bodies will remain new there, and the bodies of the holy people will not have a stench, because they took care of themselves while living on earth without sin. And they will come to the place where Adam and Eve were also, until the day of resurrection. And when the Lord will come with angels, he will lead them each with their own bodies.[131]

Although the passage is somewhat obscure, it appears to indicate that the disembodied souls of the righteous presently await their resurrection, and only at the end of time will they be rejoined to their bodies. Admittedly it is not exactly clear how to read this passage, but through comparing both the Ethiopic and Georgian versions, it seems to relate that the bodies and souls of the righteous are both gathered in Paradise, although they presently remain separate from each other. Only on the day of the resurrection will they be restored to one another. Such would be in agreement with the description of the patriarchs as souls at the text's conclusion, in any case.

Yet despite such indications that the souls of the elect currently exist without their bodies in Paradise, the resurrected Virgin remains in Paradise at the narrative's conclusion, where she clearly is not unresurrected. On the contrary, Mary remains permanently resurrected in the Garden of Paradise, where she ostensibly lives among the disembodied souls of the righteous dead. From the viewpoint of modern dogmatics, this presents a slightly complicated ending: Mary has attained the final state, resurrection, but she lives among the unresurrected souls of the just, in a place which may or may not be their final resting place. Some would resolve this tension by inventing the Virgin's eventual unresurrection, thus making Mary's final state consistent with the disembodiedness of the other inhabitants of Paradise, as well as interpreting these literary traditions as

---

[131] van Esbroeck, 'Apocryphes géorgiens', 72 (Geor.) and 75 (Lat.). See also *Liber Requiei* 10 (Arras, *De Transitu*, 6 (Eth.) and 4 (Lat.)); and Wenger, *L'Assomption*, 212–13. I have cited the Georgian version because it is slightly clearer, although the Ethiopic version is extremely close, as can be seen in the appended translations, and Wenger's early Greek narrative presents a much more condensed version of this passage.

opposed to the modern dogma of the Assumption.[132] But others, in an effort to conform this tradition to the terms of Assumption dogma, have overlooked the indications that only souls of the elect are present in Paradise, apparently without their bodies.[133] In actuality, neither dogmatic position is clearly represented in this text, whose complex understanding of Paradise contains elements that suggest and contradict both views at once.

A rather different view of Paradise and its position among the heavenly realms emerges from the early 'Bethlehem' traditions, and particularly the various Six Books narratives. Like the earliest Palm traditions, many of these narratives devote their final two books to Mary's otherworldly journey following her death, the details of which she later entrusted to the apostle John, who wrote them down. The fragmentary version from Smith Lewis's fifth-century palimpsest codex unfortunately lacks much of the tradition's apocalyptic conclusion, and so we are dependent largely on Wright's complete sixth-century manuscript for knowing this portion of the narrative in its earliest form.[134] The vision of the other world presented here is considerably more complex and contradictory than that of the preceding traditions. Moreover, it is quite an independent account, without the obvious links to traditions in the apocalypses of Peter, Paul, and later on, Mary, that characterize the apocalypse of the *Obsequies* and the *Liber Requiei*.

The celestial journey similarly begins as Christ returns Mary's lifeless body to the Paradise of Eden and rejoins it with her soul.[135] Once she has been restored to life, Christ explains that he has come to show her the glory of his Father's house. The tour begins with the Garden of Paradise itself, where Elijah, Enoch, Moses, and Peter appear to greet the Virgin. The first three, of course, were themselves rather famously brought to heaven in their bodies (see below), but Peter's presence here is somewhat

[132] Cothenet, 'Marie dans les Apocryphes', 124–5; Mimouni, *Dormition*, 81–2.

[133] See e.g. Mimouni, *Dormition*, 252. Examples of other studies built around this assumption are Manns, *Le Récit* and Testa, 'L'origine e lo sviluppo'.

[134] This point is apparently missed by Bauckham in *Fate of the Dead*, 346–60, where he treats the apocalyptic section from Smith Lewis' edition as if it were from her 5th- or 6th-century palimpsest. It is not: it has been restored from a 19th-century manuscript, and therefore must be used with caution.

[135] Wright, 'Departure', ܡ̈ܠ–ܠ (Syr.) and 155–60 (Eng.).

strange, especially given his very recent participation in the events of Mary's earthly funeral. Inside the Garden of Paradise, Christ shows his mother the things that he has 'prepared for the just', including the 'mansions of the just', the 'banquet halls of the martyrs', and 'the glorious mansion in which the righteous will live' or 'were living', depending upon how one chooses to read the Syriac at this point.[136]

Then, at the cries of the 'cherub of the sword', Mary 'ascends' from the Garden with her son, into 'the heaven in which is the glory of [the] Father', where Christ promises to show her the 'heaven of heavens and the waters which are above the heaven', and above these waters the 'decorated Jerusalem', where the Father dwells.[137] Following this announcement of their itinerary, Mary views an assortment of the heavenly territories lying outside the bounds of Paradise, eventually coming upon the souls of the just in their place of waiting:

And she saw too, in a place in that world which passeth not away, many lights shining very brightly, and mansions without number; and between one mansion and another a great scent of perfumes was diffused, and there were trumpets sounding over the mansions. And she saw the tabernacles of the just, and multitudes standing on this side of these tabernacles. My Lady Mary said to the Messiah, 'My Lord Rabbuli, what are these?' The Messiah said to my Lady Mary: 'These are the tabernacles of the just, and these lights are shining in their honour; and from a distance they behold their happiness, until the day of the resurrection, when they shall inherit their mansions.'[138]

Likewise, in this same place, still somewhere outside the Garden of Paradise, the Virgin beholds the souls of the damned as they await their final sentence:

And again my Lady Mary saw another place . . . And [people] were standing on this side of that darkness, and weeping and in sorrow, as they stood at a distance. My Lady Mary said to the Messiah: 'My Lord Rabbuli, what are those?' The Messiah said to the blessed one: 'This that is roaring is Gehenna, which is kindled for the wicked; and these who are standing and looking upon it are the sinners; and from a distance they are beholding their torment, and knowing for what they are reserved at the last day; for the day of judgment is not yet come, that

---

[136] Wright, 'Departure', ܡܢ (Syr.) and 156 (Eng.).

[137] Ibid. ܡܢ–ܩܒ (Syr.) and 156–7 (Eng.).

[138] Ibid. ܢܡ (Syr.) and 158 (Eng.).

they should receive the inheritance of darkness; and at the time of the judgment, those who have neglected my commands, which I have commanded them, and have not listened to me, shall be tormented in this Gehenna.'[139]

Immediately following their visit to these celestial way stations, the narrative reports that Jesus 'took his mother and came to the Paradise of Eden',[140] thus indicating a distinction between these places of waiting, seen during the excursion from Paradise, and Paradise itself, where 'mansions' are 'prepared for the just'. After her return to Paradise, Mary once again is not unresurrected, and despite the false indications of Jugie, Cothenet, and Mimouni to the contrary,[141] she remains in body and soul, summoning St John to come and record all the things that she has seen, so that they may also be known on the earth.[142]

The eschatological significance of Paradise, and hence of the Virgin's resurrection, is difficult to determine in this narrative, the primary issue being the ambiguity of the Syriac at a key point. As noted above, when Christ initially shows his mother around the Garden of Paradise, he points out to her 'the glorious mansion in which the righteous will live', or alternatively, 'in which the righteous were living'. The verb in question here is an active participle, and as such it does not have reference to a definite time in itself.[143] Although the form is often used with present meaning, the active participle is also used rather frequently in Syriac in place of an imperfect to express the future, even in dependent clauses such as this one.[144] Wright opted to translate the form as a present, so that in his translation the righteous are represented as actually living in the mansion already;[145] but looking at the original text, one can see the ambiguity, and in the light of various other aspects, a future meaning seems quite possible. This would seem to be the indication of the passage cited above, in which Mary beholds the

---

[139] Ibid. ܡܗ‑ܟܡ (Syr.) and 158–9 (Eng.).

[140] Ibid. ܡܟ (Syr.) and 159 (Eng.).

[141] Jugie, *La Mort*, 122–3; Cothenet, 'Marie dans les Apocryphes', 124–5; Mimouni, *Dormition*, 97.

[142] Wright, 'Departure', ܡ‑ܟܡ (Syr.) and 159–60 (Eng.).

[143] ܡܗ ܟ‑ܒܝܬܗ ܘܒ ܟܢܕܐ ܟܒܣܝܐ ܟܕܟܢܟ ܟܣܒܝ ܡܗ, ibid. ܡܗ (Syr.). On the usage, see Theodor Nöldeke, *Compendious Syriac Grammar*, 2nd edn., 211.

[144] Nöldeke, *Compendious Syriac Grammar*, 2nd edn., 213–15.

[145] Wright, 'Departure', 156 (Eng.).

righteous awaiting the day when they will inherit their mansions, which they do not yet possess.[146] Thus it is not entirely certain whether Mary saw the elect already dwelling in Paradise, as well as outside, or if instead she saw first in Paradise the places where the elect will dwell in the future, and then, outside, the elect themselves gazing upon their future home.

It may be of significance, however, that no one is present in Paradise without his or her body. The two apostles present, John and Peter, were still living when the Virgin departed this life,[147] and Enoch and Elijah had, according to biblical tradition, taken up to heaven in their bodies, without dying.[148] Moses, it is true, did die according to biblical tradition,[149] but extra-canonical traditions later developed concerning his assumption, including an apocryphal work, *The Assumption of Moses*.[150] Furthermore, according to early Christian tradition, Moses had already been resurrected in order to appear with Elijah at the Transfiguration.[151] The implication that no one is without a body might suggest that one must be embodied to be present in Paradise, and this in turn would indicate that Paradise will be home to the righteous only after their resurrection: both of these points were espoused by Ephrem, for instance, as seen above.[152]

---

[146] Such is also the assessment of Bauckham, *Fate of the Dead*, 56, 88, 347, 351; idem, 'Visiting the Places of the Dead', 85; and idem, 'Early Jewish Visions of Hell', 362. Bauckham, however, regards this as merely a confusion, and does not comment on the potential of the ambiguous Syriac form.

[147] Ibid., ܡܢܝܚ (Syr.) and 136–7 (Eng.).

[148] Gen. 5: 24 and 2 Kgs. 2: 9–12; cf. Bauckham, *Fate of the Dead*, 357–8, where he also comments on the significance of Enoch and Elijah.

[149] Deut. 32: 48–52; 34: 1–8.

[150] Johannes Tromp, ed., *The Assumption of Moses: A Critical Edition with Commentary*, Studia in Veteris Testamenti Pseudepigrapha, 10 (Leiden: E. J. Brill, 1993). See the discussion of Moses' 'assumption' on pp. 281–5.

[151] Matt. 17: 1–8 and par. This interpretation is made by writers as diverse as Tertullian (*Res.* 55 (J. G. P. Borleffs, ed., *Tertulliani Opera*, pt. 2, *Opera Montanistica*, CCL 2 (Turnhout: Brepols, 1954), 1001–3)), Origen (*sel. In Ps.* 1. 5 (PG 12. 1096); preserved in Methodius, *res.* 1. 22. 2–5 (D. G. Natanael Bonwetsch, ed., *Methodius*, GCS 27 (Leipzig: J. C. Hinrichs, 1917), 246) and Epiphanius, *haer.* 64. 14. 9 (Holl/Dummer, *Epiphanius*, ii. (GCS 31), 424)), the author of the Nag Hammadi *Treatise on Resurrection* (48. 6–19 (Harold W. Attridge, ed., *Nag Hammadi Codex I (The Jung Codex)*, 2 vols., NHS 22 (Leiden: E. J. Brill, 1985), i. 154–5), and Ephrem, *Hymni de Paradiso* 4. 6 (Beck, *Hymnen de Paradiso*, 14 (Syr.) and 13 (Germ))).

[152] See n. 119 above.

Nevertheless, as in the previous group of narratives, the precise eschatological role of the Garden of Paradise is somewhat unclear in this vision, as it sometimes is in apocalyptic traditions. Neither position on the modern dogma is clearly expressed, and the efforts of interpreters to conform these traditions to one of these two views have served only to distort their vision of Paradise. Nevertheless, if one were forced to make a decision, Mary's final state in this narrative seems more like an Assumption than not, since Mary's resurrection in Paradise is clearly both special and enduring.

In regards to Smith Lewis's early version of the Six Books, we are not completely ignorant. Although this narrative's (probable) apocalyptic conclusion is now lost, the words of Christ to his mother before her death suggest something about its views on the Virgin's bodily presence in Paradise. Just before her soul departs her body, the Saviour says to Mary:

> Now I will make thy body go into the Paradise of Eden, and there it will be until the resurrection. I will also give angels for thine honour, and they shall stand before thee holding lights and lamps until I shall come and dissolve the heaven and the earth, and shall give bliss to the righteous and torment and darkness to the wicked.[153]

The implication of this passage, which does not appear in Wright's version, seems to be that after her death, Mary's lifeless body is to be taken to heaven, where it will await reunion with her soul at 'the resurrection', presumably a reference to the general resurrection at the end of time. This narrative does not appear to relate her bodily Assumption, since there is no indication that Mary has prematurely received the reward of the just; on the contrary, the passage suggests that she must wait like everyone else. Only her inanimate body has been transferred to Paradise, which does not seem to have any particular eschatological purpose.

Several other early narratives share a similar view, including the Coptic homilies attributed to Cyril of Jerusalem and Evodius of Rome, as well as the Greek Dormition narrative attributed to the apostle John. All these narratives describe the transfer of Mary's lifeless body to Paradise, without the restoration of her soul; the fate of her soul, on the other hand, is generally

---

[153] Smith Lewis, *Apocrypha*,ܗ (Syr.) and 55 (Eng.).

unspecified, although Ps.-John's Greek narrative does mention its transfer to 'the treasures of the Father'.[154] While these texts frequently express the view, common to many of the Dormition traditions, that Paradise is a place somehow both in this world and the next, they do not assign any significant eschatological purpose to the Garden of Paradise. They merely identify it as the present location of the Virgin's inanimate body, where it awaits the general resurrection at the end of time, when it will rise together with the bodies of others among the righteous. This conclusion is somewhat unusual when compared with other Paradise traditions from the late ancient Near East: although one frequently encounters the concept of Paradise as a place where the souls of the just await their resurrection, I am aware of no other tradition in which Paradise is instead identified as a place of waiting for bodies. In contrast to the preceding traditions then, these narratives do not envision the premature redemption of Mary's body. Instead, they emphasize its special exemption from the corruption of the grave, to which all other mortal bodies are subject. This is, however, consistent with the strong emphasis throughout the early Dormition traditions on the purity of Mary's body, even after her death. It was unthinkable that this body, which had remained so pure in life, would at death lie decaying in the grave. One solution was to have Mary's body and soul rejoined in Paradise, but this final group of narratives resolves the matter differently, yet in a way still involving the Virgin's bodily presence in Paradise. Rather than being resurrected in Paradise, Mary's inanimate body is placed in the Garden, beneath the Tree of Life, where, according to an apparently unique privilege, it is preserved from decay and corruption until it will be rejoined with her soul at the general resurrection.

Although the palimpsest codex published by Smith Lewis appears to describe the preservation of Mary's inanimate body in Paradise, this view is not typical of the earliest Six Books traditions. Moreover, because the conclusion to Smith Lewis's version is lacking, it remains uncertain exactly how the complete

---

[154] Konstantin Tischendorf, ed., *Apocalypses Apocryphae* (Leipzig: Herm. Mendelssohn, 1866), 108. This it shares with the other early Bethlehem traditions, namely the Six Books, as discussed in n. 141 above. Nevertheless, unlike them, it does not continue to describe the reunion of her body and soul.

version would have proceeded to describe the moment when the Virgin gave up her soul and the fate of her body once it arrived in Paradise: we do not know if perhaps it was resurrected, even temporarily, or if instead it remained inanimate to await the final resurrection. There may be some indication of how this narrative once continued in the four palimpsest fragments published by Smith Lewis in an appendix to her edition of the codex. Two of these fifth-century fragments describe parts of the Virgin's apocalyptic journey, and while one of them is of little use for the present matter, since it describes the areas outside Paradise, the other fragment offers some tantalizing hints regarding the conclusion of these traditions during the fifth and sixth centuries. The relevant fragment unfortunately breaks off just after Christ has come to the lifeless body of his mother in the Garden of Paradise, but not before he commands his mother 'Arise' in the fragment's final words.[155] This would certainly appear to indicate her resurrection, as is described in both Wright's version and the early Palm traditions, but we cannot be sure how or if this fragment relates to Smith Lewis's early palimpsest codex.

Mary's resurrection is also described in the nineteenth-century manuscript used by Smith Lewis to complete her fragmentary palimpsest codex, a manuscript which, despite its youth, preserves a conclusion very similar to the one in the four Sinai palimpsest fragments. Moreover, Mary's resurrection as related in this modern manuscript is not temporary, but it endures until the completion of the narrative. In spite of this, however, it is still not clear in this version if Mary has prematurely attained the final reward of the just, since immediately following her resurrection in Paradise, 'she saw the just ones who were standing there. And they went before her weaving the crowns of the priests. For the garments of the just are being prepared for the day of the resurrection.'[156] The just are described as 'standing', as if perhaps already in their bodies, but their 'garments' are being prepared for the day of resurrection, suggesting that they still may not have attained their final reward in the resurrected state. Here again, the eschatological significance of Paradise is not exactly clear, and consequently, neither

---

[155] Smith Lewis, *Apocrypha*, ܡܝܚ (Syr.).

[156] Ibid. ܠ (Syr.) and 65 (Eng.).

is the position of this text regarding the question of Mary's Assumption.

The same holds true in the Ethiopic and Arabic versions of the Six Books, where the eschatological significance of Paradise, and hence the Virgin's resurrection, is equally difficult to determine. In the Ethiopic version, as in Wright's Syriac version, the righteous appear to await the resurrection simultaneously in two separate places, one in Paradise and the other somewhere outside.[157] Moreover, it is not made entirely clear in this narrative that the Virgin has been resurrected: after the separation of her body and soul, her body is taken to Paradise, and when Christ later comes to her in Paradise, her body has clearly somehow become animate. With such incoherent data, what sort of determination can one make regarding the narrative's position on the Virgin's Assumption? Traditionally this narrative has been classified, like the other Six Books narratives, among those failing to describe Mary's Assumption, but in truth the matter is not so simple. The conclusions to Wright's Six Books narrative and the Ethiopic version, for instance, seem to speak more of an 'Assumption' than not, since the Virgin has been permanently resurrected on the 'other side' in anticipation of humanity's final reward, even if she does not now reside in 'Heaven in the theological sense of the term'. Even according to the Vatican's 1950 definition, this would meet the basic criteria for an Assumption,[158] since regardless of her location, Mary clearly exists in the final state of the just, bodily resurrection. Only at the end of time will the remainder of the just attain this state, and even if she is not yet in their final resting place, her enduring, bodily resurrection speaks more of her Assumption than otherwise.

[157] Immediately following her resurrection in Paradise, the Virgin beholds there 'the good things that God has prepared for those who love him', including the 'dwelling of the saints' and the 'dwelling of the martyrs and the crowns upon their heads' (Chaine, *Apocrypha*, 45 (Eth.) and 39 (Lat.)). From the latter we may deduce that she also saw in paradise martyrs who were presently occupying their dwelling. Later in the text, after the Virgin has temporarily left Paradise and before her return, she sees the dwellings of the 'just and the good', wherein they are 'expecting the joy and happiness of the last day' (Chaine, *Apocrypha*, 47 (Eth.) and 41 (Lat.)).

[158] 'Mary was exempted from the general law for humankind which predicated that the human body must wait until the end of the world to rejoin the already glorious soul.' Pius XII, 'Munificentissimus Deus', 754; trans. Fenton, 'Munificentissimus Deus', 65.

Yet at the same time, such a formulation does not fit the understanding of the Assumption adopted by Martin Jugie and most scholars who have followed in his wake. According to Jugie's criteria, an 'Assumption' must include description of Mary's 'triumphal entry in body and soul to the special place called Heaven'.[159] The Virgin's presence in 'Heaven in the theological sense of the term' is seen as a fundamental characteristic of her Assumption, and presumably Mary's existence in the final state of the elect, resurrection, but in some eschatological waiting place, would fail to meet such a criterion. But to complicate matters even further, the Catholic tradition itself does not always distinguish clearly between 'Heaven' and the place where the souls of the righteous await their final resurrection. As Caspar Friethoff notes in his explanation of the Assumption dogma, the teaching of the Catholic church, according to the fourteenth and seventeenth General Councils, as well as Benedict XII, is that the souls of the righteous 'were, are, and shall be in heaven even before the resurrection of their bodies and the general judgement'.[160] Understood in this manner, the final judgement brings not a change of address, but an existential change, which seems to account for Pius XII's emphasis not on the Virgin's final location, but on her premature resurrection as the primary sign of her Assumption.[161]

This particular eschatological perspective is embodied in the Arabic version of the Six Books, where the souls of the just already inhabit their final resting place in a disembodied state. Their final reward then, will not be relocation to a better neighbourhood, but instead, as Christ explains to the resurrected Mary, the return of their bodies, enabling them even greater enjoyment of their blessed state: 'These are the tabernacles of the pious just, and they are the ones standing in them. . . . And on the last day . . . they will delight in it with more joy than this when their souls have been returned to their bodies, eternally and without end.'[162] Therefore, Mary's permanent resurrection

---

[159] Jugie, *La Mort*, 1.

[160] Caspar Friethoff, OP, 'The Dogmatic Definition of the Assumption', *The Thomist*, 14 (1951), 41.

[161] Pius XII, 'Munificentissimus Deus', 754.

[162] هذه مصلات الابرار الصالحين وهم وقوف فيها وهذا النور لكراميهم عندى وفىَ يوم الاخير يقّقوا لحتّ فى الخيرات ويتلذّذون بهابفرح افضل من هذا اذا رجعت ارواحهم الى اجسادهم دايمًا

establishes her prematurely in the final state of the elect, which depends not on a specific location, but on embodiment. Since she, in the words of Pius XII, 'did not have to wait until the end of time for the redemption of her body',[163] her enduring, bodily resurrection could very reasonably be viewed as an Assumption, even though this narrative too has long been classed among those that do not describe the Virgin's Assumption.

Nevertheless, such theological hairsplitting should not obscure the larger issues, namely, the eschatological diversity of the early Dormition legends and the inappropriateness of modern dogmatic categories for analysing the ancient traditions. The complex variety of the ancient traditions, and even of modern dogmatic definitions, makes such an endeavour highly questionable to say the least. We must disengage these traditions from the modern theological concerns that have often engulfed them. The effort to force these narratives to fit modern dogmatic categories is frequently distorting and confusing, particularly since the lines drawn by these more recent discussions were often quite faint, if they even existed at all, in the late fifth or early sixth century. There was, for instance, no clear notion of an Immaculate Conception urging these ancient writers to define a belief in Mary's immortality;[164] nor does a typological development of dogma seem likely, according to which these traditions passed through each of the various modern dogmatic categories along the way to their final form. Rather, the theological diversity of these traditions regarding Mary's ultimate fate probably has its source in the divergent notions of Paradise that were circulating in late antiquity. It would appear that the tradition of Mary's transfer to Paradise is in some sense primitive: it is a constant feature of these otherwise diverse traditions. What a particular writer (or community) made of this established tradition seems to depend primarily on how he or she understood the eschatological significance of Paradise. The narratives generally give

---

Maximilian Enger, ed., اخبار يوحنّا السليح فى نقلة امّ المسيح (*Akhbâr Yûhannâ as-salîh fi naqlat umm al-masîh*) لا زوال, id est *Ioannis Apostoli de Transitu Beatae Mariae Virginis Liber* (Elberfeld: R. L. Friderichs, 1854), 94.

[163] Pius XII, 'Munificentissimus Deus', 754; trans., Fenton, 'Munificentissimus Deus', 65.

[164] Although see Mimouni's hypothesis regarding Julianism as described in Ch. 4.

only a confused, if often colourful, indication of what this significance may be, without any effort to present a clear, precise dogmatic statement for or against the Virgin's Assumption. On the contrary, most narratives fit very poorly the categories offered by modern dogmatics, the overemphasis of which has led scholarship to overlook, and even occasionally modify, various details of their conclusions. This is largely because the nature of such dogmatic pronouncements is generally to contain theological diversity: we must instead develop an approach to these ancient traditions that acknowledges and represents the polyphony of their voices. This is best accomplished, I propose, by allowing them to tell us the significance of Mary's presence in the Garden of Paradise, rather than vice versa.

CONCLUSIONS

The conceptualization of the ancient Dormition legends within a narrative of either dogmatic evolution or theological decline from a single origin does not enjoy very much support from the traditions themselves. Chief among the problems is our inability to identify any one of the various extant 'types' of the Dormition legends as chronologically prior to the others. On the contrary, each of the major types first appears almost simultaneously at the moment when the Dormition traditions first come into historical view. Likewise, the related liturgical and literary traditions offer no indication that any of the topographical traditions linkedwith the ancient Dormition traditions antedate the others. To these factors may be added the eschatological diversity and complexity of the early Dormition traditions, which further complicate any effort to identify an original tradition. In the early Christian imagination, Paradise was often a fluid category, whose precise nature and purpose did not always conform to the limits of human understanding, and this is certainly the case in the visions of Paradise reported in the early Dormition traditions. Consequently, the theological diversity of the ancient Dormition legends may itself ensue from the range of ancient opinions regarding the eschatological role of Paradise. Since these narratives do not fit the dogmatic categories of a developmental typology, and it is not possible to identify an original tradition, we may conclude that the various narrative types, while they appear to have drawn upon certain common traditions, initially arose independently and not in an evolutionary succession.

4

The Prehistory and Origins of the Dormition and Assumption Traditions

As seen in the preceding chapter, an important focus of the quest for 'origins' that has occupied much previous scholarship on the early Dormition and Assumption traditions has been the effort to determine the earliest form of these diverse legends, an endeavour that has not met with very much success. In the context of this same quest, there has been similar interest in identifying the particular Christian milieu that first gave birth to these traditions, a topic that has generated much speculation. If such speculation has often been bold (and occasionally even over-bold), it is none the less warranted, at least in some degree, by the nature of the earliest extant traditions themselves. It seems altogether unlikely that these diverse traditions suddenly appeared *ex nihilo* at the very moment when they first come into our historical view. In fact, several of the earliest extant narratives themselves attest to the prior existence of written traditions that were their sources, as was already noted in Ch. 1. For instance, the earliest Bethlehem traditions, the Syriac Six Books narratives, begin by describing a global search that resulted in the miraculous 'recovery' of a text preserving the ancient traditions of Mary's Dormition, which had previously been 'lost'. Likewise, certain of the earliest Palm narratives indicate the existence of archaic written traditions, which are explicitly characterized as theologically problematic. Both the narrative of Ps.-Melito and John of Thessalonica's homilies refer to earlier, 'heretical' accounts of Mary's Dormition, which they have undertaken to revise (or 'restore') into a more 'orthodox' version.

Such data have frequently invited modern scholars to pry

behind the wall of silence that surrounds the earliest history of these traditions in an attempt to discover their original milieu. Of the various literary traditions, the Palm traditions are un-doubtedly the most intriguing in this regard, manifesting the clearest evidence of a prior existence somewhere along the theological margins of early Christianity. Perhaps the most frequently met hypothesis in regard to these narrative traditions is the notion that the Palm traditions first took shape in an early 'Jewish-Christian' group from Palestine. This view is especially associated with the Studium Biblicum Franciscanum in Jeru-salem and Bellarmino Bagatti's theories regarding the 'Church from the Circumcision', a group of theologically peculiar Jewish-Christians that he identifies as the earliest Christian community of Jerusalem. In some ways, there is much to recommend this interpretation, as we will see in a moment, but there is also much to caution us, not the least of which is the highly speculative nature of the 'Church from the Circumcision' as Bagatti identifies it. Alternatively, a few scholars have rather briefly suggested the possibility of an origin within some sort of 'gnostic' Christianity, but little serious study has been pursued along these lines. The failure to pursue this avenue is in part con-sequent, I suspect, to the theological interests of many previous scholars, who had hoped that the study of these traditions could somehow bolster the modern dogma of the Assumption. Associating these traditions with a gnostic origin would hardly help to achieve this goal. The early Dormition narratives were already viewed with a great deal of suspicion by many Catholic theologians, and any genetic connection with the gnostic Christianities of antiquity would only further discredit them in the eyes of the Roman church.[1] Consequently, this chapter will give particular consideration to the probable connections between several of the earliest narratives and the various ancient religious phenomena traditionally grouped together (for better or worse) under the label 'gnostic', exploring the possibility of their prior existence within such a heterodox form of Christianity.

Nevertheless, while the early Palm traditions betray consider-able evidence of early contact with theologically marginalized

[1] e.g. Joseph Duhr, SJ, *The Glorious Assumption of the Mother of God*, trans. John Manning Fraunces, SJ (New York: P. J. Kennedy & Sons, 1950), 36.

forms of early Christianity, the earliest narratives of the Bethlehem and Coptic traditions, as well as the earliest atypical narratives, afford no evidence of such contact. There is almost nothing in these narratives that would suggest their prior existence outside the bounds of what eventually came to be 'orthodox' Christianity, nor is there much that points towards an origin any earlier than the middle of the fifth century. The only possible exception to this would be the elaborate prologues of the earliest Bethlehem narratives, which create the appearance of some sort of a prehistory for the Six Books in their descriptions of a global search to recover the long-lost apostolic traditions. Nevertheless, it may also be the case that these prologues were instead intended to explain why the Bethlehem traditions *lacked* such a prehistory: that is, the preface may have been designed to obscure the newness of traditions that had only recently been invented, manufacturing an illusion of their antiquity.[2] Given this lack of any clear indication that these traditions had some sort of a significant pre-existence before their initial appearance in the late fifth century, this chapter will have comparatively little to say regarding a potential prehistory for the Bethlehem, Coptic, and atypical narratives, focusing, in the first part at least, on the Palm tradition.

There is, however, one issue that concerns the prehistory of all the earliest Dormition narratives, that being the rather widely held view that the origins of the Dormition and Assumption traditions were somehow connected with resistance to the council of Chalcedon. In spite of its frequent repetition, I find this almost conventional hypothesis to be not only unfounded, but seemingly contradicted by the nature of the earliest sources themselves. In reading the earliest traditions, one cannot help but be struck by the near total absence of the issues and debates generated by Chalcedon, as well as by the overall Christological banality of these narratives. The narratives give the distinct impression that, far from being anti-Chalcedonian or even pro-Chalcedonian, they have instead deliberately avoided the

---

[2] The *Apocalypse of Paul*, for instance, tells a similar account of its own discovery, presumably to explain to its readership the appearance of a relatively new apocalypse: *Apoc. Paul* 1–2 (Montague Rhodes James, ed., *Apocrypha Anecdota*, Texts and Studies, II/3 (Cambridge: The University Press, 1893), 11).

controversies and jargon that issued from the fourth council. Moreover, the few 'real' individuals that can be associated with the earliest traditions also fail to suggest an association with a particular view regarding the debates over Chalcedon. Jacob of Serug and 'Ps.-Dionysius' are both extremely difficult to identify with one party or the other,[3] and such obvious partisans as Theodosius of Alexandria and John of Thessalonica fail to use the opportunity presented by Mary's departure from this world to mull over the issues of Chalcedon. All of this suggests that these earliest traditions emerged neither within the anti- or pro-Chalcedonian camps, but if anywhere, in the context of such conciliatory movements as are represented in the various efforts to heal this theological rupture in the early Byzantine church. Indeed, as we will see, on one important occasion such a connection is made quite explicit.

Thus, while identifying the origin of these traditions lies beyond the limits of our present knowledge, there are some important traces of a prehistory to some of them. We cannot,

---

[3] Regarding Ps.-Dionysius, see Paul Rorem and John C. Lamoreaux, *John of Scythopolis and the Dionysian Corpus: Annotating the Areopagite*, Oxford Early Christian Studies (Oxford: Clarendon Press, 1998), ch. 1, where they argue against the traditional identification of Ps.-Dionysius with anti-Chalcedonianism, demonstrating convincingly that 'the Dionysian corpus . . . was being used by just about all parties in the Christian East and that at no point was it the exclusive preserve of the Monophysites'. In regards to Jacob, Constantino Vona (*Omelie mariologiche de S. Giacomo di Sarug: Introduzione, traduzione dal siriaco e commento* (Rome: Facultas Theologica Pontificii Athenaei Lateranensis, 1953), 28–35) identifies Jacob as a Chalcedonian, following the arguments put forth by Paul Peeters ('Jacques de Saroug appartient-il à la secte monophysite?' *Analecta Bollandiana*, 66 (1948), 134–98). Paul Krüger had initially adopted this view ('War Jakob von Serugh Katholik oder Monophysit?' *Ostkirchliche Studien*, 2 (1953), 199–208), but later concluded that Jacob was a moderate monophysite ('Das Problem der Rechtglaübigkeit Jakobs von Serugh und seine Lösung', *Ostkirchliche Studien*, 5 (1956), 158–76, 225–42). The issue is difficult to resolve, and perhaps does not in fact require a resolution. Despite her identification of Jacob as 'clearly a monophysite', Roberta Chesnut describes him as follows: 'Jacob, whose temperament was irenic, and whose Christian conscience was outraged by the division in the church caused by the Christological controversy, never, to my knowledge, willingly and without coercion, used the catch phrases and jargon of the monophysites' (*Three Monophysite Christologies: Severus of Antioch, Philoxenus of Mabbug, and Jacob of Sarug*, Oxford Theological Monographs (Oxford: Oxford University Press, 1976), 4, 6 n. 2). It is in my opinion better not to force such a figure to fit categories that he himself has sought to avoid.

admittedly, say much with any certainty, but we can piece together a variety of clues and perhaps catch a glimpse of their now invisible past. Such will be the approach of this final chapter: I do not aim to identify the origin or even origins of these traditions, so much as to trace backwards certain unusual theological positions embedded in the now extant texts. As a result, the first part of this chapter will be somewhat more probative than definitive. But in turning to consider the supposed anti-Chalcedonian beginnings of these traditions, the question of origins becomes much more definite. Since the earliest Dormition narratives first emerge into view during the period immediately following the council of Chalcedon, we may compare them with the various theological positions that emerged from the council and determine which if any of these the early Dormition narratives most reflect, thereby testing the hypothesis of anti-Chalcedonian origins.

EARLY CHRISTIAN HETERODOXY AND THE PREHISTORY OF THE DORMITION TRADITIONS

As Ps.-Melito begins his *Transitus Mariae*, probably written in the late fifth century, he explains his reasons for writing:

I remember that I have often written concerning a certain Leucius, who, after he had been a companion of the apostles with us, with alienated sense and rash mind departed from the way of righteousness and put into his books many things concerning the acts of the apostles, and spoke many and diverse things of their mighty deeds, but concerning their teaching lied much, affirming that they taught otherwise than they had, and establishing his own wicked position as if by their words. Nor did he account this sufficient, but also corrupted with an evil pen the departure of the blessed Mary ever-virgin, the mother of God, so that it is unlawful not only to read but even to hear it in the church of God. We therefore at your petition have written simply those things which we heard from the apostle John, and have sent them to your brotherhood, believing no alien doctrines which sprout from heretics.[4]

---

[4] Ps.-Melito, *Transitus Mariae*, prologue (Monika Haibach-Reinisch, ed., *Ein neuer 'Transitus Mariae' des Pseudo-Melito* (Rome: Pontificia Academia Mariana Internationalis, 1962), 64–5; trans. J. K. Elliott, *The Apocryphal New Testament* (Oxford: Clarendon Press, 1993), 708).

By his own admission then, Ps.-Melito was not the first to write an account of the Virgin's Dormition. In this he was preceded by a heterodox narrative that he attributes to a certain 'Leucius', who, as he remarks, was also known for composing the apocryphal acts of the apostles. Whether this Leucius actually ever even existed is neither certain nor especially important: in the early church his name became synonymous with the composition of heterodox apocrypha, and as such, Ps.-Melito's attribution may not reflect the narrative's historical origin so much as his perception of its doctrinal irregularities.[5]

About a century and a half later, John of Thessalonica reveals similar information in his homily for the Dormition, probably composed for the introduction of the 15 August feast in the liturgy of Thessalonica during the early seventh century.[6] In this situation, John was faced with the problem of explaining to his congregation why their ancestors had failed to observe this austere feast and, more generally, why this tradition had suddenly appeared only at such a late date. To assuage these concerns he offers the following explanation:

Therefore they were not neglectful or remiss, but after those who had been present then, as it has been said, wrote about her consummation, later, some of the wicked heretics, introducing their tares, twisted the writings, and on account of this, our fathers abstained from these as unfit for the catholic church. . . . But we do not spit on these truthful writings on account of their God-hated deceits, but cleansing the evil interpolations, we embrace these writings as true, to the glory of God for the sake of his saints.[7]

---

[5] Jean Gribomont, OSB, 'Le Plus Ancien *Transitus* Marial et l'encratisme', *Augustinianum*, 23 (1983), 238 n. 7. See also Eric Junod and Jean-Daniel Kaestli, eds., *Acta Iohannis*, 2 vols., CCSA 1–2 (Turnhout: Brepols, 1983), ii. 766–70.

[6] Simon C. Mimouni, *Dormition et assomption de Marie: Histoire des traditions anciennes*, Théologie Historique, 98 (Paris: Beauchesne, 1995), 136.

[7] John of Thessalonica, *dorm. BMV A* (G3) 1 (Martin Jugie, AA, ed. *Homélies mariales byzantine (II)*, PO 19. 3 (Paris: Librairie de Paris/Firmin-Didot et Cie, 1926), 376–7). Almost another century later, Andrew of Crete (*c.*660–740), in his homilies for the Dormition, still must apologize for the fact that the feast of the 'mystery' of the Dormition 'has not, in the past, been celebrated by many people': *or. 13* (PG 97. 1072B; trans. Brian E. Daley, SJ, *On the Dormition of Mary: Early Patristic Homilies* (Crestwood, NY: St Vladimir's Seminary Press, 1998), 103).

With this, John promises, as Ps.-Melito before him, to restore these legends to their original pristine state. Almost certainly, the text so full of 'tares' that stood before John as he began to compose his homily was a slightly longer version of the earliest extant Greek narrative (G1), which Wenger has convincingly identified as John's primary source.[8] Yet despite the often verbal agreement between these two narratives, John delivers, as promised, a rehabilitated narrative, 'cleansing the evil interpolations' from Wenger's earliest Greek text.

Comparison with the earliest Palm traditions suggest that John was actually using a text that had already been somewhat sanitized. As already noted in previous chapters, this earliest Greek text is very closely related to the ancient narrative witnessed in the Syriac fragments of the *Obsequies*, a more complete form of which is now known from the Ethiopic *Liber Requiei*, which as we have just seen, reliably transmits the earliest known Palm narrative.[9] The very peculiar theological atmosphere of the Ethiopic text is a further testament to its antiquity, and its narrative almost certainly represents the state of the Palm traditions before Ps-Melito, John of Thessalonica, and other like-minded individuals laboured to cleanse them. On the basis of both literary and doctrinal considerations then, we may be relatively assured that the Ethiopic version is at least as ancient as the Syriac fragments of the *Obsequies*, locating the formation of its narrative sometime in the fifth century at the latest, although as we will see, it is probably even earlier.[10] This is bolstered by the fact that nearly all the *Liber Requiei* finds parallels among any number of the early Palm narratives, which

---

[8] Antoine Wenger, AA, *L'Assomption de la T. S. Vierge dans la tradition byzantine du VIe au Xe siècle*, Archives de l'orient chrétien, 5 (Paris: Institut Français d'Études Byzantines, 1955), 31–67.

[9] See also Clayton, 'The Transitus Mariae', 76–85.

[10] See e.g. Michel van Esbroeck, 'Apocryphes géorgiens de la Dormition', *Analecta Bollandiana*, 92 (1973), 56–7; idem, 'Les Textes littéraires sur l'assomption avant le Xe siècle', in François Bovon (ed.), *Les Actes apocryphes des apôtres* (Geneva: Labor et Fides, 1981), 270; Victor Arras, ed., *De Transitu Mariae Aethiopice*, 2 vols., CSCO 342–3 (Louvain: Secrétariat du CorpusSCO, 1973), i. pp. vi–vii (Lat.); Mario Erbetta, *Gli apocrifi del Nuovo Testamento*, i. pt. 2, *Vangeli: Infanzia e passione di Cristo, Assunzione di Maria* (Casale: Marietti, 1981), 411; Bellarmino Bagatti, OFM, 'La morte della Vergine nel Testo di Leucio', *Marianum*, 36 (1974), 456–7.

further serves to confirm the general antiquity of this complete narrative.[11] Consequently, in considering the possible prehistory of the Dormition traditions, or of the Palm traditions at least, we will focus especially on the *Liber Requiei* and its fragments in Syriac and Georgian, as well as on the various early witnesses to the Palm tradition that attest to the antiquity of this version and the heterodox theolegoumena that it has preserved.

A. *The Jewish-Christian Origin of the Dormition Traditions*

The notion of a Jewish-Christian origin for the Dormition traditions first arose among a certain faculty of the Studium Biblicum Franciscanum in Jerusalem, and for the most part, the hypothesis has remained limited to that institution. Although the notion of a 'primitive' Jewish-Christianity appears to have been birthed by F. C. Baur in the nineteenth century,[12] the concept has been significantly developed in recent years by Frs. Bellarmino Bagatti and Emmanuele Testa, both of the Studium Biblicum Franciscanum. In their many publications concerning the early Jewish-Christian communities of Palestine, including especially their respective *magna opera*, Bagatti's *The Church from the Circumcision*[13] and Testa's *Il simbolismo dei Giudeo-cristiani*,[14] these two scholars have articulated the nature of this primitive Jewish Christianity in great detail. Equally fundamental in this area is the work of John (Cardinal) Daniélou

---

[11] Indeed, this is perhaps the surest indication of its antiquity: the *Liber Requiei* preserves a version of the Virgin's Dormition that explains a great deal of the variety manifest in the early Palm tradition. This is shown extensively in Arras' annotations to the *Liber Requiei*: 'Appendix II', *De Transitu*, ii. 75–105 (Lat.), and see also the table in Appendix G.

[12] See Joan E. Taylor, 'The Phenomenon of Early Jewish-Christianity: Reality or Scholarly Invention?' *Vigiliae Christianae*, 44 (1990), 314.

[13] Bellarmino Bagatti, OFM, *The Church from the Circumcision: History and Archaeology of the Judaeo-Christians*, trans. Eugene Hoade, OFM, Publications of the Studium Biblicum Franciscanum, Smaller Series, 2 (Jerusalem: Franciscan Printing Press, 1971). This English translation represents an updated version of the original French publication, idem, *L'Église de la Circoncision*, trans. Albert Storme, Studium Biblicum Franciscanum, Collectio Minor, 2 (Jerusalem: Franciscan Printing Press, 1965).

[14] Emmanuele Testa, OFM, *Il simbolismo dei Giudeo-cristiani*, Studium Biblicum Franciscanum, Collectio Maior, 14 (Jerusalem: Franciscan Printing Press, 1962).

published in his *The Theology of Jewish Christianity*. In this important and very controversial study, Daniélou, through the study of early Christian literature, arrived at many of the same conclusions that Bagatti and Testa had reached through archaeology.[15] The Cardinal's admiration for the Friars' work was mutual, and each looked to the other as having provided substantial confirmation of their own findings.[16] In the context of this larger work, Bagatti and Testa proposed the theory that the traditions of Mary's Dormition and Assumption originated among the early Jewish-Christian groups of Jerusalem.[17] Since then, Lino Cignelli, Miguel Vallecillo, and, more recently, Frédéric Manns, have all made important contributions to the hypothesis of Jewish-Christian origins, Manns in particular having developed this position quite thoroughly and along slightly different lines.[18]

At the core of this approach lies a belief that alongside the 'Church from the Gentiles', whose views are well represented in

[15] John Daniélou, *The Theology of Jewish Christianity*, trans. John A. Baker, vol. i of *The Development of Christian Doctrine before the Council of Nicaea* (London: Darton, Longman & Todd, 1964).

[16] Ignazio Mancini, OFM, *Archaeological Discoveries Relative to the Judaeo-Christians: Historical Survey*, trans. G. Bushell, Publications of the Studium Biblicum Franciscanum, Smaller Series, 10 (Jerusalem: Franciscan Printing Press, 1970), 62–3, 97–9, 111–13, 118–19, 133.

[17] Bellarmino Bagatti, OFM, 'Ricerche sulle tradizioni della morte della Vergine', *Sacra Doctrina*, 69–70 (1973), 185–214; idem, 'La verginità di Maria negli apocrifi del II–III secolo', *Marianum*, 33 (1971), 281–92; idem, 'La morte della Vergine nel Testo di Leucio', *Marianum*, 36 (1974), 456–7; B. Bagatti, M. Piccirillo, and A. Prodomo, OFM, *New Discoveries at the Tomb of Virgin Mary in Gethsemane*, Studium Biblicum Franciscanum, Collectio Minor, 17 (Jerusalem: Franciscan Printing Press, 1975), 11–18; Emmanuele Testa, OFM, 'L'origine e lo sviluppo della *Dormitio Mariae*', *Augustinianum*, 23 (1983), 249–62; idem, 'Lo sviluppo della "Dormitio Mariae" nella letteratura, nella teologia e nella archeologia', *Marianum*, 44 (1982), 316–89.

[18] Lino Cignelli, OFM, 'Il prototipo giudeo-cristiano degli apocrifi assunzionisti', in Emmanuelle Testa, Ignazio Mancini, and Michele Piccirillo (eds.), *Studia Hierosolymitana in onore di P. Bellarmino Bagatti*, ii. *Studi esegetici*, Studium Biblicum Franciscanum, Collectio Maior, 23 (Jerusalem: Franciscan Printing Press, 1975), 259–77; Miguel Vallecillo, OFM, 'El "Transitus Mariae" según el manuscrito Vaticano G. R. 1982', *Verdad y vida*, 30 (1972), 187–260; Frédéric Manns, *Le Récit de la dormition de Marie (Vatican grec 1982): Contribution à l'étude de origines de l'exégèse chrétienne*, Studium Biblicum Franciscanum, Collectio Maior, 33 (Jerusalem: Franciscan Printing Press, 1989).

most of the early Christian literature that has been preserved, there existed also a 'Church from the Circumcision', an ancient group of Palestinian Jewish-Christians whose distinctive theology and adherence to Jewish traditions separated them from the Gentile mainstream. This Jewish-Christian community was centred in Jerusalem, and continued to exist in secrecy until the early fifth century, when this 'Mother Church' was finally absorbed by the Gentile church.[19] Characteristic of this group were a subordinationist Christology, and particularly an Angel Christology; use of 'Midrash' in reading the Scriptures; an apocalyptic worldview; belief in the seven heavens and the ascent of the 'cosmic ladder'; possession of 'heavenly books'; and the use of a variety of 'mystical symbols', which Testa's *Il simbolismo dei Giudeo-cristiani* undertakes to identify and explain.[20] Within the Church of the Circumcision itself, these scholars further differentiate various sub-groups, and it is within one of these 'denominations', an Ebionite group theologically close to 'catholicism' or the 'Johannine circle', that the professors of the Studium Biblicum Franciscanum identify the origins of the Dormition traditions.[21] Testa is still more specific than his colleagues, adding that this group was led by Jesus' blood relatives, descendents of Mary's family who for centuries guarded both her tomb and the story of her life's end.[22] Bagatti and Testa, among others, have even gone so far as to identify Ps.-Melito's 'Leucius' as the actual Jewish-Christian author of the text now preserved in the Ethiopic *Liber Requiei*, which they regard as being the most ancient version.[23]

It must be recognized that this group of scholars has been

---

[19] Bagatti, *Church from the Circumcision*, 3–14, 30, 86–93, 143–7.

[20] Ibid. 137–93, 279–301; Daniélou, *Theology of Jewish Christianity*, 87–146, 173–204; Testa, *Il simbolismo, passim.*

[21] Bagatti, 'Ricerche sulle tradizioni', 186–94; idem, 'La morte', 456–7; Cignelli, 'Il prototipo', 267–8; Vallecillo, 'El "Transitus Mariae"', 194–9; Manns, *Le Récit,* 114–19.

[22] Testa, 'L'origine', 249–50, 254; idem, 'Lo sviluppo', 316, 330.

[23] Bagatti, 'La morte'; Testa, 'L'origine', 258. Arras, *De Transitu,* i. p. v (Eth.) suggests Leucius as the author of the *Liber Requiei*, without identifying him or the text as Jewish-Christian; van Esbroeck suggests that Leucius may have been the author of a hypothetical Greek narrative which was the theoretical source of several early Palm traditions, also without reference to Jewish-Christianity: 'Les Textes', 270–1.

quite successful at identifying many of the numerous heterodox concepts and themes that are present in the ancient narratives of the Palm tradition. Leaving in abeyance for the moment the highly problematic category of 'Jewish-Christianity' employed to explain the origin of these traditions, we can see that many of the beliefs and symbols identified as particularly Jewish-Christian by this group of scholars are in fact prominent in the earliest Palm narratives.

Perhaps the most significant of these ideas is the Angel Christology expressed by the earliest Palm narratives, a belief that is frequently identified with Jewish-Christianity.[24] Both the *Liber Requiei* and the earliest Greek text advance this understanding of Christ, clearly identifying him as a 'Great Angel' from the heavens.[25] In the opening sequence from these two narratives, an angel appears to the Virgin and announces her impending death; but as their conversation unfolds, it becomes apparent that this angel is also her son, Jesus Christ. When Mary asks the angel's name, he initially refuses to answer, explaining that to speak his name within Jerusalem would cause its destruction. Instead, at the angel's suggestion, they go from Jerusalem to the Mount of Olives, where the Virgin watches as the trees 'bow their heads' before this 'Great Angel',[26] in whom she suddenly recognizes her son, crying out, 'It is Jesus!' 'My Lord', she says, 'perhaps you are my Lord? For such a great miracle has come about on your account: for I see that so many trees venerate you. Behold then I say that there is no one who is capable of such a miracle, except the Lord of Glory, who has been revealed to me.'[27]

---

[24] e.g. Bagatti, *Church from the Circumcision*, 175–91; idem, 'Ricerche sulle tradizioni', 187; Cignelli, 'Il prototipo', 263–4; Daniélou, *Theology of Jewish Christianity*, 117–46; Richard N. Longenecker, *The Christology of Early Jewish Christianity*, Studies in Biblical Theology, Second Series, 17 (London: SCM Press Ltd., 1970) 26–32; Testa, 'L'origine', 251; idem, 'Lo sviluppo', 333–9; Manns, *Le Récit*, 155–61; Vallecillo, 'El "Transitus Mariae"', 212–13.

[25] *Liber Requiei* 1–3 (Arras, *De Transitu*, 1–20 (Eth.) and 1–13 (Lat.)); Wenger, *L'Assomption*, 210–15.

[26] In the Greek, however, as in most texts, the trees bow down before the palm, not the angel: Wenger, *L'Assomption*, 212.

[27] *Liber Requiei* 3 (Arras, *De Transitu*, 2 (Eth.) and 1 (Lat.)). Compare also the Greek: Ὅτε οὖν εἶδεν αὐτὸν ἡ Μαρία νομίζουσα ἥτι Ἰησοῦς ἐστιν εἶπεν· "Κύριε, μήτι σὺ εἶ ὁ Κύριός μου"; Wenger, *L'Assomption*, 212.

Addressing Mary as his mother,[28] the 'Great Angel' confirms her recognition, answering, 'there is no one who can do this miracle, except by his [the Lord of Glory's] hand, because he is powerful. . . . I am he who is in the trees and who is in the mountain. . . . Therefore, I am not the one who is above everything, but I am above the trees of the holy inheritance.'[29] Likewise in the Greek, the angel similarly affirms her recognition, answering, 'No one could work wonders except the Lord of Glory.'[30] The *Liber Requiei* here continues with a lengthy episode that is not preserved by the earliest Greek narrative, but fortunately it is known from several other early Palm narratives, including the Georgian fragments and the early Irish versions.[31] In the course of this dialogue with Mary, in a passage extant only in the Ethiopic version, the Christ-Angel speaks directly about his identity and his relation to the Father. Unfortunately, however, the two Ethiopic manuscripts disagree, and both are somewhat unclear: one reads 'I am the third that was created, and I am not the Son', and the other, 'I am the one who was created third in divinity, and I am the Son.'[32] Obviously whatever the original contents of this passage once were, they were disturbing to the theological sensibilities of the medieval copyists, who felt compelled to alter the passage, making it difficult to know what the

[28] ወይቤ፡ አምዖ፡ ኢያኅመርኪ፡ ኃይልዖ፡ ibid. 5 (Arras, *De Transitu,* 3 (Eth.) and 2 (Lat.)). See also the Greek: Καὶ λέγει αὐτῇ· "Τί γὰρ ἔχεις, μῆτερ;" Wenger, *L'Assomption,* 214.

[29] Ibid., 4 (Arras, *De Transitu,* 2–3 (Eth.) and 2 (Lat.)).

[30] Τότε εἶπεν αὐτῇ ὁ ἄγγελος "Οὐ δύναταί τις ποιεῖν σημεῖα εἰ μὴ ᾖ Κύριος τῆς δόξης·" Wenger, *L'Assomption,* 212.

[31] *Liber Requiei* 5–10 (Arras, *De Transitu,* 2–5 (Eth.) and 2–4 (Lat.)). This story is also preserved in the Georgian fragments (van Esbroeck, 'Apocryphes géorgiens', 69–72 (Geor.) and 73–5 (Lat.)), but because of their fragmentary state, we cannot be absolutely certain that the angel was identified with Christ in this version. Nevertheless, the fact that the angel addresses Mary as 'mother', as in the *Liber Requiei*, strongly suggests the angel's identity with Christ. A condensed version of this scene is also found in the Irish apocrypha (Charles Donahue, ed., *The Testament of Mary: The Gaelic Version of the Dormitio Mariae together with an Irish Latin Version,* Fordham University Studies, Language Series, 1 (New York: Fordham University Press, 1942), 28–31; and Máire Herbert and Martin McNamara, eds., *Irish Biblical Apocrypha* (Edinburgh: T. & T. Clark, 1989), 119–20), where Christ appears to Mary and announces her death, but he is never identified as an angel.

[32] *Liber Requiei* 25 (Arras, *De Transitu,* 13 (Eth.) and 8 (Lat.)). MS A: አነ፡ ውእቱ፡ ሣልስ፡ ተገብር፡ ወኢወለድ፡ MS B: አነ፡ ውእቱ፡ ዘሥልስ፡ ተገብር፡ በመለኮት፡ ወአነ፡ ወልዱ፡

ancient version actually said. Nevertheless, the reference in both versions to the Christ-Angel as a 'created' being is an interesting ante- or anti-Nicene statement that fits well with the subordinationist, Angel Christology evidenced elsewhere.

Perhaps the most striking and unambiguous expression of an Angel Christology comes later in the narrative, after the apostles have gathered at Mary's house. Overjoyed that her son's promise to reunite the apostles has been fulfilled, Mary bursts into a prayer of thanksgiving, which is extant both in the Ethiopic and the Greek versions. In the middle of her prayer, which evokes a number of heterodox concepts, Mary praises her son, saying, 'I bless the Great Cherub of Light, who dwelt for a time in my womb,'[33] confirming that the angel who appeared to her and announced her death is to be identified with her son, Jesus Christ. The verbal or near verbal agreement of the Greek and Ethiopic in this and other instances presents strong evidence that the Angel Christology belongs to an archaic stratum of the Palm traditions, on which these two very early narratives have both drawn.

Although this theme is now clearly visible only in these two narratives, the unmistakable efforts of later redactors to efface the primitive Angel Christology also attest to its antiquity. This is particularly evident in later treatments of Mary's exclamation, 'I bless the Great Cherub of Light, who dwelt for a time in my womb'. John of Thessalonica, for instance, alters this phrase to 'I bless you, the giver of light, who dwelt for a time in my womb,' and the early Latin narrative published by Wenger rewrites the statement to read, 'I bless you who sits upon the Great Cherub, because you made your dwelling place in my womb.'[34] The subtle nature of these changes attests rather strongly to the Angel Christology's antiquity. Likewise, the later transmission of the Palm tradition's opening scene confirms a primitive Angel

---

[33] εὐλογῶ τὸ μέγα χερουβὶμ τοῦ φωτός, τὸ γενόμενόν σου παροικία ἐν τῇ κοιλίᾳ μου., Wenger, *L'Assomption*, 226–9. See also the Ethiopic: ኦበረከ፡ ለዓቢይ፡ ኪሩቤል፡ ብርሃን፡ ዘኀደረ፡ ማኅደረ፡ውስተ፡ ከርሥየ፡ *Liber Requiei* 52 (Arras, *De Transitu*, 31 (Eth.) and 21 (Lat.)).

[34] See e.g. John of Thessalonica, *dorm. BMV A* 8 (Jugie, *Homélies*, 389): εὐλογῶ σέ, τὸν δοτῆρα τοῦ φωτός, τὸν γενόμενον πάροικον ἐν τῇ κοιλίᾳ μου· and Wenger's early Latin text (L4), 17 (Wenger, *L'Assomption*, 250), 'benedico te qui sedes super magnam cherubim, quia factum est tibi habitaculum in utero meo'.

Christology: in later narratives the figure who announces Mary's death is either an angel or Christ, but not both. This difference almost certain originates in the earlier identity of this figure as both Christ and an angel, a theological peculiarity that later recensions have dealt with by resolving the figure into one identity or the other.[35]

Angel Christology is regarded as a hallmark of Jewish-Christian theology by Jewish Christianity's proponents: it is present in the Ps.-Clementine literature and is ascribed to both the Ebionites and the Elchasites.[36] Nevertheless, Angel Christology was not at all limited to this particular milieu of early Christianity: in addition to these Jewish-Christian witnesses, Angel or 'Angelomorphic' Christology is met in sources as diverse as the Apocalypse of John, Justin Martyr, the *Shepherd of Hermas*, the *Ascension of Isaiah*, Tertullian, Origen, Eusebius of Caesarea, and various 'gnostic' groups, among others.[37] As a flurry of recent studies have shown, early Judaism was rife with speculation concerning a 'Great Angel', whether the 'Angel of

---

[35] Most of these traditions opt for the identification of this figure with an angel, but the early Irish narratives identify this messenger as the Son, attesting to the ambiguous nature of this figure in earlier traditions: see Donahue, *Testament of Mary*, 28–9; Herbert and McNamara, *Irish Biblical Apocrypha*, 119. The early Latin narrative published by Wenger is a particularly interesting witness in this regard. Initially, Christ appears to his mother and tells her to go to the Mount of Olives, where she will receive a palm from an angel. When Mary reaches the top and receives the palm, she asks, 'Domine, numquid tu es deus meus quoniam tanta uirtus facta est per te et quoniam omnes arbores adorauerunt te?' The angel then answers her, 'Ego angelus eius sum et missus sum ad te ut accipias hanc palmam' (Wenger, *L'Assomption*, 245). Thus, this narrative has split the Christ-Angel into two separate figures in order to resolve the issue of the earliest tradition's identity of Christ with an angel.

[36] See, in addition to n. 24 above, Longenecker, *Christology of Early Jewish Christianity*, 26–32; Daniélou, *Theology of Jewish Christianity*, 117–46; Darrell D. Hannah, *Michael and Christ: Michael Traditions and Angel Christology in Early Christianity*, Wissenschaftliche Untersuchungen zum Neuen Testament, ser. 2. Reihe, 109 (Tübingen: Mohr Siebeck, 1999), 173–9; Charles A. Gieschen, *Angelomorphic Christology: Antecedents and Early Evidence*, Arbeiten zur Geschichte des antiken Judentums und des Urchristentums, 42 (Leiden: Brill, 1998), 201–13.

[37] Charles Gieschen's recent study has carefully considered each of these sources and more quite well, obviating the need to repeat any of his work in the present study: *Angelomorphic Christology*, 187–347. See also Hannah, *Michael and Christ*, 137–213

the Lord' or one of the various named angels, who is often vaguely connected with God by nature, but is also a separate being who shares God's authority. The early Christians, in their effort to clarify Christ's relationship to Yahweh, were quick to utilize these traditions, to the effect that Angel Christologies of one sort or another are not at all uncommon in earliest Christian literature.[38]

In analysing the different early interpretations of Christ as an angel, scholars have increasingly begun to make an illuminating distinction between Christologies that are 'Angelomorphic' and true Angel Christologies. Beginning with Daniélou, scholars have sought to differentiate between early Angelomorphic Christologies, which drew on early Jewish traditions about the angels to articulate an understanding of Christ, yet without denying his divine nature, on the one hand, and actual Angel Christologies, which taught that the Son possessed an angelic, rather than divine nature.[39] It is clearly the latter of these two alternatives that we meet in the ancient Dormition traditions: Christ, the Great Angel, is explicitly identified as a created being, for instance. Nor is Christ merely seen to function in ways reminiscent of angels; he is the Great Cherub of Light. This understanding of Christ distinguishes these early Dormition narratives from the Angelomorphic Christologies of incipient

[38] In addition to the studies already mentioned by Daniélou, Hannah, Gieschen, and Longenecker, see also Christopher Rowland, *The Open Heaven: A Study of Apocalyptic in Judaism and Early Christianity* (New York: Crossroad, 1982); Joseph W. Trigg, 'The Angel of Great Counsel: Christ and the Angelic Hierarchy in Origen's Theology', *Journal of Theological Studies*, NS 42 (1991), 35–51; Peter R. Carrell, *Jesus and the Angels: Angelology and the Christology of the Apocalypse of John*, Society for New Testament Studies, Monograph Series, 95 (Cambridge: Cambridge University Press, 1997); Loren Stuckenbruck, *Angel Veneration and Christology: A Study in Early Judaism and in the Christology of the Apocalypse of John*, Wissenschaftliche Untersuchungen zum Neuen Testament, ser. 2, Reihe, 70 (Tübingen: Mohr Siebeck, 1995); Jonathan Knight, *Disciples of the Beloved One: The Christology, Social Setting, and Theological Content of the Ascension of Isaiah*, Journal for the Study of the Pseudepigrapha, Supplement Series, 18 (Sheffield: Sheffield Academic Press, 1996); and Margaret Barker's provocative and controversial *The Great Angel: A Study of Israel's Other God* (Louisville, KY: Westminster/John Knox, 1992), esp. 190–232.

[39] Daniélou, *Theology of Jewish Christianity*, 146; see also Longenecker, *Christology of Early Jewish Christianity*, 26–32; Trigg, 'The Angel of Great Counsel', 35–7; Gieschen, *Angelomorphic Christology*, 4, 15.

orthodoxy, alerting us that the earliest Palm traditions first took shape somewhere outside the ever-encroaching boundaries of proto-orthodox Christianity. While this may have been within some sort of a particularly Jewish Christianity, as Bagatti and others have proposed, we should also bear in mind the possibility of some sort of gnostic milieu, as will be explored later in this chapter.

Like the Angel Christology of these earliest narratives, the 'palm' (or 'staff') that the Christ-Angel entrusts to Mary complements the Jewish-Christian hypothesis, as does the 'book of mysteries' which appears alongside the palm or in its place in some of the earliest narratives. The palm is a fairly common symbol in early Jewish literature, and in the early Dormition narratives of the Palm tradition, the palm given to the Virgin functions in ways that are reminiscent of these Jewish traditions.[40] In the *Liber Requiei*, however, a 'book of mysteries' stands strangely in place of the palm frond that has elsewhere become the trademark of these Dormition traditions. As the *Liber Requiei* opens, the Christ-Angel, instead of giving the Virgin a palm, orders her: 'Arise Mary and take this book, which he has given to you, he who planted Paradise, and give it to the apostles, so that when they open it, they will read it before you.'[41] Only later, however, when the Virgin, as instructed, delivers the book to the apostle John, do we learn the complete significance of this book, which is full of 'mysteries': 'And she brought forth a small case that contained the book and said to him, "My father John, take this book in which is the mystery. For when he was five years old, our master revealed all of creation to us, and he also put you, the twelve in it." '[42]

More than one scholar has attributed this 'idiosyncrasy' of the *Liber Requiei* to a mistranslation of the Greek, in which the

---

[40] Manns, *Le Récit*, 122–31; Vallecillo, 'El "Transitus Mariae" ', 201–5.

[41] ተንሥኢ፡ ወንሥኢ፡ ዘንተ፡ መጽሐፈ፡ ዘወሀበኪ፡ ዘተክላ፡ ለገነተ። ወወሀብዮሙ፡ ለሐዋርያት፡ ከመ፡ ሶበ፡ ከሠትዋ፡ ወያንብብዋ፡ በቅድሜኪ። *Liber Requiei* 1 (Arras, *De Transitu*, i. 1 (Eth.) and 1 (Lat.)).

[42] ወአውፅአቶሙ፡ ቅምጠራ፡ ንዑስ፡ ዘውስቴቱ፡ ዝኩ፡ መጽሐፍ፡ ወትቤሎ፡ ኦአቡየ፡ ዮሐንስ፡ ንሣእ፡ ዘንተ፡ መጽሐፈ፡ ዘሀሎ፡ ውስቴቱ፡ ምስጢር። እስመ፡ ሀለወ፡ ህፃመት፡ ሎቱ፡ ስሲቅነ፡ አርአያነ፡ ቴሎ፡ ፍጥረት፡ ወሣመ፡ ወንሕነ፡ ላወሣ፡ ውስቴቱ። *Liber Requiei* 44 (ibid. 27 (Eth.) and 17–18 (Lat.)). Although the manuscripts read 'put us, the twelve in it', I have corrected the translation to reflect the Greek, which seems to make more sense. For the Greek parallel, see n. 48 below.

Ethiopic translator has mistakenly read βιβλίον, 'book', instead of βραβεῖον, 'palm', thereby estimating the book to be an otherwise insignificant mistake rather than evidence for a primitive tradition including a secret book of the mysteries.[43] The matter is not so simple, however. In the first place, the *Liber Requiei* persistently surrounds this object with language appropriate for a book, not a palm. Beginning with the Christ-Angel's instructions that the apostles are to 'open' and 'read' this item, the narrative context makes it highly unlikely that the Greek original from which this translation was made identified a palm in the opening sequence where we now find the book. Otherwise, one must also assume that the translator has somehow accidentally mistaken κρατήσαντες ('holding') for ἀνοίξαντες ('opening') and ὑμνήσωσιν ('they will sing') for ἀναγνώσονται ('they will read'),[44] which seems highly improbable.[45]

Any changes that were made to this passage were almost certainly deliberate, and it seems most likely that the later tradition, including the earliest Greek narrative, has altered an

---

[43] Erbetta, *Gli apocrifi*, 422–3 n. 2. This conclusion forms part of a larger argument that several 'mistranslations' indicate that the Ethiopic translator was using a Greek original. Manns has adopted this explanation, arguing that the following story, of the palm in the desert which is moved to Paradise, only makes sense if this 'book' was actually a 'palm'. In this case, the story is told to explain how this special palm tree, whose branch Mary holds, came to Paradise (Manns, *Le Récit*, 75). In the *Liber Requiei*, however, this story serves a different yet equally important narrative function. Immediately before the 'Angel' tells the story of the desert Palm, the trees on the Mount of Olives bow down before the book. The Christ-Angel then offers the story from the flight to Egypt as an example of his power to bend trees on another occasion. A similar example of this power is related in the story of the fruit trees in *Liber Requiei* 18 (Arras, *De Transitu*, i. 10–12 (Eth.) and 7–8 (Lat.)); and Wright, *Contributions*, ܡܣ‑ܠܩ (Syr.) and 50–1 (Eng.). For more on this story, see below.

[44] Compare the earliest Greek narrative with the Ethiopic in n. 41: λαβὲ τοῦτο τὸ βραβεῖον ὃ ἔδωκέν μοι ὁ φυτεύσας τὸν παράδεισον καὶ παράδος τοῖς ἀποστόλοις ἵνα κρατήσαντες αὐτὸ ὑμνήσωσιν ἔμπροσθέν σου, διότι μετὰ ἡμέρας ἀποτίθῃς τὸ σῶμα (Wenger, *L'Assomption*, 210–11).

[45] It must be noted, however, that there *are* instances in the *Liber Requiei* where a translator has confused βραβεῖον for βιβλίον. Nevertheless, it does not seem possible that such a mistake can account for the 'introduction' of a book of mysteries to this narrative: for the reasons outlined above, we must recognize that the book of mysteries is at least as primitive as the palm itself. Rather, it would seem that the simultaneous presence of two such similar sounding items (in the Greek) caused the translator to conflate them both into the book in the *Liber Requiei*. For more on this, see below.

archaic tradition preserved by the *Liber Requiei*, rather than the Ethiopic narrative's having introduced something new. Important confirmation of the book's primacy has recently come to light in the Coptic fragments of an early Dormition narrative from the Yale papyrus collection, recently published by Philip Sellew. Several of these Coptic fragments parallel the text of the *Liber Requiei*, and in the section where Mary and John first interact in the Virgin's 'inner chamber', she presents him with a 'book of mysteries', as in the Ethiopic version. These fragments provide, as Sellew emphasizes, important confirmation of both the antiquity of the *Liber Requiei* in general and the presence of a book of mysteries in the earliest traditions in particular.[46]

Moreover, the earliest Greek narrative also attests to the existence of a book of mysteries: despite the absence of such a book from its opening sequence, the narrative elsewhere identifies a book of mysteries, confirming the book's inclusion in the earliest Palm traditions. Although the Virgin originally receives a palm from the Christ-Angel instead of a book, as in the *Liber Requiei*, a book of mysteries suddenly appears alongside the palm when the apostle John arrives. As Mary surrenders the palm to John, fulfilling the Christ-Angel's command, she also presents him with the book of mysteries, which is here described exactly as it is in the *Liber Requiei*.[47] The book's appearance here alongside, rather than in place of, the palm, precludes the possibility that this book of mysteries entered the Dormition traditions simply as a translator's (or in the case of Greek transmission, a copyist's) mistake. On the contrary, this earliest Greek narrative

---

[46] Philip Sellew, 'An Early Coptic Witness to the *Dormitio Mariae* at Yale: P. CtYBR inv. 1788 Revisited', *Bulletin of the American Society of Papyrologists*, 37 (2000), 37–69, esp. 51–2, 59–60. I am not ready, however, to speak of a primitive 'pre-Palm' or 'Book' tradition (that is, one with no palm and only a book), as Sellew proposes. The only possible evidence for such a tradition at present is one of Sellew's fragments, which, as he notes, describes a book but fails to mention a palm. However, this fragment is so brief that we have no way of knowing that the palm was not included in the once complete narration. Also, the *Obsequies*, which Sellew identifies as fragments from this pre-Palm narrative, do in fact include a palm, and the *Liber Requiei*, although it does not mention a palm, has clearly mistranslated βραβεῖον as if it were βιβλίον in certain places (see n. 45 above), making both these narratives witnesses to the presence of a palm in the earliest known traditions.

[47] Wenger, *L'Assomption*, 220–3.

further verifies the book of mysteries as a tradition separate from the palm, which, judging from the verbal identity of the Greek and Ethiopic at this point, belongs to the very earliest layers of the Palm tradition.[48] Finally, this book's appearance alongside the palm in Cosmas Vestitor's early ninth-century homilies for the Dormition further confirms its existence as an independent tradition, almost certainly of great antiquity.[49]

It is admittedly difficult to explain the opening scene of the *Liber Requiei*, which in contrast to all the other known Palm traditions describes the Christ-Angel's presentation of the book rather than the palm, but as is clear from the language of the passage itself, this difference cannot be attributed simply to a translator's careless mistake. Most likely the absence of any clear parallels capable of elucidating the *Liber Requiei*'s opening sequence is largely a matter of chance, with some (not insignificant) assistance from the filter of orthodoxy. In any case, on the basis of multiple attestation in several Palm narratives, including some of the earliest, we must recognize the book of mysteries as belonging to the earliest Palm traditions.

Nevertheless, even though a translation mistake cannot account for the book of mysteries' presence in these traditions, it must at the same time be recognized that there are clear instances in the *Liber Requiei* where the book of mysteries has undeniably been confused with and replaced what was originally a palm (or βραβεῖον). Only such a mistake can in part explain the almost total

---

[48] Compare the Ethiopic, cited in n. 42 above, with the Greek: 'And she brought forth a box, in which there was a book, and she said: "Father John, take this book in which is the mystery. When he was five years old, the Master revealed all of creation, and he also put you, the twelve, in this book." ' καὶ ἐξενέγκασα γλωσσόκομον ἐν ᾧ ἦν χαρτίον εἶπεν· Πάτερ Ἰωάννη, λαβὲ τοῦτο τὸ βιβλίον ἐν ᾧ ἦν τὸ μυστήριον. Ὅτε γὰρ ἦν πενταετὴς ὁ διδάσκαλος ἐγνώρισεν πάντα τὰ τῆς κτίσεως καὶ ὑμᾶς τοὺς δώδεκα ἐν τούτῳ. ibid. 220–1. Although John of Thessalonica has eliminated this section of the text, it is preserved (in an altered form) by Cosmas Vestitor (c.810–40) in his second homily on the Dormition (see n. 49 below; for date see ibid. 147–8).

[49] See Cosmas Vestitor's second homily on the Dormition: 'Accipe autem et chartam hanc et scito cuncta subtiliter que creature sunt, ex officio apostolorum, quod a Deo predestinatum est tecum fungendum. Ecce et palmam suscipe et illam precedentem ante lectum meum' (ibid. 321). As with the later transmission of the Angel Christology, one can still sense some of the original description of the book of mysteries as found in the earliest narratives, even amidst Cosmas' (or his source's) changes in the direction of orthodoxy.

absence of the palm from the *Liber Requiei*, particularly since, in several passages, the context clearly supposes a palm rather than a book. The palm is missing, as we have already noted, from the *Liber Requiei*'s opening sequence, but it is also absent from several other key scenes where it is normally present in the early Palm narratives. The *Liber Requiei* refers to a palm only in the Jephonias episode, where Peter rather tellingly gives the healed Jephonias instructions to 'arise and take a palm-leaf from this book'.[50] Here the mistake of βιβλίον for βραβεῖον is especially clear. Comparison with the earliest Greek narrative indicates that in an earlier Greek version, on which the *Liber Requiei* depends, this passage originally described a βραβεῖον, which some translator or copyist has mistakenly transformed into a βιβλίον. While it is unquestionable that these two words have in fact been confused in this passage, it nevertheless remains equally beyond question that such a mistake *cannot* be identified as the source of the book's introduction to the narrative. Rather, it seems that the presence of both a βιβλίον and a βραβεῖον in the same narrative, as confirmed by the earliest Greek narrative, has confused a translator or copyist: the occurrence of these two similar-sounding words in the narrative, often in close proximity, is itself the source of the confusion.

This point is particularly demonstrated by *Liber Requiei* 44–5, where the Virgin twice presents John with the book of mysteries. First, according to this narrative, the Virgin 'brought forth a small case that contained the book', presenting the book to John and describing its contents; then, in the following paragraph, we are told that 'after this, she brought him to the book that had been given to her by the angel'.[51] The source of this peculiar doublet is easily identified in the earliest Greek narrative, which has preserved the same passage almost identically. In the Greek, Mary first brings John the book of mysteries (βιβλίον), exactly as described in the *Liber Requiei*; then, immediately thereafter, she brings him the palm (βραβεῖον), with instructions that he is to carry it before her at her funeral.[52] From this we can see that in an earlier version the *Liber Requiei* also included both a book and

[50] ተነሥኡ፡ ወንሣእ፡ ደጕዓሌ፡ አምዝ፡ መጽሐፍ፡ *Liber Requiei* 76 (Arras, *De Transitu*, i. 45 (Eth.) and 29 (Lat.)).

[51] *Liber Requiei* 44–5 (ibid. 27 (Eth.) and 17–18 (Lat.)).

[52] Wenger, *L'Assomption*, 220–3.

a palm, given to John in succession, just as the earliest Greek narrative relates. As it now stands, however, the *Liber Requiei* has confused the palm with a book, owing to a copyist's or translator's mistake in rendering the Greek. The error probably resulted from the close proximity of the book and palm in this passage, as well as being encouraged by the palm's absence from the opening sequence, where the Christ-Angel presents a book instead of a palm.

The comparison of these two early Palm narratives thereby demonstrates that the book and the palm are both archaic features of the Palm traditions. Admittedly, it is still not easy to understand why the *Liber Requiei* describes a book rather than a palm in its initial scene: the narrative context militates against supposing a simple confusion of Greek words in this case, and so we must find another solution. Nevertheless, despite the rather facile dismissal of the book of mysteries by most previous scholarship, the evidence of the earliest traditions demonstrates that this book almost certainly belongs to the earliest stratum of the Palm traditions.

In any case, the presence of such a book should not at all surprise us; similar books of the mysteries and other heavenly books are commonly found in both early Jewish and Christian literature.[53] In the light of their currency within both religious traditions, students of early Jewish Christianity have identified these books as a key element of Jewish-Christian belief and practice. Not surprisingly then, the presence of a book of mysteries in the earliest Palm narratives is often cited as further evidence of their Jewish-Christian origin by proponents of this theory.[54] In fact, Testa has even gone so far as to posit that such

---

[53] See e.g. van Esbroeck, 'Apocryphes géorgiens', 57. For a general survey of this feature of early Jewish and Christian literature, see Leo Koep, *Das himmlische Buch in Antike und Christentum*, Theophaneia, 8 (Bonn: Peter Hanstein Verlag, 1952). More appropriate to this particular 'kind' of book, however, is Daniélou's discussion of heavenly books in Judaism and early Christianity, where he considers particularly that type of book that reveals the mysteries of heaven and earth: Daniélou, *Theology of Jewish Christianity*, 192–204. See also Geo Widengren, *The Ascension of the Apostle and the Heavenly Book*, Uppsala Universitets Årsskrift, 1950: 7 (Uppsala: A. B. Lundequistska Bokhandeln, 1950).

[54] Daniélou, *Theology of Jewish Christianity*, 192–204; Cignelli, 'Il prototipo', 265; Vallecillo, 'El "Transitus Mariae"', 236.

a book of mysteries actually once belonged to the Ebionites of the Mount of Olives, to whom it had been entrusted by John (presumably the very book given to him by Mary). Not content to stop here, however, Testa further identifies the book as a revelation of the group's anthropological, soteriological, and eschatological mysteries, elaborating further with a detailed excursus into Ebionite eschatology.[55]

In addition to this book of the mysteries and the presence of an Angel Christology, proponents of a Jewish-Christian origin for the Dormition traditions adduce a number of additional narrative features in support of their case. Among these is the general emphasis on 'hidden mysteries' throughout the earliest narratives. One of the most basic assumptions shared by these scholars about the early Jewish Christians is that they kept secret their beliefs and the meaning of their sacred symbols, revealing them only to members of the community.[56] This is why, so the argument goes, there is so little historical evidence for these early Christians and, moreover, why their religious signs seem so peculiar and hard to interpret. Because the early Palm traditions manifest great concern for the preservation of secret teachings and revelation, these scholars argue that these texts may be identified with a Jewish-Christian milieu.[57] In addition to the book of mysteries, for instance, the Christ-Angel entrusts Mary with secret teachings, commanding that she share them only with the apostles, who are similarly forbidden from divulging them to anyone except 'those who believe'.[58] The primary content of these teachings is a secret prayer, which must be spoken at death in order to ascend from this world.

Elsewhere the narrative betrays a similar emphasis on the hidden mysteries and maintaining their secrecy, such as in Peter's all-night sermon. On the night before Mary's death,

---

[55] Testa, 'L'origine', 252–4; idem, 'Lo sviluppo', 340–5. The digression on Ebionite eschatology seems to be primarily based on Testa's article 'I Novissimi e la loro localizzazione nella teologia ebraica e giudeo-cristiana', *Liber Annuus*, 26 (1976), 121–69.

[56] Bagatti, *Church from the Circumcision*, 143–7; Testa, *Il simbolismo*, 34–40.

[57] Bagatti, Piccirillo, and Prodomo, *New Discoveries at the Tomb*, 14; Testa, 'L'origine', 252; idem, 'Lo sviluppo', 340–5; Vallecillo, 'El "Transitus Mariae"', 234–40.

[58] *Liber Requiei* 14, 24 (Arras, *De Transitu*, i. 8, 12–13 (Eth.) and 5, 8 (Lat.)); Wenger, *L'Assomption*, 214–15.

Peter suggests that someone should give a sermon, and when the apostles nominate him, he obliges them with an all-night discourse on death and the afterlife.[59] Before too long, however, Peter begins to speak too openly, and he is interrupted by a great light and a voice admonishing him not to disclose any secrets but to speak instead in terms that his audience can receive.[60] Acknowledging this divine intervention, Peter returns to his audience and apologizes for not being able to speak as he had wished, upsetting a group of virgins, who plead with Peter not to stop, but to continue leading them into the 'magnitude of Christ'. Peter reassures them that the voice was not on their account, but for 'those who stand outside of you, who are not worthy of the mystery',[61] and he promises later to reveal to them all that has been revealed to him, since the mystery 'is for all who have preserved the image of their youth'.[62]

Another example of this emphasis comes later in the narrative, as the apostles sit gathered outside the Virgin's tomb, awaiting Christ's return and the Virgin's bodily Assumption. While they wait, Paul turns to Peter and explains that since he is newly established in the Christian faith, he knew neither the Saviour

---

[59] *Liber Requiei* 54–65 (Arras, *De Transitu*, i. 32–9 (Eth.) and 21–6 (Lat.)). Paralleled most notably by the earliest Greek narrative (§30, Wenger, *L'Assomption*, 228–9), L4 (§§19–21, ibid. 251–2), John of Thessalonica's homily (§§9–11, Jugie, *Homilies*, 389–95, 419–23), L2 (§§19–21, A. Wilmart, ed., *Analecta Reginensia: Extraits des manuscrits Latins de la Reine christine conservés au Vatican*, Studi e Testi, 59 (Vatican: Biblioteca Apostolica Vaticana, 1933), 338–41). Many of these versions, however, have omitted various portions of the sermon (e.g. although G1 mentions the sermon, it omits its content). Nevertheless, John of Thessalonica's *Homily on the Dormition* has preserved what is basically a complete version of the sermon as found in the *Liber Requiei*, albeit somewhat altered in the direction of 7th-century orthodoxy. The identity of these two passages and even the nature of John's alterations make it all but certain that this episode as preserved in the *Liber Requiei* belonged to the earliest layer of these traditions.

[60] *Liber Requiei* 57 (Arras, *De Transitu*, i. 33–4 (Eth.) and 22 (Lat.)). See also Wenger's ancient Latin version (L4), 'et facta est uox dicens: "Petre uide ne reuelaris hoc, quia uobis solis datum est hec cognoscere et loqui scientiam."' (Wenger, *L'Assomption*, 251). John of Thessalonica preserves the same scene, but there the voice rebukes Peter only for speaking in terms that his audience cannot understand, without any mention of secrets (*dorm. BMV A* 9 (Jugie, *Homélies*, 390)).

[61] *Liber Requiei* 59 (Arras, *De Transitu*, i. 34 (Eth.) and 23 (Lat.)).

[62] Ibid. 59–60 (ibid. 34–5 (Eth.) and 23 (Lat.)).

nor the secret teachings that he entrusted to the apostles while still on earth. In the light of this, he asks Peter to share these secrets with him. Peter replies that although he is filled with joy that Paul has joined the Christian faith, he cannot, unfortunately, on his own authority disclose these mysteries, which he fears might frighten Paul. Instead, he encourages Paul to have patience and await the Lord's imminent return: then, if Christ approves, he will gladly reveal the mysteries.[63] When shortly thereafter Christ appears, he encourages Paul not to be upset that the apostles will not reveal the 'glorious mysteries', promising that he himself will teach Paul 'the things that are in heaven'.[64] Later, when Christ attempts to make good his promise to Paul, the devil demands that he first be given the opportunity to test Paul, to prove that he is worthy to know the mysteries. Christ agrees, and sending Peter along for help, he hands them over to the devil. After successfully facing the devil,[65] Paul and Peter are then rewarded with a journey to the

---

[63] *Liber Requiei* 78 (ibid. 45–6 (Eth.) and 30 (Lat.)); William Wright, ed., *Contributions to the Apocryphal Literature of the New Testament* (London: Williams & Norgate, 1865), ܐ (Syr.) and 43 (Eng.); Wenger, *L'Assomption*, 238–9; Donahue, *Testament of Mary*, 40–3; Herbert and McNamara, *Irish Biblical Apocrypha*, 125.

[64] *Liber Requiei* 88 (Arras, *De Transitu*, i. 52 (Eth.) and 34 (Lat.)); Wright, *Contributions*, ܠܒ (Syr.) and 46 (Eng.); Wenger, *L'Assomption*, 238–41; Donahue, *Testament of Mary*, 44–5; Herbert and McNamara, *Irish Biblical Apocrypha*, 126.

[65] At this point the *Liber Requiei* relates the rather fantastic details of the contest between Peter and Paul and the devil. This story is unparalleled, however, by any other Dormition narrative and is also known to have circulated independently in the Middle Ages in Arabic and Karshuni versions under the title *The History of Peter and Paul* (Agnes Smith Lewis, ed., *Acta Mythologica Apostolorum*, Horae Semiticae, 3–4 (London: C. J. Clay & Sons, 1904), ١٥٠.–٦٤ (Arab.) and 175–92 (Eng.); A. van Lantschoot, 'Contribution aux Actes de S. Pierre et de S. Paul, II.—Recension Karšuni des Actes de S. Pierre et S. Paul', *Le Muséon*, 68 (1955), 219–33). Both of these facts rather strongly suggest that at some point this independent narrative was probably grafted to the ancient Dormition narrative preserved by the *Liber Requiei* in an effort to fill in the details of Peter and Paul's trials. Although the early (translated probably before 716) and closely related Irish versions note the devil's request to test Paul before he learns the secrets of the universe, as well as Christ's order that Peter assist him, they do not provide the details found in this narrative and simply report the apostles' victory (Donahue, 44–5; Herbert and McNamara, 126; for date see Donahue, 27). This suggests that mention of both Paul's contending

seventh heaven, where God lives, and where they see his throne and many other cosmic wonders, thus fulfilling Christ's earlier promise to Paul.[66]

Other more minor themes have been similarly adduced by scholars as evidence of a Jewish-Christian origin, including reference to the seven heavens, a notion that is additionally linked to a supposed Jewish-Christian emphasis on the soul's ascent of the 'cosmic ladder' at its departure from the body.[67] Likewise, the power attributed the Christ-Angel's name and the fear that it would destroy the city are understood to reflect a Jewish-Christian belief in the power of divine names.[68] Michael's role as the psychopomp and even the role played by clouds in transporting the apostles from the ends of the earth have been similarly invoked as indications of a Jewish-Christian matrix.[69] But in the face of all this evidence, several fundamental questions still remain to be answered. For instance, we must ask if there are perhaps other early Christian milieux that could similarly explain the peculiar contents of the earliest Dormition traditions. More importantly, however, the entire category of 'Jewish-Christianity' as these scholars have defined it is a rather questionable construct, and as its critics have occasionally suggested, it may never even have existed as such outside the studies of its modern advocates.

Roughly forty years have passed since Daniélou, Bagatti, and Testa popularized the notion of an early 'Church from the Circumcision' that was theologically distinct from the 'Gentile' church, and during this interval, numerous studies have

---

with the devil and Peter's assistance are probably ancient, although the details provided from *The History of Peter and Paul* are not.

[66] *Liber Requiei* 132–6 (Arras, *De Transitu*, i. 81–4 (Eth.) and 52–4 (Lat.)).

[67] Bagatti, *Church from the Circumcision*, 279–93; idem, 'Ricerche sulle tradizioni', 188–9; Bagatti, Piccirillo, and Prodomo, *New Discoveries at the Tomb*, 14; Daniélou, *Theology of Jewish Christianity*, 173–81; Vallecillo, 'El "Transitus Mariae"', 228–34.

[68] Bagatti, *Church from the Circumcision*, 166–74; Daniélou, *Theology of Jewish Christianity*, 147–63; Testa, *Il simbolismo*, 361–424; Manns, *Le Récit*, 158–60; Vallecillo, 'El "Transitus Mariae"', 218–21.

[69] Michael: Manns, *Le Récit*, 156–8; Cignelli, 'Il prototipo', 265; Vallecillo, 'El "Transitus Mariae"', 223–8. Clouds: Bagatti, 'Ricerche sulle tradizioni', 189; Manns, *Le Récit*, 131–7; Cignelli, 'Il prototipo', 265; Vallecillo, 'El "Transitus Mariae"'.

appeared that are both critical and supportive of this view. Joan E. Taylor has recently surveyed both the corpus of ancient evidence for Jewish-Christianity and the reception of this category by scholars of early Christianity, eliminating the need to repeat her labour here. In *Christians and the Holy Places: The Myth of Jewish-Christian Origins*, Taylor raises a strong critique of Jewish-Christianity as identified by Daniélou, Bagatti, Testa, and others, focusing especially on the alleged archaeological evidence put forth by the two latter scholars.[70] In summary, her criticisms of this approach, with which I am in substantial agreement, are as follows. In the first place, she disputes the value of much evidence on which Bagatti and Testa have based their theories: 'Jewish-Christian' ossuaries identified by the Franciscans are in fact more likely to be simply 'Jewish', and the 'Jewish-Christian' funerary *stelai* of Khirbet Kilkish are almost certainly an elaborate forgery, of which Bagatti and Testa were the unfortunate victims.[71] Since these two archaeological assemblages formed the primary basis of Testa's *Il simbolismo dei Giudeo-cristiani*, this work must now be viewed in terms of these recent determinations.

Taylor also critiques the way in which these scholars have constructed the category of Jewish-Christianity, basing it largely on theology and ethnicity rather than on praxis.[72] As she notes, if one were to define Jewish-Christianity as a group of early Christians who utilized Jewish concepts and categories and/or were ethnically Jewish, then one must surely include Paul as a prime example of such a Jewish Christian. Yet, Paul is traditionally identified as the font of the Gentile church. Rather,

---

[70] Joan E. Taylor, *Christians and the Holy Places: The Myth of Christian Origins* (Oxford: Clarendon Press, 1993). In addition to providing a general critique of Bagatti and Testa's hypotheses, this work focuses especially on debunking their claim that these early Jewish-Christians reliably preserved the memory of the early Christian holy sites. This, the Franciscans argue, assures us that the sites venerated today, most of which were first identified after Constantine, are in fact in the correct locations.

[71] Ibid. 5–17.

[72] The following paragraph is based on ibid. 18–47, and eadem, 'Phenomenon of Early Jewish-Christianity'. See also J. Carleton Paget, 'Jewish Christianity', in William Horbury, W. D. Davies, and John Sturdy (eds.), *The Cambridge History of Judaism*, iii. *The Early Roman Period* (Cambridge: Cambridge University Press, 2000), 731–75, esp. 733–42, where similar conclusions are reached.

it seems that what distinguished Paul and the other 'Gentile' Christians from 'Jewish Christians' was neither their ethnic origin nor their use of Jewish religious ideas and symbols: it was instead their view of the Law. It cannot be denied that there were in the early church Christians who, after their conversion, observed the Jewish Law in addition to practising Christianity. But it does not seem that Gentiles were excluded from these communities, and consequently, their boundaries were not defined by ethnicity; likewise, there were certainly many Jews who, like Paul, decided that becoming Christian meant no longer following the Law. Consequently, an ethnic definition of Jewish-Christianity is not particularly meaningful.

Nor is a theologically based definition very useful, such as is presented in Daniélou's identification of Jewish-Christianity as 'the expression of Christianity in the thought forms of Later Judaism'.[73] Such a definition is exceedingly broad, even more so when one takes into consideration the remarkable breadth of Judaism during the Graeco-Roman era.[74] The use of Jewish genres and ideas cannot distinguish Jewish from Gentile Christianity, since these are equally employed by Gentile Christians, as Taylor rightly determines: 'Christianity is the child of Judaism. The notion of Christ is a Jewish concept. The Christian God is the Jewish God. The division between what is somehow exclusively Christian and what is Jewish is an impossible one to make in the early Church. Very many types of Jewish thought fed into the diversity of early Christianity. The corpus of the New Testament itself bears witness to a range of Jewish thought.'[75] Taylor then concludes that the only possibly meaningful distinction between 'Jewish' Christians and 'Gentile' Christians is one centred on the observance of the Jewish Law, a phenomenon that is known to have existed among Christians from our early sources, often transcending the boundaries of ethnicity and theology.

[73] Daniélou, *Theology of Jewish Christianity*, 10.

[74] This point is well made by R. E. Brown, 'Not Jewish Christianity and Gentile Christianity, but Types of Jewish/Gentile Christianity', *Catholic Biblical Quarterly*, 45 (1983), 74–9. See also Robert A. Kraft, 'The Multiform Jewish Heritage of Early Christianity', in Jacob Neusner (ed.), *Christianity, Judaism and Other Greco-Roman Cults: Studies for Morton Smith at Sixty*, 3 vols. (Leiden: E. J. Brill, 1975), iii. 174–99.

[75] Taylor, 'Phenomenon of Early Jewish-Christianity', 317.

From this vantage, it is indeed questionable if there ever was a specific group that espoused the peculiar Jewish-Christian theology identified by Daniélou and others. Moreover, it is further debatable whether the elements of this theology are properly regarded as Jewish: for instance, most of these scholars, and Testa especially, attribute many concepts to Jewish-Christianity that are more appropriately identified with the Christian gnostic traditions. Although there is little question that each of the heterodox themes identified as Jewish-Christian was current in early Christianity, it is not at all evident that this assortment of beliefs was ever collectively espoused by an actual group of Christians, nor, more importantly, that they are somehow uniquely Jewish. In the case of Daniélou's study, Jewish-Christian sources are identified according to the following criteria: (1) a date before the middle of the second century; (2) a literary genre common in early Judaism; and (3) ideas characteristic of Jewish Christianity, including especially apocalyptic.[76] This encompasses an enormous corpus of materials, and it is rather questionable that they all witness to the same, relatively homogenous construct that Daniélou identifies as 'the' theology of Jewish Christianity.[77] While it must be admitted that the Franciscans have done an admirable job of identifying the many heterodox theologoumena of the earliest Palm narratives, the fundamental flaws in the modern invention of a primitive Jewish-Christianity suggest that we should continue searching for other early Christian phenomena that might better illuminate the prehistory of the Dormition traditions.

B. Gnostic Christianity and the Prehistory of the Dormition Traditions

In the light of the various problems surrounding the rather dubious construct of Jewish-Christianity, it is with some trepidation that I propose the Christian gnostic traditions as a possible alternative, particularly since the work of Michael

---

[76] Daniélou, *Theology of Jewish Christianity*, 11.

[77] For such a critique of Daniélou, see Robert A. Kraft, 'In Search of "Jewish Christianity" and its "Theology": Problems of Definition and Methodology', *Recherches de Science Religieuse*, 60 (1972), 81–92.

A. Williams has recently posed a similar critique of this interpretative category.[78] It must be admitted that many of Williams's arguments for abandoning the use of 'gnosticism' are well made, and the work will undoubtedly have an impact on the understanding of both gnostic Christianities and other related religious phenomena for some time to come. The study's primary contribution is its convincing demonstration of the sometimes baffling complexity of traditions associated with 'gnosis falsely so-called': the bulk of the study successfully describes the theological menagerie that has been gathered into 'gnosticism', in which the ancient heresiologists themselves saw the many-headed hydra of Greek lore.[79] It is primarily on the basis of this diversity that Williams proposes his larger thesis: that 'gnosticism' has become 'such a protean label that it has all but lost any reliably identifiable meaning for the larger reading public'.[80] It is a 'sick sign', and as such it needs to be replaced.

In order to make his point more clear, Williams presents brief summaries of four traditionally gnostic systems: the *Apocryphon of John*, Valentinian Christianity, Justin the Gnostic's *Book Baruch*, and Marcionite Christianity. Following their descriptions, Williams observes that two things are present in all four of these systems. Firstly, all four posit 'a distinction of some sort between a truly transcendent deity and the creators of the world'. In addition, they 'all include some message sent from the higher realm, which is intended to call humans to an awareness of something more than this physical world and ascent to the transcendent realm'. Beyond these two points, however, the thought systems are remarkably diverse, in the light of which Williams concludes that such dissimilar phenomena cannot be collectively known as 'gnosticism'.[81] To replace this 'sick sign' Williams suggests as an alternative 'biblical demiurgical

---

[78] Michael A. Williams, *Rethinking Gnosticism: An Argument for Dismantling a Dubious Category* (Princeton: Princeton University Press, 1996), esp. ch. 2.

[79] Irenaeus, *haer.* 1. 30. 15 (Adelin Rousseau and Louis Doutreleau, eds., *Irénée de Lyon: Contre les hérésies*, 9 vols., SC 100, 152–3, 210–11, 263–4, 293–4 (Paris: Les Éditions du Cerf, 1969–82), bk. I, ii. (294), 385–6; Hippolytus of Rome, *haer.* 5. 11. 1 (Miroslav Marcovich, ed., *Hippolytus: Refutatio omnium haeresium*, Patristische Texte und Studien, 25 (Berlin: Walter de Gruyter, 1986), 173).

[80] Williams, *Rethinking Gnosticism*, 3.

[81] Ibid. 26–7.

traditions' for the following reasons: (1) it has a specific rather than general referent; (2) it is a modern invention, rather an ancient self-designation; (3) it is free from the prejudicial associations that gnosticism has acquired in both patristic and modern literature. Williams recognizes himself that this category fails to include all the material that has been traditionally identified as gnostic, but it was not his goal to achieve this; rather, he proposes to have developed a new construct that encompasses much traditionally gnostic material, while at the same time being both specific and useful.[82]

Unfortunately, however, this is not an altogether satisfactory solution, since, in my opinion, 'biblical demiurgical traditions' similarly fails to be very specific, and it does little to address the concern (raised by Williams) for having terminology familiar to the larger reading public. More importantly, however, this redefinition excludes far too much of the material traditionally known as 'gnostic', a problem that Williams recognizes and, in all fairness, is not concerned to resolve in his study.[83] The primary difficulty with Williams's alternative taxonomy as I see it lies in his decision to focus almost exclusively on the biblical and demiurgic components of the erstwhile gnostic traditions, while almost completely neglecting the central theme of 'gnosis' or salvific knowledge.[84] In drawing these boundaries, his definition excludes the Mandean and Manichean traditions, for instance: although these perhaps are not especially 'biblical' or 'demiurgical' traditions, they none the less have important and interesting connections with the so-called ancient gnostic traditions, similarities that demand a category capable of their expression. Moreover, in failing to emphasize the esoteric dimension of these phenomena, Williams has himself created a category that is extremely broad. Demiurgy, as Williams defines it, is a tradition that 'distinguishes between the creator(s) and controllers of the material world and the most transcendent being'.[85] Thus, the biblical demiurgical traditions encompass such disparate

---

[82] Williams, *Rethinking Gnosticism*, 51–3.

[83] Ibid. 265.

[84] Kurt Rudolph also identifies this as one of the fundamental characteristics of the gnostic traditions: *Gnosis: The Nature and History of Gnosticism*, trans. and ed. Robert McLachlan Wilson (San Francisco: Harper & Row, 1987), 55–6.

[85] Williams, *Rethinking Gnosticism*, 265.

members as Justin the Gnostic, Marcion, Philo, Valentinus, and Arius, among others. While it is certainly worthwhile to consider the possible connections among these deuterotheistic traditions, one must ask, is this assemblage any less motley and unwieldy than the one Williams so ardently insists needs replacing?

Williams himself is at least partially aware of the impact of this focus, when, for instance, in his conclusion he explains his emphasis on demiurgical traditions as follows: 'And in fact, there are scholars who would consider what I have called biblical demiurgy to be, in the final analysis, the only genuinely defining feature of "gnosticism." Nevertheless, there are some sources that many would want to call "gnostic" on the basis of other features in them, such as an orientation toward esoteric knowledge.'[86] No effort is made, however, to justify the exclusion of esoteric knowledge to those of us who fall into this second category. The concept of 'gnosis' is in fact oddly scarce in this study on 'gnosticism'. Williams devotes much consideration to various other themes that are often seen as typically gnostic, including 'protest exegesis', an anti-cosmic attitude, disdain for the body, and a belief in determinism. After demonstrating the range of opinions on these topics in various gnostic traditions, he concludes that these themes are not useful for developing a new category to represent this material, leaving us primarily with demiurgy. Nevertheless, Williams presents no similar discussion of the traditional association between secret knowledge and 'gnosticism' that would account for its exclusion from his new definition. This oversight of esoteric knowledge is even more peculiar given the fact that Williams himself demonstrates the fundamental importance of this concept from the very beginning of his study. In drawing conclusions from his initial summaries of four gnostic systems, Williams notes that, together with the demiurge, the heavenly message that enables ascent is present in all four of these otherwise very diverse traditions. Consequently, it would seem that any useful alternative to 'gnosticism' should acknowledge and include this basic component of the gnostic traditions.

A more useful category in my opinion, would identify the 'esoteric-demiurgic traditions' as a group, since it seems to me that the emphasis on saving, esoteric knowledge is a more

[86] Ibid. 265.

constant and fundamental characteristic of 'gnosticism' than the biblical tradition. This emphasis on gnosis and demiurgy would come even closer to approximating the traditional category of 'gnosticism' than Williams's alternative, yet without the disadvantages of being either vague or prejudicial. In fact, Williams seems to have discovered as much himself, when he notes the presence of both these themes in each of his exemplary traditions. Yet for some unexplained reason, he overlooks this important connection, without ever really explaining why he elects to exclude the common thread of gnosis. One particular advantage of this alternative taxonomy is its ability to address the 'semi-gnosticism', or 'gnosticizing tendencies', of certain late antique religious movements, such as Thomas Christianity or the Hermetic corpus, both of which similarly emphasize salvation through esoteric knowledge (gnosis) and the return of the soul, but either are not demiurgical or biblical. Williams acknowledges these omissions, explaining that 'connections and/ or similarities are certainly present between these bodies of fascinating phenomena [i.e. Manicheanism, Mandeism, the Hermetica] and the smaller assortment that is the focus of this book', but that 'inclusion of this wider circle of phenomena would underscore the overall point that I am making'.[87] Nevertheless, it seems to me that, to the contrary, these connections do not support Williams's argument, but highlight instead the importance of having terminology capable of including and addressing these affinities.

A possible alternative then to Williams's proposed 'biblical demiurgical traditions' would be 'esoteric-demiurgic traditions', as suggested above. This label seems to represent more accurately and encompass more completely the phenomena in question by focusing on deuterotheism and esoteric knowledge. In spite of this, I have determined to continue naming these traditions 'gnostic', for various reasons, several of which have previously been articulated by others elsewhere.[88] Although

---

[87] Williams, *Rethinking Gnosticism*, 6.

[88] See e.g. Bentley Layton, *The Gnostic Scriptures* (Garden City, NY: Doubleday & Co., 1987), 5, 8; Kurt Rudolph, ' "Gnosis" and "Gnosticism"— The Problems of their Definition and their Relation to the Writings of the New Testament', in *Gnosis und Spätantike Religionsgeschicte: Gesammelte Aufsätze*, Nag Hammadi and Manichaean Studies, 42 (Leiden: E. J. Brill, 1996), 34–52; originally printed in A. H. B. Logan and A. J. M. Wedderburn (eds.), *The New*

'gnosticism' is probably best abandoned, for reasons made clear by Kurt Rudolph almost two decades ago, it seems that the adjective 'gnostic' may be retained.[89] In the first place, as Williams himself appropriately expresses concern, we need language that can speak to the 'larger reading public'. Both 'biblical demiurgical traditions' and 'esoteric-demiurgic traditions' are rather jargonistic, technically oriented terms that will not, in my opinion, realize this goal. Gnostic, on the other hand, is a relatively familiar term, which, as Rudolph has noted, has a well-established usage in scholarship and, despite its problems, 'has proved its worth'.[90]

Moreover, 'gnostic' is in some sense an emic term. Although it is strangely absent from the Nag Hammadi literature, even Williams admits the likelihood that certain ancient groups identified themselves as gnostic.[91] In this regard, one can also point to the Mandeans, the only gnostic tradition to have survived from antiquity, whose self-designation, *Mandaiia* ('the knowers'), declares them to be gnostics. Yet even if this may not be the preferred self-designation of all the different groups that have been gathered under this rubric, the term 'gnostic' was widely used in antiquity to refer to these religious traditions, and as such it had a recognizable referent during the period here under study. Admittedly, it may have been used primarily by opponents, who in general wished to disparage these groups, but historically speaking, it is not uncommon for a group's eventual self-designation to originate among outsiders or opponents: one need only consider such names as Methodist or Quaker, or even Protestant or Christian, for that matter. Indeed, the label 'Valentinian', which Williams appears to accept, is not a self-designation encountered in any Valentinian writing; rather, it appears to be a name coined by the adversaries of Valentinian Christianity.[92]

Testament and Gnosis: Essays in Honor of Robert McLachlan Wilson (Edinburgh: T. & T. Clark, 1983), 21–37.

[89] e.g. Rudolph, ' "Gnosis" and "Gnosticism" '.
[90] Ibid. 45.
[91] Williams, *Rethinking Gnosticism*, 31–43, esp. 41–2. See also Layton, *The Gnostic Scriptures*, 5, 8.
[92] See Williams, *Rethinking Gnosticism*, 51, and Layton, *The Gnostic Scriptures*, 270.

Instead of abandoning the term 'gnostic' then, as Williams suggests, I propose that it should be retained, although in the light of the many complications identified in Williams's study, we must define its boundaries clearly. I will use the terms 'gnostic' Christianity and 'gnostic' traditions in reference to religious phenomena from the early Christian period that include both a demiurgic component and an emphasis on hidden, salvific knowledge, or gnosis. In addition, I will occasionally identify some themes as frequently or commonly 'gnostic': these are themes that, while not regular enough to be included in a definition of the gnostic traditions, are none the less commonly encountered in gnostic material. Nevertheless, their presence or absence does not impact the classification of a given phenomenon as gnostic.

According to these terms, the earliest Dormition narratives of the Palm tradition betray evidence of contact with gnostic Christianity: one meets both demiurgy and esoteric knowledge, as well as a number of commonly gnostic themes. The possibility of origins within a gnostic milieu was first suggested by W. H. C. Frend, in an impressionistic article,[93] and more recently a handful of scholars have observed the presence of many important gnostic themes in the earliest Palm narratives. Mario Erbetta, for instance, notes the presence of several key gnostic terms and ideas in his translations of several early Dormition narratives, yet without going so far as to draw conclusions regarding the traditions' origins on the basis of these connections.[94] Both editors of the Yale Coptic Dormition fragments, Leslie S. B. MacCoull and now Philip Sellew, have similarly noted elements suggesting a gnostic ambiance both in the Coptic fragments and in the early Palm narratives more generally.[95] Frédéric Manns also very briefly considers the possibility of a gnostic origin, only to reject it on the peculiar grounds that the early Dormition traditions place 'such great importance on the Scriptures'.[96] Yet given the

[93] W. H. C. Frend, 'The Gnostic Origins of the Assumption Legend', *The Modern Churchman*, 43 (1953), 23–8.

[94] Erbetta, *Gli apocrifi*, 410–11, 473 nn. 11, 17, 23.

[95] Leslie S. B. MacCoull, 'More Coptic Papyri from the Beinecke Collection', *Archiv für Papyrusforschung*, 35 (1989), 31–2; Sellew, 'Early Coptic Witness', 49–50.

[96] Manns, *Le Récit*, 115–16.

well-known gnostic fondness for the Scriptures, both Hebrew and Christian, this is hardly a serious reason for excluding this possibility.[97]

While it would certainly be going too far at this point to attribute the origin of these narratives to a particular ancient gnostic group, the earliest Palm narratives certainly betray evidence of considerable contact with such a milieu at an early stage in their history. Considering first several themes already discussed above in the context of Jewish-Christianity, we find that many of these supposedly Jewish-Christian ideas are frequently encountered in ancient gnostic literature. For instance, the Angel Christology of the earliest narratives can be explained by their development within a gnostic milieu, since a number of ancient gnostic groups identified the 'gnostic redeemer' or 'revealer' as an angel.[98] The notion that Christ was an angel appears in a number of the gnostic writings found at Nag Hammadi,[99] as well as in the famous 'Flavia Sophe' inscrip-

---

[97] Indeed, Williams has proposed a biblical orientation as one of the primary criteria for 'rethinking gnosticism'. See e.g. Williams, *Rethinking Gnosticism*, 54–79; Elaine H. Pagels, *The Gnostic Paul: Gnostic Exegesis of the Pauline Letters* (Philadelphia: Fortress Press, 1975); and eadem, *The Johannine Gospel in Gnostic Exegesis: Heracleon's Commentary on John*, Society of Biblical Literature Monograph Series, 17 (Nashville: Abingdon Press, 1973).

[98] Rudolph, *Gnosis*, 131, Layton, *Gnostic Scriptures*, 24, 52–3, 122, and 142; Trigg, 'Angel of Great Counsel', 41. Examples include, in addition to those in the following notes: *The Hypostasis of the Archons* 93. 7–97. 21 (Bentley Layton, ed., *Nag Hammadi Codex II, 2–7*, 2 vols., NHS 20–1 (Leiden: E. J. Brill, 1989), i. 250–1); *On the Origin of the World* 124. 12–14 (ibid. ii. 84–5); *Melchizedek* 14. 26–15. 7 (Birger A. Pearson, ed., *Nag Hammadi codices IX and X*, NHS 15 (Leiden: E. J. Brill, 1981), 66–9); Justin the Gnostic, *Book Baruch* (preserved in Hippolytus, *haer.* 5. 26.1–27. 5 (Marcovich, *Hippolytus*, 200–9)).

[99] In addition to those mentioned in n. 98 above, *The Sophia of Jesus Christ* 91. 12–13/78. 15–17 (Douglas M. Parrott, ed., *Nag Hammadi Codices III, 3–4 and V, 1*, NHS 27 (Leiden: E. J. Brill, 1991), 39); *Pistis Sophia* 7–8 (Carl Schmidt, ed., and Violet MacDermot, trans., *Pistis Sophia*, NHS 9 (Leiden: E. J. Brill, 1978), 12–13). See also *The Gospel according to Philip* 56. 13–15, 57. 35–58. 1 (Bentley Layton, ed., *Nag Hammadi Codex II, 2–7*, 2 vols., NHS 20–1 (Leiden: E. J. Brill, 1989), i. 54–5); *The Testimony of Truth* 68.10–20 (Birger A. Pearson, ed., *Nag Hammadi Codices IX and X*, NHS 15 (Leiden: E. J. Brill, 1981), 186–7). See in addition Carl Schmidt's discussion of the gnostic texts from the Codex Brucianus: *Gnostische Schriften in koptischer Sprache aus dem Codex Brucianus*, TU 8. 1 (Leipzig: J. C. Hinrichs'sche Buchhandlung, 1892), 433. See also Martin Werner, *The Formation of Christian Dogma: An Historical Study of its Problem*, trans. S. G. F. Brandon (New York: Harper & Bros., 1957),

tion, a gnostic epitaph found on a third-century Roman tomb. This inscription exhorts Flavia Sophe, the deceased, to 'hasten to gaze at the divine features of the aeons, the Great Angel of the great council (i.e. the Redeemer), the true Son'.[100] The inscription's explicit mention of Christ elsewhere assures us that Flavia Sophe was a Christian gnostic, and the inscription's specific reference to the bridal chamber might further suggest she was a Valentinian.[101] If this were the case, the inscription would comport with the witness of several early Christian writers who report that the Valentinians believed Christ to have been an 'angel from the Pleroma'.[102]

As important as the Angel Christology may be for identifying a gnostic context, this is not one of the two key elements that we have identified as distinguishing the gnostic traditions. Much more significant for establishing this connection are the emphasis on esoteric, soteriological knowledge and the indication of demiurgy in the earliest Palm narratives. The book of the mysteries and various other references to secret knowledge already described above certainly point in the direction of the gnostic traditions. Such heavenly books are often a feature of gnostic literature,[103] but it is the persistent emphasis on hidden

134, where he notes the identification of Christ with an angel in several Christian gnostic sources.

[100] Translation is from Rudolph, *Gnosis*, 212, where he also provides a clear photograph of the inscription. The inscription has been published with commentary in Carlo Cecchelli, *Monumenti cristiano-eretici di Roma* (Rome: Fratelli Palombi, 1944), 149–53; and in A. Ferrua, SJ, 'Questioni di epigrafia eretica romana', *Revista di archeologica christiana*, 21 (1944/5), 185–9.

[101] Rudolph identifies the bridal chamber specifically with the Valentinians in *Gnosis*, 245–7.

[102] Clement of Alexandria, *exc. Thdot.* 35. 1 (François Sagnard, ed., *Clément d'Alexandrie: Extraits de Théodote*, SC 23 (Paris: Éditions du Cerf, 1948), 136); Irenaeus, *haer.* 1. 2. 6 (Rousseau and Doutreleau, *Irénée de Lyon*, bk. I, ii (294), 48); Hippolytus, *haer.* 6. 51. 1 (Marcovich, *Hippolytus*, 271). Irenaeus also attributes this belief to the followers of Marcus: Irenaeus, *haer.* 1. 15. 3 (Rousseau and Doutreleau, *Irénée de Lyon*, bk. I, ii (294), 242–5). See also Antonio Orbe, SJ, *Estudios Valentinianos*, i. *Hacia la primera teologica de la procesion del Verbo*, Analecta Gregoriana, 99 (Rome: Gregorian University, 1958), 408–10.

[103] See e.g. *The Gospel of Truth* 19. 27–24. 9 (Harold W. Attridge, ed., *Nag Hammadi Codex I (The Jung Codex)*, 2 vols., NHS 22 (Leiden: E. J. Brill, 1985), i. 86–93); *The Gospel of the Egyptians*, III. 68. 1–69. 17 (Alexander Böhlig and Frederik Wisse, eds., *Nag Hammadi Codices III, 2 and IV, 2: The Gospel of*

mysteries that bring salvation that tips the balance strongly in favour of some kind of gnostic milieu. In the discussion of a possible Jewish-Christian origin above, we have already noted the early Palm narratives' concern for guarding secret knowledge and preventing it from being acquired by those unworthy of it: this was seen in the interruption of Peter's all-night sermon, Peter's refusal to share the mysteries with Paul, and the Christ-Angel's instructions to Mary that she share his revelations only with the apostles.

An examination of the extended revelation dialogue that took place between Mary and the Christ-Angel will lead us even further in the direction of the ancient gnostic traditions.[104] One of the first things to suggest this is the power attributed to the Christ-Angel's secret name,[105] which he eventually reveals to Mary, along with more important, specifically soteriological knowledge. The Christ-Angel reveals this salvific gnosis in response to Mary's request near the beginning of the dialogue, when she asks: 'What will we do when we rest our body, because we do not want to abandon it on earth, because it is before us? And as it suits us to dwell in this form of ours, we want our body to be with us in that place.'[106] Before answering, the Christ-Angel explains to Mary that the apostles had previously asked for

the Egyptians, NHS 4 (Grand Rapids, MI: Eerdmans, 1975), 162–6) and Pheme Perkins, *Gnosticism and the New Testament* (Minneapolis: Fortress Press, 1993), 190.

[104] This scene of course portrays Mary of Nazareth in a role very similar to that of the so-called 'gnostic Mary'. While this Mary, who appears in a number of the Coptic 'gnostic' apocrypha, is usually regarded as being Mary of Magdala, there is much evidence, from the early Dormition narratives as well as elsewhere, to suggest that the 'gnostic' Mary's identity is equally intertwined with Mary of Nazareth. For more on this, see Stephen J. Shoemaker, 'Rethinking the "Gnostic Mary": Mary of Nazareth and Mary of Magdala in Early Christian Tradition', *Journal of Early Christian Studies* (forthcoming); idem, 'A Case of Mistaken Identity?: Naming the "Gnostic Mary"', in F. Stanley Jones (ed.), *Mary(s) in Early Christian Literature* (Atlanta: Society for Biblical Literature) (forthcoming).

[105] See e.g. the extended discussion of the power of the divine name in *The Gospel of Truth* 37. 37–41. 14 (Attridge, *Nag Hammadi Codex I*, i. 110–15).

[106] *Liber Requiei* 12 (Arras, *De Transitu*, i. 7 (Eth.) and 4 (Lat.)). In the Georgian version, the Christ-Angel tells Mary of the time when this question was posed by the apostles and then answers it for her: van Esbroeck, 'Apocryphes géorgiens', 73 (Geor.) and 75 (Lat.).

this same knowledge, but were denied. Now, however, he agrees to provide her with the answer, instructing her to share the secret knowledge with the apostles when they arrive for her funeral. The primary content of this revelation is a secret prayer, which the Christ-Angel instructs Mary to recite as she goes forth from her body,[107] since one 'cannot ascend without this prayer';[108] the prayer must be observed 'with every world', for without it, 'it is not possible to pass by the beast with the head of a lion and the tail of a serpent, so as to pass through every world'.[109] The prayer, he orders Mary, must be kept secret from those who love the world and have not desired and kept word of the Lord.[110]

This secret prayer, which serves as a password enabling the soul to pass through various 'worlds' during its ascent after death, brings to mind similar notions from ancient gnostic literature. A key point of unity among the ancient gnostic traditions is their belief that a 'spark of light' from the transcendent realm lies imprisoned in the body of each gnostic believer, and that possession of the salvific gnosis enables this spark to ascend through the cosmic spheres and return to the realm of light and spirit.[111] The various regions lying between the spiritual and material worlds, however, are guarded by the demiurge and his rulers, who attempt to prevent this escape, forcing the spark of light to return to the earth, where it will live and die again. In the light of this understanding of the universe and salvation, the secret knowledge that many gnostic traditions offered their followers had a very practical content, consisting of passwords that would allow the soul to pass by the guardians of the various

---

[107] προσευχὴν ἐδεξάμην παρὰ τοῦ Πατρὸς ἐρχόμενος πρὸς σὲ καί νῦν λέγω σοι αὐτὴν ἵνα εἴπῃς ἐξερζομένη ἐκ τοῦ σώματος ἀνατέλλοντος τοῦ ἡλίου, οὕτως γὰρ ἀναπέμπεται. Wenger, *L'Assomption*, 214–15. The Ethiopic parallel is rather nonsensical, but seems to centre around the same idea: ወይእዜኒ፡ አአምሬ፡ ምግተ፡ አግበር፡ እስኩ፡ አሙ፡ አፈኑ፡ ሳዕሊኪ፡ ጸሎተ፡ ወነሣእኩ፡ አምኀበ፡ አቡየ፡ *Liber Requiei* 13 (Arras, *De Transitu*, i. 7 (Eth.) and 5 (Lat.); see also the commentary on this passage in 'Appendix II de *Libro Requiei*', Arras, *De Transitu*, i. 79–81 (Lat.).

[108] ወኢይክሉ፡ ዓሪገ፡ ዘእንበለ፡ ጸሎት፡ *Liber Requiei* 14 (Arras, *De Transitu*, i. 7–8 (Eth.) and 5 (Lat.)).

[109] ሀሎወኪ፡ ከሙ፡ ትዕቀቢ፡ምስለ፡ ቴሉ፡ ዓለም፡ ... እስሙ፡ ኢይትከሃል፡ ተዐድዎተ፡ ስሰባዕ፡ አስኩ፡ ያሐልፉ፡ ቴሉ፡ ዓለም፡ ibid. 15 (ibid. 8 (Eth.) and 5 (Lat.)).

[110] Wenger, *L'Assomption*, 214–15; *Liber Requiei* 14–15 (Arras, *De Transitu*, i. 78 (Eth.) and 5 (Lat.)).

[111] See the extensive survey of different traditions in Rudolph, *Gnosis*, 171–204, esp. 171–2.

cosmic spheres during its ascent. By speaking these words at the appropriate time and in the proper order, one could force the cosmic rulers to allow passage through the spheres and into the spiritual realm.[112] The secret prayer in the *Liber Requiei* appears to have a similar function, a connection that is under-scored by the description of the one who impedes ascent as a 'beast with the head of a lion and the tail of a serpent'. This description matches the frequent depiction of the demiurge or chief ruler in the Coptic gnostic texts as 'lion-like' or 'lion-faced', or, in the case of the *Apocryphon of John*, as a 'lion-faced ser-pent'.[113]

After the secret prayer's disclosure, the Christ-Angel con-tinues revealing mysteries to his mother, but unfortunately this part of the dialogue is extant only in the *Liber Requiei*. To make matters worse, the text becomes somewhat garbled at this point in both manuscripts (no doubt because of its heterodox content), although despite these obstacles, we can still tease the general outline and content out of the text. This section of the narrative is especially important because it refers to a common gnostic cosmological myth, including specific indication of the world's

---

[112] See Arras, *De Transitu*, ii. 81 (Lat.). Examples include *The (First) Apoca-lypse of James*, 32. 28–35. 9 (Douglas M. Parrott, ed., *Nag Hammadi Codices V, 2–5 and VI with Papyrus Berolinensis 8502, 1 and 4*, NHS 11 (Leiden: E. J. Brill, 1979), 84–9); *The Books of Jeu*, 33–8, 49–52 (Carl Schmidt, ed., and Violet MacDermot, trans., *The Books of Jeû and the Untitled Text in the Bruce Codex*, NHS 13 (Leiden: E. J. Brill, 1978), 83–8, 116–38). For a general discus-sion, see Rudolph, *Gnosis*, 172–80, 244. Cf. Irenaeus, *Adversus Haereses* 1. 21. 5 (Rousseau and Doutreleau, *Irénée de Lyon*, bk. I, ii (294), 304–8).

[113] e.g. *Apocryphon of John*, Synopsis 25 (Michael Waldstein and Frederic Wisse, eds., *The Apocryphon of John: A Synopsis of Nag Hammadi Codices II, 1, III, 1, and IV, 1 with BG 8502,2*, NHS 33 (New York: E. J. Brill, 1995), 60–1); *Pistis Sophia* 30–9, 47–57 (Schmidt and MacDermot, *Pistis Sophia*, 45–63, 86–111, *passim*); *The Hypostasis of the Archons* 94. 17 (Layton, *Nag Hammadi Codex II*, i. 252–3); *On the Origin of the World* 100.7, 26 (Layton, *Nag Hammadi Codex II*, ii. 34–5). Note also that in the *Apocalypse of Zephaniah*, Zephaniah is guided by a 'great angel', whom he worships as 'the Lord Almighty' and who is described as follows: 'His hair was spread out like the lionesses'. His teeth were outside his mouth like a bear. His hair was spread out like women's. His body was like the serpent's when he wished to swallow me.' *Apocalypse of Zephaniah* 6. 8 (Georg Steindorff, ed., *Die Apokalypse des Elias, eine unbekannte Apokalypse und Bruchstücke der Sophonias-Apokalypse*, TU 17.3a (Leipzig: J. C. Hinrichs, 1899), 46–8; trans.: James H. Charlesworth, ed., *The Old Testament Pseudepigrapha*, 2 vols. (Garden City, NY: Doubleday, 1983), i. 512).

creation by a 'demiurge'. In the following passage, the Christ-Angel describes for Mary certain events regarding the creation of Adam:

But on that day the body of Adam was in the glory that dwelled upon him, the body that remained lying on the earth, which he made with the Father, who was with him in counsel and participation. And this is that which was from the beginning and was even before the angels and the archangels, before the creation of the powers by me, until he sat and he was moved by the Ruler, when it was apparent that he could not arise. And God knew what was in the soul; and he rested and placed rest in his heart so that it would pray to him. And when the Father said this to Adam, he arose and was in the custody of the Father and the Son and the Holy Spirit until this day.[114]

As it stands now the passage is admittedly somewhat confusing; nevertheless, its content can clearly be seen to refer (however obliquely) to the events of creation as often described in the ancient gnostic traditions. According to a fairly common gnostic creation myth, some sort of 'power' from the transcendent realm has fallen into the material realm, presenting the problem of how to restore this 'spiritual power' to the 'Pleroma', as the transcendent or spiritual realm is often known. A plan is devised to effect this restoration through the creation of humanity: this 'power' is placed in humanity, through whom it will ultimately be returned to the Pleroma. In the first act of Adam's creation, the demiurge forms his physical body, and sometimes his soul as well, but at this point Adam still lies motionless. Only when a 'spiritual' component is added, consisting of the 'spiritual power' from the transcendent realm, does Adam finally come to life.[115]

These are the mythic events referred to by this extract from the *Liber Requiei*, knowledge of which can help us to understand better what is otherwise a very opaque passage. This allusion to the gnostic myth follows immediately after the Christ-Angel's revelation of the secret prayer, which he concludes with a promise that the secret prayer 'will raise the dead and give life to all, and they will behold the steadfastness of God'.[116] Given this

---

[114] *Liber Requiei* 17 (Arras, *De Transitu*, i. 9 (Eth.) and 6 (Lat.)).

[115] See the survey of different traditions in Rudolph, *Gnosis*, 67–113, esp. 76 and 94.

[116] *Liber Requiei* 16 (Arras, *De Transitu*, i. 9 (Eth.) and 6 (Lat.)).

context it would seem that the reference to Adam's body being 'in the glory that dwelled upon him' is an allusion to the final restoration to the Pleroma. In this event humanity, here represented collectively in Adam, will be returned to the glory of the transcendent realm, thus restoring to the Pleroma the lost 'spark of light' that presently lies trapped within humanity.

At first glance, the involvement of Adam's 'body' in this restoration may seem rather peculiar, given a tendency in the gnostic traditions to describe instead the ascent of the 'naked mind', 'spirit', or 'soul'. Although belief in the 'resurrection of the body' is somewhat uncommon among the ancient gnostic traditions, it is by no means unprecedented, as various writings found among the Nag Hammadi collection alert us.[117] The *Treatise on Resurrection*, for instance, a work with close connections to Valentinian Christianity, expresses belief in the resurrection in no uncertain terms:

So, never doubt concerning the resurrection, my son Rheginos! For if you were not existing in flesh, you received flesh when you entered this world. Why will you not receive flesh when you ascend to the Aeon? That which is better than the flesh is that which is for it (the) cause of life. That which came into being on your account, is it not yours? Does not that which is yours exist with you?[118]

As the tractate elsewhere makes clear, this 'flesh' is not the same material flesh that presently clothes the human soul and spirit. Rather, the author seems to have adopted Paul's notion that 'not all flesh is alike', and that at the resurrection the physical body will rise transformed into a spiritual body.[119] In this regard, one

[117] See e.g. Rudolph, *Gnosis*, 189–94; Elaine H. Pagels, ' "The Mystery of the Resurrection:" A Gnostic Reading of 1 Cor 15', *Journal of Biblical Literature*, 93 (1974), 276–88.

[118] *Treatise on Resurrection* 47. 1–13 (Harold W. Attridge, ed., *Nag Hammadi Codex I (The Jung Codex)*, 2 vols., NHS 22 (Leiden: E. J. Brill, 1985), i. 153). Regarding various points of contacts between this text and Valentinian Christianity, see Attridge, *Nag Hammadi Codex I*, i. 133; and Malcolm L. Peel, *The Epistle to Rheginos* (Philadelphia: Westminster, 1969), 175–80.

[119] 1 Cor 15: 39–44. Some have tried to interpret this tractate as expressing the more 'traditional' gnostic belief in the ascent of the naked soul, but without success in my opinion: see, e.g. Bentley Layton, *The Gnostic Treatise on Resurrection from Nag Hammadi* (Missoula, MT: Scholars Press, 1979). The text is quite clear in expressing a resurrection of the body: see the convincing arguments by Peel: Peel, *The Epistle to Rheginos*, 139–55.

is reminded of Origen's view of embodiment and resurrection, according to which an originally incorporeal 'spirit' or 'mind' has come into the body, but at the resurrection and final restoration, it will continue to be embodied, albeit in a more glorious, spiritual body.[120] Similar affirmation of a bodily resurrection occurs in the *Gospel of Philip*, a writing also identified with Valentinian Christianity. In a rather complicated passage this apocryphon similarly describes the resurrection of a spiritual body in terms also reminiscent of 1 Corinthians 15: 'It is necessary to rise in this flesh, since everything exists in it. In this world those who put on garments are better than the garments. In the kingdom of heaven the garments are better than those who have put them on.'[121] As in the *Treatise on Resurrection*, the notion of 'flesh' in this passage is clearly not limited to just the material body, but also encompasses the spiritual body that will clothe the elect after their restoration to the heavenly realm. Thus, while some Christian gnostic groups may have opposed belief in the resurrection of the body, we now know that others definitely embraced it, albeit in a slightly unusual, but very biblical, form. Consequently, it is neither surprising nor problematic to find a belief in bodily resurrection associated with the gnostic traditions of the *Liber Requiei*.

Following this brief mention of the future resurrection and restoration, the Christ-Angel next refers to Adam's creation by the chief Ruler (Archon), whom the following sentence identifies explicitly by name. After the Ruler formed Adam's body, the *Liber Requiei* reports that the body lay lifeless on the

---

[120] Origen's views regarding the resurrection are admittedly somewhat debated. Daniélou, for instance, reads Origen as believing in the mind's restoration to its original, incorporeal state (Jean Daniélou, *Origen*, trans. Walter Mitchell (New York: Sheed & Ward, 1955), 219). Other scholars, however, with whom I tend to agree, have identified the above pattern in Origen's thought: see e.g. Henri Crouzel, *Origen*, trans. A. S. Worrall (San Francisco: Harper & Row, 1989), 249–57; Henry Chadwick, 'Origen, Celsus, and the Resurrection of the Body', *Harvard Theological Review*, 41 (1948), 83–102; Thomas Corbett, 'Origen's Doctrine of the Resurrection', *Irish Theological Quarterly*, 46 (1979), 276–90.

[121] *Gospel according to Philip* 57. 18–22 (Layton, *Nag Hammadi Codex II*, i. 154–5). Regarding the resurrection in the *Gospel according to Philip*, see A. H. C. van Eijk, 'The Gospel of Philip and Clement of Alexandria: Gnostic and Ecclesiastical Theology on the Resurrection and the Eucharist', *Vigiliae Christianiae*, 25 (1971), 94–120.

earth, unable to move as in so many gnostic accounts, until Adam was somehow 'moved by the Ruler', enabling him to rise. As in other gnostic creation myths, Adam's mobility was presumably effected by the addition of some element from the transcendent realm, a spiritual substance that was probably once described by the *Liber Requiei*'s now otherwise obscure reference to 'that which was from the beginning and was even before the angels and the archangels, before the creation of the powers by me'.

Rather peculiar in this passage are the indications that the Ruler created with the 'counsel and participation' of the Father, and that the Christ-Angel was himself responsible for the establishment of the archontic powers. Nevertheless, as with the resurrection of the body, both of these concepts, while not exactly commonplace among the gnostic traditions, are attested in the ancient sources. The Valentinian tradition, for instance, is well known for having a much less negative view of the demiurge, his rulers, and the cosmos, and a number of ancient texts describe gnostic systems that portray the cosmic powers as acting in harmony (sometimes, unwittingly) with the higher powers of the transcendent realm.[122]

A good example of this tendency is the *Tripartite Tractate*, a gnostic treatise that offers some nice parallels to this passage from the *Liber Requiei*. In the *Tripartite Tractate*, it is the Logos, rather than Sophia, whose well-intended error leads to an imperfect begetting and his expulsion from the Pleroma. In

---

[122] Rudolph, *Gnosis*, 321–3. Regarding both Valentinian Christianity in general and the *Gospel according to Philip* in particular, see Einar Thomassen, 'How Valentinian is *The Gospel of Philip*?' in John D. Turner and Anne McGuire (eds.), *The Nag Hammadi Library after Fifty Years: Proceedings of the 1995 Society of Biblical Literature Commemoration*, NHS 44 (Leiden: Brill, 1997), 273. Examples of this tendency in Valentinian Christianity are found in the following sources: Ptolemy, *ep.* (in Epiphanius, *haer.* 33. 3. 1–7. 10, esp. 33. 3. 1–8 (Karl Holl, ed.; J. Dummer, 2nd edn., *Epiphanius: Ancoratus und Panarion*, 3 vols., GCS 25, 31 (2nd edn.), 37 (2nd edn.) (Leipzig: J. C. Hinrichs, 1915; Berlin: Akademie Verlag, 1980, 1985), i. 450–7)); Clement of Alexandria, *exc. Theod.* 47. 2, 49. 1, 53. 4 (Sagnard, *Clément d'Alexandrie: Extraits de Théotote*, 158–63, 168–9); Irenaeus, *haer.* 1. 5. 1–6 (Rousseau and Doutreleau, *Irénée de Lyon*, bk. I, ii (294), 77–91); Hippolytus, *haer.* 6. 28–9 (Marcovich, *Hippolytus*, 236–9). See also *A Valentinian Exposition* 34. 34–35. 37 (Charles W. Hedrick, ed., *Nag Hammadi codices XI, XII, XIII*, NHS 28 (Leiden: E. J. Brill, 1990), 130–3), where Jesus and Sophia together initiate the creation of the material world.

contrast to many other gnostic traditions, the *Tripartite Tractate* does not condemn the Logos' activity, affirming instead that 'it is not fitting to criticize the movement of the Logos'. On the contrary, the actions of the Logos brought into existence a 'system which has been destined to come about'.[123] Thus the existence of the material world is not a mistake in the *Tripartite Tractate* but is explicitly identified as the fulfilment of the 'Father's' will, as it is also in the *Liber Requiei*. Moreover, after his imperfect begetting and expulsion, the Logos creates the 'powers', appointing several 'rulers' to keep order over the material realm, including the 'chief Ruler' or demiurge, all of whom receive a positive assessment.[124] Then, the Logos and the Ruler both co-operate in the creation of humanity,[125] all of which amounts to a cosmogonic myth very similar to the one expressed in the passage from the *Liber Requiei*. If we may equate the Christ-Angel of the *Liber Requiei* with the *Tripartite Tractate*'s Logos, we find that both traditions agree in attributing the material world's existence and the creation of humanity to the will of the transcendent Father, as well as in identifying the Christ-Angel/Logos as the creator of the Rulers. Similar notions present in other writings that may be associated with Valentinian Christianity compare favourably with this feature of the *Liber Requiei*, including Heracleon's equation of the demiurge with the Logos in the Gospel according to John and Irenaeus' report that the Valentinians identified the demiurge with a 'great angel'.[126] Thus, the *Liber Requiei*'s rather positive assessment of the material creation and the demiurge in this passage find parallels in the Christian gnostic traditions, and particularly with the Valentinian traditions.

As the *Liber Requiei* continues, the Christ-Angel explains to Mary that the mystery he has just revealed was previously hidden from 'the wise, and it is not even written in the

---

[123] *The Tripartite Tractate* 75. 10–80. 11 (Harold W. Attridge, ed., *Nag Hammadi Codex I (The Jung Codex)*, 2 vols., NHS 22 (Leiden: E. J. Brill, 1985), i. 230–9).

[124] Ibid. 82. 10–24, 99. 9–12, 100. 19–101. 5 (ibid. 242–3, 272–5).

[125] Ibid. 104. 31–105. 10 (ibid. 282–3).

[126] Heracleon, *frag.* 1 (in Origen, *Jo.* 2. 14 (E. Preuschen, ed., *Origenes Werke*, iv. *Der Johanneskommentar*, GCS 10 (Leipzig: J. C. Hinrichs, 1903), 70–1)); Irenaeus, *haer.* 1. 5. 2 (Rousseau and Doutreleau, *Irénée de Lyon*, bk. I, ii (294), 80–1).

Scriptures, so that the scribes would not see it and the ignorant would not hear it among their children'.[127] Mary is in fact the first person to whom he has entrusted these secrets, and she in turn is commanded to share them with the apostles. Following this cosmological excursus, the Christ-Angel suddenly resumes discussion of the secret prayer, asking the question, 'who are they who will say this with their heart and soul completely?' In answer to his own question, he explains: 'For before creation are those who boast before humanity, saying, "We are God's." His memory arouses them as they seek recovery from their illness.'[128] Several gnostic themes are echoed in this statement. For instance, as we have already noted, the ancient gnostic traditions generally identify the human 'spirit' as something from the transcendent realm that has become imprisoned in the material realm, and more specifically, within humanity. According to many traditions, however, this 'spirit' is not present in all human beings, but only in certain people, the spiritual race, to whom the gnostic message of salvation is primarily addressed. This would seem to be implied in the *Liber Requiei*, since it appears to assume that only some of humanity is from before creation and may boast, 'We are God's.' Moreover, because this 'spirit' was originally from the spiritual world, which pre-existed the physical universe, those who possess it are truly from before the creation of the material world, as the Christ-Angel describes them.[129] The language of remembrance and the notion of material existence as an 'illness' in the passage are also reminiscent of the ancient gnostic traditions. The present condition of humanity is frequently identified in ancient gnostic texts as a 'sick' or 'drunken' state into which the spiritual essence of humanity has fallen, losing all memory of its divine origin.[130] Only by regaining the knowledge of one's divine origin can one be freed from the confines of the material world and return to the transcendent realm. This remembrance is the knowledge that the gnostic redeemer brings into the world, enabling the human spirit to be restored to the Pleroma, as seemingly described here in the *Liber Requiei*.

---

[127] *Liber Requiei* 17 (Arras, *De Transitu*, i. 9 (Eth.) and 6 (Lat.)).
[128] Ibid. 18 (ibid. 10 (Eth.) and 6 (Lat.)).
[129] Rudolph, *Gnosis*, 88–95.
[130] Ibid. 109–11, 119–21.

As the revelation dialogue between Mary and the Christ-Angel continues, the latter explains to Mary that in addition to those who are 'before creation' and can boast, 'We are God's', there are also those who make requests of God, but 'God does not hear them, because the will of God is not among them.'[131] The cryptic story that then follows is presumably an effort to explain the difference between these two peoples, and since this episode is also extant in the ancient Syriac *Obsequies* fragments, in a virtually identical version, we may be assured that it belongs to the earliest tradition.[132] The Christ-Angel asks Mary to recall the time when a 'thief . . . was taken captive among the apostles', and he begged them to intercede with their master on behalf of himself and some others. When the apostles approached Jesus on the 'thief's' behalf, he replied, 'These are the shepherds of the house of Israel, who are beseeching on behalf of the sheep, so that they will be pardoned and glorified before humanity. And they cannot sanctify themselves, because they exalt themselves like the strong. Did I not give them many signs?' The apostles still do not understand, and so Jesus subjects them to the following 'parable' in an effort to enlighten them.

Taking his apostles onto a mountain, Jesus causes them to become hungry. When they complain of hunger, Jesus commands that a grove of trees, full of fruit, come forth on the mountain-top. Jesus sends the apostles to go and pick fruit from the trees, but they return empty-handed, explaining when they came to the trees, they found no fruit on them. Jesus then persuades the apostles that they failed to see the food because the trees were too tall, telling them that if they go over again, he will cause the trees to bend so that the apostles can take their fruit. The apostles return from the trees a second time, again with no fruit, and, having become frustrated, they demand of Jesus, 'What is this, a mockery?' Jesus then bids them to go to the trees a third time and sit underneath them. When the apostles do so, 'immediately the trees released stinking worms'. When the apostles return to Jesus a third time, he offers an explanation, telling them to turn and look again at the trees. Then the apostles

---

[131] *Liber Requiei* 18 (Arras, *De Transitu*, i. 10 (Eth.) and 6 (Lat.)).

[132] This parable is found in *Liber Requiei* 18 (Arras, *De Transitu*, i. 10–12 (Eth.) and 7–8 (Lat.)); and Wright, *Contributions*, ܡܣܠܩܐ (Syr.) and 50–1 (Eng.).

see that the trees have suddenly become human beings, who 'stand and pray and are prostrate on their knees, while repent-ing', yet 'there is no fruit to God in the repentance'.

Although this parable is admittedly quite peculiar, it seems to elaborate on the Christ-Angel's identification of those whom God refuses to hear, who are distinguished from those belong-ing to God in the passage immediately preceding the parable. As the parable's conclusion explains, when those people symbolized by the trees attempt to ascend, 'they are returned to the world', and God turns away from them. These would appear to be the 'non-gnostics', who lack the spirit from the transcendent realm possessed by the gnostics and thus are unable to ascend. The division of humanity into two distinct classes, one belonging to God and another condemned to this world, is a frequent gnostic theme. Although the division between these two groups is some-times permeable in the ancient gnostic traditions, it is neverthe-less yet another important point of contact between the *Liber Requiei* and these ancient religious phenomena.[133]

The *Liber Requiei* echoes this theme in another parable, told much later in the narrative, during Peter's all-night sermon. Although this parable is not found in Wenger's early Greek text, a strikingly close parallel appears in John of Thessalonica's homily, which is a strong indication that the story was present in the sixth-century Greek Dormition narrative that was John's source. The parable, which is told by Peter, is a lengthy tale of two servants, the gist of which is that it is better to remain a virgin than to marry. In expounding its meaning, however, Peter tells the crowd that has gathered for Mary's death,

You then, the human race, are those with whom God became angry in the beginning, and he placed them in the world as in a prison and as spoils in the world for those to whom he abandoned us because of this. But the last days have come, and they will be transferred to the place where our ancient fathers Abraham, Isaac, and Jacob are. And there each one will be in the Pleroma.[134]

---

[133] Rudolph, *Gnosis*, 91–2; see also Williams, *Rethinking Gnosticism*, 189–212 on the often permeable nature of these two classes.

[134] *Liber Requiei* 65 (Arras, *De Transitu*, i. 38 (Eth.) and 25 (Lat.)). Somewhat unsurprisingly, John of Thessalonica has altered this particular passage to read as follows: '[B]eing angry with our race at the beginning, God cast Adam into this world. Under his displeasure, then, and in a kind of exile, we live in it, but

The identification of the present world as a prison is frequently met in the ancient gnostic traditions, as is the belief in the final restoration of humanity's spirit to the Pleroma.[135] The presence of both these themes in the *Liber Requiei* is further confirmation of a connection with some sort of gnostic Christianity.

Finally, the use of various gnostic 'technical terms' by the earliest Palm narratives would seem to indicate contact with the ancient gnostic traditions. These include, in the earliest Greek narrative for instance, such terms as γνῶσις, πλήρωμα, ἀνάπαυσις, ταμεῖον, and ἐπιγνῶσις, among others.[136] Consider, for example, the following prayer, spoken by Mary when she returns home after learning of her coming death:

I bless you, sign that appeared from heaven on the earth, until you chose me and dwelt in me. I bless you and all of my relatives, those who will receive me [τοὺς παραλήμπτωράς μου], who came forth invisibly before you, in order to bring you along. I bless you because you gave me a measure of virility for the parts of your body, and [because] I have been found worthy of the kiss of your bridal chamber [νυμφών], as you promised me before. I bless you so that I will be found worthy to partake of the perfect eucharist and your sweet-smelling offering, which is an abundance for all the nations. I bless you so that you will give me the garment that you promised me, saying: 'By this you will be distinguished from my relatives', and [so that] you will cause me to be taken to the seventh heaven, so that I will be found worthy of your perfect fragrance with all of those who believe in you, so that you will gather them together with me in your kingdom. For you are hidden among the hidden, observing those who are not seen. You are the hidden race [τὸ γένος τὸ κρυπτόν], and you are also the Pleroma; you are the Pleroma, and I have painfully given birth first to you and then to all of those who hope in you.[137]

Here we encounter several gnostic 'technical terms', including

we will not be allowed to remain in it. For the day of each of us is coming, and it will bring us to where our fathers and ancestors are, Abraham and Isaac and Jacob.' John of Thessalonica, *dorm. BMV A* 1 (Jugie, *Homélies*, 394–5; trans. Daley, *On the Dormition*, 61). Thus, the fall of pre-existent 'souls' has been transformed into Adam's fall, and references to the world as a prison and the restoration to the Pleroma stricken.

[135] Rudolph, *Gnosis*, 109, 196–9.
[136] See Manns, *Le Récit*, 115–16.
[137] Wenger, *L'Assomption*, 214–17. See also *Liber Requiei* 36–7 (Arras, *De Transitu*, i. 20–1 (Eth.) and 13–14 (Lat.)).

references to the Pleroma and the 'bridal chamber', as well as the 'racial' identity often espoused in the gnostic sources.[138] Particularly revealing, however, is the use of the word παραλή[μ]πτωρ, a very uncommon word in Christian Greek, but one that is frequently met in the Coptic gnostic texts. Here it appears to be used, as in the Coptic gnostic texts, as a technical term for heavenly powers that meet the soul at its separation from the body and guide it safely past the demiurge and his minions to the Pleroma.[139] Although the presence of such terms alone might not be seen as especially significant, in conjunction with the references to various gnostic themes discussed above, it seems altogether likely that this language derives from contact with some sort of gnostic milieu.

This fact alone, however, does not allow us to conclude that the Palm traditions had their origin within some sort of gnostic group: we cannot know with any certainty whether these gnostic features are 'original', or if instead they merely reflect transmission through a gnostic milieu at an earlier stage in their history. It does seem certain, however, that these legends originated somewhere off the map of early Christian history as it is presently drawn, within some sort of group, perhaps a gnostic group, that has not otherwise survived in the historical record. Moreover, some sort of early contact with gnostic ideas seems undeniable. Although certain scholars would instead identify many of these same themes with the so-called Jewish-Christian stream of early Christian thought, gnostic Christianity, in my

---

[138] Rudolph, *Gnosis*, 58. Regarding the 'bridal chamber' theme in the ancient gnostic traditions, see ibid. 245–7. On the use of 'racial' identity by ancient gnostics, see ibid. 91–2 and Williams, *Rethinking Gnosticism*, 193–202. The members of this 'race' are hidden to the extent that they themselves do not even recognize their true identity until the 'Redeemer' (Christ in gnostic Christianity) brings them to knowledge of this fact (Rudolph, *Gnosis*, 119–21).

[139] See e.g. *The Gospel of the Egyptians*, III. 64. 22, 66. 5; IV. 76. 121; 78. 7 (Böhlig and Wisse, *Nag Hammadi Codices III, 2 and IV, 2*, 149–9; 154–5); *The Second Book of Jeu* 42–3 (Schmidt and MacDermot, *The Books of Jeû*, 99. 15–16, 101. 24); *The Untitled Text in the Bruce Codex* 9 (ibid. 241. 18); *Pistis Sophia* 55. 11 and *passim* (Schmidt and MacDermot, *Pistis Sophia*, 105; see also the entry for παραλήμπτωρ in the index of Greek words, p. 790); *Zostrianos* 47. 24 (John H. Sieber, ed., *Nag Hammadi Codex VIII*, NHS 31 (Leiden: E. J. Brill, 1991), 116, and *The Apocryphon of John*, synopsis 69. 10 (Waldstein and Wisse, *The Apocryphon of John*, 148–9). On the meaning of this term, see esp. the discussion in Böhlig and Wisse, *Nag Hammadi Codices III, 2 and IV, 2*, 194–8.

opinion, provides a more useful context for understanding the rather peculiar theology of the earliest Palm traditions. Not only does gnostic Christianity present a much less dubious category than the rather questionable notion of a distinctive Jewish-Christian theology, but it can also better account for all the elements of this unusual theological assemblage, including especially the narrative's references to a demiurgical creation and its emphasis on secret, salvific knowledge.

Finally, we may draw some tentative conclusions regarding the date of the earliest Palm narratives based on their theological content. Although it must be admitted that such a method is not always consistently reliable or precise, the peculiar assortment of ideas in these early narratives does seem to suggest their existence sometime during the third or fourth century, if not even earlier, within a milieu somewhere outside proto-orthodox Christianity. This period coincides roughly with the floruit of gnostic Christianity, as well as with the relative disappearance of Angel Christology after the beginning of the fourth century.[140] The initial composition of a document centred on these ideas sometime after this point seems comparatively unlikely.

Similarly, Mary's explanation of her fear of death in *Liber Requiei* 41 bears the marks of a rather early composition, as Mary Clayton has also noted.[141] When Mary announces her impending death to her friends and family, they sense her fear of death. They are disturbed by this and ask,

O our sister, you who have become the mother of the whole world, even

---

[140] Jaroslav Pelikan considers Arianism to be the 'final, mighty upheaval' of Angel Christology in early Christianity: *The Christian Tradition: A History of the Development of Doctrine*, i. *The Emergence of the Catholic Tradition (100–600)* (Chicago: University of Chicago Press, 1971), 197–8. See also Alois Grillmeier, SJ, *Christ in Christian Tradition*, i. *From the Apostolic Age to Chalcedon (451)*, 2nd rev. edn., trans. John Bowden (Atlanta: John Knox, 1975), 46–51; Daniélou, *Theology of Jewish Christianity*, 117; Carrell, *Jesus and the Angels*, 109; Gieschen, *Angelomorphic Christology*, 187–8; Werner, *Formation of Christian Dogma*, 131–61; Joseph Barbel, *Christos Angelos: Die Anschauung von Christus als Bote und Engel in der gelehrten und volkstümlichen Literatur des christlichen Altertums*, Theophaneia, 3 (Bonn: Peter Hanstein Verlagsbuchhandlung, 1941). Regarding the floruit of gnostic Christianity, see Rudolph, *Gnosis*, 308–26, 367–8.

[141] Mary Clayton, 'The Transitus Mariae: The Tradition and Its Origins', *Apocrypha*, 10 (1999), 79, n. 18.

if we are all rightly afraid, what do you fear? You are the mother of the Lord! Woe to us! Where shall we flee, if you, incorruptible and virgin, say this? O our expectation and intercessor and our encouragement who has committed no sin, what shall we, the unworthy, do, and where shall we flee? If the shepherd fears the wolf, where will the sheep flee?[142]

Mary's response, rather shockingly, reveals that she is afraid because she has sinned! Her description of the actual sin is rather confused, no doubt because this passage proved very disturbing to the medieval translators and copyists who have preserved this narrative.[143] But the simple fact that this narrative identifies Mary as a sinner strongly suggests its composition sometime before belief in Mary's sinlessness had become widely held.[144]

A date before the end of the fourth century is additionally suggested by Richard Bauckham's studies of the apocalyptic traditions that conclude the early Palm narratives, as we have already noted in Ch. 1. Through comparison of the 'Palm apocalypse' with other ancient apocalyptic literature, Bauckham determines that the Palm narratives most probably came into existence sometime in the fourth century, if not earlier. In particular, Bauckham's recognition that the *Apocalypse of Paul*, composed around 400, has probably used the Palm apocalypse as a source suggests such a date.[145] Thus it seems quite likely that the Palm narratives were already in existence sometime before 350 CE, at a time when many of the ideas represented in the earliest narratives were at their peak. In view of this, these Dormition apocrypha should at last begin to assume their rightful place among the other apocrypha of early Christianity, company from which they have occasionally been excluded.[146]

---

[142] Quoted from the Georgian version: van Esbroeck, 'Apocryphes géorgiens', 61 (Geor.) and 65 (Lat.). See also *Liber Requiei* 40 (Arras, *De Transitu*, i. 23–4 (Eth.) and 15–16 (Lat.)).

[143] *Liber Requiei* 41 (Arras, *De Transitu*, i. 24–5 (Eth.) and 16 (Lat.)). The Georgian fragment suddenly breaks off, just as Mary confesses her sin.

[144] See Hilda Graef, *Mary: A History of Doctrine and Devotion*, i. *From the Beginnings to the Eve of the Reformation* (New York: Sheed & Ward, 1963), 82–3, 98–9, 120–2; Jaroslav Pelikan, *Mary through the Centuries: Her Place in the History of Culture* (New Haven: Yale University Press, 1996), 189–91.

[145] Richard Bauckham, *The Fate of the Dead: Studies on Jewish and Christian Apocalypses*, Supplements to Novum Testamentum, 93 (Leiden: Brill, 1998), 344–6, 360. See also the discussion in Ch. 1.

[146] These traditions are completely ignored in the collections by Hennecke

Further study of these narratives in this context will surely shed much light both on the narratives themselves and on the development of early Christianity in general. Nevertheless, we must also bear in mind that there is no way to completely exclude the possibility of a later origin. Only the existence of the fifth-century Syriac fragments, probably made from an earlier Greek version, can assure us that these traditions were almost certainly in circulation by 450 CE.

RESISTANCE TO CHALCEDON AND THE ORIGIN OF THE EARLY DORMITION TRADITIONS

Turning now from consideration of the Dormition traditions' prehistory to the context of their earliest existence, we come to a question that concerns not only the Palm traditions but the entire corpus as whole. There is a rather widely held belief that the sudden emergence of the Dormition traditions within the dominant stream of orthodox Christian discourse in the late fifth century had something to do with resistance to council of Chalcedon.[147] While some scholars holding this view appear to mean that anti-Chalcedonian Christians first shepherded numerous already existing traditions from the margins into the mainstream of Christianity, others have gone so far as to propose that the story of Mary's Dormition 'found its first written narrative expression among those communities of Syria and Palestine, in the late fifth century, which opposed as irreligious the Council of Chalcedon's description of Christ'.[148]

and Schneemelcher. J. K. Elliott (*Apocryphal New Testament*, 692–723) includes a few bits and pieces in an appendix to his collection of apocrypha, but his assemblage largely just modernizes the translations and updates the introductions and bibliographic information found in M. R. James's brief treatment of the Dormition traditions: *The Apocryphal New Testament*, corr. edn. (Oxford: The Clarendon Press, 1989), 194–227. Only Erbetta's Italian collection has done justice to these narratives so far, in giving them full representation in the collection: *Gli apocrifi*, 409–632.

[147] Here I am using the word 'orthodox' of course without reference to the council of Chalcedon itself, but rather to describe the broader grouping of both Chalcedonian and non-Chalcedonian (and even non-Ephesian) Christians that by the 6th century had emerged as the dominant form(s) of Christianity.

[148] Daley, *On the Dormition*, 7. Daley has recently repeated his belief in the

The hypothesis of some sort of a monophysite or anti-Chalcedonian origin for the Dormition traditions has been a commonplace of most previous scholarship, which on occasion has even sought to correlate individual narratives and developments within the corpus of traditions with very specific theological responses to Chalcedon. Given the initial emergence of these narratives in the midst of these doctrinal debates, as well as the Virgin's often central role in these controversies, at first glance this seems a rather obvious approach. But the evidence in favour of aligning these traditions with anti-Chalcedonianism is extremely limited to say the least. On the basis of what we have seen in this chapter so far, we may certainly exclude the possibility that these traditions first came into existence only in anti-Chalcedonian circles: their existence before the events of the fourth council seems undeniable. On the other hand, there is little to indicate that it was the opponents of Chalcedon who first embraced the already extant traditions; in fact, the narratives themselves rather strongly suggest the absence of any such connection.

It would seem that an anti-Chalcedonian origin was first proposed by Henry Chadwick, who in the year following the Assumption dogma's definition wrote:

The whole tendency of Monophysite piety was to minimize the significance of Christ's soul. As the Antiochenes clearly perceived, the result is that Christ loses solidarity with us. Is there not, then, a consequent need for popular piety to clutch at someone, with a vital part in the drama of redemption, who is beyond doubt ὁμοούσιος ἡμῖν? . . . In such a situation it would be a reassurance if there could be someone in solidarity with the rest of mankind who had risen again in the body. . . . Accordingly, there seems to be little need for surprise that such a

---

anti-Chalcedonian origins of the Dormition traditions, again without much as to why, in his lecture at the 1999 Dumbarton Oaks Symposium on Byzantine eschatology: 'The Dormition of Mary in Homilies and Legends as a Model for Christians', paper presented at the 1999 Dumbarton Oaks Symposium, 1 May, 1999. This is also Mimouni's view (*Dormition*, 664–6), and it was adopted from Mimouni by Mary Clayton, *The Apocryphal Gospels of Mary in Anglo-Saxon England*, Cambridge Studies in Anglo-Saxon England, 26 (Cambridge: Cambridge University Press, 1998), 25–6. The latter item, despite its focus on much later Anglo-Saxon texts, includes a substantial introduction that treats the early Dormition traditions.

story as the Assumption of the Virgin became current in Monophysite circles during this period.[149]

Although it is unclear whether Chadwick understood the opponents of Chalcedon to be the initial producers of Dormition narratives or instead their first known consumers, the connection with 'Monophysite circles' is here assumed, rather than demonstrated. Moreover, the logic that Chadwick deploys to comprehend this supposed relationship rests on an outmoded and stereotypical understanding of anti-Chalcedonian theology that Chadwick himself would now undoubtedly reject. Over the past fifty years, scholarship has demonstrated that the theological opponents of Chalcedon shared the council's condemnation of Eutyches' denial of Christ's consubstantiality with humanity: indeed, it was always Christ's resurrection, and never Mary's, that held the promise of eternal life for them.[150] Even more problematic for this argument, however, is the fact that many early Dormition narratives do not report Mary's resurrection. Consequently, Chadwick's early efforts to identify a 'monophysite' origin in no way successfully establishes a connection between the Dormition traditions and resistance to Chalcedon, even if such a linkage should in fact exist.

One of the primary advocates of a 'secondary' origin in an anti-Chalcedonian context is Michel van Esbroeck, who identifies the opponents of Chalcedon as the first to embrace an already existent collection of Dormition traditions. In arguing this position, van Esbroeck makes much of the events consequent to Juvenal's return to Jerusalem following the council of Chalcedon as related by the Coptic *Panegyric on Macarius of Tkōw* attributed to Dioscorus.[151] According to this report, the

---

[149] Henry Chadwick, 'Eucharist and Christology in the Nestorian Controversy', *Journal of Theological Studies*, NS 2 (1951), 163–4.

[150] See John Meyendorff, *Christ in Eastern Christian Thought* (Crestwood, NY: St. Vladimir's Seminary Press, 1975), 39–41; Aloys Grillmeier, SJ, with Theresia Hainthaler, *Christ in Christian Tradition*, ii. *From the Council of Chalcedon (451) to Gregory the Great (590–604)*, pt. 2, *The Church of Constantinople in the Sixth Century*, trans. John Cawte and Pauline Allen (Louisville: Westminster John Knox, 1995), 153–4; idem, *Christ in Christian Tradition*, ii. *From the Council of Chalcedon (451) to Gregory the Great (590–604)*, pt. 4, *The Church of Alexandria with Nubia and Ethiopia after 451*, trans. O. C. Dean, Jr. (Louisville: Westminster John Knox, 1996), 27–31.

[151] This episode and its source were previously discussed in Ch. 2.

opponents of Chalcedon had gathered at 'the shrine of holy Mary in the valley of Jehosaphat', where many were put to the sword by imperial troops on 21 Tobe (16 January).[152] Since this date holds the Coptic commemoration of Mary's Dormition, van Esbroeck concludes on the basis of this testimony that 'le sanctuaire de Gethsémani et la date à laquelle on fêtait la Dormition étaient des symboles de la résistance au concile de Chalcédoine'.[153] Despite his efforts to bolster this position with references from various scattered sources that associate 21 Tobe with resistance to Chalcedon, these do not make the case that either the tomb of the Virgin or the feast of the Dormition were somehow especially linked with resistance to Chalcedon.[154]

Although I agree with van Esbroeck (against Mimouni) that this 'shrine of Mary' where the opponents of Chalcedon had gathered was certainly the church of her tomb, the text oddly fails to specify that the gathering took place at her tomb, and there is no indication that the gathering there was connected in any way with her Dormition.[155] In this respect, the *Panegyric on Macarius of Tkōw* fails to link this anti-Chalcedonian rally with the Dormition in very obvious ways. Although the events are described as taking place on 21 Tobe, the date of the Dormition

---

[152] Ps.-Dioscorus of Alexandria, *Panegyric on Macarius of Tkōw* 7. 5 (David Johnson, *A Panegyric on Macarius, Bishop of Tkōw, Attributed to Dioscorus of Alexandria*, CSCO 415–16 (Louvain: Peeters, 1980), 49–50 (Copt.) and 38 (Eng.)).

[153] van Esbroeck, 'Les Textes', 279. See also idem, 'La Dormition chez les Coptes', in *Actes du IVe Congrès copte, Louvain-la-Neuve 5–10 septembre 1988*, ed. Marguerite Rassart-Debergh and Julien Ries, ii. *De la linguistique au gnosticisme*, Publications de l'Institut Orientaliste de Louvain, 41 (Louvain-la-Neuve: Institut Orientaliste, 1992), 436–45, and idem, 'Le Culte de la Vierge', 181–90; idem, 'Les Signes des temps dans la littérature syriaque', *Revue de l'Insitut catholique de Paris*, 39 (1991), 146–9; idem, 'Un court traité pseudo-basilien de mouvance aaronite conservé en arménien', *Le Muséon*, 100 (1987), 391–3; idem, 'Étude comparée', 6–18; idem, 'La Vierge comme véritable Arche d'Alliance', in *Colloque d'Athènes sur la Theotokos* (forthcoming); idem, 'Some Early Features in the Life of the Virgin', *Marianum* (2001).

[154] van Esbroeck, 'La Dormition chez les Coptes'.

[155] This is also the conclusion reached in Lorenzo Perrone, 'Christian Holy Places in an Age of Dogmatic Conflicts', *Proche-Orient Chrétien*, 48 (1998), 17 n. 23. See also the criticisms of Mimouni, *Dormition*, 465–71 and 637–40, many of which are valid but are also tainted by his own unfounded theories regarding the 'pro-Chalcedonian' foundation of the Kathisma, as discussed in the preceding chapter.

in the Coptic traditions, it is altogether likely that this date was invented by the later Coptic forger, who wished to intensify the drama by linking these events with the celebration of Mary's Dormition, as observed according to the Coptic calendar. This is particularly the case since the celebration of this feast on 21 Tobe (16 January) was limited to Egypt. If this gathering at the tomb had in fact been originally associated with the liturgical feast of the Dormition, one would expect it to have taken place on 15 August, since this was the date when Mary's Dormition was commemorated in Jerusalem.

In contrast to van Esbroeck, Simon Mimouni appears to argue for a 'true' anti-Chalcedonian origin, in the sense that these traditions were first produced by anti-Chalcedonian Christians. In support of this hypothesis, Mimouni offers the rather general argument that 'la croyance en la dormition aurait pris naissance dans des milieux monophysites. On sait que ceux-ci ont toujours été plus favorables aux croyances mariales que les chalcédoniens.'[156] One senses here a tacit acceptance of the (unfair) accusation by the opponents of Chalcedon that the council had returned to the teaching of Nestorius and its 'disrespect' for the Virgin Mary, a generalization that simply does not stand up under historical scrutiny.[157] Mimouni attempts to bolster his arguments, however, with a claim that the fifth- and sixth-century Syriac manuscripts preserving Dormition narratives are of 'monophysite origin', additionally identifying Jacob of Serug, the author of the earliest extant homily on the Dormition, as a monophysite. In the first place, I do not know on what basis Mimouni claims to know the Christological views of those who produced these early manuscripts: their preservation in Syriac does not alone orient them away from Chalcedon, and there is to my knowledge no clear indication of a stance regarding Chalcedon in the manuscripts themselves.[158] Moreover, as

---

[156] Mimouni, *Dormition*, 665.

[157] Consider e.g. Pulcheria, one of the driving forces behind Chalcedon, who was an ardent devotee of Mary and did much to foster her cult: see especially Kenneth G. Holum, *Theodosian Empresses: Women and Imperial Dominion in Late Antiquity* (Berkeley and Los Angeles: University of California Press, 1982), ch. 5, and now also Vasiliki Limberis, *Divine Heiress: The Virgin Mary and the Creation of Christian Constantinople* (New York: Routledge, 1994), ch. 3.

[158] In his article 'La Tradition littéraire syriaque de l'histoire de la Dormition

noted at the outset, Jacob of Serug is a figure whose theological loyalties are much debated, and he is probably best regarded as a partisan of neither side.[159] But more importantly, the ancient Dormition traditions themselves do not support this hypothesis, and as will be seen, the content of these narratives belies such efforts to connect them with resistance to Chalcedon.

Nevertheless, Mimouni's study expands significantly on the basic hypothesis of an anti-Chalcedonian origin, developing earlier suggestions by Jugie and Testa into an elaborate theory that relates the evolution of his narrative typology to subsequent developments within anti-Chalcedonian thought.[160] In what is both the most recent and detailed of such efforts, Mimouni identifies Julianism or 'Aphthartodocetism' as the historical catalyst that determined the theological and narrative evolution of the Dormition traditions, moving them from a primitive confession of the Dormition alone to the more recent belief in the Virgin's Assumption.[161] Although this reconstruction is highly

et de l'Assomption de Marie', *Parole de l'Orient*, 15 (1988–9), 167 n. 86, Mimouni cites on his behalf in this regard Anton Baumstark, *Geschichte der syrischen Literatur mit Aussluß der christlich-palästinensishen Texte* (Bonn: A. Marcus & E. Webers Verlag, 1922), 98–9. This does refer to Baumstark's description of the Syriac Dormition traditions, but contrary to Mimouni's claims, Baumstark does not here (or anywhere else to my knowledge) 'proposé que les textes syriaques pouvaient être classés en fonction de l'origine confessionelle des manuscrits', as Mimouni claims.Moreover, the preservation of these traditions in later Syriac manuscripts that are clearly Marionite (William Wright, 'The Departure of my Lady Mary from this World', *The Journal of Sacred Literature and Biblical Record*, 6–7 (1865), 418) or even Nestorian (Mimouni, *Dormition*, 101–2; Eduard Sachau, *Verzeichniss der syrischen Handschriften der Königlichen Bibliothek zu Berlin*, Die Handschriften-Verzeichnisse der Königlichen Bibliothek zu Berlin, 23 (Berlin: A. Asher & Co., 1899), 200–3) should caution us against making such an assumption without clearer evidence.

[159] See n. 3 above.

[160] Jugie, *La Mort*, 132–3, suggests that Julianism/Aphthartodocetism may have impacted the changes in the Coptic traditions of Mary's death. This was then developed by Testa in 'L'origine', 255–60 and 'Lo sviluppo', 346–52, 357–69 (see esp. 347), where he proposes that certain Dormition traditions developed among anti-Chalcedonians who were opposed to Julianism/ Aphthartodocetism.

[161] See Mimouni, *Dormition*, 666–71 for this theory. A similar proposal was earlier made by Testa: see his 'Lo svillupo', esp. 347. The main historical problem with this theory, however, is that Julianism is a much later theological

improbable, particularly given the numerous problems that have already been identified with Mimouni's developmental typology, it nevertheless merits attention because it has been adopted rather uncritically by some more recent studies of the early Dormition traditions.[162]

Julianism was a movement that developed during the early sixth century within the anti-Chalcedonian camp, named for its founder, Julian of Halicarnassus, an anti-Chalcedonian bishop from western Asia Minor. Both Julianism and the closely related view known as Aphthartodocetism were characterized especially by the idea that Christ's body was free from the mortal 'corruption' ($\phi\theta\alpha\rho\sigma\iota\alpha$) present in other human bodies, even before his resurrection. According to Julianism, all humanity is subject to bodily corruption as a consequence of Adam's original sin, and because of this corruption human beings die. But Christ, as the new Adam, possessed a body free from this mortal corruption, and consequently, he was subject to death only because he willed to die, in spite of his body's incorruption.[163] Christ's physical incorruption was attributed by Julian and his followers to his virginal conception and birth. According to the Julianist system, one did not inherit bodily corruption from one's parents; rather, it was generated by the desire present at the moment of conception, which introduced corruption to the newly formed flesh. Therefore Christ, whose conception occurred in the absence of desire, was preserved from contracting this contagion.[164]

development, as Mimouni himself has noted in criticizing the work of other scholars. See Mimouni, *Dormition*, 465–71, esp. 467.

[162] Daley, *On the Dormition*, 7–11, and Clayton, *Apocryphal Gospels of Mary*, 43–5, both of whom simply follow the arguments of Mimouni. Although Brian Daley reproduces Mimouni's hypothesis, he does note that there is no ancient evidence that Julianists asserted the incorruptibility of Mary's body: *On the Dormition*, 41, n. 29. See also idem, 'The Dormition of Mary in Homilies and Legends'.

[163] Grillmeier, *Christ*, ii. pt. 2. 93–106; Jacques Jarry, *Hérésies et factions dans l'empire byzantine du IVe au VIIe siècle*, Recherches d'archéologie, de philologie et d'histoire, 14 (Cairo: L'Institut Français d'Archéologie Orientale, 1968), 74–81; René Draguet, *Julien d'Halicarnasse et sa controverse avec Sévère d'Antioche sur l'incorruptibilité du corps du Christ*, Universitas Catholica Lovaniensis Dissertationes ad gradum magistri in Facultate Theologica consequendum conscriptae, 2/12 (Louvain: Smeesters, 1924), 100–5, 118–27, 145–51.

[164] Grillmeier, *Christ*, ii. pt. 2. 108–11; Jarry, *Hérésies*, 69; Draguet, *Julien*, 154–6.

Yet despite this rather well-known fact, Mimouni maintains that certain ancient Julianists felt it necessary to propose the incorruptibility of the Virgin's body, in order to exclude the possibility of mortal corruption passing from her body to her son's. Mimouni continues to explain that, in such a case, Mary would lack the source of human mortality, making her immortal. Using such logic, he explains, these ancient Julianists developed an 'immortalist' tradition of the end of Mary's earthly life: since she, like her son, was understood as being incorruptible and thus could not die without some miraculous intervention, a tradition was born that the Virgin was taken bodily into heaven without dying. Mimouni next imagines that the more orthodox opponents of Chalcedon, notably the followers of Severus of Antioch, responded by developing a compromise position that recognized Mary's exceptional purity in the affirmation of her bodily Assumption, but also ensured her consubstantiality with the rest of humanity by describing her prior death and resurrection.[165] The result, Mimouni posits, was the transformation of the ancient Dormition-only narratives, by way of the intermediate Coptic narratives with their interval of 206 days, into the more recent narratives including both a Dormition and Assumption.

In all of this, the resemblance of the Julianist concept of bodily corruption to the Western notion of original sin should not be missed, particularly since this similarity appears to have played a larger role in generating this theory than have the ancient sources. Both original sin and Julianist corruption are consequent to the fall of humanity and are the source of human mortality. As the sinless New Adam and conqueror of mortality, it is argued that Christ cannot be joined with such a lethal contagion, and so his body must have been either incorruptible or immaculate. In an effort to explain Christ's physical incorruptibility, Mimouni suggests that the Julianists, much like the modern Roman Catholic church, extended this freedom from corruption to his mother, whose body was purified before giving birth, lest she communicate the corruption to her son.[166] Once her flesh had been made incorruptible, Mary could no longer die, since, like the immaculate Virgin of the Roman

---

[165] Mimouni, *Dormition*, 666–8; idem, 'Genèse et évolution des traditions anciennes sur le sort final de Marie: Étude de la tradition litteraire copte', *Marianum*, 42 (1991), 119–22.   [166] Mimouni, *Dormition*, 666–7.

Catholic tradition, she lacked the cause of human mortality. Consequently, the Julianists, according to this theory, birthed the notion that Mary did not die, but was at the end of her life taken to heaven in her body.

The similarities between this historical explanation and the dogmatic arguments on which Rome has largely rested its definition of the Assumption dogma are astonishing: Mary's body is incorruptible (or 'immaculate'), because she must not transmit mortal 'corruption' (or original sin) to Christ, and because she is free from this corruption (original sin), Mary cannot die. The parallel is striking to say the least. Just as Rome has justified the definition of the Assumption dogma as a logical consequence of the Virgin's Immaculate Conception, Mimouni locates the Assumption's historical genesis in a purported Julianist belief that the Virgin's body was free from mortal corruption. In each case, Mary's bodily Assumption is professed since she lacks the source of human mortality and consequently cannot die. In both instances, the Assumption is derived from a belief that Mary lacked the source of human mortality, a corruption that was supernaturally removed lest she transmit it to her son. The correspondence of these two arguments cannot be merely coincidental, and it would seem that the modern discourse of Mary's Assumption has here again exercised a considerable influence on the modern investigation of these ancient traditions.

Such influence, whether conscious or unconscious, is particularly manifest in the distorted representation of ancient Julianism that this hypothesis manufactures. Presumably at the influence of the Roman definition, Julianism is transformed into something more closely resembling the Roman teachings on original sin and the Immaculate Conception than it appears in our ancient sources. Despite the often remarkable similarities between Julianism and the Roman understanding of original sin, there are important differences, particularly regarding the transmission of corruption or original sin. But in identifying Julianism as the source of ancient Assumptionist belief, this distinction has been obscured in an effort to make Julianism a more viable catalyst. In effect, Julianism has been recast in the image of the Roman dogma of Original Sin, in order that something like the Virgin's Immaculate Conception might be identified as the historical origin of the Assumptionist tradition.

The key point in this attempted reconstruction is Mimouni's claim that at least some ancient Julianists professed the Virgin's somatic incorruptibility; nevertheless, such belief is not ascribed to Julianism by any of the ancient sources. In contrast to the Roman understanding of original sin's transmission, ancient Julianism equated mortal corruption with concupiscence, and this corruption was understood to be transmitted through the desire that accompanies sexual reproduction.[167] If by some chance one were conceived in the absence of desire (and one ponders what this would mean for *in-vitro* fertilization!), one would not contract mortal corruption, and since Christ had been born of a virgin and conceived without concupiscence, he was in the eyes of Julianism free from mortal corruption, even if his mother was not.[168] Thus the Julianists did not base Christ's incorruptibility on Mary's freedom from mortal corruption, but rather on her virginity, which allowed his conception without the transmission of mortal corruption. In such a view, Mary's incorruption was not necessary, and in no instance of which I am aware do the ancient sources betray any evidence of a Julianist belief in the Virgin's bodily incorruption.[169]

In support of his theory, however, Mimouni appeals to a rather convoluted passage from Leontius of Byzantium's *Contra Nestorianos et Eutychianos*,[170] where the subject of the Virgin's

---

[167] While Rome understands original sin as transmitted to every human being in the process of propagation, the means by which this transmission occurs 'is a mystery that we cannot fully understand'. Concupiscence, however, is not among the causes, and is instead considered to be a primary consequence of original sin. *Catechism of the Catholic Church*, 404 (New York: Doubleday, 1995), 114. Note, however, that although Augustine, like modern Roman Catholicism, could not identify the source of Original Sin's transmission, in his debates with another Julian, Julian of Eclanum, Augustine occasionally draws near to Julian of Halicarnassus' explanation, hinting that Christ's freedom from original sin may depend on his virginal conception in the absence of concupiscence: see Elizabeth A. Clark, 'Vitiated Seeds and Holy Vessels: Augustine's Manichean Past', in *Ascetic Piety and Women's Faith: Essays on Late Ancient Christianity*, Studies in Women and Religion, 20 (Lewiston, NY: Edwin Mellen Press, 1986), 292–3, 305–6, 309–13.

[168] Grillmeier, *Christ*, ii. pt. 2. 108–11; Jarry, *Hérésies*, 69; Draguet, *Julien*, 154–6.

[169] This is confirmed by Daley, *On the Dormition*, 41 n. 29.

[170] Leontius of Byzantium, *Nest. et Eut.* (PG 86. 1325–8). Cited by Mimouni in *Dormition*, 666–7.

incorruptibility is considered in the course of a dialogue between an orthodox Christian and an Aphthartodocetist, a member of a movement related to, but not always completely identical with, Julianism.[171] The issue of Mary's bodily corruption is here raised by the orthodox participant, who asks his interlocutor whether he believes that the Virgin's body was miraculously purified from mortal corruption so that she could give birth to Christ's incorruptible body, or if instead the Virgin remained in her corrupted state, and Christ's flesh alone was miraculously transformed into incorruptibility without the Virgin's prior purification.[172] The Aphthartodocetist responds that some of the 'simple-minded' have erroneously maintained the Virgin's bodily incorruption, ascribing her more honour than is appropriate, an assessment with which his orthodox opponent agrees.[173] Rejecting this view, the Aphthartodocetist asserts instead that Christ received a corrupted body from the Virgin, which only after being joined to the Word became suddenly incorrupt.[174]

Two things from this passage in particular are significant for the present matter. Firstly, Leontius' Aphthartodocetist explicitly repudiates the notion that Mary was purified of her bodily corruption in order to preserve Christ from contact with

---

[171] There is some debate about the degree to which the Aphthartodocetist of Leontius' dialogue espouses the same teachings as Julian. For instance, Leontius' Aphthartodocetist seems to have been a Chalcedonian, whereas Julian was a monophysite. This is not particularly unusual, however, since the Julianist or Aphthartodocetist teaching on Christ's incorruptibility was popular with both monophysites and Chalcedonians and was embraced by no less a Chalcedonian than the emperor Justinian himself at the end of his life. Nevertheless, despite this and other differences, the central idea of human corruption and Christ's incorruption lies at the heart of both systems. For discussion, see Grillmeier, *Christ*, ii. pt. 2 213–16, 467–73 (on Justinian); Draguet, *Julien*, 176–8.

[172] Πότερον, ἔφην, ἆρα τοῦ σώματος τῆς Παρθένου μεταστοιχειωθέντος, καὶ τῆς ἰδίας ἐκστάντος φύσεως, ὑπὸ τῆς τοῦ Λόγου δυνάμεως οὕτως ἐξ αὐτῆς μήτρας, ἄλλως ἔχουσαν τὴν ἡμετέραν αὐτῷ φύσιν ἡνῶσθαι λέγεις; ἢ τῆς Παρθένου μὲν ἐν τοῖς ἰδιώμασι τῆς φύσεως μεινάσης, τῶνδε πρώτων ἀρχῶν, τῶν παρθενικῶν αἱμάτων λέγω, μεταποιηθέντων, ἄφθαρτον γεγενῆσθαι τὴν σάρκα; Leontius of Byzantium, *Nest. et Eut.* (PG 86. 1325D).

[173] Τινὲς μὲν, ἔφη, καὶ τῇ προτέρᾳ δόξῃ τῶν ἁπλουστέρων οἶμαι προστίθενται, πλέον ἢ προσῆκε τὴν Παρθένον ἀποσεμνύνοντες..., ibid. (PG 86. 1325D–8A).

[174] Τὸ δὲ ᾗτι φθαρτὸν ἐκ μήτρας λαβὼν τὸ ἐκ τῆς παρθένου σῶμα, εὐθέως αὐτὸ πρὸς ἀφθαρσίαν μετεκεράσατο, τῶν ᾗρθῶς ἡμῖν δοκούντων ἐστίν, ibid. (PG 86. 1329B).

corruption, an error that he attributes to the unchecked zeal of the 'simple-minded' for ascribing honours to the Virgin. Such denial can hardly stand as evidence of a Julianist or Aphthartodocetist belief in the Virgin's bodily incorruptibility, since neither participant identifies these 'simple-minded' as being either Julianists or Aphthartodocetists. But even if it were the case that there was in the sixth century some minor group that espoused this position, it does not seem very likely that such a group could be held solely responsible for the supposed introduction of Assumptionist belief in the early Byzantine church, as Mimouni proposes. Also noteworthy in this passage is the important difference between Leontius' Aphthartodocetist and the teachings of Julian regarding the means by which mortal corruption is transmitted.[175] As we have already noted, in the Julianist system, bodily corruption was transmitted by the sexual desire present at the moment of conception. In the absence of this desire, it was possible to conceive uncorrupted flesh, and since Christ's conception was believed to have been virginal, it stands to reason that he would have lacked this somatic corruption. According to Leontius' Aphthartodocetist, however, this is not the case, and despite the virginal conception, the Word was joined in his mother's womb to corrupted flesh which was not purified until after the union. Only such belief in the inheritance of corruption from one's parents would necessitate the prior purification of the Virgin's flesh. But even Leontius' Aphthartodocetist, who is represented as holding this view of transmission, explicitly rejects the possibility of the Virgin's purification before Christ's conception, asserting that the Word was joined to corrupt flesh which became incorrupt only after the union.

The Virgin's role in the transmission of mortality then is a primary point of distinction between ancient Julianism and Aphthartodocetism on the one hand, and the Roman dogma of Original Sin on the other, a difference that is seemingly overlooked by Mimouni. For Rome, Mary differs from the rest of humanity in her exemption from Original Sin, but for the Julianist, Christ alone was free from mortal corruption, and Mary shared fully the mortal corruption of human flesh.

[175] On this difference between Julianism and Aphthartodocetism, see Draguet, *Julien*, 177.

Although the somewhat different explanation offered by Leontius' Aphthartodocetist approaches the Roman understanding more nearly, it is clearly distinguished by its denial of any need to purify the Virgin's flesh in anticipation of the Incarnation and a fear that such a notion too greatly exalts the Virgin. Thus, there is no evidence to support the hypothesis that the Assumptionist traditions initially developed among a group of Julianists who maintained the Virgin's physical incorruptibility and her consequent inability to suffer death.[176] On the contrary, the current state of our evidence seems to indicate that there was no such belief among any known Julianists or Aphthartodocetists. To impute such a teaching to ancient Julianism is to read the past through Rome-coloured glasses, distorting historical Julianism into an approximation of the Roman doctrine of Original Sin.

Turning to the ancient Dormition traditions themselves, as well as now to the more general question of anti-Chalcedonian origins, there is similarly no compelling evidence to suggest a connection between the emergence of these traditions and opposition to Chalcedon, as is commonly supposed. Even Mimouni is willing to confess this, when in regards to his own theory of anti-Chalcedonian origins he admits, 'certes, pour affermir une telle hypothèse, les sources manquent'.[177] More importantly, however, the overall tenor of the early Dormition traditions themselves speaks rather strongly against such a hypothesis. With the exception of some anti-tritheist polemic in Theodosius of Alexandria's *Homily on the Dormition*,[178] the early Dormition

---

[176] Grillmeier, however, notes the existence of a belief that Christ's somatic incorruption depends on his mother's prior purification from this corruption in a *much* later Ethiopic text (16th–17th century: under Jesuit influence?): Grillmeier, *Christ*, ii. pt. 4. 351–2. The text may be found in Enrico Cerulli, *Scritti teologici etiopici dei secoli xvi–xvii*, ii. *La Storia dei Quattro Concili ed altri opusculi monofisiti*, Studi et Testi, 204 (Vatican City: Biblioteca Apostolica Vaticana, 1960), 33–4.

[177] Mimouni, *Dormition*, 665.

[178] Tritheism was the result of a mixture of Severan monophysitism with orthodox Trinitarian thought. Severan monophysitism maintained that hypostasis and nature were equivalent terms, in contrast to the Chalcedonians who distinguished the two according to the formula 'two natures in one hypostasis'. When this was joined to orthodox Trinitarian thought, which described the Trinity as 'three *hypostaseis* in one *ousia*', the result was that some opponents of Chalcedon began declaring that there were three distinct natures

legends maintain a puzzling silence concerning the most press-
ing dogmatic issues of the day, failing even to condemn
Nestorius, the Virgin's arch-enemy.[179] This is not, however, for
want of theological polemic: on the contrary, these narratives
vigorously attack, among other things, Judaism and various

in the Trinity, one corresponding to each of the three hyposteses. This teaching
was known as 'tritheism'. (Meyendorff, *Christ in Eastern Christian Thought*, 19,
29, 41; idem, *Imperial Unity and Christian Divisions: The Church 450–680 A.D.*,
The Church in History, 2 (Crestwood, NY: St. Vladimir's Seminary Press,
1989), 256–8.) As Theodosius objects in the following example, on account of
the divine unity, the incarnation involved all three members of the Trinity, by
joining their one divine nature to the flesh. Although the hypostasis of the Son
was incarnate, he brought with him the single, shared nature of the entire
Trinity, thus joining the one God, and not simply one of three gods, to
humanity: 'O My beloved mother, arise, let us go hence. My Father who liveth
and the Holy Ghost who proceedeth from the Life, wait for thy coming unto
Them; for thou didst carry their Unity, even my Godhead by nature, which
dwelt in thee.' Theodosius of Alexandria, *Homily on the Dormition* 4 (Forbes
Robinson, *Coptic Apocryphal Gospels*, Texts and Studies, IV (Cambridge:
Cambridge University Press, 1896), 104 (Copt.) and 105 (Eng.)). Similar statements to this effect may be found elsewhere in the homily.

[179] The *Homily on the Dormition* of Ps.-Cyril of Jerusalem, from before
the middle of the 6th century, might at first glance appear to be an exception
to this silence, but it is not. In E. A. W. Budge's edition (*Miscellaneous Coptic
Texts in the Dialect of Upper Egypt* (London: British Museum, 1915), 62 (Copt.)
and 639 (Eng.)) we find the following statement: 'One σύνοδος entered one
who was of two natures, and one son was brought forth, a unity of flesh without any diminution. For He was neither changed in His nature, nor reduced in
His strength, nor was he separated from His Ancient Begetter, that is to say,
the Beginning. But the oneness of the flesh of God received one Nature.' Yet
this mildly monophysite statement of faith does not appear in the other two
manuscripts, which have each inserted different credal statements at this
point (see Antonella Campagnano, ed., *Ps. Cirillo di Gerusalemme: Omelie
copte sulla Passione, sulla Croce e sulla Vergine*, Testi e Documenti per lo
Studio dell'Antichita, LXV (Milan: Cisalpiono-Goliardica, 1980), 174–6,
and Pierpont Morgan MS M 597, 60r–2v), indicating that this is probably a
later addition. Campagnano's manuscript was copied in 848, and Morgan 597
in 913/4 (Leo Depuydt, *Catalogue of Coptic Manuscripts in the Pierpont
Morgan Library*, Corpus of Illuminated Manuscripts, 4, Oriental Series, 1
(Leuven: Uitgeverij Peeters, 1993), 205, 325), and Budge's probably in the
mid-11th century (Campagnano, *Ps. Cirillo di Gerusalemme*, 17). Although
MS 597 has a similarly monophysite creed, Campagnano's manuscript, which
appears to be the earliest version (see ibid. 20), does not have such a creed and
thus does not align itself clearly with anti-Chalcedonian theology. I thank
Andrew Jabobs for sharing his translation of the key passage from Morgan MS
597.

more 'extreme' Christological errors (such as docetism and tritheism), in the light of which their silence regarding the raging controversy of the day is even more striking. While such an oversight in the *Vita* of any other saint might not command our attention, in view of the Virgin's politically charged status and her often central position in these Christological debates, this omission is surely significant. The peculiarity of the early traditions' silence is heightened by the Byzantine homilies of the eighth century, where the issues of Chalcedon suddenly make a dramatic appearance, a shift that is presumably consequent upon the seventh-century Islamic conquests, in which the major centres of anti-Chalcedonian resistance fell under Islamic rule.[180]

In so far as the early Dormition traditions betray any connections with the Christological controversies of late antiquity, they appear to be aligned primarily with the various efforts to restore the theological unity that was 'lost' in the wake of Chalcedon, a trend that is admittedly more clear in some texts than in others, but is nowhere contradicted. Despite the efforts of many ancient writers to identify the Virgin exclusively with the truth of their Christological beliefs, Mary was also frequently identified as a potential point of unity, as demonstrated by her prominent role in various early Byzantine efforts to bridge the Christological gap.[181] Like many post-Chalcedonian Mariological texts, the early Dormition narratives adopt a largely irenic tone, emphasizing the Virgin's catholicity and joining her to a rather bland Christology that deliberately avoids entering into the disputes

---

[180] See e.g. (Ps.-)Modestus of Jerusalem, *dorm.* 3, 7, 10 (PG 86. 3288B, 3296A, 3304C); Andrew of Crete, *hom. 13* (PG 97. 1085B); Germanus of Constantinople, *or. 8* (PG 98. 361A); John of Damascus, *hom. 8*, 3 (P. Voulet, ed., *Homélies dur la nativité et la dormition*, SC 80 (Paris: Les Éditions du Cerf, 1961), 88-9) and idem, *hom 9*, 4 (ibid. 136-7).

[181] For a brief survey of Mary's theological position in the post-Chalcedonian literature, see Stephen J. Shoemaker, 'Mary and the Discourse of Orthodoxy: Early Christian Identity and the Ancient Dormition Traditions', Ph.D. diss., Duke University, 1997, ch. 5, although more work remains to be done. One can also see Roberto Caro, SJ, *La Homiletica Mariana Griega en el Siglo V*, 3 vols., Marian Library Studies, NS 3–5 (Dayton, OH: University of Dayton, 1971–3), iii. 658–60. Here Caro notes the presence of Christological polemics in a number of post-Ephesian homilies: these are often crucial in his decisions about authenticity and date. Note that despite its title, this work also treats a number of 6th- and early 7th-century pseudepigraphical Marian homilies.

over Chalcedon.[182] But the most obvious indication of a connection between the early Dormition legends and the early
Byzantine efforts to restore religious unity is the presence of
henotic theolegoumena in certain narratives, namely the fifth-
and sixth-century Syriac Six Books apocrypha. Near the beginning of all three versions, one finds the following theopaschite
confession:

Blessed be Thy grace, God that didst die, King's son that wast debased,
Undying that didst will and die; who didst migrate from the Father
unto Mary, and from Mary to the manger, and from the manger to
the circumcision, and from the circumcision to bringing up, and from
bringing up to stripes, and from stripes to blows, and from blows to
the Cross, and from the Cross to death, and from death to the grave,
and from the grave to the resurrection, and from the resurrection to
Heaven, and sittest, lo, at the right hand of Thy Father.[183]

Similar emphasis on God's suffering and death in the flesh
appears in Zeno's *Henotikon*, one of the earliest efforts to
restore ecclesiastical unity, and theopaschism was later the
focus of Justinian's initial attempt to heal the divisions created
by Chalcedon.[184] The prominent affirmation of theopaschism
in these early Syriac apocrypha, as well as their otherwise
strict avoidance of the controversies over Chalcedon, suggests
dogmatic alignment with these efforts towards reunion, as other
scholars have occasionally noted.[185] Far from indicating an anti-
Chalcedonian origin, this feature points towards the development of these legends within a conciliatory milieu.

With only these exceptions, clear dogmatic alignments are
otherwise absent from the remaining early Dormition narratives,

---

[182] This tendency of post-Chalcedonian Mariological literature is discussed
by Sebastian Brock, 'Mary in Syriac Tradition', in Alberic Stacpoole, OSB
(ed.), *Mary's Place in Christian Dialogue* (Wilton, CT: Morehouse-Barlow Co.,
1983), 182–3. See also Caro, *La Homiletica,* iii. 659.

[183] William Wright, 'Departure', ܐ (Syr.) and 130 (Eng.). Agnes Smith
Lewis's version reproduces the same text with only minor variations, *Apocrypha
Syriaca,* Studia Sinaitica, XI (London: C. J. Clay & Sons, 1902), ܝܕ (Syr.) and
13–14 (Eng.). See the very similar version in Wright, *Contributions,* ܝܚ (Syr.)
and 19 (Eng.).

[184] See Grillmeier, ii. pt. 2. 317–43, and Meyendorff, *Christ,* 69–89.

[185] Testa, 'L'origine', 259–60; idem, 'Lo sviluppo', 257–69; Michel van
Esbroeck, 'Les Signes des temps', 148; idem, 'Une court traité pseudo-basilien', 393–4; idem, 'Étude comparée', 10; Mimouni, *Dormition,* 103.

although this silence may be equally telling. While the narratives frequently include various Christological statements, normally placed in the mouth of Mary or one of the apostles, these statements are distinctly innocuous and seem deliberately to avoid using the language and formulae of the controversy over Chalcedon. As one might expect, the Christological tone of most narratives is distinctly Ephesian, emphasizing the Virgin's role as Theotokos in particular.[186] Only the more primitive Angel Christology of the early Palm traditions presents a major exception, but even in the theological 'correction' of these narratives, a revision that was partly Christological, the redactors made no attempt to impose any post-Ephesian Christology onto their 'rehabilitated' narratives. In fact, only two early narratives (whose dates are somewhat questionable) even broach the questions of Christ's unity and dichotomy raised by Chalcedon. Both of these texts are preserved in Armenian, and while they may be as early as the sixth century, it is not possible to exclude a somewhat later origin. In any case, both narratives use decidedly non-partisan language to explain the relation of Christ's divinity and humanity, seeming to avoid intentionally the disputes that issued from Chalcedon.

The first of these texts is the early Armenian *Transitus*, a very free elaboration of the Palm tradition. In this narrative, after receiving the Palm from the angel, the Virgin prays:

Almighty Father, beneficent and charitable, you who sent for the salvation of the human race your only-begotten Son, who came and put on human form from your maid-servant, and formed and shaped the image of lowliness in my womb, for the glory of union with the nature

---

[186] e.g., John of Thessalonica, *dorm. BMV A* 1–2 and *B* 1 (Jugie, *Homélies mariales*, 375–8, 405–6); Theoteknos of Livias, *Homily on the Dormition* 9, 20–1 (Wenger, *L'Assomption*, 276–7; 282–3); Ps.-John, *Transitus* 3 (Konstantin Tischendorf, *Apocalypses Apocryphae* (Leipzig: Herm. Mendelssohn, 1866), 96); G1: Wenger, *L'Assomption*, 210–11; Ps.-Basil of Caesarea, *Transitus* 1–2 (Michel van Esbroeck, 'L'Assomption de la Vierge dans un *Transitus* Pseudo-Basilien', *Analecta Bollandiana*, 92 (1974), 128–9); Ps.-Evodius of Rome, *Homily on the Dormition (St Mich.)* 3–6 (Stephen J. Shoemaker, 'The Sahidic Coptic Homily on the Dormition of the Virgin Attributed to Evodius of Rome: An Edition of Morgan MSS 596 & 598 with Translation', *Analecta Bollandiana*, 117 (1999), 256–62); idem, *Homily on the Dormition (St Mac.)* 17, 19 (Paul de Lagarde, ed., *Aegyptiaca* (Göttingen: A. Hoyer, 1883; repr. Osnabrück: Otto Zeller Verlag, 1972), 59–60, 62–3).

of his divinity. And in my womb he united and joined the tremendous transformation of the incarnation into one son.[187]

This statement of the union between Christ's humanity and his divine nature to form one son could hardly be identified as either pro- or anti-Chalcedonian, since in essence the passage raises without answering the council's primary question: how does one explain the unity of Christ's humanity and his divine nature to form one son? What is unaddressed is precisely the divisive issue of whether this union occurs at the level of hypostasis (Chalcedon) or nature (opponents of Chalcedon).

The second example, Ps.-Chrysostom's encomiastic *Homily on the Dormition*,[188] draws somewhat nearer to the Chalcedonian position, explaining that in the Virgin's womb, 'the mixed human nature was united with the nature of God . . . mixed and united without confusion, and a nature was not consumed or removed, but the Word of God preserved completely the properties of both natures, uniting them in one person and in one prosopon'.[189] The emphasis in this passage on the integrity of Christ's human nature clearly tilts the homily towards Chalcedon, but in the light of the precise language adopted at

---

[187] զգեցաւ զմարդկայքին կերպարան յաղախնոյ քո,...ի փառս միաւորութեան բնութեան ատտուածունութեան իւրոյ: եւ յորովայնի իմում զսարասափելի փոխադրութիւն նեբմարդութեանն միաւորեաց և խառնեաց ի մի որդի. Esayi Tayets'i, ed., 'Բրանելրոյն Նիկողիմոսի ասացեալ յաղագս ննջման Մարիանու Աստուածածնի եւ Միշտ Կուսին (A Narration Concerning the Dormition of the Theotokos and Ever-Virgin Mary by the Blessed Nicodemus)', in Անկանոն գիրք Նոր Կտակարանաց (*Ankanon girk' Nor Ktakaranats' [Apocryphal Books of the New Testament]*), T'angaran haykakan hin ew nor dprut'eants', 2 (Venice: I Tparani S. Łazaru, 1898), 453.

[188] For the 6th-century date, see Mimouni, *Dormition*, 333–7, where, if one ignores his dubious argument that the homily's inclusion of an Assumption necessitates a date after the late 6th century, the evidence for a date slightly earlier in the 6th century is rather convincing. As Mimouni also explains, the attribution to John II of Jerusalem by van Esbroeck is rather ambitious (see Michel van Esbroeck, 'Une homélie arménienne sur la dormition attribuée à Chrysostome', *Oriens Christianus*, 74 (1990), 208).

[189] բնութիւն մարդկային խառնեալ միացաւ ընդ բնութեան Աստուծոյ: ...անշփոթ խառնեալ և միացեալ և ոչ բնութիւն ծախեալ կամ պարապարծեալ. այլ պահեաց ամբողջ բանն Աստուած զերկուց բնութեանցն զյատկութիւանն ի մի անձն և ի մի դէմս միաւորեալ. Ps.-John Chrysostom, *Homily on the Dormition* 5 (van Esbroeck, 'Une homélie arménienne', 211 (Arm.) and 223 (Fr.)).

the council, the homily's ambiguous formulations both here and elsewhere have led its editor, Michel van Esbroeck, to conclude on the basis of the homily's Christology that it is very probably a pre-Chalcedonian work.[190] Key to his determination are statements such as 'one son and one prosopon and one visage and one person, from two perfect essences, one perfect essence',[191] a passage that, despite the scent of the monophysite formula of one nature after the union, uses the category 'essence' to explain the union, in place of the Chalcedonian 'hypostasis' or the anti-Chalcedonian 'nature'.[192] This, van Esbroeck argues, is proof of the homily's origin sometime before the alternatives of nature and hypostasis had been clearly identified at the council of Chalcedon. Yet perhaps the absence of such post-Chalcedonian terminology is not an accident of chronology, but instead reflects a deliberate avoidance of theological controversy, attempting to describe the Incarnation using non-partisan language. Viewed as such, this homily converges with the general trend in the Dormition traditions to avoid the controversies arising from Chalcedon and to underscore Christian unity in the face of these divisions.

Other non-doctrinal features of these narratives also point towards an interest in Christian unity rather than partisanship. One such feature is the miraculous reunion of the apostles, an episode featured prominently in both the Palm and Bethlehem traditions.[193] The latter traditions focus especially on this event, recounting in detail the transport of each apostle from the far reaches of the known world, only to repeat these accounts again as each of the apostles describes for the others where he was and what he was doing when he was suddenly brought to Jerusalem

---

[190] Ibid. 203–4.

[191] մի որդի և մի դէմք և մի երեսք և մի անձն յերկուց կատարելոց գոյացութեանց մի կատարեալ գոյութիւն. ibid. 17 (ibid. 219 (Arm.) and 233 (Fr.)).

[192] Ibid. 203–4.

[193] It is not a feature, however, of the Coptic traditions. Although the details of this event are given much more fully in the Bethlehem traditions, this episode is also recounted by several early texts from the Palm tradition, from the 5th and 6th centuries: see Ps.-Melito, *Transitus* 3–4 (Haibach-Reinisch, *Ein neuer Transitus*, 69–72); G1 §§15 and 22 (Wenger, *L'Assomption*, 218, 223); *Liber Requiei* 42 and 46 (Arras, *De Transitu*, i. 25, 27–8 (Eth.) and 16–17, 18 (Lat.)), among others. See van Esbroeck, 'Les Textes', 268–9, where he notes this as a general feature of both families.

for the Virgin's Dormition.[194] Although the list of places varies slightly from version to version, apostles are generally imported from such places as Ephesus, Rome, Tiberias, India, Jerusalem, Armenia, Beirut, Laodicea, and the Thebaid, while Matthew is lifted from a ship at sea, and others who have died already are resurrected temporarily to witness the Virgin's Dormition. This miraculous reunion of the apostles stands as a reminder to a divided Christendom of the apostolic unity of catholic Christianity, reaching ideally from Rome to India and even beyond the grave, a notion suggesting a shared identity rooted in a common origin. Here, the unity of the apostles is portrayed as an ideal alternative to the fractious and contentious state of the contemporary church. This is particularly clear in the early Palm legends where at the moment when debate among the apostles seems immanent, Christ intervenes to restore harmony.[195] In Christ's absence, this duty would naturally fall to his earthly representative, the emperor, who generally was the agent, if not always the source, of the various attempts to restore ecclesiastical unity.[196]

Moreover, the broad geographic representation of the apostles exemplifies the Virgin's ecumenical importance, demonstrating by their presence at her Dormition that both she and her cult belong not to a particular place, but to the entire Christian world, all of which is symbolically present in the apostles. To similar effect, many of the earliest texts describe miraculous cures that were performed by the Virgin while she was in Bethlehem, most of which were worked for women throughout the world who sought her aid: 'women were coming to her from the cities and

---

[194] Smith Lewis, *Apocrypha*, ܩܝ‑ܠܡ (Syr.) and 25–33 (Eng.); Wright, 'Departure', ܟܐ‑ܠ (Syr.) and 136–41 (Eng.); idem, *Contributions*,ܠ‑ܟܕ (Syr.) and 22–4 (Eng.).

[195] *Obsequies*: Wright, *Contributions*, ܠܠ‑ܩܝ (Syr.) and 45–6 (Eng.); *Liber Requiei* 84–8 (Arras, *De Transitu*, i. 49–52 (Eth.) and 33–4 (Lat.)).

[196] Indeed, imperial religious authority is implicitly authorized in the account of a religious debate found in the early Syriac apocrypha where the Roman governor decides the outcome: see Wright, *Contributions*, ܠ (Syr.) and 27 (Eng.); Wright, 'Departure',ܠ‑ܠܟ (Syr.) and 146 (Eng.); Smith Lewis, *Apocrypha*, ܩܝ (Syr.) and 43 (Eng.). See also John Haldon, *Byzantium in the Seventh Century: The Transformation of a Culture*, rev. edn. (Cambridge: Cambridge University Press, 1997), 14, 337; Averil Cameron, 'Images of Authority: Elites and Icons in Late Sixth-Century Byzantium', *Past and Present*, 84 (1979), 17.

regions and from Rome and Athens, the daughters of kings and
procurators and prefects, and bringing presents and offerings,
and they were coming and worshipping my Lady Mary, and
every one who had a pain, and she was curing them'.[197] In addition to Rome and Athens, specific mention is also made of women
having travelled from Beirut, Alexandria, Thessalonica, and
Egypt to seek her aid. Numerous others, we are told, came from
unspecified places to receive a cure from the Virgin, who in a
single instant once cured 2,600 men, women, and children.[198]
Yet not only did Mary cure those who had made a 'pilgrimage',
but she also worked miracles for those seeking her aid from a
great distance; despite her physical location in Palestine, the
reach of her cures was unfettered by the limits of space.
Miraculously appearing throughout the Christian world, Mary
saves a total of ninety-two ships that seek her help, as well as a
group of men beset by robbers. Likewise, a woman whose son
had fallen down a well calls upon the Virgin, and she appears and
brings him up from the well. Mary also restores a merchant's lost
purse and rescues two Egyptian women confronted by a giant
snake, aiding in addition many others 'at Rome and in all
countries' who sought her assistance, all the while preparing for
her death in Jerusalem and Bethlehem.[199]

The overall impact of these worldwide miracles and the
apostolic reunion is Mary's identification as a figure belonging to all Christendom and not to one particular place or group
only. As one of the sixth-century Syriac apocrypha declares: 'All
countries are full of the glories of the blessed one.'[200] Thanks
in large part to the Dormition traditions themselves, and their
narration of the removal of Mary's body from this world, the
Virgin's cult was not, in contrast to the cult of most saints, tied to
a specific location or region where she had worked her miracles
or where her remains lay.[201] Instead, Mary was a saint with

[197] Wright, 'Departure', ܒܒ–ܪܟ (Syr.) and 141–2 (Eng.); Smith Lewis, *Apocrypha*, ܠ–ܡܠ (Syr.) and 33–4 (Eng.).
[198] Wright, 'Departure', ܠܓ–ܪܟ (Syr.) and 141–2 (Eng.); Smith Lewis, *Apocrypha*, ܠܒ–ܠ (Syr.) and 35 (Eng.).
[199] Wright, 'Departure', ܠܐ–ܪܐ (Syr.) and 147–8 (Eng.); idem, *Contributions*, ܡܙ–ܡܣ (Syr.) and 36–7 (Eng.); Smith Lewis, *Apocrypha*, ܠܒ–ܪܨ (Syr.) and 49–50 (Eng.).
[200] Smith Lewis, *Apocrypha*, ܪܨ (Syr.) and 49 (Eng.).
[201] On the special link between a saint, her or his relics, and a particular

universal appeal: although her tomb in Jerusalem and her robe and girdle in Constantinople served to link her especially with these two places, she nevertheless did not belong to any one place in particular, but was a holy person revered above all other saints throughout the Christian world. As John of Damascus, explains, addressing the significance of the Virgin's empty tomb in his eighth-century homilies on the Dormition, 'the divine power is not restricted by place, nor are the benefactions of the Mother of God. For if they were confined to the tomb alone, the divine gift would reach only a few. But now it has been freely distributed in all the regions of the world.'[202]

It is rather unsurprising then to find that the late ancient discourse of the Virgin's Dormition developed largely as a unifying discourse, rather than according to sectarian interests, particularly since these legends were a major factor in the Virgin's transformation into a holy person of universal stature. Since her body had been miraculously removed, either to some hidden place or together with her soul into Paradise, there were no relics tying her cult to a particular place. Thus, these legends effectively prevented her cult from becoming linked with a particular region, as were many other cults, enabling her to become an important locus of ecumenical and imperial Christian identity, which culminated in her adoption as the Empire's celestial patroness. Closely related to this ecumenical identity is the careful non-partisanship of the earliest Dormition traditions. The ancient narratives are guardedly silent regarding the issues of Chalcedon, a fact that militates against their identification with the anti-Chalcedonian movements. On the contrary, it suggests their historical emergence within an ideological context that was at least open, if not dedicated, to compromise on the issues of Chalcedon, a theory that is bolstered by the presence of henotic theological formula in a few of the very earliest narratives.

---

place, see Peter Brown, *The Cult of the Saints: Its Rise and Function in Latin Christianity* (Chicago: University of Chicago Press, 1981), ch. 5, and idem, 'A Dark Age Crisis: Aspects of the Iconoclast Controversy', *English Historical Review*, 88 (1973), 1–34; repr. in idem, *Society and the Holy in Late Antiquity* (Berkeley and Los Angeles: University of California Press, 1982), 251–301; see in the repr. esp. pp. 275–8.

[202] John of Damascus, *hom.* 9, 19 (Voulet, *Homélies dur la nativité et la dormition*, 168).

CONCLUSIONS

In the most literal sense, the 'origin' of the ancient Dormition traditions in an anti-Chalcedonian milieu seems to be completely out of the question. If by 'origin' one means the earliest milieu in which these traditions first took shape, it is rather clear that early Palm narratives had their origin elsewhere, in some pre-Chalcedonian theological context that is now known only imperfectly. The indication of the earliest narratives is that they were in contact with some sort of gnostic Christianity early in their development. Nevertheless, it is not at all certain that the traditions originated is such a milieu: it may be that they merely passed through such a context at some point in their now unknown prehistory. In any case, the possibility that these traditions came into existence only after the council of Chalcedon is entirely unlikely. It is a more viable possibility, however, that in the late fifth and early sixth centuries these already existing traditions were ushered into the mainstream of Christian discourse by those who were opposed to the council of Chalcedon. Nevertheless, as we have seen, there is no compelling evidence to suggest such a connection, despite its frequent repetition in scholarship on these traditions; nor is there any indication of emergence through a pro-Chalcedonian milieu, for that matter. The seemingly deliberate omission of the issues raised by Chalcedon, or the attempt to resolve them in a non-partisan manner, suggests instead that these ancient narratives were first championed and edited in a context that was opposed to (or else not affected by) the divisions sparked by Chalcedon. This hypothesis is strengthened by the presence of henotic formula in certain early narratives, as well as by the early association of these traditions with Jacob of Serug and Ps.-Dionysius, both of whom are well known for having meticulously avoided the partisanship that issued from Chalcedon. Even in the hands of such a committed opponent of Chalcedon as Theodosius of Alexandria, these traditions are not turned to the anti-Chalcedonian cause. The dogmatic neutrality of the early Dormition traditions regarding Chalcedon is really quite striking, and it coalesces with other socially and culturally integrative features of the various narratives. This generally unifying character can perhaps explain the motive for the adoption of these traditions in sixth-century Byzantium, where the need for such integrating narratives was acute.[203] As I hope to explore further in a future study, the Dormition traditions presented Mary as a potential site of unity in an increasingly divided society, which may in part explain their sudden emergence from an otherwise obscure past.[204]

---

[203] See the discussions in Haldon, *Byzantium in the Seventh Century*, 9–40 and 348–71; Cameron, 'Images of Authority', 18–35.

[204] Initial explorations in this direction were made in Shoemaker, 'Mary and the Discourse of Orthodoxy', chs. 5, 6.

Conclusion

In William Wright's introduction to *Contributions to the Apocryphal Literature of the New Testament*, where he published the important fifth-century *Obsequies* fragments, Wright cites the following passage from Heinrich Ewald's review of his previous edition of the Six Books, which may rightly be considered the earliest scholarly reception of the ancient Dormition traditions:

We can certainly affirm that this book has become from the first the firm foundation for all the unhappy adoration of Mary, and for a hundred superstitious things, which have intruded with less and less resistance into the Churches, since the 5th century, and have contributed so much to the degeneration and to the crippling of all better Christianity. The little book is therefore of the greatest importance for the history of every century in the Middle Ages, and yet today we ought to notice far more seriously than we usually do the great amount of what we have to learn from it. The whole cultus of Mary in the Papal Church rests upon this book; we might search in vain for any other foundation to it: notwithstanding the fact that it was excluded once again in early times from the list of canonical books by the *Decretum Gelasii*. The three yearly feasts in honour of Mary which the Greek Church maintains to this day, and whose number has been exceeded only by the Papal Church in the long course of centuries are ordained for the first time in this book, and are even defined by the day of the year (on which they are to be held). The delusion about the Immaculate Conception of Mary, which has in our day been elevated into a dogma finds its foundation and its certain consequences only in this book. The similarly quite unhistorical delusion about an original adoration and consecration of the Sepulchre of Christ in Jerusalem is spoken of for the first time in the beginning of the second of the six little books of this text, that is, in the beginning of the narrative about the last days of Mary, and in such a way that we can all easily understand what a deep impression such a narrative was bound to make on the world of that period even if the well-known example of Constantine's mother had not preceded it.[1]

Ewald's review is elsewhere characterized by such prejudicial vitriol, and in one instance he characterizes the form of Christianity exemplified in this narrative as so degenerate and superstitious that it is indistinguishable from Buddhism.[2] Some forty years later, however, in the introduction to her version of the Six Books narrative, Smith Lewis repeats the above passage from Ewald's review, reminding her readers that 'It is hardly necessary to say that I endorse the opinion of Dr Ewald.'[3] It would seem that with the turning of the new century, attitudes to this material had changed very little.

Nevertheless, Ewald's assessment of the Dormition traditions' importance, *mutatis mutandis*, still has much to recommend it. If we may rejoice that the discipline of Religious Studies has lost this early venom for Roman Catholicism, it has yet completely to recognize the importance of these ancient narratives for understanding the development of Marian piety, as Ewald so rightly describes it. The widespread popularity of these narratives and the related liturgical feast, both in Byzantium and the West, ensured that they would exert a profound influence on the development of Marian piety. Moreover, the regular liturgical performance of many early narratives provided a vehicle capable of communicating these traditions across a broad spectrum of society. Among other things, it would seem that these narratives are largely responsible for engendering the anti-Judaism that characterized Mary's medieval cult.[4] Likewise, they were clearly influential on the emerging belief in the effectiveness of Marian intercession. As I have argued elsewhere, and I hope to pursue

---

[1] Cited in William Wright, ed., *Contributions to the Apocryphal Literature of the New Testament* (London: Williams & Norgate, 1865), 9–10; the English translation is from the introduction to Agnes Smith Lewis, ed., *Apocrypha Syriaca*, Studia Sinaitica, XI (London: C. J. Clay & Sons, 1902), p. xvi. The original may be found in Heinrich Ewald, 'Review of "The departure of my lady Mary from this world. Edited from two Syriac manuscripts in the British Museum, and translated by W. Wright"', *Göttingische gelehrte Anzeigen* 1865, pt. 26. 1022–3. [2] Ibid. 1020–1.

[3] Smith Lewis, *Apocrypha Syriaca*, p. xvi.

[4] See Stephen J. Shoemaker, ' "Let Us Go and Burn Her Body": The Image of the Jews in the Early Dormition Traditions', *Church History*, 68 (1999), 775–823.

further in a future study, these narratives were also especially important in the identification and promotion of Mary as a kind of ecumenical saint, who, in contrast to most other saints, was not linked with any specific region that claimed her remains.[5] This feature presents a major contrast, for instance, with the Marian legends associated with Constantinople, which sought to claim Mary exclusively for the imperial capital: this difference seems particularly worthy of investigation.

The primary intention of the present volume is to establish a foundation that will facilitate future research on these and other themes from the early Dormition narratives. With this in mind, we have concerned ourselves with certain fundamental issues concerning the origins of these traditions, including in particular their probable dates and the literary relations evident among the earliest narratives. Given the abundance of traditions and their remarkable complexity, however, this is no easy task. No doubt many refinements remain to be made in regards to our understanding of these narratives: their study is very much still in its infancy. Nevertheless, given the present state of our knowledge, a number of conclusions seem relatively certain. In the first place, we may identify the period between 450 and 500 CE as the time when the ancient Dormition traditions first come into historical view from a somewhat uncertain past. Moreover, at this time, we encounter not a single, unified tradition, but instead we find several, diverse narratives, including the earliest exemplars of three major literary traditions, as well as a handful of independent or atypical narratives. One particular point on which there is simultaneously both significant unity and diversity among these earliest narratives is Mary's ultimate fate. Although all the narratives conclude with Mary's transfer to the garden of Paradise, some versions describe Mary's bodily resurrection in Paradise, while other narratives report only the transfer of Mary's lifeless body to Paradise, where it remains separate from her soul.

Various modern interpreters have occasionally sought to account for this diversity by proposing a developmental typology, according to which each narrative type develops out of

---

[5] See Shoemaker, 'Mary and the Discourse of Orthodoxy: Early Christian Identity and the Ancient Dormition Legends', Ph.D. diss., Duke University, 1997, 220–89.

and replaces an earlier type, paralleling related developments in Christian doctrine. All these developmental typologies focus tightly on the narratives' theology, with a particular concern to correlate their descriptions of Mary's ultimate fate with the modern Roman Catholic dogma of the Assumption. Narratives reporting Mary's bodily resurrection in Paradise are counted as supporting this modern doctrine, while those relating a more lasting separation of body and soul are seen as opposed to it. On the basis of this distinction, modern scholars have suggested alternatively the evolution of belief in the Assumption from a more primitive belief only in Mary's Dormition, or the corruption of an original belief in Mary's Assumption that gradually degenerated into belief only in her Dormition.

Nevertheless, as we have shown in this study, such efforts are severely misguided, in the first place because they impute the theological distinctions of modern Roman Catholic discourse to these ancient narratives, where they are inappropriate. Likewise, there is simply no historical evidence for any sort of typological or theological evolution: each type of narrative and all manner of opinions regarding Mary's ultimate fate are evident simultaneously when these narratives first appear at the end of the fifth century. Thus, the literary history of these traditions affords no evidence of any narrative type or theological position antedating the others; rather, they attest to synchronic coexistence of a variety of traditions. Moreover, their different interpretations of Mary's final presence in Paradise find an explanation in the general variety of opinion concerning the eschatological significance of Paradise that characterized both Judaism and Christianity in late antiquity. On this basis primarily, we have argued (following Antoine Wenger) that we must envision 'a great variety of original types', rather than a single point of origin.[6] Investigation of the related early liturgical traditions of Jerusalem has similarly failed to identify one tradition or another as primary. Although we are able to trace a clear development in the Palestinian cult of Mary, nothing in this pattern correlates with the early narratives in a way that would allow us to identify one type as the original source of all the others.

[6] Antoine Wenger, AA, *L'Assomption de la T. S. Vierge dans la tradition byzantine du VIe au Xe siècle*, Archives de l'Orient Chrétien, 5 (Paris: Institut Français d'Études Byzantines, 1955), 17.

Likewise, we have shown the widely held theory of a monophysite or anti-Chalcedonian origin for the early Dormition traditions to be contradicted by the evidence. On the one hand, the suggestion by some scholars that the ancient Dormition narratives were first composed only after the council of Chalcedon in circles opposed to its two-nature Christology seems untenable. Otherwise we must assume that these same opponents of Chalcedon also believed in secret, salvific knowledge and the creation of the physical universe by a demiurge, understood Christ as having been an angel, and believed that Mary had sinned, among other things. It is all but completely certain that the earliest narratives antedate the fourth council: both the peculiar theological ambience of the *Obsequies/Liber Requiei* and its literary relations with the *Apocalypse of Paul* indicate a significantly earlier existence. Yet even if we lay this evidence aside, the fact that the fifth-century Syriac versions of both the *Obsequies* and the Six Books were translated from Greek leaves little chance that these traditions came into existence only after Chalcedon.

More serious, however, is the question of whether these ancient narratives first emerged into historical view from their relatively uncertain past within an anti-Chalcedonian milieu. This theory has been advanced, particularly by Michel van Esbroeck, but there is little solid evidence to support it. On the contrary, the earliest traditions themselves seem to militate against any connection with either the opponents or advocates of Chalcedon. Their spirit is irenic rather than partisan, and they seem deliberately to avoid using the theological language that issued from the debates over Chalcedon. Moreover, in the rare instances when we find explicit reference to contemporary Christological debates, the narratives connect with theological positions that were advanced with the intention of healing the divisions created by Chalcedon. On this basis it seems most probable that the early Dormition traditions were first embraced by the party in the Byzantine church that sought theological reconciliation, rather than by the partisans of either side.

We have additionally in this study attempted to date some of the ancient Dormition traditions more precisely than the information afforded by the date of their earliest manuscripts. A major part of this effort has focused on identifying the theological peculiarities of certain early narratives, in particular the Palm traditions, that are indicative of an earlier existence. In this we have been preceded by many others, most of whom have sought to identify the origin of these traditions within some sort of early Jewish Christianity. In the light of the numerous problems with the theological construct of Jewish-Christianity as these scholars have identified it, we have instead sought to align the earliest Palm narratives with ancient gnostic Christianity, a context that we believe is a better fit. Several doctrines espoused by these narratives suggest this connection, including their emphasis on secret, salvific knowledge, demiurgy, and an Angel Christology. These and other themes point to early contact between these traditions and some form of gnostic Christianity, even if we may not be certain that this was their originary milieu. In any case, the presence of these ideas clearly seems to indicate the existence of these narratives sometime by the third or fourth century at the latest, after which time such doctrines became increasingly scarce.

This dating of the Palm traditions is confirmed by comparison with the *Apocalypse of Paul*, a text composed around 400 CE. As Richard Bauckham has noted, there is evidence of literary dependence between the *Obsequies/Liber Requiei* and the *Apocalypse of Paul*; the only question concerns which text depends on the other. For the reasons suggested by Bauckham, as well as others that we have identified, it seems altogether more likely that the *Apocalypse of Paul* has borrowed material from the earliest Palm narratives, rather than vice versa. This offers important confirmation of the date indicated by the doctrinal content of the earliest Palm narratives. Thus we may conclude with some degree of certainty that the earliest Palm traditions were already in existence sometime before 400 CE, and very probably earlier, perhaps even as early as the second century.

In a forthcoming article, Michel van Esbroeck has gathered together five previously made arguments for dating the earliest Dormition traditions *as a whole* to the fourth century at the latest.[7] Each of these arguments involves perceived relations between the Dormition traditions and other early texts, the

---

[7] See Michel van Esbroeck, 'Some Early Features in the Life of the Virgin', *Marianum* (2001) (forthcoming).

details of which are too complex to adequately reproduce here. Although van Esbroeck's arguments offer support for the proposed date of the earliest Palm traditions, I must admit that I do not find any of them especially persuasive. Two of these arguments depend on connections with texts whose dates are, in my view, rather questionable,[8] while the other arguments depend on alleged textual connections that are both convoluted and very tenuous.[9]

In contrast with the Palm traditions, we have not identified much that would allow us to date the remaining Dormition traditions much earlier than the late fifth century. The Bethlehem traditions, represented in the Syriac Six Books narratives, are indisputably from the fifth century at the latest, as attested by the manuscripts edited by Smith Lewis, including the impressive witness from the famous Syriac gospel palimpsest codex, MS Sin. syr. 30. Moreover, since these Six Books narratives identify themselves as having been translated from the Greek, a *terminus ad quem* in the early fifth century seems altogether likely. An origin much before this point, however, seems rather doubtful, at least for the form of the Bethlehem traditions preserved in the Syriac Six Books. Since the earliest Six Books narratives include material from the *Doctrina Addai* and have incorporated a rather unique account of the invention of the True Cross, they must have been composed, at least in their present form, either after or almost simultaneously with these traditions, which belong to the late fourth or early fifth century. In fact, so close in date are all three of these literary traditions, that we should probably assume

---

[8] We have already discussed the problems with van Esbroeck's dating of the Armenian homily on the Dormition attributed to John Chrysostom in Ch. 1, and his dating of the homily on the Ascension attributed to Eusebius of Alexandria does not seem sufficiently secure: see Michel van Esbroeck, 'Version géorgienne de l'homélie eusébienne CPG 5528 sur l'Ascension', *Orientalia Christiana Periodica*, 51 (1985), 277–83. Although van Esbroeck identifies some very early elements in this homily, he does not sufficiently exclude the possibility that the section referring to the Dormition is a later interpolation made during the complicated transmission of this homily.

[9] These involve alleged connections with Epiphanius of Salamis' *De mensuris et ponderibus*; the *Pistis Sophia*; and a Syriac letter on the rebuilding of the temple attributed to Cyril of Jerusalem. Although the connections proposed by van Esbroeck are possible, they are not sufficiently certain, in my opinion, to allow us to date the early Dormition traditions.

their production in some sort of common milieu.[10] In any case, based on the evidence of the earliest manuscripts and through comparison with closely related literature, it seems that we may isolate the composition of the earliest Six Books narratives during the early fifth century, at least in their present versions.

The earliest Coptic traditions were composed before the middle of the sixth century, as we know from the liturgical changes evident in Theodosius of Alexandria's homily and later texts. There is little in these narratives that would suggest an earlier date, and we cannot be certain of the existence of this type much before 500. As for the assorted atypical traditions, the earliest of these is the homily by Jacob of Serug, probably delivered before a church council in Nisibis in 489. Thus, by the year 500, it is all but certain that these four narrative types were simultaneously in existence, leaving little evidence of any sort of typological or dogmatic development.

Although I have so far resisted the temptation to identify any of the different narrative traditions as the earliest, surely it is by now fairly obvious that I regard the Palm traditions as betraying clear evidence of a significant prehistory that the other narratives lack. Although there is little to suggest the existence of any of the Bethlehem, Coptic, or atypical traditions before the end of the fifth century, there is strong indication that the earliest Palm traditions were formed by the fourth century at the latest, making these the earliest Dormition traditions. I have heretofore refrained from explicitly drawing this conclusion in the effort to dismantle the various developmental typologies that have been proposed. By no means, however, should this identification of the Palm tradition's antiquity be taken as implying that somehow all the other traditions are descended from the earliest Palm narratives. For the reasons expressed in Ch. 3, I maintain the independent origins of the different types of Dormition narratives, and I consider this understanding fundamental for future study of these traditions.

[10] On the relationship between the *Doctrina Addai* and the legends of the True Cross, see Jan Willem Drijvers, *Helena Augusta: The Mother of Constantine the Great and the Legend of Her Finding of the True Cross*, Brill's Studies in Intellectual History, 27 (Leiden: E. J. Brill, 1992), 150–62. Unfortunately, however, Drijvers's study does not take into consideration the rather distinctive accounts of the True Cross' discovery preserved in the Six Books traditions.

Recognition of the Palm traditions' antiquity should have important consequences for subsequent study both of early Christian apocrypha and of early Christianity more generally. It will be important to integrate these Dormition apocrypha more fully into the study of ancient Jewish and Christian apocrypha, an endeavour from which they have largely been excluded up to the present. Richard Bauckham's recent studies mark a notable exception to this pattern, and they present a fine example of what is to be gained from studying the Dormition traditions in this context. Moreover, as the present study has, it is hoped, demonstrated, comparison of the early Dormition traditions with other early Christian apocrypha, in this case gnostic apocrypha, has much to teach us about the nature of early Christianity.[11]

Finally, it is hoped that the antiquity of the earliest Dormition narratives will do much to erase a frequent prejudice of early Christian studies against attributing much significance to the veneration of Mary before the council of Ephesus. There is a palpable tendency in much scholarship to minimize the strong devotion to Mary evident in the ancient church,[12] exemplified, for instance, in Hans von Campenhausen's study *The Virgin Birth in the Theology of the Ancient Church*. Despite the many strengths of this work, it 'is marked by a tendency to minimize and trivialize any early mention of [Mary] so as to reduce its import for mariology'.[13] This is in fact the work's stated purpose, as von Campenhausen explains in his introduction:

---

[11] See also Stephen J. Shoemaker, 'Rethinking the "Gnostic Mary": Mary of Nazareth and Mary of Magdala in Early Christian Tradition', *Journal of Early Christian Studies* (forthcoming); and idem, 'A Case of Mistaken Identity?: Naming the "Gnostic Mary"', in F. Stanley Jones (ed.), *Mary(s) in Early Christian Literature* (Atlanta: Society for Biblical Literature) (forthcoming).

[12] See Philip Sellew's forthcoming article on the *Protevangelium*, 'Heroic Biography, Continent Marriage, and the *Protevangelium Jacobi*', *Journal of Early Christian Studies* (forthcoming), where he discusses this point with reference to the modern interpretation of the *Protevangelium*. See also Willem S. Vorster, 'The Annunciation of the Birth of Jesus in the Protevangelium of James', in J. H. Petzer and P. J. Hartin (eds.), *A South African Perspective on the New Testament* (Leiden: E. J. Brill, 1986), 39–40, cited by Sellew. See also Beverly Roberts Gaventa, *Mary: Glimpses of the Mother of Jesus*, Studies on Personalities of the New Testament (Columbia, SC: University of South Carolina Press, 1995), 16.

[13] Sellew, 'Heroic Biography', n. 73. Sellew also cites as an example Oscar

The aim of the present work is to open up a path through this scholastic wilderness, the so-called 'Mariology' of the early Church. It cannot be seriously disputed that the early Church, at any rate during its first few centuries, knew no real Marian doctrine, that is, no thematic theological concern with Mary's person and her significance in the scheme of Salvation. Nevertheless the flood of publications relating to the subject is now beyond computation, and under the pressure of present Catholic dogmatic interest it is still rising.[14]

The anti-Catholic prejudice of this passage hardly needs comment.[15] Nor is this tendency merely an isolated vestige from the past: the lingering impact of nineteenth-century Protestantism on early Christian studies continues to be seen particularly with regard to Mary.[16] Although we have fortunately begun to see more balanced views of Mary's significance in early Christian culture,[17] much work remains to be done in this regard. It is to be hoped the evidence of early devotion to Mary and concern with her theological significance afforded by the ancient Dormition traditions will help to overcome this not infrequent bias.

Cullmann's curious judgement that 'Tertullian and Origen have "more unbiased views" of the virgin birth and its implications for mariological dogma' than did the author of the *Protevangelium.* See Wilhelm Schneemelcher, ed., *New Testament Apocrypha*, rev. edn., 2 vols., trans. ed. R. McL. Wilson (Philadelphia: Westminster, 1991), 425.

[14] Hans von Campenhausen, *The Virgin Birth in the Theology of the Ancient Church*, trans. Frank Clarke, Studies in Historical Theology, 2 (London: SCM Press, 1964), 7.

[15] See also ibid., 8, n. 1, where von Campenhausen mockingly suggests that, since Catholicism knows Mariology and even Josephology, we may 'perhaps in time *per analogiam* expect an "Annalogy"'.

[16] Regarding this influence generally, see Jonathan Z. Smith, *Drudgery Divine: On the Comparison of Early Christianities and the Religions of Late Antiquity*, Jordan Lectures in Comparative Religion, 14 (Chicago: University of Chicago Press, 1990). Regarding Mary in particular, see Stephen J. Shoemaker, 'Rethinking the "Gnostic Mary": Mary of Nazareth and Mary of Magdala in Early Christian Tradition', *Journal of Early Christian Studies* (forthcoming).

[17] See e.g. Averil Cameron, *Christianity and the Rhetoric of Empire: The Development of Christian Discourse*, Sather Classical Lectures, 55 (Berkeley: University of California Press, 1991), esp. 98–106.

The Ethiopic *Liber Requiei*

1. In the name of the Father and the Son and the Holy Spirit. The Book of Mary's Repose, which is revealed about her in 5 books and in 5 heavens.[1]

When Mary heard from the Lord that her body would die, a great angel came to her and said: 'Arise Mary and take this book, which he has given to you, he who established Paradise, and give it to the apostles, so that when they open it, they will read it before you; for on the third day, your body will die. For I will send all of the apostles to you, and they will prepare your body for burial; and they will see your glory and will not depart from you until they bring you to where you were before.' And she answered and said to him, 'Why then have you brought only this one book, and you did not bring a book for each one? When one has been given to the others, they will not murmur. And what should I plan; what should I do? And what is your name? If they ask me, what should I tell them?'

2. And he said to her,[2] 'Why do you ask me my name? For it is a great wonder to be heard. When I have come, I will tell you what my name is. Then tell the apostles in secret, so that they will tell no one. And they will know my authority and the power of my strength: not because of the book alone, but also because of my name,[3] since it will be a source of great power. And it will be a revelation to all those in Jerusalem, and to

---

[1] The complete text is preserved only in Ethiopic, and has been translated from the edition by V. Arras, *De Transitu Mariae Aethiopice*, i. CSCO 342–3 (Louvain: Secrétariat du CorpusSCO, 1973). In an appendix to the Latin translation, Arras has made a number of suggestions regarding the text. I have consulted these throughout, and where they have determined my reading, or if they differ from my interpretation of the text, I have indicated this in the notes. I have also consulted the Italian translation in Mario Erbetta, *Gli apocrifi del Nuovo Testamento*, i. pt. 2, *Vangeli: Infanzia e passione di Cristo, Assunzione di Maria* (Casale: Marietti, 1981), 421–56, although this version largely reproduces Arras's Latin translation and comments, also summarizing or omitting the many very difficult passages in this text. For each of the various fragments in other languages translated below, the edition is cited at the beginning of the fragment's translation. Daggers in the translation indicate corruption in the original text.

[2] MSS: 'to me'.

[3] MS A: 'because of me'.

those who believe, it will be revealed. Go then to the Mount of Olives, and you will hear my name, because I will not speak it to you in the midst of Jerusalem, lest the whole city be destroyed. You, however, will hear it on the visible mountain; but now is not the time.'

3. And then Mary went and climbed the Mount of Olives, shining from the light of that angel and carrying the book in her hands. And when she came to the Mount of Olives, it rejoiced with all the trees. Then the trees inclined their heads and venerated the book that was in her hands. And when she saw them, Mary was startled, saying, 'It is Jesus.' And she said, 'My Lord, perhaps you are my Lord? For such a great miracle has come about on your account: for I see that so many trees venerate you. Behold then I say that there is no one who is capable of such a miracle, except[4] the Lord of Glory, who has been revealed to me.'

4. Then he said to her, 'There is no one who can do this miracle except by his hand, because he is powerful.[5] †Each[6] one of his hears what I give, which is above every place of the world.[7] I am he who is in the trees and who is in the mountain. Do not think that the trees on earth alone were astonished! And if you have tasted from it, you will die; and if they are a little careless themselves, they will die and fall to earth. For from his birth it is known that he is created; for his inheritance[8] [is] his various tree[s]. And when he has fallen upon them, they are not able to bear him; but he patiently bears everything, sitting upon them, and he is born above him. Therefore, I am not the one who is above everything, but I am above the trees of the holy inheritance.'[9] And when I saw the book, which is called 'of the inheritance', they venerated it, because I knew it.†

5. And he said, 'My mother, you did not understand my power. I

---

[4] Following the emendation suggested in Arras, *De Transitu*, i. 75–6 (Lat.).

[5] Following the suggested emendations in ibid. 76.

[6] The remainder of this section is very confusing, and its meaning is not entirely clear. Two manuscripts of John of Thessalonica's homily (the second version: G4) offer a rough parallel that is equally cryptic: Ἐγὼ γάρ εἰμι ὁ εἰς τὰ φυτὰ καὶ εἰς τὸ ὄρος ἐνεργῶν· διὸ καὶ ἐκάμφθησαν καὶ προσκύνησαν τὸ ἐν τῇ χειρί σου βραβεῖον. Καὶ ἐν τούτοις μὲν ἐνήργησαν· εἰμὶ δὲ ἐκ τῶν φυτῶν, τῆς κληρονομίας τῆς ἁγίας, ἃ καὶ αὐτὰ προσκυνοῦσιν ἐνώπιον τοῦ βραβείου. Γνοῦσα οὖν τὴν δύναμιν τοῦ βραβείου, μετάδος τοῖς ἀποστόλοις. Ἔρχονται γὰρ πρὸς σέ, καθὼς εἴρηταί σοι. Καὶ ταῦτα εἰπὼν ὁ ἄγγελος, γενόμενος ὡς φῶς ἀνῆλθεν εἰς τὸν οὐρανόν (John of Thessalonica, *dorm. BMV B* 2 [Martin Jugie, AA, ed., *Homélies mariales byzantine (II)*, PO 19. 3 (Paris: Librairie de Paris/Firmin-Didot et Cie, 1926), 407 n. 11]).

[7] Or, 'I who am above every place of this world'.

[8] MS B: 'his adornment'.

[9] See Arras, *De Transitu*, i. 76 (Lat.).

first revealed it to you at the spring, where I led Joseph.[10] He was crying, the child who is glorified because he is greater than everything, and Joseph was angry with

Ethiopic	*Georgian*
you, saying, "Give your breast to your child." At once you gave it to him, as you went forth to the Mount of Olives, fleeing from Herod. And when you came to some trees you said to Joseph, "My lord, we are hungry, and what do we have to eat in this desert place?" Then he rebuked you, saying, "What can I do for you? Is it not enough for you that I became a stranger to my family on your account; why didn't you guard your virginity, so that you would [not] be found in this; and not only you, but I and my children too; now I live here with you, and I do not even know what will happen to my seven children."	1 . . . he[11] was saying to you, "Give a breast to your child." And at once you gave him your breast, as you went forth to the mountain, fleeing from Herod. And you came beneath a single tree, and you said to Joseph, "We are hungry, and we have nothing that we could eat in this desert." 2. Then he rebuked you and said to you, "What can I do for you here and now to feed you?[12] Is it not enough for you that I became a stranger to my own things because of you,[13] because you did not guard your virginity, so that you would not be found in this;[14] not only you, but I and my children too, because I am here, and I live with you, but I do not know if something will happen to my three sons."
6. I say this to you Mary: know who I am and what power is upon me. And then he said to you, "There is no fruit that you could eat in the trees. This date-palm is tall, and I cannot climb it. I say to you that there is no one at all who has climbed, and there is nothing that a person will find in this	3. Joseph said this to you at this time. I say this to you now, Mary, so that you will know who I am and what power is with me. I am the one who announced your birth to Joachim and about John to Zechariah; and I am the one who brought the hidden mystery to you from heaven; I am

[10] A story similar to the one told in 5–9 is found in the *Gospel of Ps.-Matthew*, 20–1 (Jan Gijsel and Rita Beyers, eds., *Libri de nativitate Mariae*, 2 vols., CCSA 9–10 (Turnhout: Brepols, 1997), i. 458–70).

[11] Text in Michel van Esbroeck, 'Apocryphes géorgiens de la Dormition', *Analecta Bollandiana*, 92 (1973), 69–73.

[12] Lit., 'What can I do for you here and now, and I will feed you?'

[13] Lit., 'from your force'.

[14] MS: '[he, she, it] would not be found in this.'

Ethiopic

desert. I have been afflicted from all sides because of you, because I have left[15] my country. And I am afflicted because I did not know the child that you have; I only know that he is not from me. But I have thought in my heart, perhaps I had intercourse with you while drunk, and that I am even worse because I had determined to protect [you]. And behold, now it has been made known that I was not negligent, because there were [only] five months when I received you in [my] custody. And behold, this child is more than five months; for you embraced him with your hand. Truly, he was not from your seed, but from the Holy Spirit. And he will not leave you hungry, but he will have mercy on you; he will provide for me, and he will remember that I am a sojourner, as you are a sojourner with me."

7. Is this not everything that Joseph said to you? And the child stopped [nursing from] your breast, this one who is greater than all things, and he said to

Georgian

the one who killed the first-born sons of Egypt during the time of the Pharaoh. 4. And then Joseph said to you, "There is no tree from which we could eat in the midst of so much, except only this date-palm, and I cannot climb it. But I say to you that no one has climbed it, and no one will be found in this desert. I am afflicted from all sides, because I have left my country. And I am also burdened because I did not know this child that you have, because he is not mine. But when you were pregnant, I was thinking in my heart, by what cause am I found in this, because I had orders to protect you. 5. Behold, now it is manifest that I was not at all negligent regarding you; there are five months since I was charged[16] to protect you, and is this child not more than five months? But you love him with your spirit, and you know that he is not born from our nature, but he is from the Holy Spirit. Now, the Spirit will not abandon you in hunger, but let him have mercy on me and feed me, and he will remember that I am a sojourner with you, and you are a sojourner with me."

6. Did not Joseph say this to you? And did the child not stop [nursing] from your breast, this one who is greater than all things, and he said to Joseph, "Father,

---

[15] MSS: 'they have left.'
[16] There is a misprint in the text of მომეყვანებოდ̄ა for მომეყვანებოდა.

Ethiopic

Joseph, "My father, why don't
you climb this date-palm and
bring it to her, so that my mother
might eat from it, as was said
about it.[17] And I will feed you:
not only you, but also the fruit
that comes forth from it. I will
not be hungry even for one day."
And the child turned and said
to the date-palm, "Incline your
head with your fruit, and satisfy
my mother and father." And it
inclined immediately. And who
made it incline? Is it not because
I have power, which was because
of me?[18] And you and Joseph
were satisfied, because the date-
palm's branches were placed as
a wave of the ocean on the shore,
because I [had] joy and happiness
in my body as it appeared.[19]

8. And he said to the date-
palm, "Turn to me, O date-palm;
for the date-palm is the greatest
plant in all the land of Egypt.
Arise then and be very exalted,
because you humbled yourself
and did my will, this service. Be
exalted then, and be a sign to all
the trees, because all the holy
ones who humble themselves will
be exalted." And immediately it

Georgian

have you not come to this date-
palm from the law? Bring[20] and
let my mother eat. Believe what
I told you, 'I will feed you: not
only you, but also the fruit that
comes from it.' I will not be
hungry even for one day." 7.
And the child turned and said
to the date-palm, "I say to you,
O date-palm, incline your head
with [your] fruit to the earth, and
satisfy my mother and father."
And it inclined immediately.
8. Am I not the angel who said
this to you? But the child's power
is that which was done by me,
by which you and Joseph were
satisfied, because the date-palm's
branches with [their] fruit were
laid upon the earth, filled with
sweet fruit, which I shook with
joy and happiness at this sight.

9. And the child turned to the
date-palm and said, "O date-
palm, greater than all the plants
of Egypt, arise and be very
exalted, because you humbled
yourself and did this service.
Be exalted and be a sign more
than all the other plants, because
all my holy ones who humble
themselves will be more exalted."
10. And immediately the date-

---

[17] MS B: 'about me'.

[18] MS B: 'It was I, and what power I have, which was because of me.'

[19] Both MSS are corrupt here; I have drawn from both to reconstruct a meaning somewhat near the Georgian fragments: MS A: 'because I joy and happiness
it appeared on my body'; MS B: 'because I joy and happiness as it appeared'.
Arras (*De Transitu*, i. 77 [Lat]) suggests the following emendation: 'because joy
and happiness appeared on my body'.

[20] Reading მოართუ from მორთუმაი, instead of მუართუ, which van Esbroeck
translates 'carpe'.

Ethiopic

straightened up and became as [it was] before. And he blessed it and said to it, "This is worthy of the glory of his name. You will be called by Adam's holy name, to the splendid humanity.[21]

9. O date-palm, who expelled you from Paradise, and you emigrated to Egypt with treachery, and you were sown on the dry land, so that you would be cut down with iron? How did you come to this place, O date-palm, because you are the image of every place? Did this not happen regarding you? For when the devil went forth, after he had led Adam astray, behold, you were furious with him, and you expelled him from Paradise to the land of Mastinpanes (?).[22] Arise and give me [some] of these seeds, which are in Paradise and which are on the earth, from which one eats,[23] because you have migrated from a good place and have been sown on earth. But do not fear, trees, because just as my Father sent me for the salvation of humanity, so that they convert, he also instructed me concerning the fruit, so that my friends might eat from it, [namely,] those who receive me in my image. And you too, date-

Georgian

palm arose and became as [it was] before. And the child blessed it and said, "You who have become worthy of glorification, which has caused you to be named above both Adam and people of his race.

11. O date-palm, what happened to you that you fell from Paradise and were led to Egypt with grief, and you were transplanted to a dry place, so that iron would have dominion over you, just as the other tree[s]? How did you come to this place, unless human nature was active in all this? Behold then, how it was thus for you. 12. When the devil went forth after Adam's deception, he [the Lord?] said to him, 'Behold then, the Lord has become angry with you and is sending you out from Paradise to the earth, which is full of vegetation and the food of wild game. But arise now and give to me from all the plants that are in Paradise, and I will put them on the earth, so that when you go forth from Paradise, you will find food from them.' 13. When you passed from the good place, you were transplanted to the earth. But do not fear, plants, because just as my Father sent me for the salvation of humanity and for

[21] The end is a difficult passage; MS B suggests the following translation: 'said to it, who is worthy of the glory of his name, "You will be called by Adam's holy name . . ."'.

[22] Perhaps this originally read, 'I/he was furious . . ., I/he expelled', as in the Georgian? On 'Mastinpanes' see Arras, *De Transitu*, i. 77 (Lat.).

[23] Lit., 'from which it is eaten'.

Ethiopic

palm, migrate and descend to
the original place." And then the
date-palm arose before us and
descended into his Paradise.

10. And who carried it, Mary?
Was it not I? Not only do I raise
trees, but also those people who
humble themselves before God. I
am the one who carries them and
brings them to the place of
justice. And in one day, when you
go forth from your body, [you
will] see where your body will
rest,[24] because I am the one who
will come on the fourth day. And
they have allowed for the sake of
the one day: for our Saviour arose
on the third day, and you then
[will arise] on the fourth day.
And I will also come to all those
who have kept the Saviour's
words, and I will return them to
the Paradise of rest. Their bodies
will remain new, without
decaying, because they took care
of themselves while they were
living on earth. And there they

Georgian

their conversion, he also gave
me instruction about the plants,
so that my friends and beloved
might eat from them, [namely,]
those who receive my image and
do my command, those who were
recluses in the mountains and the
deserts. May they have you for
food. And you too, date-palm,
pass now to your original place."
Then the date-palm arose before
us and passed into Paradise.

14. And who is the one who
raised it up, Mary? Was it not
I? Not only [am I] to take plants
there, but also those people who
humble themselves before[25]
God. I raised it up[26] and carried
it to the place of the just on the
day that the souls go forth from
[their] bodies; and when you
depart from the body, I will come
myself on the fourth day; for this
extra day is allowed because our
Saviour arose on the third day.
15. And not only will I lead you
away on the fourth day, but all
those who keep the words of our
Saviour. I will come again to
those and lead them away to the
Paradise of joy. Their bodies will
remain new there, and the bodies
of the holy people will not have a
stench, because they took care of
themselves while living on earth

---

[24] Both MSS are corrupt here, although by combining readings from both,
the above sense can be construed. See also Arras, *De Transitu*, i. 78 (Lat.).

[25] წისაშე is a misprint for წინაშე.

[26] The text reads გღვიდე here, for which van Esbroeck translates, 'conduxi
eam cum candalis'(?); I could not find, however, a verb გღ-ღებაი, and so I have
translated as if the word were აღვიდე from აღ-ღებაი. Furthermore, this reading
resembles the Ethiopic and Greek versions more closely.

Ethiopic	Georgian
Ethiopic	*Georgian*
will remain until the day of the resurrection. And he will come with angels upon the earth, and they will be brought, each with their own bodies.'	without sin. And they will come to the place where Adam and Eve were also, until the day of resurrection. And when the Lord will come with angels, he will lead them each with their own bodies.'

11. And Mary said to him, 'O my Lord, with what sign will you come to them, and what is the sign of those who will be brought? Do they offer a sweet-smelling sacrifice, and thus you come to them, or when you pass among the just, and they have come, do they call your name, and you come to them? For if it is so, [tell me], so that I can do [this] and you will come to me and take me up.' And he said to her, 'What's the matter, mother?[27] For when I have been sent to you, I will not come to you alone, but with all the hosts of angels. And they will come and will sing before you. For I have been sent to tell you, so that you will then give [what I tell you] to the apostles in secret, because this is hidden from those who seek it from Jesus the Saviour.'

12. And she said, 'What will we do when we rest our body, because we do not want to abandon it on earth, because it is

16. And Mary said to him, 'O my Lord, in what manner to you come to them, or whom do you lead? Those to whom you are [coming],[28] do they offer you their aromatic sacrifice, and thus you will come to them? Or rather, do you come to the just? Or does he send [you] to the good? Or do you not come only to the elect? Or do they call on your name in prayers, and they come to you? If there is something like this, tell me, so that I can do this too, and you will come to me and lead me away on the last day. 17. And the angel said to her, 'What's the matter, mother?[29] For when I am sent to you, I will not be alone, but all the hosts of angels will come, and they will sing before you. I have been sent to reveal to you, so that you will tell the mystery to the apostles.

18. And because they were tired of seeking this from the Saviour, Jesus Christ, and they said, "What will we do when we

---

[27] The closely related, early Greek narrative has the identical construction here: Τί γὰρ ἔχεις, μῆτερ; This could also mean, 'what are you thinking?' as Daley translates the same phrase in John of Thessalonica's homily (Brian E. Daley, SJ, *On the Dormition of Mary: Early Patristic Homilies* (Crestwood, NY: St Vladimir's Seminary Press, 1998), 50).

[28] Lit., '(to/of ?) those who you are to you': რომელთა შენ ზედა ხარ (?).

[29] See n. 27.

Ethiopic

before us? And as it suits us to dwell in this form of ours, we want our body to be with us in that place.' And then the good Christ said to her,[30] 'This word [that] you seek now is great. And where I am going now, you are not able to come. But I will go and ask my Father, and I will prepare a place for your body in Paradise, where your body will remain.

Georgian

cast off our bodies, because we do not want to abandon them[31] on earth? If we are true and worthy to dwell in that [place], because he showed us the place, we do not want our body to be in this place." 19. Then the good Lord said to them, "This word that you seek now is great, and where I am going, you are not able to go now; so I will go and ask my Father, and he will prepare a place for your bodies." 20. Then it pleased the Father that your bodies will be transferred to Paradise, where your bodies will be placed, and on the last day, I will resurrect them, and they will inherit eternal life, where the Father reigns, and the Son has power, and the Holy Spirit reigns with them, and they are magnified from the age unto the age. Amen.

Ethiopic

13. †Now,[32] know what I will do when I send to you the prayer. I received [it] from my Father, as I was coming, and now I say to you:

---

[30] MS A: 'them'.

[31] Lit., 'it'.

[32] This section and the one that follows (14) are very corrupt and divergent in the two MSS. I have done my best to render what sense may be found in MS A, but I have not attempted to represent MS B, which has an equally corrupt, yet slightly different, version of this passage. I hope readers can get a sense of the topic from this translation and then come to their own judgements from the Ethiopic text and Arras's Latin translation.

The earliest Greek version helps to clarify some of what is being said here: 'Now, you want to know what you will do. When I was sent to you, I received a prayer from the Father, as I was coming to you, and now I am telling it to you so that you will say it when you go forth from the body at the rising of the sun, for thus [the prayer] is offered up. And what I tell you, share with apostles, because they too are coming. No friend of the world, who loves the world, is able to speak this prayer.' Antoine Wenger, AA, *L'Assomption de la T. S. Vierge dans la tradition byzantine du VIe au Xe siècle*, Archives de l'Orient Chrétien, 5 (Paris: Institut Français d'Études Byzantines, 1955), 36–7.

today is your departure from your body, when the sun appears. And give everything that I have told you to the apostles, because they too [are coming?]. After your body has been placed, I will come on the fourth day to their body. And they will not find it, and they will fear that they do not believe my power, and they will be seized by it, and they will go to another body which is not for the apostles.†

14. †They said, "Those who will go, how will they abandon their bodies here, because they will save another, and they will not be able to ascend without the prayer, and they will go forth from their bodies, and they will sleep for four days." And after this, I will come and awaken them. And they will not be abandoned after four days, because I, my brother, has suffered for me to receive this odour; because of this, I have been patient until the fourth day; otherwise, I would come to them on the third day. For just as a sad person cannot [say?] the prayer there, the people of his churches, who love this world and who dwell in it. Therefore tell the apostles in secret, "Do not reveal this", so that they will not come into this; because, moreover, those who have desired his word, they have not said it, those who have not kept this.†

15. Mary, know from where the prayer has come and what it is, as you will need to observe it with every world. And even if a person has gained the whole world, and he has been abandoned to the beast with the body of a lion and the tail of a snake,[33] what is his profit? And even if he is wise and richer than the whole world, and he has been abandoned to the monsters, will he not forfeit all of his possessions, even his body?[34] Truly it is thus, Mary; for it is not possible to pass by the beast with the body of a lion and the tail of a snake, so as to pass through every world, because of the hatred of Satan, which he has brought on everyone. But, the one who understands this completely will give all his possessions in order to save his body.

16. As this verdant stone that descended from heaven and appeared at the rising of the sun [?], the prayer, Mary, transcends[35] your mother's [Eve's] nature, which prevails in every creature, on account of which

---

[33] The word here is ሰብደጓት, for which Leslau offers the translations: 'viper, mythical beast with the body of a lion, tail of a snake, and the torso, arms and head of a man'. Arras suggests (*De Transitu*, i. 81 [Lat]), I think correctly, that this passage refers to the soul's ascent through the cosmic spheres after death. In this case it is likely that ሰብደጓት refers to either the Demiurge (the Archon) and/or his minions (the form is both singular and plural). Since the Demiurge is often described in the Coptic gnostic literature as 'lion-like' or 'lion-faced', or even as a 'lion-faced serpent', I have chosen the above translation to reflect this as much as possible.

[34] MS B: 'in order to save his body?'

[35] See the remarks of Arras on this passage, *De Transitu*, i. 81 (Lat.).

there is death. And it will raise the dead and give life to all, and they will behold the steadfastness of God.

17. But[36] on that day the body of Adam was in the glory that dwelled upon him, the body that remained lying on the earth, which he made with the Father, who was with him in counsel and participation. And this is that which was from the beginning and was even before the angels and the archangels, before the creation of the powers by me, until he sat and he was moved by the Ruler [Archon], when it was apparent that he could not arise. And God knew what was in the soul; and he rested and placed rest in his heart so that it would pray to him. And when the Father said this to Adam, he arose and was in the custody of the Father and the Son and the Holy Spirit until this day. And I hid this from the wise, and it is not even written in the Scriptures, so that the scribes would not see it and the ignorant would not hear it among their children. But I allowed it to be hidden among the Cherubim, and no one could see it except for the Father, the Son, and the Holy Spirit, until this day, so that it would be revealed to the wise, as it will be. And I have sent this so that you will know it, with the apostles, on that day, and they will share it with the Cherubim; but it will not be known except to the one to whom the Cherubim tell everything.

18. And today who are they who will say this with their heart and soul and mind completely? For before creation are those who boast before humanity, saying, "We are God's." His memory arouses them as they seek recovery from their illness. And those who seek a request from those [who are before creation?], God does not hear them, because the will of God is not among them. They will not be able to call upon God on their own account as on the account of others. And when they have cried out, shouting, God does not hear them.

19. Do you not recall, Mary, that thief, when he was taken captive among the apostles while he was praying and bowing his head at their feet, saying, "Beseech your master to bless us in friendship, and they will be healed from their affliction." And the apostles went and they beseeched Jesus to bless

---

[36] There are many corruptions and disagreements in both MSS for this section, but they are not as severe as in sections 13 and 14. In general, it has been possible to reconstruct a (more or less) sensible text by relying on readings of one text or the other at a given point.

Ethiopic

them, as they desired. And he
sent with the apostles—was it not
thus? And he said "Are they not
the shepherds of Israel? They
seek healing for their sheep, so
that they will be praised before
humanity. And they are unable
to heal, because they have led
astray until this day. And I gave
to you so that you will believe."
And the apostles said to him,
"Lord, behold, they bow down
and prostrate themselves and
repent.[37] Why do you not hear
them?" And he said to them,
"You want me to hear them?
But they are evil, and you know
them."

20. Then Jesus wanted to
show the apostles the reasons
why he did not hear them. And
he took them up to a mountain,
and he made them hungry. And
they came and pleaded with
Jesus and said to him, "We are
hungry, and what will we eat in
this desert?" And he ordered that
trees sprout before them and
produce fruit. Then they bore
fruit before them. And he said
to them, "When you go to these
trees in front of you, and as their
branches are numerous, so also
their foliage is beautiful to see,
eat from them." And when the
apostles went before the trees,
they did not find fruit on them.

Syriac

. . . them,[38] as they desired.
And he sent to them through
the apostles—was it not thus?
And he said, "These are the
shepherds of the house of Israel,
who are beseeching on behalf of
the sheep, so that they will be
pardoned and glorified before
humanity. And they cannot
sanctify themselves, because they
exalt themselves like the strong.
Did I not give them many signs?"
And the apostles said, "Lord,
behold, they beseech and pray
and repent and kneel on their
knees. Why have you not heard
them?" Our Lord said to them,
"I sought to hear them too, but
there is deception in them, as you
know."

And when Jesus wanted to
show the apostles the reason why
he did not hear them, he took
them up to a mountain, and he
made them hungry. And when
the apostles had gone, they asked
him and said to him, "Lord, we
are hungry; what then do we have
to eat in this desert?" And Jesus
told them to go to the trees before
them. And he said to them, "Go
to these trees that are opposite us,
these whose numerous branches
are splendid and beautiful from
a distance, and from them you
will be fed." And when the
apostles went, they did not find
fruit on their branches. And they
returned to Jesus and said,

[37] Reading ይትኔስሑ for ይትፈሥሑ.

[38] Text in William Wright, ed., *Contributions to the Apocryphal Literature of the New Testament* (London: Williams & Norgate, 1865), ⲙⲟ–ⲭⲱ.

Ethiopic

And they returned to Jesus and said, "Master, you sent us to the trees before us, and we did not find fruit on them, only their budding branches and their beautiful foliage, but there is no fruit at all." And Jesus said to them, "Did you not see it, because the trees are tall? Then go now, because the trees have inclined themselves, and you will find fruit on them and eat." And when they went, they found the trees, and they did not find fruit on them.

21. And they returned to Jesus in great sadness and then said to him, "What is this, a mockery? For first you said to us, 'You will find tall trees, full of fruit', and we did not find [any]. Why then is this like a mockery? Teach us why this is." And Jesus said to them, "Go then and sit beneath them, and you will see why this is. And when they were standing, you did not see, and also when they inclined, you did not see." And then they went and sat beneath the trees. And stinking worms came forth. And the apostles got up and said, "Master, do you want to test us?" But he turned them back to the trees,

Syriac

"Good teacher, you sent us to these trees that are opposite us, and we went and did not find fruit on them, but only branches, which are beautiful and splendid, but there is no fruit on them." And Jesus said to them, "You have not seen them because the trees are standing straight up. Go then at once, because the trees are inclining themselves, and you will find fruit on them, and you will be fed." And when they went, they found the trees inclining, but they did not find fruit on them.

And they returned to Jesus again in great distress and said to him, "What is this, teacher, that we are mocked? For first you said to us, 'You will find straight trees, and there is fruit on them'; and we found none. Why are we mocked? But it is fitting that you teach us what this is that happened. For we think that what you have sought to teach us is false; for the trees were taken hold of by a visible power and bent down. If this is a test, tell to us what it is." And Jesus said to them, "Go and sit beneath them, and you will see what it is that is on them, but you will not find them bent down again." And when the apostles went and sat beneath the trees, immediately the trees released stinking worms. And the apostles came to Jesus again, and they said to him, "Teacher, did you want to lead us astray, or to turn us away from this . . .

Ethiopic

so that they did not return to the trees.

22. And the Saviour answered them and said to them, "By no means would I tempt you, but I want you to know intelligently. Look then now: know how they are planted." And when the apostles looked, they saw that the plants had become human beings, who were praying and prostrate on their knees. And they said to Jesus, "Lord, we saw people who were dressed in white garments, praying and prostrate on their knees, and a table was before them, and bread was placed on it. And after praying, they went and wanted to eat. But they did not find the bread that was upon it, and the one who did not partake, the flames of Gehenna devoured him."[39]

23. And then Jesus said to them, "For you, my good and united children, I have reserved the table, which is eternal, and also the bread. Do you not know this one, who is the one that you seek? For as they stand and pray and are prostrate on their knees, while repenting, do you not see them then? They are standing, while there is no fruit to God in them for repentance. There is none, because they desire the world and all its fine things. And when they remember its fine things and pray to God, then he speaks to them about this table. And when they are returned to the world, he turns himself away from them."

24. Now then, Mary, give the sign to the apostles so that they will tell the mystery to those who believe. The one to whom it is given will hear: thus will my name and my power be known. And I want to show them, Mary, what power was given to me from God the Father when he sent me into the world to destroy sinners and to bless the just.

25. I am the third that was created, and I am not the Son;[40] there is no one greater than me. I am the one who destroyed every firstborn of Egypt because of the great evil that was in them, and because of the great cry, and because of the blood that was shed by them. Ask the people of the earth, Mary, why I destroyed all the firstborn in Egypt.[41] Ask those who say, "There is no one who saw us, and there is no one who knows us," as they should know. Ask then those who believe and trust in their treasures, and they will tell you why I destroyed all the firstborn of Egypt, so that they ate many lentils in the teeth of their children [?], and they will always sin, and affliction will remain on their children. And behold, these who say, "Nevertheless, we are." For this mystery is among us together, with the blood of those who were destroyed. This I tell you, Mary, so that you know about these things.

[39] Lit., 'unless Gehenna devoured him'; reading ነበልባል for ዘእንበለ፡ ከመ (MS B); አጋበ (MS A).

[40] MS B: 'I am the one who was created third in divinity, and I am the Son.'

[41] Cf. Exod. 12.

26. Listen then,[42] and I will explain for you why I destroyed the firstborn of Egypt. Was it not when the Israelites were in Egypt, under Pharaoh's yoke, and they were being tormented by those who were afflicting them? One of the Israelites named Eleazar became ill, and he could not be made to work. And the overseer came and said to him, "Why have you not come to work? Behold, your hour has come, and you are unable." And he answered nothing. And he went to the Pharaoh and said to him, "O King who lives eternally, there is one of the Israelites who is unable to do his work, saying, 'I am ill.' What order shall we give: should we pardon him or should we not pardon him?" And hearing this, the king Pharaoh gnashed his teeth, saying, "I will remove your breath and your life from you and your body if you give the Israelites rest now; make them pay their debt, their bricks. Instead, bring his wife, and she will make bricks in his place. If you have not brought his wife, and the others see this, they will abandon their bricks, and they will be devastated and will stop their work. But if they see his wife coming to make bricks, they will be afraid and will work, so that they will not stop my work and will not remember their God. Go now, overseer, to my work, because when evening comes, I will come and count every quantity of bricks of the overseers, and if I do not find the number of bricks accurate, there will be nothing else except bricks."

27. And when the overseers heard from the king Pharaoh, they went forth, being disturbed, to the house of Eleazar, the sick man. And they seized his wife, whose name was Rachel, and brought her to the brick-works. And they beat her while exacting punishment for her husband's brickwork, and they brought her close to death. And they said to her, "If you have not made these bricks, beware!" And she was very near to birth, and she was sad because of her shame, because she did not go forth from her house. And she did not allow any of the men of Egypt to see her, lest she be despised when she went forth to the brickworks.

28. And when she went forth to the works, and when she had made every brick, she was suffering very much, and she sat briefly to rest. And the overseers were there, and they beat her, saying, "Get up, make bricks. Why have you not finished for the day?" And she said to them, "I beseech you, have mercy on me, my lords; allow me to rest briefly, for my loins are pressed down." Then the overseers beat her, while saying, "We cannot have mercy on you, because today the Pharaoh will come to see the Israelite brickworks. For the king ordered me that we not help

---

[42] The story that follows, 26–31, is also known in the rabbinic literature. For parallels, see Frédéric Manns, OFM, *Le Récit de la dormition de Marie (Vatican grec 1982), Contribution à l'étude de origines de l'exégèse chrétienne*, Studium Biblicum Franciscanum, Collectio Maior, 33 (Jerusalem: Franciscan Printing Press, 1989), 76.

you; otherwise, we will make bricks in your place. Now then, we cannot [allow] you to stop." And the hour of Pharaoh's coming arrived, and they sat while they made her work. And she got up and took clay in her hands and began to make bricks. And from the multitude of her beatings, while she was afraid, the fruit of her womb fell.

29. And when the workers saw this, they were afraid and withdrew. Then, one of them arose, and he came and saw two infants, and he wept with great lamentation, while she said, "My Lord, you have repaid us according to our sin, because we have been sinners from ancient times. And now Lord, look and see our affliction, and remember the commandment that you placed on our fathers Abraham, Isaac, and Jacob, saying, 'Blessing, I bless you and your seed.' Now, even if we have sinned, do not carry out your wrath on us forever. With whom will I dwell, except with you, O Lord, and to whom shall I cry? To you, O Lord, for my affliction is very great. And I have lost this first-fruit that was in my womb, and I am powerless before the multitude of my affliction, and I do not know what I shall do. Look, O Lord, upon my infants, because they are yours."

30. And when Rachel said these things, Abraham, Isaac, and Jacob went to the good God. They bowed down and worshipped, saying, "Have mercy, Father, on our descendants, and forgive them: remember the statutes that you placed on us and on our seed." And when they said this, I was sent to her, to speak these words to her, and I said to her, "Rachel, Rachel, God has heard your grief. For just as you saw the death of your firstborn, you will see the death of the firstborn of Egypt. And just as they caused your infants to fall, I will make their infants fall similarly. Thus I will make you see the Egyptians when their firstborn are made to fall from their mothers' wombs. And now, Rachel, arise and do your work; for God has sent me to exact a blood vengeance for you." Because of this, I destroyed all the firstborn of the Pharaoh and the firstborn of the magicians; I destroyed them in the gates, in the middle of the night, by the power that was given [to me] by God.

31. †And[43] then Satan attacked, and he said to me, "Do you want me to help the Egyptians?" And then, at that moment, he blew his horn,[44] which was being made manifest, while speaking with his horn. For you have put on what power has been given to you, and you will receive

---

[43] Another very corrupt section, about which Arras says, 'Quae de occidendis primogenitis narrantur ita a normis grammaticae aberrant ut vix interpretationem dare quis possit': *De Transitu*, i. 84 (Lat.). I have done my best to translate the passage, although, admittedly, it does not make a great deal of sense.

[44] Lit., 'voice/ቃሉ', but 'horn/ቀርኑ' seems more likely. The text in this section is generally corrupt and rather difficult. See the discussion of some of the problems in Arras, *De Transitu*, i. 84 (Lat.).

vengeance against those who have sinned and whose evil is known [for] what it is. And he turned to me, and I saw him as he was warring with me. And while he was saying this with his horn, he departed from their firstborn. And seizing him, I bound [him], and I found him entering houses, teaching the sign and giving the wisdom that he has.[45] And he said, "I am not a firstborn, but in order that you save the people, so that he will not examine. There is no one like God; he made this sign of the firstborn, so that he would not forget and would not lose one who was not one of the firstborn. And the sign [is] in the right hand, just as the firstborn was not as they were saved." And there were those who cried out, saying, "Tell us; there is no firstborn among us." And they did not believe in this sign, and they extended their hands and much rebuked the darkness; while wanting to go forth, they did not see sign of their murder. And Michael blew his horn, and they were bound greatly, and then I bound.†

32. Now then, O Mary, you will see my power, because I am the one who made this sign upon the earth. I am the one who went into Sodom beforehand and saved Lot and destroyed his wife. I am also the one who caused Joseph's bones to be found, which Pharaoh had hidden.[46] For at the time when Joseph died, another king arose in Egypt. And he did not know Joseph, and he began to afflict the Israelites, and they wanted to flee from Pharaoh. And since Pharaoh knew that they would flee from him, he summoned the magicians and said to them, "I know that you are wise; now tell me, what shall I do with these people? For I heard that they were murmuring and saying, 'Let us flee from him.' " And the magicians said to Pharaoh, "If these people want to flee, do as we tell you. Take the bones of Joseph

Ethiopic	*Syriac*
and place them in a hidden place, within your power, so that they will not find them. They will not flee and abandon them. For we have heard that [Joseph], when he was dying, made them swear that they would take his bones	. . . and[47] place them in a hidden place, under the hand of your power, so that they will not find them. And when you have done this, they will not be able to flee. For we heard that Joseph, when he was dying, made the children

[45] Lit., 'and being the wisdom that he has'.

[46] The story of Joseph's bones as told in 32–5 is also known in the rabbinic literature. The Rabbinic parallels have been identified in Manns, *Le Récit*, 76–7.

[47] Text in Wright, *Contributions*, ܠܡ ܪܟܘ. Many of the verbal forms here could be either 1st or 2nd person. Wright opted to translate these as 1st person, but in the light of the Ethiopic text, as well as the sense of the passage, I have understood them as 2nd-person forms.

Ethiopic

with them. And because of this, they cannot flee unless they take them, and they will remain under your power in Egypt."

33. And then Pharaoh, the king of Egypt, arose and in his anger he made a pit in the middle of the river of Egypt. And he took the bones of Joseph and placed them in a stone box. And he covered it vigorously with pitch, and he wrote his name on a scroll, saying, "These are the bones of Joseph." And he attached it to the box and had it buried in the middle of the pit.[48] And again he brought about affliction, and he placed affliction upon the Israelites. And after this, the good God had mercy on them and heard their lamentation, and he wanted them to go forth from the land of Egypt. And he sent Moses, so that the God of Abraham, Isaac, and Jacob, the God of the living and the dead, would speak to them, because all the righteous live in him. And he came and spoke to the Israelites,

Syriac

of his people swear that when they were going up, his bones should go up with them. And when you have done this, they will not be able to flee, unless they take them with them, and they will remain under your power in Egypt."

And after these things, Pharaoh, the king of Egypt, arose and ordered that there be a pit in the middle of the river. And he took the bones of Joseph and placed them in [a stone box.][49] And he plastered it with pitch [. . .],[50] and he wrote [Joseph's][51] name on a scroll, [saying, "These] are the bones of Joseph." [And he placed] the scroll in the box and ordered that it be placed in the middle of the pit, in the middle of the river. And when Pharaoh went in, he laid hard work on the Israelites, and said to them that they should go forth. And the Israelites answered and said to Moses, "Let us go forth to the bones of Joseph, our brother of old, because he made our fathers swear that his bones would go up with the Israelites."

---

[48] Lit., 'dirt'.

[49] The Syriac MS is damaged here, and Wright gives the following reading: ܪܐ . . . ܪܬܐܠ. Based on comparison with the Ethiopic version [ገፍቀ፡ እብነ], I suggest the emendation above, supposing the Syriac to have been, perhaps: ܪܐ[ܪܒܐ] ܪܬܐܠ.

[50] Here is another lacuna. Unfortunately, the Ethiopic MSS disagree here, and do not suggest an obvious reconstruction. Wright's reconstructions, when substantial, are indicated with brackets in the translation.

[51] Or his own (Pharaoh's) name, as the Ethiopic implies.

Ethiopic   *Syriac*

saying, "Let us go; I will lead
you." And they said to him, "Let
us go then to the bones of our
brother of old, who was with us,
and who made our fathers swear
that they would remove his bones
with the Israelites."

34. And they went with Moses
to the bones of Joseph, and they
did not find them. For they
did not know that Pharaoh had
hidden them. And when they
did not find them, they rent their
garments, they and Moses, and
they wept before God, saying,
"Lord God of our fathers, why
have you abandoned us, your
people? Now then, return and
save us; and send to us your good
angel who will reveal to us; and
strengthen your mercy. And we
will not become like the land
of Kerseson,[52] from which it
happened that we had not tasted
water, and after many days a river
covered it. Now then, we have
passed from it, as is your mercy,
O Lord; for all our sin is not pure
before you. Because of this, you
have hidden the bones of Joseph
our brother, so that we would
know our wickedness. Now then,
return and have mercy on us."

But Moses went, and they did not
find them. For the Israelites did
not know that Pharaoh had taken
them away from them. And when
they did not find them, they rent
their garments and wept bitterly.
They groaned and cried out to
God, and Moses with them,
"Lord God of our Fathers, why
have you forsaken your people?
For you turned to us; and then
after you turned, you turned your
mercy away from us; and we have
become like a barren land that has
not seen water." And after a
long time, the river was
uncovered. And when it was
uncovered and had passed away,
the Israelites cried to the Lord
and said, "You have remembered
the sin and error of your people,
O Lord; therefore you have
hidden the bones of our brother
Joseph, so that we will remain in
this bondage forever. Now turn
to us, O Lord, and deliver your
people from Pharaoh's
oppression."

35. And when they were
saying these things, while the
people wept with Moses, I then
came, I, the angel, and I spoke to
Moses, saying, "Moses, Moses,

And when these things had
been said by Moses and by all the
people, I came and spoke, I,
Michael the angel. And I said to
Moses, "Moses, Moses, God has

[52] Arras suggests that this is a reference to the Wadi Kishon of 1 Chron. 18:
40–5.

Ethiopic

God has heard your grief. Arise
and go and strike the waters with
your staff, which is in your hand,
and the hidden treasure will
appear." O Mary, when Moses
struck the river, it appeared on the
mountain and came to dry water
[*sic*]. And he found the written
scroll, saying, "These are the
bones of Joseph." And he took and
brought them to the land, before he
brought forth the Israelites. Behold
then, I have shown you, O Mary,
my power;

Syriac

heard your groan. Arise and go
to the river, and strike the waters
with your staff, and the hidden
treasure will be uncovered
before you." What did you think,
Mary? As soon as Moses struck
the river, did not the box in
which the bones of Joseph were
placed appear and come to dry
land? And Moses opened it and
found the scroll on which it was
written, "These are the bones of
Joseph." And he took them and
brought them to their land [that
was given] to their fathers. And
after a long time, I have revealed
myself . . .

Ethiopic

so that you will not fear, I have spoken to you, who is before me. Hear
then my name: Adonai'el.'[53] And he also ordered that she give [the
name] to the apostles, and he said to her, 'They[54] will come to you just

[53] MS A: 'Merciful'. See the discussion of the angel's name in Arras, *De Transitu*, ii. 85.

[54] The first of several Coptic fragments, preserved by a papyrus in the Yale collection (P. CtYBR inv. 1788), offers a rough parallel to this passage. While five of the eight total fragments appear close to the present text, the others do not find obvious points of contact, although two of these are extremely fragmentary. This text has recently been published, with translation, by Philip Sellew, in an article provisionally entitled, 'An Early Coptic Witness to the *Dormitio Mariae* at Yale: P. CtYBR inv. 1788 Revisited', *Bulletin of the American Society of Papyrologists*, 37 (2000), 37–69. A preliminary edition was made by Leslie S. B. MacCoull, 'More Coptic Papyri from the Beinecke Collection', *Archiv für Papyrusforschung*, 35 (1989), 25–35, with pl. 4. Professor Sellew's edition offers a number of improved readings, and I thank him for sharing his work with me before its publication. The Coptic fragment parallel to this section reads as follows: '. . . all my apostles have been gathered to you, just as I said [to you]. And my angels will watch over you. . . .' Sellew, 'An Early Coptic Witness', 62.

As one will note, I diverge from the order of the fragments as published by Sellew in my presentation of them. This is not a criticism of Sellew's judgement, since the order that he gives is very clearly determined by the papyrus fragments themselves. The papyrus locates both this fragment and the fragment mentioned in the following note (55) after Mary's conversation with John and the presentation of the secret book (see n. 75 below). Nevertheless, comparison

as I told you, and they will go with you. Take then this book.' And the angel became light and ascended into heaven.

36. And Mary returned home. And then the house trembled on account of the glory of the book that was in her hand. And she secretly entered[55] the inner chamber, and she placed the book, wrapping it in fine cloth. And she put on blessed garments, saying, 'I bless you the firstborn,[56] who created the living, and I bless this sign that appeared from heaven on the earth, until you created us and dwelt in me. I bless your birth,[57] which illuminates and is not visible, which goes forth from you as your hand goes forth; and to you alone they come. I bless you, because you[58] counted me in what is your body. And you chose my sanctity with your word, so that you will choose me for this your coming blessing, and for the sweet-smelling sacrifice, so that I will receive that which is a statute in every age.

37. I bless you so that you will give me my garments, [about] which you told me, saying, "By this you will be distinguished from your relatives." And you have caused me to enter the seventh heaven, so that I will be found worthy of this your mystery. I bless you so that I will be found worthy of your first blessing with all those who believe in you, so that you will return them to your kingdom. For you are hidden among your hidden; you[59] see those who are not seen. And you are the son of

with the earliest narratives necessitates the order that I have indicated in these notes. As the first two translations included in this volume make clear, Mary enters her bedroom and prays to the Son *before* her conversation with John and the gathering of the apostles. I am not sure as to how this can be reconciled with the physical evidence of the papyrus; perhaps the original manuscript consisted of excepts, or was a rather free composition that drew on the earlier traditions of the Palm narrative. The fact that the final three fragments do not find close parallels with the early Palm narratives could indicate either of these possibilities.

[55] A second Coptic fragment is roughly parallel to this and the following section: '. . . Mary entered her bedroom and blessed God, saying, 'I bless you, the Son, the offspring of the Aeons, the one for whom I was a dwelling place. I bless you, the life that came forth from the Father . . .' Sellew, 'An Early Coptic Witness', 63. Although it is possible that this fragment may in fact parallel Mary's prayers in section 52 below, the indication here that she 'entered her bedroom' before praying fits best with the earliest Palm narratives at this point.

[56] MS A: 'I bless the blessed one.'

[57] Arras (*De Transitu*, i. 86 [Lat]) suggests reading ⲧⲱⲁⲅⲕ ('your generation; your family') for ⲁⲅⲧⲕ (birth), which he considers more likely in the light of the phrase τοὺς συγγενεῖς μου in the early Greek version (Wenger, *L'Assomption*, 214). Nevertheless, I have opted to translate the passage as found in the MSS.

[58] MSS: 'he'.

[59] MSS: 'I'.

the hidden one; you are the one whom I first conceived, and [then I conceived?][60] all those who believe in you.

Ethiopic	*Georgian*
Hear the prayer of your mother Mary, who cries out to you. Hear my voice and send your goodness on me, and no power will come upon me on that day, when [my soul] goes forth from my body; but fulfil for me what was said by you when I said, "What shall I do about the power that will pass upon my soul?" And you told me, saying, "Do not weep, O Mary, my mother: neither angels nor archangels, nor cherubim nor seraphim, nor any other power will come upon you, but I will come myself to your soul." And now the pain of birth[61] has drawn near. I bless you and your three servants that were sent by you to minister in the three ways. I bless the eternal light in which you dwell. I bless every plantation of your hand, which remains forever. Holy, holy, holy, you who dwells [in the heights],[62]	1. ... Hear[63] the prayer and supplication of your mother Mary, who cries out to you, my son and God and creator. 2. Hear my voice and send your goodness to me, so that no power comes before me at the time when I will go forth from the body; but fulfil what was said to me, O leader, when I was weeping before you, and I was saying, "What shall I do in order to pass by the powers that are coming upon my soul?" 3. Because you promised me and said to me, "Do not be sad and do not grieve, O Mary, my mother, because neither angels, nor cherubim, nor seraphim, nor any other power will come upon you, but I will come myself and lead you away." Now then the pain of birth has approached, which is the going forth of the soul.' 4. And she began to pray and said, 'Hear the voice of my

[60] The insertion is suggested by a similarly peculiar phrase in the earliest Greek narrative: καὶ σὲ ἐν πρώτοις ὀδύνησα καὶ πάντας τοὺς ἐλπίζοντας ἐπὶ σοί. Wenger, *L'Assomption*, 216.

[61] 'pain of birth': both MSS actually read 'way of his descent' here, but based on comparison with other narratives, it is likely that this restoration represents the original text. See Arras, *De Transitu*, i. 86 (Lat.) for an explanation of how this corruption probably entered into the MS tradition through a misreading of the Greek.

[62] In the notes to his translation, Arras reports the bracketed text as occurring in MS B at this point (Arras, *De Transitu*, i. 14 n. 12 [Lat]). In the notes to the edition, however, it is listed with previous occurrence of the Ethiopic verb 'to dwell': 'I bless the eternal light in which you dwell [in the heights]' (ibid. 22 n. 18 [Eth.]). Based on comparison with the other narratives, it would seem that the footnote reference in the edition has been misplaced, and the indication of the translation is correct.

[63] Text in van Esbroeck, 'Apocryphes géorgiens', 59–62.

Ethiopic

hear my prayer forever,
Amen.'

38. And when she had said
this, Mary went forth and said
to a maidservant of her house,
'Go and call my relatives and
those who know me, saying,
"Mary calls you."' And when
the maidservant went, she called
them. And when they came to
Mary's house, she said to them,
'My fathers and my brothers,
help me; for tomorrow I will
go forth from my body and go
to eternal rest. Arise then and
perform a great act of kindness[65]
with me: for I ask you neither
for gold nor silver, because all of
these things are vain and corrupt.
But I ask one thing of you, that
you perform an act of kindness
here, on this night. Let each of
you take a lamp, and do not let
them go out for three days, and
I will tell you all of my charity
before I depart from this place.'
And they all did as she told them.
And the news was given to all of
Mary's relatives and to those who
knew her.

39. Mary turned and she
saw all those who were standing
there, and she raised her face,
saying in a sweet voice, 'My
fathers and my brothers, let us
help ourselves, and when we have
lit our lamps, let us be vigilant,

Georgian

prayer,[64] and on the path that
evil spirits guard and control, in
peace, save my soul.'

5. And when Mary had said
this, she went forth and said to
a maidservant of her house, 'Go
and call my relatives and those
that I know, and say to them,
"Mary calls you."' The
maidservant went and called
everyone, as she had ordered her.
And when they entered, Mary
said to them, 'My fathers and my
brothers, help yourselves; for
tomorrow I am going forth from
my body, and I will depart for
my resting place, to eternal life,
to infinite light. Now, arise and
perform a great act of kindness
with me: I ask from you neither
gold nor silver, because all this
is vain and corruptible. But I ask
only this act of kindness from
you, that you remain with me for
these two nights. Each of you,
take a lamp, and do not let them
go out for two days, and I will
speak to you from my heart, until
my separation from this place.

8. And thus they all did as she
told them. And the report went
forth to all Mary's acquaintances
and her friends.

And Mary looked and saw
those surrounding her, and she
raised her face and said in a sweet
voice, 'My fathers and my
brothers, my mothers and my
sisters, let us help ourselves.
Light the lamps and be vigilant,

---

[64] Ps. 27: 2 (LXX).
[65] 'Act of kindness': ፍቅረ፡ ሰብእ = φιλανθρωπία.

Ethiopic

because I do not know the hour
when the voice will come. I do
not know, my brothers, when
I will go, and I do not know
the arrows that are in his hand.
And also, my brothers, I have
been informed when I will go
forth. And moreover, it does not
happen to everyone for a little
while. But the one who lies in
wait for everyone, the one who
makes war, he does not have
power against the just. And as
for those who do not believe, he
works his will on them. And it is
not possible for the just, because
there is nothing that he has with
them; but when he is confused,
he withdraws from them.

40. For two angels come to
a person, one of righteousness
and one of wickedness, and they
come with death.[67] And when
[death] acts on the soul that is
going forth, the two angels come
and admonish his body. And if he
has good and righteous deeds, the
angel of righteousness rejoices
because of this, because there is
no [sin] that was found upon him.
And he calls his other angels, and
they come to the soul. And they
sing before it until [they reach]
the place of all the righteous.
Then the wicked angel weeps,
because he did not find his part
in him. And if there are evil
deeds that are found in him, that
one rejoices. And he takes seven

Georgian

because you do not know the
hour when the thief will come.'[66]
9. Because I know, brothers, the
time when I will go forth, but
I do not know the arrow that is
in his hand. 10. But I have been
taught, my brothers, the time
when I will go forth. And I do not
fear, because death is universal to
all, but I fear only the enemy, the
one who wars against everyone.
11. For he is powerless against
the just and faithful, but he has
power over the unfaithful, and
he works his will on them. But
he does not conquer the just,
because he has no cause against
them, and confused, he
withdraws from them.

12. For two angels come to a
person, one of righteousness and
one of wickedness, and they come
with death. And when death
troubles the soul, the two angels
come and examine the bodies of
the people from the world. And if
he has done the work of
righteousness, the angel of
righteousness rejoices, because
that one has no business with
him. And he calls many others,
and they come to the soul and
sing before it until they arrive in
the place of all the righteous.
13. Then the wicked angel,
who is Satan, weeps, because he
has no part with him. If someone
is an evildoer, and he has done an
evil deed, the evil one rejoices

---

[66] Matt. 24: 43.
[67] Cf. *Apoc. Paul* 11–18 (Montague Rhodes James, ed., *Apocrypha Anecdota*,
Texts and Studies, II. 3 (Cambridge: The University Press, 1893), 14–21).

Ethiopic

over angels with him, and they take that soul and lead it away. The angel of righteousness weeps greatly. And now, O my fathers and brothers, let there be no evil found in you.' And when Mary had said this, the women said to her, 'O our sister, you who have become the mother of the whole world, even if we are all afraid, what has happened to you [that] you are afraid, the mother of our Lord? Then woe to us! Where should we flee when this comes to us? [You are] the hope of us all [in?] patience. And if we sinners are humble, what shall we do and where shall we flee? And if the shepherd fears the wolf, where will the sheep flee?' And then all those who were standing there wept, and Mary said to them, 'Be silent, my brothers, and do not cry; but glorify the one who is among you at this moment. I beg you, do not be cast down, because this is the joy of the virgin of God. But sing instead of weeping, so that it will be to every nation of the earth and to all the heavens of God, and there will be a blessing rather than weeping.

41. And because of this I fear: because I did not believe[68] in my God for even one day.

Georgian

him. And he brings seven more evil spirits, and he leads the spirit away, and they tear him apart. And the angel of righteousness weeps. So now, O brothers and fathers, help yourselves, and let nothing evil be found among you.' 14. When Mary had said this, the women said to her, 'O our sister, you who have become the mother of the whole world, even if we are all rightly afraid, what do you fear? You are the mother of the Lord! Woe to us! Where shall we flee, if you, incorruptible and virgin, say this? O our expectation and intercessor and our encouragement who has committed no sin, what shall we, the unworthy, do, and where shall we flee? If the shepherd fears the wolf, where will the sheep flee?' 15. And all those standing around her began to weep, and Mary said to them, 'Be silent, my brothers; do not cry, my sisters, but glorify the one who is among you in Jerusalem. I beg you, do not cry in this way for the virgin, but cry out instead of weeping, so that it may be spread to every nation of the earth and every person of God, and there will be questioning rather than weeping.

16. But I, brothers and sisters, I fear only from necessity, because I was unbelieving of my God for one day . . .

---

[68] See Arras's discussion of this passage in *De Transitu*, i. 88 (Lat.). The Georgian version confirms the presence of the negative.

Ethiopic

Behold, I will tell to you about my sin. When we were fleeing, Joseph, two of his children, and I, a terror was upon me, and I heard the voice of the infants behind me, saying, "You do not weep and you do not lament: you see and you do not see; you hear and you do not hear." And when it had said this, I turned around to see who was speaking with me. And then he had returned, and I did not know where he went. And I said to Joseph, "Let us go from this place, because I saw an infant who is not from this world." And then when I looked, he appeared to me, and I found that he was my son. And he said to me, "Mary, my mother, every[69] sin is imputed to you, because you have tasted the bitter as the sweet." I did not believe, my brothers, that I had found so much glory, until I gave him birth, since I did not at all know the menstruation of women, because of him. Now, however, I understand. And all of this took place and everything was said to me and made known to me then on the road, as was his power. And every soul hopes, both [those] of the righteous and the wicked.' When she had said this, she called her family and said to them, 'Arise and pray.' And when they prayed, they sat and began to speak among themselves about the greatness of Christ [and] the sign that he made.

42. And when it was dawn, the apostle John came and knocked on Mary's door. And he opened it and entered. And when Mary saw him, she was disturbed in spirit; she wept and was unable to restrain her tears, nor could she keep silent from her distress for a moment. And she cried out in a loud voice, saying, 'Father John, remember what our master said to you regarding me on the day that he went forth from us, and I said to him, "Where are you going, and with whom will you leave me, and where will I live?" And he said to me, while you stood and listened, "John will take care of you."[70] Now then, John, do not forget what he commanded you regarding me, and remember that he loved you more than them. Remember when you were reclining on his breast;[71] remember them too. And he spoke, and there is no one else who saw, except you and I, because you are the chosen[72] virgin. †(And[73]

[69] MS B: 'this'.

[70] Cf. John 19: 26–7.

[71] Cf. John 13: 23.

[72] The word መደሙቅ is not otherwise known in Ethiopic; 'chosen' is supplied from the various other early witnesses to these traditions. See Arras, *De Transitu*, i. 88 (Lat.) for further discussion of this matter.

[73] The text has become corrupt at this point, and although the close relationship between the *Liber Requiei* and the early Greek versions may not immediately be apparent from the translation, comparison in the original clearly indicates that the two Ethiopic MSS transmit here a garbled version of what is expressed more lucidly in the earliest Greek version. See Arras, *De Transitu*, i.

John began to be sad, because he had removed himself.) And I said to him, "If to us, tell me, John; do not abandon me," '†

43. And when Mary had said this, she wept in a quiet voice. But John could not bear it: his spirit was troubled, and he did not understand what she was saying, because she did not say that she would go forth from her body. Then he cried out in a loud voice, saying, 'Mary, our sister, who became the mother of the Twelve, I deliberately provided for you. For I left behind the one who served you, so that he would bring you food. You do not want me to transgress the command of our Lord, which he commanded us, saying, "Travel across the whole world, until sin is destroyed."[74] Now then, tell me the distress of your soul.' And she said to him, 'My father John, perform an act of kindness with me. Keep my body safe and place me in a tomb. And guard me with your brothers, the apostles. For I heard the high priests saying, "When we find her body, we will throw it into a fire, because the deceiver came forth from her." ' And when John heard this, that she said, 'I will go forth from my body', he fell in his face on his back [?] and wept, saying, 'Lord, who are we that you have shown us this tribulation, because we have not yet forgotten the previous ones so that we can encounter another tribulation. Why do I not go forth from my body, so that you might watch over me?'

44. And[75] when she heard John speaking like this and weeping, Mary begged John greatly, saying, 'My father John, be patient with me in your weeping for a moment, so that I may tell you everything that the angel imparted to me.' And then John arose and wiped away his tears. And Mary said to him, 'Come with me'; and she said to him, 'Tell the crowd to sing,' so that John could read. And while they were singing, John entered the inner chamber, and she said to him, '[Behold,] the prayer that was given to me by the angel, so that you will give it to the apostles.' And she brought forth a small case that contained the book and said to him, 'My father John, take this book in which is the mystery. For when he was five years old, our master revealed all of creation to us, and he also put you,[76] the twelve in it.' And she showed him her funeral [garments] and every preparation for her funeral, saying, 'My father John, I have shown you everything; but know that I have nothing in this

---

88 (Lat.) for a discussion of some of the problems with the text at the end of this section.

[74] Cf. Matt. 28: 19.

[75] A third Coptic fragment seems to offer a rough parallel to this section: '. . . Queen of women . . . I am not discouraged . . . But the Virgin said to John, "Be patient, my brother, and I will tell you the things that I have seen." She took him into her inner chamber to show him the book of the mysteries that [Jesus] had given her . . .' Sellew, 'An Early Coptic Witness', 59–60.

[76] MSS: 'us'.

great house except my funeral garments and two tunics. Since there are two poor people here, when I go forth from my body, give them to each one.'

45. And[77] after this, she brought him to the book[78] that had been given to her by the angel, so that the apostles would take it. And she said to him, 'My father John, take this book, so that you may carry it before my coffin, for this is why it was given to me.' And then John answered and said, 'My sister Mary, I cannot take it unless the apostles have come, because they are not here. Otherwise, when they come there will be murmuring and distress among us. For there is one who is greater than me among them; he has been appointed as our superior. And when they have come, it will be good.'

46. And after this they both entered; and when they came out of the inner chamber, there was a great tumult, so that everyone in the house was disturbed. And[79] after the tumult, the apostles descended on a cloud to Mary's door: twelve[80] of them, each seated on a cloud. First Peter and his colleague Paul—he also came on a cloud, because he was numbered among the apostles; for he had the faith of Christ with them. And the other apostles arrived on a cloud. And the others began to look at each other, and they were amazed that they had arrived together. And Peter said, 'My brothers, let us pray to God, who has gathered us with our brothers who are contending with us in the joy of the spirit. Truly, my brothers, the word of the prophet has been fulfilled which says, "Behold, it is good and pleasant when brothers are together."'[81] And

---

[77] Simon Mimouni also signals the existence of several Palestinian Syriac fragments of the this text from the 7th or 8th century, preserved in the Cairo Geniza (Mimouni, *Dormition*, 76). According to Mimouni, two of these fragments have previously been published by Agnes Smith Lewis and Margaret Dunlop Gibson in *Palestinian Syriac Texts from Palimpsest Fragments in the Taylor-Schechter Collection* (London: C. J. Clay & Sons, 1900), 75–6. I have consulted these very fragmentary texts and cannot determine on the basis of what has been published the exact relation of these fragments to the early Dormition traditions. Presumably, C. Kessler, who has provided Mimouni's information, has more carefully consulted all these fragments. The first set of fragments is reported to parallel *Liber Requiei* 45–6.

[78] This second 'book' was presumably the Palm in earlier versions of this narrative: here (but not in the preceding passages) a translator has probably confused the Greek words $\beta\rho\alpha\beta\epsilon\hat{\iota}ο\nu$ (prize/palm) and $\beta\iota\beta\lambda\acute{\iota}ο\nu$ (book). See nn. 114 and 134 below.

[79] A fourth Coptic fragment appears to have similarities with this passage: '. . . namely, the . . . And behold, immediately all of the apostles came to her . . .' Sellew, 'An Early Coptic Witness', 61.

[80] MS A: 'ten'; the early Greek traditions report eleven.

[81] Ps. 133: 1

Paul said to Peter, 'You have found the true testimony. For I am joyous, having returned to the faith of brothers.' And Peter said, 'Let us say a prayer.'[82] And all the apostles raised one voice together, saying, 'Yes, let us pray so that we will know why God has gathered us together.'

47. Then, while they were each praising their brothers according to his honour, Peter said to Paul, 'Arise and pray before us, because our spirit rejoices today in the faith of Christ.' And Paul said to him, 'Pardon me: behold, I am a neophyte, and I am not worthy to follow the dust of your feet. How shall I precede you in praying? For you are a pillar of light, and all our brothers who are present are better than I. Now then you, our father, pray for us, so that the joy of Christ will be with us.' Then the apostles rejoiced at his humility, and they also said [to Peter], 'You pray before us.' They confessed,[83] saying, 'We are present because of you; each of us has been sent, as he commanded, each one according to his own ordinance. And we ought to observe the glory of prayer that our master taught us and say it in our hearts. Where is Peter, the bishop, our father, so that he may speak this glory of prayer: O that he will listen and will pray here.'

48. And then Peter prayed, saying, 'God our Father and our Lord Jesus Christ, has glorified me in so far as my ministry has been glorified; for I am the least, brothers, and I do this as it has been chosen. And in this way we too are one congregation that is among us all: each one glorifies the place of the others, and not a human being. For this is a command that we have received from our master, that we will love one another.[84] Bless me then, because this is what is pleasing to you.'

49. And he stretched out his hands and said, 'I give thanks to you, ruler of the whole world, who is seated upon the chariot of the cherubim[85] and dwells in the heights and who looks[86] upon the lowly, who dwells in light[87] and gives rest to the world, in a hidden mystery that you revealed by the cross. We do this too when we raise our hands in the image of your cross, so that by its form we will receive rest and everyone will receive rest, and you will give [rest] to those who must suffer. You loosen the hard labour; you are the one who has revealed the hidden treasure;[88] you have established your Messiah among us. And

---

[82]   I have followed Arras's suggestion (*De Transitu*, i. 89 [Lat]) to read ለፕፕር or ·በ·ı ፕፕር instead of በ·ır, which is present in both MSS.

[83]   See the discussion of this passage in Arras, *De Transitu*, i. 89 (Lat.).

[84]   John 15: 12.

[85]   Cf. 2 Kgs. 19: 15.

[86]   Lit., 'knows'; nevertheless, the early Greek versions support this translation, as does the Psalm being cited: 112: 5–6 (LXX).

[87]   Cf. 1 Tim. 6: 16.

[88]   Cf. Isa. 45: 3.

who of the gods is as merciful as you? Your power is not distant from us. Who is as merciful as you, just as your Father? And he saves those who believe in him from evil; your will has conquered desire; your faith turns away error; there is nothing more beautiful than your beauty; your humility has cast down the proud. You are the living one and you vanquished death; you are rest and you have eradicated the darkness, the glory of the unique one who is with the Father, the glory of mercy that was sent from the spirit of the Father of truth. Maruyal,[89] Maruyal, Marenatha, Beyatar, from now unto the age of the age, Amen.'

50. And[90] when they said 'Amen', they embraced each other. And when they had embraced together, then, when Andrew and Peter were together, John came into their midst and said, 'Bless me, all of you.' Then they all embraced him, each one in his order. After they had embraced, Peter said, 'Andrew and John, beloved of the Lord, how did you come together here? How many days have you been here?' And John said to him, 'Listen then to what happened to me. When we[91] were in a foreign land,[92] while I was teaching the twenty-eight who believed in our Saviour, who had taken hold of me, I was raised up before them, at the ninth hour. And the cloud descended to the place where we[93] were gathered and it snatched me up before all those who were with me. And it brought me here. And I knocked on the door, and a girl opened it for me. And I found people with Mary, our sister, and she said to me, "I will go forth from my body." And I did not remain among those people who were standing with her, and my grief weighed down on me. Now then, my brothers, when you go forth tomorrow, do not weep, and there will be no disturbance: for if you weep, there will be a great disturbance. For this is what our master taught me when I was reclining on his breast at the supper: if the people who have come into her company see us weeping, they will revile us in their hearts and say, "They also fear death." But let us soothe Mary with a saying of love.'

51. And then the apostles began to enter Mary's house, and they said with one voice, 'Mary, our sister and also the mother of those who are saved, joy be with you.' And Mary said, 'How have you entered in here, and who here has told you that I will go forth from my body? And how have you come together? For behold, I see that you are sad.' And they told, each one, the region where they were dwelling, and how a cloud came and snatched them up and brought them here. And then they all

---

[89] See the discussion of these names in Arras, *De Transitu*, i. 90–1 (Lat.).

[90] The second set of Palestinian Syriac fragments indicated by Mimouni (see n. 77 above) is reported to parallel *Liber Requiei* 50–2.

[91] MSS: 'you (pl.)'.

[92] Lit., 'the city/region of Nerdo/Nador'; see the discussion in Arras, *De Transitu*, i. 91 (Lat.), where he suggests the above emendation.

[93] MSS: 'you (pl.)'.

praised her, from Peter to Paul, saying, 'May God, who is able to save everyone, bless you.'

52. And then Mary rejoiced in spirit and said, 'I bless the one who has power over every blessing. I bless the Great Cherub of Light, who dwelt in my womb. I bless every work of your hands, which obey every command. I bless the love [with which] you loved me. I bless the word of life that you have sent forth from your body, which has truly been given to us. Moreover, I believe that everything that you told me is happening to me. For you said to me,[94] "I will send all the apostles to you when you go forth from your body"; and behold, they have gathered, and I am in their midst, as a vine that bears fruit in its time, just as when we were with you, just as [you were] a vineyard in the midst of your angels, subduing your enemies with all their works. I bless you with every blessing; what you told me is happening. For you told me, "You will see me with my apostles when you go forth from your body."'

53. And when she had said this, Mary called Peter and all of the apostles. And she brought them into her inner chamber and showed them her funeral [garments], in which they were to bury her. And after this, they went forth and sat in the midst of everyone who had lit a lamp [and] did not allow it to be extinguished, just as Mary had commanded them.

54. And when the sun had set on the second day, as the third day was beginning, when she was to go forth from her body, Peter said to all the apostles, 'My brothers, let the one who has learned discourse[95] speak all night until the sun rises.' And the apostles said, 'Who is wiser than you? For we are all small before you.'

55. Then Peter began to speak to them, 'All my brothers, you who are in this place, at this hour, for this lover of humanity, our mother Mary, you who have lit lamps that are visible from earth, this you have done well. And I also desire that each receive the lamp of humanity: this is the lamp of the one who put on humanity, which is the three-wicked[96] lamp that is our soul, our body, and our spirit, which three shine from

---

[94] A fifth Coptic fragment parallels the text rather nicely at this point: ' ". . . my angels and my apostles will gather on the day of your departure from the body." Behold, they have gathered to me, and I am in their midst, as a vine surrounded by its fruit. I bless you [with?] every blessing and all sweetness. For there are no words in . . . today . . .' Sellew, 'An Early Coptic Witness', 64. See also nn. 54 and 55 above.

[95] Lit., 'discourse of a child': ⲛⲅⲁ: ⲇⲧⲧ. This is probably a corruption of the Greek λόγον παιδείας, present in the earliest Greek narratives. See Wenger, *L'Assomption*, 228 and Jugie, *Homélies mariales byzantines (II)*, 389.

[96] See the discussion in Arras, *De Transitu*, i. 92 (Lat.) of this otherwise unknown word, ⲛⳋ. I have followed Arras's suggestion, based on comparison with other early, related Dormition narratives.

the true fire. I now boast and am not ashamed, because you will enter into marriage, and moreover, you will enter and rest with the bridegroom. Thus the light of our sister Mary's lamp fills the world and will not be extinguished until the end of days, so that those who have decided to be saved will receive assurance[97] from her. And if they receive the image of light, they will receive her rest and her blessing.

56. My brothers, do not think that this is death. It is not death, but eternal life, because the death of the righteous will be blessed before God.[98] For this is their glory, and the second death cannot subdue them. And believe [what] has been revealed to me and the apostles with me. And when you know the first death, behold, I will tell you about the second death. But I will tell you about the second death, that there is no one who will hear. But God the Father, whose spirit is[99] now in our midst, is also concerned for his ministry. Moreover it is fitting that we hear what is not heard by those who are not worthy and do not want to hear.'

57. Then Peter raised his hands and said, 'From where is the first death?' And while he was speaking, a great light shone in the house in the midst of them all, so that it made the light of their lamps seem dark. And a voice came, which said, 'Peter, there is no one to whom you can tell this, because you are not alone. Speak this discourse in a sign that they can bear. For a doctor heals the sick person according to his illness, and a nurse raises an infant to a child.'

58. Peter raised his voice and said, 'I bless the blessed one; I bless you who saved our souls, so that you would have mercy on us. You have led us well, so that we do not suffer in the evil abyss. I bless the horn of our knowledge,[100] whose faith we have known.' And he turned and said to them, 'My brothers, we are not able to say what we wanted without the practice of every good thing. He directs us in every good thing, so that we will take care of our duty among ourselves.'

59. And when he had said these things, twenty-one virgins arose one by one and fell at Peter's feet, saying, 'We beg you, our father, bring us into the greatness of Christ and those who are known to him.' And then Peter made them rise, saying, 'Listen to me, our joy, and the glory of our honour: do not think that the speaking voice was revealed on your account. It is not so; rather [it is for] those who are standing outside, who are not worthy of the mystery. You are worthy, and [so is] everyone

---

[97] 'assurance': lit., 'faithful, believer, one to be relied on'; see the discussion in Arras, *De Transitu*, i. 92 (Lat.).

[98] Ps. 116: 15.

[99] 'whose spirit is': MSS: 'the spirit is not'. As Arras explains, there has probably been a misunderstanding of οὐ for οὗ: *De Transitu*, i. 93 (Lat.).

[100] Lit., 'horn of our tongue'. As Arras explains (*De Transitu*, i. 93 [Lat.]), probably the result of confusion between γνῶσις and γλῶσσα.

[who] has preserved the image of their infancy. For your glory is not of this world.

60. Listen then and learn what our master says to you: "The kingdom of heaven is like a virgin."[101] He did not say, "it is like time", because time passes. Nor is it like rich people, because wealth passes; but a virgin remains. But know that [a virgin] is glorious; therefore [a virgin] is artfully like the kingdom of heaven. And therefore there is nothing that you should worry about, because when he sends [death] to you, you will not say, †"Make us [know?] where will we ascend and where will we descend; our affliction, children, and great riches, and whose fields will sprout; whose luxury is great,"†[102] because there is nothing in this that you worry about. You have no concerns except for your virginity. And when [death] is sent to you, then you will be found ready, since you have nothing.[103] And what you have is light, your virginity. Be patient then, and I will reveal to you what has been revealed to me. And be certain that you know that there is nothing that is lighter than the name of virginity, and there is nothing that is heavier than a person of the world, so that you will rejoice.

61. There was a certain rich man in a city who had great wealth. And the servants of his house were charged with a crime: when they did not obey his order, their master became angry, and he sent them away to a distant land for a long time. And then later he called those who had committed the crime and had gone away. One had built a house for himself and planted a vineyard and also [built] a bakery. And he had produced much additional wealth. Now the other servant, [what] he produced, he converted into gold, which is enduring.[104] And he summoned a goldsmith and had him make a crown[105] of gold for him, saying to the goldsmith, "I am a servant, and I have a master and [he

---

[101] Cf. Matt. 25: 1.

[102] The homilies of John of Thessalonica are helpful for understanding the gist of this very garbled passage: ' "Woe to us—where shall we flee, and leave our poor children or our great wealth or our planted fields or our large possessions?" ' (Jugie, *Homélies mariales byzantines (II)*, 391; trans. Daley, *On the Dormition*, 59).

[103] 'since you have nothing': this translation is suggested by the similar statement below, but perhaps one should not rule out 'since there is nothing that you are [lacking]', which comparison with John of Thessalonica's homily suggests; see the notes in Arras, *De Transitu*, i. p. 23 n. 10 and p. 93 (Lat.).

[104] The text is somewhat difficult at this point, and some things have probably fallen out in transmission, as comparison with John of Thessalonica's homily suggests. See the remarks of Arras, *De Transitu*, i. 93 (Lat.).

[105] See Arras, *De Transitu*, i. 93–4 (Lat.) concerning this difficult word, ፍሕስ, and why it is perhaps best translated as 'crown'.

has] a son, and the crown that I have made [is for them]."[106] And when the goldsmith heard, he worked his craft.

62. And after this, their time was finished, and their master sent someone. And he said to him, "If you do not bring them in seven days, you and not I, it will be on you." Then the one who was sent went forth with haste, and he went to that region, in order to find them, whether it be day or night. And when he apprehended them, he said to them, "Your master has sent me to you." And he said to the one who had acquired a house, a vineyard, and additional wealth, "Let us go, servant." And he said, "Let us go; but be patient with me, until I sell all the wealth that I have acquired here." And then he said to the one that he was sent to meet, "I cannot wait for you and be patient with you, because I have received seven days time, and it is passing. I cannot wait for you." Then that servant wept, saying, "Woe is me, for I will abandon all this. Woe is me, for I have been found unprepared." The overseer said to him, "O wicked servant, your greed has been revealed. And when your master wanted [you] and sent to you, why did you plant a vineyard for yourself in this land, and you were found unprepared, when I came to you?" Then the servant wept and said, "Woe is me! I thought [that] I would remain in this exile forever. And if I had known that my master wanted me, I would not have produced so much wealth in this land." Then the messenger brought him forth, bringing nothing with him.

63. While he was leading him, the other servant heard that he had been sent for him. And he arose and placed the crown on his head. And he went to the road along which the messenger was travelling, looking for him. And when the messenger came, he said to him, "Your master has sent me to you." And he said, "Let us go, because I have nothing here, and what I have is light. Let us go with joy. What I have is as nothing, because I have nothing at all here except this crown of gold. I had it made for this reason, hoping every day and praying that mercy would come upon me, and that my master would send and receive me from this land. For there are some who hate me and would take this crown from me. Now he has heard my prayer. Let us arise and go."

64. Then both servants went forth with the steward. When their master saw them, he said to the one who had acquired farms, "Where is the produce of such a long time in exile?" The servant answered and said, "My master, you sent to me a soldier, who would have no mercy on me. I begged him to be patient with me, so that I could sell what I had

---

[106] Although the Ethiopic here is garbled, John of Thessalonica's Greek is clear: 'I am a servant and have a master who has a son; form their images in a gold crown.' Jugie, *Homélies mariales byzantines (II)*, 392; trans. Daley, *On the Dormition*, 59.

and not be ashamed and acquire in my hands the things that you deserve." Then his master said to him, "O wicked servant, now you remember to sell, when I have sent for you. Why did you not consider it in exile? You were not thinking of me there because of your wealth." And he became angry and ordered that his hands and feet be bound, and that he be sent to another land. And then he called the one who was crowned with the crown and said, "O good and faithful servant, you have longed for freedom, on account of which you made the crown, because it is the crown of the free. And you did not dare to wear it unless it was written to you by your master. For a servant cannot be set free except by his master. As you desired freedom, you will find it with me." Then he freed him, and he was placed in charge of many.'

65. And Peter said this to the brothers who were with Mary, and he turned to them and said, 'Listen, my brothers, to the things that will come upon you. For the virgin belongs to the true bridegroom, to the God of all creation. You then, the human race, are those with whom God became angry in the beginning, and he placed them in the world as in a prison and as spoils in the world for those to whom he abandoned us because of this. But the last days have come, and they will be transferred to the place where our ancient fathers Abraham, Isaac, and Jacob are. And there each one will be in the Fullness [the Pleroma]. And he will send the severe angel of death to us. And when he comes upon the souls of sinners, he afflicts them with pain for their many sins and makes them work very hard. Then he pleads with God, saying, "Have patience with me for a brief moment, until I redeem my sins, which have been sown in my body." But death will not allow it. How [could he]? And everyone who is full of sin, having no righteousness, will be brought to the valley of damnation. If he has works of righteousness, he will rejoice, saying, "There is nothing that owns me, because I have nothing here except my virginity." And he will plead, saying, "Do not abandon me on this earth, because there are those who hate me on this earth, and they would take from me the name of my virginity." Then his soul will go forth from his body, and he will be brought to bridegroom with psalms, until [they reach] the place of the Father. And when the Father sees the soul, he will rejoice and place it with the other souls. Now then, my brothers, know that we will not remain in this world.'

66. And when Peter had said this all night, while the crowd was steadfast, the sun rose. And Mary arose and went outside, and she prayed, saying her prayer. And after her prayer, she went in and lay down. And she fulfilled the course her life.[107] And Peter sat at her head,

---

[107] Lit., 'And the ministry was completed by her.' It seems likely that መልእክት ('letter, message, duty, business, service, mission, ministry, function, office') represents what was originally οἰκονομία, which appears here in the early Greek

John at her feet, and the rest of the apostles encircled her bier. And at that hour of the day, there was a tumult and a sweet, pleasant smell, like the odour of Paradise. And all those who were standing near Mary began to sleep, except only the virgins: he kept them from sleeping so that they would be witnesses of Mary's funeral and of her glory.

67. And our Lord Jesus Christ came on a cloud with an innumerable multitude of angels. And Jesus entered the inner chamber, where Mary was; Michael and the angels stood outside the inner chamber, singing. And when he entered the place

Ethiopic	*Syriac*
and found the apostles with Mary, he embraced them. And after this, Mary embraced [him] and opened her mouth, and she blessed, saying, 'I bless you, the one who spoke with me and did not deceive me, and furthermore who told me, saying, "I will not allow the angels [to come] upon your soul," and he came to me himself. And it has happened to me, O Lord, according to your word.[108] Who am I, a wretch, that I have been found worthy of such glory?' And when she said this, she fulfilled the course of her life,[109] not turning her face from the Lord. And then the Lord took her soul and placed it in Michael's hands, and they wrapped it in a fine garment, so splendid that one could not keep silent.	... and[110] found the apostles with Mary, he greeted them and Mary. And Mary opened her mouth and said, 'I magnify you, my Lord, my master ... ... And when Mary had said these things, her soul went forth from her body, and grace covered her face in front of them. And then our Lord took her soul and placed it in Michael's hands. And they wrapped it in a pure garment, whose splendour was indescribable.

narratives. Although Dillmann's lexicon unfortunately offers no evidence of this correspondence, መልእክት appears again in the section below (see n. 109), where the Greek texts also use οἰκονομία in the context of Mary 'fulfilling the course of her life'. See additionally the discussion in Arras, *De Transitu*, i. 94 (Lat.), where he prefers the reading of MS B in this passage, 'And the angels will pass her by,' but comparison with other early witnesses in this literary tradition makes this reading much less likely in my opinion.

[108] Cf. Luke 1: 38.
[109] See n. 107 above.
[110] Fragment in Wright, *Contributions*, 14.

Ethiopic

68. And the apostles saw Mary's spirit as it was given into Michael's hands: a perfect form, but its body was both male and female, and nevertheless one, being similar to every body and seven times white.[111]

69. And Peter rejoiced and asked our Lord, saying, 'Who among us [has] a soul as white as Mary's?' And he said to him, 'O Peter, all the elect who were sent here [had] such souls, because they went forth from a holy place. But, when they go forth from their bodies, they are not found [thus], and they are not white, because in one way they were sent, and in another they are found.[112] Because they have loved [evil] deeds, their soul has become dark from many sins.[113] And if someone guards himself as in the first days, when he comes forth from the body, he will be found white.'

70. And the Saviour said to Peter, 'Bring forth Mary's body, departing quickly, and go out from the left of the city, and you will find a new tomb. Place her body there and guard it as I commanded you.' And when he said this, her body cried out from splendour, saying, 'Remember me, O Lord, king of glory, because I am your image. Remember me, because I guarded the great treasure that was given to me.' And then Jesus said to her body, 'I will not abandon you, pearl of my new treasure: by no means will I abandon you, the closed sanctuary of God! By no means will I abandon the one who is truly the guarantee! By no means will I abandon the one who led five guards! [?] By no means will I abandon the treasure [that was] sealed until I sought it!'

71. When he had said this, there was a loud noise. And Peter, the other apostles, and the three virgins prepared Mary's body for burial and placed it on a bier. And after this, those who were sleeping awoke. And Peter brought the book[114] and said to John, 'You are a virgin, and you must sing before the bier, so take [it].' John said to him, 'You, our father and bishop, must take up the book before her, until we come to the place [of burial].' And Peter said to him, 'So that none of us will grieve, let us tie [it to] Mary's bier.' And then the apostles got up and

---

[111] Lit., 'and white seven cubits', but the earliest Greek narrative reads: 'λευκότητος ἑπταπλασίως' (Wenger, *L'Assomption*, 232). John of Thessalonica's homily reads λευκότητος τοῦ ἡλίου ἑπταπλασίως (Jugie, *Homélies mariales byzantines (II)*, 396–7), perhaps the original reading. See also the discussion in Arras, *De Transitu*, i. 94–5 (Lat.).

[112] Lit., 'others were sent, and others were found'(?).

[113] Reading አኪት (evil, sin) instead of ካልእ (other). John of Thessalonica's homily supports such a reading. See the discussion in Arras, *De Transitu*, i. 95 (Lat.).

[114] In other early narratives, this is the palm (or staff). This is probably another instance of mistaking βραβεῖον for βιβλίον (see n. 78 above).

carried Mary's bier. And Peter sang, saying, 'When Israel went out of Egypt, hallelujah.'[115]

72. And the Lord and his angels were going alongside the bier, singing and not being seen. And they heard the sound of many people. And many people came out from Jerusalem.

Ethiopic	*Syriac*
And the high priests heard the sound of the tumult and the voice of those who were singing and not seen; they heard the voice of many, and many people went out. And those who heard the voice were disturbed, saying among themselves, 'What is this tumult?' And there was one of them who said, 'Mary has gone forth from her body, and the apostles are singing alongside her.' Then Satan entered into their hearts,[116] and they said, 'Arise, let us go and kill the apostles and burn the body of the one who bore the deceiver.'	... And[117] when the high priests heard the great voice of those who were singing, they were troubled and saying among themselves, 'What is this great tumult?' And one of them answered and said to them, 'Mary has gone forth from the world, and the apostles are singing before her.' ...
73. And when they had got up, they went forth with swords and spears,[118] in order to kill them. †And then the angels in the clouds attacked them [with blindness?], and they smashed their heads into the wall, since they could not see [where] they were going—except for [those who found] the way to go out, to report what had happened to them.[119] And when they drew	... the angels went forth from the cloud at God's command, and they struck them with hallucinations, and they were all blinded. And they smashed their heads into the walls, because they did not know how to go out. But one of them found the way out,

---

[115] Ps. 113: 1 (LXX).

[116] Cf. John 13: 27.

[117] Fragment in Wright, *Contributions*, 14–15.

[118] Cf. Matt. 26: 47, 55 and par.

[119] Lit., 'And then the angels in the clouds attacked them, and they smashed their heads into the wall, since those who were going could not see, except their way, so that they would go forth and tell what happened.' The Syriac fragments,

Ethiopic

near to the apostles and saw the
crowned bier, the apostles were
singing and saying, 'A great
victory[120] has been accomplished.
Behold the Dormition, which
has blessed us, the people: how
much glory we receive!'[121]†
And they got up and went forth
with great wrath, and they were
wanting to [over]throw the bier
and grasp it where the book was.
And they pulled and wanted to
send it down into a pit. Then one
of them touched the bier with
his hands, and they were cut off
from his shoulder blade. And
they remained, and he saw them
hanging from the bier, and other
[parts] of them remained hanging
from their body.

Syriac

and he went out. And when he
drew near to the apostles and saw
the crowned bier and the apostles
singing, he answered and said
to them with great wrath, 'Why
have you troubled the people
with what you have done?' And
his anger rose, and he[122] ran
to the bier and took hold of it,
and he tried to throw it down to
the ground. And he took hold
where the staff[123] was, in order
to throw the body down to the
ground. And at once his hands
clung to the bier and were cut off
from his [arms]. And his hands
remained hanging from the bier,
and another half remained on his
body.

however (opposite column), preserve the text rather well. Through comparison
with other early narratives, I have tried to reconstruct a passage that is at least
readable, with as little change to the original wording as possible. Note, however, that in the other related early texts only 'one of them' finds the way out
(see the Syriac), rather than the plural evident in the Ethiopic version. Also note
that the other early traditions describe the angels as having smitten them with
blindness, rather than just the generic attack indicated in the Ethiopic (again,
see the Syriac version).

[120] Reading መእት as መኡእት instead of, as Arras, መዐት ('wrath'), which is spelled
'correctly' just two lines beneath. The *Liber Requiei* has significantly altered this
passage, based on comparison with other early narratives (see n. 121 below), and
the reading adopted above (of መኡእት/victory) better suits the context of the *Liber
Requiei*'s alterations of this episode, while Arras's reading has more support in
the ancient literary traditions.

[121] Obviously the Jewish attacker's cry against the Virgin, which usually
appears here in other early narratives (e.g. see the Syriac, opposite column),
was just too offensive for some medieval copyist. Subtle changes have been
made in the text preserved by both MSS to revise the attacker's outrage so that
it becomes praise of Mary's Dormition. The text as it appears in other early
witnesses is generally as follows: 'When he approached the apostles, he saw
them carrying the crowned bier and singing hymns. And he was enraged and
said, "Behold, the dwelling place of the despoiler of our people: what glory she
receives today!"' Wenger, *L'Assomption*, 234.   [122] MS: 'they'.

[123] See below, n. 137.

Ethiopic

74. Then the man wept before the apostles, begging them and saying, 'Do not repay me with such torment. Remember, Peter, my father,
because he was the doorkeeper and your disciple,[124] and I said to you,
"You are this man's disciple."[125] How I beseech you now and ask you,
do not repay me!'[126] And Peter said to him, 'This is not my act, that I
will heal you, nor another one of them. Now then, if you believe that
Jesus is the Son of God, whom you seized and killed, and those who are
without the law did not believe[, then you will be healed(?)].' And he
said, 'We did not believe? Yes, truly we believed that he was the Son of
God. But what shall we do with our[127] pride, which darkens our eyes?

75. [When] they [our fathers] were about to [die],[128] they summoned
us and said to us, "Behold children, God has chosen us from every tribe,
so that we would be before his people with power, so that you would
[not?] labour in another land.[129] This [is your] task: that you will build
up the people, so that you will receive from them tithes, and first-fruits,
and every firstborn that the womb brings forth. But take care, children,
lest the place of their places [i.e. the temple] should be too abundant
for you, and they will rise up and go against it. [Do not] anger God,[130]
but give from what you have to the poor, the orphans, and the widows
of the people, and save the soul of the blind." But we did not listen to
our fathers' instruction. When we did not believe [them], the place was
very abundant, and we put the firstborn of all the sheep and cattle and
of all of the beasts on the table of those who sell and buy. And the Son of
God came, and he expelled them all from that place, and he said to
those who were selling doves, "Take this out of this place, and do not
make my father's house a house of commerce.[131] You have established
it in corruption, you who have been accustomed to evil." And we were

---

[124] Arras suggests the possibility of reading here 'and he heard you', instead
of 'and your disciple'. See *De Transitu*, i. 96–7 (Lat.).

[125] Cf. Matt. 26: 69 and par.

[126] Wenger's early Greek narrative reads here: 'O Peter, remember my
father, when the doorkeeper, the maidservant, questioned you and said to you,
"You are one of this man's disciples", and how and in what manner I questioned
you.' Wenger, *L'Assomption*, 234.

[127] MSS: 'their'.

[128] In this section the words in brackets are supplied from the earliest
Greek narrative and John of Thessalonica's homily, both of which have better
preserved this story: they are absent from the Ethiopic version.

[129] John of Thessalonica's homily reads here: 'so that you would not have to
work in the mud of this earth'. Jugie, *Homélies mariales byzantines (II)*, 399.

[130] Both MSS: ወተምዒፀየ፡ ለአግዚአብሔር [?]. The suggested interpretation is
based on comparison with the earliest Greek traditions.

[131] John 2: 16.

plotting in our hearts, and we rose up against him and killed him, knowing that he was the Son of God. But do not remember our evil and ignorance; but forgive us, because our beloved has come, who is from God, so that we will be saved.'

76. Then Peter ordered that they put down the bier, and he said to the high priest, 'Are you listening now with your whole heart? Go then and embrace Mary's body, saying, "I believe in you and in the one who came forth from your womb."' Then the high priest of the Jews blessed Mary in his language for three hours, and he allowed no one to approach her while he was prophesying and bringing forth testimonies from the 100 books of Moses,[132] where[133] it was written about her that God was born in glory, so that the apostles heard the magnificence of what was given by him, which they had not heard at all. And Peter said to him, 'Go then and touch her bier with your hands.' He touched [it], saying, 'In the name of Jesus, the son of Mary, the son of the dove, who was crucified, with goodness my hands have touched your bier.'

Ethiopic	*Syriac*
Then they became as they were before, and they were patient [?]. And Peter said to him, 'Arise and take a palm-leaf from this book,[134] and go into the city, and you will find blind people who do not see and do not recognize the	... And[135] he did as he had been ordered by him ... his hands as they were before, and nothing about them had changed. And when he had been healed, Peter said to him, 'Arise and take a branch[136] from this staff[137] and go

---

[132] See the note in Arras, *De Transitu*, i. 97 (Lat.).

[133] Lit., 'from when'.

[134] This is one of the clearest pieces of evidence that a translator has confused the Greek words βραβεῖον and βιβλίον (see n. 78 above). Both items appear together in the earliest Greek text, and the Coptic fragments also include a 'book of the mysteries' in equivalent places, ruling out Erbetta's suggestion that the book appears in the Ethiopic text only as a result of this mistranslation (Erbetta, *Gli Apocrifi*, i. pt. 2. 423 n. 2). Rather, it seems that the presence of two such similar sounding items (in the Greek) led the translator to conflate them both into the book.

[135] Fragment in Wright, *Contributions*, 15.

[136] ܡܘܝܩܐ: normally this word means 'ridicule, scoffing', which is clearly incorrect here. It would seem instead that this is the Greek word θαλλός (branch) which appears in the form θαλλεῖον at approximately this point in the earliest Greek texts.

[137] One would expect to find a word for 'palm' here, as in the many other narratives of the 'Palm of the Tree of Life' literary tradition, of which these Syriac fragments are in fact the earliest extant witness. Instead we find the word ܚܘܛܪܐ, which generally means 'rod, staff, or sceptre', although it could also mean

way. And tell them what has happened to you,

into the city, and ... you will find blind people, around 5,000, who do not know the way to go out. Speak with them and say ... what has [happened] to you ...

Ethiopic

and for those who believe, place the palm-leaf on their eyes, and then they will see. And if they do not believe, they will not see.'

77. And he went just as Peter ordered him, and he found many people in a crowd, weeping and saying, 'Woe to us! What has happened [to us] is as Sodom. Woe to us! It has surpassed [Sodom], because at first he attacked them [with blindness],[138] and after that, he brought down fire from heaven, and it consumed them. Woe to us, because the

---

'stick' or even 'branch'. The underlying Greek, however, is complicated. The word used here in the Greek narratives is βραβεῖον, and although it is usually understood to mean a 'palm' in the Dormition traditions, elsewhere it is more commonly used to mean either a 'prize' or a 'rod'. In the Latin and Irish traditions the object is clearly identified as a Palm, but in the East the identification is more complex. In the other early Syriac and Arabic narratives, which are not from the same literary family, the object is also identified as a 'staff', the Syriac narratives using a different word than this narrative, ܫܒܘܩܐ (William Wright, 'The Departure of my Lady Mary from this World', *The Journal of Sacred Literature and Biblical Record*, 6–7 (1865), ܡܠ; Agnes Smith Lewis, ed., *Apocrypha Syriaca*, Studia Sinaitica, XI (London: C. J. Clay & Sons, 1902), ܡܗ) and the Arabic عصاة (Maximillian Enger, ed., اخبار يوحنّا السليح في نقلة امّ المسيح (*Akhbâr Yûhannâ as-salîh fi naqlat umm al-masîh*), id est *Joannis apostoli de transitu Beatae Mariae Virginis liber* (Eberfeld: R. L. Friderichs, 1854), 72).

It would seem then that there were two ancient traditions of interpretation, one that the βραβεῖον was simply a 'palm', and another, represented here, that the βραβεῖον was a staff either made from palms or having palms attached. The ambiguity is probably best explained by the religious traditions of the ancient Near East, according to which kings and other authorities (such as Moses) held as a symbol of their authority a rod or staff that was in fact a branch from the Tree of Life. In many of these contexts, the Tree of Life was believed to be a date palm as it is here in the earliest Dormition traditions. See Geo Widengren, *The King and the Tree of Life in Ancient Near Eastern Religion (King and Saviour IV)*, Uppsala Universitets Årsskrift, 1951: 4 (Uppsala: A. B. Lundequistska bokhandeln, 1951), 20–41; and E. O. James, *The Tree of Life: An Archaeological Study*, Studies in the History of Religions, Supplements to Numen, 11 (Leiden: E. J. Brill, 1966), 93–129.

[138] The other early narratives again refer specifically to blindness, making the parallel with Sodom more exact: see n. 119 above.

end has come for us, in the coming fire!'[139] Then that man took the book, the palm-leaf, and he spoke with them concerning the faith. And whoever believed, his eyes were opened; and whoever did not believe, his eyes were not opened, but he remained in his blindness. And the apostles immediately brought Mary to the tomb.

78. And when they had set her down, they all sat together, waiting for the Lord to come and take Mary's body. Mary was lying down, and the apostles were sitting at the entrance of the tomb, as the Lord had commanded them. And Paul said to Peter, 'Our father, you know that I am a neophyte and this is the beginning of my faith in Christ. For I did not meet the master, so that he could tell me the great and glorious mystery. But I have heard that he revealed it to you on the Mount of Olives. Now then, I beg you to reveal it to me too.' And Peter said to Paul, 'Paul, my brother, [it is clear][140] that we rejoice now that you have come into the faith of Christ, but we cannot reveal this mystery to you. For we fear that perhaps hearing this, you would be afraid. But be patient, and behold, we will remain here for three days, and our Lord will come with his angels to take Mary's body, and if he orders us, we will gladly tell you.

79. †And while they were deliberating among themselves, behold, two men passed from Jerusalem to Kidron, and when they came to a vineyard, they said, 'Let us go inside, {my[141] brothers; if no one answers me, I will plant a vineyard.' And Paul said to the apostles, 'If you will not reveal our Saviour's words to me, you will go, and I will hear the words of those two men, so that I will not tell you how those two men ridicule us, O our father.' And Peter said to him, 'We have found its interpretation for you, while you were speaking, Paul, the storehouse of wisdom, and you are in this with us.' And when he knew that Peter had confessed, humbling himself, he said, 'He confessed.' And he said, 'Forgive me, O our father Peter, because we have not been found wise according to you, but it is given from creation. And now command me to speak.' And then all the apostles answered with one voice, and they said to him, 'Speak Paul, our beloved.' And Paul said, 'They are demons who have ridiculed humans.' And Paul said to them, 'Listen to me and hear the end of these words.}†

80. [There was a time] when Solomon was judging a man and his son

---

[139] Cf. Gen. 19: 11, 24.

[140] A main verb is missing here; this has been supplied from the earliest Greek narrative.

[141] The section in braces is preserved only in MS B. MS A, which omits this material, resumes the narrative at the beginning of section 80 below. Perhaps a scribe omitted the passage because it is corrupt; nevertheless, its omission does not improve the sense of the narrative at this point.

regarding his mother's property.[142] And after she died, his father took two wives; then his son seized him, saying, "Give me my mother's property." And together they came and spoke to Solomon in court. And while he was judging them, a demon came into their midst and laughed a great laugh. And Solomon got up from the judge's seat, and he seized the demon in his hand and removed him by himself, so that he could punish him because he had laughed. And Solomon said to him, "What is this that you dare to laugh in our midst, in the midst of the courtroom, while I am judging all the people?" The demon said, "Do you want to know why I laughed at this man, who is accusing his son over property? Because another day will not come [before] his son will die." And Solomon said, "O unclean spirit, how then do you know what is in the heavens?" And the demon said to him, "We are condemned angels. God has become angry with us and placed us in the clouds. And we ascend, but we do not reach heaven: we knock on the door, and we see their places, because there are guards at the door, so that we do not enter the heights. And we hear them speaking. Perhaps we hear them saying that they will bring an order from the place of great power, so that they will go to a soul. And they just come to the door, and they speak with the doorkeepers, and they say to them, 'Open for us, because we are going to a soul.' And we go forth ahead of them. And we go and enter the house of that person, and we listen carefully for them. And when we have heard them, we laugh at them, since we know." And when Solomon realized that this was true, he sent the man and his son to their house, saying to them, "Come in seven days; go to your house, and in seven days, come and I will pass judgement on you and your lawsuit." And when they entered their house together, the boy became sick. And he wept and looked at his father, and he said to him, "I am dying, and you have made me sad; and you[143] made me go up to King Solomon so that I would be judged as a child. And you did not remember the good words of my mother,

[142] A similar, but much briefer, version of what appears to be the same story is preserved in the *Testament of Solomon* 20 (C. C. McCown, ed., *The Testament of Solomon, Edited from Manuscripts at Mount Athos, Bologna, Holkham Hall, Jerusalem, London, Milan, Paris and Vienna* (Leipzig, J. C. Hinrichs, 1922), 60*–63*).

[143] MSS: 'he'.

Ethiopic

saying to you herself when she
went forth from her body, 'Do
not act unjustly against my
beloved son.' And behold now,
father, you have made me sad and
you have brought me to death."

81. And then his father wept,
saying, "I give you everything,
my son, because you are a boy;
for Abraham gave a sign to Levi,
his father, so that he might know
God." And he said to his father,
"I beg of you, my father, if I have
found favour before you, bring
me a small amount of wealth and
give it to those who are drawing
out my soul. Then perhaps they
will leave me alone." And then
his father went and brought
exactly half his property and
placed it before his son. And
he cried out in a loud voice and
said, "I beg you who are drawing
out my son's soul, take all these
possessions, and leave my son's
soul." Then his son was severely
afflicted. And he said to his
father, "My father, they have
not withdrawn from me, while

Syriac

". . . saying[144] to you, 'Do not
cause any grief for [my] beloved
[son]', when she went forth
from the world. And behold,
you have made me sad unto
death."

And after these things, his
father wept over his son, saying
to him, "[I give] you everything
that I have, [my son] . . . there
was . . . a boy, from the offspring
of Abraham and his father[145]
Levi. And he gave his father
a sign, so that he might know
God." And the son answered
and said to this father, "I beg of
you, my father, if I have found
favour in your eyes, bring a little
of our earnings and give it to the
one who is afflicting my soul,
so that perhaps he will leave
me alone, and I will not die."
Then his father brought half his
property, and he placed it before
his beloved son. And he answered
and said in a loud voice, "I beg
of him who is afflicting my son's
soul, take these possessions, and
leave me my son's soul." And

---

[144] This section is paralleled by what are presented as two separate fragments
in Wright's *Contributions*. The primary fragment is the largest fragment of the
Obsequies, published by Wright on pp. ܟܘ–ܡܝ. This fragment is preceded by a
very badly damaged fragment, published by Wright in his preface, pp. 12–13. I
have not translated it in its entirety, due to its very fragmentary state, but only
the end, where it is more readable. The traces preserved on the folio, however,
clearly identify its contents as having once been very similar to that of section
80 above. It is a testament to Wright's codicological skills that, with very
little knowledge of these literary traditions, he identified this leaf as 'the leaf
immediately preceding' the larger fragment that follows in the translation
above.

[145] Here ends the fragment on pp. 12–13 and begins the lengthy fragment
published on pp. ܟܘ–ܡܝ.

Ethiopic

afflicting my soul. Perhaps these possessions are too little; bring then what will be sufficient for them. Because [he saw what] you have placed, he has afflicted me severely."

82. Then his father got up and brought everything that he had, and he borrowed still more [adding?] to it. And he placed [it] before his beloved son and wept, saying, "I beg you who are afflicting my son's soul, take everything, but leave me my son." But the son was afflicted and began to die. And he turned and said to his father, "You see that neither gold nor silver is ransom for my soul, but only a heart that is sincere towards God. Arise then, father, and take these possessions, and give to the poor and orphans, and build houses for strangers, †so that they will not pay me interest [?].†[146] And we will find rest for our souls." And saying this, when he had spoken, he died.

83. And his father did as his son had ordered. And eight days passed, and he did not return to king Solomon, according to the agreed time, which gave him

Syriac

after this, the boy was severely afflicted. And again he answered and said to his father, "My father, the one who is afflicting my soul has not withdrawn from me; perhaps what you have brought him is far too little for him. And because he saw that it is too little for him, he has afflicted me severely."

And his father got up and brought everything that he owned; and he brought with it other things [that] he borrowed. And he placed it before his beloved son, and said in a loud voice, "I beg of him who is afflicting the soul of my son, take everything that I have, and leave me only my son." But the boy was severely afflicted. And when he was near death, he turned to his father and said to him, "My father, you see that neither gold, nor silver, nor anything else can be given for my life, except for a heart that is sincere towards God. Arise then, my father, and take these possessions, and build with them places for strangers, so that they may enter into them, and dwell and rest in them. And also give from them to the poor and orphans, and we will find rest for our souls." The son said these things, and his life ended.

And his father did everything that his son had told him. And when eight days had passed, and they did not come to king Solomon, according to the

---

[146] See the discussion of this passage in Arras, *De Transitu*, i. 98 (Lat.).

Ethiopic

seven days. Nine days passed,
and he did not come. And
Solomon sent for them, saying,
"Why have you not come, so that
I will deliver your judgement to
you, as I said to you?" And he
said to him, "My lord, do you not
know that our agreed time was
seven days, and that my
unfortunate son is dead? And
I gave all my possessions on
his behalf, so that he would not
grieve. But I have done
everything as he ordered." And
then Solomon understood what
he said: "The demons know what
will happen. Because of this,
people say, 'We are the ones at
whom they laugh', not knowing
what it is that will come upon
them."'

84. Then the apostles agreed
with what had been said by Paul,
for they proposed that he speak to
them again, so that he would not
ask them to reveal the mystery to
him. And all the apostles turned
to him and said, 'Our brother
Paul, speak to us with your
pleasant words, because God
has sent you to us to gladden us
for these three days.' And Paul
answered and said, 'Peter, [since]
you are not willing to reveal the
greatness of Christ our Saviour
to me, tell me, when you go forth
to preach, what will you teach, so

Syriac

agreement that they had made
before him, that after seven days
they would go to him. And the
eighth [day] passed, and the
ninth, and they did not go to king
Solomon. The king sent after
them, saying, "Why have you not
come, so that I will settle [things]
among you, as I said to you?"
And the boy's father answered
and said, "My lord, behold, it
is eight days since my son went
forth from the world. For if I
had known that he was dying,
I would have given everything
that I had to my son, so as not
to cause him grief. But I have
done everything that he said to
me." And when Solomon heard
this from the man, he said, "The
demons know what will happen.
Because of this, humans say,
'They are not the ones who
laugh at us', because they know
the things that are said by
them."'

Then the apostles agreed with
what Paul said, for they were
asking him to speak with them
again, so that he would not press
them, and they would not reveal
to him the glorious mysteries that
our Saviour taught. And again all
the apostles answered and said to
Paul, 'Our brother Paul, speak
with us in words, because we are
listening to you with delight. For
our Lord has sent you to us to
gladden us for these three days.'
And Paul answered and said to
Peter, 'Since you were not willing
to reveal the great things of Jesus

Ethiopic

that I will teach from your
doctrine?'

85. And Peter said to him,
'My brother Paul, this word
that you have spoken is good.
Because you want to learn about
the doctrine that we will teach,
listen, and I will tell you. When
I have gone to preach, I will say
that whoever does not fast every
day will not see God.' And Paul
said to Peter, 'Our father Peter,
what is this word that you have
spoken? For when they hear, they
will rise up and kill us, because
they worship gods and do not
believe in God, nor in fasting.'
And Paul turned to John and said
to him, 'Tell your doctrine too,
our father John, and we will teach
thus.'

86. And John said, 'When I
have gone forth to teach, I will
say that if there is anyone who
is not continent until his repose,
he will not see God.' And Paul
answered and said to John, 'What
is this word? For they will not
believe this word that you speak,
because they are people who
worship trees and stones. If they
hear this from us, they will stone
us.' And again Paul turned to
Andrew and he said to him, 'Tell
me your opinion too, our father
Andrew: as Peter thinks and
believes that he is a great bishop,
and John believes that he is a
virgin, and because of this, they

Syriac

to me, tell me, when you go forth,
what will you preach and teach,
so that I too will know how to
teach with your doctrine?'
    Peter said to him, 'My brother
Paul, this word that you have
spoken is good. Since you have
asked to know and hear what we
are going to teach and preach to
people, listen, and I will tell you.
When I go forth to preach, I will
say that anyone who does not fast
all of his days will not see God.'
Paul said to Peter, 'Our father
Peter, what is this word that you
have spoken? For they will not
hear your word, and they will rise
up and kill you, because they are
wicked and unacquainted with
God or fasting.' And again Paul
turned to John and said to him,
'Tell us your doctrine too, our
father John, so that I too may
teach and preach thus.'
    John said to him, 'When I
go forth to teach and preach, I
will say that anyone who is not
a virgin all of his days will not
be able to see God.' And Paul
answered and said to John, 'Our
father John, what are these words
to people who do not know God?
For if people who worship stones
and trees hear these things from
you, they will throw us in prison
and lock us up.' And again Paul
turned to Andrew and said to
him, 'Our father Andrew, tell us
what your opinion is too, so that I
too may teach and preach [thus],
lest perhaps Peter should think
that he is great and a bishop, and

Ethiopic

speak heavy words.' And Andrew said to him, 'When I have gone forth to preach, I will say that whoever does not leave his father and mother, and his brothers and his children, and his possessions,[147] he has not followed God, and he will not be able to see him.' And Paul said to Andrew, '[The words] of Peter and John are much lighter than yours, Andrew, because you have separated everyone from the earth in one moment. What is this word of yours? †For at this time there is no one who can bear upon him the burden that he has placed on an infant, Andrew.'†[148] And Peter answered, as before, and said, 'Paul, beloved of our soul, tell us how you would want us to preach.'

87. And Paul said to them, 'What you hear from me, this I advise you to do, so that we may ascertain something that will be possible for people to bear, because they are just beginning with these things.[149] Let us say, "Let each man remain with his wife, because of adultery; and let each woman remain with her husband." And let us establish a fast for them, [and] they will not fast again in the week. And let us not give them doubt [about]

Syriac

John also be proud that he is a virgin, and because of these things they have spoken grand things.' And Andrew said to Paul, 'When I go forth to preach, I will say that everyone who does not leave father and mother, and brothers and sisters, and children and houses, and everything that he has, and go forth after our Lord, he will not be able to see God.' And Paul said to Andrew, 'Our father Andrew, the words of Peter and John are light compared with yours, for you have separated everyone from the earth in one moment. For who will hear your words at this time and place a heavy burden on himself?' And Peter and Andrew answered and said to Paul, 'Paul, friend of our soul, tell us how you want us to go forth and preach.'

Paul said to them, 'If you will listen to me, do these things, and let us think of things that they will be able to do, because they are new and do not know the truth. Let us say these things to them: "Let every man take his wife," so that they will not commit adultery; and "let a woman take her husband, that she may not commit adultery." And let us establish one or two days [of fasting] in the week for them, and let us not be too hard

---

[147] Cf. Luke 14: 26.

[148] The sentence is very difficult, and its meaning somewhat unclear. I have tried to make some sense of it as it stands, but see the discussion in Arras, *De Transitu*, i. 98 (Lat.).

[149] Lit., 'because they have them from the beginning'.

Ethiopic	*Syriac*
fasting, lest they waver and turn away. But if they have fasted today and are a little weary, they will still persevere, saying, "Tomorrow we will [not] fast again." And if they come to mealtime, and they have rested, they will give to the poor, saying, "Why this fast, which comes?" and they will ponder God in their hearts. And let us also say to them, "Let the one who is not able fast until the second hour, and the one who is average until the ninth, and the perfect one until evening." And when we have trampled on their wings a little, we will know that they are able to bear this. And then we can give them milk to drink, and we will tell them the glorious things.' Then the apostles murmured, not agreeing with the words in Paul's advice.	on them, lest they become negligent and turn away. But if they fast today and are a little weary, they will persevere for the time and say, "Tomorrow we will not fast." And if they come to the time when they eat, and they find a poor person and give to him, they will say, "Why do we fast, if we do not give to the poor?" and they will know God in their hearts. And let us also say to them, "Let the one who is weary fast until the sixth hour, and the one who is able, until the ninth, and the one who is still able, until evening." And when we have given them to drink as with milk, and we have turned them to us, then we will tell them the great and glorious things, words that will be useful to them.'[150] Then all the apostles murmured, and would not agree with Paul's words.

| 88. The 16th Day: The coming of our Lord to his disciples, so that they would bring the holy one's body into Paradise.[151] | And as all the apostles were sitting in front of the entrance to Mary's tomb, disputing Paul's words, behold, our Lord Jesus Christ came from heaven with the angel Michael. And he sat among the apostles as they were debating over Paul's word. |
| And while Paul was sitting at the entrance and speaking with them, behold, the Lord Jesus came from heaven with Michael. And he sat among the apostles, while they were denouncing Paul's words. And he said, 'Greetings Peter, the bishop, and John, the virgin: you are my | And Jesus answered and said, 'Greetings Peter, the bishop, and greetings John, the virgin, you who are my heirs. Greetings Paul, the adviser of good things. Truly I say to you, Peter, that your advice was always |

---

[150] Cf. 1 Cor. 3: 2.
[151] MS A: 'The 18th Day: Reading'.

Ethiopic

inheritance. Greetings Paul, who
advises good things. Truly I say
to you that your advice will not
be understood, neither Peter's,
nor John's, nor Andrew's, except
for Paul's: now all these words
will be understood. And I see
the whole world in a net, and
that Paul will find them in nets.
Then all your words will be made
known on the last day.' And our
Lord turned to Paul: 'My brother
Paul, do not be sad because the
apostles have not revealed the
glorious mystery to you. And
to whom has it been revealed in
doctrine, that which I will teach
in the heavens?'

89. Then our Lord made a
sign to Michael, and Michael
answered in the voice of faithful
angels. And they descended on
three clouds, and the number
of angels on a cloud appeared
to be ten thousand angels in the
presence of the Saviour. And our
Lord said to them, 'Let them
bring the body of Mary into the
clouds.' And when her body had
been brought, our Lord said to
the apostles that they should come
to him. And they ascended into
the cloud, and they were singing
with the voice of angels. And
our Lord told the clouds to go to
the East, to the area of Paradise.
And when they arrived together
in Paradise, they placed Mary's
body beside the tree of life. And
they brought her soul and placed
it in her body. And our Lord sent
his angels to their places.

Syriac

destructive: yours and Andrew's
and John's. But I say to you that
you should receive that of Paul.
For I see that the whole world
will be caught in Paul's net, and
it will precede them. And then,
after these things, your words
will become known at the end of
time.' And the Lord turned to
Paul and said to him, 'My brother
Paul, do not be sad that the
apostles, your fellows, will not
reveal the glorious mysteries to
you. For to them I have revealed
the things that are on earth; but I
will teach you the things that are
in heaven.

And after these things our
Lord made a sign to Michael,
and Michael answered in the
voice of a mighty angel. And
the angels descended on three
clouds; and the number of angels
on each cloud was 1,000 angels,
singing praises before Jesus. And
our Lord said to Michael, 'Let
them bring Mary's body to the
clouds.' And when Mary's body
entered the clouds, our Lord said
to the apostles, 'Come near to
the clouds.' And when they came
into the clouds, they were singing
with the voice of angels. And our
Lord told the clouds to depart for
the gate of Paradise. And when
they entered Paradise, Mary's
body went to the tree of life. And
they brought her soul and made it
enter into her body. And
immediately our Lord sent the
angels away to their places.

Ethiopic

90. Then the apostles said to the Saviour, 'Lord, did you not say to us when you were with us and we beseeched you that we would see the torments?' And he said to them, 'Is this what you want? Then be patient on this day of her body's departure, and I will make you ascend, and I will show it to you.' And while he was speaking with the apostles, our Lord made a sign with his eyes to the clouds, and they snatched up the apostles and Mary and Michael with our Lord. And they led them to where the sun sets, and they left them there. And our Lord spoke with the mighty angels, and the earth leapt up, and Gehenna was opened. And the Lord gave place to the apostles, so that they could see, as they wanted. And they saw the damned people. And when they saw Michael,[152] they wept with great tears. And they said, 'Michael, our angel Michael, Michael our king, Michael our archangel, who intercedes every day on our behalf. Have you forgotten us now forever? Why do you not beseech [the Lord] on our behalf?' And the apostles and Mary fell down from the distress of those in the torments, and they fell on their faces.

Syriac

And after these things the apostles said to our Lord, 'Lord, you said to us, when you were with us, and when we persuaded you, that we would see Mary's grave, that it would be good for us. And you said to us, "If you want to see this, wait until the day of Mary's departure, and I will lead you, and you will see the depths." '

The terrible place of torment which the Disciples begged our Lord to see

And when these things had been said by the blessed apostles, our Lord made a sign with his eyes, and a cloud snatched up the apostles and Mary and Michael and our Lord with them, and it brought them to where the sun sets and left them there. And our Lord spoke with the angels of the pit, and the earth leapt up, and the pit was revealed in the midst of the earth. And our Lord gave place to the apostles, so that they could see, as they wanted. And when they approached and looked into the pit, those who were in the pit saw Michael. And there was great weeping and groaning; and they answered and said to Michael, 'Michael the

---

[152] Compare sections 90–4, 99–100 with the *Apoc.Paul* 43–4 (James, *Apocrypha Anecdota*, 34–6).

Ethiopic

Syriac

archangel, Michael our strength,
Michael, the captain of the host,
were you victorious today in your
struggle on our behalf? For you
have forgotten us for all this time.
Why do you not beseech the
Lord on our behalf, that he give
us a little relief from torment?'
And as soon as Mary and the
apostles saw, they fell to the
ground from the distress of those
in the pit.

91. And the Lord raised
them up, saying, 'My apostles,
arise, my disciples; for I told
you that you would not be able
to endure this, and you were not
able to endure this. What if I
had brought you to the interior
place, where no human being
is known—what would have
happened to you?' Then Michael
spoke to those who were in the
torments, to those who were
weeping: 'The Lord lives. He
lives who is worthy. He lives who
will soon judge the living and the
dead. He lives who will judge the
damned. And there are twelve
hours in the day, and twelve
hours in the night, which are the
number of psalms [?]. And when
each of the psalms is finished,
those who offer up the sacrifices
fall and worship the good God,
interceding on behalf of all
creation and all humanity.'

And our Lord raised them up
and said to them, 'O you apostles,
arise and learn; for I told you
before that you would not be able
to endure when you have seen
these things. For if I had brought
you to the outer place where
there is not even a human breath,
and where there are many
torments that differ from one
another, what would have
become of you?' Then Michael
spoke to those who were in the
pit, and he said to them, 'My
children, the Lord lives, the Lord
lives. He lives who will soon
judge the dead and living. He
lives who has power over all
creatures. For there are twelve
hours in the day, and twelve in
the night, and these are
numbered with praise. The
sacrifice ascends to God, and the
angels fall down and
worship his grace, and they
intercede on behalf of all creation
and all humanity.'

92. And the angels of the
waters beseeched, saying, 'Have
mercy on them, Father, so that

And the angel who is placed
over the waters approached and
beseeched God, saying, 'Let

Ethiopic

the fruit of the waters will be abundant for the sake of the human race, because they are your image and likeness. Because of this, I beseech you to hear me, your angel, that there be mercy upon the waters, that they will be abundant.'

Syriac

springs of water be abundant for the sake of the human race, because they are your image and likeness, Lord. Because of this, I beseech you to hear me, I who am your minister. Let your mercy be upon the waters, and let them be abundant in all the earth.' . . .

Ethiopic

And the angels of the winds worshipped and said, 'We beseech you, the good God, for the sake of humanity, let the winds blow, and let your mercy be abundant upon them, because of the fruit of the trees and because of that which sprouts meat [?]' And the angels of the clouds also worshipped, saying, 'We beseech you, the good God, do not abandon humanity, so that the clouds will overshadow them, and we will cease revealing to them. But let your goodness cause us to serve them.' And many angels were terrified on account of [these] people.

93. And Michael, who is over every soul, said, 'I repeatedly fell down, beseeching at every hour, but all your labor is as nothing, because you did not keep the commandments that were given to you.' And Michael went and saw for himself the folly of those who had been seduced, and he too fell before the Lord Jesus and said, 'I beseech you Lord, give[153] the people rest from this torment, and do not make me look at them and think that I have condemned them.'

94. Then Jesus made Michael rise, saying, 'Michael, my chosen one, rest from your weeping. Do you love them more than the one who created them, or will you be more merciful to them than the one who gave them breath? And before you asked on their behalf, Michael, I did not spare my blood, but I gave it for their sake. O Michael, was there not one who remained in pain, having abandoned the pleasure of Jerusalem? I was conceived in the womb for their sake, to give them rest, and I wept before my Father. And you, Michael, for one moment you have beseeched my Father on their behalf. But my blood has not rested, beseeching the Father day and night on their behalf. And when the Father wants to show them mercy from torment, they will be returned to the right hand. And I saw those who are in the interior place, who are immersed in blood, and my mercy has been turned away from them. And the cherubim are disturbed by the weeping and petitions, and they clap their hands together from my petition to the Father on behalf of the souls of those who are in torment. And the

[153] MSS.: 'Lord who gives . . .'.

Father turned and said to me, "I desire mercy, and my mercy is great; but what is placed before you is as great as your blood." Now then Michael, arise and we will show the apostles what is.'

95. And when Michael got up, the Lord said, 'Arise, apostles, and see what is.'[154] And then they saw a man in whose mouth was a flaming razor,[155] which burned, and he was not able to speak. Then Mary and the apostles cried out, saying, 'Who is this man who is in torment?' And he said, 'He is a reader, who spoke glorious words, and he did not do [them]. Because of this, he is in great torment.' And then they saw another person who had been led from afar, with a great punishment of fire in his hand, and he was not allowed to speak. And young children were biting him on his sides, with many others. And the apostles said, 'Who is this one who does not receive mercy, while there is fire in his hands, and they bring him and bite him?'

96. And the Saviour said, 'This is the one who said, "I am a deacon," and he took the glorious blood and did not care for it as he should have. †And[156] those who eat him are those who perished and did not see; those who did what they should not have, and they returned from the temple and did not have mercy; those who do not sin from now, but who see them who have no sin, because they were serving in sin; and this [will be?] with them until they finish their sin. And for this reason they come and eat here, as they eat them.'†

97. And then we saw another person who was bound in torment, and [there were] two [who] kept him in darkness. And they were striking him in his face with round stones as *hobet*,[157] and they did not have mercy on him. And they did not turn away, but they were striking him from the right and the left. And Mary said, 'Lord, who is this who has a great punishment, more terrible than the others, and he receives no mercy at all? Why are they beating him with round stones as *hobet*,[157] and his bones do not fall to the earth?' And he[158] said to her, 'Every person has sinned: the one whom the two from the darkness beat with rocks in his face, how will they not be as dust? But he knows

---

[154] The following section (94–8) should be compared with the *Apoc. Paul* 34–6 (James, *Apocrypha Anecdota*, 29–30).

[155] ሀበት; Arras suggests 'palm' as a translation for this otherwise unknown word: see his explanation in Arras, *De Transitu*, i. 101 (Lat.). Comparison with the *Apoc. Paul* 36 (James, *Apocrypha Anecdota*, 30) very strongly suggests 'razor'.

[156] The remainder of this section is very corrupt and cannot be translated well. Moreover, there is no clear parallel in the Old Irish narratives as there is for sections 92–5. See Arras's comments: *De Transitu*, i. 101 (Lat.).

[157] MS A: ኋበት; MS B ሀበት. This word's meaning is unknown; see the discussion in Arras, *De Transitu*, i. 101 (Lat.).

[158] MSS: 'I'.

the affliction of human flesh, and if he gets up from this, a stone will be a great and horrible affliction upon him, and he will not be dissolved.'

98. And the Saviour said to her, 'Mary, know who this is, and then I will tell you how his form[159] is not dissolved. This is a priest whom the poor, destitute, and afflicted trusted, and he ate the memorials and first offerings; and not only by himself, but he gave them to those who were not worthy. And because of this they beat him in his face. And if you want to know how his face is not dissolved, it is because he was an infidel from the place of believing. And his soul will not die, and it will be in torment while not dying or being dissolved.'

99. And when Jesus had said this, he gave them a way by which they could arise from the torment. And the Saviour looked at Michael, and he separated himself from them, and he left Mary and the apostles, so that they would understand them. Then those who were in the torments cried out and said, 'Mary, we beseech you, Mary, light and the mother of light; Mary, life and mother of the apostles; Mary, golden lamp, you who carries every righteous lamp; Mary, our master[160] and the mother of our Master; Mary, our queen, beseech your son to give us a little rest.' And others spoke thus: 'Peter, Andrew, and John, who have become apostles.' For they knew that each of them had been appointed as priests over the cities. And they said to them, 'Where did you place our doctrine that we taught you? For the day is still coming when Christ will appear to you; and the Lord has appointed everything. And after everything we fear God and all of his commandments.' And they were very ashamed and could not reply to the apostles.

100. The Saviour arose and came to the place of torment, and he said to them, 'Where did you place what they taught you? Did you not hear everything that they said?' †And they[161] did not answer, and they spat at him and did not listen. 'Am I not able, with a wink of my eye, to smash heaven and earth to pieces, onto the sinners who have sinned

---

[159] Lit., 'his beauty/goodness'.

[160] Although the form here is feminine (እግዝእትነ), 'mistress' and 'lady' both have connotations in English that make them problematic for translation here. Although 'master' is often used as a gendered term in English, it is here employed in a neuter sense. In other words, while 'master' most appropriately expresses in English the meaning of the Ethiopic word used here, it should not be taken as suggesting the use of masculine forms in reference to the Virgin in the ancient text.

[161] MSS: 'he'. Comparison with early Latin and Irish versions suggests that this passage may have been significantly altered in transmission. These western texts preserve an earlier version that seems to have been changed in subtle ways to yield the text translated above, particularly through change of subject. See the examples cited in Arras, *De Transitu*, i. 102 (Lat.).

against me. But I[162] have not done [this], in order to show you my plan, and so that you will know that you will go just like them. Nevertheless, you have not done this, except for their condemnation, which you have done. You [were] reviled,[163] you persevered, and you were oppressed. Because of this you will be repaid. And what joy have I prepared for you!† Because of the tears of Michael, my holy apostles, and my mother Mary, because they have come and they have seen you, I have given you nine hours[164] of rest on the Lord's day.'

101.　Then he made a sign to the mighty angels with his eyes, and he made it appear as the earth. And then something unexpected happened, and the apostles came to Paradise, and they sat under the tree of life. And the soul of Abraham was there, and the soul of Isaac, and the soul of Jacob, along with many others [whom] the Saviour had brought from death to life by his resurrection and placed in the Paradise of the living. David was there with his harp, making music, and Elizabeth was there with them, although there was another place for women. And the Magi[165] were there, those who went up because of the Saviour, and the little children were there, because of the Saviour. And we also saw great and wonderful things, namely, all the souls of the good people who had gone forth from their bodies, all those who went forth and are reclining in the bosom of Abraham, Isaac, and Jacob.

102.　And we also saw Enoch and the olive tree, [which was there?] at the time when Enoch cut off [a branch] from its foliage and gave [the branch] to the dove, so that it would take [the branch] to Noah on the ark.[166] For in the days of the flood, Noah sent the dove to Paradise to

---

[162]　MSS: 'you'.

[163]　The form here is actually active, but in the light of the following verbs it seems that the best translation is as a passive.

[164]　MS A: 'three days'.

[165]　The term here is ማራስ, which Arras fails to translate, instead transcribing it as if it were a proper name. Nor does he provide any explanation, as he usually does with unusual words that are present in the text. In the translation published by Erbetta, however, the term is rendered 'i magi', also without any explanation. Presumably, ማራስ is understood to be a corrupt form (hardly infrequent in this text) of ማሪ, ማርይ, ማርይ (plural: ማርያን, መራይት, መራይት), meaning 'magician, pagan priest, seer, or spiritual leader'. This seems to me a likely solution, particularly given the relative instability of this word even in the lexical entry.

[166]　Richard Bauckham, *The Fate of the Dead: Studies on Jewish and Christian Apocalypses*, Supplements to Novum Testamentum, 93 (Leiden: Brill, 1998), 344, has the following to say about this tradition: 'The tradition that the olive branch came from Eden is found in rabbinic literature: GenRab 33:6; LevRab 31:10; CantRab 1:15:4; 4:1:2. That Enoch was in Eden at the time of the Flood, from which it was protected, is found in Jubilees 4:23–24. [This] text seems to be unique in connecting these traditions.'

petition his father's ancestor. And God had mercy on the earth and looked upon it. And when the dove went forth, it petitioned Enoch, and it found his words severe, and it returned Noah, with nothing. And Noah sent it a second time, and it went and petitioned Enoch, and it found that God had had mercy on the earth. And he cut off a branch from the olive tree and gave [it] to [the dove], saying, 'Take the sign to Noah and say to him, "This olive branch is a sign and is what we saw on a tree." '

103. And the Lord said to them, 'Do not be amazed at this. And if you have prepared yourselves on the earth, then will you find a better inheritance. And again I say to you, remain here with Mary and with all those who are here until I have made Paul ascend and shown him everything, just as I told him.' And the Lord ascended onto a cloud, and he called Paul to his side, while making him ascend onto the cloud with him. And the Devil cried out in the heights, saying, 'Jesus, Son of God, who came into the world and preached before Jerusalem and gave a commandment to your apostles that they preach to the whole earth in Jerusalem, how do you make this one named Paul ascend, before he contends with me, in your greatness, and defeats me? And it is fitting that you have shown everything to the twelve, since they were worthy, and they have contended with me and defeated me. But this one has not contended with me and has not defeated me. How do you make him ascend? Let him come then: first he will contend with me, and if he defeats me, bring him and show him everything.'

104. Then our Lord said to Paul, 'My brother Paul, prepare yourself for battle, so that he will find nothing against you.' And Paul said, 'I do not know him, but I know that I must contend with him.' And our Lord said to him, 'I will send Peter with you, and he will teach you to fight with him.' Then he descended to Paradise, where the apostles were, and our Lord said to Peter, 'Arise and go with Paul and teach him to fight with the enemy, because he asked that you fight with him.' And Peter said, 'Lord, where will we fight with him again: on a mountain or in the middle of a crowd?' And he said, 'In the middle of a crowd, so that they will know his affliction and his shame. You will fight with him where the cloud sets you down.'

[The two then went and fought the devil, who fell at their hands.][167]

---

[167] I have omitted an extensive section here (105–31), which accounts for approximately 25% of the *Liber Requiei* as it has been preserved. This section details the contendings of Peter and Paul with the devil, in an account that circulated separately during the Middle Ages and has been preserved in an Arabic version entitled *The History of Peter and Paul*, edited by Agnes Smith Lewis, with accompanying English translation: Agnes Smith Lewis, ed. *Acta Mythologica Apostolorum*, Horae Semiticae, 3–4 (London: C. J. Clay & Sons,

132. And then we apostles arrived in Paradise, with our companions the apostles, and we greeted them, telling them everything that happened to us. And then our Lord brought us to a white river and he washed us together with Mary. And he led us up to the seventh heaven, where God sits. And we wanted to enter in to him, so that we could embrace him, and we were afraid, because [God is] entirely fire. But we saw two seraphim standing, each one having six wings: with two they covered their feet, and with two they flew. And they did not touch the face of God, because [God is] completely perfect: for they could not see the face of God, because [God was] entirely fire. And the other two wings of the seraphim covered their faces, both of them covering. And with two they were suspending the feet of God, lest they make an impression on the heights and on the earth; for at that moment, when his feet touch the earth, [that will be] the time of the world's consummation. †For[168]

1904), ١٥٠–٧٤ (Arab.) and 175–92 (Eng.). In addition to this Arabic version, there is also a Karšuni version, published in A. van Lantschoot, 'Contribution aux Actes de S. Pierre et de S. Paul, II.—Recension Karšuni des Actes de S. Pierre et S. Paul', *Le Muséon*, 68 (1955), 219–33. In another article (A. van Lantschoot, 'Contribution aux Actes de S. Pierre et de S. Paul', *Le Muséon*, 68 (1955), 17–46) van Lantschoot published an Ethiopic fragment of the *Liber Requiei* which he identified with the *History of Peter and Paul*: although he was aware of the fragment's parallels with the *History of Peter and Paul*, he did not know of the *Liber Requiei*'s existence. Just before van Lantschoot's fragment breaks off, however, we see that it continues with the heavenly journey of the apostles, told exactly as in the *Liber Requiei*, clearly identifying it as a fragment of the Dormition narrative, rather than the *History of Peter and Paul*.

There are several reasons for the omission of this section, the most important of these being that, unlike the remainder of the *Liber Requiei*'s contents, there is no ancient witness (or any other witness, for that matter), indicating that these traditions were joined with the traditions of Mary's Dormition in antiquity. On the contrary, there is every reason to assume that these traditions were combined at a later date by someone who recognized that this account of Peter and Paul's contention with the Devil was well suited to fill out the brief mention of this event that was present in the ancient Dormition traditions. Nevertheless there is support in the early Irish narratives for the dialogue between Peter, Paul, Jesus, and the Devil in sections 103–4, making for a strong possibility that this part, or at least something like it, was found in the ancient Dormition traditions. The sentence inserted between sections 104 and 132 is the outcome described in the Irish traditions, which has been cited from the translation by Máire Herbert and Martin McNamara, *Irish Biblical Apocrypha* (Edinburgh: T. & T. Clark, 1989), 126. Note, however, that in the early Irish narratives this episode occurs at a different point: immediately following the debate among the apostles over how to preach, when Jesus promises to reveal the mysteries to Paul in heaven.

[168] See the discussion of this difficult section in Arras, *De Transitu*, i. 104–5 (Lat.).

[there is] still a little [time?], and they will touch the earth, because from twelve days he comes in twelve, except for a little.

133. Our Saviour hurried, intending to show us[169] everything, as we came to announce everything, saying 'God is the beginning of knowledge.' But we were not able to go in to the Father, since there is no one who speaks with another seraph, who has six wings, who appeared to us from our Saviour, saying, 'This then is what is appropriate for the just in the days of his kingdom; and he will cover you with his wings, and he will gather you to him.' And we wanted to worship and embrace him, but we were not permitted, saying, 'It is difficult now: wait a little longer[170] and embrace my hands, because the one who has embraced my body will not die.' And Mary, because she has gone forth from her body, she has embraced him. And we saw our Lord Jesus Christ and Mary sitting at the right of God. And we saw every sign of God that was on his side, and the sign on his hands, which was on that day when we were with him.†

134. And Peter asked our Lord, saying, 'This is marvellous: the body is similar to the spirit.' And Peter said to him, 'Have you not healed the wound of that spear, the stab of the sword? Are you unable to heal it? Until you teach us this and tell us this teaching, I will not rest.' And he said to us, 'Until the day of judgement, when he will rebuke the children of Israel, if there is someone who wants to deny this sign, [let him know that?] it was revealed, because he wanted to send his son at every time. And if there are some people from the city who want to rise up against him and beat him and tear his purple garment, the son will show his father and he will protect him. And on that day, when the king wanted to bestow delights on every city, then he ordered that nothing would be given to that city. And the people of that city will speak, saying, "Why have we not found delights?" And he will answer them, saying, "Why did you rise up against my son?" Then they will deny, saying, "We have not risen up against him, and we did not know him." Then his father will order that the purple garment be brought, and the son will show his father the evidence of their rebellion. Thus then it will be for the children of Israel.'

135. And after these words, our Lord turned his face to a seraph that had two wings, and he made a sign to him. And the seraph left two words, which no one could understand. Then a great gathering of angels came with a pure, adorned throne, and there was no end to its glory. Myriads of angels were surrounding it, each one on his own throne. Then they said to us, 'Go to the earth and proclaim everything that you have seen.' And they brought another throne for Mary, and

---

[169] MSS: 'you (pl.)'.

[170] 'wait a little longer': lit., 'reside again'.

there were 10,000 angels and three virgins surrounding it. And she sat [on it] and went into Paradise, and they remained in the third heaven, singing.

136. But Michael made us descend, so that we would inhabit the earth. And we saw other wonders, because we saw every power. And we also saw the sun and its light, while eagles were circling and carrying the sun. And a light appeared in the eagles' midst, so that we asked Michael and said to him, 'How is the light of the sun different here, and it appears different on the earth?' And he taught us, saying, 'Light is upon all creatures. And when the first sin took place, when blood was shed on the earth, a seventh part of the sun's light was removed from it. And because of this the eagles remain here, surrounding the light at this part.' And we also saw the powers of the stars. And when we saw these great wonders, we came together with Michael to the Mount of Olives, by the order of our Lord, to whom be glory and power, unto the age of the age. Amen.

The Earliest Greek Dormition Narrative

Narrative by St John, the Theologian and Evangelist, concerning the Dormition of the All-Holy Theotokos and How the Undefiled Mother of Our Lord Was Translated.[1]

1. Great and worthy of amazement, above all discourse and beyond all understanding are the affairs of Mary, the holy and ever-virgin mother of our true God and Lord, Jesus Christ: the seedless conception, the uncorrupted birth, and God's incarnation from her, coming forth into the world in the form of a human being. But no less so is the mystery of her glorious and wondrous Dormition.

2. When Mary heard from the Lord that she was to come forth from the body, a great angel came to her and said, 'Rise Mary, and take this palm-staff,[2] which was given to me by the one who planted Paradise,

---

[1] This translation is based on the editions published by Antoine Wenger, *L'Assomption de la T. S. Vierge dans la tradition byzantine du VIe au Xe siècle*, Archives de l'Orient Chrétien, 5 (Paris: Institut Français d'Études Byzantines, 1955), 210–41; and Frédéric Manns, OFM, *Le Récit de la dormition de Marie (Vatican grec 1982), Contribution à l'étude de origines de l'exégèse chrétienne*, Studium Biblicum Franciscanum, Collectio Maior, 33 (Jerusalem: Franciscan Printing Press, 1989), 'Synopse des textes'. In preparing the translation, I have consulted the commentaries of both editors and the reproduction of MS Vatican Greek 1982 that accompanies Mann's study.

[2] The word here is βραβεῖον, which is usually translated as 'palm', following Lampe's indication in the *Patristic Greek Lexicon* (304) that this word is used by John of Thessalonica in his homily for the Dormition to refer to a 'palm'. The more usual meaning of this word, as indicated by Lampe, Liddell and Scott's *Greek–English Lexicon*, and Sophocles' *Greek Lexicon of the Roman and Byzantine Period*, is 'a prize', or, as Liddell and Scott note, 'a wand or baton'. In the light of this, it appears that βραβεῖον's usage for 'palm' in John of Thessalonica's homily, and consequently, in the early Greek Dormition traditions, is exceptional. Yet there is little in these narratives that would clearly identify their βραβεῖον as a palm. Near the end of the narrative, we learn that Peter gives a 'palm-leaf' from the βραβεῖον to Jephonias, with which he heals the blinded Jews. Undoubtedly this has led many previous readers to identify this object as a palm, rather than a 'prize' or 'rod'.

Although 'prize' does not seem a likely translation, there is good reason to

and deliver it to the apostles, so that while holding it they may sing
before you, because in three days you will lay aside the body. For
behold, I will send all the apostles to you, and they will bury you and
will not leave you until they have carried you to the place where you will
soon be in glory.'

reconsider 'rod' or 'staff' as an appropriate translation. This is in fact suggested
by the Syriac fragments published last century by William Wright. Among
his fragments of the *Obsequies of the Holy Virgin*, generally regarded as the
earliest extant Dormition narrative, are several badly damaged fragments
that were published without translation in the preface to his *Contributions
to the Apocryphal Literature of the New Testament* (London: Williams &
Norgate, 1865), 11–15. In Wright's time the Dormition traditions were
insufficiently known to be able to make much sense of these fragments, but now,
many of them are very useful as the earliest witness to the 'Palm of the Tree of
Life' traditions of Mary's death, so-called after this βραβεῖον. It is interesting
that in this earliest witness to the Palm tradition, the 'palm' is not a palm, but
rather a ܚܘܛܪܐ, a word that usually means 'a rod, staff, or sceptre', although
it could also mean 'stick' or even 'branch'. It would seem that this 5th-cen-
tury Syriac translator was unaware that in this special instance βραβεῖον was to
be translated as 'palm', and instead he understood a more common meaning,
'rod'.

In the light of this, we may want to reconsider whether or not the modern
decision to translate βραβεῖον as 'palm' is appropriate, particularly in view of its
ancient usage for 'rod', recorded by Liddell and Scott. The earliest witness to
these traditions, the *Obsequies*, has understood the object as a staff, which was
presumably made from palms or had them attached in some way. This is also
true of the other early Syriac and Arabic narratives, which, although they are
not from the same literary family, represent this object as a staff, the Syriac
using ܫܒܝܠܐ (William Wright, 'The Departure of my Lady Mary from this
World', *The Journal of Sacred Literature and Biblical Record*, 6–7 (1865), ܡܠ;
Agnes Smith Lewis, ed., *Apocrypha Syriaca*, Studia Sinaitica, XI (London:
C. J. Clay & Sons, 1902), ܡܗ) and the Arabic عصاة, (Maximillian Enger, ed.,
اخبار يوحنّا السليح في نقلة اُم المسيح) *Akhbâr Yûhannâ as-salîh fi naqlat umm al-masîh*),
id est Joannis apostoli de transitu Beatae Mariae Virginis liber (Eberfeld: R.L.
Friderichs, 1854), 72) both of which mean 'staff or rod'. The Coptic version uses
the word ⲂⲀ, which conveniently means both 'palm' and 'staff' (E. Revillout,
ed., *Évangile des douze apôtres*, PO 2. 2 (Paris: Librairie de Paris/Firmin-Didot
et Cie, 1907), 176). The Latin tradition, however, very clearly describes this
object as a 'ramus palmae' (Monika Haibach-Reinisch, ed., *Ein neuer 'Transitus
Mariae' des Pseudo-Melito* (Rome: Pontificia Academia Mariana Internationalis, 1962), 66) or 'palma' (Wenger, *L'Assomption*, 245), and the Irish
narratives refer to the object as a 'pailm' (Charles Donahue, ed., *The Testament
of Mary: The Gaelic Version of the Dormitio Mariae together with an Irish
Latin Version*, Fordham University Studies, Language Series, 1 (New York:
Fordham University Press, 1942), 28). In the light of this complex mass of
witness, it has seemed best to me to translate βραβεῖον as 'palm-staff', since this
represents both ancient interpretative traditions, as well as paying homage to

3. Mary answered and said to him, 'Why have you brought only this palm-staff to me and not one for each of the apostles, lest it be given to one, and the others will murmur? And what do you want me to do, or what is your name, so that if they should ask me, I can tell them?' And the angel said to her, 'Why do you seek my name? For it is wondrous, and you cannot hear it. But when I am about to ascend, I will tell it to you, so that you may share it with the apostles secretly, so that they will not repeat it to others and will know the power of my authority. Only do not hold on to[3] the palm-staff, because many miracles will come to pass through it, and it will be a test for all the people of Jerusalem. To the one who believes then, it will be revealed, and to the one who does not believe, it will be hidden. Go to the mountain then, and there you will learn my name, because I will not speak it inside Jerusalem, lest it be completely devastated. But you will hear it on the Mount of Olives.[4] Yet

the ancient usage of this word for 'rod'. For more on this topic, see the discussion in Ch. 1.

[3] The text is slightly problematic here: the phrase is *Μὴ μόνον περὶ τοῦ βραβείου περικρατήσῃς*, which Wenger translates without comment as 'ne sois pas inquiète au subject de la palme' (*L'Assomption*, 211), and Manns as 'Ne te préoccupe pas de la palme' (*Le Récit*, 240). Nevertheless, *περικρατέω* is not elsewhere used with the meaning 'to be anxious'; among its more common meanings are 'to have full command of, hold fast, prevail over, control, master, maintain, support'. John of Thessalonica's homily, however, uses either *διστάσῃς* (most MSS) or *ἀγωνιάσῃς* (MSS B and O), which mean 'be in doubt, hesitate' and 'be distressed, agonize' respectively. The only other version in which the angel addresses the Virgin's concerns about the palm is the early Irish translation, which reads, 'Let no terror be upon thee, nor fear, at taking this palm from me' (*na bith omon ort-sa na eagla na pailme sea do gabail uaim-sea*: Donahue, *Testament*, 28–9; see also Máire Herbert and Martin McNamara, eds., *Irish Biblical Apocrypha* (Edinburgh: T. & T. Clark, 1989), 119).

The immediately preceding phrase, *περὶ τοῦ βραβείου*, seems to suggest some sort of concern 'about the palm', but this is just not within the range of meanings for *περικρατέω*. A possible solution is that *περικρατήσῃς* is a corruption of *περικηδέσῃ[s]*, from *περικήδομαι*, which means 'to be very anxious or concerned about', in which case the text would have read originally 'Only do not be so concerned about the palm . . .'. Nevertheless, I have attempted above to translate the text as it stands in the manuscript.

[4] The Greek is slightly unusual here: *ἐν τῷ ὄρει τῷ φερομένῳ τῷ ἄνωθεν τῶν ἐλαίων* (thus in both Wenger's and Mann's editions, although in the reproduction of the MS included with Mann's study, the text appears to read *τὸ ἄνωθεν*, rather than *τῷ ἄνωθεν*). Clearly, however, the Mount of Olives is indicated, and so Wenger opts, as I do, for this simple translation. Nevertheless, Manns translates: 'le Mont célèbre et élevé des Oliviers' (*Le Récit*, 240), and I would also suggest the possibility of translating: 'the mountain bearing an abundance of olives'.

you cannot tell it to the apostles,[5] as I am about to tell you, because the time has come for you to put off the body.'

4. Then Mary, holding the palm-staff in her hand, went to the Mount of Olives, with the angel's light shining ahead of her. And when she came to the mountain, it rejoiced greatly, along with all of its trees, so that its trees bowed their heads and venerated the palm-staff that was in her hand.

5. When Mary saw this, she thought that it was Jesus and said, 'Lord, are you not my Lord?' Then the angel said to her, 'No one can work miracles except the Lord of Glory. For just as my Father sent me for the salvation of humanity, to convert those whom he has entrusted to me,[6] so also [he has sent?] from the trees, so that my friends will eat from them and receive the likeness, which he has entrusted to me. And not only do I transfer trees, but I also carry people who humble themselves before God; I transfer them to the place of the just on the day that they come forth from the body. And so when you come forth from the body, I will come to it myself on the fourth day: because our Saviour

---

[5] As Wenger notes (*L'Assomption*, 213 n. 2), this strangely seems to contradict the angel's previous statement that she is to share his name with the apostles in secret.

[6] According to Wenger (*L'Assomption*, 35, 213 n. 4), the second part of this comparison is lacking in the MS, which suddenly continues with 'And not only do I transfer . . .'. In Mann's edition, however, he gives the following text, which we have translated above: Καὶ ἐκ τῶν φυτῶν ἵνα φάγωσιν ἐξ αὐτῶν οἱ φίλοι μου λαμβάνοντες τὴν ὁμοίωσιν ἣν ἐνετείλατό μοι. This inclusion of this text is confirmed by the reproduction of the MS at the end of his study. Presumably, in making his transcription, Wenger committed the common copyist's mistake often known as 'saut du même au même': the passage omitted ends with the same two words as the locus where Wenger's omission begins: ἐνετείλατό μοι. Moreover, a very similar statement occurs in the *Liber Requiei* and the Georgian fragments of this same text, both of which illuminate what is otherwise a rather cryptic reference to the trees. It would seem that a long episode has largely fallen out here, leaving only this trace. The episode concerns the story of a date-palm from which the Holy Family fed during their flight into Egypt. As a reward for feeding his family, Christ transfers the tree to Paradise, offering this assurance: 'because just as my father sent me for the salvation of humanity, so that they convert, he told me also about the fruit, so that my friends might eat from it, [namely,] those who receive me in my image' (*Liber Requiei* 9 (Victor Arras, ed., *De Transitu Mariae Aethiopice*, 2 vols., CSCO 342–3, 351–2 (Louvain: Secrétariat du CorpusSCO, 1973) i. 5 (Eth.) and 3–4 (Lat.)); and 'because just as my father sent me for the salvation of humanity and for their conversion, he also gave me a command about the plants, so that my friends and beloved might eat from them, [namely,] those who receive my image and do my command' (Michel van Esbroeck, 'Apocryphes géorgiens de la Dormition', *Analecta Bollandiana*, 92 (1973), 71).

was resurrected on the third day, so I will raise you up also on the fourth day. And not only you, but I also transfer all who observe the commandments of God to the sweet-smelling Paradise, because they have kept themselves perfect on earth.'

6. Mary said to him, 'Lord, how do you come to them, or who are those that you transfer? Do they distinguish themselves and offer sweet-smelling sacrifices, and thus you come to them? Or rather do you come to the righteous or to the elect? Or, when you are sent, do you come to those who call upon your name while praying? You must tell me about this, so that I too can do thus, and you will come and take me up.'

7. And he said to her, 'What's the matter, mother?[7] When I am sent to you,[8] I will not be alone, but all the hosts of angels will come, and they will sing before you. I have been sent to you now to [make] you know[9] [what to do?[10]], in order that you will share [this] with the apostles in

---

[7] *Tί γὰρ ἔχεις, μῆτερ;* this could also mean, 'what are you thinking?' as Daley translates the identical phrase found in John of Thessalonica's homily (Brian E. Daley, SJ, *On the Dormition of Mary: Early Patristic Homilies* (Crestwood, NY: St Vladimir's Seminary Press, 1998), 50).

[8] The word here is *ἀποστελῶ*, for which Manns suggests we must understand *ἀποσταλῶ*, a 1st person 2nd aorist passive subjunctive (*Le Récit* 241 n. *a*). Comparison with the Ethiopic (ተፈነውኩ *Liber Requiei* 11 (Arras, *De Transitu*, i. 6 (Eth.))) and Georgian versions (მოვივლინები: van Esbroeck, 'Apocryphes', 71) suggests this as well. Nevertheless, the future active form found in the MS is also possible: for this rather unusual use of *ἀποστέλλω* in the active meaning 'to visit', see Lampe, *Patristic Greek Lexicon*, 209. Moreover, the more usual translation remains an outside possibility: 'When I send for you . . .'.

[9] As Wenger explains (*L'Assomption*, 215 n. 1), *ἐπιστῆσαί*, 'to know', is not the word that one would expect here: instead, a verb meaning 'to make to know', seems more appropriate. This is the case in the Ethiopic *Liber Requiei*: ተፈነውኩ ከመ እንግርክሙ አንቲኒ ከመ ተህቦሙ ለሐዋርያት በኅቡእ 'I have been sent to tell you so that you will give to the apostles in secret' (Arras, *De Transitu*, i. 6–7 (Eth.)) and the Georgian fragments: მოვივლინები შენდა გულისხმისყოფად რათა ჯერხრა ჵენ მოციქულთა საიდუმლოთ, 'I have been sent to you to make known to you, so that you will tell the apostles' (van Esbroeck, 'Apocryphes', 73). Both these texts, it should be noted, were unavailable to Wenger. Manns, however, understands the form to be from *ἐφίστημι*, rather than from *ἐπίσταμαι* (*Le Récit*, 89). This is a possibility, in which case this may mean, 'I have been sent to attend to you', although we should note that in early Byzantine usage *ἐφίστημι* had taken on distinctly intellectual associations, meaning, among other things, 'to understand, wonder, consider, perceive, observe, explain': see Lampe, *Patristic Greek Lexicon*, 587b.

[10] Wenger has added 'my name' as the object of the verb, but this does not appear in the Greek text (nor is an object present in the Georgian and Ethiopic versions of this same text—see above, n. 9). There seems to be a need for some sort of object, and in the light of the preceding conversation, 'my name' seems a strong possibility. As I have construed it, however, what Mary will know and

secret. Now, you want to know what you will do. When I was sent to you, I received a prayer from the Father, as I was coming to you, and now I am telling it to you so that you will say it when you go forth from the body at the rising of the sun, for thus [the prayer] is offered up. And what I tell you, share with apostles, because they too are coming. No friend of the world, who loves the world, is able to speak this prayer.'

8. When he had said these things, the angel ordered her to share this prayer with the apostles, 'For they are coming to you, as I have told you, and they will sing before you and they will bury you. Therefore, take this palm-staff.' And when Mary had received the palm-staff, the angel became as light, ascended into the heavens.

9. Then Mary returned to her house, and at once the house trembled on account of the glory of the palm-staff in her hand. And after the tremor, she went into her secret, inner room and put it away in fine cloth. And when she had undressed, she took water and washed, and she put on different garments while blessing, saying,

10. 'I bless you, sign that appeared from heaven on the earth, until you chose me and dwelt in me.[11] I bless you and all my relatives, those who will receive me,[12] who came forth invisibly before you, in order to

transmit to the apostles is the answer to her question above: what she is to do at death. The answer is then given in the secret prayer that must be spoken when going forth from the body, a solution also adopted by Manns (*Le Récit*, 241).

[11] The meaning of the phrase ἕως ἂν ἐκλέξῃ με καὶ κατοικήσῃς ἐν ἐμοί is not entirely clear here. Although Manns (*Le Récit*, 241) has chosen to understand it as an expression of purpose, which it may in fact be, Wenger (who also notes that the meaning of the passage is obscure (*L'Assomption*, 215 n. 4)), opts for the somewhat more usual temporal meaning. I have chosen the latter, based primarily on the strong temporal sense in the other earliest versions that include this phrase: ⲗⲛ̅ⲏ: ⲗⲁⲡ ('until, so long as' (Arras, *De Transitu*, i. 21 (Eth.))) and 'donec' (Wenger, *L'Assomption*, 246).

[12] This is a somewhat unusual expression: τοὺς παραλήμπτωράς μου. Presumably this is from the word παραλή[μ]πτωρ, in which case one would expect the form παραλήμπτορες, meaning 'inheritors, receivers', as translated above. While this word is very uncommon in Greek usage, it occasionally appears in Coptic literature, for instance, in Theodosius of Alexandria's homily for the Dormition (Forbes Robinson, ed., *Coptic Apocryphal Gospels*, Texts and Studies, IV (Cambridge: Cambridge University Press, 1896), 100). Its most frequent usage, however, is in the Coptic 'gnostic' texts of late antiquity, where it is also attested in the grammatical form understood by the author of our text, ⲠⲀⲢⲀⲖⲎⲘⲠⲦⲰⲢⲟⲤ: *The Gospel of the Egyptians*, III. 64. 22; 66. 5; IV. 76. 121, 78. 7 (Alexander Böhlig and Frederik Wisse, eds., *Nag Hammadi Codices III, 2 and IV, 2: The Gospel of the Egyptians*, NHS 4 (Grand Rapids MI: Eerdmans, 1975) 148–9, 154–5); *The Second Book of Jeu* 42–3 (Carl Schmidt, ed., and Violet MacDermot, trans., *The Books of Jeû and the Untitled Text in the Bruce Codex*, NHS 13 (Leiden: E. J. Brill, 1978), 99. 15–16, 101. 24); *The*

bring you along. I bless you because you gave me a measure of virility for the parts of your body, and [because] I have been found worthy of the kiss of your bridal chamber, as you promised me before. I bless you so that I will be found worthy to partake of the perfect eucharist and your sweet-smelling offering, which is an abundance for all the nations.'

11. 'I bless you so that you will give me the garment that you promised me, saying: "By this you will be distinguished from my relatives", and [so that] you will cause me to be taken to the seventh heaven, so that I will be found worthy of your perfect fragrance with all those who believe in you, so that you will gather them together with me in your kingdom. For you are hidden among the hidden, observing those who are not seen. You are the hidden race, and you are also the Pleroma; you are the Pleroma, and I have painfully given birth[13] first to you and then to all of those who hope in you.'

12. 'Hear the prayer of your mother Mary crying out to you. Listen to my voice and send forth your favour on me, so that no power will come to me in that hour when I go forth from my body; but fulfil what you said when I was weeping before you, saying, "Let me pass by the powers that will come upon my soul." And you made a promise to me, saying, "Do not weep, O Mary, my mother: neither angels nor archangels, nor cherubim nor seraphim, nor any other power will come

Untitled Text in the Bruce Codex, 9 (ibid. 241. 18); *Pistis Sophia* 55. 11 and *passim* (Carl Schmidt and trans. Violet MacDermot, *Pistis Sophia*, NHS 9 (Leiden: E. J. Brill, 1978), 105; see also the entry for παραλήμπτωρ in the index of Greek words, p. 790); *Zostrianos* 47. 24 (John H. Sieber, ed., *Nag Hammadi Codex VIII*, NHS 31 (Leiden: E. J. Brill, 1991), 116), and *The Apocryphon of John*, synopsis 69. 10 (Michael Waldstein and Frederic Wisse, eds., *The Apocryphon of John: A Synopsis of Nag Hammadi codices II,1, III,1, and IV,1 with BG 8502,2*, NHS 33 (New York : E. J. Brill, 1995), 148–9). In these texts παραλήμπτωρ is a 'gnostic' technical term for the heavenly powers that meet the soul at its separation from the body and guide it safely past the Demiurge and his minions to the Pleroma (see also the discussion of this word in Böhlig and Wisse, *Nag Hammadi Codices III, 2 and IV, 2*, 194–98). Here the idea seems to be that Mary's relatives will fill this role when she goes forth from the body.

[13] The word in Wenger's text here is ἠδύνησα: 'I have caused pain.' But MSS B and O of the interpolated version of John of Thessalonica's closely related homily for the Dormition preserve a nearly identical text at this point, where the word is instead ὠδίνησα: 'to suffer birth pains; bring forth with pain' (see Martin Jugie, AA, ed., *Homélies mariales byzantine (II)*, PO 19. 3 (Paris: Librairie de Paris/Firmin-Didot et Cie, 1926), 408 n. 15; other MSS omit this passage entirely). A similar reading is found in the Ethiopic *Liber Requiei* 37 (ኣጸነስኩ 'I conceived you'; Arras, *De Transitu*, i. 21 (Eth.)). In the translation above I have understood ἠδύνησα as a corruption of ὠδίνησα. Wenger seems to have reached a similar decision (although he does not explain himself), translating the word 'engendré'.

upon you, but I will come myself to your soul." But now pain has come upon her who gives birth. I bless you and the three servants sent by you for the service of the three ways. I bless you and the eternal light in which you dwell. I bless every plantation of your hands, which will endure unto the ages. Holy, holy, you who rests among the holy ones, hear the voice of my supplication.'[14]

13. When she had said these things, she went out and said to the maidservant of her house, 'Go out and call all my relatives and acquaintances, saying, "Mary calls you."' The maidservant went out and called them, just as Mary had ordered her. And when they had come, Mary said, 'Fathers and brothers, let us help ourselves through good works and faith in the living God. For tomorrow I will go forth from the body and will depart for my eternal rest. Arise then and do a great act of kindness with me: I ask you neither for gold nor silver, because all these things are vain and corruptible. But I ask you only for piety,[15] that you guard what I say to you and remain with me for these two days and nights. Each of you, take a beautiful lamp, and do not let them go out for the three days, so that I can tell you my thoughts before I depart this place.' And they all did as she commanded them.

14. The report was spread to all Mary's acquaintances and friends, and Mary called all those closest to her and said to them, 'Arise and let us pray.' And after the prayer they sat down, discussing with one another the mighty works of God, signs and wonders that he worked through his mother.

15. As Mary was praying and saying Amen, behold, suddenly the apostle John arrived on a cloud. And he knocked on Mary's door, opened it, and went in. When Mary saw him, her spirit was disturbed, and sighing, she did not have the strength to restrain her tears, nor could she keep silent her great lamentation. She cried out in a loud voice and said, 'Father John, remember the words of the teacher, what he advised you for my sake on that day when he went forth from us and I wept, saying, "You are going away; with whom do you leave me and

---

[14] Ps. 27: 2 (LXX).

[15] Another difficult word: φιλοθεσίαν. I have chosen the translation above based on a presumed relationship between this form and the more routine words φιλοθεΐα and φιλόθεος. John of Thessalonica uses φιλανθρωπίαν (Jugie, *Homélies mariales byzantine (II)*, 381), as similarly found in the closely related Latin (*humanitas*), Georgian (კაცთმოყუარებისა), and Ethiopic (ፍቅረ፡ ሰብእ፡) texts (Wenger, *L'Assomption*, 246; van Esbroeck, 'Apocryphes', 60; and Arras, *De Transitu*, i. 22 (Eth.), respectively). The also closely related early Irish versions, however, offer some support for the reading found in the earliest Greek text: here one finds the Virgin asking for 'constant prayer' (*urnaithe gressach*: Donahue, *Testament*, 32 and Herbert and McNamara, *Irish Biblical Apocrypha*, 123).

with whom will I live?" And he said to me, while you stood and listened, "John is the one who will take care of you."[16] Now then, father John, do not forget what has been commanded to you regarding me. Remember that he loved you more than the others. Remember that, while you were reclining on his breast,[17] he spoke to you alone the mystery that no one else knows, except you and I, because you are a chosen virgin, and he did not want me to grieve, because I am his dwelling place. Then I said to him, "Tell me what you said to John." And he said to you what you imparted to me. Now then, father John, do not abandon me.'

16. When she had said these things, Mary wept in a quiet and desolate voice. But John could not bear it: his spirit was troubled, and he did not know what to say to her. For he did not know that she was about to go forth from the body. Then John cried out in a loud voice, 'Mary, my sister, who became the mother of the twelve branches, what do you want me to do for you? For indeed, I left behind my servant to provide you with food. You would not want me to transgress the command of my Lord, which he commanded us, saying, "Go throughout the whole world, until the sin of the world is abolished"?[18] Now then, tell me what you need.'

17. She said to him, 'Father John, I have no need for the things of this world, but after tomorrow, I will go forth from the body. I ask you, father John, to perform an act of kindness for me: watch over my body and place it in a tomb. And guard me with your brothers, the apostles, on account of the high priests. For with my own ears I have heard them say, "When we find her body, we will commit it to fire, because from her the deceiver came forth." '

18. When John heard her say, 'I will come forth from the body', he fell at her knees and wept, saying, 'Lord, who are we that you have shown us these tribulations? For we have not yet forgotten the previous ones, so that we can endure yet another tribulation. Why, O Mary, do I not go forth from the body, so that you might watch over me?'

19. When she heard John weeping and saying these things, she asked those present to be quiet, and she restrained John, saying, 'Father John, be patient with me in [your][19] weeping for a moment, so that I may tell you what the angel imparted to me.' Then John wiped away his tears,

---

[16] Cf. John 19: 26–7.

[17] Cf. John 13: 23.

[18] Cf. Matt. 28: 19.

[19] As Wenger explains (*L'Assomption*, 221 n. 3), although the text reads 'my weeping' (κλαυθμῷ μου), clearly, in the light of the sentence that follows, 'your weeping' must be understood, as found in John of Thessalonica's homily (κλαυθμοῦ σου: Jugie, *Homélies mariales byzantine (II)*, 385) and the *Liber Requiei* (Arras, *De Transitu*, i. 26 (Eth.)).

and Mary said to him, 'Come with me, and tell the crowd to sing psalms.' And while they were singing psalms, she brought John into her inner chamber and told him the prayer that had been given to her by the angel.

20. And she brought forth a small case that contained a book and said, 'Father John, take this book in which is the mystery. For when he was five years old the teacher revealed all the things of creation, and he also put you, the twelve, in it.'[20] And she showed him her funeral garments and every preparation for her body,[21] saying, 'Father John, you know everything that I have in this big house except my funeral garments and two tunics. There are two widows here: when I go forth from the body, give one to each.'

21. After she said these things, she brought him to where the palm-staff was, which had been given to her by the angel, so that the apostles would take it. And she said to him, 'Father John, take this palm-staff, so that you may carry it before me, for this is why it was given to me.' Then John said to her, 'Mary, my mother and sister, I cannot take this by myself, without my fellow apostles being present. Otherwise, when they come, murmuring and resentment will arise among us: for there is one among us who has been appointed the superior. But when we come together, the approval of our Saviour will be upon us.'

22. After these things they both came out, and while they were coming out of the inner chamber, behold, suddenly there was thunder, so that those in that place were disturbed. And after the sound of the thunder, behold, suddenly the apostles descended on a cloud, from the corners of the world to Mary's door. Being eleven in number, they were seated on clouds. First Peter, second Paul—he was also carried on a cloud and numbered among the apostles; for at that time he had the beginnings of the faith of God. After them the rest of the apostles also met one another in the clouds at Mary's door. And they embraced one

[20] The odd phrase, 'and he also put you, the twelve, in it', is also present in the *Liber Requiei*, which reads almost identically at this point in the text: አስመ፡ ህለዉ፡ ፮ግመት፡ ሎቱ፡ ለሊቅነ፡ አርአያነ፡ ኵሎ፡ ፍጥረት፡ ወሚመ፡ ወገሕነ፡ ፲ወ፪ ውሙቱቱ (Arras, *De Transitu*, i. 27 (Eth.).

[21] τοῦ σκηνώματος. Wenger and Manns translate this phrase as 'de sa maison' and 'dans sa tente' respectively. Nevertheless, it would seem that Mary here refers to the funeral preparations that lay ready for her corpse. σκήνωμα is frequently used in reference to the body generally or to a corpse in particular. It is used in reference to Mary's corpse specifically in John of Damascus' *carm. dorm. BVM* 6 (PG 96. 1365A): although Daley translates the word here as 'tabernacle', the passage unmistakably refers to her corpse (*On the Dormition of Mary*, 243). This interpretation is confirmed by the *Liber Requiei*, which reads here, 'every preparation for her funeral' (ወኵሎ፡ ተድላ፡ ግንዛታ፡, Arras, *De Transitu*, i. 27 (Eth.)).

another, gazing at each another and marvelling at how they suddenly
came to meet in the same place.

23. Peter answered and said, 'Brothers, let us pray to God, who has
gathered us together, especially because our brother Paul, the delight
of our souls, is with us. Truly brothers, the scripture and the word of
the prophet has been fulfilled which says, "Behold, how beautiful and
pleasant it is for brothers to dwell together!" '[22] Paul said to Peter, 'You
have found the appropriate testimony: for I was separated, and now I
have been brought[23] into the community of the apostles.' Then Peter
encouraged them to say a word of prayer. And the apostles raised their
voice, saying, 'Yes, let us pray that it be made known to us why God has
brought us together.' When those nearby[24] realized that they should
pray, they said to Peter, 'Father Peter, you have been appointed over
us: therefore, you pray for us!' And Peter said, 'God our Father and
our Lord Jesus Christ will glorify you, just as my ministry has been
glorified. Therefore bless me in this, if it is pleasing to you.'

24. Then Peter stretched out his hands and said, 'Lord God, who
is seated upon the chariot of the cherubim,[25] who is seated in the
heights and looks upon the lowly,[26] who dwells in unapproachable
light[27] in eternal rest, the hidden mystery in which the saving cross was
revealed.[28] We do this very same thing when we raise our hands in the
image of your cross, so that by recognition of this we will receive rest:
for you are rest for weary limbs; you loosen the hard labours; you are
the one who reveals hidden treasures;[29] you have planted your goodness

---

[22] Ps. 133: 1.
[23] Both Wenger's and Manns' text have misprinted ἀνήθχην here: Mann's
reproduction of the MS clearly shows the correct form ἀνήχθην.
[24] Δοξαζόντων τῶν πλησίον: again, both Manns and Wenger give this reading, but in a textual note beneath Wenger's edition, we find the phrase printed
Δοξαζόντων τῶν πλησίων, which is the form that one would expect with the
article. Manns' reproduction of the MS is somewhat more difficult to read at this
point, but it too seems to confirm the latter reading.
[25] Cf. 2 Kgs. 19: 15.
[26] Ps. 112: 6 (LXX).
[27] 1 Tim. 6: 16.
[28] Wenger (*L'Assomption*, 225) suggests translating this phrase as follows:
'toi mystère caché qui as été révélé par la croix du salut'. This translation finds
some support in the interpolated version of John of Thessalonica's homily
(Jugie, *Homélies mariales byzantine (II)*, 416), but, as Wenger notes, it differs
from his Greek text, ἐν ᾧ ὁ σωτήριος σταυρὸς ἐδείχθη, which I have rendered
above. The *Liber Requiei* reads, 'in a hidden mystery that you revealed by the
cross' (በምሥጢር፡ ኅቡእ፡ ዘአመስቀል፡ አርአይከ፥), according to one MS, and 'the hidden
mystery that you revealed to us by the cross' (ምሥጢረ፡ ኅቡእ፡ ዘአመስቀል፡ አንተ፡
አርአይከነ፥) in the other MS (Arras, *De Transitu*, i. 29 (Eth.)).
[29] Cf. Isa. 45: 3.

in us. For who of the gods is as merciful as your Father? And you do not remove your benevolence from us.[30] Who is as merciful as you, just as your Father is very merciful, because he saves those hoping in him from evil.'

25. 'Your will has conquered every desire; your faith has crushed falsehood; your beauty has vanquished comeliness; your humility has cast down every arrogance. You are the living one and the one who has vanquished death, our rest that has uprooted death, the glory of your mercy, which was sent from the Spirit of the Father of truth. Emmanuel, Emmanuel, Maranatha, from now unto the ages of ages. Amen.'

26. When they said Amen, Peter and Andrew embraced one another, and John was in their midst, saying, 'Bless me, all of you.' Then they all embraced each another, according to the proper order. After embracing, Peter and Andrew said, 'John, beloved of the Lord, how did you come here, and how many days have you been here?' John answered and said, 'Listen to what happened to me. It happened when I was in the city of Sardis, with twenty-eight disciples, who believed in the Saviour: I was raised up on a cloud from their midst. It was the ninth hour, and behold, when the cloud descended upon the place where we were, it snatched me up and brought me here. When I knocked on the door, they opened it for me, and I found a great crowd around our mother Mary, who was saying, "I will come forth from the body." I did not remain among those surrounding her, but my grief weighed down on me.'

27. 'Now then, my brothers, when we go in tomorrow, do not weep, lest she be troubled—for this is what our teacher taught me when I reclined on his breast at the supper—lest the crowd around her, seeing us in tears, should be divided in their hearts, saying, "They also fear death." But let us encourage each other with the sayings of the beloved.'

28. Then, when the apostles went into Mary's house, they said with one voice, 'Mary, our sister, mother of all the saved, the grace of the Lord be with you.' When she saw them, she was filled with joy and cried out, saying, 'And grace be with you. How have you come here together? For I see you gathered together.' And they said, each one, how, in an instant, they were gathered together from every land by clouds; for each one told the country from which he had been brought. Then they all greeted her, from Peter to Paul, saying, 'May the Lord, the Saviour of all, bless you.'

29. Then Mary rejoiced in spirit and said, 'I bless you, the master of every blessing. I bless the dwelling places of your glory. I bless the Great Cherub of Light, who dwelt for a time in my womb. I bless all

---

[30] Cf. 2 Macc. 6: 16.

the works of your hands, which obeyed with complete submission. I bless your love, with which you loved us. I bless all the words of life that come forth from your mouth and give us the truth. For I believe that the things that you told me have happened to me. You said, "I will send all the apostles to you when you go forth from the body"; and behold, they have been brought together, and I am in their midst, just like a fruit-bearing vine, just as when I was with you, and you were like a vine in the midst of your angels, binding the enemy in chains, with all of his workings. I bless you [with every blessing],[31] because the things that were spoken to me have happened. For you said, "You will be able to see me with the apostles when you come forth from the body." Behold then, Lord, they have been gathered together.'

30. When she had said these things, Mary called Peter and all the apostles, and she brought them into her inner chamber and showed them her funeral garments. And after this, she went out and sat down in their midst. The lamps were still lit, and they did not allow them to be extinguished, just as Mary had commanded them. When the sun set on the second day, at the beginning of the third day, on which she went forth,[32] Peter said to the apostles, 'Brothers, let the one having learned discourse speak throughout the night, until the sun rises, exhorting the crowd.' And the apostles said to him, 'Who is wiser than you? We would be delighted to hear your learning.'

31. Then Peter began to speak: 'Brothers and all you who have come

---

[31] Wenger completely omits this second occurrence of the phrase ἐν πάσῃ ἐνεργείᾳ from his translation, suspecting that a copyist has mistakenly copied it twice (*L'Assomption*, 229 n.3). Nevertheless, it would seem that instead a copyist has written ἐνεργείᾳ where the original probably read εὐλογίᾳ; following the readings found in John of Thessalonica's homily (ἐν πάσῃ εὐλογίᾳ; Jugie, *Homélies mariales byzantine (II)*, 389) and the Ethiopic *Liber Requiei* (እንበለ፡ በኵሉ፡ በረከት፡, Arras, *De Transitu*, i. 32 (Eth.)), I offer the emended translation given above. Moreover, one need not suppose, as does Manns (*Le Récit*, 89), that something of the order of διὰ τό has fallen out of the text here: the following phrase is an accusative absolute.

[32] Ὅταν οὖν ἔδυ ὁ ἥλιος ἐν τῇ δευτέρᾳ ἡμέρᾳ εἰς τὴν τρίτην ἐξερχομένης αὐτῆς. This passage is somewhat difficult. Both Wenger and Manns seem to understand ἐξερχομένης αὐτῆς as referring back to ἡμέρᾳ, but it is also possible that it refers to Mary, as I have rendered the passage. Comparison with other closely related, early Dormition traditions supports the translation that I have made, although this then makes the phrase εἰς τὴν τρίτην a little elliptic. Examples from the earliest text supporting my translation are found in: Arras, *De Transitu*, i. 32 (Eth.); Jugie, *Homélies mariales byzantine (II)*, 389; Donahue, *Testament*, 40; Herbert and McNamara, *Irish Biblical Apocrypha*, 124; A. Wilmart ed., *Analecta Reginensia: Extraits des manuscrits Latins de la Reine christine conservés au Vatican*, Studi e Testi, 59 (Vatican: Biblioteca Apostolica Vaticana, 1933), 338.

here at this hour for the benevolence of our mother Mary, you who have
lighted the lamps that shine with the fire of the visible earth, you have
performed a noble service. But I also desire that each virgin will receive
her lamp in the immaterial firmament of heaven. This is the three-
wicked lamp of the more glorious[33] human being, that is, the body,
the mind, and the spirit. For if these three shine with the true fire, for
which you are struggling, you will not be ashamed when you enter into
marriage and rest with the bridegroom. So it is for our mother Mary:
the light of her lamp has filled the world and it will not be put out until
the end of the age, so that all those wishing [to be saved][34] will take
courage from her, and you will receive the blessings of rest. Now then,
brothers, struggle, recognizing that we will not remain here forever.'

32. After Peter had said these things and exhorted the crowd until
dawn, the sun rose, Mary got up and went outside, and she recited the
prayer that the angel had given her. And after praying, she went in and
lay down on her bed, and she fulfilled the course her life.[35] Peter sat at
her head, and John at her feet, and the others were in a circle around
her bed.

33. And at about the third hour of the day, there was a great thunder
and a sweet-smelling fragrance, so that everyone was driven off to sleep
by the exceedingly sweet smell, except for only the three virgins.[36] He

---

[33] ἐνδοξοτέρου. Wenger translates here, 'de l'homme intérieur', preferring
the reading found in John of Thessalonica's homily, ἐνδοτέρου (Jugie, *Homélies
mariales byzantine (II)*, 390). The *Liber Requiei* is slightly different here and
cannot assist.

[34] Wenger suggests (*L'Assomption*, 231 n. 1) that this should be supplied
from comparison with John of Thessalonica, who includes σωθῆναι (Jugie,
Homélies mariales byzantine (II), 390), a reading also found in the *Liber Requiei*:
እስ፡ መስፉ፡ ይድኅኑ፡ (Arras, *De Transitu*, i. 33 (Eth.)).

[35] Actually, her οἰκονομία. Note, however, that this does not seem to refer to
the actual moment of her death: see below.

[36] Here is the first hint that two separate traditions of the moment of the
Virgin's death may have been harmonized, more or less, as will become increasingly apparent. Although this statement would seem to imply that the apostles
also fell asleep, it is apparent later in the narrative that the apostles remained
awake, since Christ embraces them and speaks with Peter. Nevertheless, still
later in the narrative, after Christ has departed with the Virgin's soul, we are told
that the three virgins woke the apostles up! (See below, section 37 and n. 41.)
This could be explained by the incomplete blending of two separate traditions:
(1) one in which the apostles are all put to sleep, and only the three virgins
witness the separation of Mary's body and soul, and (2) another version in which
the apostles are awake and embrace and converse with Christ. The *Liber Requiei*
also preserves this reading: ወጼና፡ መዓዛ፡ ሥናይ፡ ከመ፡ ዘእምገነት፡ ጼናሁ፡ ወአንዘሙ፡ ገዋግም፡
እኵሎሙ፡ እለ፡ ይቀውሙ፡ ጎበ፡ ማርያ፡ እንበለ፡ ባሕቲቶን፡ ደናግል፡ ገብራ፡ ከመ፡ ኢይኑማ፡ ከመ፡ ስምዐ፡
ይኩና፡ በእንተ፡ ግዝፋ፡ ለማርያም፡ ወበእንተ፡ ሰብሐቲሁ። ('. . . and a sweet, pleasant smell,

caused them to remain awake so that they could testify concerning the funeral of Mary the mother of our Lord and her glory. And behold, suddenly the Lord Jesus arrived on clouds with an innumerable multitude of holy angels. And he entered into the inner room, where Mary was, along with Michael and Gabriel, while the angels sang hymns and remained standing outside the inner room. And as soon as the Saviour entered, he found the apostles gathered around Mary, and he embraced them.

34. And Mary opened her mouth and gave thanks, saying, 'I bless you, because you have done what you promised, and you have not grieved my spirit. You promised me that you would not allow angels to come to my soul, but that you would come to it. And it has happened to me, Lord, according to your word.[37] Who am I, a lowly one, that I have been found worthy of such glory?' And when she had said these things, she fulfilled the course of her life,[38] with her face smiling at the Lord.

35. The Lord embraced her, and he took her holy soul and placed it in Michael's hands, wrapping it in indescribably splendid skins. And we, the apostles, beheld the soul of Mary as it was given into Michael's hands: it was perfect in every human form, except for the shape of male or female, with nothing being in it, except for a likeness of the complete body and a sevenfold whiteness.[39]

like the odour of Paradise. And all those who were standing near Mary began to sleep, except only the virgins: he kept them from sleeping so that they would be witnesses of Mary's funeral and of her glory.'; Arras, *De Transitu*, i. 39 (Eth.)), as does the early Latin text edited by Wenger: 'tonitruum factum est et odor suauitates, ita ut a multa suauitate somnum occuparet omnes qui stabant circa mariam, exceptis tribus uirginibus quas fecit uigilare ut testificarent de gloria qua suscepta est beata maria' (Wenger, *L'Assomption*, 252–3). Other early texts, however, including John of Thessalonica, the early Irish version, and Ps.-Melito, specify that all were put to sleep except for the three virgins *and* the apostles. This would appear to be a later smoothing out of the confusion generated by this imperfect blending. For more on this feature of the earliest traditions, see Stephen J. Shoemaker, 'Gender at the Virgin's Funeral: Men and Women as Witnesses to the Dormition', *Studia Patristica* (forthcoming). The three virgins who remain awake are presumably the same three virgins who lived with Mary (particularly in the Bethlehem traditions: e.g. Wright, 'Departure', (ܠܡܦܩ (Syr.) and 135–6 (Eng.))). These women are occasionally present in the iconography, along with the apostles.

[37] Cf. Luke 1: 38.

[38] Again, her οἰκονομία.

[39] John of Thessalonica's homily reads λευκότητος τοῦ ἡλίου ἑπταπλασίως: 'seven times whiter than the sun' (Jugie, *Homélies mariales byzantine (II)*, 395–6), which is the basis of Wenger's translation. The *Liber Requiei* reads, 'and a whiteness seven cubits [measures?; i.e. "sevenfold"]': መዐልፀ፡ ሰብአ፡ ሰብዐት፡ (Arras, *De Transitu*, i. 40 (Eth.)).

36. And the Saviour said to Peter, 'Guard Mary's body, my dwelling place, diligently. Go out from the left side of the city, and you will find a new tomb. Place the body in it, and remain there until I speak to you.' When the Saviour had said these things, Mary's body cried out, saying, 'Remember me, king of glory; remember that I am your creation; remember that I guarded the treasure that was entrusted to me.' Then the Lord said to the body, 'I will not abandon you, my pearl, the inviolate treasure: by no means will I abandon the treasury that was sealed until it was sought.' And when he had said these things, the Saviour suddenly ascended.

37. Peter, John, and the others were vigilant,[40] and the three virgins attended to Mary's body and placed it on a bier. After that, they woke up the apostles.[41] Then Peter took the palm-staff and said to John, 'You are a virgin, John, and you must sing hymns before the bier while holding this.' John said to him, 'You are our father and bishop; you must be before the bier until we bring it to the place [of burial].' And Peter said to him, 'So that none of us will grieve, let us crown the bier with it.' And the apostles got up and carried Mary's bier. And Peter said the hymn, 'Israel went out of Egypt, hallelujah.'[42]

38. And the Saviour and the angels were in the clouds, invisibly singing hymns before the bier at a distance. One heard only the sound of a great crowd, such that all Jerusalem came out. And when the high priests heard the clamour and the sound of the hymns, they were disturbed and said, 'What is this clamour?' And someone told them, 'Mary has gone forth from the body, and the apostles are gathered around her, singing hymns.' And immediately Satan entered into them,[43] saying, 'Let us get up and go out, and kill them and burn the body that bore that deceiver.' And they got up immediately and went out with weapons and shields[44] to kill them.

39. And immediately the invisible angels struck them with blindness, and they smashed their heads into the walls, since they could not see where they were going—except for only one among them,[45] who

---

[40] Or possibly, 'were awake' (ἐγρηγόρησαν)?

[41] διύπνησεν τοὺς ἀποστόλους. See n. 36 above. Wenger suggests that we read instead διύπνησεν τοὺς ἄλλους (*L'Assomption*, 232–3 n. 3 and critical apparatus; 47–8). This would bring the text roughly into agreement with John of Thessalonica and the *Liber Requiei*. But I suggest that this may be another seam, signalling an incompletely harmonized tradition in which the apostles were asleep during the events of the Dormition.

[42] Ps. 113: 1 (LXX).

[43] Cf. John 13: 27.

[44] Cf. Matt. 26: 47, 55 and par.

[45] Wenger suggests (*L'Assomption*, 48), based on comparison with John of Thessalonica's homily, that the word ἀρχιερέως has fallen out here, a

took the road that went out [from the city], in order to see what was happening. When he approached the apostles, he saw them carrying the crowned bier and singing hymns. And he was enraged and said, 'Behold, the dwelling place of the despoiler of our people: what glory she receives today!' And in his rage he came upon the bier, wanting to overturn it, and he took hold of it where the palm-staff was. And instantly his hands clung to the bier, cut off from his arms. And they remained hanging from the bier.

40. Then the man cried out and begged the apostles, saying, 'Do not abandon me in such great pain. O Peter, remember my father, when the doorkeeper, the maidservant, questioned you and said to you, "You are one of this man's disciples",[46] and how and in what manner I questioned you.' Then Peter said, 'I do not have the power to help you, nor does anyone here. Therefore, believe that Jesus is the Son of God, the one against whom you rose up, whom you imprisoned and killed, and it will put an end to this lesson at once.'

41. Jephonias answered and said, 'It is not that we did not believe: yes, truly we know that he is the Son of God. But what are we to do, since avarice darkens our eyes? For our fathers, when they were about to die, summoned us and said, "Behold children, God has chosen you from all the tribes to build up this people and to take tithes and first-fruits. But take care, children, lest the place be increased by you, and you go into business for yourselves; do not anger God, but give your surplus to the poor and orphans." But we did not listen, and when we saw that that place was extremely abundant, we set up[47] tables in the temple for buying and selling. And when the Son of God came into the sanctuary, he threw them all out, saying, "Do not make my Father's house a house of commerce."[48] But considering only the practices that he had abolished, we plotted evil among ourselves and killed him, knowing that he is the Son of God. But forgive our ignorance and pardon me: for this has come upon me, I who am loved by God, in order that I might live.'

42. Then Peter had the bier set down and said, 'If now you believe

---

reconstruction supported later in the text (section 42), where this character is explicitly identified as the high priest.

[46] Cf. Matt. 26: 69 and par.

[47] Here the text reads ἐπελαθόμεθα, 'we forgot'. I have followed Wenger's suggested emendation (*L'Assomption*, 237 n. 2) ἐθέμεθα, which he has taken from John of Thessalonica's homily. John's text is paralleled almost exactly at this point in the *Liber Requiei*, indicating that this is probably the earlier reading: በከ፡ረ፡ ከሎ፡ ዓባግዕ፡ ወአልሕም፡ ት፡ ወዘእንገሰ፡ አንበርነ፡ ማዕደ፡ ለእለ፡ ይሰይጡ፡ ወይሳየጡ፡ 'We put the firstborn of all the sheep and cattle on the table for those who buy and sell.'

[48] John 2: 16.

with your whole heart, go and kiss Mary's body, saying, "I believe, O virgin Theotokos, pure mother, in the one who was born from you, our Lord and God." Then, raising his voice, the high priest spoke in the Hebrew language, and while weeping, he blessed Mary for three hours. And he did not allow anyone to touch the bier, while he brought forth testimonies from the holy scriptures and the books of Moses that it was written about her that she will be called the temple of God and the gate of heaven, such that the apostles heard great and wonderful things from him.[49]

43. And Peter said to him, 'Go and join your hands together.' And Jephonias ran and said eagerly, 'In the name of the Lord Jesus Christ, the Son of God and of Mary the pure dove, the one hidden in his goodness, let my hands be joined together without defect.' And immediately they became as they were before. And Peter said to him, 'Rise up and take [a branch][50] from the palm-staff, which I will give you, and when you enter the city, you will find a great crowd that cannot find their way out. Tell them what happened to you, and for whomever believes, place this branch on that one's eyes, and immediately that person will see again.'

44. And when Jephonias went back, just as Peter had commanded him, he found a great crowd weeping and saying, 'Woe to us, because what happened to the Sodomites has also happened to us. For first he struck them with blindness, and then a fire fell and consumed them. Woe to us, for behold, we have been blinded: next, the fire will come.'[51] Then Jephonias took the branch and spoke to them about the faith, and whoever believed saw again.

45. The apostles brought Mary to the tomb, and after they placed her inside, they sat down to wait for the Lord together, as he had commanded them. And Paul said to Peter, 'Father Peter, you know that I am a neophyte, and that this is the beginning of my faith in Christ Jesus. For I did not gain possession of the teacher,[52] so that he could tell

---

[49] Wenger considers this passage 'corrupt', and suggests that, based on comparison with John of Thessalonica, the word θαυμάζειν must have fallen out, leading him to translate: 'en sorte que les apôtres étaient dans l'admiration des grandeurs et des merveilles qu'il disait' (*L'Assomption*, 236–7 n. 6) Nevertheless, above I have translated the Greek as it stands in the MS, which does not seem corrupt to me.

[50] Other early narratives, including the *Liber Requiei* 76 (Arras, *De Transitu*, i. 45 (Eth.)), John of Thessalonica's homilies (Jugie, *Homélies mariales byzantine (II)*, 401), and the early Syriac fragments (Wright, *Contributions*, 15), among others, support the insertion of this word (θαλλεῖον) here.

[51] Cf. Gen. 19: 11, 24.

[52] This somewhat strange expression, κατέλαβον τὸν διδάσκαλον, which troubled Wenger (*L'Assomption*, 239, n. 2), is similar in the *Liber Requiei*:

me the precious mysteries. But I have heard that he revealed everything to you on the Mount of Olives. Therefore I implore you to reveal them to me.' Then Peter said to Paul, 'It is clear that we rejoice greatly that you have come to the faith of Christ, but we cannot reveal these mysteries to you: you are not able to hear them.[53] But wait, for behold, we will remain here for three days, just as the Lord told us. For he will come with his angels to take up Mary's body, and if he orders us, then we will gladly reveal these things to you.'

46. And while they were seated at the doors of the tomb, debating with each other about doctrine, faith, and many other things, behold, the Lord Jesus Christ came from the heavens, and Michael and Gabriel with him. He sat in the midst of the apostles and said to Paul, 'Paul, my beloved, do not be distressed that my apostles have not revealed the glorious mysteries to you. For I revealed them to them on earth: I will teach them to you in the heavens.'

47. Then he nodded to Michael, [and Michael spoke][54] in a truly angelic voice, and the clouds descended to him. And the number of angels on each cloud was a thousand angels, and they uttered praises[55] before the Saviour. And the Lord told Michael to take the body of Mary up onto the cloud and to set it down in Paradise. And when the body was taken up, the Lord told the apostles to come closer to it. And when they came onto the cloud, they were singing with the voice of angels, and the Lord commanded the clouds to depart for the East, to the regions of Paradise.

48. And when they came to Paradise, they placed the body of Mary under the tree of life. And Michael brought her holy soul, and they placed it in her body. And the Lord returned the apostles to their places for the conversion and salvation of humankind. For to him are due glory, honour, and power, unto the ages of ages. Amen.

አረቀብዎ፡ ለሊቱን፡ 'I did not gain possession our master.' (Arras, *De Transitu*, i. 46 (Eth.)).

[53] Reading, as Wenger suggests (*L'Assomption*, 239 n. 3), χωρεῖς for χωρὶς.

[54] Wenger has restored this text from the earliest Syriac fragments (ܪܠܐܘ ܠܪܟܝܡ; Wright, *Contributions*, ܠܝ), with which the *Liber Requiei* is in agreement (ወአውሥአ፡ ሚካኤል፡, Arras, *De Transitu*, i. 53 (Eth.)).

[55] Although this is not a usual meaning of παραινέω, its use here is clearly similar to that of its root αἰνέω and other derived forms, as the Syriac fragments of this passage indicate: ܡܫܒܚܝܢ ܗܘܘ (Wright, *Contributions*, ܠܝ).

Fifth-Century Syriac Palimpsest Fragments of the Six Books

[S. P. f. 151a][1] . . . born in Jerusalem. And James, the first bishop of Jerusalem made me a deacon, he who was the first bishop of Jerusalem while the apostles were alive. I have written . . . this volume with my own hand in the month of Haziran, in the year 336 . . . on the third day of the week at the middle of the day, concerning the Jewish man who was an authority.[2] And he struck the bishop James, and he died, because the Jews hated the bishop James very much, since he was called the brother of our Lord.' And the bishop and his clergy asked . . . blessed, and not . . . they found . . . the volume [of] the end which was written in the handwriting of the bishop: 'I, James the bishop, write thus, that in the year 345 my master Mary[3] went forth from this world. And I, James, bear witness that the apostles who were still living came, and those who were buried arose and came, and creatures above with those below, to greet the Blessed One, and then she went forth from this world. And six books were written about her (two of the apostles wrote each book) and all the signs and wonders and glories from heaven and from the earth which happened before her. And the creation gave thanks to the Lord and the glory[4] of his mother who bore him with the adoration of the earthly beings and with the blowing of the seraphim's trumpets. And I, James, have written with my own handwriting in this volume, and these books that were written, John the younger, who is

---

[1] The fragments in this appendix were published in Agnes Smith Lewis, ed., *Apocrypha Syriaca*, Studia Sinaitica, XI (London: C. J. Clay & Sons, 1902), ܡܘ‎; date, p. iii. The folio numbers appear in brackets in the text.

[2] Reading ܟܐܡܐ‎ from Smith Lewis, *Apocrypha Syriaca*, ܠܒ‎ (hereafter SL). S. P. 151 reads ܟܬܡܘ‎, which would translate 'fuller'.

[3] Although the form here is feminine (ܡܪܬܝ‎), 'mistress' and 'lady' both have connotations in English that make them problematic for translation here. Although 'master' is often used as a gendered term in English, it is here employed in a neuter sense. In other words, while 'master' most appropriately expresses in English the meaning of the Syriac word used here, it should not be taken as suggesting the use of masculine forms in reference to the Virgin in the ancient text. This principle has been applied throughout the translation.

[4] ܐܝܩܪ ܐܠܗ‎? SL: ܐܝܩܪ ܐܡܗܘ‎ܬ: 'who returned to the mother'.

very blessed, carried [them. And the] [S. P. f. 151b] hand[writing of all the apostles][5] is in these books that they wrote. And they celebrated my master Mary at the time when there were memorials and offerings for her, three times in the year. And Paul and Peter and John the young, who is very blessed, know where these books about the death of my master Mary are, because they came from Jerusalem with them, and . . .' the bishop and his clergy read this volume, and they wrote a letter to Mount Sinai thus: 'From Cyrus the bishop of Jerusalem and all the clergy to our brothers, the priests and our fathers who are on Mount Sinai, may peace be great. We have received the letter of your charity, and we have made enquiries in all Jerusalem concerning the departure of my master Mary, and we have not found it. But we have found an autograph of James the bishop, which he has written thus: "These six books that were written when my master Mary died, John the young carried them, and he came . . . we [have made known][6] to your holiness, the fathers, that there are letters to Rome, to the hands of . . . holy Peter and Paul, [when][7] these holy books were found. And also write letters to Ephesus where my lord John was, who is very blessed; perhaps the book of the Theotokos has been found there. And if your holiness should find the book, let us know in a letter . . .

[S. P. f. 156a] '. . . an offering to the Lord. Let [Nisan?] come . . . carry-ing . . . bearing . . . bearing . . . Let Haziran come . . . Let Tamuz come, bearing thanks because of human beings, who sing . . . full of joy. Let Ab come, giving worship, which I[8] have blessed and given it the unripe fruit and the ripe. Let Ilul come, glorifying him and giving thanks to Christ, who brought and gave all the believers to the Father in humanity. Let Teshrin come, thanking and praising the one who heard the voice of the husbandman, who has sown with the plough of the cross. Let Teshrin come and its good things with it, [in] which dew comes and rejoicing from heaven to the earth and its inhabitants.[9] Let Kanun come, and its joys with it, dark clouds and lightning and thunder, which pour forth upon . . . creation. Let Kanun come and with it the snow and ice, which gladden the earth. Let Shebat come, bearing on its shoulders good things which give birth to joys. Let Adar come,

---

[5] Text in brackets supplied from SL.

[6] Text in brackets supplied from SL.

[7] Text in brackets supplied from SL.

[8] S. P. 156a: ܚܘܣܝܐ ܚܕܬܐ; but Wright, 'Departure', 108–60 (hereafter W): ܘܚܣܐ ܕܛܒ ܐܠܗܐ.

[9] S. P. 156a: ܡܢ ܐܠ [.] ܘܣܐ ܐܕܗ ܐܕܪܝܢ; SL: ܐܕܗ ܐܕܗ ܕܗ ܘܒܢܝܐ ܘܥܡܪܗ ܐܝܟ ܡܢ ܕܒܪܟ ܥܡ; W: ܘܥܡܪܗ ܡܢܗܘ ܘܒܢܝܐ ܡܢ ܫܡܝܐ ܐܠܗܐ. ܘܒܢܝܐ ܐܝܟ

bringing offerings to the Lord, choice[10] lambs and sheep, giving thanks.'

Thus the apostles prayed and said, 'O Lord God, who sent his son to us, in order to save[11] the world from its youth, let your blessing be upon the earth and its inhabitants, when an offering is made to my master Mary, who gave birth to you. And let your grace be [upon us][12] [S. P. f. 156b] at this time.'

Then the voice of the prayers of the apostles ascended into heaven, and our Lord Jesus Christ came to them on a luminous cloud, and he spoke with them and said to them, 'Be strong, have courage, and be valiant; do not be afraid and do not tremble, because everything that you have asked will be heard. And at all times your wishes will be unto your Father who is in heaven.' Then the apostles bowed their heads, and they were blessed by our Lord. And the apostles arose from the place where they were praying, and they said, 'Come, let us go down from the Mount of Olives to the cave of the valley. And there let us write how my master Mary was snatched away on a luminous cloud, and our Lord Jesus carried her to the Paradise of Eden.'

And the apostles went down from the Mount of Olives to the cave of the valley, and they prayed and burned incense. And they commanded that they should write in this book thus: 'We all, the apostles, witness before our Lord Jesus Christ and before the Holy Spirit that our Lord Jesus Christ did these wonders, these miracles, and these signs before the one who bore him, my master Mary, when she went forth from this world. And all those of the faithful who believe in the words that are written in this book will live; and whoever does not believe will be judged. And this is the woman who was chosen from us from before the foundation of the world . . .

[S. P. f. 160a] . . . who/that he/we will sleep . . . the day of resurrection, and they gave . . . the holy departed . . . and they heard . . . and they were made to rest . . . for their bodies ... of the exalted heights . . . their spirits,[13] with the prayers of the prophets and the apostles, and of the martyrs and confessors, and of the righteous and the priests, and everyone who believes in the Father and in the Son and in the Holy Spirit and in my master Mary, the Theotokos. And in the church . . . of Christ . . . of the just. May we receive a blessing from God and from Jesus Christ, who was born from the holy Virgin. Whoever makes a commemoration for my master Mary, the mother of our Lord, may his commemoration be in heaven and on earth. And every assembly that hears these holy

---

[10] Reading ܪܚܬ from SL; S. P. 156a reads: ܪܚܟܘ.
[11] S. P. 156a: ܡܘܫܐ; W: ,ܡܘܫܐ.
[12] Words supplied from comparison with SL and W.
[13] Or, 'their deliverance, relief': ܚܘܢܕܘܐܬ.

words, the Lord will have compassion and . . . to the ages of ages, Amen.

[Book Five][14]

And when the Blessed One had been placed in the Paradise of Eden and crowned with this great glory, and the apostles had departed for every region, our Lord Jesus Christ came to her from heaven to Paradise. And the chariot of spiritual beings descended from heaven . . . who have no end. And all the Paradise of Eden was covered, and all the mountains that were surrounding it. And nothing was heard there except the cherubim crying out and the angels who were shining . . . [S. P. f. 160b] of light that had no end. Because the Paradise of Eden is on the earth, at the outer edge . . . its great mountain. And its foundations are placed on the earth, and four rivers go forth from it: Gihon, Pishon, Daklat, and Euphrates.[15] And when there was a flood, it went up to the lower parts of the mountain, and at once it was covered by a sign. For the flood did not dare to dishonour that sacred mountain. For the Lord of Paradise has fixed his glory on the Paradise of Eden, and he was standing in it and beheld the flood that was scourging those on the earth and the human beings who were on the earth. And when the flood approached the outer edge of the Paradise of Eden, it bowed its head and worshipped the Lord of creation, who was standing in Paradise and turned it behind him. For this Paradise is a meeting place of the exalted beings and a dwelling place of the heavenly beings . . . was before the times of the world to be . . . a dwelling place for Adam, the head of the race . . . God [came down] and walked among the delightful trees in Paradise. And to this Paradise came the body of this holy Virgin, the bearer of our Lord. . . . And when our Lord Jesus Christ came to my master Mary . . . and he said to her, 'Mary, arise, and . . . from humanity there is not in heaven . . .

[S. P. f. 155a] . . . [the Virgin saw][16] the servants of the Lord preaching about him, the house of the rain and dew and heat [?], the house of winds and lightning, the house of breezes and darkness. And she saw there wrath and peace, which, when ordered, go forth to creation. And she saw the place where Elijah the prophet stood and prayed, because it is in this outer heaven. And my master Mary saw [these things] in these outer heavens. And she was snatched up and ascended to the heaven of heavens. And she saw the creation of spiritual beings[17] who had no

[14] Not in S. P. 106a; supplied from SL and W. There is, however, a break in the text in S. P. 106a.

[15] Cf. Gen. 2: 10–14.

[16] In the other narratives this is a list of things that the Virgin saw in the heavens, after leaving Paradise with her son.

[17] S. P. 155a: ܪ̈ܘܚܢܐ ܕܒ̈ܪܝܬܐ. SL: ܪ̈ܘܚܢܐ ܣܕ̈ܪܐ, 'ranks of spiritual beings' seems to make more sense.

number, a rank with a host of seraphim with horns, which [there was] no limit, but . . . he did not know their number. But the powers of the Lord approached and worshipped my master Mary. Above them he sat in the chariot. And they stood glorifying the Blessed Virgin. Who will see and not be afraid, when the exalted beings are standing, glorifying and exalting the daughter of earth, his mother, whom he took to the heights? And she ascended unto him, while the exalted beings were saying, 'Holy, holy, holy, Son of God, to whom this holy Blessed One gave birth without intercourse!' And my master Mary stretched forth her hand, and she gave praise to the Lord who had exalted the holy mother who gave him birth, and she ascended above the heaven of heavens and saw there ranks of angels standing above the waters. And they were spreading their wings, and their eyes were looking upward, because they were not able to behold . . . the glory. They did [this] without ceasing. [S. P. f. 155b] Behold, thus she saw above the angels. And she ascended and saw the heavenly Jerusalem, in which the Father is worshipped by his Son and the Spirit. And she saw that it had twelve gates. And the twelve gates were in the name of the twelve apostles. And an apostle was standing on every gate . . . with angels and archangels standing and giving praises. But the two sons of Zebedee were at the inner gates: John the younger and his brother James at another gate on the right. And then the apostles were coming[18] on the gates. And on the outer gate of Jerusalem were standing spiritual beings without end and without number, who were giving praises to the city of the great King. And all the prophets were standing with their harps; and Abraham and Isaac and Jacob and David the psalmist. And they worshipped Christ the King and his mother. When she entered to worship in the heavenly Jerusalem, she entered by the first gate, and she was worshipped by the angels . . . and the powers. She entered the second gate, and the worship of the cherubim of the Lord was offered to her. She entered the third gate, and the prayer of the seraphim . . . She entered the fourth gate, and she was worshipped by the family of arch[angels].[19] She entered the fifth gate, and the thunder and lightning sang praises before her. She entered the sixth gate, and they cried out before her, 'Holy, holy, holy!' She entered the seventh gate, and fire worshipped her. . . .

---

[18] S. P. 155b: ܦܕܗܪ. SL: ܚܬܐܣ, 'arranged' seems to make better sense.
[19] S. P. 155b: ܪܒܬܐ. W: ܕܐܘܠܐ ܕܬܐ; SL: ܕܐܠܚ ܕܬܐ.

The Ethiopic Six Books

[23] On the 16th of the Month of Nahase, the Departure of Mary[1]

Christ my God and my hope, and Mary my master,[2] intercede for me through this narrative of the holy and pure Mary, the mother of Christ our God, and her departure from this world into heaven.

And on the third day, at midday, Mary went forth from her house and went to pray at her son's tomb, because thus she used to go every day to the tomb of Golgotha to pray there. But after the death of Christ, the Jews placed a great stone at the mouth of the tomb, and they sealed it with a seal.[3] And they placed guards and ordered them not to allow anyone to pray there, and if anyone should come to pray, they should stone and kill that person. And then the Jews took the cross of Christ, the two crosses on which the thieves were crucified, the spear with which they pierced his side, the clothes that he was wearing, the crown of thorns with which they crowned him, and the nails with which they nailed him to the cross. And they took them and hid them together in the earth; for they feared lest someone should come and ask them concerning everything that happened to Christ, and because of this they hid them in the earth.

And the Jews saw Mary going to the tomb every day to pray. And she bowed down and remained for a long time, saying, 'My Lord and my God, send someone who will take me from this wicked world, for I am very afraid of the Jews, your enemies and mine. When they came to me long ago, I expelled them and sent them away; and by the word that came forth from my mouth, their eyes were blinded and their hearts

---

[1] Translation made from the edition by Marius Chaine, ed., *Apocrypha de Beata Maria Virgine*, CSCO 39 (Rome: Karolus de Luigi, 1909), 21–49. The numbers in brackets refer to the page numbers in Chaine's edition.

[2] Although the form here is feminine (**አእግዚእትነ**), 'mistress' and 'lady' both have connotations in English that make them problematic for translation here. Although 'master' is often used as a gendered term in English, it is here employed in a neuter sense. In other words, while 'master' most appropriately expresses in English the meaning of the Ethiopic word used here, it should not be taken as suggesting the use of masculine forms in reference to the Virgin in the ancient text. This principle has been applied throughout the translation.

[3] Cf. Matt. 27: 66.

were darkened by the power of my God who was born from me according to his will. For they were not able to work evil against me, and they
made me drink the water of trial.[4] And when they saw me coming and
praying at the tomb, they rebuked me and raised themselves against
me.' Then the guards went to the priests and said to them, 'No one has
come to pray at the tomb of Golgotha, except only Mary, and she comes
to pray for the whole day, from dawn until dusk.' [24] And the priests
answered and said to the guards, 'When she comes again, stone her.'
And the guards said to the priests, 'We will not stone her! But when she
comes to the tomb, we will tell you: do to her what you will.' And the
priests said to the guards, 'Stone her severely, for she deserves great
punishment, because she has she has put the children of Israel to
shame.'

And on Friday Mary came to pray at the tomb of Golgotha, and as she
prayed, she raised her eyes to heaven with the fragrant perfume of fine
incense. And then the angel Gabriel came to Mary, and he venerated
her and said to her, 'Hail, you who are blessed among women, the Lord
is with you,[5] Theotokos. Behold, your prayer has reached and been
received by our Lord Jesus Christ. Therefore, you will go forth from
this world and enter into life eternal. Amen. For because of this I have
been sent to you: to tell you and inform you that in the hour that you
prayed on earth, your prayer was heard in heaven. And everything that
you have sought from Christ, who sits to the right of the Father, he will
grant to your petition, and he will fulfil your wish for you in heaven and
on earth, so that his name will be blessed forever, Amen.' And the
guards came again to the priests, and they told them that Mary had
come and prayed at the tomb, and then she returned and departed for
her house. And behold, there was a great tumult in Jerusalem concerning Mary. And the priests went to the governor, and they said to him,
'Send notice to Mary that she may not go to the tomb of Golgotha and
may not pray there.'

And while they were concerned over this matter, behold, a message
came from Abgar, the king of Edessa, to the emperor Tiberius.[6] 'Know
that an apostle from the seventy-two disciples[7] built a church in the city
of Edessa. He healed me from the illness that had settled upon me, and
he told me the miracles that Christ had worked, and then his love

---

[4] Cf. *Protev.* 16 (Konstantin Tischendorf, ed., *Evangelia Apocrypha*, 2nd
edn. (Leipzig: 1876; repr. Hildesheim: Georg Olms, 1966), 30–1).

[5] Luke 1: 28.

[6] Compare the events of this paragraph to the account in the *Doctrina Addai*
(George Howard, trans., *The Teaching of Addai*, Society of Biblical Literature
Texts and Translations, 16, Early Christian Literature Series, 4 (Chico, CA:
Scholars Press, 1981), ۰ (Syr.) and 13 (Eng.)).

[7] Cf. Luke 10: 1, 7.

entered into my heart. And I desired to see him and that he be with me in my city. And when I heard that the Jews had seized him and crucified him, I was very sad. Therefore I arose and mounted my horses, and I came to the [25] Euphrates, in order to go to Jerusalem and make war, so as to destroy it and kill those who were living in it, because they had killed Christ. But while I was going along the way, I thought in my heart and said, "If I have crossed over the Euphrates, which does not belong to me, Tiberius will think in his heart to arise, and there will be an army and a battle between us." For this reason, I turned around and came back to my own territory. Now then I want you to punish the Jews, who crucified Christ, who was innocent. If I had known ahead of time that they were going to crucify Christ, I would have come to you, so that they would not crucify him.' Thus wrote Abgar the king of Edessa to Tiberius. And when the emperor Tiberius read the letter, he trembled and was astonished and was very afraid. And he wanted to kill the Jews.

And when the people of Jerusalem heard, fear gripped them. And then they went to the governor and said to him, 'All of this happened because of Mary, and because of the one who was born from her, the temple was destroyed. Now send notice to Mary that she may not go to the tomb of Golgotha and may not pray there.' The governor answered and said to them, 'Go, tell her yourselves as you wish.' And then the priests went to Mary and said to her, 'Behold, from now on, take care neither to come again nor to pray at the tomb of Golgotha. O Mary, we have said to you: remember the sin that you have committed before God. And if you wish to pray, pray with the people and observe the laws of Moses, so that the sins that you have committed will be forgiven. And on the Sabbath, go with the people to the synagogue. And the priests will place the Book of the Law on your head, so that your sin will be forgiven. And if you do this, we will not reject you, nor will we despise you. And if you are ill, we will cry out with the sound of the horn, and at the proper time, you will be cured, and we will ask God to have mercy on you and pardon you. And if you do not heed our words, leave Jerusalem and go to Bethlehem, because we will not allow you to pray again at the tomb of Golgotha.' And Mary answered and said to them, 'It is not fitting for you to speak these words with me: I will not accept your commands, nor will I hear your voice, and I will not follow your perverse way.' And then the Jews went away from Mary with great wrath and indignation, and they went to [26] their homes, for the sun had set. And on the following day, they came to Mary and said to her, 'O Mary, behold, we have already spoken with you, but you have not accepted our commands, nor have you heard our voice, and you have had disdain for our words.' And Mary was silent, and she did not answer them anything. Then Mary became ill, and she called all the women of her neighbourhood, and she said to them, 'Peace be with you.

Behold, I want to go to Bethlehem, to live in my house there, because the Jews have prevented me from praying at the tomb of Golgotha. If there are any who wish to come with me, do not delay in coming, because the Lord God is with me, my God who is in heaven, and everything that I ask of the Lord, he will grant me, and he will do my bidding.'

And Mary's heart rejoiced again on account of the message that the angel Gabriel revealed to her while she was praying at the tomb, saying, 'O you who are blessed among women, behold, you will go forth from this transitory world and enter into life eternal, which has no end nor consummation, because your prayer and petition have been heard in the ears of the Lord God Sabaoth.' And then the three virgins who were ministering to her came to her and said, 'Do not be sad, our master! Behold, we will come with you, so that we will find mercy and clemency before God, who was born from you; for we have abandoned family and everything that we had for your sake. We have chosen you and we have come to you, so that we will live and die with you.' The virgins spoke thus to Mary, and they joined themselves to Mary, ministering to her day and night. And they asked her to tell them how the Lord Jesus Christ, the Son of living God, was born from her without marriage to a man. And Mary, the mother of light, loved the virgins very much, and she told them everything that they wanted to be taught by her. And they accepted her service, and they did her will. And they washed her feet and made her clothes fragrant with incense. And Mary was blessed by them, because they saw the miracles and wonders that Mary performed before them day and night. And this is the first miracle that the virgins saw. Like waves of the sea, the smell of fragrant incense filled the house where Mary was, and all the sick and afflicted who had come [27] to her. And they received a blessing from her and venerated her, and they recovered from their illness. And the virgins were amazed when they saw that a great glory was upon her. And then many men and women came to Mary, and they prostrated themselves before her, saying, 'Have mercy on us and forgive us, and do not cast us away, O master.'

And the blessed one, having extended her arms, blessed them and said, 'May the Lord receive your prayer and your petition before the Lord Jesus Christ. And moreover, may he bless these virgins who have come with me in order to minister to me, because of all the people of Israel, there is no one who has followed me except for them.' And then the angel of the Lord Gabriel appeared to the blessed Mary and said to her, 'Be strong and do not fear,[8] O Theotokos! Arise and go to Bethlehem, and remain there until you see armies of angels, the

---

[8] Cf. Luke 1: 30.

apostles, and every creature coming to you to pray to you and proclaim you blessed.' And when the virgins saw the angel of the Lord speaking with Mary, they were very afraid.

And then the blessed Mary summoned the virgin women and said to them, 'Bring incense and clothing so that I may make an offering to God.' And the virgins were the children of the elders of Jerusalem, and their names were as follows. The first was Anna, and its interpretation is the church, the assembly of the people, which is the heavenly Jerusalem. And the second is Absa, and its interpretation is Christ the Son of the Living God, who sits at the right hand of the Father. And the name of the third is Saga, and its interpretation is the Holy Spirit, who gives eternal life to all those who believe in the heavenly Christ. And on the morning of the fifth day, Mary went forth with the virgins, and they went to Bethlehem, and they dwelt there that night. And on Friday at dawn, Mary became ill, and then she said to the virgins, 'Bring me a censer, because I want to make an offering to God, our Lord Jesus Christ, who is in heaven.' And they brought her one, and she placed incense in the censer and prayed thus, saying, 'My Lord and my God, Jesus Christ, who dwells in heaven, hear my prayer and my petition, [28] and send to me John the lesser, because I want to see him and to rejoice with him. And also send to me all the apostles, his brothers, and I trust in your grace, with which you have favoured me, because I believe that you hear me and give me everything that I want from you.'

And when she finished the prayer, the Holy Spirit spoke to John in Ephesus and said to him, 'Behold, the mother of your teacher wants to see you. Go forth at dawn and go to Bethlehem. I will go to your brothers the apostles, and I will gather them from all the regions, and I will revive from their tombs those who have fallen asleep. And I will bring them all together to greet the holy and blessed Mary.' Thus the Holy Spirit spoke to John, and he departed. And on the next day, John arose and began to instruct his followers not to stop ministering in the sanctuary, but to pray at all times. And he also told them what the Holy Spirit said to him concerning Mary. Then he went forth from Ephesus and prostrated himself; and he prayed and he said, 'My Lord and my God, Jesus Christ, the Son of God, give me your aid and strength in this journey, which I am about to undertake in order to see your mother before she dies.' And while he was praying, the Holy Spirit suddenly came and snatched him up into a cloud of light, and it brought him to Mary's house.

And it seemed to him that he went on land to Bethlehem, and he opened the door of Mary's house. And he entered to her and bowed down at her feet, and he said, 'Hail, you who are blessed among women, the Theotokos! Do not be sad: behold, you will go forth from this world with joy and happiness, with great honour and glory.' And then the three virgins came to John and were blessed by him. And Mary said to John, 'Put incense in the censer', and he did as she commanded him. And he prayed thus, saying, 'My Lord and my God, perform signs and wonders for your mother, before she goes forth from the world, so that all those who do not believe in you will be ashamed and disgraced, and they will praise your name among those who love your name and believe that you are Christ, the Son of God. Behold, heaven and earth witness that holy Mary is your mother, and you are Christ, the [29] Son of the living God. And all who believe in you will live forever. Amen.'

And when John had finished his prayer, holy Mary said to him, 'Behold, your teacher said to me, "When you want to go forth from the world, I will come to with all the armies of angels."' John answered and said to her, 'Behold, he will come and you will see him, just as he told you.' And the blessed one answered and said to him, 'Behold, the Jews have been plotting among themselves to burn my body when I die.' John said to her, 'Fear not: the Lord is with you, because there is no one who has been given power over you.' And the Blessed one answered and said to him, 'When I die, where will you bury me?' And John said to her, 'Where Christ has ordered me.' At that time the Blessed one wept and flowed tears. And when John saw her crying, he was very sad. And he cried with the virgins and drew near to her. And he said to her, 'If you, the Theotokos, fear death and the departure from this world, how will the just and righteous fare when they depart this world? So do not fear: behold, the Holy Spirit said to me in Ephesus, "Arise and go to the blessed Mary, and [remain with her] until the apostles come and venerate her."' And Mary answered and said to him, 'Put incense in the censer and pray.' And he did as she commanded him. And he prayed, saying, 'My Lord, Jesus Christ, hear my prayer. Receive my petition and receive the petition of your mother. Grant that she see you while still living, as you said with your holy mouth, when you came to her according to your will and the will of your Father, and according to the benevolence of the one who is in the heavens. Just as you descended from heaven and dwelt in her, visit now with the armies of angels, so that your name will be praised in heaven and on earth.' And while John was praying thus, a voice came from heaven and said, 'Amen.'

And while John was marvelling at the word that he heard, the Holy Spirit said to him, 'The voice that you heard is to summon the apostles from everywhere, so that they will greet the holy Virgin Mary.' And then the Holy Spirit went to the apostles and said to them, 'Go to Bethlehem and receive the blessing of Mary.' And behold, Simon Peter was wanting to go into the sanctuary [30] and celebrate the Eucharist. The Holy Spirit came to him and said to him, 'As soon as you have completed the Eucharist, go to Bethlehem, because the time has come for the departure of Mary, the mother of your Lord.' And he also spoke with Paul, in the region whose name is Teryo, which is fifty stadia distant from Rome. And he found the Jews chiding him and blaspheming against him, and they were saying to him, 'We will not hear your words, because you are from the men of Tarsus, and you preach concerning Christ. And behold, we know that you are a poor man.' And while the Jews were chiding him thus, the Holy Spirit said to Paul, 'Behold, the time has come for the departure of your teacher's mother from this world: arise and go to her.' And the Holy Spirit also spoke to Thomas in the region of India, while he was sitting on the bed of the king's daughter, and he said to him, 'The time has arrived for the departure of Mary, the mother of your teacher: go to her quickly.' And then Thomas arose and entered a church. And he put incense in a censer and prayed for her. And the Holy Spirit also spoke to Matthew, and he said to him, 'The time has come for the departure of Mary, the mother of your Lord: go to her quickly.' And thus spoke the Holy Spirit to James in Jerusalem. And to those who were sleeping, Andrew, the brother of Simon Peter, Luke, and Simon the Zealot, the Holy Spirit came and said to them in their tombs, 'Do not think that the resurrection of the dead has come, nor that time has come to an end. Rather, arise today from your tombs and go to Bethlehem to receive the blessing of Mary.' Thus the Holy Spirit spoke to all the apostles.

And they were thinking and saying, 'How can we arrive in Bethlehem quickly?' Then the Holy Spirit came to them and snatched them up into clouds, and the winds blew the clouds from everywhere. And heaven and earth were shining from much lightning, from dawn until midday on the fourth day. And in that hour the apostles came to Bethlehem. And there was a great fear because of their awesome majesty, because they came riding on clouds of light. And their clothes were white as snow and crowns of glory shone on their heads. And the angels brought cloud-chariots, and those riding on them [31] were the apostles. And the Holy Spirit guided the clouds among heaven and earth. And behold, David the son of Jesse came with them, speaking and saying, 'Glory to the Father, the Son, and the Holy Spirit'; thus he sang before them. And then the archangels Michael and Gabriel came, and they stood before the apostles, saying to them, 'Greetings to you, the disciples of the great King, who chose you of his own will.' And the apostles also said to the angels, 'Greetings to you, angels of our Lord Jesus Christ, who guard the holy mysteries.' Then the Holy Spirit spoke to John and said to him, 'Go forth and welcome the apostles; behold, they have come to Bethlehem.' And then John went and welcomed them and bowed down before them. And Peter said to John, 'Has she died, the holy and blessed mother of light, or not?' John answered and said to him, 'No, she has not died.' And then John prayed before them, and a scent of delightful fragrance filled Bethlehem. And then the apostles and angels entered the blessed and holy woman's house together, and they bowed down at her feet and said to her, 'Hail, you who are full of grace and joy! Do not fear or be disturbed, you who are blessed among women, because the one who was born from you will lead you from this world with great joy and glory. And he will lead you to the treasury of light, because you have power over all of them and over all of the just.'

Then Mary arose and sat on her bier, and she said to the disciples, 'Behold, I now know and believe that my Lord will come from heaven. I will see him before I die, just as you have appeared to me. Tell me, who told you that I was sick, and from which region you have come to me, and on what you rode and suddenly arrived here. Behold, I want to glorify God, who has spoken to you about me.' And Peter answered and said to John and the disciples, 'Let each one tell how he came to her.' The disciples responded and said to John, 'Behold, you came first: tell how you came.' And John answered and said, 'While I was in Ephesus, the Holy Spirit came and [32] said to me, "Behold John, the time has come for the departure of your teacher's mother from this world, and she desires to see you." And again the Holy Spirit said to me, "Behold, I will travel around and go to every region, and I will inform the apostles, the living and the dead, and I will tell them about Mary, so that they will go to her in Bethlehem and greet her." Behold, the Holy Spirit suddenly snatched me up into a cloud of light, and in that hour it brought me to Mary's house.' Peter answered and said, 'While I was in Rome, wanting to celebrate the Eucharist of the body of our Lord and Saviour, Jesus Christ, which effects the forgiveness of sins, the Holy Spirit came to me and said to me, "The time has come for the departure of your Lord's mother Mary from this world; go to her in Bethlehem." And then the Holy Spirit snatched me up into a cloud of light, and he brought me here, where I saw all the apostles, riding on clouds and coming towards me.'[9] Paul answered and said, 'While I was arguing with the Jews, the Holy Spirit suddenly snatched me up and brought me to you.' Thomas answered and said, 'While I was in the land of India, behold, the Holy Spirit came and snatched me up and brought me to you.' Mark said, 'While I was standing and praying in Alexandria, the Holy Spirit came to me and said to me, "Behold, the time has come for the departure of your Lord's mother from this world. Arise and go to Bethlehem." And then the Holy Spirit snatched me up and brought me here.' James answered and said, 'While I was burning incense at the tomb of Golgotha, the Holy Spirit came to me and said to me, "The holy and blessed one will go forth from this world." And the Holy Spirit snatched me up and brought me here.' Matthew said, 'While I was on a

---

[9] Chaine suggests the possibility of reading 'toward her' instead.

boat, praising and glorifying God, waves surrounded me from all sides. I wept and prayed, and the Holy Spirit snatched me up into a cloud of light and brought me to you.' Philip said, 'I was dead, and I heard the voice of a messenger, crying out and saying, "Philip, Philip, arise and go forth from the grave." And when I arose, behold, the Holy Spirit snatched me up and brought me to you.' Simon the Zealot said, 'After I was dead, [33] I arose from the tomb. Behold, I saw the hand of an extended arm: it came to me and raised me up from among the dead. And the Holy Spirit snatched me up into a cloud of light and brought me to you.' And Luke said, 'While I was in the grave, I heard the sound of a horn,[10] blown by an angel. And a light came and entered into me in the tomb, and it seemed to me that it was the resurrection of the dead. And behold, the Holy Spirit came and snatched me up and brought me to you.' Andrew answered and said, 'I arose from the dead, because I heard the voice of the Son of God, saying, "Andrew, Andrew, arise and come with the disciples to Bethlehem. Behold, I have come to you with all the tribes of angels, because the time has come for the departure of the holy and blessed Mary with glory and honour. And she will go forth from this world and will be brought to the Father's treasuries of light, and she will remain there until I come to judge the living and the dead."' Bartholomew said, 'While I was asleep in the name of the Lord Jesus Christ and trusting in the wealth of his grace, the Holy Spirit came to me and snatched me up and brought me to you.' Thus the apostles spoke to holy Mary, and each one told her how they came to her.

And when holy Mary heard the words of the apostles, she praised the God of heaven and earth, saying, 'I bow down before you, my Lord and my God. I trust in you; I glorify and magnify you; I praise you in song; I bless you; I declare you holy, you who did not make a mockery of me to the people. And you also put to shame the perverse Jews, who were plotting evil against me, to burn my body in a fire. And now I glorify your name and magnify your power forever, Amen. And I will continuously send praises before you, who sent your disciples to me.' And when Mary finished her prayer, she said to the disciples, 'Put incense in the censer and pray.' And they did as Mary ordered them: they prayed and prostrated themselves on the earth. And behold, the sound of thunder came from heaven, like the sound of wheels that were running side by side. And behold, a fragrant and sweet smell came from heaven. And then the angels and the heavenly host without number descended and covered the house where the holy and blessed Mary was, [34] and they crowned her with their wings, saying, 'Holy, holy, holy, the Lord our God, before whom heaven and earth bow down.' And then there

[10] Cf. 1 Cor 15: 52.

was great fear in Bethlehem, and miracles and wonders were manifest there. And the army of the Lord's host did not cease ascending into heaven and descending to that house. And there came into their midst one like the Son of Man, who spoke in the midst of the chariot of cherubim, and he said, 'Go, enter Mary's house.'

Then the guards went from Bethlehem to Jerusalem and told the elders and priests of all the miracles and wonders that happened for holy Mary's sake. And then, when the guards and the people of Bethlehem entered, they told the people all the signs and miracles that they saw done before the holy one. But they did not believe them until they sent others who had examined what had happened for her sake. And when they came there, behold, they saw the gates of heaven opened and angels of God descending and entering into the house of Mary. And lightning and thunder also went forth from Mary's house and ascended into heaven. Then they saw the disciples ministering to the holy one. And they also saw clouds coming from heaven and drizzling moisture and mist on Bethlehem. And they also beheld stars descending from heaven and bowing down before holy Mary. And they also saw the sun and moon, which were illuminating the whole world, descending from heaven and bowing down before Mary. And they also saw the holy one lying on her bier, with the angel Gabriel standing at her head and Michael at the foot of her bed, and they were fanning the holy one with the fans in their hands. And then they beheld the apostles standing by her bier with fear and trembling, raising their hands to heaven. Peter and John wiped away her tears with their clothes. And they also saw the smoke of incense, going forth as waves of the sea from the foundations of the house, and cohorts of angels without number standing with fear and trembling and giving glory to God, who dwelt in the Virgin Mary's womb. And they spread their wings and bowed down before the holy [35] and blessed Mary, the one who bore Christ, crying out and saying, 'Hail, you who are blessed among women! Blessed is the one who was born from you, our Lord and God, our Saviour, Jesus Christ.' And the heavenly host glorified Mary with song, and the spiritual beings rejoiced, and powers blessed holy Mary. And they were not able to approach her, because of the great light that was shining over her.

And they also saw people who were mute, deaf, blind, afflicted, and in distress coming to the holy one's house, crying out and saying, 'Holy and blessed Mary, have mercy on us and forgive us: heal us with your prayer and petition.' And then they were healed from their illnesses. And women also came to her from every land: from Rome, Egypt, and from all Alexandria. And the daughters of kings and rulers brought gifts and venerated Mary, and they believed in Christ, her son. And they said to her, 'Tell us how our Lord Jesus Christ was born from you without the seed of a man.' And Mary told them everything that happened to her. And when they returned to their lands, she blessed them and gave them a sweet and beautiful fragrance, so that their families would believe that the report concerning holy Mary was accurate. And behold, there came to her two women, whom demons had made ill, and they wailed and said to her, 'Have mercy on us, O holy and pure one, and heal us from our illness.' And the holy one prayed before them and blessed them, and at that moment they recovered from their illness. And a woman from Egypt also came to her, suffering from a great fever. She venerated Mary, and immediately she was cured. Another woman, whose right eye had been blinded by a demon, came to Mary and pleaded with her, saying, 'Have mercy on me, my master.' And she placed her hand on her eye, and she healed her instantly. And there came another woman, who was beset by many demons, and she cried out to Mary with a great voice, saying, 'Have mercy on me, my master.' She extended her hand and prayed, saying, 'I adjure you, in the name of the Lord Jesus Christ, come out of this soul, and do not afflict her again.' And at that moment, the demons went forth from that woman, crying out and saying, 'What do you have against us Mary,[11] the one who bore Christ? Behold, we were scattered into [36] every region by the great power of the one who was born from you, because we were not able to resist him, and he cast us down into the depths of the earth. But just like him, you have banished us with your prayer from this soul.' Then Mary plunged them into the depths of the sea. And behold, there came to Mary Safnon, king of Egypt, whose head had been attacked by a lion, and he cried out and said, 'My master, have mercy on me with your prayer.' And she stretched forth her hand and placed it on his head, and in that instant, he was healed from his illness. And then many people gathered in Jerusalem, and they were sick and afflicted, pleading and saying, 'Where is the blessed Mary?' And they answered and said, 'She is not here; she is dwelling in Bethlehem.' And behold, this crowd of people, which was without number, went [to Bethlehem], and they fell down on their faces while on the way to Bethlehem. They cried out in a great voice, saying, 'Holy Mary, the one who bore Christ, have mercy on us and heal us, and do not put us to shame.' And when she heard their words, she prayed for them and said, 'My Lord Jesus Christ, in your great magnificence, receive my prayer and petition, and heal the souls of the afflicted who have come to you.' And immediately they were all healed, and they were in number 2,008 men, excluding the women and children. And there was great glory in the whole region of Bethlehem.

---

[11] Lit., 'What is in us with you, Mary?' From the context, it is not clear whether the sense of the passage is 'why have you done this?' or 'how have you done this?'

At that time the leaders and elders of Jerusalem went to Bethlehem. And they called together the men who had been healed by Mary, and they asked them and said to them, 'Tell us what Mary did for you.' And they answered and said, 'When Mary prayed for us, a great power came from her, and we were healed from our illnesses.' And when the Jews heard this, their eyes became blind. And their priests were afraid and their leaders astonished, and they said with a great voice, 'Behold, great fear, affliction, and devastation have come upon us because of Mary.' And there were those who said, 'Let us now expel Mary from Bethlehem. Do not allow her to remain among you.' And when evening fell, the Jews came to Mary's house, in order to seize Mary and the disciples. And when they reached Mary's house, they were unable to enter, because at that moment the doors of heaven opened and a great light [37] came forth. Then they returned to the leaders and priests, and they told them what had happened. And they ordered the governor to go forth with 30 soldiers and seize Mary and the disciples. And then the Holy Spirit descended to the apostles and said to them, 'Behold, the governor is coming with 30 soldiers from Jerusalem to seize you, the disciples and Mary. Now, go forth from this place and do not fear. Behold, I will cause you to pass between heaven and earth, and no one will be able to see you, because the power of the Lord is with you.' And then the apostles went forth, carrying Mary's bier. And behold, the Holy Spirit came, and he snatched them up and brought them to Jerusalem.

Then the governor came to Mary's house with his soldiers, and when he went inside, he found no one at all. And the governor became very angry, and he said to the people of Bethlehem, 'Did you not come to the leaders and tell them that the disciples of Jesus were with Mary, with great glory and angels of the God ascending and descending to Mary's house? Now, come to the rulers to tell them what you want.' And they went with them and entered Jerusalem, and they spoke with the rulers, saying, 'When we entered Bethlehem, we found neither Mary nor the disciples, nor anyone.' And the priests said to them, 'Do you not understand that the disciples have made an incantation on your eyes, so that you did not see? Now, as soon as you hear a reliable report of them, seize them and bring them to us.'

And after five days, the people of Jerusalem saw angels of the Lord entering and going forth from Mary's house. And behold, her neighbours gathered. They cried out, saying, 'Holy Mary, Theotokos, we hope in you. Beseech Christ to send us salvation from him.' And on the next day the priests summoned her neighbours and said to them, 'What is this outcry and wailing that we hear among you?' And they answered and said, 'Behold, Mary the Theotokos has returned to her house, and the angels of the Lord are praising her.' Then the priests went to the governor and said to him, 'Behold, there will be great conflict and tumult in Jerusalem because of [38] Mary.' And the governor answered and said to them, 'What then shall we do?' And the people of Jerusalem responded and said to him, 'Let us take fire and wood and burn the house where she dwells.' And the governor answered and said to them, 'Do what you will.' Then the people of Jerusalem took fire and wood, in order to burn the house where Mary was dwelling. And when they came to where Mary was dwelling, they began to close the doors of Mary's house.[12] And then an angel of the Lord descended and struck them in their faces with his wings, and he burned all those who had drawn near to the doors of the house. And a large multitude died there, and there was great fear in Jerusalem. And when the governor saw this miracle, he stretched forth his hands to heaven and said, 'Glory to the Son of God, who was born from the Virgin Mary: I praise him, I glorify him, and I worship him, unto the ages.'

And on the next day, the governor sent word that the priests should assemble all the people of Jerusalem, and he said to them, 'O you evil people who crucified Christ, who descended from heaven for the salvation of the whole world! But I believe in him, because I am neither one of you nor from the people of your nation; rather, the emperor Tiberius has appointed me as governor over you, because of your evil deeds. Behold, from now on, I say to you, no one shall draw near to the house of the blessed and holy Mary.' Then arose a faithful man named Caleb, who believed in Christ, and he spoke to the governor in secret, and he said, 'O governor, make them swear this oath, "by the living God, who brought forth the Israelites from the land of Egypt, and by the holy Law of Moses", so that they will not speak lies, but will instead honestly tell whom they say that Christ, who was born of Mary, is: a prophet, or the Son of God, or a man who was begotten through intercourse; then they will speak the truth. For behold, I know that they are wise, and they will be able to make known the word of the Scriptures.'

And then the governor arose and sat on his exalted throne, and he ordered that all the people of Jerusalem assemble and swear by the oath that Caleb had said. And he said to them, 'O Israelites, I adjure you by the holy Law of Moses to divide yourselves according to those who believe in Christ, who was born from Mary, [39] and those who do not believe in him.' And when they heard this, they divided, each one from

[12] The text is a little peculiar here, but comparison with the early Syriac apocrypha helps to make sense of the narrative: 'And when they came to the house, the doors were closed. And when they laid hands on them to break them down, straightaway an angel dashed his wings in their faces . . .' Wright, 'The Departure', ܡܒ–ܟܐ (Syr.) and 143 (Eng.). See also Agnes Smith Lewis, ed., *Apocrypha Syriaca*, Studia Sinaitica, XI (London: C. J. Clay & Sons, 1902), ܠܘ (Syr.) and 38 (Eng.).

the other, with great fear. The governor answered and said to them, 'Do you believe in Christ, who was born from Mary, or do you not?' And the elders said to the governor, 'We believe in him, that he is the Son of God, the maker of heaven and earth and all that is in them.' But others who did not believe said to the governor, 'We know that Christ's coming has not drawn near.' The lovers of Christ responded and said, 'Did our father Adam not order his son Seth, before he died, saying, "Behold, a sacrifice and an offering are placed in the cave of treasures, gold, incense, and myrrh, which the Magi brought before the Son of Man, who was born in Bethlehem." '[13] The infidels, who did not believe, answered and said, 'Is Christ greater than Abraham, for whom God opened the heavens, and to whom God spoke?' The lovers of Christ answered and said, 'You certainly are infidels who are lacking in knowledge. Nevertheless, we believe with certainty that the one who was born of Mary is the creator of the entire world, and before Abraham was created in the womb, Christ was before every creation.' The infidels said, 'Christ, in whom you believe, is he greater than Isaac, who was a worthy sacrifice to God?'[14] And the lovers of Christ said, 'If Isaac had been sacrificed, then it would be known as an individual sacrifice. But, it was in fact a symbol of the Son, and Christ's crucifixion on a wooden cross was a sacrifice for the entire world, and through him they will draw near to God.' And the infidels who would not believe said, 'Is Christ greater than Jacob, who saw the heavenly ladder, and the angels of God ascending and descending by means of that ladder?'[15] The lovers of Christ said, 'The angels and ladders that Jacob saw in the midst of heaven and earth were prophecies concerning the coming of Christ.' The infidels who would not believe said, 'Is Christ greater than Elijah, who ascended into heaven and in whom God flourished in all his deeds?'[16] The lovers of Christ said, 'Elijah was on a cloud that is below heaven, where the sun and the moon appear. But when Elijah ascended to heaven, no one venerated him, except for [40] his disciple Elisha. When Christ ascended above the heavens, every creature in heaven and on earth venerated him.' The infidels said, 'Is Christ greater than Moses, who submerged Pharaoh and his army in the sea and established the waters like a wall on both sides and saved the Israelites?'[17] The lovers of Christ said, 'Did Christ not rebuke the demons and submerge them in the sea? And he also extended his hands and saved Simon Peter

---

[13] *Testament of Adam* 3. 7 (Stephen Edward Robinson, ed., *The Testament of Adam: An Examination of the Syriac and Greek Traditions*, Society of Biblical Literature Dissertation Series, 52 (Chico, Calif.: Scholars Press, 1982), 64–5).

[14] Cf. Gen. 22: 1–19.

[15] Cf. Gen. 28: 12.

[16] Cf. 2 Kgs. 2: 9–12.

[17] Cf. Exod. 14: 21–25.

from the waters of the sea.[18] For he has power over all creation, on the dry land and in the sea.' And when the governor heard this, he believed in Christ, and he ordered that forty men who did not believe should be whipped with a great whip.

And when it became evening, at the time when the cock crew, the governor went to Mary with two of his children. And behold, another of the governor's children became ill. And when he arrived and knocked on the door of Mary's house, one of the virgins who were serving Mary came to him. And the governor said to her, 'Speak to the holy one on my behalf.' And when the holy one heard him, she ordered that they open the door of her house. And when the governor entered unto her, he wept and said to her, 'Mother of God, peace to you and to Christ who was born from you, and peace to heaven, which bears the throne of his power. Behold, from now on I will worship you, and I believe in Christ, who was born from you; stretch forth your right hand and bless me, O mother of light, and pray for my son, that he recover from his illness, and pray also for the city of Rome. And also pray for me, so that I will depart from this place in peace, and I will go peacefully to see my family.' Then the holy one stretched forth her hands and blessed him, and she said to him, 'Remain here.' And when the governor saw the apostles standing in Mary's presence, he bowed down at their feet and said to them, 'Peace to you, O holy ones of God, whom he chose by his will, so that you would preach his name in all the world.' And then the apostles blessed the governor, and immediately his son became well. And he went to his city, Rome, and he proclaimed all the things that he saw in Mary's presence. And there were disciples of Paul there, and they wrote down all the miracles and wonders that came upon those who were invoking Mary's name.

And when it was dawn, [41] the Holy Spirit spoke to the apostles, 'Take up Mary and bring her forth from Jerusalem and bring her to the path that leads to the place where there are three caves and a bed towards the east; take her up and place her on the bier, and read before her until dawn.' And when it was dawn, they brought Mary forth from Jerusalem. And then many Jews gathered and they said to Tafonya [Jephonias?], 'We know that you are strong and powerful; now then, go and seize Mary's bier and throw it to the ground, and we will burn her body with fire, lest the disciples think that they have conquered us and the people of Jerusalem.' Then Tafonya arose and stretched forth his hands to destroy Mary's bier. And at that moment, an angel of the Lord descended and struck him with a sword of fire and severed both his hands from his shoulders, and [his hands] were hanging on the bier. And then he wept and cried out to the apostles and said to them, 'Have

---

[18] Cf. Matt. 8: 24–32 and par.

pity and mercy on me; and you too, Christ the Son of God, have mercy on me according to your great mercy.' The apostles answered and said to him, 'Pray to Mary, whose bier you wished to destroy.' Then Tafonya said, 'O mother of God, have mercy on me.' And Mary answered and said to Peter, 'Restore to him these severed hands that are hanging on the bier as [they were] before.' And then Peter took both the severed hands and said, 'In the name of our Lord Jesus Christ and in the name of holy Mary, be restored as before', and immediately he was healed. Then Peter took a stick, and he gave it to Tafonya and said to him, 'Go, and from now on make manifest the power of God before all the Jews, and tell them what Mary did for you, because they revile Mary greatly and hate her. And they say, "She has conquered us in her life; let us burn her body with fire." For the infidels are ignorant and do not understand that our Lord Jesus Christ will not abandon his mother's body in this world. Behold then, I tell you, O lovers of Christ: all those who love Mary and celebrate her commemoration and believe in her son will not be friends with the Jews; otherwise they are far from the love of Christ.'

And while the apostles were reading over Mary in [42] the cave, the Holy Spirit spoke to them and said, 'The angel Gabriel was sent to Mary his mother in the sixth month in order to announce the good news to her concerning the one who was born from her for the salvation of the whole world. On the first day Christ was born in Bethlehem from the Virgin Mary; and on the first day the aged and the infants praised and glorified him; and also on the first day he will come again to judge the living and the dead; and on the first day he will come with every power of heaven and earth in order to transfer Mary and to manifest glory on her.'

And on the first day Eve, the mother of the human race, came, and Anna, the mother of Mary, and Elizabeth, the mother of John the Baptist, and they approached Mary and bowed down at her feet and said, 'Blessed be the Lord, who chose you to be the dwelling place of his glory.' And when Peter saw the patriarchs coming to Mary, he said to the women, 'Depart from here.' And then Adam came, and his son Seth, and Noah, and Shem, and they bowed down at the holy one's feet. The other fathers also came: Abraham, Isaac, and Jacob, and David the prophet, and they bowed down before Mary. And then the prophets came with censers in their hands, and they bowed down before Mary. And then the doors of heaven opened, and thence a multitudes of the hosts of angels without number came forth to see Mary's departure from this world. And behold, Enoch and Moses and Elijah came, riding on a chariot of fire, and they stood in the midst of heaven and earth in order to see the descent of our Lord Jesus Christ. And then 12 armies of archangels came, and their number was 12 myriads. Then our Lord

Jesus Christ appeared, seated on a chariot of seraphim and cherubim; he came to Mary while all the creatures were praising and glorifying him. And he said to the holy one, 'O Mary', and she answered and said, 'Here I am, my Lord and my God.' Jesus said to her, 'Behold then the great glory that has been given to me by my Father.' And behold, Mary saw a glorious wonder that no one could describe. And our Lord said to her, 'Now I will lead your body to the garden of Eden, so that it will remain there until the resurrection of the dead, [43] and I will order the angels to minister to you.'

Then the apostles came to Mary and said to her, 'O mother of light, pray for the world from which you are going forth, and for all those who observe your commemoration and offer up sacrifices in your name, and for those who believe in God, who sent his beloved son and dwelt in you.' Then Mary prayed and said, 'Lord God, who dwells in heaven, by your will you sent your son Jesus Christ, and he dwelt in my womb. I beseech and pray you on behalf of all the sons of baptism who observe my commemoration and offer up sacrifices to me: hear, O Lord, their prayers and receive their petitions and put away captivity and sadness from them. And [in] the places where they offer sacrifices to me, preserve their labour from mice and locusts, from crickets and hail, from frost and from grasshoppers. And all the afflicted who invoke my name will recover from their illness, and those who are possessed by a demon and are in pain will be cured in my name. And likewise keep those who travel on the sea in ships and call on my name safe from the surges[19] and waves of the sea and from the violent winds. And also hasten the return of those who have gone to a faraway land and called upon my name. And the fields that bring forth fruit, and [from them] they offer sacrifices in my name, may they [the fields] be blessed. And the harvest of the vine, from which they offer a sacrifice in my name, may it be blessed. And all those who observe my commemoration, may they be blessed unto the age of the age, Amen.'

And then our Lord answered and said to her, 'Everything that you have asked for has been given to you; and I will have pity and mercy on all who have called upon your name, and I will forgive their sins. And everyone who offers up a sacrifice and an offering in your name will send up a fragrant smell into heaven before the throne of the Father and before the throne of the Son Jesus Christ, unto the ages of ages, Amen.' And every creature answered and said, 'Amen.' And then our Lord ordered Peter and said to him, 'Speak to all the heavenly and earthly creatures so that they will sing a musical psalm with joy and gladness.'

---

[19] The text here reads ማዕበር, but it would seem that this is a misprint. I have read instead ማዕበል, 'wave', as seems to be indicated by Chaine's translation: 'undis'.

At that time Mary's soul went forth, and he brought it to the treasuries of the Father. Then John stretched forth his hand and straightened her out and closed her eyes. Peter and Paul [44] straightened her hands and feet, but the clothes that she was wearing did not go forth, for the Holy Spirit clothed her with a great light, which cannot be comprehended.

Then the 12 apostles carried her, and 12 clouds of light carried the apostles and brought them to Paradise. And behold, Eve our mother came before us, and Anna the mother of Mary, and Elizabeth the mother of John the Baptist. And after them came Adam and Seth, Noah and Shem; and after them came Abraham and Isaac and Jacob. And after them came Enoch and Elijah and Moses, and after these, the chariot of our Lord Jesus Christ. And then as the 12 apostles were carrying holy Mary, they brought her into the Paradise of delight and placed her there. Then all the creatures turned around and returned to their dwellings. And the apostles went to Mount Sinai, riding on clouds, and no one was separated from them, and then they prayed, saying, 'We praise you, our Lord Jesus Christ, who gathered us from the ends of the world and made us worthy to receive the blessing of holy Mary your mother before she went forth from this world, just as you told us with your holy mouth and said, "Behold, I have given you power to trample on vipers and scorpions and to sit upon 12 thrones and judge the 12 tribes of Israel who do not believe in you and in Mary your mother."'

And when they had finished the prayer, the apostles said, 'Let us write then everything that we have seen and heard and observed concerning the departure of Mary from this world. The departure of the holy one was in the year 345.[20] And behold, we have established and commanded that there should be a commemoration of the holy and blessed Mary three times every year. And the first day of her commemoration is after the Nativity, because on this day, on which she is commemorated, they will be saved from the locusts that cover the earth, and their seeds will be blessed, and also by her prayers the kings will be saved from murder and there will not be hate among them, nor will human blood be shed upon the earth.' Next the apostles ordered that there be a commemoration of her in the month of Ayar, because through her prayers the birds will not eat the fruit of the earth, nor will the worms, nor the black moths, nor the grasshoppers destroy the fruit of the earth, and there will not be hunger for the people. And then the Holy Spirit said to the apostles, 'I say [45] to you, in the land where God has wished to send punishment of his wrath, the locusts will come upon

---

[20] This is year 345 of the Seleucian or Greek era. An identical date appears in Wright's Syriac version of the 'Six Books', and he identifies this date as equivalent to either 33 or 34 CE: Wright, 'Departure', ܟ (Syr.) and 133 (Eng.).

that place in the blink of an eye.' And therefore the apostles ordered that
they make supplication and pray to God that they be preserved from
destruction. Next the apostles ordered that there be a commemoration
of Mary on the 17th of the month Nahase on account of the harvest and
the fruit of the vine and the trees that bear fruit. And then the apostles
ordered those who want to make offerings to bring flour and wheat at
night and to remain pure and keep vigil in the church until dawn. And
the priests will pray over it, saying, 'O Mother of God, hear the prayers
of those who remember you and your name, and receive this sacrifice,
which they offer to you.' And while the priests pray thus, Mary the
mother of light [will] come and bless this sacrifice and those who faithfully receive this table, unto the ages, Amen.

After the apostles finished this mandate, a voice came to them from
heaven, saying, 'Each one of you, take the written letter of the commemoration of Mary and return to his land.' Then cloud chariots came
to them, and they snatched up each one and brought them to their lands,
and the dead returned to their tombs.

After this, our Lord Jesus Christ came to Mary in Paradise and said
to her, 'Behold then the good things that God has prepared for those
who love him.' Then the holy one raised her eyes and saw the dwelling
place of the saints, beautiful and greatly adorned. And she also saw the
dwelling place of the martyrs and the crowns upon their heads. And
there were trees of beautiful fragrance, and sweet perfume went forth
from them. Then our Lord took the fruit of these trees and gave it to
Mary. And then he said to her, 'Arise so that you will see what is in
Heaven.'

And the holy one ascended, and behold, she saw the water that is
above the third heaven and above the heavenly Jerusalem. And our
Lord commanded the sun to stand at the door of heaven so that its light
would reach into Paradise, whose foundations were on the earth and
whose walls reach to heaven. And four rivers go forth from it: Euphrates,
Tigris, Gihon, and Pishon.[21] For when the flood was [46] upon the
earth, the power of God did not allow it to ascend near to Paradise. And
our Lord Jesus Christ was seated on his chariot of light above the sun.
And behold, Mary saw the treasuries of God: the treasury of hail and
snow; the treasury of dew and mist; the treasury of cold and snow and
rain; the treasury of lightning and thunder. And she also saw the place
where all the good were, and the place where Elijah was standing and
praying in the first heaven. And she also saw in the second heaven angels
extending their wings and their eyes looking upward, and they did not
cease praise with their voices, saying, 'Holy, holy, holy, God Sabaoth.'

And she also saw in the third heaven twelve walls and in them twelve

[21] Cf. Gen. 2: 10–14.

doors with the names of the 12 apostles, and on each door stood one of the apostles with an army of angels and powers who were giving praise. And through the exalted door is the heavenly Jerusalem, and she saw standing there Abraham, Isaac, and Jacob, and David the prophet, bowing down before the great king Jesus Christ. And then she entered to see the heavenly Jerusalem, and when she reached the first door, the angels bowed down before her. And at the second door the seraphim praised her. And at the third [door][22] the cherubim exalted her. And at the fourth door the powers bowed down before her. And at the fifth door thunder and lightning glorified her. And at the sixth door the angels cried out before her, saying, 'Holy, holy, holy, God Sabaoth.' And at the seventh door the fiery lights bowed down before her. And at the eighth door the rains, the dew, and the mist bowed down before her. And at the ninth door Michael and Gabriel bowed down before her. And at the tenth door the lights of the sun and moon and stars glorified her. And at the eleventh door all the apostles bowed down before her and glorified her. And at the twelfth door all the powers of the Lord glorified her. And there she saw the one who was born from her. Thus was Mary's entrance into the heavenly Jerusalem. And at that time she bowed down before God [47] the Father, and then the holy one saw the holy Father and his beloved Son and the Paraclete, the Holy Spirit, while the Father was glorified by the Son, the Son by the Father, and the Holy Spirit by the Father and the Son.

And then Christ showed Mary the hidden mysteries, which no eye has seen, no ear has heard, nor has any human heart thought them, which God has prepared for those who love him and believe in his name. And on the last day he will reveal to them the joy that has no end or completion. And he also showed her the place where Enoch prayed. Then Mary raised her eyes and she saw innumerable dwelling places, and they shone brightly, and the smell of sweetly fragrant incense came forth from there. The sound of the horn's blast was heard in those places, and many men and women were dwelling in them. Then Mary said, 'Tell me, my Lord and my God, who are they who dwell in these dwelling places?' And the Lord answered and said to her, 'They are the just and good; behold, the light shines upon them because of their greatness, and they expect the joy and happiness of the last day.' And she also saw the place of darkness, from which came forth smoke, whose rotten smell and great fiery flames burned in it, and many men and women were standing beside the darkness, crying out and wailing. And Mary answered and said to him, 'Tell me, my Lord, who are they who are

---

[22] The text actually reads 'heaven' here, but I have followed the pattern established in the text by choosing to translate 'door'. Chaine does the same, but does not identify the problem in the text.

standing beside the place of darkness?' And our Lord answered and said, 'This place is Gehenna, and those who stand beside it are the sinners who await the judgement that they deserve. And moreover, all those who refuse to observe my commandments will be cast into this fire.' Then holy Mary heard the voice of the good saying, 'Glory to you, our Lord and God Jesus Christ, who repays much in return for little to those who call on you and have faith in you.' And when she heard the voice of the good, Mary rejoiced. And she also heard the cries of the sinners and the wails of those who were standing near the darkness, saying, 'Have mercy on us and forgive us, Jesus Christ, the Son of the living God, when you come to judge the living and the dead.' And when Mary heard [48] this, she was very sad and said, 'My Lord and my God, have mercy on them and forgive the sinners, and do not neglect the work of your hands when you come to judge them. For I have heard their weeping and lamentation, and I have become sad because of them.' And then our Lord raised up Mary and brought her into the Paradise of delights with all the inhabitants of heaven.

And behold, Mary told John the lesser everything that our Lord Jesus Christ showed her, and she said to him, 'Preserve this narrative, which your teacher revealed to you, until it is revealed at the right time to those who observe my commemoration and call upon my name. For on the last day, sadness will increase among humanity, and there will be murder and fear and famine on account of the many sins and wicked deeds. On that day affliction will be multiplied upon the earth, and the power of heaven will be moved, and the day will be changed, and signs and wonders will appear, and corruption will come upon humanity, and a great illness will come upon them. On that day the only Son, Jesus Christ, will come, and he will find neither faith nor good works.' And our Lord Jesus Christ revealed all this to Mary, and Mary told it to John the lesser.

And then our Lord said to Mary, 'O beatific and blessed one, all those who call upon your name and observe your commemoration will be preserved from affliction.' Mary answered and said to Christ, 'You have spoken truly, my Lord and my God, just as the mouth of your holy Father and your living voice has spoken. For everything that you have promised me upon the earth has been given to me, and everyone who believes in you will live forever and will inherit the heavenly kingdom that you have prepared for those who love you, and also those who believe that you are Christ who was born from me by your will in the last days. Because of love for the first Adam, your creature, may there be glory to your living name, from now unto the ages of ages, Amen and Amen. Let it be so.

Here ends the narrative of holy Mary, through the assistance of the Holy Spirit. Glory to the Father, glory to the Son, glory to the Holy

Spirit, unto the ages of ages, Amen and Amen.

And especially for the one who caused this book to be written, Tanse'a [49] Krestos, on account of love for Mary the mother of light, so that there would be hope for all the faithful who hear it. And now, my master [Mary], grant standing on the right side in the new time, when Christ will rule over the just and he will hear the voice of blessing with the blessed and the good. Protect him with your right hand, now from Satan and later from bitter sadness, and make him recline in the place of Armageddon, Amen, with its scribe and its reader and its hearers, unto the ages of ages, Amen and Amen. Let it be so, let it be so.

APPENDIX E

The Sahidic Coptic *Homily on the Dormition* Attributed to Evodius of Rome

1. A homily delivered by Apa Evodius, the Archbishop of the great city of Rome, the second after the apostle Peter.[1] And he delivered it in the first of the churches recently built in the name of the holy Theotokos and true Bearer of God, Mary. And he proclaimed a few praises in honour of the holy Virgin Mary, which he told us on the day of her departure, the twenty-first of the month of Tobe. In the peace of God, Amen.

2. It is proper and right that we give every honour and every blessing to the master[2] of us all, the holy Theotokos Mary, our intercessor who continuously intercedes on our behalf before God, the Queen of the entire race of women and the mother of the King of Kings, our Lord Jesus Christ. For if a king of this world wants to make a marriage for his son, his people gather to him. They dress in white and put on royal garments: the governors, the generals, the dignitaries, the scholars, the local governors, the government officials in general, down to the humble earring-wearers, who are servants to those who serve. The others similarly dress in white according to their honour and come to the marriage of the king's son. The standard-bearers set up standards in the praetorium. The friends of the people honour the groom and his bride. The scribes are gathered, and they stand according to order. The couriers prepare themselves, and they summon those who are worthy of

---

[1] A more technical version of this translation can be found, together with the critical edition from which it was made, in Stephen J. Shoemaker, 'The Sahidic Coptic Homily on the Dormition of the Virgin Attributed to Evodius of Rome: An Edition of Morgan MSS 596 & 598 with Translation', *Analecta Bollandiana*, 117 (1999), 241–83.

[2] Although the form here is feminine (**TENXOEIC**), 'mistress' and 'lady' both have connotations in English that make them problematic for translation here. Although 'master' is often used as a gendered term in English, it is here employed in a neuter sense. In other words, while 'master' most appropriately expresses in English the meaning of the Coptic word used here, it should not be taken as suggesting the use of masculine forms in reference to the Virgin in the ancient text. This principle has been applied throughout the translation.

coming to the wedding. The actors prepare theatres and perform plays. The mimers prepare places for miming and perform shows. The gladiators prepare fights with wild beasts, and they bring forth wild beasts, which they are bold to fight well. The cithara players play the cithara in melodies that are sweet and pleasing to those who listen. The lute players sing with instruments. Dining couches are set up in the marketplaces. The people of the marketplace, those who sell things, crown their seats with palms and fragrant branches. They hang banners and fine linen cloths in the streets of the city, rejoicing at the marriage of the king's son. Not only will the rich and the dignitaries rejoice so at this marriage, but also the poor and those who are in need, and the strangers and the sojourners. They too rejoice on account of the joy of the marriage of the king's son. Likewise, those in prison forget the troubles that beset them, and they rejoice greatly that the king had mercy on them in the troubles that had befallen them, on account of the joy of the marriage of the king's son. But when the king beholds this great joy that is spread forth on his behalf, he is in great royal authority. Then he prepares places for drinking, and he gives great sanctions and extends great charities to everyone in need.

3. And all these things are on account of a marriage of this world— for truly their joy turns to grief after a little while because of death. How great then is the joy that spreads forth today among all the orders of heaven: the angels and archangels, the cherubim and seraphim, the thrones and dominions, the powers and authorities! They rejoice, adorn themselves, and dance at the wedding of the King's son. Blessed are you, O Mary, the Queen of women and the mother of the King of life and the King of Kings, the one about whom Solomon prophesied in the Song of Songs, saying, 'Arise and come beside me, my bride, my dove, who is beautiful among women.'[3] And not only the inhabitants of heaven, but also those on earth are very glad, and they rejoice in your joy. Those who are in the heaven of heavens and those upon the earth rejoice with you, O Virgin Mary. And not only do the men rejoice, but also the women rejoice that a woman has given birth to this great one in his days, and it did not damage her virginity. Because of this, he has changed the shame of woman into an honour, through that God-bearing Virgin.

4. Let our ancient fathers gather and come here today and glorify that holy Virgin, the true bride who gave birth to the true, undefiled bridegroom. And when he came forth from her, the bonds of her virginity were not undone. Come to us today, O Isaiah, whose voice is great among the prophets, and see the Virgin about whom you prophesied a long time ago, when you said through the prophetic spirit

---

[3] Cf. S. of S. 1: 8, 2: 10–14, 5: 9, 6: 1.

that was in you: 'Behold, the virgin will conceive and bear a son, and they will call his name Emmanuel, that is, God with us.'[4] Come now and see Emmanuel, God raised upon her knees, feeding on virgin milk. O David, come and see the honoured Queen standing at the right hand of the King and clothed in the many-coloured garment.[5] O Solomon, the wise king, come and see the true bride about whom you prophesied in the Song of Songs, saying: 'My bride, my dove, who is beautiful among women, arise and come from the trees of Lebanon.'[6] O Ezekiel, arise and come into our midst today and behold the closed gate, through which the ruler entered and also came forth, and it was closed as it was before,[7] namely, the holy Virgin Mary, from whom the King of Kings came forth, and the bonds of her virginity remained sealed as they were before.

5. O Mary, you are more blessed than every female creature that God has created.[8] I wish that I could have seen you, O Mary, when you gave birth to God, without change or illusion, even though we saw him as he grew in years, in the way of every human being, and we were worthy to eat with him and see all the wonders that he worked. I saw them with my own eyes, I Evodius, the least, who is speaking now in this exposition: I and my fathers the apostles and the seventy-two disciples.[9] But, in all these things, I was wishing that I had been worthy to see him when he was raised up on your knees, gazing at your face and laughing at you with his divine laughter. I wanted to see you, O undefiled lamb, holding the hand of Emmanuel, your son, and talking with him, saying, 'Walk, walk, my son', in the way that all little children are taught to walk. He, Jesus my Lord, would not take step on step with his little feet while walking, following like all little children. I wanted to see you, O beautiful treasure, when he was looking at your face, as if saying to you, 'Pick me up, O my mother, because I have become weary from walking.' I wanted to see you, O beautiful dove, when he stretched forth his hand, taking hold of your undefiled breast and placing it in his divine mouth.

6. Truly you are blessed! You are many times blessed, O beautiful treasure that has been found, hidden in the field.[10] To what shall I compare you, or what is equal to you in all the creation that God has created? If I compare you to heaven, truly, you are exalted above it, because he who created heaven and earth desired and dwelled in you for nine months. You are more exalted than the sun. You are more exalted than the moon. You are more exalted than the angels. You are more

---

[4] Isa. 7: 14.

[5] Cf. Ps. 44: 10 (LXX).

[6] Cf. S. of S. 1: 8, 2: 10–14, 4: 8, 5: 9, 6: 1.

[7] Cf. Ezek 44: 2–3.

[8] Cf. Luke 1: 42.

[9] Cf. Luke 10: 1, 7.

[10] Cf. Matt. 13: 44.

honoured than the archangels. You are more exalted than the cherubim. You are more honoured than the seraphim. O swift cloud, on which God was mounted![11] O golden jar, in which the manna is hidden![12] O new vessel, whose salt seasons our souls,[13] which are insipid from sin! O holy ark, within which are the tablets of the covenant![14] O chosen lampstand of gold,[15] whose lamp shines for those who dwell in the darkness and shadow of death![16] O honoured bush whose intellectual fire did not burn the bonds of her virginity![17] Blessed are you, who is beautiful among women![18] O honoured turtledove, which signals to us that summer has drawn near,[19] which is the season of our salvation!

7. Where are you now, O ignorant Jew, the murderer of his Lord? This one who does evil to those who do good to him, let him come here today and be ashamed of himself, hearing all these testimonies, which those of his own people have previously prophesied concerning this Virgin and her blessed birthing. For instance, one is 'Behold the virgin will conceive and bear a son, and they will call his name "Emmanuel", that is, God with us.'[20] Another is 'The queen stood at your right hand in a gilded garment, clothed with many colours.'[21] Another is 'Arise, you who are beautiful among women,[22] because the king desired your beauty, because he is your lord,'[23] and 'he wanted your breasts more than wine'.[24] And another is 'I saw a sealed scroll in the hand of the angel, and no one could open it, except the victorious lion from the tribe of Judah.'[25]

8. Since you do not receive these testimonies, O defiled Jew— because you heard them often with your ears, and you touched with your hands the blind that the son of the holy Theotokos Mary made to see, the lame that he made to walk, and the dead that he raised, things to which your very own hands bore witness when you took the stone from the mouth of the tomb with them, so that he came forth, living again— are you not, O ignorant one, the one who loosened the grave-clothes that were wrapped around his body and the towel that was bound to his head[26]—I am speaking of Lazarus—and you released him, and he went forth again, after he had been in the tomb for four days—

---

[11] Cf. Isa. 19: 1.

[12] Cf. Heb. 9: 4.

[13] Cf. 2 Kgs. 2: 20–21.

[14] Cf. Exod. 25: 16, Deut. 10: 3–5, 1 Kgs. 8: 9, Heb. 9: 4.

[15] Cf. Exod. 25: 31–39, Rev. 1: 12–2.1.

[16] Cf. Isa. 9: 1 (LXX), Matt. 4: 16 and par.

[17] Cf. Exod. 3: 2.

[18] Cf. Luke 1: 42.

[19] Cf. S. of S. 2: 11–12.

[20] Isa. 7: 14.

[21] Ps. 44: 10 (LXX).

[22] Cf. S. of S. 1: 8, 2: 10–13, 5: 9, 6: 1.

[23] Ps. 44: 12 (LXX).

[24] Cf. S. of S. 1: 2, 1: 4, 7: 9 (LXX).

[25] Cf. Rev. 5: 1–5.

[26] Cf. John 11: 38–45.

[then][27] will not your children testify against you on the day of judgement, O ignorant Jew, since they took palm-branches and went forth to meet him, saying, 'Hosanna! Blessed is he who comes in the name of the Lord'?[28] Indeed, your children have confessed his divinity, but you have denied it.

9. Was not I, Evodius, the least, there when you invited Jesus, the son of the Virgin, to the wedding? We ourselves, the disciples, and his mother were following him, and you saw the miracle that took place.[29] When they were lacking wine, his mother, the holy Virgin, went and sat at the feet of her blessed son, and she said to him, 'My son, my Lord, and my God, they have no wine.' And he turned his face, which poured forth every joy upon her, and said to her, 'Woman, what do you want from me? My hour has not yet come.' She said to him, 'My son, my beloved, this is the time for your holy name to be glorified. They have summoned you as a man, O my son: reveal to them the glory of your divinity. For everyone who comes to the marriage, each one brings gifts according to his or her wealth and also according to the honour of the marriage. And you, O my blessed son, favour them with the honour above every honour, that is, the honour of your divinity. Reveal to them the glory of your divinity, so that your holy name will be glorified and all those who are at the marriage will believe in you, along with your blessed apostles, that you are truly the Son of God. Listen to me: I am your virgin mother. Grant me this gift which is above every gift, that is, the honour of your divinity.' And when he heard these things, namely the one in whom are the storehouses of mercy, he said, 'Let them fill the water jars with water.' And they filled them to the rim. He caused the waters to change their nature: they became superior wine.

10. Did you not see all these things that were done by him, this Son of God, to whom this holy Virgin gave birth? Why are you now ignorant, so as not to believe that it is in fact a holy birth in which the Virgin gave him birth? Why did your tongue not dry up in your mouth, O defiled Jew, when you said to Pilate with your tongue, which is worthy of being cut out, 'It is through fornication that Mary gave birth to Christ'?[30] Why do you not remember the voice of the archangel Gabriel, saying, 'The Holy Spirit will come upon you, and the power of

---

[27] The syntax of this passage is a little complex and difficult to translate. I have understood the entire passage as a lengthy conditional sentence, having a somewhat convoluted protasis and an apodosis that begins only at this point.

[28] Matt. 21: 9 and par.

[29] Cf. John 2: 1–10.

[30] Cf. *A. Pil* A 2. 3–6 (Konstantin Tischendorf, ed., *Evangelia Apocrypha*, 2nd edn. (Leipzig: 1876; repr. Hildesheim: Georg Olms, 1966), 224–8); also, *b. Šabb.* 104b and *b. Sanh.* 67a.

the Most High will overshadow you. Because of this the one to whom
you will give birth is holy, and he will be called the son of the Most
High.'[31] O those who were given the law and have denied the lawgiver!
O those who say, 'We know the law well', but deny the one who has
given them the law and his commandments! Why have you not believed
these shepherds who saw the birth-star of the son of the Virgin,[32] when
she gave birth to the one who is consubstantial with the Father? Indeed,
are these not eyes of some from your own people? Why have you not
asked them? Truly, those who were there will proclaim to you the truth
concerning the voices of the angels singing hymns for the birth of the
Son of God, crying out and saying, 'Glory to God in the heights; his
peace on earth among people of his will.'[33]

11. O lawless one who is more defiled than every menstruous
woman, why have you not imitated these Magi, pagans and greatest
sinners of the whole earth, these who saw the star in the east?[34] They
set out from their country and came to Judaea, and they worshipped
the King: 'O Son of God, the Almighty and also the son of the holy
Virgin, Saint Mary!' They knew truly that the one to whom the Virgin
Mary gave birth was divine, and they worshipped him and gave him
frankincense as a king. They knew that he was a human being whose
humanity had joined with his divinity, and they worshipped him with
myrrh as a human. Why have you not, O ignorant Jew, remembered
these things that were attested to you concerning the birth of God the
Word and believed in him? But you have abandoned all these things and
done evil, and you have turned from the way of truth. You cried out to
Pilate, saying, 'He is a man who has fashioned himself God',[35] and also,
'He is the product of fornication.'[36]

12. What is the repayment that you shall receive on that day of
requital for all the things that you have done? I say to you that the blame
that will be put on you will not be worse for you than the punishments
into which you will be cast with the severe sentence: 'these enemies of
mine, who did not want me to rule over them, bring them and slay them
in my presence',[37] and also: 'let the sinners return to Hell, all the nations
that forget God'.[38] O Jews, who are the most defiled of the whole earth,
why have you denied your life and your inheritance and received a curse
upon your head, not a blessing?[39] But rightly he has spoken to you thus:
'God is able to raise up sons to Abraham from these stones.'[40] But you,

---

[31] Luke 1: 35.   [32] Cf. Luke 2: 8–14.
[33] Luke 2: 14.   [34] Cf. Matt. 2: 1–12.
[35] Cf. John 10: 33, 19: 7.
[36] Cf. *A. Pil* A 2. 3–6 (Tischendorf, *Evangelia Apocrypha*, 224–8).
[37] Luke 19: 27.   [38] Ps. 9: 18 (LXX).
[39] Cf. Deut. 11: 26–8.   [40] Matt. 3: 9, Luke 3: 8.

O defiled Jews, will be cast into the outer darkness, where there will be weeping and gnashing of teeth.[41]

13. But let us abandon matters of this sort and return to the greatness of this Virgin, the Bearer of God, and tell you about the day of her honourable departure, so that the faithful will hear and will praise God. And all the things that I will say, no one else who saw them has told me about them, but I saw them with my own eyes, and I touched them with my own hands:[42] for the sight of eyes is more trustworthy than the hearing of ears.

14. And it happened when the apostles had completed everything that the Lord Jesus Christ had commanded them, and they gathered together secretly, so that each one would depart for the region that he was allotted and preach the gospel of the kingdom of heaven. And they also cast lots for us, the lesser disciples. The lot fell to me, Evodius, to continue journeying with my father and teacher, Peter, the chief of the apostles and the first ordained by the hands of God the Word and the Creator of all. When the lot of this region, that is, Rome, fell to him, we prepared ourselves, each one for his region.

15. But my father, Peter the apostle, said to the apostles, 'Let us all gather in a single place tomorrow and assemble together and celebrate the mystery which our Lord taught to us.' And we were gathered for the breaking of bread, all of us, the apostles and the other disciples, and Mary the mother of the Lord was gathered with us, and Salome and the other women who followed the Lord Jesus Christ, and we were in a single place out of fear of the Jews, but we were full of joy: behold, the Lord Jesus, the Life of us all stood in our midst and said to us, 'Peace to you; let the peace which my Father has given to me be with you.'[43] For that day was the twentieth of Tobe. And when the apostles and the other lesser disciples saw the teacher, Jesus, they rejoiced greatly, and such great happiness came upon us. We advanced to him, one by one: first the apostles, and then the lesser disciples. Then we ourselves bowed down before him and kissed his hands, his feet, and his breast. And the women who were with us did likewise. But Mary, his mother, came in a rush, and she advanced to him and kissed him, mouth on mouth.

16. And when Jesus saw his virgin mother, he smiled at her with a spiritual smile and said to her, 'You are more blessed, O my mother, than every creature that my Father has created. You are exalted above

---

[41] Matt. 8: 12, 22: 13, 25: 30.

[42] Cf. 1 John 1: 1.

[43] Grammatically this sentence is a series of circumstantial clauses describing the circumstances of Jesus' sudden appearance, and strictly speaking one should translate: 'And as we were gathered . . . behold, the Lord Jesus, the Life of us all stood in our midst . . .'

heaven, more esteemed than the earth, because God resided in your holy womb. Blessed are you, O beautiful dove, my bride without blemish. Arise and come beside me, because my time has drawn near, when I will eat my bread with you[44] and drink the sweet-smelling wine in my garden,[45] my holy Paradise. O my mother, if you spent nine months carrying me in your holy womb, I too will carry you in the bowels of my mercy. And if you nursed me on knee and arm, I too will raise you upon a glorious throne to the right of me and my good Father. If you wrapped me in rags on the day that you gave birth to me, and you put me in a manger, and an ox and an ass made shade for me, I too will cover you with the wings of the seraphim. And if you kissed me with your mouth and nourished me with your virgin milk, I too will kiss you in the presence of my Father in heaven, and my Father will feed you with the bread of truth. O Mary, my mother, the time has come for you to come forth from the body in the way of all humanity, because there is no one upon the earth exempt from tasting death, including me, the one whom you formed, so that I redeemed my form.[46] Do not be distressed, O Mary my mother, that you are coming forth from the body. For you will leave this world behind you and go to the place of eternal gladness and joy.'

17. And the Saviour turned to my father Peter and the rest of the apostles and said to them, 'O my excellent fellow-members,[47] these whom I have chosen and not the whole world,[48] when it is dawn, I will gather you together in my body and my blood, and I will give you my peace and that of my Father and that of the Holy Spirit. Prepare yourselves, because my Father will send a multitude of angels for Mary, my mother and the mother of you all. And she will be taken up into heaven, to the place of rest that is in that eternal place.'

18. And when the Saviour had said these things to us, the sun rose on the twenty-first of the month of Tobe. And the Saviour gathered us together by his own hands, we and the women who were with us. Then he said to Peter, 'Arise and go onto the altar, beside which I have now gathered you together, and bring me these linen garments that I have brought from the heavenly things, which my Father has sent to you to bury my beloved mother in, since it is not possible for a garment of this world to befit her body, because it was the dwelling place of his beloved Son, namely, me.'

19. And our father Peter went, and he brought the garments. The

---

[44] Or perhaps, 'will eat my bread of truth'; but see Cant. 5: 1 (LXX).
[45] Cf. S. of S. 4: 16–5: 1 (LXX).
[46] Or perhaps, 'until I redeemed my form'.
[47] Cf. Rom. 12: 4–5, 1 Cor. 12: 27.
[48] Cf. John 15: 19.

Saviour went inside and spread them out with his own hands. And he said, 'O my mother, arise and lie down in the midst of these garments, because the time has come for you to come forth from the body, and I will take you up to heaven, beside my Father.' And then we all kissed her, and she went into the midst of the garments that the Saviour had spread out with his own hands, and she turned her face to the east. The Saviour went outside, and we all followed him, since it is not possible for Death to come to a place where Life is. And while he sat for a little while, the Saviour spoke with us of the mysteries of the height. And while we were still sitting, we heard the women inside, where the Virgin was lying, weeping and crying out greatly. And Salome and Joanna came to us and said to the Saviour, 'Our Lord and our God, your mother and the mother of us all has died.' Then the Saviour arose immediately and went in to the place where she was lying, and he stretched forth over her and wept. Afterward, he kissed her precious mouth and said, 'You are many times blessed, O my mother. Blessed are your breasts, which nursed me, and blessed also is your womb, which bore me, and blessed is the womb of your mother, which also bore you. This is the day that the prophecy of my father David has been fulfilled: "Virgins will be brought to the king behind her, in a garment that is gilded."'[49]

20. And when the Saviour had said these things, he took hold of his mother, the holy Virgin, and with his own hands he prepared her for burial in the garments that he had spread out. He sat beside her for a long time. And my father Peter and all the apostles and also the women who were in our company all wept over the departure of the holy Virgin Mary, the Theotokos. And the Saviour said to the apostles, 'Why are you grieving when I, the joy of all creation, am with you?' The apostles said to the Saviour, 'We are grieving because of the departure of the master of us all, the holy Theotokos Mary, because she gives us consolation in everything. Do you not now have the power that she not die, until we all die?' The Saviour said to the apostles, 'Is not everything possible for me? But it is not possible that a person remain upon the earth forever, that she not taste death. Even I tasted death, and I rose from the dead and freed all those who have died in Adam.'[50]

21. While the Saviour was still saying these things to us, we heard the sound of great multitudes, like the sound of waterfalls, and we were afraid. The Saviour said, 'Do not be afraid. It is Mary my mother, whom my good Father has sent to you, so that you will see her yet once more, and she will comfort you in your grief.' And while we were saying these things, behold, a great chariot of light came into our midst, with a multitude of angels surrounding it. A glorious and exalted throne was

---

[49] Cf. Ps. 44: 14–15 (LXX).   [50] Cf. 1 Cor. 15: 22.

raised up on the chariot. The master of us all was sitting on the throne, and she reached out over us, saying, 'The peace of my son be with you all.' And when we advanced to her, we all kissed her, and also the women who were with us. She said to us, 'Blessed are you, because you have become worthy of following my son and the Son of the living God, the Saviour of the entire world.'

22. But our teacher, Jesus, said to us, 'Raise my mother's body upon a bier and crown it well with palms and fragrant branches. And sing before it the hymn that I taught you when I rose from the dead until [you reach] the place where I will order you to stop.' And when the Saviour had said these things, he got on the chariot with his virgin mother, and the angels of God sang hymns before him until they reached heaven gloriously and honourably, while we were watching them. And we raised the body of his virgin mother upon a bier, and we sang Psalms before her, there also being a crowd of Jews with us.[51] When we reached the place that is called the Valley of Josaphat, outside Jerusalem, a multitude of angels came forth from heaven, and they seized the Virgin's body. The angels of light flew with her to the

---

[51] The meaning of this last phrase is not entirely clear, and it is likely that something is wrong with the text here. With only one other exception (the homily on the Dormition attributed to Modestus of Jerusalem), every other ancient narrative of the end of the Virgin's life includes at this point an episode in which the Jews attack the Virgin's bier in an attempt to destroy her body. Its absence here is very peculiar, and I am convinced that this phrase once marked the beginning of this scene in an earlier version of this homily. Somehow in the course of transmission, the remainder of this episode must have fallen out.

I strongly disagree with Gonzalo Aranda Pérez's assessment of this passage, in which he concludes: 'Además EvSah1 [St Mich.] transforma radicalmente el episodio de los judíos que atacan el féretro, presente en la gran mayoría de los relatos de la Dormición, convirtiendolo en un dato favorable a los judíos. No refleja por tanto un ambiente antijudío': Gonzalo Aranda Pérez, *Dormición de la Virgen: Relatos de la tradición copta*, Apócrifos christianos, 2 (Madrid: Editorial Ciudad Nueva, 1995), 103. Given the fact that almost one-third of this homily is devoted to violent anti-Jewish polemic, conclusions that this text 'does not reflect an anti-Jewish atmosphere' or that it can be read as somehow favourable to Judaism are not very persuasive. Indeed, for its sheer quantity of anti-Jewish invective, the St. Michael homily stands apart as among the most particularly anti-Jewish of the ancient Dormition traditions. In the light of this, I repeat my suggestion that the anti-Jewish episode involving the Virgin's funeral procession has most probably somehow been lost during the transmission of this homily, and its absence is not indicative of any sort of favouritism on the part of this homily towards Jews. For more on the anti-Judaism of the early Dormition traditions, see Stephen J. Shoemaker, ' "Let Us Go and Burn Her Body": The Image of the Jews in the Early Dormition Traditions', *Church History*, 68 (1999), 775–823.

heights, singing hymns before her, while we watched until they were hidden in the air. And we returned to the house, glorifying God.

23. And when we continued to be troubled in heart concerning her body, because it was hidden from us, Christ appeared to us again, with his virgin mother to his right. He said to us, 'When you go forth into the world, preach the good news of the departure of my mother Mary. And regarding her body, my Father has ordered that it be placed beneath the fragrant tree of life,[52] which is the resting place of his beloved Son, namely, me.'

24. And as for me, Evodius, the disciple of my father Peter, the great apostle, no one else told me these things, but I was there just as all these things were happening. And the day of the departure of the master of us all, the holy Theotokos Mary, is the twenty-first of the month of Tobe. Our Lord has commanded us to celebrate a feast every month in the name of the Virgin Mary, and especially on the twenty-first of the month of Tobe. Glory to the Father and the Son and the Holy Spirit unto the ages of ages. Amen.

[52] Cf. *4 Ezra* 2: 12.

Jacob of Serug, *Homily on the Dormition*

The 81st festal homily of St Mar Jacob, concerning the burial, that is, the departure, of the holy Virgin Mary, the Theotokos, and how she was buried by the apostles, which was spoken by him when there was an enquiry about it at the synod, while it was meeting in the church of St Mar Cyriacus the Martyr in the city of Nisibis, on the fourth day of the week, on the fourteenth of the month Ab [August].[1]

Son who in his love inclined his exaltedness and descended to earth,
  put on the body and became a human being from the daughter of
  David,
Mystically begotten one, of whom the heights and depths are full,
  fill me with learning, you whose concealment created the universe.
Only Son who formed Adam from nothing,
  form in my humble mind a homily to sing to you.
Son who planted the ten senses in the mortal body,
  gather my thoughts and bring them to your Father's place.
Christ, who gave the spirit of life to Adam, whom you created,
  pour into me the life of your discernment, full of wonder.
[710] Hidden one, who is concealed even from the watchers, so that they
do not see him,
  rise in me quietly, and I will openly cry out concerning your mother.
O you who healed the unclean[2] man that approached him,
  restore and heal the body and soul of those who wait for you.
Light, Christ, who illuminated eyes that were darkened,

---

[1] This translation has been prepared from the edition by P. Bedjan, ed., *S. Martyrii, qui et Sahdona, quae supersunt omnia* (Leipzig: Otto Harrassowitz, 1902), 709–19, in consultation with A. Baumstark's Latin translation of a different MS: A. Baumstark, 'Zwei syrische Dichtungen auf das Entschlafen der allerseligsten Jungfrau', *Oriens Christianus*, 5 (1905), 91–9. The numbers in brackets refer to the page numbers from Bedjan's edition.

[2] Baumstark's text reads 'leprous' (ܓܪܒܐ) instead of 'unclean' (ܛܡܐܐ), perhaps the correct reading, since this would make the reference to Matt. 8: 1–4 (and par.) somewhat more clear.

let your light rise upon my weakness, and I will be enlightened by
you.

Lord of humanity, who willed to become a human being in the flesh,
 and dwelt and resided in the pure mother, the daughter of lights,

O you who dwelt in her for nine months and came to birth,
 let my mind bring forth gifts of splendour for your mystical birth.

O you who was cherished by the lullabies of his chosen mother,
 let my tongue bring forth all the praises of your sweetness.

Son who visited us and perfected all of his economy,
 allow me to speak concerning the burial of the faithful woman.

Your mother endured great suffering on your account;
 every sorrow beset her at your crucifixion.

How many sighs and tears of grief her eyes shed,
 when they were preparing you for burial, and they carried you and
 placed you in the tomb!

What horrors the mother of mercy beheld at your burial,
 when the guards at the tomb seized her, lest she draw near you!

She suffered sorrow when she saw you suspended on the cross,
 [711] and they pierced your side with a spear on Golgotha,

and when the Jews sealed the tomb in which was lain
 your living body, life-giving and debt-forgiving.

And this mother, who suffered these things on your account,
 the end drew near for her, so that she would pass into the world full
 of blessings.

The time had come for her to journey along the way of all generations,
 who have journeyed and gone forth to the end with great trembling.

Adam, the beginning of all generations, journeyed on it,
 and noble Seth, and the generations of his righteous, ancient sons.

The pure and innocent generation of righteous Noah journeyed on it,
 and that of Shem, and of Japheth, and of Ham, the sons who were on
 the earth.

The good labourers Abraham and Isaac went forth after them,
 and also the just that were on the earth in every generation.

The righteous and humble Jacob journeyed along this way,
 and after him the twelve patriarchs, his noble sons.

Joseph journeyed on it, and the sons of Ephrem and Judah,
 and with them Moses the humble and the illustrious Hur.

After him came Joshua the son of Nun, a marvellous man,
 Aaron the priest, and all the tribe of the sons of Levi;

King David and the entire generation of the kingdom,
 [the Kings Hezekiah, and Josiah, and Asa;][3]

---

[3] A line is missing from Bedjan's text here. The reading given is from
Baumstark's Latin translation of the version of the homily found in MS

and Daniel, the beloved man,[4] in the land of Babylon,
  [712] and with him the three innocent children in the furnace;
and Jephte the just and the great Gideon, who divided the people,[5]
  and the elect Samson, who lost his life because of a woman;
the twelve prophets who have passed on and gone forth with the ancients,
  and death consumed their generations along with their times;
the pure Samuel, with the most famous Jeremiah,
  and Ezekiel, marvellous in the revelations of prophecy.
Isaiah passed on, the faithful rebuker,[6]
  and the entire company of prophecy came to an end.
The ancients passed on, and the age of the sons of iniquity came,
  and the Lord has descended in order to save them from error.
He dwelt and resided in the womb, pure and full of grace,
  of this Virgin, whose story, behold, will now be told by us.
He inhabited and dwelt in her for nine months without impediment,
  and the time came for his birth, according to the order of things.
He willed it and was born, and he received baptism in the Jordan,
  and he performed miracles and healed the sick and cleansed lepers.
He endured the temptations of the Devil, and he trampled upon him and overcame him,
  and the children and the infants praised him with their hosannas.
He chose for himself the company of the illustrious twelve,
  from which the betrayer Judas sprang forth, the evil demon.
[713] He handed over his master, and he lost his soul and became disgraceful,
  and from the rank of the apostolate he fell, because of what he chose.
Then our Lord came unto death, as we have said,
  and he died and redeemed us, and he rose from the grave and has raised us with him.

Jerusalem Syriac 43, from which he gives the following text: ܐܦ ܣܝܡ ܐܦ ܩܪ̈ܐ. ܘܐܪܬ ܟܠܝܐ. (Baumstark, 'Zwei syrische Dichtungen', 93 n. 2.)

---

  [4] Dan. 10: 11.
  [5] Cf. Judg. 7: 2–8.
  [6] The phrase ܡܟܣܢܐ ܕܫܪܬܐ has proved somewhat difficult to translate. Literally, the phrase means, 'the rebuker of truth'. Vona has translated the phrase 'quell'indicatore di verità [the guide of truth]', and Baumstark suggests 'sera veritatis [the bolt of truth]', neither of which seems to be exactly correct. Baumstark's translation is supported by Brockelman's *Lexicon Syriacum* (337a), where the meanings 'sera, claustrum' are suggested for ܡܟܣܢܐ, based on comparison with ܡܘܟܠܐ, which has the meaning 'bar, bolt' (J. Payne Smith, *A Compendious Syriac Dictionary*, 251a). Both R. and J. Payne Smith give 'reprover, rebuker, chider, confuter' as meanings for ܡܟܣܢܐ, and these I have followed.

The mother of this Jesus Christ, the Son of God,
  death came unto her so that she might taste its cup.
The Lord commanded the exalted hosts above
  and the blazing legions, the Seraphim of light.
The watchers descended by companies in their raiment,
  and they sang the praise of their hallelujahs in raised voice.
The just from every age came and assembled,
  along with the righteous and the patriarchs from long ago.
The thunder of the company of the prophets sang praise,
  one to another as beholders of the truth.
The ancient priests and all the company of the sons of Levi,
  with their sacrifices, their holocausts, and their offerings.
The company of the twelve chosen apostles arose,
  and prepared the virgin body of the Blessed One for burial.
John drew near, as the master of the house of truth,
  and prepared the glorious body of the Blessed One for burial.
Two of the illustrious, chosen apostles of the covenants,
  [714] were entrusted with this treasure of truth.
The just Nicodemus prepared the body of her son for burial,
  and the chosen, virgin son of thunder,[7] the body of this woman.
The pastors and their flocks came to the top of the mountain,
  the glorious priests, and the deacons with their censers.
The winds struck the vault [of heaven] more forcefully than whirlwinds,
  and the height and the depth sang praise with their harps.
Light shone upon the place where they were gathered,
  the humans and watchers, to prepare the one full of grace for burial.
And as the Lord descended and prepared his servant Moses for burial,
  so with these he prepared his mother according to the flesh for burial.
On top of the mountain, within luminous clouds,
  the prophet Moses was prepared for burial by God.
So also, Mary, on that mountain of the Galileans,[8]
  the watchers and angels, along with God, prepared her for burial.
John, the young virgin, drew near and embraced her,
  the pure mother who was entrusted to him by our Saviour.
He was a mediator between God and humanity,
  when the watchers descended with great, ineffable pomp.
Into a cave of stone, the new tomb of Nicodemus,
  [715] they brought and laid the son of this blessed woman.
And also this pure mother of the Son of God,
  into a cave, a tomb, a cavern of stone they brought and laid her.
The entire company of the apostles gathered and stood by,

---

[7] Cf. Mark 3: 17.   [8] i.e. the Mount of Olives.

as their master truly prepared her for burial with them.
The ranks and companies and host of the sons of light;
    the tumult of the watchers and the fiery assemblies of flame;
the fiery Seraphim, with their dense wings of flame,
    with legions and their heavenly battalions;
the mighty Cherubim, who were yoked to his chariot;
    they trembled with wonder while singing praises with their
    hosannas.
The followers of Gabriel, assemblies more fiery than flame,
    were variously changed in their natures.
The followers of Michael, full of motion in their descent,
    were keeping the feast, exulting and rejoicing this day with their
    halleluiahs.
Heaven and the air were filled with the praise
    of the heavenly ones, who went forth and descended to the place of
    earth.
A sweet and pure fragrance came forth from the censers
    of the exalted assemblies, when they went forth to descend to the
    earth.
The demons and the powers, the sons of darkness, fled,
    and all the afflicted souls were given rest.
[716] The demons fled from the souls that they were upon,
    and there was rest for those who were being afflicted with their
    cruelty.
The evil demons were troubled and disturbed,
    because they saw a sign that could only be accomplished by our Lord.
They saw heaven sending forth assemblies of hosts,
    and all the air was sanctified by a sweet fragrance.
The new voices of all the singing birds,
    who were singing in ranks according to their natures.
All the animals in their places joyfully shouted praise,
    and the whole earth was shaken by their joyful shouts.
The heights and mountains and all the adorned plains
    sent forth praise when the virgin body was prepared for burial.
All the trees with their fruits and produce
    sprinkled dew, the sweet fragrance of their pleasantness.
All the beautiful flowers in their variety,
    sent forth their fragrance like fragrant aromatics.
The waters and the fish and all the creeping things in the seas
    were aware of this day, and they trembled because of the glory.
All the silent and speaking creatures
    bestowed the praise that was due, according to their natures.
On this day Adam and Eve his wife rejoice,
    [717] because their daughter dwells where they are gathered.

On this day the just Noah and Abraham rejoice,
    because their daughter has visited them in their mansions.
On this day noble old Jacob rejoices,
    because the daughter who sprang from his root has called him to life.
On this day the twelve just sons of the maimed one[9]
    rejoice greatly and exult because of her who has visited them.
On this day Judah also rejoices greatly,
    for behold, the daughter who has given life came forth from his loins.
On this day Joseph rejoices, and the great Moses,
    because one young woman has called all his race to life.
On this day Aaron and Eleazar rejoice,
    and all the tribe of Levi with their priesthood.
On this day the renowned father David rejoices,
    because his daughter has placed a beautiful crown on his head.
On this day Samuel rejoices with Jeremiah,
    because the daughter of Judah has sprinkled dew on their bones.
Come Ezekiel, skilled in prophetic revelation,
    if this event is described in your prophecy.
On this day the prophet Isaiah rejoices,
    because she about whom he prophesied, behold, she has visited him
    in the place of the dead.
On this day all the prophets from their graves
    [718] lifted up their heads, because they saw that the light shone
    upon them.
They saw that death was troubled and fleeing from their midst,
    and the gates of the heights and the depths of the earth were opening
    again.
The prophets, the apostles, the priests, and the martyrs were
assembled,
    and the teachers, the patriarchs, and the just of long ago.
In the height, the watchers, in the depth, humanity, in the air, glory,
    when the Virgin Mary was buried as one of the deceased.
A light shone on the assembly of the disciples,
    and also on her companions, her relations, and her kindred.
The heavenly assemblies led with their cries of 'Holy'
    to the glorious soul of the mother of the Son of God.
The fiery Seraphim were surrounding the soul that was translated
    and were raising a loud cry of jubilation.
They cried out and said, 'lift up all your heads, O gates,[10]
    because the mother of the King desires to enter into the bridal
    chamber of light.'
The height was filled with the sweet song of the angels,

---

[9] Jacob: cf. Gen. 32: 25, 31.   [10] Ps. 27: 4, 9.

and the depth was disturbed with the disciples, who were full of
grief.
The assemblies of the heights and depths cried out in one song,
　whose message neither heavenly beings nor mortals could tell
　completely.[11]
The ranks of the heavenly assembly cried aloud
　one to the other, shouting joyfully in their praises.
The air poured forth the rain of life upon the bones
　[719] of the sons of the Church, the daughter of the pagans,[12] who
　did not deny her.
She wove and placed on her exalted head a beautiful crown,
　on which precious pearls were arranged.
The name of Christ the King, who was crucified on Golgotha,
　gives life and sheds forth mercy to those who call upon it,
and to me, a sinner, who is inadequate for the praises
　of the mother of mercies, who gave birth to you according to the
　flesh.
Through her prayers, make your peace to dwell, Son of God,
　in the height and the depth, and among all the counsels of her sons.[13]
Bring an end to wars and temptation, and remove the scourges,
　and grant calm weather and tranquillity to those traversing the sea.[14]
Heal the sick, restore the infirm, satisfy the hungry,
　and be a father to the orphans, whom death has deprived.
In your mercy drive away the demons that vex humankind,
　and lift up your church in the four corners of the world, so that it
　will sing your praise.
Preserve the priests and purify the deacons,
　and be a guide to the old and the young.
O Christ, the bridegroom, glory to you from every mouth,
　and mercy upon us in every time. Amen and Amen.

[The homily] of Mar Jacob concerning the departure of the holy
Theotokos is finished.

---

[11] Or 'bring to an end': ܡܣܝܟ.

[12] Lit., 'the Arameans': ܐܪܡܝܐ.

[13] Baumstark's MS reads ܟܠܗܘܢ ܡܠܟܝܗ ܕܐܪܥܐ, 'all the kings of the earth',
which perhaps makes more sense than Bedjan's text: ܟܠܗܘܢ ܡܠܟܝ ܕܒܢܝܗ.

[14] ܘܗܒ ܢܝܚܐ ܘܡܫܝܢܘܬܐ ܠܕܥܒܪ ܒܝܡܐ which actually translates 'and grant rest
and tranquillity to those dwelling in the sea'. Bedjan, however, suggests understanding, ܠܒܝܡܐ for ܒܝܡܐ, which is in fact the reading preserved in Baumstark's
MS. Nevertheless, we should not rule out the version preserved in Bedjan's
MS, which could make some sense, especially in the light of the previous
reference to 'the waters and the fish and all the creeping things in the seas'.

Parallels to the *Liber Requiei* from the Early Palm Narratives

The following list is not meant to be exhaustive: only those parallels most valuable from a text-critical vantage have been included. Numerous additional parallels exist among the early Western (Latin and Irish) narratives, but since these narratives are usually highly compressed, the parallels are often only to a general point or a particular phrase expressed in the earlier Eastern narratives. While these Western witnesses are, of course, quite valuable for understanding the early history of these traditions, it seemed more useful to focus on the earliest and most complete parallels. On some occasions, however, the Western narratives are particularly important witnesses, and in these cases they have been signalled in the chart below. Further examples, especially with regard to individual phrases, can be found in Arras, *De Transitu*, i. 75–105 (Lat.). The references below include a letter and number combination, followed by a section number where such numbers exist in the printed edition. In cases where the printed edition does not contain section numbers, I have referred to the page number in the edition. The letter-number combinations follow those assigned by van Esbroeck in his 'Les Textes', and they are keyed to the different Dormition narratives in the bibliography that follows.

Liber Requiei	Parallels
1	**G1** 2; **G3** 3
2	**G1** 3; **G3** 3
3	**G1** 4–5; **G3** 3
4	**G4** 2 (partial: esp. codices BO); **G1** 5 (partial); **G3** 3 (partial)
5	**I1** 1–2; **H1** 3 (partial); **H2** 3 (partial)
6	**I1** 3–5; **H1** 3 (partial); **H2** 3 (partial)
7	**I1** 6–8; **H1** 4 (partial); **H2** 3 (partial)
8	**I1** 9–10; **H1** 4 (partial); **H2** 3 (partial)
9	**I1** 11–13; **H1** 5 (partial); **H2** 3 (partial)
10	**I1** 14–15; **G1** 5 (partial); **G3** 3 (partial) ; **H1** 6 (partial); **H2** 3 (partial)
11	**I1** 16–17; **G1** 6–7; **G3** 3

12	**I1** 18–20
13	**G1** 7–8 (partial)
14	**G1** 7 (partial)
15	
16	
17	
18	
19	**S1** (Wright, *Contributions*, ܡܣ–ܝܣ and 50–1)
20	**S1** (Wright, *Contributions*, ܡܣ–ܝܣ and 50–1)
21	**S1** (Wright, *Contributions*, ܡܣ–ܝܣ and 50–1)
22	
23	
24	**G1** 3 (partial)
25	
26	
27	
28	
29	
30	
31	
32	**S1** (Wright, *Contributions*, ܝܣ–ܪܣ and 48–50)
33	**S1** (Wright, *Contributions*, ܝܣ–ܪܣ and 48–50)
34	**S1** (Wright, *Contributions*, ܝܣ–ܪܣ and 48–50)
35	**S1** (Wright, *Contributions*, ܝܣ–ܪܣ and 48–50)
36	**G1** 9–10; **G3** 4 (partial)
37	**G1** 11–12; **I3** 1–4; **G3** 4 (partial)
38	**G1** 13–14; **I3** 5–8; **G3** 5
39	**I3** 8–11; **G3** 5
40	**I3** 12–15; **G3** 5
41	**I3** 16 (partial); **G1** 14 (partial); **G3** 6 (partial)
42	**G1** 15; **G3** 6
43	**G1** 16–18; **G3** 6
44	**G1** 19–20; **G3** 6
45	**G1** 21; **G3** 6; Palestinian Syriac Fragments (Mimouni, *Dormition*, 76)
46	**G1** 22–3; **G3** 7; Palestinian Syriac Fragments (Mimouni, *Dormition*, 76)
47	**G3** 7
48	**G3** 7
49	**G1** 24–5; **G3** 7
50	**G1** 26–7; **G3** 8; Palestinian Syriac Fragments (Mimouni, *Dormition*, 76)
51	**G1** 28; **G3** 8; Palestinian Syriac Fragments (Mimouni, *Dormition*, 76)

52	**G1** 29; **G3** 8; Palestinian Syriac Fragments (Mimouni, *Dormition*, 76)
53	**G1** 30; **G3** 8
54	**G1** 30; **G3** 9
55	**G1** 31; **G3** 9
56	**G3** 9 (partial)
57	**G3** 9
58	**G3** 9 (partial)
59	**G3** 10 (partial)
60	**G3** 10
61	**G3** 10
62	**G3** 10
63	**G3** 10
64	**G3** 10
65	**G3** 11
66	**G1** 32–3; **G3** 12
67	**G1** 33–5; **G3** 12; **S1** (Wright, *Contributions*, 14)
68	**G1** 35; **G3** 12
69	**G3** 12
70	**G1** 36; **G3** 12
71	**G1** 37; **G3** 13
72	**G1** 38; **G3** 13; **S1** (Wright, *Contributions*, 14–15)
73	**G1** 38–9; **G3** 13; **S1** (Wright, *Contributions*, 14–15)
74	**G1** 40–1; **G3** 13 (partial)
75	**G1** 41; **G3** 13
76	**G1** 42–3; **G3** 13; **S1** (Wright, *Contributions*, 15)
77	**G1** 44–5; **G3** 13
78	**G1** 45
79	
80	**S1** (Wright, *Contributions*, ܚ‍ܝ‍ܐ and 42–8, partial)
81	**S1** (Wright, *Contributions*, ܚ‍ܝ‍ܐ and 42–8)
82	**S1** (Wright, *Contributions*, ܚ‍ܝ‍ܐ and 42–8)
83	**S1** (Wright, *Contributions*, ܚ‍ܝ‍ܐ and 42–8)
84	**S1** (Wright, *Contributions*, ܚ‍ܝ‍ܐ and 42–8)
85	**S1** (Wright, *Contributions*, ܚ‍ܝ‍ܐ and 42–8)
86	**S1** (Wright, *Contributions*, ܚ‍ܝ‍ܐ and 42–8)
87	**S1** (Wright, *Contributions*, ܚ‍ܝ‍ܐ and 42–8)
88	**S1** (Wright, *Contributions*, ܚ‍ܝ‍ܐ and 42–8); **G1** 46 (partial)
89	**S1** (Wright, *Contributions*, ܚ‍ܝ‍ܐ and 42–8); **G1** 47–8
90	**S1** (Wright, *Contributions*, ܚ‍ܝ‍ܐ and 42–8); **H1** 30 (partial); **H2** 51 (partial); **L2** (MS N 2, Wenger, *L'Assomption*, 258–9; partial)

91   **S1** (Wright, *Contributions*, ܚܡܘ ܘܥ and 42–8); **L2** (MS N 2–3, Wenger, *L'Assomption*, 258–9; partial)

92   **S1** (Wright, *Contributions*, ܚܡܘ ܘܥ and 42–8)

93   **H1** 30 (partial); **H2** 51 (partial)

94   **H1** 30; **H2** 51–2; **L2** (MS N, 3, Wenger, *L'Assomption*, 258–9; partial)

95   **H1** 31; **H2** 53

96

97   **H1** 32 (partial); **H2** 53 (partial)

98

99   **H1** 33 (partial); **H2** 54 (partial); **L2** (MS N, 4, Wenger, *L'Assomption*, 258–9; partial)

100   **H1** 33–4 (partial); H2 54 (partial); **L2** (MS N, 5, Wenger, *L'Assomption*, 258–9; partial)

101   **H1** 34–5 (partial); **H2** 54–5 (partial); **L2** (MS N, 6, Wenger, *L'Assomption*, 258–9; partial)

102

103

104

105–31   [Agnes Smith Lewis, *Acta Mythologica Apostolorum*, Horae Semiticae 3 and 4 (London: C. J. Clay & Sons, 1904), 150–64 (Arab.) and 175–92 (Eng.).]

132

133

134

135

136

BIBLIOGRAPHY

NARRATIVES OF THE DORMITION OF THE VIRGIN
FROM BEFORE THE TENTH CENTURY

After Michel van Esbroeck, 'Les Textes littéraires sur l'assomption avant le Xe siècle', in François Bovon (ed.), *Les Actes apocryphes des apôtres* (Geneva: Labor et Fides, 1981), 266–8. The numbers assigned to the different narratives are borrowed from van Esbroeck's earlier catalogue, as are many of the 'titles' and references to unpublished manuscripts. For a more complete listing of manuscripts, see the entries for individual works in Simon C. Mimouni, *Dormition et assomption de Marie: Histoire des traditions anciennes*, Théologie Historique, 98 (Paris: Beauchesne, 1995).

A. Arabic Traditions

AB1 (= S 3) 'The Six Books'
    ENGER, MAXIMILLIAN, ed., اخبار يوحنّا السليح في نقلة امّ المسيح (*Akhbâr Yûhannâ as-salîh fi naqlat umm al-masîh*), *id est Joannis apostoli de transitu Beatae Mariae Virginis liber* (Eberfeld: R. L. Friderichs, 1854).

AB2 Cyril of Alexandria, *Homily for 21 Tobe*
    'ABD AL-MASIH SULAIMAN, ed., *Kitâb mayâmir 'agâ'ib is-sayyidat il-'adhra Miryam* (Cairo, 1916 (1st edn.), 143–68; 1927 (2nd edn.), 210–48; 1947 (3rd edn.), 169–90). [I have been unable to locate a copy of this work. Reference is from Mimouni, *Dormition*, 222 n. 40.]

AB3 Cyril of Alexandria, *Homily for 16 Mesore*
    'ABD AL-MASIH SULAIMAN, ed., *Kitâb mayâmir 'agâ'ib is-sayyidat il-'adhra Miryam* (Cairo, 1916 (1st edn.), 169–86; 1927 (2nd edn.), 248–60; 1947 (3rd edn.), 192–200). [I have been unable to locate a copy of this work. Reference is from Mimouni, *Dormition*, 224 n. 46.]

AB4 (= C 5) Theodosius of Alexandria, *Homily on the Dormition*
    Unedited. Vaticanus arabicus MS 698, fol. 85–102.

AB5 *Transitus* from Paris ar. 150
    Unedited. Bibliothèque National, Paris, MS arabe 150, fol. 157r–170v.
    LEROY, L., 'La Dormition de Marie', *Revue de l'Orient Chrétien*, 15 (1910), 162–72 (French translation).

AB6 (= G 8) Theophilus of Landra, *Homily on the Dormition*
    Unedited. Vaticanus arabicus MS 698, fol. 41–8.

AB7 (= E 5) Sermon of Cyriacus of Behnasa (Oxyrhynchus), *Homily on
    the Dormition*
    Unedited. Vaticanus arabicus MS 170, fol. 317–39.

AB8 Euthymiac History
    ESBROECK, MICHEL VAN, 'Un témoin indirect de l'Histoire
    Eutymiaque dans une lecture arabe pour l'Assomption', *Parole de
    l'Orient*, 6–7 (1975–6), 485–8.

AB9 *Transitus* of John the Evangelist
    Unedited. Vaticanus arabicus MS 698, fol. 51–84.

AB10 MS Cairo, Coptic Museum 105 (Hist. 477)
    Unedited. Coptic Museum, Cairo, MS 105 (Hist. 477), fol.
    145r–154v.

B. Armenian Traditions

AM1 'Standard *Transitus*'
    TAYETS'I, ESAYI, ed., ' Երանելւոյն Նիկողիմոսի առաքեալ յաղագս
    ննջման Մարիանու Աստուածածնի եւ Միշտ Կուսին (A Narration
    concerning the Dormition of the Theotokos and Ever-Virgin Mary
    by the Blessed Nicodemus)', in Անկանոն գիրք Նոր Կտակարանաց
    (*Ankanon girk' Nor Ktakaranats' [Apocryphal Books of the New
    Testament]*), T'angaran haykakan hin ew nor dprut'eants', 2 (Venice:
    I Tparani S. Łazaru, 1898), 451–77.
    VETTER, PAUL, 'Die armenische "Dormitio Mariae"', *Theologische
    Quartalschrift*, 84 (1902), 321–49 (German translation of a more
    critical text; Armenian text not given).

AM2 (= S 4) Jacob of Serug, *Homily on the Dormition*
    Unedited. Bibliothèque National, Paris, MS arméniene 117, fol.
    156–8.

AM3 Ps.-John Chrysostom, *Homily on the Dormition*
    ESBROECK, MICHEL VAN, 'Une homélie arménienne sur la dormi-
    tion attribuée à Chrysostome', *Oriens Christianus*, 74 (1990): 199–
    233.

AM4 (Ps.-)Moses Chorenatsi, 'Reply to the Letter of Isaac'
    Պատասխանի թղթոյն Սահակայ (Reply to the Letter of Sahak),
    in Սրբոյ Հորն մերոյ Մովսեսի Խորենացւոյ մատենագրութիւնք
    (*Srboy horn meroy Movsesi Khorenats'woy matenagrut'iwnk' [The
    Writings of our Holy Father Moses Khorenatsi]*), 2nd edn. (Venice: I
    Tparani S. Łazaru, 1865), 283–96.
    DASNABEDIAN, THAMAR, 'L'histoire de l'icône de Hogeac'

Vank'. Une attribution à Moïse K'ert'oł', *Handes Amsoreay*, 107 (1993), 149–66; repr. in *La Mère de Dieu: Études sur l'Assomption et sur l'image de la très-sainte Mère de Dieu* (Antelias: Catholicossat Armenien de Cilicie, 1995), 9–50 (French translation).

AM5 Zachariah the Catholicos, *Homily on the Dormition*

ESBROECK, MICHEL VAN, 'L'homélie Ա‍րարիչ ա‍րարածոց, ses attributs et sa métamorphose', *Hask*, NS 6 (1994), 47–66.

DASNABEDIAN, THAMAR, 'Une homélie arménienne sur le transitus de la Mère de Dieu et sur son image', *Bazmavep*, 1–4 (1992), 217–35; repr. in *La Mère de Dieu: Études sur l'Assomption et sur l'image de la très-sainte Mère de Dieu* (Antelias: Catholicossat Armenien de Cilicie, 1995), 73–102 (French translation of a closely related version that has combined the traditions of AM 3 and AM 4).

AM6 (= G 6) Résumé of John of Thessalonica

DASNABEDIAN, THAMAR, 'Une récit arménien du Pseudo-Jean l'Évangéliste sur la Dormition', *Armach*, 1 (1992), 27–38; repr. in *La Mère de Dieu: Études sur l'Assomption et sur l'image de la très-sainte Mère de Dieu* (Antelias: Catholicossat Armenien de Cilicie, 1995), 51–72.

AM7 Letter of Pseudo-Dionysius the Areopagite to Titus

SRUANDZTEANTS', GAREGIN, ed., Թուղթ Դիոնեսիոսի Ա‍րիսպագացւոյ (The Letter of Dionysius the Areopagite), in Հնոց եւ նորոց պատմունֆիւն վասն Դաւֆի եւ Մովսեսի Խորենացւոյ (*Hnots' ew norots' patmut'iwn vasn Dawt'i ew Movsesi Khorenats'woy [History of the Old and New concerning David and Moses Khorenatsi]*), (Constantinople: Tpagrut'iwn E. M. Tntesean, 1874), 110–15.

VETTER, PAUL, 'Das apocryphe Schreiben Dionysius des Areopagiten an Titus über die Aufnahme Mariä', *Theologische Quartalschrift*, 69 (1887), 133–8 (German translation of text published in article below).

—— 'Ա‍պախերապական Թուղթ Դիոնեսիոսի Ա‍րիսպագացւոյ առ Տիտոս վասն ննջմ‍ան Մարեմայ (The Apocryphal Letter of Dionysius the Areopagite to Titus concerning the Dormition of Mary)', in J. Dashian (ed.), Հայկական աշխատասիրութիւնք (*Haykakan ashkhatsirut'iwnk' [Armenian Studies]*), Azgayin matenadaran, 17 (Vienna: Mkhit'arean Tparan, 1895), 11–17 (Armenian translation of the above article, including original Armenian text of the letter).

C. Coptic Traditions

C1 'Standard *Transitus*' (= E1 = S1 = I1)

MacCOULL, LeslieS.B., 'MoreCopticPapyrifromtheBeineckeCollection', *Archiv für Papyrusforschung*, 35 (1989), 25–35, with pl. 4.

REVILLOUT, E., ed., *Évangile des douze apôtres*, PO 2. 2 (Paris: Librairie de Paris/Firmin-Didot et Cie, 1907), 174–83.

SELLEW, PHILIP, 'An Early Coptic Witness to the *Dormitio Mariae* at Yale: P. CtYBR inv. 1788 Revisited', *Bulletin of the American Society of Papyrologists*, 37 (2000), 37–69.

C2 Ps.-Cyril of Jerusalem, *Homily on the Dormition*

BUDGE, E. A. W., ed., *Miscellaneous Coptic Texts in the Dialect of Upper Egypt* (London: British Museum, 1915), 49–73 (Copt.) and 626–50 (Eng.).

CAMPAGNANO, ANTONELLA, ed., *Ps. Cirillo di Gerusalemme: Omelie copte sulla Passione, sulla Croce e sulla Vergine*, Testi e Documenti per lo Studio dell'Antichita, LXV (Milan: Cisalpiono-Goliardica, 1980), 151–95.

ROBINSON, FORBES, ed., *Coptic Apocryphal Gospels*, Texts and Studies, IV (Cambridge: Cambridge University Press, 1896), 24–41.

Unedited. Pierpont Morgan Library, New York, MS M 597 fol. 46r–74v.

C3 Evodius of Rome, *Homily on the Dormition ('Sahidic version'; St Mich. version)*

SHOEMAKER, STEPHEN J., 'The Sahidic Coptic Homily on the Dormition of the Virgin Attributed to Evodius of Rome: An Edition of Morgan MSS 596 & 598 with Translation', *Analecta Bollandiana*, 117 (1999), 241–83.

C4 Evodius of Rome, *Homily on the Dormition ('Bohairic version'; St Mac. and W. Mon. versions)*

DE LAGARDE, PAUL, ed., *Aegyptiaca* (Göttingen: A. Hoyer, 1883; repr. Osnabrück: Otto Zeller Verlag, 1972), 38–63 (text of St Mac. version).

ROBINSON, FORBES, ed., *Coptic Apocryphal Gospels*, Texts and Studies, IV (Cambridge: Cambridge University Press, 1896), 45–67 (English translation of St Mac. version); 67–89 (text and translation of W. Mon. version).

WHITE, H. G. E., ed., *The Monasteries of the Wadi 'n Natrûn*, i. *New Coptic Texts from the Monastery of Saint Macarius* (New York: The Metropolitan Museum of Art, 1926), 54–8 (fragments).

C5 (= AB 4) Theodosius of Alexandria, *Homily on the Dormition*

BELLET, P. M., 'Theodosio de Alejandria y su homilia copta sobre la Asunción de la Virgen', *Ephemerides Mariologicae*, 1 (1951), 243–66.

CHAÎNE, MARIUS, 'Sermon de Théodose Patriarche d'Alexandrie sur la Dormition et l'Assomption de la Vierge', *Revue de l'Orient*

Chrétien, 29 (1933–4), 272–314.

ROBINSON, FORBES, ed., *Coptic Apocryphal Gospels*, Texts and Studies, IV (Cambridge: Cambridge University Press, 1896), 90–127.

WHITE, H. G. E., ed., *The Monasteries of the Wadi 'n Natrûn*, i. *New Coptic Texts from the Monastery of Saint Macarius* (New York: The Metropolitan Museum of Art, 1926), 60–2 (fragments).

C6 Ps.-Theophilus of Alexandria, *Homily on the Dormition*
WORRELL, W. H., ed., *The Coptic Texts in the Freer Collection* (New York: Macmillan, 1923), 249–321 (Copt.) and 359–80 (Eng.).
Unedited. Pierpont Morgan Library, New York, MS M 600, fol. 46–63.

C7 Bohairic Fragments
WHITE, H. G. E., ed., *The Monasteries of the Wadi 'n Natrûn*, i. *New Coptic Texts from the Monastery of Saint Macarius* (New York: The Metropolitan Museum of Art, 1926), 55–8.

D. Ethiopic Traditions

E1 (= S1 = C1 = I1) *Liber Requiei*
ARRAS, VICTOR, ed., *De Transitu Mariae Aethiopice*, 2 vols., CSCO 342–3, 351–2 (Louvain: Secrétariat du CorpusSCO, 1973), i. 1–84 (Eth.) and 1–54 (Lat.).
LANTSCHOOT, A. VAN, 'Contribution aux Actes de S. Pierre et de S. Paul', *Le Muséon*, 68 (1955), 17–46.

E2 (= S3) The Six Books
CHAINE, MARIUS, ed., *Apocrypha de Beata Maria Virgine*, CSCO 39–40 (Rome: Karolus de Luigi, 1909), 21–49 (Eth.) and 17–42 (Lat.).

E3 Résumé of The Six Books
ARRAS, VICTOR, ed., *De Transitu Mariae Aethiopice*, 2 vols., CSCO 342–3, 351–2 (Louvain: Secrétariat du CorpusSCO, 1973), i. 85–100 (Eth.) and 55–66 (Lat.).

E4 Cyril of Jerusalem, *Homily on the Dormition*
ARRAS, VICTOR, ed., *De Transitu Mariae Aethiopice*, 2 vols., CSCO 342–3, 351–2 (Louvain: Secrétariat du CorpusSCO, 1973), ii. 1–33 (Eth.) and 1–25 (Lat.).

E5 (= AB 7) Cyriacus of Behnesa (Oxyrhynchus), *Homily on the Dormition*
ARRAS, VICTOR, ed., *De Transitu Mariae Aethiopice*, 2 vols., CSCO 342–3, 351–2 (Louvain: Secrétariat du CorpusSCO, 1973), ii. 34–55 (Eth.) and 26–42 (Lat.).

E6 John the Metropolitan, *Homily on the Dormition*
    ARRAS, VICTOR, ed., *De Transitu Mariae Aethiopice*, 2 vols., CSCO
    342–3, 351–2 (Louvain: Secrétariat du CorpusSCO, 1973), ii. 56–61
    (Eth.) and 43–6 (Lat.).

E7 A Reading concerning the Apostle Thomas
    ARRAS, VICTOR, ed., *De Transitu Mariae Aethiopice*, 2 vols., CSCO
    342–3, 351–2 (Louvain: Secrétariat du CorpusSCO, 1973), ii. 62–72
    (Eth.) and 47–55 (Lat.).

E. Greek Traditions

G1 The Greek *Transitus*
    WENGER, ANTOINE, AA, *L'Assomption de la T. S. Vierge dans la
    tradition byzantine du VIe au Xe siècle*, Archives de l'Orient Chrétien,
    5 (Paris: Institut Français d'Études Byzantines, 1955), 210–41.

    MANNS, FRÉDÉRIC, OFM, *Le Récit de la dormition de Marie
    (Vatican grec 1982), Contribution à l'étude de origines de l'exégèse
    chrétienne*, Studium Biblicum Franciscanum, Collectio Maior, 33
    (Jerusalem: Franciscan Printing Press, 1989) (in appendix; includes
    reproduction of Vatican Greek 1982).

G2 (= I4) *Transitus* of John the Evangelist
    TISCHENDORF, KONSTANTIN, ed., *Apocalypses Apocryphae*
    (Leipzig: Herm. Mendelssohn, 1866), 95–110.

    JAMES, MONTAGUE RHODES, *The Apocryphal New Testament*, corr.
    edn. (Oxford: Clarendon Press, 1989), 201–9 (English translation).

    ELLIOTT, J. K., *The Apocryphal New Testament* (Oxford:
    Clarendon Press, 1993), 701–8 (English translation).

G3 (1st version), G4 (2nd version) and G5 (various alternative endings)
    John of Thessalonica, *Homily on the Dormition*
    JUGIE, MARTIN, AA, ed., *Homélies mariales byzantine (II)*, PO
    19. 3 (Paris: Librairie de Paris/Firmin-Didot et Cie, 1926), 344–
    438.

    DALEY, BRIAN E., SJ, *On the Dormition of Mary: Early Patristic
    Homilies* (Crestwood, NY: St Vladimir's Seminary Press, 1998), 47–
    70 (English translation of 1st version [G3]).

G6 (= AM6) Résumé of John of Thessalonica
    HALKIN, F., 'Une légende byzantine de la Dormition: L'Epitomé
    du récit de Jean de Thessalonique', *Revue des Études Byzantines*, 11
    (1953), 156–64.

G7 (= I7) Euthymiac History
    Unedited. Sinaiticus Codex 491, fol. 246v–251.

    KOTTER, BERNARD, ed., *Die Schriften des Johannes von Damaskus*,

v. *Opera homiletica et hagiographica* (Walter de Gruyter: Berlin, 1988), 536–9.

G8 (= AB6) Theoteknos of Livias, *Homily on the Dormition*
  WENGER, ANTOINE, AA, *L'Assomption de la T. S. Vierge dans la tradition byzantine du VIe au Xe siècle*, Archives de l'Orient Chrétien, 5 (Paris: Institut Français d'Études Byzantines, 1955), 271–91.
  DALEY, BRIAN E., SJ, *On the Dormition of Mary: Early Patristic Homilies* (Crestwood, NY: St Vladimir's Seminary Press, 1998), 71–81 (English translation).

G9 (Ps.-)Modestus of Jerusalem, *Homily on the Dormition*
  PG 86. 3277–312.
  DALEY, BRIAN E., SJ, *On the Dormition of Mary: Early Patristic Homilies* (Crestwood, NY: St Vladimir's Seminary Press, 1998), 83–102 (English translation).

G10 Andrew of Crete, *Homilies on the Dormition*
  PG 97. 1045–110.
  DALEY, BRIAN E., SJ, *On the Dormition of Mary: Early Patristic Homilies* (Crestwood, NY: St Vladimir's Seminary Press, 1998), 103–52 (English translation).

G11 John of Damascus, *Homilies on the Dormition*
  PG 96. 697–762.
  ALLIES, MARY H., *St. John Damascene on Holy Images followed by Three Sermons on the Assumption* (London: Thomas Baker, 1898) (English translation).
  DALEY, BRIAN E., SJ, *On the Dormition of Mary: Early Patristic Homilies* (Crestwood, NY: St Vladimir's Seminary Press, 1998), 183–239 (English translation).
  KOTTER, BERNARD, ed., *Die Schriften des Johannes von Damaskus*, v. *Opera homiletica et hagiographica* (Walter de Gruyter: Berlin, 1988), 461–555.
  Voulet, P., ed., *Homélies dur la nativité et la dormition*, SC 80 (Paris: Les Éditions du Cerf, 1961), 80–197.

G12 Germanus of Constantinople, *Homily on the Dormition*
  PG 98. 340–72.
  DALEY, BRIAN E., SJ, *On the Dormition of Mary: Early Patristic Homilies* (Crestwood, NY: St Vladimir's Seminary Press, 1998), 153–81 (English translation).

G13 Cosmas Vestitor, *Four Homilies on the Dormition*
  WENGER, ANTOINE, AA, *L'Assomption de la T. S. Vierge dans la tradition byzantine du VIe au Xe siècle*, Archives de l'Orient Chrétien, 5 (Paris: Institut Français d'Études Byzantines, 1955), 315–33.

F. Irish Traditions

H1 The Testament of Mary

DONAHUE, CHARLES, ed., *The Testament of Mary: The Gaelic Version of the Dormitio Mariae together with an Irish Latin Version*, Fordham University Studies, Language Series, 1 (New York: Fordham University Press, 1942).

H2 *Transitus Mariae*

HERBERT, MÁIRE, and MCNAMARA, MARTIN, eds., *Irish Biblical Apocrypha* (Edinburgh: T. & T. Clark, 1989), 119–31 (English translation).

Unpublished. *Liber Flavus Fergusiorum*. Royal Irish Academy, Dublin, MS 23 O 48.

G. Georgian Traditions

I1 (= E1 = S1 = C1), I2, and I3 (= E1 = S1 = C1), Early Fragments from the Klardjeti Homiliary

ESBROECK, MICHEL VAN, 'Apocryphes géorgiens de la Dormition', *Analecta Bollandiana*, 92 (1973), 55–75.

MGALOBLIŠVILI, TAMILA, ed., კლარჯული მრვალთავი *(K'larjuli mravaltavi [The Klardjeti Homiliary])*, Zveli kartuli mcerlobis zeglebi, 12 (Tbilisi: 'Metsnieba', 1991), 420–5.

I4 (= G2) *Transitus* of John the Evangelist

Unedited. Athos Iviron MS 11, fol. 156rb–162rb; Tiflis MS A-144, fol. 195vb–201vb; Jerusalem Georgian MS 178, fol. 142v–148v.

I5 *Transitus* of Pseudo-Basil of Caesarea

ESBROECK, MICHEL VAN, 'L'Assomption de la Vierge dans un Transitus Pseudo-Basilien', *Analecta Bollandiana*, 92 (1974), 128–63.

I6 Reading for 13 August

ESBROECK, MICHEL VAN, 'Nouveaux Apocryphes de la Dormition conservés en Géorgien', *Analecta Bollandiana*, 90 (1972), 363–9.

I7 (= G7) Euthymiac History

Unedited. Kutaïs MS 3, fol. 377–9.

I8 (Ps.-?)Maximus the Confessor, *Life of the Virgin*

ESBROECK, MICHEL VAN, ed., *Maxime le Confesseur: Vie de la Vierge*, CSCO 478–9 (Louvain: Peeters, 1986).

H. Latin Traditions

L1 *Transitus* of Pseudo-Melito

ELLIOTT, J. K., *The Apocryphal New Testament* (Oxford: Clarendon Press, 1993), 708–14 (English translation).

HAIBACH-REINISCH, MONIKA, ed., *Ein neuer 'Transitus Mariae' des Pseudo-Melito* (Rome: Pontificia Academia Mariana Internationalis, 1962).

JAMES, MONTAGUE RHODES, *The Apocryphal New Testament*, corr. edn. (Oxford: The Clarendon Press, 1989), 209–16 (English translation).

TISCHENDORF, KONSTANTIN, ed., *Apocalypses Apocryphae* (Leipzig: Herm. Mendelssohn, 1866), 124–36.

L2 *Transitus* 'W'

CAPELLE, BERNARD, 'Vestiges grecs et latins d'un antique "Transitus" de la Vierge', *Analecta Bollandiana*, 67 (1949), 21–48.

WENGER, ANTOINE, AA, *L'Assomption de la T. S. Vierge dans la tradition byzantine du VIe au Xe siècle*, Archives de l'Orient Chrétien, 5 (Paris: Institut Français d'Études Byzantines, 1955), 258–9. ('Type N')

WILMART, A. ed., *Analecta Reginensia: Extraits des manuscrits Latins de la Reine christine conservés au Vatican*, Studi e Testi, 59 (Vatican: Biblioteca Apostolica Vaticana, 1933), 323–62.

L3 *Transitus* of Pseudo-Joseph of Arimathea

TISCHENDORF, KONSTANTIN, ed., *Apocalypses Apocryphae* (Leipzig: Herm. Mendelssohn, 1866), 113–23.

L4 'The Archaic *Transitus*'

WENGER, ANTOINE, AA, *L'Assomption de la T. S. Vierge dans la tradition byzantine du VIe au Xe siècle*, Archives de l'Orient Chrétien, 5 (Paris: Institut Français d'Études Byzantines, 1955), 245–56.

L5 Cosmas Vestitor, *Homilies on the Dormition*

WENGER, ANTOINE, AA, *L'Assomption de la T. S. Vierge dans la tradition byzantine du VIe au Xe siècle*, Archives de l'Orient Chrétien, 5 (Paris: Institut Français d'Études Byzantines, 1955), 315–44.

L6 John of Arezzo, *Homily on the Dormition*

WENGER, ANTOINE, AA, *L'Assomption de la T. S. Vierge dans la tradition byzantine du VIe au Xe siècle*, Archives de l'Orient Chrétien, 5 (Paris: Institut Français d'Études Byzantines, 1955), 337–62.

L7 Gregory of Tours, *In gloria Martyrum*

KRUSCH, B. ed., *Gregorii Episcopi Turonensis miracula et opera minora*, 2nd edn., Monumenta Germaniae Historica, Scriptores Rerum Merovingicarum, 1/2 (Hanover: Impensis Bibliopolii Hahniani, 1969), 39 and 43.

L8 (= G 2) *Transitus* from the Laurentienne MS

WENGER, ANTOINE, AA, *L'Assomption de la T. S. Vierge dans la tradition byzantine du VIe au Xe siècle*, Archives de l'Orient Chrétien, 5 (Paris: Institut Français d'Études Byzantines, 1955), 357–62.

I. Syriac Traditions

S1 (= E1 = C1 = S1) *Obsequies*
WRIGHT, WILLIAM, ed., *Contributions to the Apocryphal Literature of the New Testament* (London: Williams & Norgate, 1865), ‎ܡܘ—ܡܠ‎ and 42–51.

S2 *Transitus Mariae*
WRIGHT, WILLIAM, ed., *Contributions to the Apocryphal Literature* (London: Williams & Norgate, 1865), ‎ܐܝ—ܝܚ‎ and 18–41.

S3 The Six Books
BUDGE, E. A. W., ed., *History of the Blessed Virgin Mary and the History of the Likeness of Christ which the Jews of Tiberias Made to Mock at* (London: Luzac & Co., 1899), 3–153 (Syr.) and 3–168 (Eng.).
SMITH LEWIS, AGNES, ed., *Apocrypha Syriaca*, Studia Sinaitica, XI (London: C. J. Clay & Sons, 1902), ‎ܡܝܩ—ܓ‎ (Syr.) and 12–69 (Eng.).
WRIGHT, WILLIAM, 'The Departure of my Lady Mary from this World', *The Journal of Sacred Literature and Biblical Record*, 6 (1865), 417–48 and 7 (1865), 108–60.

S4 Jacob of Serug, *Homily on the Dormition*
BAUMSTARK, ANTON, 'Zwei syrische Dichtungen auf das Entschlafen der allerseligsten Jungfrau', *Oriens Christianus*, 5 (1905), 91–9 (Latin translation of a second manuscript).
BEDJAN, PAUL, ed., *S. Martyrii, qui et Sahdona, quae supersunt omnia* (Leipzig: Otto Harrassowitz, 1902), 709–19.

S5 John of Birtha, *Homily on the Dormition*
BAUMSTARK, ANTON, 'Zwei syrische Dichtungen auf das Entschlafen der allerseligsten Jungfrau', *Oriens Christianus*, 5 (1905), 100–25.

OTHER PRIMARY SOURCES

The Acts of Pilate, ed. Konstantin Tischendorf, *Evangelia Apocrypha*, 2nd edn. (Leipzig: 1876; repr. Hildesheim: Georg Olms, 1966), 211–322.

ADAMNAN, *De locis sanctis*, ed. Denis Meehan, *Adamnan's De locis sanctis*, Scriptores Latini Hiberniae, 3 (Dublin: Dublin Institute for Advanced Studies, 1958).

AMBROSE, *Expositio evangelii secundum Lucam*, ed. C. & H. Schenkl, *Expositio evangelii secundum Lucam*, CSEL 32.4 (Leipzig: G. Freytag, 1902; repr. New York: Johnson Reprint Co., 1962).

(Ps.-)ANTONINUS PLACENTIUS, *Itinerarium*, ed. P. Geyer, *Itineraria et alia Geographica,* CCL 175 (Turnhout: Brepols, 1965) 127–74; third recension: ed. T. Tobler and A. Molinier, *Itinera Hierosolymitana,* 2 vols. (Geneva: J.-G. Fick, 1879), i. 89–138 and 360–91.

The (First) Apocalypse of James, ed. Douglas M. Parrott, *Nag Hammadi Codices V,2–5 and VI with Papyrus Berolinensis 8502, 1 and 4,* NHS 11 (Leiden: E. J. Brill, 1979), 65–103.

The Apocalypse of Paul, ed. Montague Rhodes James, *Apocrypha Anecdota,* Texts and Studies, II/3 (Cambridge: The University Press, 1893), 11–42.

The Apocalypse of Zephaniah, ed. Georg Steindorff, *Die Apokalypse des Elias, eine unbekannte Apokalypse und Bruchstücke der Sophonias-Apokalypse,* TU 17. 3a (Leipzig: J. C. Hinrichs, 1899), 34–65.

The Apocryphon of John, ed. Michael Waldstein and Frederic Wisse, *The Apocryphon of John: a synopsis of Nag Hammadi codices II,1, III,1, and IV,1 with BG 8502,2,* NHS 33 (New York : E. J. Brill, 1995).

The Armenian Jerusalem Lectionary, ed. A. Renoux, *Le Codex arménien Jérusalem 121,* 2 vols., PO 35. 1 and 36. 2 (Turnhout: Brepols, 1971).

The Ascension of Isaiah, ed. Paolo Bettiolo and Enrico Norelli, *Ascensio Isaiae,* 2 vols., CCSA 7–8 (Turnhout: Brepols, 1995).

The Assumption of Moses, ed. Johannes Tromp, *The Assumption of Moses: A Critical Edition with Commentary,* Studia in Veteris Testamenti Pseudepigrapha, 10 (Leiden: E. J. Brill, 1993).

AUGUSTINE, *De natura et gratia liber,* ed. C. F. Urba and J. Zycha, *Sancta Aureli Augustini Opera,* sect. VIII. pt. I, CSEL 60 (Leipzig: G. Freytag, 1913), 233–99.

—— *Tractatus in evangelium Ioannis,* ed R. Willems, *Tractatus in evangelium Ioannis,* CCL 36 (Turnhout: Brepols, 1954).

The Books of Jeu, ed. Carl Schmidt and trans. Violet MacDermot, *The Books of Jeû and the Untitled Text in the Bruce Codex,* NHS 13 (Leiden: E. J. Brill, 1978), 1–141.

Brevarius de Hierosolyma, ed. R. Weber, *Itineraria et alia Geographica,* CCL 175 (Turnhout: Brepols, 1965), 105–12.

The Capture of Jerusalem, ed. Gérard Garitte, *La Prise de Jérusalem par les Perses en 614,* CSCO 202–3 (Louvain: Secrétariat du CorpusSCO, 1960) (Georgian version); idem, *Expugnationis Hierosolymae A.D. 614,* 2 vols., CSCO 340–1, 347–8 (Louvain, Secrétariat du Corpus SCO, 1973–4) (Arabic version).

CHRYSIPPUS OF JERUSALEM, *Encomium in Mariam Deiparam,* ed. Martin Jugie, AA, *Homélies mariales byzantines (II),* PO 19. 3 (Paris: Librairie de Paris/Firmin-Didot et Cie, 1926), 336–43.

CLEMENT OF ALEXANDRIA, *Excerpta ex Theodoto,* ed. François Sagnard,

Clément d'Alexandrie: Extraits de Théodote, SC 23 (Paris: Éditions du Cerf, 1948).

Commemoratorium de casis Dei, ed. Titus Tobler, *Descriptiones Terrae Sanctae ex saeculo VIII. IX. XII. et XV.* (Leipzig: J. C. Hinrichs'sche Buchhandlung, 1874).

CYRIL OF SCYTHOPOLIS, *Vita Euthymii*, ed. Eduard Schwartz, *Kyrillos von Skythopolis*, TU 49. 2 (Leipzig: J. C. Hinrichs, 1939).

—— *Vita Sabae*, ed. Eduard Schwartz, *Kyrillos von Skythopolis*, TU 49. 2 (Leipzig: J. C. Hinrichs, 1939).

—— *Vita Theodosii*, ed. Eduard Schwartz, *Kyrillos von Skythopolis*, TU 49. 2 (Leipzig: J. C. Hinrichs, 1939).

DANIEL THE ABBOT, *The Life and Journey of Daniel, Abbot of the Russian Land*, ed. Klaus-Dieter Seemann, Хожение *[Khozhdenie]: Wallfahrtsbericht*, Slavische Propyläen, 36 (Munich: W. Fink, 1970); trans. John Wilkinson, Joyce Hill, and W. F. Ryan, *Jerusalem Pilgrimage 1099–1185*, Works Issued by the Hakluyt Society, 2nd series, 167 (London: The Hakluyt Society, 1988), 120–71.

Decretum Gelasianum, ed. Ernst von Dobschütz, *Das Decretum Gelasianum de libris recipiendis et non recipiendis*, TU 38. 4 (Leipzig: J. C. Hinrichs, 1912).

Ps.-DIONYSIUS THE AREOPAGITE, *De divinis nominibus*, ed. Beate Regina Suchla, *Corpus Dionysiacum*, i. *Pseudo-Dionysius Areopagite De divinis nominibus*, Patristische Texte und Studien, 33 (Berlin/New York: Walter de Gruyter, 1990); trans. Colm Luibhéid (and Paul Rorem), *Pseudo-Dionysius: The Complete Works*, The Classics of Western Spirituality (New York: Paulist Press, 1987).

Ps.-DIOSCORUS OF ALEXANDRIA, *Panegyric on Macarius of Tkōw*, ed. David Johnson, *A Panegyric on Macarius, Bishop of Tkōw, Attributed to Dioscorus of Alexandria*, CSCO 415–16 (Louvain: Peeters, 1980).

Doctrina Addai, trans. George Howard, *The Teaching of Addai*, Society of Biblical Literature Texts and Translations, 16, Early Christian Literature Series, 4 (Chico, CA: Scholars Press, 1981); Syriac text repr. from George Phillips, ed., *The Doctrine of Addai, the Apostle* (London: Trübner & Co. 1876).

EPHREM, *Hymns on Paradise*, ed. Edmund Beck, *Des Heiligen Ephraem des Syrers Hymnen de Paradiso und Contra Julianum*. CSCO 174–5 (Louvain: CSCO, 1957).

Ps.-EPHREM, *Hymns on Mary*, ed. Thomas Josephus Lamy, *Sancti Ephraem Syri hymni et sermones*, 4 vols. (Mechliniae: H. Dessain, 1882–1902), ii.

EPIPHANIUS HAGIOPOLITA, *Itinerarium*, ed. Herbert Donner, 'Die Palästinabeschreibung des Epiphanius Monachus Hagiopolita', *Zeitschrift des Deutschen Palästina-Vereins*, 87 (1971), 42–91.

EPIPHANIUS OF SALAMIS, *Panarion*, ed. Karl Holl; 2nd edn., J. Dummer, *Epiphanius: Ancoratus und Panarion*, 3 vols., GCS 25, 31 (2nd edn.), 37 (2nd edn.) (Leipzig: J. C. Hinrichs, 1915; Berlin: Akademie Verlag, 1980, 1985); trans. Frank Williams, *The Panarion of Epiphanius of Salamis*, NHS 36 (Leiden: E. J. Brill, 1994).

EPIPHANIUS THE MONK, *Life of the Virgin*, PG 120. 185–216.

EUTYCHIUS OF ALEXANDRIA (Sa'id ibn Batrîq), *Annales*, ed. M. Breydy, *Das Annalenwerke des Eutychios von Alexandrien*, CSCO 471–2 (Louvain: Peeters, 1985); Antiochene recension: ed. L. Cheikho, *Eutychii Patriarchae Alexandrini Annales*, 2 vols., CSCO 50–1 (Louvain: L. Durbecq/CSCO, 1954, 1960); Latin trans.: PG 111. 889–1156.

FABRI, FELIX, OP, *Evagatorium in Terrae Sanctae, Arabiae et Egypti peregrinationem*, ed. C. D. Hassler, 3 vols., Bibliothek des Literarischen Vereins in Stuttgart, 2–4 (Stuttgart: sumtibus Societatis literariae stuttgardiensis, 1843–9).

The Fourth Book of Ezra, ed. Robert Weber, OSB, Bonifatio Fischer, OSB, Johannes Gribomont, OSB, H. F. D. Sparks, W. Thiele, and H. J. Frede, *Biblia sacra iuxta vulgatam versionem*, 3rd edn. (Stuttgart: Deutsche Bibelgesellschaft, 1983), 1931–74.

The Georgian Jerusalem 'Chantbook' (Iadgari), ed. E. Metreveli, C'. Cankievi, and L. Xevsuriani, უძველესი იადგარი (*Uzvelesi Iadgari [The Oldest Chantbook]*), Zveli k'art'uli mcerlobis zeglebi, 2 (Tbilisi: Mec'niereba, 1980).

The Georgian Jerusalem Lectionary, ed. Michel Tarchnischvili, *Le Grand Lectionnaire de l'église de Jérusalem*, 2 vols. CSCO 188–9, 204–5 (Louvain: CSCO, 1959–60).

The Gospel according to Philip, ed. Bentley Layton, *Nag Hammadi Codex II, 2–7*, 2 vols., NHS 20–1 (Leiden: E. J. Brill, 1989), i. 131–217.

The Gospel of Bartholomew (Coptic)/The Book of the Resurrection of Jesus Christ by Bartholomew the Apostle, ed. E. A. W. Budge, *Coptic Apocrypha in the Dialect of Upper Egypt* (London: British Museum, 1913), 1–49 (Copt.) and 179–215 (Eng.) (complete); fragments: ed. Pierre Lacau, *Mémoires publiés par les membres de l'institut français d'archéologie orientale du Caire*, ix. *Fragments d'apocryphes coptes* (Cairo: Imprimerie de l'institut français d'archéologie orientale, 1904), version A: 25–32 (Copt.) and 33–7 (Fr.); version B: 43–66 (Copt.) and 67–77 (Fr.).

The Gospel of Pseudo-Matthew, ed. Jan Gijsel and Rita Beyers, *Libri de nativitate Mariae*, 2 vols., CCSA 9–10 (Turnhout: Brepols, 1997), i.

The Gospel of the Egyptians, ed. Alexander Böhlig and Frederik Wisse, *Nag Hammadi Codices III, 2 and IV, 2: The Gospel of the Egyptians*, NHS 4 (Grand Rapids, MI: Eerdmans, 1975).

The Gospel of Truth, ed. Harold. W. Attridge, *Nag Hammadi Codex I (The Jung Codex)*, 2 vols., NHS 22 (Leiden: E. J. Brill, 1985), i. 55–122.

GREGORY OF NYSSA, *De virginitate*, ed. V. W. Callahan, J. P. Cavarnos, and W. Jaeger, *Gregorii Nysseni Opera*, viii. pt. 1, *Opera Ascetica* (Leiden: E. J. Brill, 1952).

GRETHINOS THE ARCHIMANDRITE, *Pilgrimage of Grethinos the Archimandrite*, trans. Sophia Khitrovo, *Itinéraires russes en Orient*, Publications de la Société de l'Orient latin, Série géographique, 5 (Geneva: J-G. Fick, 1889), 165–91 (trans. of MS 329/1426, fol. 106–23, Museum of Ecclesiastical Archaeology, Kiev).

HESYCHIUS OF JERUSALEM, *Sermones*, ed. Michel Aubineau, *Les Homélies festales d'Hésychius de Jérusalem*, 2 vols., Subsidia Hagiographica, 59 (Brussels: Société des Bollandistes, 1978–80).

HIPPOLYTUS OF ROME, *Refutatio omnium haeresium*, ed. Miroslav Marcòvich, *Hippolytus: Refutatio omnium haeresium*, Patristische Texte und Studien, 25 (Berlin: Walter de Gruyter, 1986).

The History of Peter and Paul, ed. Agnes Smith Lewis, *Acta Mythologica Apostolorum*, 2 vols., Horae Semiticae, 3–4 (London: C. J. Clay & Sons, 1904), 150–64 (Arab.) and 175–92 (Eng.) (Arabic version); A. van Lantschoot, 'Contribution aux Actes de S. Pierre et de S. Paul, II.—Recension Karšuni des Actes de S. Pierre et S. Paul', *Le Muséon*, 68 (1955), 219–33 (Karshuni version); idem, 'Les Textes palimpsest de B. M., Or. 8802', *Le Muséon*, 41 (1928), 225–47 (Coptic fragments).

The Hypostasis of the Archons, ed. Bentley Layton, *Nag Hammadi Codex II, 2–7*, 2 vols., NHS 20–1 (Leiden: E. J. Brill, 1989), i. 220–59.

IRENAEUS, *Adversus Haereses*, ed. Adelin Rousseau and Louis Doutreleau, *Irénée de Lyon: Contre les hérésies*, 9 vols., SC 100, 152–3, 210–11, 263–4, 293–4 (Paris: Les Éditions du Cerf, 1969–82).

JOHN OF DAMASCUS, *Carmen in dormitionem BMV*, PG 96. 1364–8.

JOHN OF SCYTHOPOLIS (Ps.-Maximus the Confessor), *Scholia in Dionysius the Areopagite, De divinis nominibus*, PG 4. 185–416.

The Klardjeti Homiliary, ed. Tamila Mgaloblišvili, ქართული მრავალთავი *(K'larjuli mravalt'avi [The Klardjeti Homiliary])*, Zveli k'art'uli mcerlobis zeglebi, 12 (Tbilisi: Mec'niereba, 1991).

LEONTIUS OF BYZANTIUM, *Contra Nestorianos et Eutychianos*, PG 86. 1267–396.

Melchizedek, ed. Birger A. Pearson, *Nag Hammadi Codices IX and X*, NHS 15 (Leiden: E. J. Brill, 1981), 19–85.

METHODIUS, *De resurrectione*, ed. D. G. Natanael Bonwetsch, *Methodius*, GCS 27 (Leipzig: J. C. Hinrichs, 1917).

NICCOLÒ DA POGGIBONSI, OFM, *Libro d'Oltramare*, ed. Alberto Bacchi,

Libro d' Oltramare, 2 vols., Scelta di curiosita letterarie inedite o rare dal secolo XIII al XVII, 182–3 (Bologna: G. Romagnoli, 1881).

NICEPHORUS CALLISTUS, *Historia ecclesiastica*, PG 147. 9–448.

OECUMENIUS, *Commentarius in Apocalypsin*, ed. H. C. Oskier, ed., *Commentary of Oecumenius of Tricca on the Apocalypse*, University of Michigan Humanistic Series, 23 (Ann Arbor: University of Michigan Press, 1928).

On the Origin of the World, ed. Bentley Layton, *Nag Hammadi Codex II, 2–7*, 2 vols., NHS 20–1 (Leiden: E. J. Brill, 1989), ii. 12–134.

ORIGEN, *Commentarii in Ioannem*, ed. E. Preuschen, *Origenes Werke*, iv. *Der Johanneskommentar*, GCS 10 (Leipzig: J. C. Hinrichs, 1903).

——*De principiis*, ed. Henri Crouzel and Manli Simonetti, *Origène. Traité des Principes*, 5 vols., SC 252–3, 268–9, 312 (Paris: Les Éditions du Cerf, 1978, 1980, and 1984).

——*Selecta in Psalmos*, PG 12. 1054–686.

The Palestinian Georgian Calendar, ed. Gérard Garitte, *Le Calendrier palestino-géorgien du Sinaiticus 34 (Xe siècle)*, Subsidia Hagiographica, 30 (Brussels: Société des Bollandistes, 1958).

Pistis Sophia, ed. Carl Schmidt and trans. Violet MacDermot, *Pistis Sophia*, NHS 9 (Leiden: E. J. Brill, 1978).

Ps.-PROCHORUS, *Acta Joannis*, ed. Theodor Zahn, *Acta Joannis* (Erlangen, 1880; repr. Hildesheim: Georg Olms, 1975).

PROCOPIUS OF CAESAREA, *De aedificiis*, ed. Jacobus Haury, rev. Gerhard Wirth, *Opera Omnia* (Leipzig: Teubner, 1964), iv.

Protevangelium of James, ed. Konstantin Tischendorf, *Evangelia Apocrypha*, 2nd edn. (Leipzig: 1876; repr. Hildesheim: Georg Olms, 1966), 1–50.

QUODVULTDEUS, *Sermones de symbolo*, ed. R. Braun, *Opera Quodvultdeo Carthaginiensi episcopo tributa*, CCL 60 (Turnhout: Brepols, 1976), 303–63.

Qur'an, trans. N. J. Dawood, *The Koran with a Parallel Arabic Text* (London: Penguin Books, 1994).

SEVERIAN OF GABALA, *Orationes sex in mundi creationem*, PG 56. 429–500.

The Sinai Homiliary of the Year 864, ed. Akaki Šanize, სინური მრავალთავი 864 წლისა (*Sinuri mravalt'avi 864 c'lisa [The Sinai Homiliary of the Year 864]*), Zveli k'art'uli enis kat'edris šromebi, 5 (Tbilisi: T'bilisis Stalinis saxelobis saxelmcip'o universitetis gamomc'emloba, 1959).

Slavonic Apocalypse of Enoch, ed. A. Vaillant, *Le Livre des secrets d'Hénoch* (Paris: Institut d'études slaves, 1952); trans. F. I. Anderson, in James H. Charlesworth (ed.), *The Old Testament Pseudepigrapha* (Garden City, NY: Doubleday, 1983), i. 102–221 (trans. of MSS. 13.

434   *Bibliography*

3. 25 and 45. 13. 5, Library of the Academy of Sciences of the USSR, Leningrad).

The Sophia of Jesus Christ, ed. Douglas M. Parrott, *Nag Hammadi Codices III, 3–4 and V, 1*, NHS 27 (Leiden: E. J. Brill, 1991).

SOPHRONIUS OF JERUSALEM, *Carmina anacreontica*, PG 87. 3733–838.

Syriac Apocalypse of Baruch, ed. Michael Kmosko, *Liber Apocalypseos Baruch Filii Neriae*, Patrologia Syriaca, 1/2 (Paris: Firmin-Didot et Socii, 1907), 1056–306.

TERTULLIAN, *De anima*, ed. J. H. Waszink, *Tertulliani Opera*, pt. 2, *Opera Montanistica*, CCL 2 (Turnhout: Brepols, 1954), 779–869.

—— *De resurrectione*, ed. J. G. P. Borleffs, *Tertulliani Opera*, pt. 2, *Opera Montanistica*, CCL 2 (Turnhout: Brepols, 1954), 919–1012.

Testament of Adam, ed. Stephen Edward Robinson, *The Testament of Adam: An Examination of the Syriac and Greek Traditions*, Society of Biblical Literature Dissertation Series, 52 (Chico, CA: Scholars Press, 1982).

Testament of Solomon, ed. C. C. McCown, *The Testament of Solomon, Edited from Manuscripts at Mount Athos, Bologna, Holkham Hall, Jerusalem, London, Milan, Paris and Vienna* (Leipzig, J. C. Hinrichs, 1922).

The Testimony of Truth, ed. Birger A. Pearson, *Nag Hammadi Codices IX and X*, NHS 15 (Leiden: E. J. Brill, 1981), 101–203.

THEODORE OF PETRA, *Vita Theodosii*, ed. Hermann Usener, *Der heilige Theodosius, Schriften des Theodoros und Kyrillos* (Leipzig: Teubner, 1890).

THEODOSIUS, *De situ terrae sanctae*, ed. P. Geyer, *Itineraria et alia Geographica*, CCL 175 (Turnhout: Brepols, 1965), 113–25.

TIMOTHY OF JERUSALEM, *In Simeonem et Annam*, PG 86. 237–54.

Treatise on Resurrection, ed. Harold W. Attridge, *Nag Hammadi Codex I (The Jung Codex)*, 2 vols., NHS 22 (Leiden: E. J. Brill, 1985), i. 123–57.

The Tripartite Tractate, ed. Harold W. Attridge, *Nag Hammadi Codex I (The Jung Codex)*, 2 vols., NHS 22 (Leiden: E. J. Brill, 1985), i. 159–337.

The Tübingen Theosophy, ed. Hartmut Erbse, *Theosophorum Graecorum Fragmenta* (Stuttgart: Teubner, 1995), 1–56.

The Untitled Text in the Bruce Codex, ed. Carl Schmidt and trans. Violet MacDermot, *The Books of Jeû and the Untitled Text in the Bruce Codex*, NHS 13 (Leiden: E. J. Brill, 1978).

A Valentinian Exposition, ed. Charles W. Hedrick, *Nag Hammadi codices XI, XII, XIII*, NHS 28 (Leiden: E. J. Brill, 1990), 89–172.

Vision of Ezra, ed. Otto Wahl, *Apocalypsis Esdrae—Apocalypsis Sedrach—Visio beati Esdrae*, Pseudepigrapha Veteris Testamenti Graece, 4 (Leiden: E. J. Brill, 1977).

Vitae Prophetarum, ed. Theodor Schermann, *Prophetarum vitae fabulosae indices apostolorum discipulorumque Domini Dorotheo, Epiphanio, Hippolyto aliisque vindicate* (Leipzig: Teubner, 1907).

ZACHARIAH OF MITYLENE, *Ecclesiastical History*, ed. E. W. Brooks, *Historia Ecclesiastica Zachariae Rhetori vulgo adscripta*, 2 vols., CSCO 83–4, 87–8 (Louvain: E Typographeo I.-B. Istas, 1919–24).

Zostrianos, ed. John H. Sieber, *Nag Hammadi Codex VIII*, NHS 31 (Leiden: E. J. Brill, 1991), 7–225.

SECONDARY SOURCES

AHARONI, Y., *Excavations at Ramat Rahel*, 2 vols., Serie archeologica, 2 and 6 (Rome: Universita degli studi, Centro di studi semitici, 1962, 1964).

—— 'Excavations at Ramath Rahel, 1954: Preliminary Report', *Israel Exploration Journal*, 6 (1956), 102–11, 137–57.

AVIGAD, NAHMAN, 'The Nea: Justinian's Church of St. Mary, Mother of God, Discovered in the Old City of Jerusalem', in Yoram Tsafrir (ed.), *Ancient Churches Revealed* (Jerusalem: Israel Exploration Society, 1993), 128–35.

AVNER, RINA, 'Birth Pangs on the Bethlehem Road (in Hebrew)', *Judea and Samaria Research Studies: Proceedings of the Eighth Annual Meeting 1998* (Kedumim-Ariel: The Research Institute, College of Judea and Samaria 1999), 155–60; English summary, pp. XVIII–XIX.

—— 'Jerusalem, Mar Elias', *Excavations and Surveys in Israel*, 13 (1993), 89–92.

—— 'ירושלים מר אליאס–כנסיית הקתיסמה', *Hadashot Arkheologiyot*, 108 (1998), 139–42.

BAGATTI, BELLARMINO, OFM, *Alle origini della chiesa*, i. *Le comunità giudeo-cristane* (Vatican City: Libreria Editrice Vaticana, 1981).

—— *The Church from the Circumcision: History and Archaeology of the Judaeo-Christians*, trans. Eugene Hoade, OFM, Publications of the Studium Biblicum Franciscanum, Smaller Series, 2 (Jerusalem: Franciscan Printing Press, 1971).

—— *L'Église de la Circoncision*, trans. Albert Storme, Studium Biblicum Franciscanum, Collectio Minor, 2 (Jerusalem: Franciscan Printing Press, 1965).

—— 'La morte della Vergine nel Testo di Leucio', *Marianum*, 36 (1974), 456–7.

—— 'Ricerche sulle tradizioni della morte della Vergine', *Sacra Doctrina*, 69–70 (1973), 186–94.

—— 'La verginità di Maria negli apocrifi del II–III secolo', *Marianum*, 33 (1971), 281–92.

BAGATTI, BELLARMINO, OFM, PICCIRILLO, M., and PRODOMO, A., OFM, *New Discoveries at the Tomb of Virgin Mary in Gethsemane*, Studium Biblicum Franciscanum, Collectio Minor, 17 (Jerusalem: Franciscan Printing Press, 1975).

BALDI, DONATO, OFM, *Enchiridion Locorum Sanctorum* (Jerusalem: Typis PP. Franciscanorum, 1935).

—— 'I santuari mariani in Terra Santa', *Liber Annus*, 3 (1952–3), 219–69.

—— and MOSCONI, ANACLETO, OFM, 'L'Assunzione di Maria SS. negli apocrifi', in *Atti del congresso nazionale mariano dei Fratei Minori d'Italia (Roma 29 aprile–3 maggio 1947)*, Studia Mariana, 1 (Rome: Commissionis Marialis Franciscanae, 1948), 75–125.

BALDOVIN, JOHN F., *The Urban Character of Christian Worship: The Origins, Development, and Meaning of Stational Liturgy*, Orientalia Christiana Analecta, 228 (Rome: Pont. Institutum Studiorum Orientalium, 1987).

BALIĆ, CAROLUS, OFM, *Testimonia de Assumptione Beatae Virginis Mariae ex omnibus saeculis*, pt. 1, *Ex aetate ante concilium tridentine* (Rome: Academia Mariana, 1948).

BARBEL, JOSEPH, *Christos Angelos: Die Anschauung von Christus als Bote und Engel in der gelehrten und volkstümlichen Literatur des christlichen Altertums*, Theophaneia, 3 (Bonn: Peter Hanstein Verlagsbuchhandlung, 1941).

BARKER, MARGARET, *The Great Angel: A Study of Israel's Other God* (Louisville, KY: Westminster/John Knox, 1992).

BAUCKHAM, RICHARD, 'Early Jewish Visions of Hell', *Journal of Theological Studies*, NS 41 (1990), 355–85.

—— *The Fate of the Dead: Studies on Jewish and Christian Apocalypses*, Supplements to Novum Testamentum, 93 (Leiden: Brill, 1998).

—— 'Visiting the Places of the Dead', *Proceedings of the Irish Biblical Association*, 18 (1995), 78–93.

BAUER, WALTER, *Orthodoxy and Heresy in Earliest Christianity*, trans. eds. Robert A. Kraft and Gerhard Krodel (Philadelphia: Fortress Press, 1971).

BAUMSTARK, ANTON, 'Die leibliche Himmelfahrt der allerseligsten Jungfrau und die Lokaltradition von Jerusalem', *Oriens Christianus*, 4 (1904), 371–92.

—— 'Zwei syrische Dichtungen auf das Entschlafen der allerseligsten Jungfrau', *Oriens Christianus*, 5 (1905), 100–25.

—— *Geschichte der syrischen Literatur mit Aussluß der christlich-palästinensishen Texte* (Bonn: A. Marcus & E. Webers Verlag, 1922).

BEATRICE, PIER FRANCO, 'Pagan Wisdom and Christian Theology According to the *Tübingen Theosophy*', *Journal of Early Christian Studies*, 3 (1994), 403–18.

——'Traditions apocryphes dans la *Théosophie de Tübingen*', *Apocrypha*, 7 (1996), 109–22.

BECK, EDMUND, OSB, 'Die Mariologie der echten Schriften Ephräms', *Oriens Christianus*, 40 (1956), 22–39.

——*Ephraems Hymnen über das Paradis*, Studia Anselmiana, 26 (Rome: Herder, 1951).

BENSLY, ROBERT L., HARRIS, J. RENDEL, BURKITT, F. CRAWFORD, and SMITH LEWIS, AGNES, *The Four Gospels in Syriac* (Cambridge: The University Press, 1894).

BLACK, MATTHEW, ed. (in consultation with James C. VanderKam), *The Book of Enoch, or, I Enoch: A New English Edition with Commentary and Textual Notes*, Studia in Veteris Testamenti Pseudepigrapha, 7 (Leiden : E. J. Brill, 1985).

BLAKE, ROBERT P., 'La Littérature grecque en Palestine au VIII siècle', *Le Muséon*, 78 (1965), 367–80.

BROCK, SEBASTIAN, 'From Antagonism to Assimilation: Syriac Attitudes to Greek Learning', in Nina G. Garsoïan, Thomas F. Mathews, and Robert W. Thomson (eds.), *East of Byzantium: Syria and Armenia in the Formative Period* (Washington: Dumbarton Oaks, 1982), 17–34.

——*The Luminous Eye: The Spiritual World Vision of Saint Ephrem the Syrian*, rev. edn., Cistercian Studies, 124 (Kalamazoo, MI: Cistercian Publications, 1992).

——'Mary in Syriac Tradition', in Alberic Stacpoole, OSB (ed.), *Mary's Place in Christian Dialogue* (Wilton, CT: Morehouse-Barlow Co., 1983), 182–91.

——*St. Ephrem the Syrian: Hymns on Paradise* (Crestwood, NY: St Vladimir's Seminary Press, 1990).

BROWN, PETER, *The Cult of the Saints: Its Rise and Function in Latin Christianity* (Chicago: University of Chicago Press, 1981).

——'A Dark Age Crisis: Aspects of the Iconoclast Controversy', *English Historical Review*, 88 (1973), 1–34; repr. in *Society and the Holy in Late Antiquity* (Berkeley and Los Angeles: University of California Press, 1982), 251–301.

BROWN, R. E., 'Not Jewish Christianity and Gentile Christianity, but Types of Jewish/Gentile Christianity', *Catholic Biblical Quarterly*, 45 (1983), 74–9.

BUCHHOLZ, DENNIS D., *Your Eyes Will Be Opened: A Study of the Greek (Ethiopic) Apocalypse of Peter*, Society of Biblical Literature Dissertation Series, 97 (Atlanta: Scholars Press, 1988).

BURGHARDT, WALTER J., SJ, *The Testimony of the Patristic Age Concerning Mary's Death* (Westminster, MD: The Newman Press, 1957).

CAMERON, AVERIL, *Christianity and the Rhetoric of Empire: The Development of Christian Discourse*, Sather Classical Lectures, 55 (Berkeley: University of California Press, 1991).

—— 'Images of Authority: Elites and Icons in Late Sixth-Century Byzantium', *Past and Present*, 84 (1979), 3–35.

—— 'The Theotokos in Sixth-Century Constantinople', *Journal of Theological Studies*, NS 29 (1978), 79–108.

CAMPENHAUSEN, HANS VON, *The Virgin Birth in the Theology of the Ancient Church*, trans. Frank Clarke, Studies in Historical Theology, 2 (London: SCM Press, 1964).

CAPELLE, BERNARD, 'Les anciens récits de l'Assomption et Jean de Thessalonique', *Recherches de Théologie ancienne et médiéval*, 12 (1940), 209–35.

—— 'La Fête de l'Assumption dans l'histoire liturgique', *Ephemerides Theologicae Louvanienses*, 3 (1926), 33–45.

—— 'La Fête de la Vierge à Jérusalem au Ve siècle', *Le Muséon*, 56 (1943), 1–33.

—— 'Les Homélies liturgique de prétendu Timothée de Jérusalem', *Ephemerides liturgicae*, 63 (1949), 5–26.

CARLETON PAGET, J., 'Jewish Christianity', in William Horbury, W. D. Davies, and John Sturdy (eds.), *The Cambridge History of Judaism*, iii. *The Early Roman Period* (Cambridge: Cambridge University Press, 2000), 731–75.

CARO, ROBERTO, SJ, *La Homiletica Mariana Griega en el Siglo V*, 3 vols., Marian Library Studies, NS 3–5 (Dayton, OH: University of Dayton, 1971–3).

CAROZZI, CLAUDE, *Eschatologie et au-delà: Recherches sur l'*Apocalypse de Paul (Aix-en-Provence: Université de Provence, 1994).

CARRELL, PETER R., *Jesus and the Angels: Angelology and the Christology of the Apocalypse of John*, Society for New Testament Studies, Monograph Series, 95 (Cambridge: Cambridge University Press, 1997).

Catechism of the Catholic Church (New York: Doubleday, 1995).

CERULLI, ENRICO, *Scritti teologici etiopici dei secoli xvi–xvii*, ii. *La Storia dei Quattro Concili ed altri opusculi monofisiti*, Studi et Testi, 204 (Vatican City: Biblioteca Apostolica Vaticana, 1960).

CHABOT, J.-B., 'Deux *Lychnaria* chrétiens avec inscriptions greques', *Journal Asiatique*, 9/16 (1900), 271–2.

CHADWICK, HENRY, 'Eucharist and Christology in the Nestorian Controversy', *Journal of Theological Studies*, NS 2 (1951), 145–64.

—— 'Origen, Celsus, and the Resurrection of the Body', *Harvard Theological Review*, 41 (1948), 83–102.

CHAISE, FILBERT DE LA, OFM Cap., 'A l'origine des recits apocryphes du "Transitus Mariae"', *Ephemerides Mariologicae*, 29 (1979), 77–90.

CHARLES, R. H., *The Ascension of Isaiah* (London: Adam & Charles Black, 1900).

CHARLESWORTH, JAMES H., ed., *The Old Testament Pseudepigrapha*, 2 vols. (Garden City, NY: Doubleday, 1983).

CHESNUT, ROBERTA, *Three Monophysite Christologies: Severus of Antioch, Philoxenus of Mabbug, and Jacob of Sarug*, Oxford Theological Monographs (Oxford: Oxford University Press, 1976).

CHITTY, DERWAS, *The Desert a City: An Introduction to the Study of Egyptian and Palestinian Monasticism Under the Christian Empire* (Oxford: Basil Blackwell, 1966).

CIGNELLI, LINO, OFM, 'Il prototipo giudeo-cristiano degli apocrifi assunzionisti', in Emmanuelle Testa, Ignazio Mancini, and Michele Piccirillo (eds.), *Studia Hierosolymitana in onore di P. Bellarmino Bagatti*, ii. *Studi esegetici*, Studim Biblicum Franciscanum, Collectio Maior, 23 (Jerusalem: Franciscan Printing Press, 1975), 259–77.

CLARK, ELIZABETH A., 'Vitiated Seeds and Holy Vessels: Augustine's Manichean Past', in *Ascetic Piety and Women's Faith: Essays on Late Ancient Christianity*, Studies in Women and Religion, 20 (Lewiston, NY: Edwin Mellen Press, 1986), 291–349.

CLAYTON, MARY, *The Apocryphal Gospels of Mary in Anglo-Saxon England*, Cambridge Studies in Anglo-Saxon England, 26 (Cambridge: Cambridge University Press, 1998).

—— 'The Transitus Mariae: The Tradition and Its Origins', *Apocrypha*, 10 (1999), 74–98.

CORBETT, THOMAS, 'Origen's Doctrine of the Resurrection', *Irish Theological Quarterly*, 46 (1979), 276–90.

CORBO, VIRGILIO, OFM, 'The Church of the House of St. Peter at Capernaum', in Yoram Tsafrir (ed.), *Ancient Churches Revealed* (Jerusalem: Israel Exploration Society, 1993), 71–6.

COTHENET, ÉDOUARD, 'Marie dans les Apocryphes', in Hubert du Manoir, SJ (ed.), *Maria: Études sur la Sainte Vierge*, 7 vols. (Paris: Beauchesne et ses Fils, 1961), vi. 71–156.

CROUZEL, HENRI, *Origen*, trans. A. S. Worrall (San Francisco: Harper & Row, 1989).

DALEY, BRIAN E., SJ, 'The Dormition of Mary in Homilies and Legends as a Model for Christians', paper presented at the 1999 Dumbarton Oaks Symposium, 1 May, 1999.

—— *On the Dormition of Mary: Early Patristic Homilies* (Crestwood, NY: St Vladimir's Seminary Press, 1998).

DANIÉLOU, JEAN, *Origen*, trans. Walter Mitchell (New York: Sheed & Ward, 1955).

DANIÉLOU, JEAN, 'Terre et paradis chez les pères de l'église', *Eranos-Jahrbuch*, 22 (1953), 433–72.

—— *The Theology of Jewish Christianity*, trans. John A. Baker, vol. i of *The Development of Christian Doctrine before the Council of Nicaea* (London: Darton, Longman, & Todd, 1964).

DELUMEAU, JEAN, *History of Paradise: The Garden of Eden in Myth and Tradition*, trans. Matthew O'Connell (New York: Continuum, 1995).

DEPUYDT, LEO, *Catalogue of Coptic Manuscripts in the Pierpont Morgan Library*, Corpus of Illuminated Manuscripts, 4, Oriental Series, 1 (Leuven: Uitgeverij Peeters, 1993).

DRAGUET, RENÉ, *Julien d'Halicarnasse et sa controverse avec Sévère d'Antioche sur l'incorruptibilité du corps du Christ*, Universitas Catholica Lovaniensis Dissertationes ad gradum magistri in Facultate Theologica consequendum conscriptae, 2/12 (Louvain: Smeesters, 1924).

DRIJVERS, JAN WILLEM, *Helena Augusta: The Mother of Constantine the Great and the Legend of Her Finding of the True Cross*, Brill's Studies in Intellectual History, 27 (Leiden: E. J. Brill, 1992).

DUGGAN, PAUL E., 'The Assumption Dogma: Some Reactions and Ecumenical Implications in the Thought of English-Speaking Theologians', STD diss., International Marian Research Institute, University of Dayton, 1989.

DUHR, JOSEPH, SJ, *The Glorious Assumption of the Mother of God*, trans. John Manning Fraunces, SJ (New York: P. J. Kennedy & Sons, 1950).

EHRMAN, BART D., *The Orthodox Corruption of Scripture: The Effect of Early Christological Controversies on the Text of the New Testament* (New York: Oxford University Press, 1993).

EIJK, A. H. C. VAN, 'The Gospel of Philip and Clement of Alexandria: Gnostic and Ecclesiastical Theology on the Resurrection and the Eucharist', *Vigiliae Christianiae*, 25 (1971), 94–120.

ELLIOTT, J. K., *The Apocryphal New Testament* (Oxford: Clarendon Press, 1993).

ERBETTA, MARIO, *Gli apocrifi del Nuovo Testamento*, i. pt. 2. *Vangeli: Infanzia e passione di Cristo, Assunzione di Maria* (Casale: Marietti, 1981).

ERNST, J., *Die leibliche Himmelfahrt Mariä, historisch-dogmatisch nach ihrer Definierbarkeit beleuchtet* (Regensburg, 1921).

ESBROECK, MICHEL VAN, *Aux origines de la Dormition de la Vierge: Études historique sur les traditions orientales* (Brookfield, VT: Variorum, 1995).

—— 'Bild und Begriff in der Transitus-Literatur, der Palmbaum und der Tempel', in Margot Schmidt (ed.), *Typus, Symbol, Allegorie bei den östlichen Vätern und ihren Parallelen im Mittelalter* (Regensburg: Freidrich Pustet, 1982), 333–51.

—— 'Un court traité pseudo-basilien de mouvance aaronite conservé en arménien', *Le Muséon*, 100 (1987), 385–95.

—— 'Le Culte de la Vierge de Jérusalem à Constantinople aux 6e–7e siècles', *Revue des Études Byzantines*, 46 (1988), 181–90.

—— 'Deux listes d'apôtres conservées en syriaque', in René Lavenant, SJ (ed.), *Third Symposium Syriacum 1980*, Orientalia Christiana Analecta, 221 (Rome: Pont. Institutum Studiorum Orientalium, 1983), 15–24.

—— 'La Dormition chez les Coptes', in Marguerite Rassart-Debergh and Julien Ries (eds.), *Actes du IVe Congrès copte, Louvain-la-Neuve 5–10 septembre 1988*, ii. *De la linguistique au gnosticisme*, Publications de l'Institut Orientaliste de Louvain, 41 (Louvain-la-Neuve: Institut Orientaliste, 1992), 436–45.

—— 'Étude comparée des notices byzantine et caucasiennes pour la fête de la Dormition', in *Aux origines de la Dormition de la Vierge: Études historique sur les traditions orientales* (Brookfield, VT: Variorum, 1995), item II, 1–18.

—— 'Le Manuscrit sinaïtique géorgien 34 et les publications récentes de liturgie palestinienne', *Orientalia Christiana Periodica*, 46 (1980), 125–41.

—— *Les Plus Anciens Homéliaires géorgiens: Étude descriptive et historique*, Publications de l'Institut orientaliste de Louvain, 10 (Louvain-la-Neuve: Universite catholique de Louvain, Institut orientaliste, 1975).

—— 'La Première Église de la Vierge bâtie par les apôtres', *Festschrift Paul Devos* (forthcoming).

—— 'Die Quelle der Himmelfahrt Muhammeds vom Tempel in Jerusalem aus', in *Deutscher Orientalistentag in Bamberg März 2001* (forthcoming).

—— 'Les Signes des temps dans la littérature syriaque', *Revue de l'Insitut catholique de Paris*, 39 (1991), 113–49.

—— 'Some Early Features in the Life of the Virgin', *Marianum* (2001) (forthcoming).

—— 'La Structure du répertoire de l'homéliaire de Mush', in G. B. Jahykyan (ed.), Միջազգային Հայերենագիտական գիտաժողով. Զեկուցումները *(Mijazgayin hayerenagitakan gitazhoghov: zekuts'umner [International Symposium on Armenian Linguistics: Proceedings])* (Yerevan: Haykakan SSH GA Hratarakch'ut'yun), 282–306.

—— Les Textes littéraires sur l'assomption avant le Xe siècle', in

442   *Bibliography*

François Bovon (ed.), *Les Actes apocryphes des apôtres* (Geneva: Labor et Fides, 1981), 265–85.

ESBROECK, MICHEL VAN, 'Version géorgienne de l'homélie eusébienne CPG 5528 sur l'Ascension', *Orientalia Christiana Periodica*, 51 (1985), 277–303.

—— 'La Vierge comme véritable Arche d'Alliance', in *Colloque d'Athènes sur la Theotokos* (forthcoming).

EWALD, HEINRICH, 'Review of "The Departure of my Lady Mary from this World. Edited from two Syriac MSS. in the British Museum, and translated by W. Wright"', *Göttingische gelehrte Anzeigen* 1865, pt. 26. 1018–31.

FALLER, OTHONE, SJ, *De priorum saeculorum silentio circa Assumptionem b. Mariae virginis*, Analecta Gregoriana, Series Facultatis Theologicae, 36 (Rome: Gregorian University, 1946).

FENTON, JOSEPH C., 'Munificentissimus Deus', *The Catholic Mind*, 49 (1951), 65–78.

FERRUA, A., SJ, 'Questioni di epigrafia eretica romana', *Revista di archeologica christiana*, 21 (1944/5), 165–211.

FOERSTER, GIDEON, and TSAFRIR, YORAM, 'City Center (North); Excavations of the Hebrew University Expedition', *Excavations and Surveys in Israel*, 11 (The Bet She'an Excavation Project (1989–1991)) (1993), 3–32.

FREND, W. H. C., 'The Gnostic Origins of the Assumption Legend', *The Modern Churchman*, 43 (1953), 23–8.

FRIETHOFF, CASPAR, OP, 'The Dogmatic Definition of the Assumption', *The Thomist*, 14 (1951), 41–58.

GAVENTA, BEVERLY ROBERTS, *Mary: Glimpses of the Mother of Jesus*, Studies on Personalities of the New Testament (Columbia, SC: University of South Carolina Press, 1995).

GÉHIN, PAUL, and FRØYSHOV, STIG, 'Nouvelles découvertes sinaïtiques: à propos de la parution de l'inventaire des manuscrits grecs', *Revue des Études Byzantines*, 59 (2000), 167–84.

GIAMBERARDINI, GABRIELE, OFM, *Il culto mariano in Eggito*, i. *Sec. I–VI*, 2nd edn., Pubblicazioni dello Studium Biblicum Franciscanum, Analecta, 6 (Jerusalem: Franciscan Printing Press, 1975).

GIBSON, MARGARET DUNLOP, *Catalogue of the Arabic MSS in the Convent of S. Catharine on Mount Sinai*, Studia Sinaitica, III (London: C. J. Clay & Sons, 1894).

GIESCHEN, CHARLES A., *Angelomorphic Christology: Antecedents and Early Evidence*, Arbeiten zur Geschichte des antiken Judentums und des Urchristentums, 42 (Leiden: Brill, 1998).

GIJSEL, JAN, *Libri de natiuitate Mariae: Pseudo-Matthei Euangelium*, CCSA 9 (Turnhout: Brepols, 1997).

GIL, MOSHE, *A History of Palestine, 634–1099*, trans. Ethel Broido (Cambridge: Cambridge University Press, 1992).

GILDEMEISTER, JOHANN, *Theodosius de situ Terrae Sanctae im ächten Text und der Brevarius de Hierosolyma vervollstäandigt* (Bonn: Adolph Marcus, 1882).

GRAEF, HILDA, *Mary: A History of Doctrine and Devotion*, i. *From the Beginnings to the Eve of the Reformation* (New York: Sheed & Ward, 1963).

GRIBOMONT, JEAN, OSB, 'Le Plus Ancien *Transitus* Marial et l'encratisme', *Augustinianum*, 23 (1983), 237–47.

GRIFFITH, SIDNEY, 'From Aramaic to Arabic: The Languages of the Monasteries of Palestine in the Byzantine and Early Islamic Periods', *Dumbarton Oaks Papers*, 51 (1997), 11–31.

—— 'The Monks of Palestine and the Growth of Christian Literature in Arabic', *The Muslim World*, 78 (1988), 1–28.

GRILLMEIER, ALOIS, SJ, *Christ in Christian Tradition*, i. *From the Apostolic Age to Chalcedon (451)*, 2nd rev. edn., trans. John Bowden (Atlanta: John Knox, 1975).

—— with Theresia Hainthaler, *Christ in Christian Tradition*, ii. *From the Council of Chalcedon (451) to Gregory the Great (590–604)*, ii. *The Church of Constantinople in the Sixth Century*, trans. John Cawte and Pauline Allen (Louisville: Westminster/John Knox, 1995).

—— *Christ in Christian Tradition*, ii. *From the Council of Chalcedon (451) to Gregory the Great (590–604)*, pt. 4, *The Church of Alexandria with Nubia and Ethiopia after 451*, trans. O. C. Dean, Jr. (Louisville: Westminster/John Knox Press, 1996).

HALDON, JOHN, *Byzantium in the Seventh Century: The Transformation of a Culture*, rev. edn. (Cambridge: Cambridge University Press, 1997).

HANNAH, DARRELL D., *Michael and Christ: Michael Traditions and Angel Christology in Early Christianity*, Wissenschaftliche Untersuchungen zum Neuen Testament 2/109 (Tübingen: Mohr Siebeck, 1999).

HANSBURY, MARY, *Jacob of Serug: On the Mother of God* (Crestwood, NY: St Vladimir's Seminary Press, 1998).

HEINE, RONALD E., 'Can the Catena Fragments of Origen's Commentary on John be Trusted?' *Vigiliae Christianae*, 40 (1986), 118–34.

HENNESSEY, LAWRENCE R., 'The Place of Saints and Sinners after Death', in Charles Kannengeisser and William L. Peterson (eds.), *Origen of Alexandria: His World and His Legacy* (Notre Dame: University of Notre Dame Press, 1988), 295–312.

HILLGARTH, J. N., 'The East, Visigothic Spain, and the Irish', *Studia Patristica*, 4 (1961), 442–56.

HIMMELFARB, MARTHA, *Tours of Hell: An Apocalyptic Form in Jewish and Christian Literature* (Philadelphia: University of Pennsylvania Press, 1983).

HOADE, EUGENE, OFM, *Guide to the Holy Land* (Jerusalem: Franciscan Printing Press, 1984).

HOLUM, KENNETH G., *Theodosian Empresses: Women and Imperial Dominion in Late Antiquity* (Berkeley and Los Angeles: University of California Press, 1982).

HURST, THOMAS R., 'The "Transitus" of Mary in a Homily of Jacob of Sarug', *Marianum*, 52 (1990), 86–100.

JAMES, E. O., *The Tree of Life: An Archaeological Study*, Studies in the History of Religions, Supplements to Numen, 11 (Leiden: E. J. Brill, 1966).

JAMES, MONTAGUE RHODES, *The Apocryphal New Testament*, corr. edn. (Oxford: The Clarendon Press, 1989).

——'A New Text of the Apocalypse of Peter', *Journal of Theological Studies*, 12 (1911), 36–55, 157, 362–83, 573–83.

JARRY, JACQUES, *Hérésies et factions dans l'empire byzantine du IVe au VIIe siècle*, Recherches d'archéologie, de philologie et d'histoire, 14 (Cairo: L'Institut Français d'Archéologie Orientale, 1968).

JUGIE, MARTIN, AA, *L'Immaculée Conception dans l'Écriture sainte et dans la tradition orientale*, Collectio Edita Cura Academiae Marianae Internationalis, Textus et Disquisitiones, Bibliotheca Immaculatae Conceptionis, 3 (Rome: Academia Mariana/Officium Libri Catholici, 1952).

——*La Mort et l'assomption de la Sainte Vierge: Étude historico-doctrinale*, Studi e Testi, 114 (Vatican City: Biblioteca Apostolica Vaticana, 1944).

——'La Mort et l'assomption de la Sainte Vierge dans la tradition des cinq premiers siècles', *Échos d'Orient*, 25 (1926), 5–20, 129–43, and 281–307.

JUNOD, ERIC, and KAESTLI, JEAN-DANIEL, *L'Histoire des actes apocryphes des Apôtres du IIIe au IXe siècle: Le Cas des Actes de Jean*, Cahiers de la revue de théologie et de philosophie, 7 (Lausanne: La Concorde, 1982).

—— ——eds., *Acta Iohannis*, 2 vols., CCSA 1–2 (Turnhout: Brepols, 1983).

KLAMETH, GUSTAV, *Die neutestamentlichen Lokaltraditionen Palästinas in der Zeit vor den Kreuzzügen*, Neutestamentliche Abhandlungen, 5/1 (Münster: Aschendorffsche Verlagsbuchhandlung, 1914).

KNIBB, MICHAEL A., *The Ethiopic Book of Enoch: A New Edition In Light of the Aramaic Dead Sea Fragments*, 2 vols. (Oxford: Clarendon Press, 1978).

KNIGHT, JONATHAN, *Disciples of the Beloved One: The Christology, Social Setting, and Theological Content of the Ascension of Isaiah*, Journal for the Study of the Pseudepigrapha, Supplement Series, 18 (Sheffield: Sheffield Academic Press, 1996).

KOEP, LEO, *Das himmlische Buch in Antike und Christentum*, Theophaneia, 8 (Bonn: Peter Hanstein Verlag, 1952).

KRAFT, ROBERT A, 'In Search of "Jewish Christianity" and its "Theology": Problems of Definition and Methodology', *Recherches de Science Religieuse*, 60 (1972), 81–92.

—— 'The Multiform Jewish Heritage of Early Christianity', in Jacob Neusner (ed.), *Christianity, Judaism and Other Greco-Roman Cults: Studies for Morton Smith at Sixty*, 3 vols. (Leiden: E. J. Brill, 1975), iii. 174–99.

KRETZENBACHER, LEOPOLD, *Sterbekerze und Palmzweig-Ritual beim "Marientod": Zum Apokryphen in Wort und Bild bei der κοίμησις, dormitio, assumption der Gottesmutter zwischen Byzanz und dem mittle-alterlicher Westen*, Österreichische Akademie der Wissenschaften, Philosophisch-Historische Klasse, Sitzungsberichte, 667 (Vienna: Verlag der Österreichischen Akademie der Wissenschaften, 1999).

KRONHOLM, TRYGGVE, 'The Trees of Paradise in the Hymns of Ephraem Syrus', *Annual of the Swedish Theological Institute*, 11 (1978), 48–56.

KRÜGER, PAUL, 'Das Problem der Rechtglaübigkeit Jakobs von Serugh und seine Lösung', *Ostkirchliche Studien*, 5 (1956), 158–76, 225–42.

—— 'War Jakob von Serugh Katholik oder Monophysit?' *Ostkirchliche Studien*, 2 (1953), 199–208.

LANTSCHOOT, A. VAN, 'L'Assomption de la Sainte Vierge chez les Coptes', *Gregorianum*, 27 (1946), 493–526.

LAUSBERG, H., 'Zur literarischen Gestaltung des Transitus Beata Mariae', *Historisches Jahrbuch*, 72 (1935), 25–49.

LAYTON, BENTLEY, *The Gnostic Scriptures* (Garden City, NY: Doubleday & Co., 1987).

—— *The Gnostic Treatise on Resurrection from Nag Hammadi* (Missoula, MT: Scholars Press, 1979).

LEEB, HELMUT, *Die Gesänge im Gemeingottesdienst von Jerusalem (vom 5. bis 8. Jahrhundert)*, Wiener Beiträge zur Theologie, 28 (Vienna: Verlag Herder, 1970).

LIMBERIS, VASILIKI, *Divine Heiress: The Virgin Mary and the Creation of Christian Constantinople* (New York: Routledge, 1994).

LINDER, AMNON, 'Christian Communities in Jerusalem', in Joshua Prawer and Haggai ben-Shammai (eds.), *The History of Jerusalem: The Early Muslim Period, 638–1099* (New York: New York University Press, 1996), 121–62.

LIPSIUS, RICHARD A., ed., *Die apokryphen Apostelgeschichten und Apostellegenden*, 2 vols. (Brunswick, 1883–90; repr. Amsterdam: Philo Press, 1976).

LOFFREDA, STANISLAO, OFM, *Lucerne Bizantine in Terra Santa con Iscrizioni in Greco*, Studium Biblicum Franciscanum, Collectio maior, 35 (Jerusalem : Franciscan Printing Press, 1989).

LOMBARDI, G., *La tomba di Rahel*, Pubblicazioni dello Studium Biblicum Franciscanum, Collectio Minor, 11 (Jerusalem: Franciscan Printing Press, 1971).

LONGENECKER, RICHARD N., *The Christology of Early Jewish Christianity*, Studies in Biblical Theology, 2/17 (London: SCM Press, 1970).

LOUTH, ANDREW, *Maximus the Confessor* (New York: Routledge, 1996).

—— 'Recent Research on St Maximus the Confessor: A Survey', *Saint Vladimir's Theological Quarterly*, 42 (1998), 67–84

MACALISTER, R. A. S., and DUNCAN, J. GARROW, *Excavations on the Hill of Ophel, Jerusalem, 1923–25*, Palestine Exploration Fund Annual, 1923–1925, 4 ([London]: Published by order of the committee, 1926).

MAGEN, YITZHAK, 'The Church of Mary Theotokos on Mt. Gerazim', in Yoram Tsafrir (ed.), *Ancient Churches Revealed* (Jerusalem: Israel Exploration Society, 1993), 83–9.

MAGNESS, JODI, 'Illuminating Byzantine Jerusalem: Oil Lamps Shed Light on Early Christian Worship', *Biblical Archaeology Review*, 24/2 (March/April 1998), 40–7, 70–1.

—— *Jerusalem Ceramic Chronology, circa 200–800 CE*, Journal for the Study of the Old Testament/American Schools of Oriental Research Monographs, 9 (Sheffield: Sheffield Academic Press, 1993).

MAISURAZE, M., MAMULAŠVILI, M., GAMBAŠIZE, A., and C'XENKELI, M., ათონის მრავალთავი *(At'onis mravalt'avi [The Athos Homiliary])* (Tbilisi: Georgian Academy of Sciences, K. Kekelidze Institute of Manuscripts, 1999); English summary, 283–5.

MANCINI, IGNAZIO, OFM, *Archaeological Discoveries Relative to the Judaeo-Christians: Historical Survey*, trans. G. Bushell, Publications of the Studium Biblicum Franciscanum, Smaller Series, 10 (Jerusalem: Franciscan Printing Press, 1970).

MANNS, FRÉDÉRIC, OFM, 'La Mort de Marie dans les textes de la Dormition de Marie', *Augustinianum*, 19 (1979), 507–15.

—— *Le Récit de la dormition de Marie (Vatican grec 1982), Contribution à l'étude de origines de l'exégèse chrétienne*, Studium Biblicum Franciscanum, Collectio Maior, 33 (Jerusalem: Franciscan Printing Press, 1989).

METREVELI, E. (Métrévéli, Hélène), 'Les Manuscrits liturgiques géorgiens des IXe–Xe siècles et leur importance pour l'étude de l'hymnographie byzantine', *Bedi Kartlisa*, 35 (1978), 43–8.

——CANKIEVI, Cʻ. (Tchankieva, Ts.), XEVSURIANI, L. (Khevsouriani, L.), 'Le Plus Ancien Tropologion géorgien', trans. Michel van Esbroeck, *Bedi Kartlisa*, 39 (1981), 54–62.

——and JGAMAIA, L., ქართულ ხელნაწერთა აღწერილობა, სინური კოლექცია *(K'art'ul xelnacert'a agceriloba, sinuri kolek'c'ia [Description of Georgian Manuscripts, Sinai Collection])*, 3 vols. (Tbilisi: Mec'niereba, 1978).

METZGER, BRUCE M., *The Early Versions of the New Testament: Their Origin, Transmission, and Limitations* (Oxford: Clarendon Press, 1977).

MEYENDORFF, JOHN, *Byzantine Theology*, 2nd edn. (New York: Fordham University Press, 1979).

——*Christ in Eastern Christian Thought* (Crestwood, NY: St. Vladimir's Seminary Press, 1975).

——*Imperial Unity and Christian Divisions: The Church 450–680 A.D.*, The Church in History, 2 (Crestwood, NY: St Vladimir's Seminary Press, 1989).

MGALOBLIŠVILI, TAMILA, კლარჯული მრავალთავი *(K'larjuli mravalt' avi [The Klardjeti Homiliary])*, Zveli kartuli mcerlobis zeglebi, 12 (Tbilisi: Mec'niereba, 1991); English summary, 466–90.

MIAN, FRANCA, *Gerusalemme città santa: Oriente e pellegrini d'Occidente (sec. I~IX/XI)*, (Rome: Il Cerchio, 1988).

MILANI, CELESTINA, *Itinerarium Antonini Placentini: Un viaggio in Terra Santa del 560–570 d.C.* (Milan: Vita e Pensiero, 1977).

MILIK, J. T., 'Notes d'épigraphie et de topographie palestiniennes' *Revue Biblique*, 67 (1960), 550–97.

——'Problèmes de la littérature hénochique à la lumière de fragments araméens de Qumran', *Harvard Theological Review*, 64 (1971), 333–78.

——ed. (with Matthew Black), *The Books of Enoch: Aramaic Fragments of Qumrân Cave 4* (Oxford: Clarendon Press, 1976).

MIMOUNI, SIMON C., 'Les *Apocalypses de la Vierge*: État de la question', *Apocrypha*, 4 (1993), 101–12.

——*Dormition et assomption de Marie: Histoire des traditions anciennes*, Théologie Historique, 98 (Paris: Beauchesne, 1995).

——'La Fête de la dormition de Marie en Syrie à l'époque byzantine', *The Harp*, 5 (1992), 157–74.

——'Genèse et évolution des traditions anciennes sur le sort final de Marie. Étude de la tradition litteraire copte', *Marianum*, 42 (1991), 69–143.

448 *Bibliography*

MIMOUNI, SIMON C., " "Histoire de la Dormition et de l' Assomption de Marie": Une nouvelle hypothèse de recherche', *Studia Patristica*, 19 (1989), 372–80.

—— 'Histoire de la Dormition et de la Assomption de Marie: Recherche d'histoire littéraire,' Thèse de diplôme, École Pratique des Hautes Études, Section des Sciences Religieuses, 1988.

—— 'La Lecture liturgique et les apocryphes du Nouveau Testament. Le Cas de la Dormitio grecque du Pseudo-Jean', *Orientalia Christiana Periodica*, 59 (1993), 403–25.

—— 'La Synagogue "judéo-chrétienne" de Jérusalem au Mont Sion', *Proche-Orient chrétien*, 40 (1990), 215–324.

—— 'La Tradition littéraire syriaque de l'histoire de la Dormition et de l'Assomption de Marie', *Parole de l'Orient*, 15 (1988–9), 143–68.

—— 'Les Transitus Mariae sont-ils vraiment des apocryphes?' *Studia Patristica*, 25 (1993), 122–8.

—— 'Les *Vies de la Vierge*: État de la question', *Apocrypha*, 5 (1994), 211–48.

MONTAGNA, D. M., 'Appunti critice sul Transitus B. V. Mariae dello Pseudo-Melitone', *Marianum*, 27 (1965), 177–87.

MURRAY, ROBERT, *Symbols of Church and Kingdom: A Study in Early Syriac Tradition* (Cambridge: Cambridge University Press, 1975).

NEWMAN, JOHN HENRY, 'The Theory of Developments in Religious Doctrine', in *Conscience, Consensus, and the Development of Doctrine* (New York: Image Books, 1992), 1–29.

NICHOLS, AIDAN, OP, *Byzantine Gospel: Maximus the Confessor in Modern Scholarship* (Edinburgh: T. & T. Clark, 1993).

ORBE, ANTONIO, SJ, *Estudios Valentinianos*, i. *Hacia la primera teologica de la procesion del Verbo*, Analecta Gregoriana, 99 (Rome: Gregorian University, 1958).

ORTIZ DE URBINA, IGNATIUS, SJ, 'Maria en la patristica siriaca', *Scripta de Maria*, 1 (1978), 29–114.

—— 'Le Paradis eschatologique d'après Saint Ephrem', *Orientalia Christiana Periodica*, 21 (1955), 467–72.

—— *Patrologia Syriaca*, 2nd edn. (Rome: Pont. Institutum Orientalium Studiorum, 1965).

OUTTIER, BERNARD, 'Deux homélies pseudo-chrysostomiennes pour la fête mariale du 15 Août', *Apocrypha*, 6 (1995), 165–77.

PAGELS, ELAINE H., *The Gnostic Paul: Gnostic Exegesis of the Pauline Letters* (Philadelphia: Fortress Press, 1975).

—— *The Johannine Gospel in Gnostic Exegesis: Heracleon's Commentary on John*, Society of Biblical Literature Monograph Series, 17 (Nashville: Abingdon Press, 1973).

—— ' "The Mystery of the Resurrection:" A Gnostic Reading of 1 Cor 15', *Journal of Biblical Literature*, 93 (1974), 276–88.

Palestine Archaeological Museum Gallery Book, iii. *Persian, Hellenistic, Roman, Byzantine Periods* (Jerusalem: n.p., 1943).

PEEL, MALCOLM L., *The Epistle to Rheginos* (Philadelphia: Westminster, 1969).

PEETERS, PAUL, 'Jacques de Saroug appartient-il à la secte monophysite?' *Analecta Bollandiana*, 66 (1948), 134–98.

PELIKAN, JAROSLAV, *The Christian Tradition: A History of the Development of Doctrine*, i. *The Emergence of the Catholic Tradition (100–600)* (Chicago: University of Chicago Press, 1971).

——*Mary through the Centuries: Her Place in the History of Culture* (New Haven: Yale University Press, 1996).

PERADZE, G., 'An Account of the Georgian Monks and Monasteries in Palestine', *Georgica*, 1 (1937), 181–246.

PÉREZ, GONZALO ARANDA, *Dormición de la Virgen: Relatos de la tradición copta*, Apócrifos christianos, 2 (Madrid: Editorial Ciudad Nueva, 1995).

PERKINS, PHEME, *Gnosticism and the New Testament* (Minneapolis: Fortress Press, 1993).

PERRONE, LORENZO, 'Christian Holy Places and Pilgrimage in an Age of Dogmatic Conflicts: Popular Religion and Confessional Affiliation in Byzantine Palestine (Fifth to Seventh Centuries)', *Proche-Orient Chrétien*, 48 (1998), 5–37.

PIOVANELLI, PIERLUIGI, 'Les Origines de l'*Apocalypse de Paul* reconsidérées', *Apocrypha*, 4 (1993), 25–64.

PIUS XII, 'Munificentissimus Deus', *Acta Apostolicae Sedis*, 42 (1950), 753–71.

PIXNER, BARGIL, 'Church of the Apostles Found on Mt. Zion', *Biblical Archaeology Review*, 16/3 (1990), 16–35, 60.

PLONTKE-LÜNING, ANNEGRET, 'Über einige Jerusalemer Einflüsse in Georgien', in Ernst Dassmann and Josef Engemann (eds.), *Akten des XII. Internationalen Kongresses für Christliche Archäologie, Bonn 1991*, Jahrbuch für Antike und Christentum, Ergänzungsband, 20 (Münster, Germany: Aschendorffsche Verlagsbuchhandlung, 1995), 1114–18.

RAES, A., SJ, 'Aux origines de la fête de l'Assomption en Orient', *Orientalia Christiana Periodica*, 12 (1946), 262–74.

RAHMANI, L. Y., '*Eulogia* Tokens from Byzantine Bet She'an', '*Atiqot*, 22 (1993), 109–19.

RAHNER, KARL, 'Zum Sinn des Assumpta-Dogmas', in *Schriften zur Theologie* (Einsiedeln: Benziger, 1967), 239–52.

REICH, RONNY, AVNI, GIDEON, and WINTER, TAMAR, *The Jerusalem Archaeological Park* (Jerusalem: Israel Antiquities Authority, 1999).

REISS, K. VON, 'Kathisma Palaion und der sogenannte Brunnen der Weisen bei Mar Eljas', *Zeitschrift des Deutschen Palästina-Vereins*, 12 (1889), 19–23.

RIVIÈRE, J., 'Le Plus Vieux "Transitus" latin et son dérivé grec', *Recherches de Théologie ancienne et médiévale*, 8 (1936), 5–23.

RENOUX, CHARLES, 'De Jérusalem en Arménie: L'Heritage liturgique de l'église arménienne', in Thomas Hummel, Kevork Hintlian, and Ulf Carmesund (eds.), *Patterns of the Past, Prospects for the Future: The Christian Heritage in the Holy Land* (London: Melisende, 1999), 115–23.

—— 'La Fête de l'assomption dans le rite arménien', in A. M. Triacca and A. Pistoia (eds.), *La Mère de Jésus-Christ et la communion des saints dans la liturgie* (Rome: Edizioni Liturgiche, 1986), 235–53.

ROREM, PAUL, and LAMOREAUX, JOHN C., *John of Scythopolis and the Dionysian Corpus: Annotating the Areopagite*, Oxford Early Christian Studies (Oxford: Clarendon Press, 1998).

ROWLAND, CHRISTOPHER, *The Open Heaven: A Study of Apocalyptic in Judaism and Early Christianity* (New York: Crossroad, 1982).

RUDOLPH, KURT, *Gnosis: The Nature and History of Gnosticism*, trans. and ed. Robert McLachlan Wilson (San Francisco: Harper & Row, 1987).

—— ' "Gnosis" and "Gnosticism"—The Problems of their Definition and their Relation to the Writings of the New Testament', in A. H. B. Logan and A. J. M. Wedderburn (eds.), *The New Testament and Gnosis: Essays in Honor of Robert McLachlan Wilson* (Edinburgh: T. & T. Clark, 1983), 21–37; repr. in *Gnosis und Spätantike Religionsgeschicte: Gesammelte Aufsätze*, NHS 42 (Leiden: E. J. Brill, 1996), 34–52.

SALLER, SYLVESTER J., OFM, *Excavations at Bethany (1949–1953)*, Publications of the Studium Biblicum Franciscanum, 12 (Jerusalem: Franciscan Press, 1957).

—— 'The Tombstone Inscription in the Church of Mary's Tomb at Gethsemane', in Virgilio Corbo, OFM (ed.), *Richerche archeologiche al Monte degli Ulivi*, Publicazioni dello Studium Biblicum Franciscanum, 16 (Jerusalem: Tip. dei Padri Francescani), 76–80.

SCHAFFER, CHRISTA, *Koimesis, Der Heimgang Mariens: Das Entschlafungsbild in seiner Abhängigkeit von Legende und Theologie*, Studia Patristica et Liturgica, 15 (Regensburg: Kommissionsverlag Friedrich Pustet, 1985).

SCHICK, ROBERT, *The Christian Communities of Palestine from Byzantine to Islamic Rule: A Historical and Archaeological Study*, Studies in Late Antiquity and Early Islam, 2 (Princeton: The Darwin Press, 1995).

SCHMIDT, CARL, *Gnostische Schriften in koptischer Sprache aus dem Codex Brucianus*, TU 8. 1 (Leipzig: J. C. Hinrichs'sche Buchhandlung, 1892).

SCHNEEMELCHER, WILHELM, ed., *New Testament Apocrypha*, rev. edn., 2 vols., trans. and ed. R. McL. Wilson (Philadelphia: Westminster, 1991).

SCHNEIDER, A. M., 'Die Kathismakirche auf Chirbet Abu Brek', *Journal of the Palestine Oriental Society*, 14 (1934), 230–1.

SÉD, NICHOLAS, 'Les Hymnes sur le Paradis de Saint Ephrem et les traditions juives', *Le Muséon*, 81 (1968), 455–501.

SELLEW, PHILIP, 'Heroic Biography, Continent Marriage, and the *Protevangelium Jacobi*', *Journal of Early Christian Studies* (forthcoming).

SEYMOUR, JOHN D., 'Irish Versions of the Transitus Mariae', *Journal of Theological Studies*, 23 (1921–2), 36–43.

SHOEMAKER, STEPHEN J., 'A Case of Mistaken Identity?: Naming the "Gnostic Mary"', in F. Stanley Jones (ed.), *Mary(s) in Early Christian Literature* (Atlanta: Society for Biblical Literature) (forthcoming).

—— 'Gender at the Virgin's Funeral: Men and Women as Witnesses to the Dormition', *Studia Patristica* (forthcoming).

—— ' "Let Us Go and Burn Her Body": The Image of the Jews in the Early Dormition Traditions', *Church History*, 68 (1999), 775–823.

—— 'Mary and the Discourse of Orthodoxy: Early Christian Identity and the Ancient Dormition Legends', Ph.D. diss., Duke University, 1997.

—— 'The (Re?)Discovery of the Kathisma Church and the Cult of the Virgin in Late Antique Palestine', *Maria: A Journal of Marian Studies*, 2 (2001), 21–72.

—— 'Rethinking the "Gnostic Mary": Mary of Nazareth and Mary of Magdala in Early Christian Tradition', *Journal of Early Christian Studies* (forthcoming).

SMITH, JONATHAN Z., *Drudgery Divine: On the Comparison of Early Christianities and the Religions of Late Antiquity*, Jordan Lectures in Comparative Religion, 14 (Chicago: University of Chicago Press, 1990).

SMITH LEWIS, AGNES, *Catalogue of the Syriac MSS. in the Convent of S. Catharine on Mount Sinai*, Studia Sinaitica, I (London: C. J. Clay & Sons, 1894).

—— and GIBSON, MARGARET DUNLOP, *Palestinian Syriac Texts from Palimpsest Fragments in the Taylor-Schechter Collection* (London: C. J. Clay & Sons, 1900).

STUCKENBRUCK, LOREN, *Angel Veneration and Christology: A Study in Early Judaism and in the Christology of the Apocalypse of John*, Wissenschaftliche Untersuchungen zum Neuen Testament, 2/70 (Tübingen: Mohr Siebeck, 1995).

TAYLOR, JOAN E., *Christians and the Holy Places: The Myth of Jewish-Christian Origins* (Oxford: Clarendon Press, 1993).

—— 'The Phenomenon of Early Jewish-Christianity: Reality or Scholarly Invention?' *Vigiliae Christianae*, 44 (1990), 313–34.

TEIXIDOR, JAVIER, 'Le Thème de la descente aux enfers chez Saint Éphrem', *L'Orient Syrien*, 6 (1961), 25–40.

TESTA, EMMANUELE, OFM, 'I Novissimi e la loro localizzazione nella teologia ebraica e giudeo-cristiana', *Liber Annuus*, 26 (1976), 121–69.

—— 'L'Origine e lo sviluppo della *Dormitio Mariae*', *Augustinianum*, 23 (1983), 249–62.

—— *Il simbolismo dei Giudeo-cristiani*, Studium Biblicum Franciscanum, Collectio Maior, 14 (Jerusalem: Franciscan Printing Press, 1962).

—— 'Lo sviluppo della "Dormitio Mariae" nella letteratura, nella teologìa e nella archeologìa', *Marianum*, 44 (1982), 316–89.

THOMAS, CHARLES, *The Early Christian Archaeology of North Britain* (London: Oxford University Press, 1971).

THOMASSEN, EINAR, 'How Valentinian is *The Gospel of Philip?*' in John D. Turner and Anne McGuire (eds.), *The Nag Hammadi Library after Fifty Years: Proceedings of the 1995 Society of Biblical Literature Commemoration*, NHS 44 (Leiden: Brill, 1997), 251–79.

THOMSEN, PETER, 'Die lateinischen und griechischen Inscriften der Stadt Jerusalem', *Zeitschrift des Deutschen Palästina-Vereins*, 44 (1921), 1–61 and 90–168.

THOMSON, ROBERT W., 'Jerusalem and Armenia', *Studia Patristica*, 18 (1985), 77–91.

TRIGG, JOSEPH W., 'The Angel of Great Counsel: Christ and the Angelic Hierarchy in Origen's Theology', *Journal of Theological Studies*, NS 42 (1991), 35–51.

ULLENDORFF, EDWARD, *The Ethiopians: An Introduction to Country and People* (London: Oxford University Press, 1960).

VALLECILLO, MIGUEL, OFM, 'El "Transitus Mariae" según el manuscrito Vaticano G. R. 1982', *Verdad y vida*, 30 (1972), 187–260.

VANDERKAM, JAMES C., *Textual and Historical Studies in the Book of Jubilees*, Harvard Semitic Museum, Harvard Semitic Monographs, 14 (Missoula, MT: Scholars Press, 1977).

VIKAN, GARY, *Byzantine Pilgrimage Art*, Dumbarton Oaks Byzantine Collection Publications, 5 (Washington: Dumbarton Oaks, 1982).

VINCENT, HUGHES, and ABEL, F.-M., *Jérusalem: Recherches de topo-*

graphie, d'archéologie et d'histoire, ii. *Jérusalem Nouvelle*, (Paris: J. Gabalda, 1926).

VONA, CONSTANTINO, *Omelie mariologiche de S. Giacomo di Sarug: Introduzione, traduzione dal siriaco e commento* (Rome: Facultas Theologica Pontificii Athenaei Lateranensis, 1953).

VÖÖBUS, ARTHUR, *Early Versions of the New Testament: Manuscript Studies*, Papers of the Estonian Theological Society in Exile, 6 (Stockholm: Estonian Theological Society in Exile, 1954).

VORSTER, WILLEM S., 'The Annunciation of the Birth of Jesus in the Protevangelium of James', in J. H. Petzer and P. J. Hartin (eds.), *A South African Perspective on the New Testament* (Leiden: E. J. Brill, 1986).

WENGER, ANTOINE, AA, *L'Assomption de la T. S. Vierge dans la tradition byzantine du VIe au Xe siècle*, Archives de l'Orient Chrétien, 5 (Paris: Institut Français d'Études Byzantines, 1955).

—— 'Ciel ou Paradis: Le Séjour des âmes, d'après Phillipe le Solitaire, Dioptra, Livre IV, Chapitre X', *Byzantinische Zeitschrift*, 44 (1951), 560–9.

WERNER, MARTIN, *The Formation of Christian Dogma: An Historical Study of its Problem*, trans. S. G. F. Brandon (New York: Harper & Bros., 1957).

WIDENGREN, GEO, *The Ascension of the Apostle and the Heavenly Book*, Uppsala Universitets Årsskrift, 1950: 7 (Uppsala: A. B. Lundequistska Bokhandeln, 1950).

—— *The King and the Tree of Life in Ancient Near Eastern Religion (King and Saviour IV)*, Uppsala Universitets Årsskrift, 1951: 4 (Uppsala: A. B. Lundequistska bokhandeln, 1951).

WILKEN, ROBERT L., *The Land Called Holy: Palestine in Christian History and Thought* (New Haven: Yale University Press, 1992).

WILKINSON, JOHN, *Jerusalem Pilgrims Before the Crusades* (Warminster: Aris & Phillips, 1977).

WILLARD, R., 'The Testament of Mary: The Irish Account of the Death of the Virgin', *Recherches de Théologie ancienne et médiévale*, 9 (1937), 341–64.

WILLIAMS, MICHAEL A., *Rethinking Gnosticism: An Argument for Dismantling a Dubious Category* (Princeton: Princeton University Press, 1996).

WRIGHT, J. EDWARD, *The Early History of Heaven* (New York: Oxford University Press, 2000).

WRIGHT, WILLIAM, *Catalogue of the Syriac Manuscripts of the British Museum Acquired Since the Year 1838*, 3 vols. (London, 1870).

Index

458   *Index*